LEADERSHIP
Resources

A GUIDE TO TRAINING AND DEVELOPMENT TOOLS

D1599866

8th Edition

L E A D E R S H I P
Resources

A GUIDE TO TRAINING AND DEVELOPMENT TOOLS

Edited by
Mary K. Schwartz
Kinsey G. Gimbel

Center for Creative Leadership
Greensboro, North Carolina

The Center for Creative Leadership is an international, nonprofit educational institution founded in 1970 to advance the understanding, practice, and development of leadership for the benefit of society world-wide. As a part of this mission, it publishes books and reports that aim to contribute to a general process of inquiry and understanding in which ideas related to leadership are raised, exchanged, and evaluated. The ideas presented in its publications are those of the author or authors.

The Center thanks you for supporting its work through the purchase of this volume. If you have comments, suggestions, or questions about any Center publication, please contact John R. Alexander, President, at the address given below.

Center for Creative Leadership
One Leadership Place
Post Office Box 26300
Greensboro, North Carolina 27438-6300

Center for
Creative Leadership

leadership. learning. life.

CCL No. 348

ISSN No. 1529-742X
ISBN No. 1-882197-57-7

To
Frank H. Freeman

As Library Director at the Center for Creative Leadership for thirty years, Frank Freeman developed an unequaled expertise in the subject area of leadership resources—reading materials, training tools, and the people and organizations involved in leadership education. One venue for sharing his expertise was *Leadership Education: A Source Book.* The first edition resulted from a 1986 CCL conference for experienced and novice leadership educators to exchange success stories and good ideas as well as their syllabi and favorite resources. Frank, along with Visiting Fellow Robert Gregory and leadership scholar Miriam Clark, organized this information into a loose-leaf notebook as a permanent record of the conference and a tool for future planners of leadership education courses and programs.

As the field of leadership education grew, so did the number of resources and the demand for more source books. Frank continued as Library Director and source book editor for six more editions. The book underwent many changes including a division into two separate titles—*Leadership Education: A Source Book of Courses and Programs* and *Leadership Resources: A Guide to Training and Development Tools.* Frank retired recently but his legacy to put good information into the hands of leadership educators everywhere carries on. Thank you, Frank, for your wise counsel and living example of professionalism in the field where leadership education meets information science.

CONTENTS

ABOUT THE EDITORS

Mary K. Schwartz, Research Librarian, develops the special collection of leadership resources at the Center for Creative Leadership Information Center. Since 1991, she has participated as an assistant and editor of *Leadership Education: A Source Book of Courses and Programs* and *Leadership Resources: A Guide to Training and Development Tools.* She holds an M.L.S. in library and information science from the University of North Carolina at Greensboro.

Kinsey G. Gimbel is the Library Resources Specialist at the Center for Creative Leadership Information Center. She is currently pursuing a master's degree in public administration from the University of North Carolina at Greensboro.

ACKNOWLEDGMENTS

The production of this book requires a team effort to gather, review, edit, check facts, check again, and assure the readability of an enormous amount of information. Many thanks to:

Joanne Ferguson for her discriminating eye and substantial patience as we submitted completed sections, added items, changed details, and changed again.

Vinnie Gordy for finding precious time to write annotations for the bibliography.

Karen Hardie for meticulous copyediting and double- or triple-checking every detail.

Carol Keck and **Peggy Cartner**, our Information Center colleagues who cheered us on and suggested wonderful sources of leadership materials to add to this collection.

Pete Scisco and **Kelly Lombardino** for planning the strategy around the book's concept, audience, and production.

Carol Slattery for contributing her teaching expertise to the bibliography annotations, particularly those about educational leadership, and for verifying and editing information about organizations.

And a heartfelt thanks to the many **leadership educators** who responded to our survey with their favorite classroom-tested resources.

INTRODUCTION

Leadership Resources: A Guide to Training and Development Tools is prepared by the Center for Creative Leadership for people who are responsible for leadership development, including HRD professionals, corporate trainers and consultants, educators, student activity directors, and organizers of youth and community leadership programs.

It contains descriptions of reading materials, instruments, exercises, videos, websites, organizations, and conferences. First published as part of *Leadership Education: A Source Book* in 1986, this book has been a forum for sharing favorite resources that enhance leadership lessons. As the field of leadership education grows, so do the number and quality of resources that support it.

Sources of Information

The resources described in this book were suggested by leadership educators who responded to our survey, Center for Creative Leadership staff, and a thorough search of library sources. These include:

- Databases such as PsychLit®, ABI/Inform®, Books In Print, ERIC, and Social Sciences Abstracts.
- Standard reference materials.
- Catalogs from book publishers, film distributors, and vendors of instruments and exercises.
- Tables of contents of more than 100 journals and newsletters and numerous reviews.
- Listserv discussion groups and Internet websites.

The editors examined hundreds of articles, books, instruments, exercises, and Internet resources. From the enormous amount of material found, we selected about sixty percent for inclusion in this book. As such, these resources provide a core, not an exhaustive list, of materials available.

Criteria for Selection

Annotations of each resource are descriptive rather than evaluative. However, an element of evaluation may be assumed as each item must meet certain criteria to be included in the book. Some criteria apply more to some sections than others. To be selected, items must:

- Be explicitly related to leadership theory or practice or be implicitly related to leadership learning. For instance, an article about 360-degree feedback is useful in understanding leadership development.
- Have a sound conceptual base and accurately reflect the concept that it claims to teach.
- Be clearly and interestingly presented.
- Conform to one of the book's subject headings.
- Include appropriate support materials for facilitators.
- Be easily available.

New Materials

Materials that appeared in previous editions but are still referenced and widely used remain in this edition. However, about one-half of the book is new. Dated items have been removed and replaced with more current information. The *New* tag above a title identifies an item that is new to this edition.

Changes in This Edition

In this edition we attempt to simplify the book's arrangement. With one exception, all sections are arranged in alphabetical order by title. The Bibliography is divided by very broad categories and arranged by author. For ease of subject browsing, every item is tagged with a subject descriptor and, as always, the subject index may be used as a detailed guide.

The Websites section was previously titled Internet Resources and contained information about listserv discussion groups. We have discovered that these groups often go dormant, get flamed, or stray off topic, so we have chosen to eliminate them. However, some enduring, moderated groups are available through the websites that are included in this section.

We have strengthened the focus of our selections and descriptions to meet the needs of HRD professionals and corporate trainers. There is additional information on executive education programs, trends, and support materials. We hope that leadership educators in academia and student affairs, as well as planners of community leadership programs, will also find these resources helpful.

The editors invite your suggestions for improving the next edition. We are especially interested in short film clips that illustrate a leadership lesson. Please send recommendations for format changes or favorite resources to:

Mary Schwartz, Research Librarian
Center for Creative Leadership
One Leadership Place
Post Office Box 26300
Greensboro, NC 27438-6300
Phone: (336) 286-4086
Fax: (336) 286-4087
E-mail: schwartzm@leaders.ccl.org

BIBLIOGRAPHY

The annotations in this bibliography describe textbooks, research reports, essays, program models, debates of existing theory or introduction of new theory, training materials, fiction, biographies, and self-development tools. They are organized by subject headings, then by the first author's last name using American Psychological Association-style citations.

The subject sections have been significantly changed for this edition, condensed from over thirty specific subjects to nine more general ones. We found a great deal of crossover—items that cover multiple subjects and don't fit neatly into the old sections. The new, simplified organization will help readers easily browse the entries for a good overview. Where we previously used the term Leadership Processes and Skills, we now use the term Leadership Competencies. We use this term in a general sense to describe the skills, attitudes, and behaviors practiced by competent leaders, although it is understood that competencies vary from one leadership situation to another. Below is an outline of what is included in each section.

Leadership Overviews
• Definitions of effective leadership
• Textbooks or introductions for new readers
• Future of leadership
• Quotations

Leadership in Context
• Community leadership
• Corporate – CEOs, boards, executives, managers, supervisors, selection, strategic leadership
• Educational leadership – schools, colleges, and universities
• Military leadership
• Political leadership – elected officials, heads of state
• Public administration – federal agencies, state, county, and city governments

Leadership in History, Biography, and Literature
• Profiles of past and present leaders
• Examples of leadership in classic works of literature

Leadership Competencies
• Communication, negotiation, and conflict management
• Creativity, vision, innovation, and change
• Decision making and problem solving
• Empowerment, collaboration, and shared leadership
• Ethics, values, spirit, and servant leadership
• Learning and experience
• Power, charisma, influence, and motivation

Research, Theories, and Models
• Overviews and comparisons of existing leadership theories
• Introductions of new models
• Reports on research projects

Training and Development
• Coaching, mentoring, and 360-degree feedback
• Leadership development programs and training models
• Program evaluations
• Resources for trainers
• Self-development and career development

Social, Global, and Diversity Issues
• Leadership that impacts society
• Diversity issues in the workplace
• Leadership issues specific to women and minorities
• Cross-cultural issues and leadership practices in non-U.S. cultures

Team Leadership
• Group dynamics
• Team building
• Self-managing teams

Organizational Leadership
• Organizational culture
• Learning organizations
• Systems in organizations

CONTENTS

LEADERSHIP OVERVIEWS

New
Albrecht, K. (1996). *Creating leaders for tomorrow*. Portland, OR: Productivity Press.

This one-hour reader, part of the Management Master Series, provides an introduction to leadership. Brief chapters discuss leadership at all organizational levels, leader capabilities, service leadership, shared meaning, and action learning. Albrecht recommends several steps for releasing one's leadership potential. Includes bibliographical references.
Subject(s): Future of leadership

Bass, B. M. (1990). *Bass and Stogdill's handbook of leadership: Theory, research, and managerial applications* (3rd ed.). New York: Free Press.

Intended for students of leadership, this edition of the handbook covers a broad range of leadership definitions, concepts, and theories. Shifts in the content and method of leadership studies resulted in new chapters on executive studies, leader/follower relations, and women in leadership. Also featured are chapters on personal traits, charisma, intellect, and political tactics. Seventy-five hundred references include some unpublished reports that offer fresh ideas. Includes bibliographical references, a glossary of terms, and author and subject indexes.
Subject(s): Leadership overview

Bennis, W. (1997). *Managing people is like herding cats*. Provo, UT: Executive Excellence Publishing.

Bennis says that cats, like people, "won't allow themselves to be herded. They may, however, be coaxed, cajoled, persuaded, adored, and gently led." Bennis applies these principles in the three sections of this book, which address the leadership crisis, what makes a leader, and leading change. The book's chapters originally appeared as articles in *Executive Excellence* and include such titles as "Leadership Pornography and Optional Ethics," "Four Competencies of Great Leaders," "Ten Traits of Dynamic Leaders," "Dealing with the Way Things Are," and "Winning and Losing." Includes index.
Subject(s): Leadership effectiveness

New
Bennis, W. (1999). **The end of leadership: Exemplary leadership is impossible without full inclusion, initiatives, and cooperation of followers.** *Organizational Dynamics, 28*(1), 71-80.

In this *Organizational Dynamics* issue on management in the 21st century Bennis describes the end of leadership as we know it. *TOPdown* leadership is making room for the *new leadership* that: practices the power of appreciation, reminds people of what's important, and sustains trust. In the new leadership the leader and the led are intimate allies. Bennis finds examples of new leadership in the corporate sector,

politics, history, popular media, and literature.
Subject(s): Future of leadership

Bennis, W. G. (1994). *On becoming a leader* (2nd ed.). Reading, MA: Addison-Wesley.

From the author of *Why Leaders Can't Lead*, this report examines the dynamics and difficulties in becoming a leader. Bennis presents the idea that every person has the capacity for leadership. Discussions with leaders in politics, business, and the arts include such topics as knowing oneself, knowing the world, moving through chaos, and creating change. Includes a bibliography and index.
Subject(s): Leadership effectiveness

Boone, L. E., & Bowen, D. D. (1987). *The great writings in management and organizational behavior* (2nd ed.). New York: Random House.

An anthology of seminal essays written by individuals whose works have become the cornerstones for contemporary management and organizational theory. From pioneers Weber, Fayol, and Follet, to second-generation contributors Mayo, Barnard, and Maslow, the text is chronological and gives the reader a historical point of reference. Part three, "The Paradigm Creators," includes McGregor's "The Human Side of Enterprise," "One More Time: How Do You Motivate Employees" by Herzberg, and Likert's "An Integrating Principle and an Overview." The final section, "Major Current Contributions," includes essays by McClelland, Vroom, and Schein. Includes indexes.
Subject(s): Leadership overview

Burns, J. M. (1978). *Leadership.* New York: Harper & Row.
The "dynamic reciprocity" theme is presented in a highly readable volume of leadership analysis. History, biographies, and a sociopsychological approach combine to provide a highly innovative study of the elements of leadership. Teaching and learning leadership are discussed in narrative format. This book could well be used as a follow-up text to the study of leadership theory. Includes bibliographical references and index.
Subject(s): Leadership overview

New
Campbell, D. P. (1999). **The complete inklings: Columns on leadership and creativity.** Greensboro, NC: Center for Creative Leadership.

In 1982 David Campbell began writing a column called "Inklings" for *Issues & Observations*, the Center for Creative Leadership's newsletter. This book contains all 61 of Campbell's columns, which over the years have addressed such wide-ranging topics as risk-taking, decision making, corporate taboos, travel, technology, health, and creativity.
Subject(s): Leadership overview, creativity

Clark, K. E., & Clark, M. B. (Eds.). (1990). *Measures of leadership.* West Orange, NJ: Leadership Library of America.

This is an introduction to a wide variety of measures of leadership, with detailed information on their characteristics and their validity. The book includes 29 research reports from well-known contributors to the study of leadership; they describe leaders' abilities, personalities, and behaviors. Included are an introduction that summarizes and interprets the findings and a report of the proceedings of the conference on which the book is based. Includes bibliographical references and index.
Subject(s): Leadership overview, assessment

Clark, K. E., & Clark, M. B. (1996). *Choosing to lead* (2nd rev. ed.). Greensboro, NC: Center for Creative Leadership.

Those who aspire to lead must be aware of the responsibilities involved and must make a conscious decision to commit. The Clarks call this "choosing to lead." The key is to identify and develop leaders who will choose to be dedicated. The authors review 15 years of theory and research to support this premise. They analyze existing leadership programs and discuss the role of experience and cultural differences in leadership development. Includes bibliographical references and index.
Subject(s): Leadership overview, commitment

Clark, K. E., Clark, M. B., & Campbell, D. P. (Eds.). (1992). *Impact of leadership.* Greensboro, NC: Center for Creative Leadership.

The impact of leadership was the subject of a 1991 conference sponsored by the Center for Creative Leadership. The 42 research papers in this book represent the range of discussion at that conference from the outcomes of good leadership to the ways of producing those effects. Other leadership impact issues include power, influence, authority, perceptions, stereotypes, customs, and expectations. Includes bibliographical references and index.
Subject(s): Leadership effectiveness

Cleveland, H. (1985). *The knowledge executive: Leadership in an information society.* New York: Dutton.

This book builds on the premise that more than half of all work now done in the United States is information work, and discusses the differences between information and other kinds of resources. Cleveland says that "tomorrow's leaders will be those with a taste for paradox, a talent for organizational ambiguity, and the capacity to hold new and dissimilar ideas comfortably in the managerial mind." Includes bibliographical references and index.
Subject(s): Leadership overview, ambiguity

New
Cottrell, D. (1997). *Birdies, pars, bogies: Leadership lessons from the links.* Dallas, TX: CornerStone Leadership Institute.

Leadership consultant and avid golfer David Cottrell suggests that there are leadership lessons to be learned on the golf course. In this brief book Cottrell walks readers through a round of 18 holes and 44 lessons. For instance, advice from his caddy reminds him that a good leader listens to employees and has the courage to act on others' suggestions. Cottrell also comments on keeping cool under pressure, staying focused on a goal, having the courage to take risks, and continually developing.
Subject(s): Leadership effectiveness

New
Covey, S. R., Merrill, A. R., & Jones, D. (1998). *The nature of leadership.* Salt Lake City, UT: Franklin Covey.

In leadership, as in nature, there are fundamental principles. This book combines the power of natural beauty and the wisdom of thought leaders to prove that point. Stunning photographs by Roger Merrill and Dewitt Jones dramatically illustrate leadership principles such as interdependence, change, growth, diversity, and inspiration. Jones says, "From the time I first picked up a camera, I have celebrated nature through my lens. And nature has responded by teaching me some extraordinary lessons."
Subject(s): Leadership overview, nature, photographs

Culp, K., & Cox, K. J. (1997). **Leadership styles for the new millennium: Creating new paradigms.** *Journal of Leadership Studies, 4*(1), 3-17.

This literature review provides an overview of both the study of leadership and of the development of leadership practices throughout history. The authors profile the different ways scholars have defined leadership, explain different theories of how leadership is developed, and present a table of the evolution of leadership, from Genghis Khan to Ronald Reagan. Also included is a table showing the effects of time and environment on leadership styles. Seven leadership paradigms are then presented as alternative styles of leadership that may arise in the next century: administrative, catalytic, collegial, humanitarian/activist, innovative, religious, and visionary. Includes references.
Subject(s): Leadership overview

New
Daft, R. L. (1999). *Leadership: Theory and practice.* New York: Dryden Press.

This textbook for undergraduate students covers a broad range of leadership topics. Chapters focus on: the differences between management and leadership; traits, behaviors, and relationships; vision and strategic direction; communication; culture and values; teams; learning organizations; and more. Daft offers examples of leadership in practice, such as Phil Jackson's Chicago Bulls practicing selfless team leadership and the love-inspired leadership that built the Hard Rock Café. Each chapter includes a theoretical overview, synopses of relevant readings, discussion questions, a self-test, and a case study. Includes bibliographical references and name, company, and subject indexes.
Subject(s): Leadership overview, textbook

Drucker, P. F., Dyson, E., Handy, C., Saffo, P., & Senge, P. M. (1997). **Looking ahead: Implications of the present.** *Harvard Business Review, 75*(5), 18-32.

To commemorate the 75th anniversary of *Harvard Business Review* five noted business writers—Peter Drucker, Esther Dyson, Charles Handy, Paul Saffo, and Peter Senge—were asked to describe the problems and challenges they see for executives in the next century. Drucker discusses the demographic changes taking place that will result in the "collective suicide" of the world's developed nations and a rapid rise in the power of current Third World countries. Dyson says that the Internet has narrowed the boundaries of what can be held private and shrunk the distance between a company and its employees and customers. She says companies must learn to accept and use the "involuntary feedback" the Internet allows. Handy describes a model for a "citizen contract" in which corporations are not considered the property of stockholders but communities of common purpose. Saffo addresses the need for new technology that not does not simply produce more information but helps us make sense of it. Finally, Senge discusses the need to abandon hierarchical leadership and develop a community of leaders through research, capacity building, and practice.
Subject(s): Future of leadership

Du Brin, A. J. (1995). *Leadership: Research, findings, practice, and skills.* Boston: Houghton Mifflin.

This textbook is intended for use in undergraduate and graduate leadership courses in business management or public administration. It reviews basic leadership theories, emphasizes skill development, and suggests effective leadership practices. Each chapter includes self-assessments, case studies, skill-development exercises, and questions to initiate discussions.
Subject(s): Leadership overview, textbook

New
Fairholm, G. W. (1998). *Perspectives on leadership: From the science of management to its spiritual heart.* Westport, CT: Quorum Books.

Fairholm identifies five "virtual environments" or ways of thinking about leadership: leadership as management, leadership as excellence, values leadership, trust leadership, and spiritual leadership. This book addresses the theoretical and practical ramifications of these perspectives, providing a historical background and examples of everyday applications for each. Includes bibliographical references and index.
Subject(s): Leadership overview

Farson, R. E. (1996). *Management of the absurd: Paradoxes in leadership.* New York: Simon & Schuster.

Farson draws on his experience as a psychologist, naval officer, and CEO to examine the dilemmas faced every day by managers and leaders. Farson's long-time collaboration with famed psychologist Carl Rogers taught him that life is difficult, that human relations are complex, and that for every action there is an opposite reaction. He expects readers to be disturbed by the paradoxes here, but hopes that disagreement will lead to thought and discussion. The paradoxes include: effective managers are not in control, people we think need changing are pretty good the way they are, we learn not from our failures but from our successes, and individuals are very fragile.
Subject(s): Leadership effectiveness

Fitton, R. A. (Ed.). (1997). *Leadership: Quotations from the world's greatest motivators.* Boulder, CO: Westview Press.

Fitton has compiled memorable words spoken by leaders and about leadership. Statesmen, military leaders, executives, philosophers, and poets from ancient history through the present day are represented. For example, Napoleon Bonaparte said, "A leader is a dealer in hope." Quotations are arranged by subject and indexed by author for easy access. Subjects include: adversity, boldness, character, duty, humor, mistakes, physical presence, truth, and victory. This book is a handy reference for writers, researchers, speakers, or leaders who practice reflection.
Subject(s): Quotations

Gardner, H., & Laskin, E. (1995). *Leading minds: An anatomy of leadership.* New York: BasicBooks.

Gardner's research of the human brain and his passion for history and current events led to this study of the mind of the leader. He questions which type of leadership has greater influence, the direct leadership of a president or prime minister or the indirect leadership of a creative mind. For example, during World War II, were Franklin Delano Roosevelt's and Winston Churchill's creation of an allied force more influential than Albert Einstein's theory of nuclear reaction? Gardner examines other great minds in politics, religion, anthropology, business, and the military. Includes bibliographical references and index.
Subject(s): Leadership effectiveness

New
Grint, K. (Ed.). (1997). *Leadership: Classical, contemporary, and critical approaches.* Oxford, England: Oxford University Press.

This collection of writings uses five different perspectives to answer the question, "What is leadership?" Classical leadership is addressed by writers including Plato and Machiavelli, while chapters by Chester Barnard and R. M. Stogdill describe traditional leadership. The section on modern leadership includes articles on democratic leadership and the glass ceiling, and the mythical leadership section includes a chapter by Manfred Kets de Vries. Finally, alternative leadership is addressed with chapters on Martin Luther King, Jr., and the feminist and post-modernist construction of leadership. Includes bibliographical references and index.
Subject(s): Leadership lessons in literature

New
Gronn, P. (1999). **Substituting for leadership: The neglected role of the leadership couple.** *Leadership Quarterly, 10*(1), 41-62.

This article describes the concept of a leadership couple, in which two people share leadership of a group or organization. Like partners in a marriage, a leadership couple balances between trust and mutual dependence. Their values must align and temperaments must blend. Labor is divided according to expertise so that each complements the other. Each partner gives the other enough space to exercise responsibilities. Each understands that one's personal accountability reflects on the other. The case of Timbertop, a school in Australia, tells the story of one successful leadership couple. Includes bibliographical references.
Subject(s): Substitutes-for-Leadership Theory

New
Handy, C. (1999). *Waiting for the mountain to move: Reflections of work and life.* San Francisco: Jossey-Bass.

Handy shares his reflections on the meaning of life and work in 65 essays taken from his "Thought for the Day" segment on BBC's radio show *Today.* Handy encourages listeners and readers to think holistically about life, work, and spirit. A theme of active reflection—alignment of one's being with one's doing—runs throughout the book.
Subject(s): Leadership reflections

New
Hesselbein, F., & Cohen, P. M. (Eds.). (1999). *Leader to leader: Enduring insights on leadership from the Drucker Foundation's award-winning journal.* San Francisco: Jossey-Bass.

This collection of articles from the journal *Leader to Leader* is divided into seven sections: on leaders and leadership, leading innovation and transformation, leadership in the new information economy, competitive strategy in a global economy, leading for high performance, building great teams, and leadership across the sectors. Contributors include John P. Kotter, Sally Helgesen, Peter Drucker, Margaret Wheatley, Warren Bennis, Stephen Covey, and Max De Pree. Includes index.
Subject(s): Leadership overview

Hesselbein, F., Goldsmith, M., & Beckhard, R. (Eds.). (1996). *The leader of the future: New visions, strategies, and practices for the next era.* San Francisco: Jossey-Bass.

This is a collection of original essays written by the most recognized names in the field of leadership. Future visions of our schools, our jobs, and our society are described in works by: Peter Senge, "Leading Learning Organizations: The Bold, the Powerful, and the Invisible"; Stephen Covey, "Three Roles for the Leader in the New Paradigm"; James Kouzes and Barry Posner, "Seven Lessons for Leading the Voyage to the Future"; David Noer, "A Recipe for Glue"; and many others. The Drucker Foundation supported the creation of this

book, which leads off with a foreword by Peter Drucker. Includes an index.
Subject(s): Future of leadership

New
Hesselbein, F., Goldsmith, M., & Somerville, I. (1999). *Leading beyond the walls.* San Francisco: Jossey-Bass.

This collection of writings addresses how leaders can develop and maintain relationships both within and outside their organizations, a necessary skill in today's fast-paced global market. The articles are divided into four sections: New Strategies for a World Without Walls, Transforming Organizations for New Realities, The New Requirements of Leadership, and Leading the Larger Community. Contributors include Peter Senge, Sally Helgesen, Stephen Covey, William Bridges, Jim Belasco, and Peter Drucker. Includes index.
Subject(s): Leadership effectiveness

Hitt, W. D. (Ed.). (1992). *Thoughts on leadership: A treasury of quotations.* Columbus, OH: Battelle Press.

This anthology of quotations supports the theory that leaders are fully functioning persons. In a generic leadership model, 25 competencies comprise five leadership dimensions: reasoning, coping, knowing, believing, and being. Ideas regarding creative thinking, excellence, integrity, knowing the organization, visioning, team-building, valuing, responsibility, and courage are capsulized in the words of original authors. Quotations are indexed by author and by subject. Includes bibliographical references.
Subject(s): Quotations

Hogan, R., Curphy, G. J., & Hogan, J. (1994). **What we know about leadership: Effectiveness and personality.** *American Psychologist, 49*(6), 493-504.

This article reviews current literature and contemporary definitions of leadership. The major themes identified are: the link between personality and leadership, what leaders do, teamwork, if leadership really matters, how leaders are chosen, and leadership failures. The appendix describes the "Big Five Dimensions of Personality" that are critical to leadership: 1) surgency—social inclination and assertiveness, 2) emotional stability, 3) conscientiousness, 4) agreeableness, and 5) intellectance—imagination, culture, and curiosity. Includes bibliographical references.
Subject(s): Leadership effectiveness, personality

New
Jones, P. (1998). **The new business age: Delivering exceptional performance.** *Monash Mt. Eliza Business Review, 1*(2), 54-61.

Jones states that society's transition from Industrial Age to Information Age necessitates a transition in performance management. She offers a performance prism model to demonstrate the complexity of this transition. At the base of the prism is the context for organizational management, which includes culture, environment, intent, and capability. The prism's four sides represent: 1) a management style that is enabling and inspirational, 2) relationships, 3) integrated systems, and 4) successful teams. Jones describes how the prism works in several companies. Includes bibliographical references.

Subject(s): Future of leadership

Kellerman, B. (Ed.). (1984). *Leadership: Multidisciplinary perspectives.* Englewood Cliffs, NJ: Prentice Hall.

This book represents cooperative work in leadership studies. It provides a comprehensive range of perspectives on the interactions between those labeled leaders and those labeled followers. It serves as both an introduction to the subject and as a forum for related ideas that may be expected to stimulate more advanced discussion and study. The volume consists of a series of original essays by scholars from different disciplines, each considering leadership issues. Includes bibliographical references and index.

Subject(s): Leadership overview

New
Kellerman, B. (1999). *Reinventing leadership: Making the connection between politics and business.* Albany: State University of New York Press.

Kellerman argues that although business leadership and political leadership are generally addressed separately, they are actually similar and intertwined processes. She offers a historical perspective, tracing how the different worlds of politics and business have moved closer together since the 1950s until today they are "joined at the hip." Kellerman also describes the barriers of technology, race, class, and power that continue to separate the two groups of leaders. She concludes that business and political leaders must learn to work together in order to solve the problems facing them both. Includes index.

Subject(s): Leadership effectiveness, corporate leadership, political leadership

Kets de Vries, M. F. R. (1993). *Leaders, fools, and impostors: Essays on the psychology of leadership.* San Francisco: Jossey-Bass.

From a psychoanalytic viewpoint Kets de Vries offers a collection of essays on the leader-follower relationship. Beginning in childhood we all seek leaders in life. When called upon to lead we often fall into traps. Examples of successful and failed leaders in history, literature, the arts, and business help to define several leader types. Mirroring, narcissism, disengagement, and emotional illiteracy are among the leadership pitfalls to avoid. Includes bibliographical references and index.

Subject(s): Psychology of leadership, negative views of leadership

New
Klein, E. B., Gabelnick, F., & Herr, P. (Eds.). (1998). *The psychodynamics of leadership.* Madison, CT: Psychosocial Press.

Essays discuss the evolving nature of the new workplace in which organizations are complex, ever changing, and widely dispersed systems. Employment has become disconnected and impersonal. The authors suggest that leaders of the near future will be project- or team-oriented rather than company-oriented and will take personal responsibility for tasks, performance, and relationships. Their leadership styles will necessarily be collaborative, requiring sensitivity and psychological maturity. They call this a psychodynamic approach that is suitable for open systems that include learning, risk, creativity, and change. Seven essays discuss organizational theory and visions of leadership. Seven chapters address transformational leaders, their vulnerability, diversity, and connection. Includes bibliographical references and indexes.

Subject(s): Psychology of leadership

New
Komives, S. R., Lucas, N., & McMahon, T. R. (1998). *Exploring leadership: For college students who want to make a difference.* San Francisco: Jossey-Bass.

This source advocates relationships as the key to leadership. Komives proposes the idea that leadership, like many other skills, needs to be learned and practiced. Intended mainly for students, this four-part book uses an educational and psychological perspective to first enhance self-awareness before exploring relationships with others. This is accomplished through the *Relational Leadership Model,* as well as an exploration of leadership evolution. The second part of the source delves into self-exploration and relationships with others, focusing on character, interaction, and learning. Leadership settings and complex organizations are profiled in the following part with a focus on collaborative processes. Finally, the book concludes with a section relating to the importance of group and individual renewal. Includes bibliographical references and index.

Subject(s): Leadership effectiveness

New
Kotter, J. P. (1999). *John P. Kotter on what leaders really do.* Boston: Harvard Business School Press.

This collection of Kotter's work from the *Harvard Business Review* contains articles published from 1977 to 1995, including "Leading Change" and "Managing Your Boss." In the introduction written for this book Kotter describes his "ten observations about managerial behavior" and how changes in the workforce are affecting the nature of management. Includes index.

Subject(s): Leadership overview

Kouzes, J. M., & Posner, B. Z. (1995). *The leadership challenge: How to keep getting extraordinary things done in organizations* (2nd ed.). San Francisco: Jossey-Bass.

In this revision of the popular 1987 work Kouzes and Posner continue to explore the practices and commitments of exemplary leaders. Chapters include: "Confronting the Status Quo," "Learning from Mistakes and Successes," "Inspiring a Shared Vision," "Sharing Power and Information," and "Building a Commitment to Action." The work is research-based, with data originating from the authors' collaborative leadership project begun in 1983 and resulting in the instrument, *The Leadership Practices Inventory*. Includes bibliographical references and index.
Subject(s): Leadership effectiveness

New
Kouzes, J. M., & Posner, B. Z. (1999). *Encouraging the heart: A leader's guide to rewarding and recognizing others.* San Francisco: Jossey-Bass.

Kouzes and Posner say that motivating people to higher standards of performance is at "the heart of effective leadership," and they identify "Seven Essentials of Encouraging" that leaders can use to energize and recognize people: 1) set clear standards, 2) expect the best, 3) pay attention, 4) personalize recognition, 5) tell the story, 6) celebrate together, and 7) set the example. The book's final chapter lists "150 Ways to Encourage the Heart," including everything from clarifying organizational values to attending clown school. Includes index.
Subject(s): Leadership effectiveness, motivation

New
Krass, P. (Ed.). (1998). *The book of leadership wisdom: Classic writings by legendary business leaders.* New York: Wiley.

This collection includes speeches and essays by business leaders including Katherine Graham, Ross Perot, J. Paul Getty, Bill Gates, Andrew Carnegie, Michael Eisner, Henry Ford, William Randolph Hearst, and Ray Kroc. The writings are divided into sections addressing necessary leadership qualities, dealing with adversity, perspectives on labor, company culture, motivators and mentors, and leading revolution. Includes index.
Subject(s): Leadership overview

New
Kurtzman, J. (Ed.). (1998). *Thought leaders: Insights on the future of business.* San Francisco: Jossey-Bass.

This is a collection of interviews that were originally printed in the quarterly business journal *Strategy & Business*. Selected for inclusion in this book are interviews with thought leaders who have a global perspective and whose ideas about business strategy, change, and new social contracts in the workplace are shaping the future of business. Among them are the scholars Charles Handy, professor at London Business School; Warren Bennis, professor at the

University of Southern California; John Kao, professor at Harvard Business School; and C. K. Prahalad, professor at the University of Michigan. Includes index.
Subject(s): Future of leadership, corporate leadership

New
Lissack, M., & Roos, J. (1999). *The next common sense: Mastering corporate complexity through coherence.* London: Nicholas Brealey.

Lissack and Roos say that the business practices of the past were designed to work in a complicated business world made up of many independent units. But these practices don't work in today's complex environment, which is characterized by interwoven and interconnected events. This book uses the chaos and complexity theories to describe how organizations can reach coherence, a state of alignment of purpose and action that helps make sense of a complex world. The authors offer a five-step plan for mastering complexity: 1) identify yourself and your goals, 2) use the right language, 3) create the right context, 4) turn people loose and then get out of their way, and 5) use communication that works. Includes index.
Subject(s): Future of leadership, complexity, chaos

Nahavandi, A. (1997). *The art and science of leadership.* Upper Saddle River, NJ: Prentice Hall.

This textbook presents a broad review of leadership not limited to business organizations. The author's basic assumption is that leadership can be learned, focusing this book on practical application. He looks at various definitions of leadership and effectiveness, the wave of organizational change in recent years, individual attributes, the link between power and leadership, contingency theories, and leadership training and development. Each chapter contains tables and models, discussion questions, and exercises. Includes bibliographical references and index.
Subject(s): Leadership overview, textbook

New
O'Toole, J. (1999). *Leadership A to Z.* San Francisco: Jossey-Bass.

This book contains 92 brief entries, arranged alphabetically, that address topics and behaviors essential to leadership. O'Toole says that, taken together, the entries "identify clearly what leaders need to do in order to create high-performing, self-renewing organizations." Entries offer examples from business, literature, and politics and include bibliographical references. Subjects covered include commitment, ego, inequality, obsession, power, resilience, sound bites, and vision.
Subject(s): Leadership overview

Reckmeyer, W. (Ed.). (1995). *Leadership readings.* Stanford, CA: American Leadership Forum.

This volume includes the essays and writings of some of the world's foremost thinkers on leadership. Authors include

Stephen Covey, *The Seven Habits of Highly Effective People* (1989); John Gardner, *On Leadership* (1990); Robert Greenleaf, *The Servant as Leader* (1990); Barbara Kellerman, *Leadership for a Shrinking Planet* (1991); Deborah Tannen, *You Just Don't Understand* (1990); Peter Vaill, *Managing as a Performing Art* (1989); and Margaret Wheatley, *Leadership and the New Science* (1992). The collection also includes Martin Luther King's *I Have a Dream* speech (1963) and his *Letter from a Birmingham Jail* (1963).
Subject(s): Leadership overview

Rost, J. C. (1991). *Leadership for the twenty-first century.* New York: Praeger.

A critique of 150 writings on leadership since 1930, this book explores old definitions of leadership and proposes a new one. Fundamental concepts of great-man theories, facilitators, psychological traits, behavior, situation, and excellence are criticized for oversimplifying a complex set of relationships. Rost suggests that a study of followership will help scholars, trainers, and practitioners to better understand leader/follower relationships. Includes bibliographical references and index.
Subject(s): Leadership overview

Safire, W., & Safire, L. (Eds.). (1990). *Leadership.* New York: Simon & Schuster.

This is a collection of leadership quotations from ancient Greek and Chinese philosophers, former and current politicians, executives, and sports heroes. The editors suggest searching for the verb or action in each bit of wit and wisdom. Quotations are arranged by leadership traits such as excellence, intelligence, loyalty, and strength. Names of leaders quoted are indexed.
Subject(s): Quotations

New
Sayles, L. R. (1999). *Managerial Behavior and a journey through time. Leadership Quarterly, 10*(1), 7-11.

Sayles tells of the academic and personal context that led to his research for the seminal book, *Managerial Behavior* (1964). Sayles credits his colleagues at MIT and the work of Kurt Lewin to help him understand the complexities of management relationships as they existed in the 1960s. Jerry Hunt, Richard Osborn, Rosemary Stewart, and Blake Ashforth comment on the book's enduring themes and Sayles's evolving leadership theories throughout his career (pp. 1, 13-24). Includes bibliographical references.
Subject(s): Leadership overview

New
Shelton, K. (Ed.). (1997). *A new paradigm of leadership: Visions of excellence for 21st century organizations.* Provo, UT: Executive Excellence.

Shelton discusses a management shift toward empowerment driven by competition, change, and employee expectations. He edits this collection of information from renowned leaders and executives sharing their thoughts concerning a new paradigm of leadership. Divided into four sections, this source contains individually authored chapters depicting leadership for the 21st century and delving into such topics as change, leadership qualities, the ability to be both a leader and a follower, and the soul of leadership. Leaders see the changing times with an increase in globalization and a decrease of hierarchies. Servant leadership, credibility, and entrepreneurial spirit are among the leadership qualities perceived as necessary. Leaders also advise adopting new roles for effective management in emerging team environments. Finally, spiritual connections between leaders and employees are recommended to obtain inspirational leadership.
Subject(s): Future of leadership

Shepard, I. S., Farmer, R. F., & Counts, G. E. (1997). **Leadership definitions and theorists: Do practitioners and professors agree?** *Journal of Leadership Studies, 4*(1), 26-45.

Countless definitions of leadership exist. The authors of this study identified 11 definitions, developed by Fiedler, Zaleznik, Rost, Sergiovanni, Bennis, Burns, Nicoll, Hersey and Blanchard, Covey, and Bates, and then asked professors and practitioners of leadership programs whether or not they agreed with the definitions. Five tables present the results, but ultimately the authors concluded that no one definition has widespread support. The authors argue that developing an accepted definition of leadership within a school or organization is essential, or serious conflicts can emerge over hiring, policy development, and policy implementation. Includes references.
Subject(s): Leadership overview

Shriberg, A., Lloyd, C., Shriberg, D. L., & Williamson, M. L. (1997). *Practicing leadership: Principles and applications.* New York: Wiley.

This textbook uses the metaphor of a journey to move students through the evolution of leadership theory. The technique of parable is woven throughout the text to illustrate the journey and leadership development of fictional college students. Each chapter employs a variety of teaching tools: book summaries, questions to spark discussion, cases, exercises, and biographical sketches of people who exemplify one leadership style. The subjects of globalism and diversity are integrated throughout the book to affirm their importance throughout all theories, attributes, and applications. Some chapters are: "Pre-Industrial Paradigms of Leadership," "The Disciplinary Roots of Leadership," "Modern Leadership Theories," and "The Hero's Journey: A New Leadership Model." Includes bibliographical references and index.
Subject(s): Leadership overview, textbook

Tulgan, B. (1995). *Managing Generation X: How to bring out the best in young talent.* Santa Monica, CA: Merritt Publishing.

A Generation X'er himself, Tulgan interviewed over 100 up-and-coming workers born between 1963 and 1981 to find out

if the "slacker" stereotypes are true and to determine how managers can best handle this new population of workers. Quotes from his subjects on issues such as technology, corporate culture, career security, and their best and worst managers fill the book. Tulgan shares a list of recommendations for managers who supervise X'ers. Includes index.
Subject(s): Leadership effectiveness, Generation X

Ulmer, W. F. (1997). *Inside view: A leader's observations on leadership.* Greensboro, NC: Center for Creative Leadership.

Ulmer, a retired U.S. Army three-star general and former president of the Center for Creative Leadership, shares his insight on the subject of leadership. This book is a compilation of *Inside View* columns that Ulmer wrote for CCL's quarterly newsletter *Issues & Observations* and an adapted essay written for the Kellogg Leadership Studies Project. Ulmer addresses the difficulty of defining leadership, the differences between military officers and civilian leaders, current selection and promotion systems, assessment, change, and his passion—learning. Includes bibliographical references.
Subject(s): Leadership reflections

New
Vaill, P. B. (1998). *Spirited leading and learning: Process wisdom for a new age.* San Francisco: Jossey-Bass.

This collection of writings by Peter Vaill contains both previously published essays and new material, including "The Purposing of High-performing Systems," "The Learning Challenges of Leadership," and "Executive Development as Spiritual Development." The essays are divided into four sections: Process Wisdom for a New Age, Leading, Learning, and Spirit. Includes bibliographical references and index.
Subject(s): Leadership overview

New
Vecchio, R. P. (Ed.). (1997). *Leadership: Understanding the dynamics of power and influence in organizations.* South Bend, IN: University of Notre Dame Press.

This six-part text for management students and executive MBA candidates discusses key theories in the management field. The book introduces the concept of leadership in its true form, dispelling the myths and acknowledging the ambiguity. Power, politics, and influence are discussed in terms of game playing and leader-subordinate influence. One chapter is devoted to the dysfunctions of leadership including self-destructive or narcissist leaders. The predominant models of leadership are reviewed and updated in part four of the text. This section delves into the path-goal theory as well as managerial intelligence, transformational and situational leadership, and the contingency model. The following section offers alternative views of leadership such as self-managing work teams, superleadership, and servant leadership. The final chapter explores leadership in a time of continuous change. Includes bibliographical references.
Subject(s): Leadership overview, textbook

Wells, S. (1997). *From sage to artisan: The nine roles of the value-driven leader.* Palo Alto, CA: Davies-Black.

"Leadership opportunities are inevitably embedded in the context of management issues." Wells argues that no distinction should exist between managers and leaders, and describes nine roles in which the leadership process intersects with the focused responsibilities of a manager—Sage, Visionary, Magician, Globalist, Mentor, Ally, Sovereign, Guide, and Artisan. Both a self-scoring role assessment and a free mail-in assessment are included with the book. The chapter on each role includes tables of ways to identify a person's role, tips for learning the skills of a specific role, and warning signs to indicate if you have gone overboard in a role. Includes bibliographical references and index.
Subject(s): Leadership overview

Wheatley, M. J. (1992). *Leadership and the new science: Learning about organization from an orderly universe.* San Francisco: Berrett-Koehler.

How does "new science"—revolutionary discoveries in quantum physics, chaos theory, and molecular biology—affect the fundamental issues of organizing work, people, and life? Wheatley suggests we tear down 17th-century Newtonian thinking about our universe and adopt new perspectives from our natural world. A new perspective can help to find order in a chaotic world; differentiate order from control; create more participative, open, and adaptive organizations; and reconcile individual autonomy and organizational control. Includes bibliographical references and index.
Subject(s): Scientific perspective, chaos

White, R. P. (1997). **Seekers and scalers: The future leaders.** *Training & Development, 51*(1), 20-24.

White dismisses the idea that leadership can be learned by following a set of simple steps, arguing instead that leadership and innovation come from "difficult learning," or searching for knowledge without having a specific goal or "right answer" in mind. White says that children are the best role models for leaders because they are not afraid of difficult learning. He also offers a whimsical scale for assessing leadership and learning potential, with couch potatoes on the bottom, passengers in the middle, and explorers on top.
Subject(s): Future of leadership

Wren, J. T. (Ed.). (1995). *The leader's companion: Insights on leadership through the ages.* New York: Free Press.

This is a collection of the principal works on leadership, which are assigned readings in the Foundations course at the Jepson School of Leadership Studies at the University of Richmond. Included are excerpts from the classic writings of James MacGregor Burns, Robert Greenleaf, Bernard Bass, Plato, Ann Morrison, Geerte Hofstede, John Gardner, Warren Bennis, and many others. Wren's selection and organization of these readings supports his premise that leadership is central to the human condition, that leadership is timeless and current—not a fad, and that leadership should be understood

and practiced by all—not by a privileged few. Includes bibliographical references and index.
Subject(s): Leadership overview

New
Yukl, G. (1999). **An evaluative essay on current conceptions of effective leadership.** *European Journal of Work and Organizational Psychology*, *8*(10), 33-48.

Theories of transformational and charismatic leadership have flourished in the last 20 years, but these theories often have serious conceptual flaws such as reliance on simplistic two-factor models, a focus on dyadic processes, and an overuse of weak measurement techniques. Yukl describes an exploratory study he did to determine whether various two-factor theories held up when they were tested together. He administered a survey covering a wide range of leadership behaviors explained by these popular theories to over 300 workers, and found that none of the dyadic models was adequate to explain the variance in findings. Yukl concludes by encouraging readers to acknowledge the value of new leadership theories but not to overrate their importance. Includes bibliographical references.
Subject(s): Leadership effectiveness

LEADERSHIP IN CONTEXT

Ashbaugh, C. R., & Kasten, K. L. (1995). *Educational leadership: Case studies for reflective practice* (2nd ed.). White Plains, NY: Longman.

This book presents 62 case studies based on educational leaders who have experienced value conflicts and controversies due to differences in beliefs and attitudes. The cases are written for graduate students who are planning administrative careers in levels from kindergarten through high school. The authors give procedures for analyzing and reflecting on situations dealing with culture, program design, resources, and politics. The importance of values in decision making is stressed, along with the idea that educational administration can be never be value-free. Includes bibliographical references and index.
Subject(s): Educational leadership

New
Austin, J. E. (1998). **Business leadership lessons from the Cleveland turnaround.** *California Management Review*, *41*(1), 86-106.

Between 1978 and 1996 the city of Cleveland rose from the bankrupt "mistake on the lake" to a thriving, prosperous city. This article describes how Cleveland Tomorrow, an organization of local CEOs, contributed to the city's revival and argues that urban problems cannot be solved without the involvement of business leaders. Four central questions are considered: What is the role of business leaders in urban revitalization? How can these leaders organize themselves for action? What are the key factors in formulating a community development strategy? And how can this strategy be implemented? Austin emphasizes the importance of business leaders' going beyond just philanthropy and becoming actively involved in city issues, and in institutionalizing the community building process to ensure the involvement of future leaders. Includes bibliographical references.
Subject(s): Community leadership

Bahrami, H., & Evans, S. (1997). **Human resource leadership in knowledge-based entities: Shaping the context of work.** *Human Resource Management*, *36*(1), 23-28.

A growing number of companies today are knowledge-based entities, organizations characterized by intensity, novelty, and collaborative teamwork. What role can HR play in these organizations? This article argues that HR should take an active leadership role based on a new model for HR teams. The model identifies four roles HR needs to play in these knowledge-based entities: 1) the "orgitecht" who leads organizational design, 2) the vendor who handles HR transactions, 3) the hub who acts as an information base, and 4) the glue who handles communications and executive development.
Subject(s): Human resources managers

Baldwin, J. N. (1996). **The promotion record of the United States Army: Glass ceilings in the officer corps.** *Public Administration Review*, *56*(2), 199-206.

Baldwin studied the promotion records of over 123,000 Army officers between 1980 and 1993 and compared the promotion rates of female and minority officers with those of male and white officers. He found that "those promoted and considered for promotion in the Army are disproportionately men and Caucasian." Relative to the Army's "Uniform Guidelines on Employee Selection Procedures," the promotion rates are respectable, but when compared to other public agencies the Army's record is not good. Baldwin attributes the inequality in promotion not only to gender and race issues but to the interactions of "socioeconomic, educational, cultural, and institutional factors."
Subject(s): Men as military leaders, women as military leaders

New
Beck, L. G. (1999). **Metaphors of educational community: An analysis of the images that reflect and influence scholarship and practice.** *Educational Administration Quarterly*, *35*(1), 13-45.

Because of the debates concerning the meaning of community in educational settings, Beck advocates an expansion of the understanding of this term. The discussion begins with a historical perspective of community in education and describes the dilemmas resulting from the attempt to attach one meaning of community. Citing work from several cognitive scientists, Beck argues that embracing multiple metaphors of community will enhance learning environments and future research. This article describes the types of scholarship that have provided the various meanings of community, analyzes the language, and concludes with a discussion of implications. Includes bibliographical references.
Subject(s): Educational leadership

Bennis, W., & Townsend, R. (1995). *Reinventing leadership: Strategies to empower the organization.* New York: William Morrow.

This book is for companies seeking new leadership styles to suit their new downsized status. It probes the old command-and-control style of leadership that no longer works, and suggests ways to create guiding visions and to empower employees. Bennis and Townsend present their ideas in dialogue form and offer dialogue starters at the end of each section to stimulate new ideas. There are role-playing dialogues, partner analyses, debate questions, what-if discussions, management evaluations, and group dialogues. At the end of the book a 21-day planner helps readers to transfer new learnings into practical application.
Subject(s): Corporate leadership, empowerment

Beyle, T. L. (1995). **Enhancing executive leadership in the states.** *State and Local Government Review*, 27(1), 18-35.

Beyle explains three decades of reform in state governments that has led to increased gubernatorial authority—greater power to make appointments in executive positions, veto legislation, and write state budgets. Two polls, one of constituents and one of political scientists and journalists, report on the job performance of 50 governors serving in the summer of 1994. When the numbers were correlated six governors received exceptionally high ratings and five received very low ratings. Beyle analyzes the factors that determine good job performance at this level: the institutional powers of governorship in a given state; a governor's personal power; and how a governor works with administrators, the state legislature, and the media. Includes bibliographical references.
Subject(s): Governors

Bogue, E. G. (1994). *Leadership by design: Strengthening integrity in higher education.* San Francisco: Jossey-Bass.

Bogue's belief is "that the principal challenge to leadership effectiveness in colleges and universities is more than a challenge of intellect—to acquire and use good ideas. It is a challenge of character—to learn and apply constructive ideals." An aspect of his thesis is that leaders are designers. Each chapter of the book centers on a design ideal: honor, dignity, curiosity, candor, compassion, courage, excellence, and service. Bogue also believes that effective leadership is a "conceptual, moral, and performing art form—one in which ideas and ideals are tested, integrated, and utilized in the act, the performance." His audience is academic administrators, mentors for collegiate leaders, those selecting collegiate leaders, and leaders in corporate and civic sectors. Includes bibliography and index.
Subject(s): Leadership in higher education, integrity

Bolman, L. G., & Deal, T. E. (1994). *Becoming a teacher leader: From isolation to collaboration.* Thousand Oaks, CA: Corwin Press.

Bolman and Deal, authors of *Reframing Organizations: Artistry, Choice and Leadership* (1991), expand their theory of reframing into the field of education. They believe that new and veteran teachers can become more successful when they divide their classroom perspectives into four frames: structural, human resource, political, and symbolic. Using several frames helps a teacher view a situation from different angles and find new ways to deal with issues of power or relationships. For example, teachers can use the human resource frame to bond with troublesome students or balance work and family responsibilities. They can use the political frame to view conflict as a source of energy and renewal rather than a source of stress. Includes bibliographical references.
Subject(s): Teacher as leader

New
Bowen, W. G., & Shapiro, H. T. (1998). *Universities and their leadership.* Princeton, NJ: Princeton University Press.

This anthology consists of essays originally presented at the Princeton Conference on Higher Education in March 1996. The essays address four general topics: the university overall, the presidency, the faculty, and the planning and oversight of science. The section on the university overall contains writings on higher education and accountability and on critics of universities. The presidency is discussed in two essays reviewing the history of the position in the United States. The third section, on the faculty, includes chapters on professional conduct of faculty, how universities can teach professional ethics, and European universities in the era of "mass higher education." Finally, essays on the planning and oversight of science discuss new policies science has demanded in universities and the growth of scientific enterprises. Includes index.
Subject(s): Leadership in higher education

New
Bradshaw, H. H. (1998). *4 x 4 leadership and the purpose of the firm.* New York: Haworth Press.

According to Bradshaw, "business is the business of trade" and "executive leadership is charged with the responsibility of moving the enterprise toward increased trade." In this book he identifies four organizational elements that leaders can use as levers to increase trade: assets, systems, people, and organization. Bradshaw also describes the impact of self-esteem on performance, and says that leaders must energize four elements of employees' self-esteem to ensure successful trade: achievement, recognition, influences, and values. Includes index.
Subject(s): Executive leadership

Brubaker, D. L., & Coble, L. D. (1997). *Staying on track: An educational leader's guide to preventing derailment and ensuring personal and organizational success.* Thousand Oaks, CA: Corwin Press.

This guide is an assessment tool for educational leaders who want to avoid derailment and, at the same time, develop in their career. Brubaker and Coble discuss real issues that face leaders in education, which potentially could result in a response that leads them to derailment. The authors present cases built around themes of avoiding or dealing with derailment, which can be thought through individually or discussed in a group. Lessons learned through this guide enable leaders to get on the right track as well as help their staff and colleagues stay on track. Includes bibliographical references and indexes.
Subject(s): Educational leadership

New
Buckingham, M., & Coffman, C. (1999). *First, break all the rules: What the world's greatest managers do differently.* New York: Simon & Schuster.

Over the last 25 years the Gallup Organization has surveyed thousands of managers and, in this book, Buckingham and Coffman present that research to a general audience, hoping to answer the question, "What makes a great manager?" Using survey data and some specific real-life examples, the authors identify four keys to great managing: 1) select for talent, 2) define the right outcomes, 3) focus on strengths, and 4) find the right fit. They then offer a practical guide on "turning the keys," including advice on interviewing for talent and performance management. Appendices include "A Selection of Talents" listing talents commonly found by managers and a meta-analysis of the data.
Subject(s): Corporate leadership

New
Callahan, K. L. (1997). *Effective church leadership: Building on the twelve keys.* San Francisco: Jossey-Bass.

In previous books Callahan describes 12 characteristics of effective churches. This book focuses on the three characteristics related to leadership: mission, decision making, and organization. Callahan claims that the ministry has changed as society has changed from the "churched culture" of the 1950s to the "unchurched culture" of recent years. Ministers no longer serve as distinguished yet bureaucratic professionals in their communities. They have assumed missionary roles with community outreach programs and dynamic worship services. They practice participatory decision making and relationship building. Effective church leadership doesn't resemble a bureaucracy with ample resources. Effective church leaders live at the edge of their resources, stretching their budgets and staffs for maximum impact. An appendix helps readers design an action plan for adopting this new style of church leadership.
Subject(s): Religious leadership

Campbell, C., & Rockman, B. A. (Eds.). (1996). *The Clinton presidency: First appraisals.* Chatham, NJ: Chatham House.

Contributing authors share their assessments of President William Clinton's first presidential campaign and first term in office. Barbara Sinclair describes Clinton's relationship with Congress. David O'Brien writes of Clinton's effect on the judicial arm of government. Joel Aberbach analyzes the executive branch through selection of political appointees and the use of permanent officials. Other essays describe Clinton's ability to mobilize support, his domestic and foreign policy, his lack of influence on mid-term elections, and the state of executive leadership in the U.S. Includes bibliographical references in chapter notes and an index.
Subject(s): U.S. presidents: Clinton, W. J.

Campbell, D. W., & Greene, D. (1994). **Defining the leadership role of school boards in the 21st century.** *Phi Delta Kappan, 75*(5), 391-395.

The National School Boards Association formed a task force with the California School Boards Association to develop a definition of the governance responsibilities of school boards. They determined that content function should be: vision and climate for excellence, superintendent appointment and evaluation, budget adoption and fiscal accountability, curriculum development and program accountability, governance and policy, and collective bargaining. Tenets of effective boardsmanship are: understanding, teamwork, support, respect, trust, communication, professionalism, and fairness.
Subject(s): School boards

Card, M. A. (1997). **Toward a middle-range theory of individual-level strategic leadership transitions.** *Leadership Quarterly, 8*(1), 27-48.

Case studies of three state-level agency directors, including the directors of Ohio's Departments of Health and Employment Services, are used to examine the importance of the initial actions of a new official. Card identifies three stages in the leadership transition process: the crisis of appointment as a new leader tries to secure his or her position, the crisis of leadership as the leader tries to establish influence and authority with subordinates, and the crisis of autonomy and control as the new leader arrives on the job. This article attempts to offer potential agency leaders a guide for easing these difficult organizational transitions.
Subject(s): Public service leadership

Carter, G. R., & Cunningham, W. G. (1997). *The American school superintendent: Leading in an age of pressure.* San Francisco: Jossey-Bass.

The authors, one of whom is a former Superintendent of the Year, talked to over 40 superintendents of school districts around the nation in preparation for writing this in-depth look at the challenges faced by the leaders of American schools. Sections of the book address current dilemmas for superintendents, responses and remedies, and new directions and responsibilities in the schools. In addition to describing the current situation of school superintendents the book also tries to "chart the way for pioneers, champions, and catalytic agents to create the future of American education." Includes bibliographical references and index.
Subject(s): Educational leadership, superintendents

Carver, J. (1997). *Boards that make a difference: A new design for leadership in nonprofit and public organizations* (2nd ed.). San Francisco: Jossey-Bass.

Carver presents his policy governance model and explains how nonprofit and public agency leaders can implement it in their organizations. Carver defines four categories of policies that boards should focus on: 1) ends to be achieved, 2) means to those ends, 3) the board-staff relationship, and 4) the process of governance itself. The second edition includes

updated policy samples and a chapter on the process of policy development. Includes bibliographical references and index.
Subject(s): Nonprofit boards

Chrislip, D. D., & Larson, C. E. (1994). *Collaborative leadership: How citizens and civic leaders can make a difference.* San Francisco: Jossey-Bass.

Three challenges facing communities are: complex societal issues such as poverty and crime, frustrated citizens, and bureaucratic gridlock. Chrislip and Larson share case studies to demonstrate how five communities faced these challenges with collaborative leadership and achieved successful results. Baltimore organized BUILD (Baltimoreans United in Leadership Development) to deal with its overwhelming poverty, illiteracy, school dropout, teen pregnancy, unemployment, and housing problems. Its mission is to prepare young people to be responsible, contributing citizens. Phoenix, Newark, Denver, and Roanoke also addressed and overcame their communities' problems through collaboration. Includes bibliographical references and index.
Subject(s): Community leadership, collaboration

New
Clarke, K. (1996). **Kick out the image makers.** *New Statesman, 128*(4423), 8-9.

Clarke, former British Chancellor of the Exchequer for Margaret Thatcher, denounces the current practice of political image-making. He believes that spin doctors, focus groups, image consultants, and pollsters encourage shallow policy-making. Politicians who speak in sound bites and respond to changing popular opinion tend to avoid the controversial decisions that are required of true leaders. Clarke suggests that Prime Minister Tony Blair practices popular policy-making as opposed to Margaret Thatcher who made tough choices despite popular opinion.
Subject(s): Prime ministers, media influence

Collins, J. C., & Porras, J. I. (1994). *Built to last: Successful habits of visionary companies.* New York: HarperBusiness.

Collins and Porras researched 18 companies they define as visionary, including 3M, American Express, Nordstrom, and Walt Disney, and identified the factors that made them successful. These include establishing a company's core values and sticking to them, setting "Big Hairy Audacious Goals," and being willing to both experiment and fail. Very reader-friendly, the book includes interviews with the CEOs of visionary companies, charts, graphs, index, and Frequently Asked Questions.
Subject(s): Corporate leadership, vision

New
Conger, J., Finegold, D., & Lawler, E. E., III. (1998). **CEO appraisals: Holding corporate leadership accountable.** *Organizational Dynamics, 27*(1), 7-20.

This article addresses the importance of CEO evaluations and the role of corporate boards in such evaluations. Boards must possess five key elements to perform effective CEO appraisals: 1) varied background and knowledge among members, 2) information from multiple sources, 3) power to make decisions and hold the CEO accountable, 4) motivation in the form of long-term options, and 5) time to become well informed and make good decisions. The authors suggest that boards consider how well a CEO formulates and implements strategy, leads employees, develops external relations, and keeps the board informed. The financial performance of the organization is, of course, another important factor. Includes bibliographical references.
Subject(s): CEOs, corporate boards, accountability

New
Crainer, S. (1998). *The ultimate book of business gurus: 110 thinkers who really made a difference.* New York: AMACOM.

In the introduction Crainer explains the phenomenon of business gurus who are theorists who advise managers how to better run their businesses. The rest of the book contains profiles of the 50 gurus whose ideas, whether sound advice or hype, have most influenced business leaders. Each profile details a guru's personal career and contribution to management science. Although management science is primarily a 20th-century discipline dominated by American business models, Crainer's gurus represent consultants, executives, and academics across time and national boundaries. Another 60 gurus are briefly profiled in the appendix. Includes bibliographical references and index.
Subject(s): Corporate leadership

New
Crow, G. M., & Matthews, L. J. (1998). *Finding one's way: How mentoring can lead to dynamic leadership.* Thousand Oaks, CA: Corwin Press.

According to Crow and Matthews, having a mentor is essential for school principals both in the beginning and middle of their careers. This book first places mentoring in a theoretical framework by analyzing the socialization process of school administrators, and then offers strategies for mentoring interns, assistant principals, and new and mid-career principals. The authors use the metaphor of a journey to illustrate the mentoring process, describing the terrain, destination, directions, and mile markers found in each mentor/protégé relationship. Includes bibliographical references and index.
Subject(s): Principal as leader, mentoring

Cunningham, W. G., & Gresso, D. W. (1993). *Cultural leadership: The culture of excellence in education.* Needham Heights, MA: Allyn and Bacon.

Cunningham and Gresso provide an overview of school reform through success stories from several school districts. Instead of providing a formula for success they support the idea that every community is unique and needs to formulate its own success story. The school culture, not the structure, must change to bring reform. There are examples of success-

ful school reform through such program themes as Quality, Information and Improvement; School-University Partnerships; and Visioning in Schools. In Norfolk, Virginia, public schools were successful using visioning techniques to change the way administrators, teachers, and students viewed each other. At the same time they were able to raise test scores and attendance levels. Includes bibliographical references and indexes.
Subject(s): Educational leadership, school reform

Dart, R., Bradshaw, P., Murray, V., & Wolpin, J. (1996). **Boards of directors in nonprofit organizations: Do they follow a life-cycle model?** *Nonprofit Management & Leadership*, 6(4), 367-379.

Several theoretical models exist that apply a life cycle to nonprofit boards. This study used survey data from 1,200 Canadian nonprofits to empirically test these models. Results showed that some of the broader life-cycle hypotheses did apply to most boards—boards tended to grow in size and use more structure and formal procedures as they aged. However, the authors found that their research did not support more specific hypotheses about board behavior, and they caution against applying these models without considering more variables than just board age.
Subject(s): Nonprofit boards

New
Dauphinais, G. W., & Price, C. (Eds.). (1998). **Straight from the CEO: The world's top business leaders reveal ideas that every manager can use.** New York: Fireside.

The CEOs of companies such as Royal Dutch/Shell, Chase Manhattan, Compaq Computer, Enron Corporation, and British Airways contributed to this collection of writings that addresses six main issues: globalization, leadership, radical change, culture, customer relationships, and creativity. Specific chapter topics include creating a culture of continuous renewal, communicating in the information age, strategic roots of innovation, and creative marketing. Includes index.
Subject(s): CEOs

De Pree, M. (1997). **Leading without power: Finding hope in serving community.** San Francisco: Jossey-Bass.

De Pree says that for-profit companies could learn from America's nonprofit community because volunteers "allow no room in their work for the deceptive simplicity of the single bottom line." Instead nonprofits are places where people "realize their potential and do so continually." This collection of essays offers leaders inspiration and advice on how to transform their organizations into "movements" that attract people not with money but with the promise of meaningful work and a fulfilled life. De Pree's topics include potential, service, vision, and moral purpose.
Subject(s): Nonprofit leadership

New
Deal, J. J., Sessa, V. I., & Taylor, J. J. (1999). **Choosing executives: A research report on the Peak Selection Simulation.** Greensboro, NC: Center for Creative Leadership.

In 1995 the Center for Creative Leadership began using the Peak Selection Simulation (PSS) in its Leadership at the Peak training program. PSS uses a multimedia presentation to simulate the decision-making processes of those who select executives. In this study researchers used data collected from over 600 executives to examine what information they considered in their selection process and how it affected their ranking of candidates. Appendices provide a literature review, statistical information, and a description of PSS. Includes bibliographical references.
Subject(s): Corporate leadership, selection, research report

Deal, T. E., & Peterson, K. D. (1994). **The leadership paradox: Balancing logic and artistry in schools.** San Francisco: Jossey-Bass.

Deal and Peterson bemoan the changing roles of school principals. In years past, a principal was a community figure of moral authority who exerted positive influence on young minds. In recent years, principals have become disciplinarians who run schools like assembly lines. The leadership paradox in this book refers to a principal's need to rely on both knowledge and wisdom—knowing about and knowing how—to run schools and impact young minds at the same time. They compare management and leadership issues, as well as technical and spiritual methods, that a principal may employ to balance dual roles. Includes bibliographical references and index.
Subject(s): Principal as leader

DeGregorio, C. A. (1997). **Networks of champions: Leadership, access, and advocacy in the U.S. House of Representatives.** Ann Arbor: University of Michigan Press.

The author states that lawmaking is a team effort among legislators, their staffs of experts, and the lobbyists who seek to influence them. In the U.S. House of Representatives, where each team member has personal interests to protect, the teams must work together against incredible odds. While researching this book the author discovered that congressional leadership emerges from obscure positions. Those who possess substantive knowledge and informal influence, but do not hold positions of power, practice an "earned style of leadership." These are the leaders who can "turn warring factions into winning coalitions" and who "champion policy in the face of adversity." Legislators seek alliances with and lobbyists are quick to ferret out these leaders. To illustrate congressional team leadership in context, DeGregorio cites several recent policy issues including: welfare reform, international trade policy, farm credit, nuclear test ban, and the anti-drug bill. Includes bibliographical references and indexes.
Subject(s): Congressional leadership

New

Deluga, R. J. (1998). **American presidential proactivity, charismatic leadership, and rated performance.** *Leadership Quarterly: Special Issue: Political Leadership, 9*(3), 265-291.

This study examines the relationship between American presidents and proactive personalities. Biographical information and the results of prior studies on charisma and performance were used to construct profiles for 39 American presidents, Washington through Reagan. Using the profiles only, with no names attached, three raters applied the *Proactive Personality Scale* (Bateman & Crant, 1993) to each president. Factors included creativity, war entry, war avoidance, great decisions, and consensus of greatness. John Adams received the highest ranking for proactivity. A strong correlation was found between perceived charisma and proactive presidential leadership. Includes bibliographical references.

Subject(s): U.S. presidents

Denton, R. E., Jr., & Holloway, R. L. (1996). *The Clinton presidency: Images, issues, and communication strategies.* Westport, CT: Praeger.

Contributing authors analyze William Clinton's skills as a "rhetorical president." Beginning with the 1993 inaugural address they examine town hall meetings, political advertising, unsuccessful health care reform, and a roller coaster relationship with the media throughout his first term in office. Craig Allen Smith's essay suggests that Clinton's middle-class appeal is based on his message that we can make tomorrow better than today, and we all have a responsibility to make it happen. The Republican cry for family values is described as using a passive noun. In contrast, Clinton used active verbs when demanding a government that values families and promotes family leave, health care, and job training. The book also includes content analysis of political cartoons, an essay on the communication style of Hillary Rodham Clinton, and a critique of the Clinton administration e-mail system. Includes bibliographical references and index.

Subject(s): U.S. presidents: Clinton, W. J.

New

Devos, G., Van den Broeck, H., & Vanderheyden, K. (1998). **The concept and practice of a school-based management contest: Integration of leadership development and organizational learning.** *Educational Administration Quarterly, 34* (Supplemental Issue), 700-717.

With the recent popularity of decentralization and school-based management, training programs for principals have proved ineffective. Training programs for school leaders have neglected the elements of empowerment and organizational learning. Several attempts have been made to rectify this dilemma including mentoring programs and computer simulations; however, these did not encourage a team approach that has been deemed effective. Following a history of principal-training programs, this article describes the development of the School-based Management Contest, which originated in a Belgian university. This approach uses

team assignments within schools as a learning experience. Assessment and evaluation are discussed. Includes bibliographical references and an appendix.

Subject(s): Educational leadership

New

Dimmock, C., & Walker, A. (1998). **Comparative educational administration: Developing a cross-cultural framework.** *Educational Administration Quarterly, 34*(4), 558-595.

The current trend toward multiculturalism supports the need for school leadership analysis. The development of comparisons across different contexts, known as comparative educational administration, remains underdeveloped according to Dimmock and Walker. They advocate a need for a cross-cultural approach to comparative administration and present a framework to serve as a starting point. The integral pieces of the framework include cultural concepts, organizational structures, leadership and management processes, curriculum, teaching, and learning. Implications and challenges related to this framework conclude the article. Includes bibliographical references.

Subject(s): Educational leadership, cultural context

New

Dobel, J. P. (1998). **Political prudence and the ethics of leadership.** *Public Administration Review, 58*(1), 74-81.

Political achievement and moral virtue often seem to be mutually exclusive, but in this article Dobel presents a practical framework of political prudence that he says can help leaders reconcile the two. Prudence requires leaders to "achieve moral self-mastery, to attend to the context of a situation, and . . . to seek concrete outcomes that are legitimate and durable." To be politically prudent, leaders must attend to seven dimensions or capacities: 1) disciplined reason and openness, 2) foresight, 3) deploying power, 4) timing and momentum, 5) means and ends, 6) durability and legitimacy, and 7) building community. Includes bibliographical references.

Subject(s): Political leadership, ethics

New

Downs, A. (1997). *Beyond the looking glass: Overcoming the seductive culture of corporate narcissism.* New York: American Management Association.

Downs discusses a corporate disease that has inflicted malady upon organizations. *Corporate narcissism* is defined as "obsession with the image of success," *image* being the keyword. A narcissistic manager will go to extremes to present the surface image of leading a successful organization. Underneath the facade, all is not well with the style of leadership or the morale of employees. This type of person has a hidden agenda to quench an excessive thirst for power and approval. Often the goals of the organization will be sacrificed to attain this "image." The author presents several techniques that are useful in helping to create an environment that is intolerant of excessive narcissistic behavior. Also

included are methods for surviving a narcissistic manager. Includes bibliographical references and index.
Subject(s): Negative views of corporate leadership

Drucker, P. F. (1969). ***The effective executive.*** New York: Harper & Row.

Drucker presents findings of a systematic study on what effective executives do that the rest do not do, and what they do not do that the rest tend to do. Findings show that effectiveness can be learned and, more importantly, that it must be learned. This book presents, in simple form, the elements of this practice.
Subject(s): Executive leadership

Drucker, P. F. (1982). ***The changing world of the executive.*** New York: Times Books.

This book provides insights into, and an understanding of, the world of the executive. It also provides a useful "executive agenda" to stimulate both thought and action. The book should be read with this overriding question in mind: "How can I, and we in my organization, use this idea or these insights to perform more effectively—to do a better job, and above all, to welcome and accommodate the new and the different?"
Subject(s): Executive leadership

New
Drucker, P. F. (1998). **Management's new paradigms.** *Forbes, 162*(7), 152-177.

Drucker reviews 100 years of management paradigms to explain how we arrived at current theories and practices. Assumptions about American business, its customers, and its workforce were once focused internally on production and profit. To succeed in a rapidly changing global and techno-logical environment, the managerial mind-set is shifting to an external focus on non-customers, partnerships, knowledge, innovation, and the lessons that can be learned from organi-zations outside the corporate sector. Drucker claims that "the center of modern society is the managed institution" that does not exist to react but exists to create results. Includes photographs.
Subject(s): Corporate leadership

Duerst-Lahti, G., & Kelly, R. M. (Eds.). (1995). ***Gender power, leadership, and governance.*** Ann Arbor: University of Michigan Press.

This book merges theory with empirical research and incorporates feminism into political ideology. The primary concept is gender power—"the power that results from our gendered (e)valuation of things and behaviors, our ways of being, behaving, and structuring social relations." Contribut-ing authors link power and traditional leadership to masculin-ity and link sex-role identity to decision-making style. There is an analysis of the 1992 elections and a popular media slogan, "the year of the woman." Authors examine the number of times during this "year" that women were

represented as leaders in articles of the *New York Times* and the *Washington Post.* The editors conclude that acceptance of gender power would contribute to the understanding of public governance and leadership. Includes bibliographical references.
Subject(s): Political leadership, gender diversity

New
Duke, D. L. (1998). **The normative context of organizational leadership.** *Educational Administration Quarterly, 34*(2), 165-195.

This article serves to view educational leadership from an organizational context. The first portion of the article depicts differing views of organizations as cited by various authors. In the next section trends are reviewed that call for studying leadership at the normative level. Following is a depiction of the elements of a normative context and a model of norma-tive structure. The conclusion discusses implications for leadership research and the need for a balanced approach. Includes bibliographical references.
Subject(s): Educational leadership

Dunlap, D. M., & Schmuck, P. A. (Eds.). (1995). ***Women leading in education.*** Albany: State University of New York Press.

Essays in this book urge women to take leadership positions in the field of education where women dominate the workforce. Personal narratives of women who have risen to leadership roles tell of their journeys of struggle and success. Other essays describe successful mentoring programs, the glass ceiling, gender consciousness, advocacy organizations, accounts of women of color in educational leadership, and feminist leadership theories. A ten-year study of 142 female administrative aspirants reports that 58% of the women achieved their career goals. Dunlap proposes a new agenda for a new century. She suggests that educational leadership practice, policy, and research focus on: gender and leader-ship, schools as organizations, social congruence, support, and action. Includes bibliographical references and index.
Subject(s): Educational leadership

Dutton, G. (1996). **Future shock: Who will run the com-pany?** *Management Review, 85*(8), 19-23.

Many companies have no formal succession plan, and if top-management members leave suddenly the organization can be thrown into turmoil. Dutton recognizes that succession plans can cause problems within the organization if they become political, but she emphasizes their necessity. Four types of succession plans are described—simple replacement of the CEO, full replacement of top management, creating an internal talent pool, and creating an extended talent pool both inside and outside the organization. The succession plans of companies including Wal-Mart, Coca-Cola, Goodyear, and Texas Instruments are described.
Subject(s): Corporate leadership, succession

Eadie, D. C. (1997). *Changing by design: A practical approach to leading innovation in nonprofit organizations.* San Francisco: Jossey-Bass.

Written for the leaders of nonprofits, this book offers a model for designing and implementing change initiatives. The author focuses on three key areas: coordinated leadership on the part of the chief executive and the board, creative innovation in establishing what needs to be changed and how, and effective implementation of new ideas and programs. Real-life case studies are used to illustrate concepts, and chapters address issues including building boards, nurturing creativity, and strategic management.
Subject(s): Nonprofit leadership, change, innovation

Eldersveld, S. J., Stromberg, L., & Derksen, W. (1995). *Local elites in Western democracies: A comparative analysis of urban political leaders in the U.S., Sweden, and the Netherlands.* San Francisco: Westview Press.

The authors tested the premise that in a healthy society, political elites form strong relationships with community groups to help them understand the communities' problems and values and to respond with the appropriate actions. Intermediate-sized cities—population 29,000 to 163,000—were selected for comparison: 20 in the U.S., 15 in Sweden, and 20 in the Netherlands. Interviews were conducted with the top public administrators in each city to determine their evaluation of and effectiveness in dealing with their city's problems. Cultural diversity, the power of local leaders in business and other institutions, and the variations between the cities themselves complicated efforts at generalization. The research did identify some uniformity in the areas of perceived problems and priorities. Includes bibliographical references and index.
Subject(s): Political leadership, multicultural context

Ellis, S., Nadler, A., & Rabin, A. (1996). **Political leaders in the SYMLOG space: Perceptions of right and left wing leaders by right and left wing constituencies.** *Leadership Quarterly, 7*(4), 507-526.

This study used the *Systematic Multiple Level Observation of Groups (SYMLOG®)* measure to determine how different constituent groups felt about the friendliness, task-orientation, and dominance of right- and left-wing Israeli politicians. Right-wing voters rated right-wing leaders higher on friendliness and task-orientation, while left-wing voters rated left-wing leaders higher on those traits. Each group of constituents saw leaders affiliated with their political party as closer to their image of the ideal leader than leaders from the opposing party.
Subject(s): Political leadership

Ellis, S. J. (1996). *From the top down: The executive role in volunteer program success* (Rev. ed.). Philadelphia: Energize.

This book addresses leadership issues for organizations that depend on volunteers to deliver service. This revised edition designates different types of volunteers: student interns, stipended workers, corporate volunteers, technical assistance volunteers, groups, those who give a few hours of support, court-refereed community-service workers, residents of community homes, those with vested interest in a program, national service workers, unemployed or disabled volunteers, and virtual volunteers. Ellis makes recommendations about how to handle legal issues, determine the dollar value of volunteer work, and foster volunteer/staff relationships. One appendix outlines the major functions of volunteer administration. Another appendix lists resources including support organizations and a bibliography. Includes index.
Subject(s): Volunteers

Ettorre, B. (1996). **Changing the rules of the board game.** *Management Review, 85*(4), 13-17.

Corporate governance, according to the author, has long consisted of "rubber-stamp boards, overpaid directors, and interlocking directorships." This article outlines some of the recent reforms that companies have instituted to make their boards more accountable and more effective. Type of compensation, board diversity, self-evaluation, the mission and values of a board, and board size are all addressed. Examples of board reforms from companies such as American Express, General Electric, and Kimberly-Clark are included.
Subject(s): Corporate boards

Farkas, C. M., & De Backer, P. (1996). *Maximum leadership: The world's leading CEOs share their five strategies for success.* New York: Henry Holt.

After interviewing more than 160 CEOs of multinational corporations, Farkas and Backer identified the five approaches to leadership used most by executives: strategic, human assets, expertise, box, and change-agent. The strengths and weaknesses of each approach are addressed, and examples of leaders, from companies including Gillette and ITT, who succeeded and failed with each strategy are given. Includes index.
Subject(s): CEOs

Farquhar, K. W. (1995). **Not just understudies: The dynamics of short-term leadership.** *Human Resource Management: Special Issue on Transitional Leadership, 34*(1), 51-70.

Interim and acting CEOs—are they junior leaders? Do they aspire to reach the top without much chance of actually getting there? Or is temporary leadership a strategic window to practice skills in crisis management, support of organizational goals, and paving the way for new leadership? Farquhar defines the three styles of interim leadership and their potential for success. A case study of interim leadership in an educational setting illustrates Farquhar's model of the dynamics of short-term leadership.
Subject(s): CEOs

Firstenberg, P. B. (1996). *The 21st century nonprofit: Remaking the organization in the post-government era.* New York: Foundation Center.

Firstenberg, a long-time nonprofit executive and board member, applies his years of experience to developing a plan for managing tax-exempt organizations. He addresses the importance of accountability and describes a way that nonprofits can prove their productivity to the public. Other chapters address how to expand an organization's revenue base and managing human resources in nonprofits. Three leaders of nonprofits are also profiled—McGeorge Bundy, former president of the Ford Foundation; former Princeton president William Bowen; and Joan Ganz Cooney, a founder of *Sesame Street*. Includes index.
Subject(s): Nonprofit leadership, accountability

Fisher, J., & Koch, J. V. (1996). *Presidential leadership: Making a difference.* Phoenix: Oryx Press.

The authors recommend a transformational style of leadership in institutions of higher learning. They explain how a charismatic president with a powerful vision can transform a university. They also discuss total quality management in the context of higher education, race and gender issues, fundraising, presidential searches, and salary negotiation. Includes bibliographical references and index.
Subject(s): Leadership in higher education

Floyd, S. W., & Wooldridge, B. (1996). *The strategic middle manager: How to create and sustain competitive advantage.* San Francisco: Jossey-Bass.

Traditional definitions of middle managers focus on their operating responsibilities and management duties, but Floyd and Wooldridge argue that in today's business world middle managers must take on more strategic leadership roles. They recount the history of middle management from World War II on, describe the possibilities for leadership that exist in mid-level positions today, and then offer hands-on advice on applying the book's ideas. Specific chapters address issues faced by those in middle management, how top managers can better work with middle managers, and how those aspiring to middle-management positions can use leadership skills. Includes two self-assessment tests and an index.
Subject(s): Mid-level managers

New
Forbes, D. P., & Milliken, F. J. (1999). **Cognition and corporate governance: Understanding boards of directors as strategic decision-making groups.** *Academy of Management Review, 24*(3), 489-505.

This article introduces a model of corporate board effectiveness. The complexity of board dynamics is affected by the characteristics of board members and by the processes of their work. Increased diversity among members' job backgrounds, knowledge, and skills paves the way for improved group dynamics. However, members must exercise their diverse insights and expertise to be effective. Boards that

have demographic diversity, actively engaged members, and cognitive conflict are well positioned for optimal decision making. The outcomes are board cohesiveness without the danger of groupthink and a higher level of firm performance. Includes bibliographical references.
Subject(s): Corporate boards, decision making

New
Fullan, M. (1998). **Leadership for the 21st century: Breaking the bonds of dependency.** *Educational Leadership: Association for Supervision and Curriculum Development, 55*(7), 6-10.

This special edition titled *Reshaping School Leadership* focuses on school and district administration during this time of increasing pressures on educators. The article by Fullan states the need for education leaders to dismiss the fallacy of easy solutions in leadership and instead create their own theories in a trial-and-error manner. Fullan discusses four guidelines leading to greater success. The adjacent article, "Telling All Sides of the Truth," focuses on the leadership styles of superintendents and their rapport with individual schools. Leadership styles are also the focus of an article depicting schools as mirrors of a leader's own value system.
Subject(s): Educational leadership

New
Fulmer, R. M., & Wagner, S. (1999). **Leadership: Lessons from the best.** *Training & Development, 53*(3), 28-32.

In early 1998 a benchmarking study examined the best leadership practices of six organizations: Arthur Andersen, General Electric, Hewlett Packard, Johnson & Johnson, Shell International, and The World Bank. The article highlights the study's significant findings, which include that competencies matter, leadership development needs action learning, development must link to succession planning, and it's best to grow your own leaders. Includes lists of the ten keys to productive leadership and 20 leadership talents or "themes."
Subject(s): Corporate leadership, best practices

New
Garubo, R. C., & Rothstein, S. W. (1998). *Supportive supervision in schools.* Westport, CT: Greenwood Press.

This book serves as a guide for creating positive relations between teachers and administrators. Garubo and Rothstein observe a need for these groups to engage in a "cooperative effort to learn what is really happening in classrooms." This source depicts a method for accomplishing this called *supportive supervision.* The specialized conferencing method takes place between teachers and administrators for the goal of improving communication. Garubo and Rothstein describe leadership behavior in schools, including group dynamics and interpersonal skills as well as psychological insights. The final portion of the book describes the supportive supervisory and administrative processes. Includes bibliographical references.
Subject(s): Educational leadership

Gertzog, I. N. (1995). *Congressional women: Their recruitment, integration, and behavior* (2nd ed.). Westport, CT: Praeger.

In Gertzog's first edition of this book, published in 1984, he examined the women who served in Congress from 1916 to the late 1970s. He updated his study with new interviews after the 1992 "Year of the Woman" elections, and in great detail describes the background and experiences that successive generations of Congresswomen have brought to their offices. There are direct quotes from past and present Congresswomen and charts showing the most common characteristics of Congresswomen and the issues they have faced. Includes bibliographical references and index.
Subject(s): Congressional leadership, women leaders

Ghoshal, S., & Bartlett, C. A. (1995). **Changing the role of top management: Beyond structure to processes.** *Harvard Business Review, 73*(1), 86-96.

The hierarchical-management structure that built large corporations in the 1970s no longer works in the competitive business environments of the 1980s. This article discusses 20 U.S., European, and Japanese companies that changed their vertical structures and reaped rewards. Three processes highlight their success stories: an entrepreneurial process, a competence-building process, and a renewal process.
Subject(s): Corporate leadership

Glasman, N. S., & Glasman, L. D. (1997). **Connecting the preparation of school leaders to the practice of school leadership.** *Peabody Journal of Education, 72*(2), 3-20.

The authors believe that the behaviors that characterize school leadership should be the focus of training programs for educational leaders, and in this article they provide a theoretical background for their argument. First they offer common definitions of leadership and the behaviors associated with those definitions, and then they describe the content and history of educational leadership training programs. One element—problem solving—is identified as a link between preparation and practice, and a problem-solving module worksheet is included as an appendix. Includes bibliographical references.
Subject(s): Educational leadership

New
Gobel-Kobialka, S. (1998). **Reaching business excellence through sound people management.** *European Journal of Work and Organizational Psychology, 7*(4), 549-558.

In a business environment of continuous change, managing people is key to organizational success. This article describes the personnel development concept German company Siemens Nixdorf Informationssysteme AG (SNI) uses to encourage personal and organizational development. The SNI model is made up of six parts: job profiles, career models, a skills database, assessment and feedback procedures, a database of high-potentials, and a company-wide human resources market advertising internal jobs. Identifying and

developing high-potential employees is a critical part of this model, and strategic personnel reviews and training are used in this process. Includes bibliographical references. Commentary by Tony Keenan follows the article.
Subject(s): Corporate leadership

Goodsell, C. T., & Murray, N. (Eds.). (1995). *Public administration illuminated and inspired by the arts.* Westport, CT: Praeger.

Fifty years ago, a commentary in the journal *Public Administration Review* suggested that novels provide a useful medium for deeper understanding of public administration. This book takes that idea further by recommending novels, short stories, poetry, classical literature, films, and paintings to enhance leadership lessons in public administration. These works of art reflect the complexities of human nature and provide opportunities to learn about unfamiliar cultures. The editors call these connections "bridges." Some chapters are: "Leadership Lessons from Shakespeare" by C. R. Gira; "How Imagination Transforms Leaders" by S. R. Kuder; "Art and Transformation in *Murder in the Cathedral*" by M. R. Carey; "Poetry and Leadership" by D. H. Nelson; and "Lessons in Leadership from *Lonesome Dove*" by P. R. Russell and D. B. Tinsley. An index guides readers to subjects, authors, artists, and works of art. Includes bibliographical references.
Subject(s): Public service leadership, artist as leader

Green, J. C., & Griesinger, D. W. (1996). **Board performance and organizational effectiveness in nonprofit social services organizations.** *Nonprofit Management and Leadership, 6*(4), 381-402.

The authors surveyed the leaders and board members of 16 nonprofits serving developmentally disabled adults to determine whether board performance was related to organizational effectiveness. Itemizing board activities and using accreditation surveys to determine effectiveness, the study found a significant relationship between the two factors. Board activities most strongly correlated with effectiveness included policy formation, financial planning and control, program monitoring, resource development, and dispute resolution.
Subject(s): Nonprofit boards

Green, M. F., & McDade, S. A. (1991). *Investing in higher education: A handbook of leadership development.* Washington, DC: American Council on Education.

Directed to governing boards, chief executive officers, senior administrators, faculty, and others who make decisions about duties, performance, and professional lives of faculty and staff, this book serves as a guide to developing individuals who can lead institutions of higher education in their quest for excellence. It focuses on a very practical question: How can colleges and universities develop leadership capacity and effectiveness to the fullest extent possible? With chapters organized by specific positions (academic deans, department chairs, faculty, etc.), it is well suited for selective reading.

Includes bibliographical references and index.
Subject(s): Educational leadership, leadership development

New
Griffith, J. (1999). **The school leadership/school climate relation: Identification of school configurations associated with change in principals.** *Educational Administration Quarterly*, 35(2), 267-291.

Organizational climate has been determined as an element in leadership effectiveness, and is also linked to educational aspects. Griffith conducted a study to determine the relationship between school leadership and school configuration. His question proposed, "Do schools having a change in principals have identifiable organizational configurations?" The results provided an affirmative answer to this question with the supporting opinions of students and parents that schools changing leaderships were less disciplined, and parents felt less empowerment. Standardized test scores were also reportedly lower in schools that had experienced a change in leadership. The article also discusses the implications of effective principal leadership characteristics. Includes five tables and bibliographical references.
Subject(s): Educational leadership

Grove, A. S. (1996). *Only the paranoid survive: How to exploit the crisis points that challenge every company and career.* New York: Doubleday.

Grove shares his experiences as a manager at Intel before becoming chairman of the board. He describes "strategic inflection points," which are "the times in the life of a business when its fundamentals are about to change." Although these changes are often brought on by technological changes, they are not restricted to technological industries; they can affect any business. Grove tries to teach leaders and others to cope with such change by "shaping an energetic and efficient team that is capable of responding to the unanticipated as well as to any ordinary event."
Subject(s): Corporate leadership, change

Gullatt, D. E. (1997). **Teachers taking the lead.** *Schools in the Middle*, 6(5), 12-14.

Gullatt states that teachers play key leadership roles when developing programs, climate, and curriculum that help students learn to their maximum capability. Predictors of teacher leadership are: a broad range of skills, interests, and experiences; involvement in curriculum teaching and development; administrative and organizational experience; knowledge of community concerns; risk-taking temperament; and interpersonal skills. Gullatt suggests methods for developing leadership skills in middle school teachers. Includes bibliographical references.
Subject(s): Teacher as leader

New
Gundry, L. K. (1997). **The leadership focus of women entrepreneurs at start-up and early-growth stages.** *A Leadership Journal: Women in Leadership—Sharing the Vision*, 2(1), 69-77.

Over 300 women entrepreneurs were surveyed to learn what skills and information they needed to take their businesses to the next level. The author found that women had different needs at different stages in their businesses. In the start-up phase women typically work alone and need to implement their ideas and identify sources of financing, while in the early-growth stage entrepreneurs are often managing employees and are looking for information on expansion and organizational structure. Gundry suggests that future analysis should segment entrepreneurs according to state-of-business development. Includes bibliographical references.
Subject(s): Entrepreneurship

New
Haass, R. N. (1994). *The power to persuade.* New York: Houghton Mifflin.

Haass, a veteran of prominent federal positions and a professor at Harvard University's school of government, hopes this book will help "individuals working in and with governments and other large, often unruly, organizations." Each individual is advised to design a personal compass with superiors to the North, direct reports to the South, internal peers to the East, and external colleagues to the West. Finding your center means shaping your own agenda while finding balance with the agendas of all other compass points. Doing so allows public-sector leaders to exert influence through five principles: 1) focus on a narrow agenda, 2) look for opportunities to act, 3) act with integrity, 4) be careful and thorough, and 5) develop relationships. Includes bibliographical references.
Subject(s): Public service leadership, persuasion

New
Hecht, W. D., Higgerson, M. L., Gmelch, W. H., & Tucker, A. (1999). *The department chair as academic leader.* Phoenix: Oryx.

Responsibilities of department chairs have grown complex in recent years. Chairs must handle schedules, budgets, strategic planning, and a multitude of student and faculty issues. Most importantly, the authors claim, chairs are responsible for establishing the department's culture and morale. This book aims to guide chairs through the operations and relationships—internal and external—required in this leadership position. Includes bibliographical references and index. Part of the American Council on Education Series on Higher Education.
Subject(s): Educational leadership in higher education

New

Hein, E. C. (Ed.). (1998). *Contemporary leadership behavior: Selected readings* (5th ed.). New York: Lippincott.

Written for professional nurses, this anthology addresses both the culture of nursing and the leadership skills nurses need in their day-to-day work. This newest edition contains all new articles written largely by leaders in the field of nursing and includes study questions at the end of each section. A chapter on leadership behaviors includes selections on assertiveness, advocacy, mentoring, power, and change. A concluding section describes leadership as it applies to the field of health care. Includes index.

Subject(s): Nursing leadership

New

Hennessey, J. T. (1998). **"Reinventing" government: Does leadership make the difference.** *Public Administration Review*, *58*(6), 522-532.

In 1993 President Clinton launched a major initiative to "reinvent" the federal government; changing the organizational culture of federal agencies was a key part of this effort. This study examined the role leadership played in the "reinvention" of offices in the Veterans Administration and the Department of Defense. The author first examined the connection between organizational culture and reinvention and found that an organization's leader was critical in the success of any organizational change. The leaders of the nine organizations in the study were then evaluated in terms of Bennis's four competencies of leadership: the ability to manage attention, meaning, trust, and self. The author found that no one competency was most important but that leaders needed a combination of skills to effectively guide their organizations through reinvention and culture change. Includes bibliographical references.

Subject(s): Public service leadership

Henton, D., Melville, J., & Walsh, K. (1997). *Grassroots leaders for a new economy: How civic entrepreneurs are building prosperous communities.* San Francisco: Jossey-Bass.

Joint Venture: Silicon Valley was a collaborative regional alliance, formed in 1992, that united business, government, education, and community leaders for the purpose of strengthening the economy and improving the area's quality of life. Three Joint Venture advisors wrote this book to describe their efforts and other examples of civic entrepreneurship around the country. They explain how any community can implement a program like theirs, outlining the steps of initiation, incubation, implementation, and improvement. Includes bibliographical references and index.

Subject(s): Grassroots leadership

Herman, R. D. (Ed.). (1994). *The Jossey-Bass handbook of nonprofit leadership and management.* San Francisco: Jossey-Bass.

Nonprofit scholars and executives write about the unique management skills necessary in nonprofit organizations. Their intent is to provide a comprehensive and in-depth picture of this sector. They discuss the nature of philanthropy, political influence, legal issues, lobbying, program development, fund-raising and financial management, recruiting and retaining volunteers, staff and board relationships, and the future of nonprofits. Includes bibliographical references.

Subject(s): Nonprofit leadership

Herman, R. D., Renz, D. O., & Heimovics, R. D. (1997). **Board practices and board effectiveness in local nonprofit organizations.** *Nonprofit Management & Leadership*, *7*(4), 373-385.

How do nonprofits judge the effectiveness of their boards? This study of 64 Kansas City agencies examined the relationship between the extent to which boards used prescribed board practices and stakeholder judgments of their effectiveness. The prescribed practices, drawn from the growing literature on boards, include having a board manual, holding an annual board retreat, and using a board self-evaluation. The study found that the methods used to evaluate boards vary so widely that making any generalizations is dangerous, but the authors believe that using prescribed board practices may increase overall effectiveness.

Subject(s): Nonprofit boards

New

Hickok, T. A. (1999). *Workforce reductions: An annotated bibliography.* Greensboro, NC: Center for Creative Leadership.

Workforce reductions have become a part of life in today's unstable business environment. It is essential for managers to recognize the effects that these changes have on both individuals and organizations. These annotations review sources addressing three aspects of downsizing: organizational factors, such as strategy and decision making; the organizational-individual relationship; and the individual perspective, including how both those who leave and downsizing "survivors" react. The literature promotes the idea that leaders can take steps to minimize negative effects, particularly by encouraging communication and planning. Includes index and an appendix with citations of further resources.

Subject(s): Corporate leadership

Hodgkinson, C. (1991). *Educational leadership: The moral art.* Albany: State University of New York Press.

Hodgkinson claims that "values constitute the essential problem of leadership and that the educational institution is special because it both forms and is formed by values." The special problem for educational leadership is a lack of goal specificity, or divergent interests at two levels—the personal level where the teaching-learning process occurs and the organizational level that determines collective purpose and achievement. The solution for educational leadership lies in the theory and practice of values, which Hodgkinson calls the moral art. In the final chapter, "Prescriptions and Practicalities," Hodgkinson suggests that educational leaders

observe leaders in other fields to understand personal values and those in other contexts. Includes bibliographical references and index.
Subject(s): Educational leadership, values

Hollenbeck, G. P. (1994). *CEO selection: A street-smart review.* Greensboro, NC: Center for Creative Leadership.

Although selecting a CEO may be the single most important event an organization must face, there is little practical literature available on the subject. In this report the author, a management psychologist specializing in executive development and succession planning and former human resources executive, reviews several practically oriented books and articles on CEO selection. The reviews are critical and evaluative and reflect the author's own views, tempered by his experience. Includes bibliographical references and index.
Subject(s): CEOs, selection

New
Humes, J. C. (1997). *Nixon's ten commandments of leadership and negotiation: His guiding principles of statecraft.* New York: Scribner.

Nixon's guiding principles for handling presidential power first appeared in his book *The Real War* (Simon & Schuster, 1980). In this new book Humes, speech writer for Richard Nixon and three other U.S. presidents, explains how Nixon lived and led by these principles. Each one is reinforced with stories of other statesmen. An example is commandment number seven, "Always leave your adversary a face-saving line of retreat," a principle practiced by both Nixon and General Douglas MacArthur. Includes an index.
Subject(s): U.S. presidents: Nixon, R. M.

New
Hunt, J. W., & Laing, B. (1997). **Leadership: The role of the exemplar.** *Business Strategy Review, 8*(1), 31-42.

The Exemplar model of leadership is similar to charismatic or transformational models, but it focuses primarily on managers in organizational/work settings. Hunt and Laing use this model in their study of what traits define leadership. They administered a 360-degree-feedback instrument to 105 senior executives attending a London Business School program, looking for five traits: vision, differentiation, values, transmission, and a characteristic flaw. Analysis showed that leaders rated more competent by their colleagues possessed these traits, but the authors also say that the picture that emerges of these leaders "is not particularly attractive." Successful leaders tended to be forceful and aggressive and were viewed by subordinates with respect rather than affection. Survey responses and quotes from interviews with the executives are used to illustrate the findings. Includes bibliographical references.
Subject(s): Corporate leadership

New
Immelman, A. (1998). **The political personalities of 1996 U.S. presidential candidates Bill Clinton and Bob Dole.** *Leadership Quarterly: Special Issue: Political Leadership, 9*(3), 335-366.

This is an analysis of the personality-based leadership characteristics of the two 1996 United States presidential candidates. A personality assessment instrument was compiled from the work of Theodore Millon and titled the *Millon Inventory of Diagnostic Criteria (MIDC)* (Immelman, 1993). Applied to published information about the two candidates, the *MIDC* revealed patterns of control, assertion, sociability, agreeability, complaining, conforming, hesitation, introversion, distrust, and instability. Democratic incumbent Bill Clinton's results indicate a self-promoting and gregarious personality that is consistent with a leadership style filled with ethical troubles, lapses of judgment, a drive to achieve, and self-confidence in the face of adversity. Republican candidate Bob Dole's results indicate a controlling and conforming personality that is consistent with a dogmatic leadership style. Appendices outline each candidate's results on each scale. Includes bibliographical references.
Subject(s): U.S. presidents: Clinton, W. J.

New
Ireland, R. D., & Hitt, M. A. (1999). **Achieving and maintaining strategic competitiveness in the 21st century: The role of strategic leadership.** *Academy of Management Executive, 13*(1), 43-57.

Strategic leadership helps firms compete in complex and turbulent environments such as those created by the global economy. This leadership style is an interactive relationship among all organizational citizens who assume responsibility for and reap rewards from organizational success. Within this style "great groups" collaborate internally, form external partnerships, and share knowledge throughout the organizational community. The great group that includes a CEO and top management team practices six key functions of strategic leadership: 1) establishing an organizational vision, 2) developing and leveraging core competencies, 3) developing human capital, 4) sustaining an effective organizational culture, 5) emphasizing ethical practices, and 6) establishing the balance of controls that nurture creativity and productivity. Includes bibliographical references.
Subject(s): Strategic leadership

Isachsen, O. (1996). *Joining the entrepreneurial elite: Four styles to business success.* Palo Alto, CA: Davis-Black.

Isachsen identifies four styles of entrepreneurs, two who do the work of managers and two who are leaders. The administrator and tactician are responsible, persistent, and know how to best deliver goods and services. The strategist and idealist are spiritual, maintain their sense of purpose, build trust, and enable their employees to deliver superior performance. There is a brief self-scored test for the reader to determine his or her dominant entrepreneurial style. To support his framework, Isachsen tells the stories of entrepreneurs who

became successful. Some of them are: administrator Bob Lowe, CEO of Lowe Enterprises, a real-estate firm; tactician Beverly Trupp, CEO of Color Design Art, Inc., one of the largest interior decorating firms in the U.S.; strategist Delores Kesler, Chair of Accustaff temporary employment agency; and idealist Barbara Edwards, CEO of the public relations firm California Host. Includes index.
Subject(s): Entrepreneurship

Jack, E. T. (1996). **Philosophical foundation of citizen leadership.** *Journal of Leadership Studies, 3*(4), 54-60.

Jack claims that in the last 25 years Americans have distanced themselves from their neighbors by being less involved in civic associations and religious communities. He believes that it is this distancing that causes the social problems of divorce, alcoholism, poverty, and crime. Jack recommends that citizens join forces to solve local problems and cites several historical and current examples of successful citizen action. Public benefits of such citizen leadership are: strangers meeting on public ground, mutual responsibility for our world, the fear of strangers faced and dealt with, and conflict resolution.
Subject(s): Civic leadership

New
Jackson, P., & Delehanty, H. (1995). *Sacred hoops: Spiritual lessons of a hardwood warrior.* New York: Hyperion.

Phil Jackson writes about his life in basketball, both as a team member and a coach. Readers are given a glance at his leadership style through this autobiographical sketch emphasizing the importance of compassion and selflessness for a successful team. Spirituality is an integral point of Jackson's journey as he demonstrates his knowledge of critical leadership skills. This source discusses strategies employed by Jackson, which are applicable to all managers. Through experience and relationships with team members, the book discusses the inspirational role of a leader as well as coping with chaos, gaining team support, empowerment, trust, and intuition.
Subject(s): Sports leadership

James, G. (1996). *Business wisdom of the electronic elite: 34 winning management strategies from CEOs at Microsoft, COMPAQ, Sun, Hewlett-Packard and other top companies.* New York: Times Business.

From industry-wide research and personal interviews with leaders of successful high-tech companies, James describes what the *electronic elite* have to teach other business leaders. He reveals their management strategies that unleash creativity, increase responsiveness, respect individuals, and build communities. The new corporate culture practiced by the electronic elite can be adopted by traditional organizations if leaders and employees shift into six new mind-sets: 1) business is an ecosystem, not a battlefield; 2) the corporation is a community, not a machine; 3) management is service, not control; 4) employees are peers, not children; 5) motivate

with vision, not fear; and 6) change is growth, not pain. Throughout the book are quotations—tidbits of wisdom from the electronic elite, exercises, and self-assessments to test the reader's alignment with the new culture. Includes bibliography and index. Appendices summarize key learnings.
Subject(s): Technical leadership

Jaques, E., & Clement, S. D. (1991). *Executive leadership: A practical guide to managing complexity.* Arlington, VA: Cason Hall.

This book defines what leadership is, who can be a leader, and how managerial leadership affects the success or failure of an organization. Jaques and Clement examine the internal, personal world of human intent and the external world of human interaction in the workplace. They offer five components of capability to evaluate effective and accountable leaders. Examples are drawn from the U.S. Army leadership training and doctrine. Includes bibliographical references and index.
Subject(s): Military leadership

New
Johnson, C. B. (1997). **Are we losing potential leaders at an early age?** *A Leadership Journal: Women in Leadership—Sharing the Vision, 2*(1), 125-132.

Former middle school teacher Johnson administered two instruments, the *16 Personality Factor Questionnaire* and the *Basic Assessment of Cognitive Organization*, to groups of gifted students categorized as achievers and underachievers. She found that the underachieving students were at risk for failure in their academic work because they showed personality traits or learning styles that traditional education does not recognize. Johnson says that teachers must recognize these different learning styles and offer at-risk students leadership opportunities to ensure that they develop the necessary academic and leadership skills. Includes bibliographical references.
Subject(s): Educational leadership

Juckes, T. J. (1995). *Opposition in South Africa: The leadership of Z. K. Matthews, Nelson Mandela, and Stephen Biko.* Westport, CT: Praeger.

This book presents a sociopsychological retrospective of 20th-century political activities in South Africa. Three key individuals led an apartheid-opposition movement that restructured a society and earned one of them a Nobel Peace Prize. Zachariah Matthews led the intellectual movement that stressed liberation through education. Nelson Mandela, who was imprisoned for his leadership of the militant movement, became a symbol of black hope and strength. Stephen Biko's dedication to integrated education spawned the Black Consciousness movement. A chronology of events runs from the 1652 settlement of Dutch colonists to Nelson Mandela's 1990 release from prison, 1993 Nobel Peace Prize, and 1994 election as president of South Africa. Includes bibliographical references and index.
Subject(s): Political leadership in South Africa

New
Kaarbo, J., & Hermann, M. G. (1998). **Leadership styles of prime ministers: How individual differences affect the foreign policymaking process.** *Leadership Quarterly: Special Issue: Political Leadership*, *9*(3), 243-263.

The authors explore how leadership studies of the American presidential system might apply to the leadership study of prime ministers in parliamentary systems. Links are formed between leadership style and foreign-policy decision making. Some of the variables are: interest and experience in foreign policy, building support and developing good policy within the cabinet, managing information, managing conflict, and managing the locus of decisions. A pilot study of four prime ministers—Margaret Thatcher, John Major, Konrad Adenauer, and Helmut Kohl—is reported. Includes bibliographical references.
Subject(s): Prime ministers

Kahn, S. (1991). *Organizing: A guide for grassroots leaders* (Rev. ed.). Silver Spring, MD: NASW Press.

As a songwriter and folksinger Si Kahn focuses on struggle and social change in America. This written guide teaches how to unite people to effect change and existing power structures. Social workers set the example, serving as agents of change and preserving the worth, dignity, and uniqueness of each individual. Kahn calls for grassroots organizations to address the issues of homelessness, violence, drug abuse, poverty, and health care. Includes bibliographical references and index.
Subject(s): Grassroots leadership

Kanter, R. M. (1997). *Rosabeth Moss Kanter on the frontiers of management.* Boston: Harvard Business School Press.

Kanter, former editor of the *Harvard Business Review*, presents her classic essays as a refresher course for managers who are scrutinizing their organizational structures and aspiring to innovative futures. The essays cover a variety of topics: strategy, innovation, global trends, strategic alliances, and community responsibility. But there is a unifying theme: "the importance of providing the tools and conditions that liberate people to use their brainpower to make a difference in a world of constant change and challenge." In Chapter 5 Kanter describes six certainties for CEOs to achieve success in an uncertain world: keep learning, focus on processes—not products, maintain standards of excellence, understand the politics of business, develop interdependent and intercompany relationships, and be prepared for rising levels of discomfort. Chapter 19 describes the 1991 *World Leadership Survey* distributed through business journals in 25 countries. Responses came from 11,678 managers representing all 25 countries. Includes index.
Subject(s): Corporate leadership

New
Kanter, R. M. (1999). **Change is everyone's job: Managing the extended enterprise in a globally connected world.** *Organizational Dynamics*, *28*(1), 7-23.

Kanter introduces the future of corporate leadership—a geographically dispersed team that shares knowledge, rewards innovation, and thrives on disagreement. Her fictional team is actually a composite of trends that she currently sees among CEOs, boards, and senior executives. In this article Kanter shares some of the best practices that she's observed in extended enterprises. Such companies offer seed grants for innovation, develop high-potential change agents, champion knowledge networks, and train collaboration ambassadors. Kanter sums up the best practices as the 3Cs: concepts, competence, and connections. Includes bibliographical references.
Subject(s): Corporate leadership, change

New
Karl, K. A., & Sutton, C. L. (1998). **Job values in today's workforce: A comparison of public and private sector employees.** *Public Personnel Management*, *27*(4), 515-527.

To determine what job values workers found most important and whether public and private employees valued different things, the authors surveyed over 200 workers in a range of public and private jobs. While similar studies in the 1970s and 1980s found that employees valued interesting work most highly, these data show that good wages and job security are the most important factors for today's workers. But while public and private employees valued job security equally, wages were more important to private workers. Public employees were more likely to rate doing interesting work as the most important job value. Includes bibliographical references.
Subject(s): Public service leadership

Keithly, D. M. (1996). **Leadership in doctrine.** *Journal of Leadership Studies*, *3*(4), 129-138.

Keithly, an associate professor at the National Defense University, explains the U.S. Navy's military doctrine for learning and practicing leadership. During times of peace, Naval commanders have little opportunity to practice the skills necessary for combat leadership. They rely on a leadership doctrine, a set of standards written by senior officers. Recognizing that leadership is complex, the standards are not commandments. They are a touchstone from which an officer may use personal judgment, take initiative, and develop a personal style. The doctrine recognizes that leadership hinges on personalities and situations.
Subject(s): Military leadership

Kellerman, B. (Ed.). (1986). *Political leadership.* Pittsburgh, PA: University of Pittsburgh Press.

This is a sourcebook for the study of political leadership. All of the essays address some aspect of leadership, yet among the authors are philosophers, psychologists, sociologists, political scientists, historians, mythologists, literary figures, activists, and public officials. The collection is particularly rich in political psychology—work that explicitly connects political life to the psychology of individuals and groups. Includes bibliographies.

Subject(s): Political leadership

New

Kets de Vries, M. F. R., & Florent-Treacy, E. (1999). *The new global leaders: Richard Branson, Percy Barnevik, and David Simon.* San Francisco: Jossey-Bass.

Branson of Virgin, Barnevik of BPP, and Simon of British Petroleum are business leaders who have used innovative methods to expand their companies into the global marketplace. This book first profiles the men, describing their backgrounds and business experiences, and then provides a transcript of an interview conducted with each man. A concluding section uses the profiles to identify leadership best practices used by these leaders, including expressing the vision, gaining power by sharing power, and choosing complementary colleagues. Includes index.

Subject(s): Corporate leadership, global leadership

New

Keyes, M. W., Maxwell, C. H., & Capper, C. A. (1999). **"Spirituality? It's the core of my leadership": Empowering leadership in an inclusive elementary school.** *Educational Administration Quarterly*, 35(2), 203-237.

Education legislations have included individuals with disabilities. Most recently, the law has mandated that special needs students be educated in a least restrictive environment. The outcome of this mandate varies according to individual districts and schools. This article presents an ethnographic study to determine the role of the principal in an inclusive elementary school. The framework for the study consisted of three particular behaviors: creating a supportive environment, facilitation of critique, and the possibilities for staff development. The study was conducted in one particular school using data from observations and interviews with students, staff, district administration, and the principal. The discussion notes the effects of the framework behaviors as well as six spiritual beliefs based in each of the behaviors. The results advocate the crucial role of principal leadership in an inclusive school through five conclusions. Includes bibliographical references.

Subject(s): Principal as leader

Koehler, J. W., & Pankowski, J. M. (1997). *Transformational leadership in government.* Delray Beach, FL: St. Lucie Press.

This book is a response to public cynicism of government bureaucracies that consume tax dollars, stifle innovation, and deliver far fewer outcomes than citizens demand. The authors draw parallels between government agencies and corporations and their leadership. Corporations have been moving toward smaller, more responsive, and efficient organizational structures with empowered employees. The authors suggest

that government agencies implement such transformational style leadership to improve their own organizations. This book outlines the principles, skills, and behaviors of transformational leadership. It suggests steps for creating a vision, empowering employees, and inspiring change. Includes bibliography and index.

Subject(s): Public service leadership, transformational leadership

Kotter, J. P. (1988). *The leadership factor.* New York: Free Press.

In a very precise and direct manner the components that allow effective leadership to occur are presented. This book covers such factors as: why effective leadership is increasingly important and what does effective leadership really mean to business outcomes, profits, and products? Companies that have shown superior leadership are presented to illustrate the elements present in real situations that promote the growth of effective leadership. The appendix offers an *Executive Resources Questionnaire* helpful to those who may be curious to know where their business falls in the effective leadership spectrum. Includes bibliography and index.

Subject(s): Corporate leadership

Kotter, J. P. (1990). *A force for change: How leadership differs from management.* New York: Free Press.

Kotter reports on a two-phase research program to determine the differences between leadership and management. First, 200 senior executives from 12 successful organizations were interviewed and surveyed regarding executive history and behavior. Then, 12 cases of "highly effective leadership in business" were identified and studied. Kotter indicates that early experiences form intelligence, drive, mental health, and integrity—factors that separate leaders from managers. Vision, alignment, and motivation are defined. Examples illustrate what these factors look like in practice and how they are created. Includes bibliographical references and index.

Subject(s): Corporate leadership

Kotter, J. P. (1995). *The new rules: How to succeed in today's post-corporate world.* New York: Free Press.

A tracking study of 115 MBAs from the Harvard Class of 1974 reveals changes in the path to a successful career. Over 20 years the study participants responded to annual questionnaires indicating their personal and professional choices, actions, successes, and failures. Kotter's assessment of the data indicates that career paths have changed drastically in 20 years. The globalization of markets and competition has caused a huge shift in economic forces, the structure and function of organizations, and wage levels. The path to a successful career has shifted away from big business toward entrepreneurship. Currently the requirements for success are speed and flexibility, exceedingly high standards, a strong competitive nature, and lifelong learning. Includes bibliographical references and index.

Subject(s): Entrepreneurship

Lakey, B., Lakey, G., Napier, R., & Robinson, J. (1995). *Grassroots and nonprofit leadership: A guide for organizations in changing times.* Philadelphia: New Society Publishers.

The authors believe that social change is like a river, at various times running fast, slow, dangerous, and calm. They use this metaphor to structure their book, which addresses the organizational issues nonprofits face. Chapter topics include starting a social movement (gathering the rafting party), handling growth (finding a big enough raft), developing a board (coordinating paddling), and avoiding burnout (pacing yourself for the journey). Includes index.
Subject(s): Grassroots leadership, nonprofit leadership

New
Lashway, L. (1997). *Leading with vision.* Eugene, OR: ERIC Clearinghouse on Educational Management.

Lashway synthesizes the literature on educational vision to explain how to define a vision, its content and purpose, alignment with school structure and culture, the roles of various stakeholders, and the effort it takes to implement a vision. Administrators, teachers, parents, and community leaders may also read this book to help plan their personal visions. Includes bibliographical references and a sample vision statement.
Subject(s): Educational leadership, vision

New
Leithwood, K., Lawrence, L., & Sharratt, L. (1998). **Conditions fostering organizational learning in schools.** *Educational Administration Quarterly, 34*(2), 243-276.

The National Commission on Teaching and America's Future reported the inadequacy of current school structures to support organizational learning. This article presents three particular studies of organizational learning pertaining to schools in British Columbia, Ontario, and Newfoundland. The purpose was to increase the small amount of known evidence concerning conditions affecting professional development of school personnel. The studies consisted of restructuring teaching and learning processes, changes in school-based management, and an increase in technology use in the curriculum. Teachers identified factors within the school, within the community, and in the administration that impact their organizational learning. The authors delve into the organizational learning process as it relates to these three studies and report the methodology and results. Includes bibliographical references.
Subject(s): Educational leadership

LeVeness, F. P., & Sweeney, J. P. (Eds.). (1987). *Women leaders in contemporary U.S. politics.* Boulder, CO: Lynne Rienner.

Based on personal interviews, this book is a collection of biographical sketches of nine women who have achieved success in politics. It focuses on their career paths, their unique areas of involvement, and their positions on women's issues. Shared character traits are identified as supportive

families, strong values, religious upbringing, and educational achievements. Among the women studied are Shirley Chisolm, Dianne Feinstein, Geraldine Ferraro, and Sandra Day O'Connor. Includes bibliographical references and index.
Subject(s): Political leadership, women leaders

Lewis, P. V. (1996). *Transformational leadership: A new model for total church involvement.* Nashville, TN: Broadman & Holman.

Lewis addresses the need for change in the leadership of today's churches. He outlines leadership traits and styles to help pastors identify their current practices and learn new ones. Transformational leadership style is most closely aligned with Christian leadership. It builds on the strengths of others, raises awareness about issues of consequence, and enables people to transcend their own self-interest. Lewis cites examples of transformational leadership from business, sports, music, and scripture. At the end of each chapter are questions to encourage discussion and reflection.
Subject(s): Religious leadership, transformational leadership

Lucas, A. F. (1994). *Strengthening departmental leadership: A team-building guide for chairs in colleges and universities.* San Francisco: Jossey-Bass.

Lucas offers advice for those who move from subject-specific faculty positions into roles as department chairs with leadership responsibilities. She outlines nine key responsibilities: creating a shared vision, motivating faculty to enhance productivity, motivating faculty to teach effectively, handling faculty evaluation and feedback, motivating faculty to increase scholarship, motivating faculty to increase service, building a creative climate for communication, managing conflict, and developing chair survival skills. She suggests a method to rate individuals, then use the feedback to build skills. A Leadership Matrix graphs an individual's skill development against each skill's importance to the department. Using the matrix allows an individual to see strengths and weaknesses and to plan opportunities for leadership development. Includes bibliographical references and index.
Subject(s): Leadership in higher education

Lynch, R. (1993). *Lead! How public and nonprofit managers can bring out the best in themselves and their organizations.* San Francisco: Jossey-Bass.

Managers are often so overwhelmed by everyday tasks that they forget the more fundamental task of leadership. Lynch describes how the leadership role transcends managerial tasks and explains how public and nonprofit leaders can enhance their organizations through bringing out the best in themselves, their organizations, and their people. Case studies are used to illustrate how managers can optimize their personal influence, establish a sense of collective purpose, design jobs that reward employees for meaningful tasks, create a more streamlined organizational structure, foster and sustain

meaningful values, keep employees hopeful in hard times, and create a positive organizational climate. Includes bibliographical references and index.
Subject(s): Public service leadership, nonprofit leadership

Maghroori, R., & Rolland, E. (1997). **Strategic leadership: The art of balancing organizational mission with policy, procedures, and external environment.** *Journal of Leadership Studies, 4*(2), 62-81.

This article examines strategic leadership and the assessment of the right leadership style for an organization's condition. Strategic leadership is defined as the art of creating a balance between external environment, corporate mission, and the corresponding system of implementation. External effectiveness occurs when an organization's mission is congruent with its external environment. Internal effectiveness suffers when policies and procedures are not aligned with the mission. Four leadership strategies for internal effectiveness are: status quo, total quality management, reengineering, and mission institutionalization. Four strategies for external effectiveness are: long-term survival, mission maintenance, mission realignment, and mission creation.
Subject(s): Strategic leadership

New
Maor, M. (1999). **The paradox of managerialism.** *Public Administration Review, 59*(1), 5-18.

Governmental reforms over the last 20 years have given public administrators more managerial control over programs. As a result political executives have lost control over program implementation and have attempted to compensate by fighting for more power over the bureaucracy. This has set up an interesting paradox: giving public administrators more power to administer programs tends to decrease both their job security and their influence in policy-making. This article illustrates the paradox by analyzing the changes in public officials' tenure security in Australia, New Zealand, Canada, the United Kingdom, Austria, and Malta between 1980 and 1996. Includes bibliographical references.
Subject(s): Public service leadership

Marano, R. (1997). **Young volunteers: Providing service and making an impact on communities.** *NASSP Bulletin, 81*(591), 45-48.

Marano describes the Prudential Spirit of Community Awards created in partnership with the National Association of Secondary School Principals in 1995. The awards recognize young heroes who initiate outstanding volunteer projects. So far 10,000 young people have been honored. Every U.S. school may name one honoree per every 1,000 students. From that pool each state selects two winners who each receive $1,000, a silver medal, and an expense-paid trip to the national awards in Washington, DC. Five national winners each receive $5,000 and a gold medal. One 1997 winner is Brian Harris of Cypress, California, who paired 20,000 global pen pals to promote interracial understanding.

Another is Kristin Deaton of Putnam City, Oklahoma, who founded a softball league for children with special needs. More than fame or prizes, the awards serve to focus on the contributions of young people and to encourage all citizens to get involved in their communities.
Subject(s): Youth leadership, volunteers

Marquis, B. L., & Huston, C. J. (1996). *Leadership roles and management functions in nursing: Theory and application* (2nd ed.). Philadelphia: Lippincott.

This is a textbook for students of nursing administration and leadership. It is divided into units covering advocacy, conflict resolution, ethical issues, time management, staffing, motivating, and controlling. The authors walk through the evolution of leadership styles from trait theories to visioning to the integrated leader. Decision-making tools such as decision grids and pay-off tables are provided. Each chapter contains learning exercises to enhance critical-thinking skills and promote discussion.
Subject(s): Nursing leadership, textbook

Mason, D. E. (1996). *Leading and managing the expressive dimension: Harnessing the hidden power source of the nonprofit sector.* San Francisco: Jossey-Bass.

Mason states that voluntary, nonprofit organizations are "instruments for people who want something done and arenas for people who seek expressive involvement." This expression may take the form of fostering innovation, the pleasure of performing, socializing, or alignment with an ideology. Among the competencies for developing an organization's expressive dimension are: forming and articulating a vision, building trust, communicating, innovating, understanding political activity, persuading, recruiting, fund-raising, emphasizing ethics, inspiring, exploiting opportunities, and maximizing cohesion. This book is written for leaders, volunteer coordinators, board members, researchers, educators, and consultants in the independent sector. Includes bibliographical references, name index, and subject index.
Subject(s): Nonprofit leadership

Matusak, L. R. (1997). *Finding your voice: Learning to lead—Anywhere you want to make a difference.* San Francisco: Jossey-Bass.

This book is written for people who do not hold positions of power but who do choose to lead. Matusak states that every day we all have opportunities to be creative, act with purpose, and encourage others to work together toward positive change. Through her work at the Kellogg Foundation Matusak has identified hundreds of people who make a difference in their communities without getting their names in the headlines. In this book she shares many of their stories. A resource section recommends leadership development programs, books, and films for people who want to find their voices and begin leading. Includes index.
Subject(s): Community leadership

McGovern, S. J. (1997). **Mayoral leadership and economic development policy: The case of Ed Rendell's Philadelphia.** *Policy and Politics*, *25*(2), 153-172.

McGovern describes the popularity and success of Philadelphia mayor Ed Rendell as a leadership phenomenon. Rendell was responsible for leading his city out of a fiscal crisis and pursuing economic growth, gaining an exceptional 80% approval rating among constituents. He has consulted with mayors throughout the country to share his leadership expertise. His methods include: collaboration with the city council and state legislature, personal involvement in large and small community affairs, bringing an influx of state aid and HUD money, and eliminating budget deficits without raising taxes. Rendell's leadership style served his city well in times of crisis. McGovern examines Rendell's ability to lead the city in *normal* times. Includes bibliographical references.

Subject(s): Mayors

New

McKinney, J. B., & Howard, L. C. (1998). *Public administration: Balancing power and accountability* (2nd ed.). Westport, CT: Praeger.

This textbook is designed for students aspiring to hold public administrative positions. Targeted toward middle- and lower-level managers, McKinney and Howard advocate greater accountability and empowerment among public servants in middle management. Their method of instruction includes relating theories to actual practice using case studies, and presents the context of administration including a definition of power and accountability. Various organization theories are discussed as well as processes and practices, supporting and controlling functions, and areas of policy. The final chapter argues that middle-level managers have considerable power and should utilize this in promoting a higher level of accountability.

Subject(s): Public service leadership, power, accountability, textbook

McNally, J. A., Gerras, S. J., & Bullis, R. C. (1996). **Teaching leadership at the U.S. Military Academy at West Point.** *Journal of Applied Behavioral Science*, *32*(2), 175-188.

The authors, professors in the Department of Behavioral Sciences and Leadership at West Point, describe their method for teaching their cadets leadership. They teach the Intellectual Procedure in which cadets identify what is happening, account for what is happening, and formulate leader action. The course also includes a theoretical section that addresses individuals, groups, leadership, and organizational systems. In addition the article describes the West Point grading and course-evaluation procedure, and the seven-week workshop on teaching military leadership that new faculty must attend. The authors have used the Intellectual Procedure when training police departments around the country and believe that it applies in both civilian and military settings.

Subject(s): Military leadership

Menzel, D. C. (Ed.). (1996). *The American county: Frontiers of knowledge.* Tuscaloosa: University of Alabama Press.

Most studies of leadership in public administration avoid discussion of county governments. This level of public administration is responsible for unglamorous services such as corrections, welfare, indigent health care, road maintenance, vital statistics, property taxes, and garbage collection. The essays in this book address a transformation of county governments in recent decades. They acknowledge that counties have rapidly growing populations to serve, are moving away from old-style political machines to new-style management structures, and are initiating coordinated services across intergovernmental boundaries. Challenges that face the elected and appointed officials who want to modernize county governments are: partisanship, fragmented authority, and the relationship between county commissioners and county managers. Includes bibliographical references and index.

Subject(s): County governments

Menzel, D. C. (1997). **Teaching ethics and values in public administration: Are we making a difference?** *Public Administration Review*, *57*(3), 224-230.

Beginning in the 1970s many schools offering master's degrees in public affairs and administration began requiring students to take ethics courses. This study surveyed the graduates of four such schools to determine whether they faced ethical dilemmas on the job and whether their ethics education helped them resolve these dilemmas. The author concluded that although students at three of the schools reported that their classes had helped them resolve ethical problems, overall these classes are not doing enough to address the real-life issues that public administration leaders face.

Subject(s): Public service leadership, ethics

New

Mertz, N. T., & McNeely, S. R. (1998). **Women on the job: A study of female high school principals.** *Educational Administration Quarterly*, *34*(2), 196-222.

This study was conducted to examine the leadership of females in a predominantly male occupation of school administration, specifically, principalship. Two female high school principals were chosen for the study, which consisted of close examination of their behaviors in this role. Results indicate little difference between the styles of the two women when compared to males in the same position; however, the surprising differences occurred between the styles of the two women. The article details the leadership of both women and follows with a discussion of the results. Includes bibliographical references.

Subject(s): Principal as leader

New

Meyer, C. (1997). ***Relentless growth: How Silicon Valley's innovative secrets will work for you.*** New York: Free Press.

Drawing on his experience as a consultant and educator for Silicon Valley firms, Meyer attempts to answer two questions: 1) How does Silicon Valley grow successfully through innovation, and 2) How can this innovation methodology be adapted to work in other companies? Meyer says that Silicon Valley leaders actively encourage their managers to innovate by generating competitive paranoia, getting employees focused externally, and setting "stretch" goals. He then describes a five-part model for integrating the innovation process with daily operations, focusing on: 1) the role of leadership in creating growth, 2) strategic alignment, 3) the innovation process and development paradigm, 4) the application of predictive and balanced metrics, and 5) the people. Includes index.

Subject(s): Technical leadership, innovation

Michaels, J. E. (1997). ***The president's call: Executive leadership from FDR to George Bush.*** Pittsburgh, PA: University of Pittsburgh Press.

Arguing that presidents are "judged by the company they keep," Michaels examines presidential leadership in the context of Senate-confirmed presidential appointees (PASs). She surveyed and interviewed current and former PASs, mainly from the Bush administration, and uses the responses to analyze the leadership of both presidents and PASs within their departments. Chapters describe the people who become PASs, the nomination and confirmation process, interbureaucratic relations, and how presidents use political appointments. Advice is also offered to future PASs. Includes bibliographical references and index.

Subject(s): U.S. presidents

Miles, R. H. (1997). ***Leading corporate transformation: A blueprint for business renewal.*** San Francisco: Jossey-Bass.

According to Miles, the corporate transformation process can be broken down into four steps: generating energy for transformation, developing a vision of the future, aligning the organization and culture, and orchestrating the transformation. The author also divides corporate transformations into four categories—repositioning, revitalizing, merging businesses and cultures, and managing leadership succession—which he illustrates with case studies of organizations including National Semiconductor and the PGA Tour. Includes bibliographical references and index.

Subject(s): Corporate leadership

New

Mintzberg, H., Ahlstrand, B., & Lampel, J. (1998). ***Strategy safari: A guided tour through the wilds of strategic management.*** New York: Free Press.

Strategy formation is the proverbial blind man's elephant that seems to be a different beast from every angle. This book identifies the various parts and puts together a coherent big picture. Readers journey on a safari of ten schools of strategic management: design, planning, positioning, entrepreneurial, cognitive, learning, power, cultural, environmental, and configurational. A critique of each considers its contributions and limitations. The entrepreneurial school contributes the concept of vision manifested in visionary leadership. In the end two figures illustrate the beast of strategic management with all its parts. One is a map that juxtaposes the messages of all schools. The other splits the process. The authors contend that understanding both outcomes is the only way to understand strategic management. Includes bibliographical references and index.

Subject(s): Strategic management

New

Moon, M. J. (1999). **The pursuit of managerial entrepreneurship: Does organization matter?** *Public Administration Review, 59*(1), 31-43.

Public organizations are increasingly encouraging entrepreneurial tactics as a way to improve service and management. This article identifies three types of entrepreneurship that managers use in organizations: product-based (enhancing customer satisfaction), process-based (reducing red tape), and behavior-based (promoting risk-taking). The authors used survey data from the National Administrative Studies Project to determine what organizational factors facilitate entrepreneurship. Findings suggest that three sets of factors—structural, cultural, and environmental—affect whether workers use entrepreneurial strategies. To facilitate these strategies leaders must reduce hierarchy and formalization and increase trust and mission clarity. Includes bibliographical references.

Subject(s): Public service leadership, entrepreneurship

New

Morris, M. H. (1998). ***Entrepreneurial intensity: Sustainable advantages for individuals, organizations, and societies.*** Westport, CT: Quorum Books.

Morris says that entrepreneurship is not just about starting a small business but is a bottom-up way of thinking about business and life centered around the idea of individual responsibility and choice. The book begins by listing 13 common myths about entrepreneurship and then describes the resources and environment necessary for the entrepreneurial process to succeed. Morris also addresses entrepreneurship at different levels, including the individual, organizational, and societal levels. Final chapters discuss government and entrepreneurship and the possible future for entrepreneurs. Includes bibliographical references and index.

Subject(s): Entrepreneurship

Murphy, J. A., & Pimentel, S. (1996). **Grading principals: Administrator evaluations come of age.** *Phi Delta Kappan, 78*(1), 74-84.

This article examines a results-based, profit-sharing evaluation program used in the Charlotte-Mecklenburg Schools

(CMS), North Carolina. It is similar to evaluation programs found in the corporate world. CMS moved from evaluations based on a principal's compliance, to a checklist of rules, to a system that focuses on a principal's effectiveness. The system is based on performance incentives—bonuses for staff who have made improvements or have met set goals. Examples of questions from evaluation surveys given to teachers, staff, parents, and students are provided. Addie Moore and Fred Slade, two CMS principals, share their personal accounts of the new evaluation system's effect on their work.

Subject(s): Principal as leader

New

Nalbandian, J. (1999). **Facilitating community, enabling democracy: New roles for local government managers.** *Public Administration Review*, *59*(1), 187-197.

Open-ended survey questions and in-depth panel discussions were used to identify how the roles of city management professionals have changed over the last ten years. Four major changes are identified: 1) city managers are now responsible for community building, 2) managers are expected to facilitate and develop partnerships, 3) the council-manager system is no longer seen as the "best" way of government, and 4) managers' administrative roles are becoming more process oriented. Includes bibliographical references.

Subject(s): City managers

New

Nanus, B., & Dobbs, S. M. (1999). *Leaders who make a difference: Essential strategies for meeting the nonprofit challenge.* San Francisco: Jossey-Bass.

Leaders of nonprofit organizations must play a unique role: while handling all of the managerial and strategic responsibilities of a business leader, they also bear a responsibility for making society a better place. This book describes the six roles that the authors say nonprofit leaders must play to ensure their organization's success—visionary, strategist, change agent, coach, politician, and fund-raiser—and devotes a chapter to each. Each chapter includes descriptions of the competencies and skills needed to fulfill that role and a profile of a successful nonprofit leader. Includes bibliographical references and index.

Subject(s): Nonprofit leadership

Neustadt, R. E. (1990). *Presidential power and the modern presidents: The politics of leadership from Roosevelt to Reagan* (Rev. ed.). New York: Free Press.

The president is vested with the powers of our country's highest office. How does he make those powers work for him? Neustadt defines power in politics: what it is, how to get it, how to keep it, how to lose it. This revised edition reexamines Franklin D. Roosevelt, Truman, and Eisenhower and then examines Kennedy, Johnson, Nixon, Ford, Carter, and Reagan. It is intended as a learning device for corpora-

tion presidents, union leaders, clergy, and students of government and politics. Includes bibliographical references and index.

Subject(s): U.S. presidents

New

Nice, D. C. (1998). **The warrior model of leadership: Classic perspectives and contemporary relevance.** *Leadership Quarterly: Special Issue: Political Leadership*, *9*(3), 321-332.

The author uses examples of warrior leaders in classic philosophy and literature to explain some behaviors demonstrated in political leaders today. His sources are: Machiavelli's *The Prince* (1514), Clausewitz's *On War* (1832), Musashi's *A Book of Five Rings* (1645), Sun Tzu's *The Art of War* (c. 400 B.C.), the book of Sirach (c. 180 B.C.) from the Apochrypha, and the writings of Baltasar Gracián (1658). A common theme is that warrior leadership is dependent on conflict and opposition. Warrior leaders control the flow of information and believe that success is more important than how it is achieved. Warrior leaders regard the world as a dangerous place and know their adversaries well enough to exploit their vulnerabilities. Nice connects these behaviors to specific and generalized behaviors at the presidential and congressional level of the American political system. Includes bibliographical references.

Subject(s): Political leadership, leadership lessons in literature, Eastern philosophy

Oliver, D., Jr. (1992). *Lead on! A practical approach to leadership.* Novato, CA: Presidio Press.

Drawing on years of experience in America's nuclear-powered submarine fleet, Rear Admiral Dave Oliver's leadership successes have far-reaching implications for civilian management. His stories and examples of leadership at work in military situations show how leadership makes individual efforts better and melds individuals into superior teams. The final chapter encapsulates the book with a checklist for leadership effectiveness. Includes bibliographical references.

Subject(s): Military leadership

Pagonis, W. G., & Cruikshank, J. L. (1992). *Moving mountains: Lessons in leadership and logistics from the Gulf War.* Boston: Harvard Business School Press.

Pagonis recounts his logistical operation that moved unprecedented numbers of people, vehicles, fuel, ammunition, food, shelters, medical supplies, and mail during the Gulf War. Citing Alexander the Great as his inspiration, Pagonis describes the leadership lessons found in logistical operations. He credits his success on building blocks—leadership support from many directions: 1) the civilian leadership of President Bush and Secretary of Defense Cheney; 2) military leadership of Generals Schwartzkopf, Powell, Yeosock, Luce, and Franks; 3) corporate leadership of the 12,000 Americans working in Saudi Arabia; 4) global leadership of

the host country; and 5) the hands-on leadership among his troops. Includes bibliographical references and index.
Subject(s): Military leadership

New
Palmer, P. J. (1998). *The courage to teach: Exploring the inner landscape of a teacher's life.* San Francisco: Jossey-Bass.

Palmer says that good teaching comes from the identity and integrity of the teacher because "we teach who we are." Therefore "good teaching requires self-knowledge." He asserts that when teachers truly examine their own motives and fears they will be better able to be present with their students and make the most of learning opportunities. He specifically addresses common fears teachers share and describes how teachers can create a learning community that will allow them to teach in a supportive environment. Palmer uses examples from his own teaching career to show the importance of self-knowledge, and says that the ideas in this book can apply to all teachers, from kindergarten to college. Includes index.
Subject(s): Educational leadership, courage

New
Palmer, P. J. (1998). **Evoking the spirit in public education.** *Educational Leadership: Association for Supervision and Curriculum Development, 56*(4), 6-11.

The author is also a traveling teacher who advocates teaching for meaning. Palmer believes that the focus of current education ignores the important aspect of spirituality. He promotes the openness of teachers and students to seek a connection between themselves and life. The latter part of the article exemplifies spirituality for teachers and methods to help them with spiritual education. This entire issue is dedicated to *The Spirit of Education* with Palmer as the lead author. The adjacent article explores spirituality as natural experiences in schools. Other articles present opposing viewpoints concerning the role of spirituality and religion in schools.
Subject(s): Educational leadership, spirit

Parkay, F. W., & Hall, G. E. (1992). *Becoming a principal: The challenges of beginning leadership.* Needham Heights, MA: Allyn and Bacon.

This book presents the findings of the Beginning Principals Study (BPS) through case studies on 12 first-year principals. The purpose of the BPS is to show the development of a principal's professional identity. It also describes his or her expectations, fears, and common problems. Directed to graduate students, the discussion questions and activities at the end of each chapter examine the basics of a successful foundation: visibility, communication, and an effective administrative team. The authors offer advice for new principals on decision making, relationships with staff, and empowerment. Veteran principals share their reflections. The experiences of principals in Canada, the United Kingdom,

and Australia are compared to those in the U.S. Includes bibliographical references and index.
Subject(s): Principal as leader

Parry, A. E., & Horton, M. J. (1997). **Board leadership when there is no leader.** *Journal of Leadership Studies, 4*(2), 55-61.

This case study is a model for universities that are facing the crisis of operating without a president and with only a board of directors. Friends University, a small private university in Kansas, shares its story of finding a replacement for a resigned president and dealing with the challenge of balancing the budget and reducing the deficit at the same time. The college approached the situation by learning how the outside world perceived the school and accepting the results of this critical research. Then the board worked together to find a qualified president while successfully reducing the school's deficit.
Subject(s): University boards

New
Pascale, R. (1998, April-May). **Grassroots leadership.** *Fast Company,* (14), 110-120.

Steve Miller, a group managing director at Royal Dutch/Shell, shares his philosophy of grassroots leadership in a corporate environment. Specifically, he describes the efforts to empower people "at the coal face," those in the field and on the frontline in the company. A series of boot camps, work sessions "in a fishbowl," and follow-up sessions to discuss breakdowns and breakthroughs develop leaders who will develop more leaders. Channeling managerial egos into teaching efforts improves company performance from the bottom up.
Subject(s): Corporate leadership

Peters, R. M., Jr. (Ed.). (1994). *The speaker: Leadership in the U.S. House of Representatives.* Washington, DC: Congressional Quarterly.

In the foreword, former speaker Tom Foley describes changes in the U.S. House of Representatives over the past 30 years. Primarily, there has been a movement away from a monopoly of power in the hands of senior members to a distribution of power to all members. Ironically, as power was redistributed in the House, the role of the speaker grew more influential. This book provides a history and insightful analysis of this role. Topics include: selecting a speaker, the speaker as party leader, the speaker's relationship with the minority party, and the speaker's influence on the national budget and foreign policy. Former speakers Carl Albert, Thomas P. "Tip" O'Neill, Jr., and Jim Wright share their insights and advice to those who follow in their footsteps. Includes bibliographical references and index.
Subject(s): Congressional leadership

New

Pettigrew, A., & McNulty, T. (1998). **Sources and uses of power in the boardroom.** *European Journal of Work and Organizational Psychology, 7*(2), 197-214.

This study used interviews, surveys, and documentary materials to examine how the boards of the top 50 British corporations perceived and used their power. The authors focused specifically on how the power of part-time board members compared to that of full-time members. A four-part conceptual model describes the interaction of context, structure, power sources, and the "will and skill" members have to use power. Two case studies illustrate how boards can use their power to dismiss influential members. Includes bibliographical references.
Subject(s): Corporate boards, power

Pfeffer, J. (1994). *Competitive advantage through people: Unleashing the power of the work force.* Boston: Harvard Business School Press.

Pfeffer documents his belief that unleashing the power of the workforce is essential in the success of any organization. Written as a textbook for an organizational behavior course, a chapter on effective firms highlights 16 practices for managing people, such as employee ownership, information sharing, training and skill development, and promotion from within. A chapter on wrong heroes and wrong theories describes real-world examples of bad human-resource practices. The final chapter, "Making the Change," explains how all industries can dramatically improve their performance by redefining relationships with workers. This book is recommended for organizations undergoing restructuring, implementing new programs, or considering downsizing. Includes bibliographical references and index.
Subject(s): Corporate leadership, textbook

New

Pfeffer, J. (1998). *The human equation: Building profits by putting people first.* Boston: Harvard Business School Press.

Pfeffer argues that "the culture and capabilities of an organization—derived from the way it manages people—are the real and enduring sources of competitive advantage." This book describes mistakes organizations make in managing people, such as inadequate compensation and incompetent dealings with unions. Pfeffer also identifies seven characteristics of successful organizations: 1) employment security, 2) selective hiring of new personnel, 3) self-managed teams and decentralized decision making, 4) high compensation contingent on organizational performance, 5) extensive training, 6) reduced status distinctions and barriers, and 7) extensive sharing of performance and financial information. Includes index.
Subject(s): Corporate leadership

New

Pillai, R., & Williams, E. A. (1998). **Does leadership matter in the political arena? Voter perceptions of candidates' transformational and charismatic leadership and the 1996 U.S. presidential vote.** *Leadership Quarterly: Special Issue: Political Leadership, 9*(3), 397-416.

This study examines various influences on voter behavior: political ideology, party affiliation, intent to vote, and candidates' perceived leadership styles and abilities. A survey of 262 working students was taken one week before the 1996 U.S. presidential election. Students judged Democratic incumbent Bill Clinton and Republican candidate Bob Dole on factors of transformational and charismatic leadership. Students also provided data on party affiliation, intent to vote, and demographics. A post-election survey collected voting data. The results indicate that the evaluation of leadership has a significant impact on voting behavior even after party affiliation is considered. Includes bibliographical references.
Subject(s): U.S. presidents, transformational leadership, charismatic leadership

New

Pitcher, P. (1997). *Artists, craftsmen, and technocrats: The dreams, realities, and illusions of leadership* (2nd ed.). Toronto: Stoddart.

Pitcher studied the CEOs of 15 global financial corporations to determine what type of leaders they were: artists, craftsmen, or technocrats. This book uses the metaphor of a play—complete with actors, plot, and staging—to illustrate how these different types of leaders interact and the problems that result when the wrong type of leader fills a particular role. Appendices include an adjective checklist and guidelines for interpretation, the history of Pitcher's leader-as-artist theory, and data from his research. Includes index.
Subject(s): CEOs

Pynes, J. E. (1997). *Human resources management for public and nonprofit organizations.* San Francisco: Jossey-Bass.

Written by a professor of public administration, this is the first book to address integrating human resources management and strategic mission in the context of public and nonprofit agencies. In addition to discussing recruitment, performance evaluation, and compensation, the author addresses issues unique to nonprofits, such as managing volunteers. Figures and exhibits provided include wage schedules, sample interview questions, National Labor Relations Board Standards, and a grid for matching present and potential board members.
Subject(s): Nonprofit leadership, public service leadership

New

Ragsdale, L. (1998). *Vital statistics on the presidency.* Washington, DC: Congressional Quarterly.

Ragsdale presents a comprehensive statistical picture of the presidency, from Washington to Clinton. While the book does offer background information on the individuals who have held the office, it primarily emphasizes the importance of the presidency as an institution. Over 150 tables and figures present data on presidential selection, elections, public appearances, public opinion, the executive branch, presidential policy-making, congressional relations, and the presidency and the judiciary. Includes bibliographical references and index.

Subject(s): U.S. presidents

New

Ramsden, P. (1998). *Learning to lead in higher education.* New York: Routledge.

Ramsden describes the present state of academic leadership as challenging and alludes to increasing difficulties in the future. This source is aimed specifically toward department heads in higher education who are in need of leadership training. Part one introduces six principles and four responsibilities of academic leadership. Part two delineates a leadership improvement plan including vision, planning, and general management. Beginning in the second part, Ramsden uses real-life examples to enhance his teachings. The final portion of the book discusses the fostering of academic leadership for the future. Includes bibliographical references, appendix, and index.

Subject(s): Leadership in higher education

Reed, T. K. (1996). **A new understanding of "followers" as leaders: Emerging theory of civic leadership.** *Journal of Leadership Studies, 3*(1), 95-104.

Reed presents the new theory of civic leadership and how it has transformed the shape of leadership and democratized society. During the last three decades social movements have fostered civic learning among followers of grassroots leaders. This learning has equipped followers to take a critical look at the world around them and to take action against injustice. In this article civic leaders are defined as are the differences between civic participation and civic leadership. One impact of civic leadership is that leaders are no longer universally trusted simply by virtue of position. Reed challenges leadership study programs to learn more about this emerging leadership role and the new theory of societal leadership.

Subject(s): Civic leadership, followership

Rejai, M., & Phillips, K. (1996). *World military leaders: A collective and comparative analysis.* Westport, CT: Greenwood.

This analysis covers 45 military leaders from 13 countries. Rejai and Phillips look at sociodemographic, psychological, and situational variables that accounted for the development of each military leader, using a quantitative and qualitative approach. Some of the variables analyzed are: urban or rural birthplace; number of siblings and age rank among them; ethnicity; religious affiliation; education level; father's primary occupation; membership in legal or revolutionary organizations; arrest, imprisonment or exile; and foreign

travel. The authors also look at six psychological or motivational dynamics that propel men toward military careers: nationalism; conservative (or ultra-) nationalism; relative deprivation; love deprivation; marginality; and vanity, egotism, and narcissism. Includes bibliographical references and index.

Subject(s): Military leaders, multicultural context

New

Renett, D., & McLure, H. (1998). **New partnerships: Federal managers and the human resources office.** *The Public Manager, 27*(2), 44-48.

In 1998 the Center for Human Resources Management at the National Academy of Public Administration began holding a series of workshops for line managers and human resources (HR) officials. The goal of the workshops was to identify the strengths and weaknesses of the line/HR relationship and determine how to encourage proactive, collaborative interactions. While both groups agreed that line managers are responsible for many HR functions and need support from HR staff, line managers were less positive about the current state of the business relationship. This article describes exercises used in the workshop and some of the action plans participants developed, which focused on the need for improved communication between HR and line managers.

Subject(s): Public service leadership, line managers, human resources managers

New

Renshon, S. A. (1998). **Analyzing the psychology and performance of presidential candidates at a distance: Bob Dole and the 1996 presidential campaign.** *Leadership Quarterly: Special Issue: Political Leadership, 9*(3), 377-395.

Renshon explains why the public finds it difficult to make sound judgments about candidates campaigning for political office. There are too many candidates to evaluate in too little time, and political advisors control the information released to the public. This article suggests a framework for journalists and the public to understand the character, leadership, and judgment of U.S. presidential candidates. Comparative psychoanalytic theory is applied to an analysis of three presidential tasks: decision making, leadership, and politics. To demonstrate the framework Renshon analyzes 1996 Republican presidential candidate Robert Dole. Includes bibliographical references.

Subject(s): Political leadership

New

Riggs, F. W. (1998). **Public administration in America: Why our uniqueness is important.** *Public Administration Review, 58*(1), 22-31.

Riggs describes his work during the 1960s with the American Society for Public Administration's Comparative Administration Group, which studied how American public administration practices could be applied in developing countries. He argues that the American experience is so unique that

American management techniques are often useless in other contexts. He advocates studying the American public service from a comparative perspective, which will allow scholars to better understand the U.S. system and will help practitioners improve their efforts overseas. Examples from Riggs's work in Thailand, and from American and British history, support his argument. Includes bibliographical references.
Subject(s): Public service leadership

New
Rinehart, J. S., Short, P. M., Short, R. J., & Eckley, M. (1998). **Teacher empowerment and principal leadership: Understanding the influence process.** *Educational Administration Quarterly, 34* (Supplemental Issue), 630-649.

Increased teacher empowerment is a goal for many educators. The attainment of this shift is thought to be greatly influenced by the leadership of principals. This article depicts a study conducted to determine the influence of principals on teacher empowerment. The authors examined the relationship between teacher empowerment and the influence of principals, focusing on three elements of the *social influence theory*: trustworthiness, attractiveness, and expertness. The findings are presented in three particular conclusions supporting the notion that empowerment levels are influenced by trustworthiness and social attractiveness. Includes bibliographical references and three tables.
Subject(s): Principal as leader, empowerment

Rockman, B. A. (1997). **The limits of executive power.** *The World & I, 12*(1), 22-31.

Rockman claims that the American president appears to be more powerful than he really is. In public he is surrounded by media and Secret Service personnel. Streets are blockaded to let his motorcade pass. When he approaches a podium to speak, a band plays "Hail to the Chief." These symbols create an illusion of power for a president who is head of state but limited by constitutional checks and balances. Rockman compares the real power of modern American presidents to past presidents and to heads of state in other countries. In other countries heads of state do not have the same constraints imposed by the American Congress and Supreme Court.
Subject(s): U.S. presidents

Rose, G. L. (1997). *The American presidency under siege.* Albany: State University of New York Press.

Rose observes that in the past 25 years presidential elections have become a routine exercise in politics more than "a coming to power of a new national leader." He contends that presidential candidates no longer touch the hearts and souls of American citizens, not because of voter apathy but because of a post-Watergate phenomenon—a decline in presidential power. Rose sees the American presidency as under siege by special interest groups, the media, an oversized federal bureaucracy, and a reactionary Congress. He documents this hostile environment, describes the contributions of America's best presidents, and proposes the restoration of creative

presidential leadership. An appendix suggests debate issues for students of political science. Includes bibliographical references and index.
Subject(s): U.S. presidents

New
Rosenthal, C. S. (1998). *When women lead: Integrative leadership in state legislatures.* New York: Oxford University Press.

An integrative style of leadership is characterized by a sharing of power, mutuality, cooperation, and lack of competitiveness. According to Rosenthal, women tend to employ this style in their leadership of state legislative committees. This source serves as an exploration of gender differences in political leadership. It describes the theoretical roots of gender leadership styles in legislatures while presenting origins of committee styles. After defining the components of integrative leadership, Rosenthal presents case studies from Colorado, Ohio, and Oklahoma to demonstrate geographical influence on leadership styles. Includes bibliographical references, appendix, and tables.
Subject(s): Women as political leaders

New
Rothwell, W. J., Prescott, R. K., & Taylor, M. W. (1998). *Strategic human resource leader: How to prepare your organization for the six key trends shaping the future.* Palo Alto, CA: Davies-Black.

This book works as an action-planning guide for reinventing the human resources (HR) function and turning HR practitioners into visionary, strategic leaders. There are six challenges facing organizations of the near future: technology, globalization, cost containment, speedy market changes, knowledge capital, and change. HR leaders must anticipate each trend, plan strategies to deal with each, and develop competencies to implement the strategies. Interviews with renowned HR leaders and exercises throughout the book help readers apply learnings to their own organizations. Four appendices include two research reports, an organizational assessment tool, and an HR competency assessment tool. Includes bibliographical references and index.
Subject(s): Strategic leadership, human resources managers

Sapienza, A. M. (1995). *Managing scientists: Leadership strategies in research and development.* New York: Wiley-Liss.

This book is for managers who administer R&D organizations and direct the work of creative scientists. Their leadership challenges are unique—the cognitive work of scientists is unpredictable and scientists are often trained to be solo contributors. Sapienza discusses methods for improving human interaction and, thus, inspiration and collaboration among these knowledge workers. There are techniques for communicating, understanding organizational culture, designing systems to foster innovation, and managing change. Exercises help the reader identify personal leadership styles as well as strengths and weaknesses. Includes bibliographical references and index.

Subject(s): Technical leadership

New

Scarbrough, H. (1998). **The unmaking of management? Change and continuity in British management in the 1990s.** *Human Relations, 51*(6), 691-716.

Focusing on British organizations, this article describes the significant changes that have occurred in management over the last decade. The author challenges Charles Handy's late-1980s writings on management, arguing that developments in the business world since then are leading to the "unmaking of management." Scarborough says that as a result of shifts toward total quality management, lean organizations, and worker empowerment, managerial work has diffused through organizations, and that the very cultural definition of management is changing. Includes bibliographical references.

Subject(s): Corporate management

Scharfstein, B. (1995). *Amoral politics: The persistent truth of Machiavellism.* Albany: State University of New York Press.

The author uses the term *Machiavellism* to represent a "disregard of moral scruples in politics, that is, the political use . . . of every kind of deception and force." A comparison of political practice in Ancient China and India, Renaissance Italy, tribal cultures, and the 20th century indicates that Machiavellism is fundamental to societies and a human condition as common as love and hate. Scharfstein questions citizen acceptance of amoral politicians and some scholars' reluctance to include Machiavellism in studies of politics and ethics. He struggles with the question, "Does the prevalence of Machiavellism rule out the likelihood of a better political future?" but determines that it is impossible to answer. Includes bibliographical references and index.

Subject(s): Negative views of political leadership

Scher, R. K. (1997). *Politics in the new South: Republicanism, race and leadership in the twentieth century.* Armonk, NY: M. E. Sharpe, Inc.

While Scher disputes the existence of a "New South," in this book he describes three political changes that have shaped the South this century: the rise of the Republican party (and consequently two-party politics), the entry of blacks into mainstream politics, and the changing nature of gubernatorial leadership. In the section on Southern governors Scher offers both a historical background of the office and a theoretical model for Southern gubernatorial leadership. Charts, tables, and figures are included in this extensively researched book. Includes bibliographical references and index.

Subject(s): Political leadership

New

Scherer, M. (1998). **The discipline of hope: A conversation with Herb Kohl.** *Educational Leadership: Association for Supervision and Curriculum Development, 56*(1), 8-13.

In an interview with the founder of the Open School Movement, Scherer converses with Herb Kohl on the highlights of his newest book, *The Discipline of Hope.* Kohl formulates the requirements of a positive school climate, focusing on the importance of giving students hope. This article is the lead in a special issue titled *Realizing a Positive School Climate.* A neighboring article, "How Leaders Influence the Culture of Schools," emphasizes the critical role that principals, teachers, and parents play in creating a positive school climate. Other articles exemplify techniques used within the school to create a positive atmosphere.

Subject(s): Educational leadership

New

Schmitt, D. P., & Winter, D. G. (1998). **Measuring the motives of Soviet leadership and Soviet society: Congruence reflected or congruence created?** *Leadership Quarterly: Special Issue: Political Leadership, 9*(3), 293-307.

It is assumed that elected leaders of a democratic society reflect the will of the people and that dictators and totalitarian leaders impose their will upon the people. This study examines that assumption by considering three motives of political leaders—achievement, affiliation, and power—and their correlation to political behavior and the psychological convergence between the leader and the led. Speeches of four Soviet leaders—Stalin, Khrushchev, Brezhnev, and Gorbachev—are measured against societal profiles before, during, and after the time of the speeches. It is determined that in Soviet society leaders shaped rather than reflected the will of the people. Includes bibliographical references.

Subject(s): Political leadership in the Soviet Union, speeches

Schneider, M., Teske, P., & Mintrom, M. (1995). *Public entrepreneurs: Agents for change in American government.* Princeton, NJ: Princeton University Press.

Public entrepreneurs are political leaders who spearhead sweeping movements, introduce new policies, and create dynamic change. Entrepreneurs see unfilled needs and create new ways to meet those needs. Entrepreneurs seize opportunities even when the outcome is uncertain. And entrepreneurs assemble teams that have the talents and resources necessary to create a desired change. Includes bibliographical references and index.

Subject(s): Public service leadership

Scully, J. A., Sims, H. P., Jr., Olian, J. D., Schnell, E. R., & Smith, K. A. (1994). **Tough times make tough bosses: A meso-analysis of CEO leader behavior.** *Leadership Quarterly, 5*(1), 59-83.

Mid-level managers at 56 technology firms were asked to rate their CEOs' leadership behaviors. When compared to each firm's financial data the study showed that CEOs

respond to the bottom line with specific leadership styles. In firms with low performance, CEOs acted as tough bosses utilizing instruction-, command-, and reprimand-type behaviors. In firms with high performance, CEOs practiced encouraging, motivating, and inspiring behaviors.
Subject(s): CEOs

Selsky, J. W., & Smith, A. E. (1994). **Community entrepreneurship: A framework for social change leadership.** *Leadership Quarterly: Special Issue: Leadership for Environmental and Social Change*, 5(3/4), 277-296.

Community entrepreneurship occurs when a community-based leader organizes a group that influences social change. These situations are characterized by turbulent social environments, temporary and fluid alliances, and fast-paced events. Three qualities coexist in community entrepreneurs: the ability to envision and articulate a multiframe perspective, an entrepreneurial spirit, and a reflective and learning nature. Two case studies are documented in this research report, both concerned with community development in Philadelphia's nonprofit sector in the 1980s.
Subject(s): Community leadership, entrepreneurship

Sergiovanni, T. J. (1992). *Moral leadership: Getting to the heart of school improvement.* San Francisco: Jossey-Bass.

Sergiovanni introduces the idea of building school leadership on the basis of moral authority. This book for school administrators and principals examines a traditional view of leadership called *direct leadership* and its failure to improve schools. Sergiovanni suggests using substitutes for direct leadership such as creating a sense of community and promoting professionalism as a virtue. He believes that leaders should be servants and ministers to those whom they lead. Leadership needs to be based on shared values—in the sense of a community rather than an organization. Community leadership builds motivation through emotions, values, and connections with other people. Includes bibliographical references and index.
Subject(s): Educational leadership

Sergiovanni, T. J. (1994). *Building community in schools.* San Francisco: Jossey-Bass.

Sergiovanni focuses on the theory of community in schools as an alternative to a traditional, formal organizational structure. Community is a sense of connection and commitment. It binds teachers and students together with shared values and ideals. Educators interested in community are introduced to ideas for building relationships, transforming discipline policies, and encouraging citizenship. Key elements for a curriculum that supports community are: setting educational priorities, the social significance of students' learnings, and school climate. Principals and teachers who are struggling to build community share their ideas and stories. Includes bibliographical references and index.
Subject(s): Educational leadership

New
Sergiovanni, T. J. (1996). *Leadership for the schoolhouse: How is it different? Why is it important?* San Francisco: Jossey-Bass.

Sergiovanni argues against the perceived effectiveness of current educational leadership theories. Since schools belong to a unique institution, management of this institution should also be unique. An erroneous practice for educational leadership is to import styles and theories from business management. This source delineates the misuse of several popular corporate theories and lists criteria for ideal educational leadership theories. Sergiovanni advocates community building to aid in the establishment of "a moral voice" necessary for effective leadership. Other issues addressed include school size, decision making, staff development, and politics. This book proposes a new theory of change that accounts for the reality of the educational environment rather than the ideal of corporate theory. Includes bibliographical references and index.
Subject(s): Educational leadership

New
Sergiovanni, T. J. (2000). *The lifeworld of leadership: Creating culture, community, and personal meaning in our schools.* San Francisco: Jossey-Bass.

"Good schools" and "good school leadership" are both hard to define, but Sergiovanni says that they are both based on the accountability and involvement of the community. He argues that it is critical for schools to develop a sense of institutional character, and that this must happen at the local level in order to create the layered loyalties and sense of community accountability that lead to successful schools. This book describes how a strong school character can affect teachers, assessment, school leadership, and building a diverse community. Excerpts from reviews of two schools illustrate ways of evaluating teaching and learning. Includes bibliographical references and index.
Subject(s): Educational leadership

New
Sergiovanni, T. J., Burlingame, M., Coombs, F. S., & Thurston, P. W. (1999). *Educational governance and administration.* Boston: Allyn and Bacon.

This textbook serves as an introduction to educational administration and governance. The five parts each contain several chapters delving into an introduction to educational administration and governance, political issues, cultural aspects, and legal considerations. Part one discusses school policy and public values. Part two focuses on general administration including roles, theories, and leadership. Part three presents a cultural view of the educational environment emphasizing the people involved. Part four depicts the governance role in educational administration and delineates the role of local, federal, and state governments. The final part of the book considers the legal and financial aspects of

educational administration. Includes bibliographical references and index.
Subject(s): Educational leadership

Sessa, V. I., & Campbell, R. J. (1997). *Selection at the top: An annotated bibliography.* Greensboro, NC: Center for Creative Leadership.

In this era of rapidly changing organizational environments, the task of executive selection is critical. Compiled by researchers at the Center for Creative Leadership, these summaries direct the reader to over 100 books and articles on such issues as how to do selection, how to avoid costly mistakes, and how to predict executive success. Includes bibliographical references and index.
Subject(s): Corporate leadership, selection

New
Sessa, V. I., Kaiser, R., Taylor, J. K., & Campbell, R. J. (1998). *Executive selection: A research report on what works and what doesn't.* Greensboro, NC: Center for Creative Leadership.

What does it mean to be successful in today's organization? How can we select executives who are more likely to be successful? These are questions currently being asked of organizational researchers. This study addresses these queries as well as the larger issue of modern organizational executive selection. The purpose of this study was to determine the judging criteria of executive performance as well as methods of selection. The research report describes the Executive Selection Framework and follows with seven research questions. The findings are presented in extensive tables with results from each question. The discussion mirrors the questions introduced in the beginning and the report concludes with scientific and practical implications. Includes bibliographical references and appendices.
Subject(s): Corporate leadership, selection, research report

New
Sessa, V. I., & Taylor, J. K. (1999). **Choosing leaders: A team approach for selection.** *Leadership in Action*, *19*(2), 1-6.

The authors discuss their research on executive selection at the Center for Creative Leadership. Several studies with CEOs and top-level executives reveal two findings. First, selection decisions made by teams are more effective than those made by individuals. Second, there is a system for effective selection. The system begins with preparation—organizational assessment and position analysis. The next step is to assemble a selection team that represents diversity in terms of jobs and demographics. The system proceeds to plan a recruitment strategy, develop a rich candidate pool, and find the right match. Important final steps are to facilitate the new executive's transition into alignment with organizational values and to monitor behaviors for performance feedback. The authors state that executive selection itself is a crucial leadership activity. Includes bibliographical references.
Subject(s): Corporate leadership, selection

New
Shamir, B., Zakay, E., & Popper, M. (1998). **Correlates of charismatic leader behavior in military units: Subordinates' attitudes, unit characteristics, and superiors' appraisals of leader performance.** *Academy of Management Journal*, *41*(4), 387-409.

The authors tested a theory of charismatic leadership in the Israel Defense Forces. A representative sampling of infantry, tank, and engineering companies included 1,642 participants. Data were collected from military records, performance appraisals, and questionnaires. At the individual and unit levels, subordinates reported that charismatic leadership existed in units with strong identities, culture, and trust. Company leaders reported that charismatic leadership existed among superiors with a strong ideology and exemplary performance. Includes bibliographical references.
Subject(s): Military leadership

New
Shoemaker, C. C. J. (1998). *Leadership in continuing and distance education in higher education.* Boston: Allyn and Bacon.

This is a handbook for those who administer continuing education programs in higher education. Such programs are increasingly popular among workers needing to update skills and adults eager for lifelong learning. Continuing education leaders must build academic, marketing, and management expertise to develop relevant and meaningful programs. Chapters address challenges, trends, power, change, visions, decisions, teamwork, and problem solving as well as management functions. Special attention is paid to the unique needs of distance learning courses. The appendices include samples of a mission statement, market plan, and annual report. Includes bibliographical references and index.
Subject(s): Leadership in higher education, distance education

Short, P. M. (1997). **Reflection in administrator preparation.** *Peabody Journal of Education*, *72*(2), 86-99.

This article identifies reflection as a tool that school administrators can use to improve their leadership skills. After reviewing the literature and research on reflection Short describes techniques that can promote it, including group reflection, reflective journals, educational platforms, case stories, and reflective shadowing and interviewing. Includes bibliographical references.
Subject(s): Educational leadership, reflection

Short, P. M., & Greer, J. T. (1997). *Leadership in empowered schools: Themes from innovative efforts.* Upper Saddle River, NJ: Merrill.

This is a report of two studies that examined leadership and empowerment in 26 newly restructured schools. The chapters describe the dimensions of leadership identified in the research and the specific behaviors of teachers and principals who exhibited or failed to exhibit each leadership dimension.

Examples of these dimensions are: leading change, focusing on structure, building trust, stimulating risk, empowering teachers and students, and evaluating empowered leadership. Following most of the case studies are discussion questions for students of educational leadership. The authors recommend two assessment instruments for practitioners who want to identify their school's leadership strengths and weaknesses. Includes index.
Subject(s): Educational leadership, empowerment

Sifonis, J. G., & Goldberg, B. (1996). *Corporation on a tightrope: Balancing leadership, governance, and technology in an age of complexity.* New York: Oxford University Press.

Sifonis and Goldberg identify three major forces that affect corporations—governance, technology, and leadership—and describe how businesses must confront these factors aggressively and concurrently. Chapters address how governing boards can help and hurt a company, how CEOs must lead technological changes, and how to build multilevel leadership. Examples from companies including Motorola, General Electric, and Federal Express illustrate the concepts. Contains an index and bibliography.
Subject(s): Corporate leadership, corporate boards

New
Simonton, D. K. (1998). **Introduction: Political leadership: Part I.** *Leadership Quarterly: Special Issue: Political Leadership, 9*(3), 239-242.

Simonton acknowledges the importance of political leadership and the inadequate attention it receives in leadership research. He, as guest editor, and the contributors to this special issue try to remedy that situation. Part I addresses political leadership outside the U.S. There are articles about prime ministers, presidents, leaders of the former Soviet Union, and hereditary monarchs around the world. Part II, which considers political leadership in the U.S., is introduced on pages 333-334.
Subject(s): Political leadership

New
Simonton, D. K. (1998). **Political leadership across the life span: Chronological versus career age in the British monarchy.** *Leadership Quarterly: Special Issue: Political Leadership, 9*(3), 309-320.

Based on a long history of life-span developmental psychology, this study considers the age and outstanding achievements of British monarchs over a period of 550 years. Histories and biographies were consulted to determine such factors as: war years, battles fought, victories, invasions, truces, territorial gains and losses, alliances, and reforms. In five-year periods, the rulers' chronological age, career age (years since coronation), historical data, and leadership criteria are analyzed to determine if age impacts leadership ability. The findings are complex and no significant pattern is identified across 17 leadership criteria. Includes bibliographical references.
Subject(s): Monarchs

Sinclair, B. (1995). *Legislators, leaders, and lawmaking: The U.S. House of Representatives in the postreform era.* Baltimore: Johns Hopkins University Press.

Sinclair discusses the changing role of congressional leadership following reforms of the past 25 years. In the 1970s both parties lost identity and power, leaving congressional candidates to win elections and develop leadership on their own rather than depending on party loyalty. In the 1980s House majority-party leadership developed its own cohesion and regained lost power. When the 1994 elections put Republicans in the majority seat for the first time in 40 years, political scholars predicted a show of strong leadership. Sinclair analyzes the "anomaly of strong congressional party leadership in an era of relatively weak parties." She describes House leadership functions and their considerable influence on the legislative process. Analysis of leadership function and influence are reported in tables throughout the text. Includes bibliographical references and index.
Subject(s): Congressional leadership

Smilor, R. W., & Sexton, D. L. (Eds.). (1996). *Leadership and entrepreneurship: Personal and organizational development in entrepreneurial ventures.* Westport, CT: Quorum Books.

This collection of writings examines the entrepreneurial leader from the personal, organizational, and multidimensional perspectives. Chapters include "Leadership Skills of Entrepreneurs" by John Eggers and Raymond Smilor, "Creating the Uncommon Company" by Ewing Kauffman, "Leading the Virtual Corporation" by William Davidow, and "Making the Entrepreneurial Team Work" by Lee Bolman and Terrence Deal. Includes bibliographical references and index.
Subject(s): Entrepreneurship

Smith, C. A., & Smith, K. B. (1994). *The White House speaks: Presidential leadership as persuasion.* Westport, CT: Praeger.

Persuasive speech is central to the position of president. Speech is used to unify varied interests, legitimize the president's power, resolve conflicts, and implement policies. To illustrate the persuasive power of presidential speechmaking, the authors discuss Gerald Ford's pardon of Richard Nixon, Ronald Reagan's debate over the Panama Canal treaties, Jimmy Carter's energy program, and William Clinton's 1992 campaign. Includes bibliographical references and index.
Subject(s): U.S. presidents, speechmaking

Smith, G. E., & Huntsman, C. A. (1997). **Reframing the metaphor of the citizen-government relationship: A value-centered perspective.** *Public Administration Review, 57*(4), 309-318.

Past theories of the relationship between citizens and government have included the citizen-as-customer and citizen-as-owner models. Both of these have been criticized—the customer model limits citizens to the role of passive consumers, and government is too large for most individuals

to relate to it as owners. The authors propose a value-centered model, which emphasizes the worth of government to its citizens and the investments citizens make. A study of the government of a Northeast city illustrates how public administrators and leaders can reframe their view of government services and think in terms of their value, not their cost.
Subject(s): City managers

Smith, S. C., & Piele, P. K. (Eds.). (1997). *School leadership: Handbook for excellence* (3rd ed.). Eugene, OR: ERIC Clearinghouse on Educational Management.

The essays in this book suggest how a leader, especially a principal, can inspire all members of a school community to work toward the goal of excellence in education. It approaches leadership from four perspectives: the person, the values, the structure, and the skills. Chapters include: "Portrait of a Leader"; "Leadership Styles and Strategies"; "Ethical Leadership"; "Cultural Leadership"; "School-based Management"; and "Building Coalitions." The authors synthesize theoretical literature on school leadership and interviews with practitioners to recommend action and continuous learning. Includes bibliographical references.
Subject(s): Educational leadership

Steers, R. M., Porter, L. W., & Bigley, G. A. (1996). *Motivation and leadership at work* (6th ed.). New York: McGraw-Hill.

Previous editions of this graduate-level textbook were titled *Motivation and Work Behavior*. The new title and contents reflect an increased interest in the relationship between leadership and organizational behavior (OB), particularly leadership and motivation. The text focuses on a blend of theoretical frameworks, major research, real-world applications, and selections authored by leading OB scholars. They explain the nature of work, goal-directed work attitudes and performance, the fairness of reward systems, social interaction, personal identity, and the development of employees as learners. Includes bibliographical references and indexes.
Subject(s): Corporate leadership, motivation, textbook

New
Strike, K. A. (1999). **Can schools be communities? The tension between shared values and inclusion.** *Educational Administration Quarterly*, 35(1), 46-70.

Strike argues that a criterion for educational community is shared values. This article serves to discuss a dilemma created with these values. Two extreme types of values are constitutive and nonconstitutive. Strike advocates the establishment of a middle ground between these two types. In support of this notion, the article discusses concepts and examples of educational communities and constitutive values. Liberal neutrality is then presented in terms of inclusiveness. Following this is the discussion of three possible school-community values—comprehensive doctrines, caring, and democracy. The conflicting element presented in this discussion centers on the degree of these

values. Strike suggests a continuum. Includes bibliographical references.
Subject(s): Educational leadership, values

Sullivan, G. R., & Harper, M. V. (1996). *Hope is not a method: What business leaders can learn from America's Army.* New York: Times Books.

The authors are former U.S. Army senior officers and are currently affiliated with Boston University's CEO Leadership Forum. They played key roles in reinventing Army leadership from the command-and-control style that served the military so well during World War II and then corporate America during the 1950s and 1960s. They lay out five challenges that needed to be addressed: 1) the competitive environment changed rapidly, 2) emerging technology posed new opportunities and problems, 3) teamwork and technical skills needed to be upgraded, 4) stakeholders demanded new and unexpected tasks, and 5) financial pressure forced massive cost cutting and downsizing. Sullivan and Harper believe these challenges can be met by "creating the future" through strategic leadership. They share their guidelines for leading change, emphasizing values, building teams, being flexible, and developing leaders. Appendices chart the changes in Army personnel and budgets since 1989. Includes bibliographical references and index.
Subject(s): Military leadership

New
Sumser, R. (1998). **New options, new talent.** *The Public Manager*, 27(3), 37-40.

Changes in the American workforce have resulted in more and more public agencies turning noncore work over to supplemental workers, reducing the number of permanent, full-time employees. Workforce options include temporary employees, temporary help companies, consulting firms, independent contractors, and professional employer organizations. This article compiles data from several sources to offer a statistical picture of supplemental workers. Part two of the study, published in *The Public Manager*, 27(4), describes why workers and managers choose supplemental options and how to best manage these workers. Includes bibliographical references.
Subject(s): Managing supplemental workforce

New
Sumser, R. (1998-99). **New options, new talent: Part two.** *The Public Manager*, 27(4), 45-48.

Part one of this study defined supplemental workers. Part two describes some of the reasons managers use these workers, such as changing workloads, cost controls, and to protect core employees. Workers also may prefer the independence and work/life balance that supplemental work offers. Sumser describes a ten-step plan for managing supplemental workers. Steps include: prepare accurate specifications, communicate with core employees, offer interesting work, and evaluate the workforce plan annually. Eight recommendations more

specifically focused on the federal civil service are also provided. Includes bibliographical references.
Subject(s): Managing supplemental workforce

New
Svara, J. H. (1999). **The shifting boundary between elected officials and city managers in large council-manager cities.** *Public Administration Review, 59*(1), 44-53.

Traditionally in council-manager governments the elected council members provide political leadership while appointed administrators serve as administrative leaders. Today these boundaries have begun to blur, especially in large city governments, which typically face complex problems and media scrutiny. Svara surveyed council members and city managers in 31 large U.S. cities to examine the roles the two groups played, comparing his results to similar studies done in 1985 and 1989. While Svara argues that the line between council and manager still exists, he says that it is becoming more common for council members to be involved in administrative decisions and managers to contribute to mission and policy formulation. Includes bibliographical references.
Subject(s): Mayors, city councils, city managers

Svara, J. H., & Associates. (1994). *Facilitative leadership in local government: Lessons from successful mayors and chairpersons.* San Francisco: Jossey-Bass.

In a city run by a council-manager style of government a mayor has little official power. The same is true for the chairperson of a county commission. Svara shares actual cases where chief elected officials exhibited leadership skills to become more than figureheads in: Decatur, Georgia; Greensboro, North Carolina; Montgomery County, Ohio; Roanoke, Virginia; College Station, Texas; and San Diego, California. Svara's Facilitative Model ranks a mayor's or chairperson's perception as a ceremonial figure, spokesperson, educator, goal setter, and team builder. Includes bibliographical references and index.
Subject(s): Mayors, city councils, county government

New
Tacheny, S. (1999). **If we build it, will they come?** *Educational Leadership: Association for Supervision and Curriculum Development, 56*(6), 62-65.

Accountability is a current issue of reform in educational issues. Tacheny reminds readers that accountability is a value rather than a system. Educational leaders need to cultivate a culture that embraces this value through supportive strategies such as professional development and formal accountability. Relative storytelling is another proposed technique in creating an accountable atmosphere. Finally, Tacheny believes that it is important to replace blame and judgment with cooperation and problem solving, and that every person in the organization has a role to play.
Subject(s): Educational leadership, accountability

Taylor, R. L., & Rosenbach, W. E. (Eds.). (1996). *Military leadership: In pursuit of excellence* (3rd ed.). Boulder, CO: Westview Press.

Contributing authors from within and outside the military compare the special nature of military leadership with the universal concept of leadership in general. In his foreword, Walter Ulmer states that "warfare and the institutions dedicated to preparation for war have given us the richest lode to mine in our quest for understanding . . ., routinely exposing the bedrock of character that underlies leader behavior." Essays stress the importance of followership, credibility, and personal values in concert with organizational values. New to this edition are portraits of military heroes of the past and leadership lessons learned from current events. New images of leadership have emerged from downsized corporate America, the end of the Cold War, technological innovations, and women in the military. Lee Smith describes how the "new" U.S. Army is adapting. Includes bibliographical references.
Subject(s): Military leadership

Teitel, L. (1997). **Understanding and harnessing the power of the cohort model in preparing educational leaders.** *Peabody Journal of Education, 72*(2), 66-85.

In 1995 the University of Massachusetts at Boston began using the cohort model in which students are admitted in groups and work together toward their degrees, in all of their educational leadership programs. This article describes the change, using quotes from students and faculty, to illustrate the benefits and drawbacks of the cohort model. The author identifies five issues this model raises, including increased connections among students and unbalanced power relationships with faculty members, and offers recommendations on how schools and students can deal with them. Includes bibliographical references.
Subject(s): Educational leadership, cohorts

Terry, L. D. (1995). *Leadership of public bureaucracies: The administrator as conservator.* Thousand Oaks, CA: Sage.

Bureaucratic leadership is defined as "institutional leadership in the administration of public bureaucracies within the executive branch of all levels of government." The American public has lost faith in many of these bureaucracies, giving way to discussions about reorganization and privatization. In this book, Terry affirms the legitimacy of bureaucratic leadership by drawing on research from law, management, and sociology. He believes that, when guided by constitutional principles, public administrators can earn public trust and maintain governmental stability. A model of administrative conservatorship defines how bureaucrats can conserve institutional mission, integrity, stakeholder support, and authority. Some of the agencies discussed are: FAA, FBI, Federal Reserve Bank, IRS, NASA, and HUD. This book is part of the "Advances in Public Administration Series," which encourages critical rethinking of public administration. Includes bibliographical references and index.
Subject(s): Public service leadership

Terry, L. D. (1997). **Public administration and the theater metaphor: The public administrator as villain, hero, and innocent victim.** *Public Administration Review, 57*(1), 53-61.

The theater metaphor has always been a powerful tool in American political discourse. This article describes how Ronald Reagan used the metaphor during the 1980s to portray public administrators as evil villains. The supporters of the administrative state fought back by casting civil servants in the roles of hero and innocent victim, but the author believes that all of these characterizations are dangerous. He says that they limit the abilities of public administrators because "the villain is incapable of positive action, the hero lacks an understanding of limitations to power, and the victim is ignorant of responsibility."

Subject(s): Public service leadership, performing art as metaphor for leadership

Thomas, J. C. (1995). *Public participation in public decision: New skills and strategies for public managers.* San Francisco: Jossey-Bass.

Since the 1960s American citizens have become increasingly involved in managing public organizations, and Thomas states that this trend is growing. He wrote this book primarily for public managers seeking guidelines for grassroots collaboration and also for citizen leaders who want to learn about policy-making. He reviews the history of the public-participation movement, theories of public management, and mechanisms for gaining public acceptance. An Effective Decision Model suggests criteria for collaboration. Case studies in each chapter enhance the lessons on how to and how not to collaborate. Includes bibliographical references and index.

Subject(s): Public service leadership

Tichy, N. (1996). **Simultaneous transformation and CEO succession: Key to global competitiveness.** *Organizational Dynamics, 25*(1), 45-59.

A change in leadership and organizational transformation are two of the biggest challenges a company can face, especially when they occur at the same time. This article illustrates this with the story of Ameritech, a company that named a new CEO and completely reorganized its internal structure between 1991 and 1995. As Tichy relates the process Ameritech went through he also describes old and new frameworks for CEO succession and the "three-act drama" of organizational change—awakening, envisioning, and re-architecting.

Subject(s): CEOs, succession

Tichy, N. M., & Cohen, E. (1997). *The leadership engine: How winning companies build leaders at every level.* New York: HarperBusiness.

Tichy uses examples from companies including GE and Ameritech to illustrate how good leaders develop more leaders within their organization, creating an ever-turning "leadership engine." He identifies four areas in which good

leaders help others develop: generating positive energy, making tough decisions, developing good business ideas, and instilling values that will help support those ideas. A "Handbook for Leaders Developing Leaders" also offers over 100 pages of hands-on development activities leaders can use in their organizations. Includes bibliographical references and index.

Subject(s): Corporate leadership

Tropman, J. E. (1997). *Successful community leadership.* Washington, DC: NASW Press.

Social services and community organizations are rapidly and profoundly changing. Tropman uses practical how-to advice to explain how to take leadership in community groups, how to conduct effective community group meetings, and the rewards of community leadership. Chapters are divided to quickly find information about group leadership, community group membership, the community facilitator, decision management, discussions, evaluations, and other subjects. A section is also devoted to using the library and the Internet to search for information about the community and leadership issues. The appendices show a sample agenda, sample options memo, and sample minutes from a meeting. Includes bibliographical references and index.

Subject(s): Community leadership

Tschirhart, M. (1996). *Artful leadership: Managing stakeholder problems in nonprofit arts organizations.* Bloomington: Indiana University Press.

This book explains how and why leaders of nonprofit arts organizations choose their strategies for dealing with stakeholders. Predictors and themes in problem management are analyzed, and insight is given into why specific problems arise, why certain strategies are chosen, and how effective those strategies are. Although targeted primarily toward students and scholars this book may also be used by the practitioners in nonprofit organizations. There are chapters on managing relationships with stakeholders, predicting responses to problems with stakeholders, finding patterns in the management of problems, and exploring challenges associated with stakeholder groups. Appendices explain study methodology and tables used throughout the book. Includes bibliographical references and index.

Subject(s): Nonprofit leadership

Tucker, R. C. (1995). *Politics as leadership* (Rev. ed.). Columbia: University of Missouri Press.

The original edition (1981) was based on a series of lectures on leadership ethics. The lectures are reprinted in this revised edition with additional commentary on key events of the past 15 years in which political leadership caused sweeping reform. Tucker cites Mikhail Gorbachev and Nelson Mandela as recent political leaders who effected positive change and Rwandan President Habyariamana as a political leader responsible for the genocidal slaughter of one million of his compatriots. Includes bibliographical references and index.

Subject(s): Political leadership

Ulrich, D. (1997). *Human resource champions: The next agenda for adding value and delivering results.* Boston: Harvard Business School Press.

This book doesn't address the tasks of human resources professionals. Rather, it studies the challenges they face and the results they must deliver. One important challenge is the development of intellectual capital. Businesses must become learning organizations that can respond quickly to rapidly changing environments. To achieve this, HR professionals act as change agents. Another challenge is balancing the tension between serving as a strategic management partner and as an employee champion. To achieve this, HR professionals must facilitate communication, build trust, and offer development opportunities. Includes bibliographical references and index.
Subject(s): Human resources managers

New
van Linden, J. A., & Fertman, C. I. (1998). *Youth leadership: A guide to understanding leadership development in adolescents.* San Francisco: Jossey-Bass.

The authors say that adult leadership models are inappropriate for teenagers, who have unique development needs. They describe three stages in adolescent leadership development—awareness, interaction, and mastery—and offer strategies on how to nurture leadership in teens. Case studies from high schools and nonprofits illustrate how organizations and communities can support adolescents' leadership efforts, and an appendix provides a list of national organizations that promote youth leadership. Includes bibliographical references and index.
Subject(s): Youth leadership

New
Villani, S. (1999). *Are you sure you're the principal? On being an authentic leader.* Thousand Oaks, CA: Corwin Press.

From her 20 years as a school principal Villani offers "craft knowledge," experience supplemented with analysis. Her stories tell of first-year challenges and the evolution of leadership over time. Along the way Villani learned to work through conflict, adapt to multiple roles, build community, find mentors, be a mentor, and maintain her authenticity. She hopes that aspiring principals and female leaders in all fields will use this book as a learning tool.
Subject(s): Principal as leader, storytelling

New
Vogelsang-Coombs, V., & Miller, M. (1999). **Developing the governance capacity of local elected officials.** *Public Administration Review, 59*(3), 199-217.

Local elected officials (LEOs) play a critical role in communities but often neglect their learning, choosing not to develop their governance capacity. This study examined the effectiveness of LEO education using the "human performance improvement" methodology, which collects both cross-sectional and longitudinal data. First, approximately

100 LEOs in northeast Ohio were surveyed to determine their learning needs and performance gaps. Then, Cleveland State University's College of Urban Affairs created an advanced development program for the LEOs with units on team building, board leadership, personal development, and regional cooperation. Finally, the authors gathered data on the LEOs' perceptions of the training. Based on their analysis, the authors offer a job description for LEOs consisting of six competencies: 1) developing decision patterns that support responsible policies, 2) maintaining sound municipal organizations, 3) bringing together diverse citizens, 4) envisioning the future to strengthen communities, 5) connecting political entities, and 6) actively engaging in personal development. Includes bibliographical references.
Subject(s): Mayors, city councils, county government

Walsh, D. F., Best, P. J., & Rai, K. B. (1995). *Governing through turbulence: Leadership and change in the late twentieth century.* Westport, CT: Praeger.

In the past three decades, major political and economic changes have compounded the difficult task of leading a national government. In this book the authors present case studies of seven world leaders who have governed in times of turbulence. Three were leaders of communist states undergoing transitions: Lech Walesa, president of Poland; Mikhail Gorbachev, president of the Soviet Union; and Boris Yeltsin, president of the Russian Republic. Two were leaders of Third World countries: Deng Xiaoping, de facto leader of the Communist Party of China; and Rajiv Gandhi, prime minister of India. Two were leaders of advanced industrial nations: Margaret Thatcher, prime minister of the United Kingdom; and Helmut Kohl, chancellor of Germany. Includes bibliographical references and index.
Subject(s): Political leadership

Weems, L. H., Jr. (1993). *Church leadership: Vision, team culture, and integrity.* Nashville, TN: Abingdon Press.

Pastors are leaders, and their leadership takes on greater significance in difficult times. If the task of leadership is change, what are the stages of the journey for the leader to become change master? Weems suggests the first stage is creating a vision that embodies people's hopes and desires, where imagination and courage are essential. Next, change masters must have the power to advance their vision by involving and influencing a team culture where people will devote their considerable time and energy to make the vision a reality. Finally, change masters must maintain the momentum and keep faith and hope alive during the inevitable frustrations inherent in execution. Weems asserts the best way for institutions to endure and prosper is to encourage leaders who will build on the past by envisioning an even better future. Includes bibliographical references.
Subject(s): Religious leadership

New

Welch, E., & Wong, W. (1998). **Public administration in a global context: Bridging the gaps of theory and practice between Western and non-Western nations.** *Public Administration Review, 58*(1), 40-49.

The authors argue that substantial gaps exist between traditionalist and revisionist theories in public administration, and between Western and non-Western perspectives of public management. This article attempts to bridge those gaps by presenting a framework that identifies the global forces, such as advancing information technology and demands for public-sector efficiency, that affect all nations. Both theorists and practitioners should act "both globally and locally" in order to fully understand how global factors affect bureaucratic structure and behavior. Includes bibliographical references.

Subject(s): Public service leadership, multicultural context

New

Westphal, J. D. (1998). **Board games: How CEOs adapt to increases in structural board independence from management.** *Administrative Science Quarterly, 43*(3), 511-537.

A recent trend is for corporate boards to add members and leaders who are loyal to shareholders rather than to their organizations. This article analyzes how that type of board structure affects organizational performance and a CEO's influence, ingratiation, and compensation. One conclusion is that independent boards encourage stronger interpersonal relations with a CEO. The loss of a structural power base increases a CEO's motivation to use persuasion to gain approval for organizational strategy and personal compensation. Westphal determines that this influence relationship generally has positive outcomes on every count. Includes bibliographical references.

Subject(s): Corporate boards, CEOs

Whitaker, G. P., & Jenne, K. (1995). **Improving city managers' leadership.** *State and Local Government Review, 27*(1), 84-94.

In 28,000 American municipalities the city manager is the top administrator. This article reviews the power of authority typically held by city managers, challenges to their roles as leaders, and the results of sharing authority. The authors suggest that city managers who practice facilitative leadership are most effective. The key elements of facilitative leadership are: promoting staff development, cooperating with elected officials, championing change, committing to community awareness and responsiveness, and facilitating the flow of information.

Subject(s): City managers

White, M. C., Smith, M., & Barnett, T. (1997). **CEO succession: Overcoming forces of inertia.** *Human Relations, 50*(7), 805-828.

An earlier study by Smith and White (1987) of executive succession from 1957 to 1981 found that the career special-izations of new CEOs tended to be the same as their predecessor's, and were typically in line with the company's past strategies. The current study analyzed the succession of 138 CEOs of *Business Week 1000* companies between 1981 and 1990. The authors found that these CEOs were more likely to have different career specializations than their predecessors, and past corporate strategy had less influence on their selection. The authors believe that as technology and globalization forced industries to change quickly in the 1980s, many companies used the entrance of a new CEO to facilitate organizational adaptation.

Subject(s): CEOs, succession

White, R. P., Hodgson, P., & Crainer, S. (1996). *The future of leadership: Riding the corporate rapids into the 21st century.* London: Pitman.

The authors assert that the days of corporate certainty, when leaders understood their roles and direction was predictable, are gone. Leadership in the 1990s and beyond is more about responding to change and learning to balance. They suggest five key skills necessary for leaders of the future: 1) learning the difficult lessons means seeking change and taking risks; 2) maximum energy helps when trial-and-error approaches drain physical and emotional energy; 3) simplicity is essential to deliver important messages in times of chaos and complexity; 4) multiple focus allows leaders to balance multiple objectives that are often in opposition; and 5) trusting one's inner sense (a combination of experience, timing, instinct, and flexibility) enables leaders to respond quickly and with confidence. Includes bibliographical references.

Subject(s): Corporate leadership, chaos

New

Winkler, J. D., Shukiar, H. J., Dewar, J. A., Lewis, M. W., Benjamin, B., Sollinger, J. M., Peters, J. E., & Thie, H. J. (1998). *Future leader development of army noncommissioned officers: Workshop results.* Santa Monica, CA: Rand.

The conference proceedings of the *Noncommissioned Officer Professional Development Workshop* are presented in this source. The purpose of the week-long workshop was to examine the professional development of the enlisted force. This book divides the results of this conference into four areas. One part is devoted to the summarization of the results of the main workshop. A smaller conference proposed a vision and policy implications, which are detailed in the third section of this book. The fourth section identifies needs of research. Extensive appendices illustrate particular aspects of the workshop as well as the results. Includes bibliographical references.

Subject(s): Military leadership

New

Winter, D. G. (1998). **A motivational analysis of the Clinton first term and the 1996 presidential campaign.** *Leadership Quarterly: Special Issue: Political Leadership, 9*(3), 367-376.

Winter analyzes the changing nature of President William Clinton's political motives from the 1992 campaign, through

his first term in office, and in the 1996 campaign. Select speeches were analyzed for images of power, affiliation, and achievement. Early Clinton speeches rated higher in achievement than in power, which is usually associated with idealism but not with political success. Following a low point in 1994 when Clinton's proposed health care reform failed and Republicans won new Congressional seats, a new Clinton emerged. He won a budgetary showdown and blamed Republicans for the 1995 government shutdown. Popular issues such as Medicare and education gained support and restored Clinton's confidence. By the 1996 campaign Clinton's motive profile measured higher in power, which positively impacted his re-election. Includes bibliographical references.
Subject(s): U.S. presidents: Clinton, W. J.

Wood, M. M. (Ed.). (1996). *Nonprofit boards and leadership: Cases on governance, change, and board-staff dynamics.* San Francisco: Jossey-Bass.

This book is made up of 13 teaching cases based on real-life leadership issues faced by nonprofit organizations. Each case includes exhibits, an annotated bibliography, and discussion questions, and requires the reader to make a decision based on the information provided. Organizations described in the cases include a United Way allocations committee, a nonprofit hospital, a museum, a university, a women's shelter, and AIDS Project Los Angeles. Includes index.
Subject(s): Nonprofit boards

New
Wood, S., & de Menezes, L. (1998). **High commitment management in the U.K.: Evidence from the Workplace Industrial Relations Survey, and Employers' Manpower and Skills Practice Survey.** *Human Relations, 51*(4), 485-516.

Unlike previous research this study treats high commitment management (HCM) as a matter of degree. Seventeen indicators from the 1990 U.K. Workplace Industrial Relations Survey were used to measure whether organizations had low, medium, or high degrees of HCM. Indicators included internal recruitment, merit pay, appraisal, information disclosure, and direct communication. The authors then examined how organizations with high HCM compared on performance factors such as productivity, turnover, and financial performance. They found few overall differences between high HCM organizations and others but advocate further research and an increased focus on organizations with medium HCM levels. Includes bibliographical references.
Subject(s): Corporate leadership

Woodward, B. (1991). *The commanders.* New York: Simon & Schuster.

Woodward chronicles in great detail U.S. military decision making from the election of George Bush as president in 1988 until 1991 when the Persian Gulf War began. The relationships between leaders including Bush, Dick Cheney,

Colin Powell, and James Baker are described, and their decisions in military actions including the invasion of Panama are explained. Based mainly on interviews with people involved in these decisions, Woodward says that "this book falls somewhere between newspaper journalism and history." Includes index and photographs.
Subject(s): Military leadership

Yeung, A. K., & Ready, D. A. (1995). **Developing leadership capabilities of global corporations: A comparative study in eight nations.** *Human Resource Management, 34*(4), 529-547.

More than 1,200 managers from large corporations around the world responded to a survey about leadership competence. There was general agreement in the areas of facilitating strategic change, articulating a vision, and empowering others. In other areas, cultural influences affected perceptions of leadership competence. French, Italian, and Australian managers rated a leader's ability to be a catalyst of cultural change as most important. German and Korean managers emphasized integrity and trust. Japanese managers stressed empowerment, British managers stressed quality, and American managers stressed action to get results.
Subject(s): Corporate leadership, global leadership

Zaleznik, A. (1992). **Managers and leaders: Are they different?** *Harvard Business Review, 70*(2), 126-135.

While performing very different roles, managers and leaders are vital to the success of business. They must be cultivated and trained to achieve success. Managers defuse conflict and ensure day-to-day business gets done. Their goals arise from necessity rather than desires. Leaders define goals from personal attitudes, inspire creativity, and seek new opportunities for organizations. A solid organizational framework must be in place to realize the potential of our most gifted leaders. This article originally appeared in the May-June 1977 issue of *Harvard Business Review, 55*(3), 67-78.
Subject(s): Corporate leadership

Zlotkowski, E. (1996). **Linking service-learning and the academy: A new voice at the table?** *Change, 28*(1), 20-27.

The interest in service learning on college campuses has grown in recent years, but this kind of experience has not yet been effectively linked to traditional academic learning. Do service-learning proponents, asks the author, "represent a movement of socially and morally concerned activists operating from an academic base or a movement of socially, morally, and pedagogically concerned academicians?" He believes there is a place on campus for both civic/moral concepts and the academic but says that service-learning enthusiasts have not successfully presented their case to academia. Leaders in this area must now establish pedagogical rationales for service learning in specific disciplines and integrate the movement into all areas of higher education.
Subject(s): Educational leadership, service learning

LEADERSHIP IN HISTORY, BIOGRAPHIES, AND LITERATURE

Ashby, R., & Ohrn, D. D. G. (Eds.). (1995). *Herstory: Women who changed the world.* New York: Viking.

Herstory details the historical and social significance of over 100 women and gives overviews of the times in which they lived and led. It contains diverse women from all areas of the world with political, religious, social, and artistic influence. Some of the more well-known women are: Sappho, Sojourner Truth, Susan B. Anthony, Eleanor Roosevelt, and Bessie Smith. Some less recognizable women are: The Trung Sisters, who led a Vietnamese uprising against the Chinese in 39 A.D.; Sister Juana Ines de la Cruz of Mexico, who entered a convent in order to continue her broad education and defend the right of women to pursue a scholarly life; and Mairead Corrigan and Betty Williams, who won the 1976 Nobel Peace Prize for their efforts to stop the violence in Northern Ireland. The book includes a selected bibliography and suggested further reading as well as geographical, alphabetical, and occupational indexes.
Subject(s): History of women's leadership

New
Beatty, J. (1998). *The world according to Peter Drucker.* New York: Free Press.

Peter Drucker is a pioneer in the fields of management and management theory, coining such terms as "privatization" and "management by objectives." With Drucker's cooperation Beatty has written both a biography and "intellectual portrait" covering topics including Drucker's childhood and education in Europe, his early anti-fascist writings, his work with GM, and his more recent post-capitalist writings.
Subject(s): Biography: Drucker, P.

Boyes, R. (1994). *The naked president: A political life of Lech Walesa.* London: Secker and Warburg.

Boyes chronicles the political rise and fall of a revolutionary-turned-president. Walesa's charismatic, street-style leadership qualities met the needs of the Polish working class in 1990. But when his Solidarity Party couldn't influence parliament sufficiently to serve effectively, he lost popularity and his bid for reelection. Includes bibliographical references and index.
Subject(s): Biography: Walesa, L.

Burns, J. M. (1956). *Roosevelt: The lion and the fox.* San Diego, CA: Harcourt-Brace Jovanovich.

This is a highly readable, two-volume biography (the second volume is *Roosevelt: Soldier of Freedom*). Burns describes the 32nd president as a man of "no fixed convictions about methods and policies" whose chief tenet was "improvise."
Subject(s): Biography: Roosevelt, F. D.; U.S. presidents: Roosevelt, F. D.

Clemens, J. K., & Mayer, D. F. (1987). *The classic touch: Lessons in leadership from Homer to Hemingway.* Homewood, IL: Dow Jones-Irwin.

This book taps the collective wisdom found in the classic works of Western philosophy, history, biography, and drama and applies it to the problems of modern managers and leaders. It addresses such issues as how to build a team and keep it together, how to manage an acquisition once it's in place, how to eliminate daily distractions, and how to better trust your intuition. Includes bibliography and index.
Subject(s): History, leadership lessons in literature

New
Corrigan, P. (1999). *Shakespeare on management: Leadership lessons for today's managers.* London: Kogan Page.

Corrigan states that in William Shakespeare's plays there are leadership lessons about the rise and fall of powerful characters. Richard II demonstrates a leader's misguided faith in positional power that costs the king his crown and his life. King Lear foolishly gives up his land, the source of his authority, and unwittingly precipitates turbulent changes that wreak havoc on all he rules. Antony is a leader who abuses power, rightfully earned as a Roman general but wrongfully usurped through his relationship with Cleopatra, empress of Egypt. Macbeth's king suffers the consequences of developing a violent and immoral culture that rewards the act of murder. Shakespeare's one heroic king, Henry V, learns to lead by listening to his followers. Corrigan also describes the important leadership competencies of playing the fool—telling unpopular truths to the king—and paying attention to subplots. Includes bibliographical references and index.
Subject(s): Leadership lessons in literature

New
Datta, R. (1999). Gender, leadership, and development: A profile of Indira Gandhi. *A Leadership Journal: Women in Leadership—Sharing the Vision, 3*(2), 63-70.

This profile of Indira Gandhi describes her childhood, education, and political rise to become prime minister of India. Gandhi's father was Jawaharlal Nehru, the country's first prime minister, and both he and Mahatma Gandhi were important influences on Indira. However, Datta says that once Gandhi became prime minister she followed her own agenda and often used an autocratic or authoritarian leadership style. Datta also says that although Gandhi was committed to social equality, she did not actively address gender issues as prime minister, focusing instead on a nationalist agenda. Includes bibliographical references.
Subject(s): Biography: Gandhi, I.

New

Davis, A. M. (1997). **Liquid leadership: The wisdom of Mary Parker Follett (1868-1933).** *A Leadership Journal: Women in Leadership—Sharing the Vision, 2*(1), 11-17.

Mary Parker Follett was a widely respected speaker, scholar, and historian who served as a management consultant to British and American business leaders during the early 1900s. In this article Davis describes Follett's views on leadership as a "philosophy of interrelatedness" in which the differences between people who are linked together in relationships lead to the continuous development of the group. Davis also outlines Follett's theories on leadership in communities and emphasizes the importance Follett placed on followership. Includes bibliographical references.
Subject(s): Biography: Follett, M. P.

Davis, M. A., Jr. (1997). **Matilda of Tuscany and Daimbert of Pisa: Women's leadership in medieval Italy, 1054-1092.** *A Leadership Journal: Women in Leadership—Sharing the Vision, 1*(2), 31-38.

In this brief look at the political life of Maltilda, Marchioness of Tuscany (1054-1116), the author makes two main points about leadership in the Middle Ages: women were key players in the political events of the time and the "great person" theory of history has been overused in medieval studies. By describing the complex alliance that Matilda formed with Tuscan nobility, the papacy, and Daimbert, the archbishop of Pisa, Davis illustrates both Matilda's political power and the complex interplay of people and circumstances that determined the course of history. Includes bibliographical references.
Subject(s): Biography: Matilda of Tuscany

New

Endress, W. L. (1999). **Searching for influence and vision: Life histories reflect leadership development.** *A Leadership Journal: Women in Leadership—Sharing the Vision, 3*(2), 71-82.

This article uses profiles of three women leaders—Jill Ker Conway, Mary McLeod Bethune, and Wilma Mankiller—to analyze Astin and Leland's theoretical construct of women's leadership development (*Women of Influence, Women of Vision*, 1991). Their theory identified several factors important to women's development, including family of origin, mentors, education, and work. Endress compares the lives of the three women profiled to the theory and found that these women experienced significant life-changing events that the model did not account for. She says that this shows the complexity of analyzing the lives of individuals, and says that Astin and Leland's theory may not apply to emerging women leaders today. An appendix offers biographical information on Conway, Bethune, and Mankiller. Includes bibliographical references.
Subject(s): Biography, women as leaders

Erikson, E. H. (1970). *Gandhi's truth: On the origins of militant nonviolence.* New York: Norton.

Erikson reveals that what has always been thought of as a relatively minor episode in Gandhi's life—the Abmedabad Mill strike of 1918 and Gandhi's first fast—was in fact an event of crucial importance in his rise as a natural leader and as the originator of militant nonviolence. Bibliographical references included in notes.
Subject(s): History: India

Freeman, D. S. (1942). *Lee's lieutenants.* New York: Scribner.

This is a three-volume study of the Confederate commanders who served with and under General Robert E. Lee in the Civil War. "The necessary qualities of high military command manifestly are military imagination, initiative, resourcefulness, boldness coupled with a grasp of practicality, ability to elicit the best of men, and the more personal qualities of character, endurance, courage and nervous control." Includes bibliography and index.
Subject(s): History: Civil War

New

Garland, L. (1999). *Byzantine empresses: Women and power in Byzantium, A.D. 527-1204.* New York: Routledge.

Garland chronicles seven centuries of powerful women in the medieval Mediterranean empire of Constantinople, also known as Byzantium. Although power was technically vested in the ruling emperor, some women ruled with their husbands or served as regents for their young sons. A few were officially acknowledged as heads of state. This book tells the stories of 13 empresses, their rise to power, on-the-job training, and their great achievements in political and social affairs. Includes bibliographical references, genealogy tables, a glossary, and index.
Subject(s): History of women's leadership

Goodwin, D. K. (1991). *Lyndon Johnson and the American dream.* New York: St. Martin's Press.

Kearns has taken her observations and what LBJ told her during their years together as part of the White House Fellows Program and distilled them into an anecdotal-analytical picture of his personality and his accumulation of power. The author discusses how this power was put to use in light of the nature of political power in general and the changing character of U.S. government since the 1930s. Includes bibliographical references and index.
Subject(s): Biography: Johnson, L. B.; U.S. presidents: Johnson, L. B.

Greenstein, F. I. (1991). **The president who led by seeming not to: A centennial view of Dwight Eisenhower.** *Antioch Review, 49*(1), 39-44.

In polls following his presidency, experts ranked Eisenhower 29th in terms of greatness. In the 1980s another poll ranked Eisenhower in the top ten. Newly acquired documents reveal that Eisenhower intentionally played up his role as head of state while downplaying his role as political leader. He greeted the public and press with great warmth, muddled speech, scrambled syntax, and sparse substance. Yet his official papers indicate that he was shrewd, well informed, analytical, and on top of the issues. His hidden-hand style of leadership was employed to keep his strategies private and to avoid blame for unpopular decisions.

Subject(s): Biography: Eisenhower, D. D.; U.S. presidents: Eisenhower, D. D.

Greenstein, F. I. (1994). **The two leadership styles of William Jefferson Clinton.** *Political Psychology, 15*(2), 351-361.

President Clinton exhibits two distinct styles—one is a passion to make numerous sweeping policy changes without attention to detail and the other is salesmanship to gain support for a pet project with infinite attention to detail. Greenstein analyzes the factors contributing to these alternate styles: the policy issues during Clinton's term, his political drive, fluency, charm, energy, intelligence, lack of discipline, and his capacity to learn from his mistakes.

Subject(s): Biography: Clinton, W. J.; U.S. presidents: Clinton, W. J.

Gyatso, T. (Dalai Lama XIV). (1990). *Freedom in exile: The autobiography of the Dalai Lama.* New York: HarperCollins.

In 1940 a six-year-old child was proclaimed the 14th Dalai Lama of Tibet. He served as a spiritual and political leader until an army of the People's Republic of China forced his exile in 1959. He has continued to lead the 100,000 refugees who followed him to India as the Tibetan Government in Exile. His Five-Point Peace Plan in 1987, proposing the restoration of Tibet and the protection of its citizens' fundamental human rights, earned him the Nobel Peace Prize in 1989.

Subject(s): Biography: Dalai Lama

New
Hayward, S. F. (1997). *Churchill on leadership: Executive success in the face of adversity.* Rocklin, CA: Forum.

Hayward says that Winston Churchill should be the model for today's business leaders, who can apply Churchill's political strategies to management and commercial competition. This book uses Churchill's letters, speeches, and writings to illustrate his philosophy of leadership and to show how he put that philosophy into practice. Specific chapters address how Churchill saw administration and organization, managing people, his decision-making process, and his view of communication. Each chapter concludes with several leadership lessons. For example, Churchill's career in public office taught him to define the job, not simply to learn it, and to always look for opportunities to advance new initiatives. An appendix offers a biographical sketch of Churchill's executive career. Includes bibliographical references and index.

Subject(s): Biography: Churchill, W. S.

Heifetz, R. A. (1994). **Some strategic implications of William Clinton's strengths and weaknesses.** *Political Psychology, 15*(4), 763-768.

Heifetz comments on William Clinton's presidential style. He states that Clinton's ebullience and dynamism reflect a belief in an enormous personal power to solve complex problems and heal others' personal pain. Clinton's desire to be up close and personal with the public, his verbal and organizational skills, and his persistence are considered both strengths and weaknesses. Heifetz notes that President Clinton's style during his first nine months in office closely parallels his style during his first term as governor of Arkansas, which was consumed with setbacks but served as a valuable learning experience.

Subject(s): Biography: Clinton, W. J.; U.S. presidents: Clinton, W. J.

Iacocca, L., & Novak, W. (1984). *Iacocca: An autobiography.* New York: Bantam Books.

This book provides an autobiographical account of Lee Iacocca's life in leadership, from his 32 years with Ford Motor Company to his taking over the helm of Chrysler. It is filled with personal reflections on his experiences and views of corporate and national leadership. Includes index.

Subject(s): Biography: Iacocca, L.

Isaacson, W. (1992). *Kissinger: A biography.* New York: Simon & Schuster.

Henry Kissinger has as many critics as admirers. This biography attempts to remain unbiased in the account of the teenage refugee who fled Nazi Germany and became Richard Nixon's secretary of state. He is an undisputed political genius and statesman, but his role in the public spotlight made him a celebrity with enormous power in domestic and foreign affairs. Extensively researched, this book describes Kissinger's influence on the Vietnam War; on peace summits in Moscow, Beijing, and the Mideast; and on Watergate. Includes bibliographical references and index.

Subject(s): Biography: Kissinger, H.

Keegan, J. (1987). *The mask of command.* New York: Viking.

Historian Keegan recognizes "the leader of men in warfare can show himself to his followers only through a mask, but a mask made in such form as will mark him to men of his time and place as the leader they want and need." It is the intent of the author to penetrate behind the mask. The following are discussed: "Alexander the Great and Heroic Leadership"; "Wellington: The Anti-hero"; "Grant and Unheroic Leadership"; and "False Heroic: Hitler as Supreme Commander." He concludes with a provocative "Post-heroic: Command in the Nuclear World." Includes bibliography and index.

Subject(s): History of military leaders

King, M. L., Jr. (1964). *Why we can't wait.* New York: Harper & Row.

An inside account of the nonviolent movement for civil rights, which achieved its greatest victory to date with the demonstration in Birmingham in the summer of 1963. Rejecting both planned gradualism and unplanned spontaneity, King here reveals himself as a master-strategist in conducting civil rights demonstrations.

Subject(s): Civil rights leadership

New
Kotter, J. P. (1997). *Matsushita leadership: Lessons from the 20th century's most remarkable entrepreneur.* New York: Free Press.

Konosuke Matsushita rose from poverty to found Matsushita Electric Corporation, one of Japan's largest and most powerful companies. Kotter traces Matsushita's life, from his apprenticeship as a child, through the trials of the Great Depression and World War II, to the growth of his company and his philanthropic work. The book also describes the management and leadership practices Matsushita used, many of which he pioneered, that helped make his company a global success. Includes index.

Subject(s): Biography: Matsushita, K.

Krause, D. G. (1995). *The art of war for executives.* New York: Perigree.

Twenty-five hundred years ago, a Chinese warlord collected the teachings of a military strategist named Sun Tzu. In this book Krause applies a modern translation of those teachings to the business world, explaining that "today's battlefields are not physical places . . . today's battles occur within the minds of those who comprise the constituents of an organization." Sun Tzu's writings address subjects including planning, gathering intelligence, and maneuvering, and are based on his ten basic principles: learn to fight, show the way, do it right, know the facts, expect the worst, seize the day, burn the bridges, do it better, pull together, and keep them guessing.

Subject(s): Leadership lessons in literature, Eastern philosophy

Luecke, R. A. (1994). *Scuttle your ships before advancing: And other lessons from history on leadership and change for today's managers.* New York: Oxford University Press.

Luecke differentiates between the hard sciences, which accumulate knowledge from each generation to the next, and the moral sciences, which need to be continually relearned. The moral sciences—leadership, diplomacy, and negotiation—occur in difficult and ambiguous situations. Luecke's historical references to leaders in such situations provide lessons for today's leadership studies. Included are Hernan Cortes, Aztec emperor; Louis XI, King of France; Martin Luther, religious reformer; Hadrian, Roman emperor; Thomas Hutchinson, British loyalist; and Lyndon Johnson, U.S. president. Includes bibliographical references and index.

Subject(s): Leaders in history

Manchester, W. (1978). *American Caesar: Douglas MacArthur, 1880-1964.* Boston: Little, Brown.

General of the Army Douglas MacArthur "was a great thundering paradox of a man, noble and ignoble, inspiring and outrageous, arrogant and shy, the best of men and the worst of men, the most protean, most ridiculous, and most sublime." Includes bibliographical references and index.

Subject(s): Biography: MacArthur, D.

Manchester, W. (1983). *The last lion: Winston Spencer Churchill.* Boston: Little, Brown.

Working with diaries, memoranda, government documents, the private correspondence of Churchill and others, and interviews with Churchill's surviving colleagues and members of his family, the author provides a narrative recreating the past and private life of Churchill. This is the first of a two-volume biography. Includes bibliography and index.

Subject(s): Biography: Churchill, W. S.

Mankiller, W., & Wallis, M. (1993). *Mankiller: A chief and her people.* New York: St. Martin's Press.

Wilma Mankiller tells the story of the Cherokee people and of her emergence as their first female chief. Like her ancestors before her, Mankiller was forced to leave her family home in Oklahoma during a government relocation program. And like her ancestors she returned to her ancestral home. Her journey in the years between reflects the history of her people—facing prejudice and fighting for their heritage. During the Native American occupation of Alcatraz from 1969 to 1971 Mankiller experienced a political awakening and began her work in the revitalization of tribal communities. She later raised funds for Native American causes, formed government relations, met her mentor Ross Swimmer, and rose through the leadership ranks of the Cherokee Nation. In 1985 Mankiller became chief of the Cherokees upon Swimmer's resignation and was subsequently reelected to serve two more terms. Her leadership resulted in the legal and moral recognition of Native American nations and their self-governance.

Subject(s): Biography: Mankiller, W.; Native American leadership

McFeely, W. S. (1981). *Grant: A biography.* New York: Norton.

This biography of Ulysses S. Grant, Union Army Commander and 18th president of the United States, tells "a story of the quest of an ordinary American man in the mid-nineteenth century to make his mark. Grant failed as a peacetime army officer, a farmer, a minor businessman, a store clerk—and still he wanted to be taken into account." Includes bibliography and index.

Subject(s): Biography: Grant, U. S.; U.S. presidents: Grant, U. S.; military leadership

New

McNeilly, M. (1996). *Sun Tzu and the art of business*. New York: Oxford University Press.

This book of strategic principles is based on Sun Tzu's *The Art of War*, which was created for the military in 400 B.C. Six pertinent principles are: 1) win all without fighting; 2) avoid strength; 3) attack weakness, deception, and foreknowledge; 4) use speed and preparation; 5) shape your opponent; and 6) practice character-based leadership. Each chapter contains examples of one principle's effective application in a business setting. Includes a translation of *The Art of War*, bibliographical references, index, and figures.
Subject(s): Leadership lessons in literature, Eastern philosophy

Meier, A. (1965). **On the role of Martin Luther King.** *New Politics, 4*, 52-59.

Martin Luther King, Jr.'s combination of militancy and conservatism led to his great success. King better than anyone else could articulate the desires of blacks both to the blacks and to white America. This, along with his ability to hold the center position between conservative and radical groups, made King an effective leader.
Subject(s): Biography: King, M. L., Jr.; civil rights leadership

Morgenthau, H. J., & Hein, D. (1983). *Essays on Lincoln's faith and politics: Volume 4.* Lanham, MD: University Press of America.

Morgenthau approached Lincoln's view of ethics and religion from the vantage point of the political scientist and historian. Hein has approached the study of Lincoln's faith as a theologian and religious historian. Lincoln's religious and political ethics represented the core values in the American political tradition.
Subject(s): Biography: Lincoln, A.; U.S. presidents: Lincoln, A.; religious history

Nair, K. (1994). *A higher standard of leadership: Lessons from the life of Gandhi.* San Francisco: Berrett-Koehler.

Although he never held public office, Gandhi had enormous influence on his country. His religious principles drove him to seek equality for the millions of "untouchables" at the bottom of India's caste system. Nair believes that Gandhi's heroism, which stemmed not from violence but from bravery and moral purpose, provides a fine example for young people. Gandhi's higher standard of leadership was based on fundamental values and commitment to his fellow citizens. Includes bibliographical references and index.
Subject(s): Biography: Gandhi, M.

Oates, S. B. (1983). *Let the trumpet sound: The life of Martin Luther King, Jr.* New York: New American Library.

This is a magnificent recreation of a life—of a boy dominated by the minister father who "ruled his home like a fierce Old Testament patriarch"; of a young scholar passionately caught up in the teachings of Thoreau and Gandhi; of a man driven by his vision of racial equality. Stephen Oates portrays the forces that shaped "a very human man"—parental, cultural, spiritual, and intellectual—into the right person for a crucial moment in American history. Includes bibliographical references and index.
Subject(s): Biography: King, M. L., Jr.

Phillips, D. T. (1992). *Lincoln on leadership: Executive strategies for tough times.* New York: Warner Books.

Taking a historical perspective in search for tomorrow's leadership solutions, Phillips explores the qualities that made Abraham Lincoln one of America's most revered leaders. Lincoln's talent with people, his character, management style, and communicative abilities are analyzed to identify keys that will serve today's leaders. Phillips explains why we should seize the initiative and never relinquish it, wage only one war at a time, encourage risk-taking while providing job security, make requests or suggestions instead of issuing orders, and, once in a while, let things slip. Includes bibliographical references and index.
Subject(s): Biography: Lincoln, A.; U.S. presidents: Lincoln, A.

Phillips, D. T. (1997). *The founding fathers on leadership: Classic teamwork in changing times.* New York: Warner.

Phillips combines history lessons with examples of team leadership in this book on America's founding fathers. Samuel Adams is described as a rabble-rouser whose passionate indignation painted a vision for America's independence. George Washington inspired followers when he read the Declaration of Independence to the soldiers of the Continental Army. Benjamin Franklin built strong alliances to shore up the new country's weaknesses and lift morale. These leaders and dozens more provide leadership lessons for present-day executives and teams. Includes a bibliography and index.
Subject(s): History: U.S. presidents; team leadership

New

Phillips, R. D. (1999). *The heart of an executive: Lessons on leadership from the life of King David.* New York: Doubleday.

Phillips says that the Biblical story of King David is actually one of a career executive, consisting of "preparation leading to advancement, trials and challenges serving to build character and hone skills, advancement leading to achievement, and finally the passing on of the torch to others." This book uses Biblical passages and analysis to describe David's life, from his defeat of Goliath through his rise to power and the establishment of his successor. Each chapter identifies leadership lessons readers can learn from David, such as the importance of personal loyalty, that the integrity of an organization and its leader are inseparable, and that executive leadership is about developing and integrating systems for sustained performance. Ultimately, Phillips concludes that leadership is built upon love, and says that David was a great leader because he held God, his people, and his dream in his heart.

Subject(s): Biography: King David; religious history

Powell, C. (1995). *My American journey.* New York: Ballantine.

Colin Powell is one of this country's premier military leaders. In this book he tells the story of his life, from his childhood in Harlem to his marriage, to his experiences in Vietnam, Panama, and Desert Storm. Includes index and photographs.

Subject(s): Biography: Powell, C.; military leadership

Roberts, W. (1985). *Leadership secrets of Attila the Hun.* New York: Warner Books.

The history books describe Attila the Hun as a 5th-century tyrant who ruled a band of rapists and murderers as they plundered their way across the Roman Empire. Roberts suggests that we view Attila as an entrepreneur who forged a cohesive team from an uncivilized horde of barbarians. Roberts explains why he considers Attila to have been a successful negotiator, field marshal, and visionary leader.

Subject(s): Biography: Attila the Hun

Salinger, P. (1997). *John F. Kennedy, Commander in Chief: A profile in leadership.* New York: Penguin Studio.

Salinger, former press secretary to President Kennedy, shares his account of Kennedy's military leadership. In this book he tells how it felt to be an insider at the behind-the-scenes decision making during the Bay of Pigs, the building of the Berlin Wall, the beginnings of U.S. involvement in Vietnam, the space race, and the Cuban missile crisis. Salinger tells his stories through fond memories, excerpts from speeches, and many photographs. Includes index.

Subject(s): Biography: Kennedy, J. F.; U.S. presidents: Kennedy, J. F.; military leadership

Scott, R. F. (1923). *Scott's last expedition: Captain Scott's own story.* Philadelphia: Transatlantic.

This work contains the personal journals of Captain Robert Falcon Scott on his 1910 to 1912 expedition to the South Pole. "Had we lived, I should have had a tale to tell of the hardihood, endurance, and courage of my companions which would have stirred the heart of every Englishman." Includes charts and illustrations.

Subject(s): Biography: Scott, R. F.

Simonton, D. K. (1994). *Greatness: Who makes history and why.* New York: Guilford Press.

This book is grounded in the psychology of history. The author considers psychological factors such as birth order, personality, madness, and genius to identify characteristics of those who influence society. Artists, authors, composers, politicians, scientists, inventors, military heroes, movie stars, and criminals serve as examples to support his theories. Includes bibliographical references and indexes.

Subject(s): History

Skowronek, S. (1997). *The politics presidents make: Leadership from John Adams to Bill Clinton* (New ed.). Cambridge, MA: Belknap Press.

Originally published in 1993, this new edition has an updated preface and afterword with insights on President Bill Clinton's leadership. The book examines recurring leadership patterns in presidential history and links modern presidents to their predecessors by similarity of political style or situation. In particular, presidents are considered as agents of change. Three types of presidential change agents are discussed in detail. *Reconstruction* represents an opposition to the previous administration and the most promising of all situations for the exercise of political leadership. Thomas Jefferson, Abraham Lincoln, and Franklin Roosevelt fall into this category. *Articulation* represents a stable situation in which a president has the opportunity to be innovative. James Monroe, Theodore Roosevelt, and Lyndon Johnson are examples in this category. *Disjunction*-type presidents assume power in impossible situations. Their affiliation with failed commitments can lead only to lost credibility. John Quincy Adams, Herbert Hoover, and Jimmy Carter are described as disjunction-type presidents. Includes bibliographical references in notes and an index.

Subject(s): History: U.S. presidents

New

Strock, J. M. (1998). *Reagan on leadership: Executive lessons from the great communicator.* Rocklin, CA: Forum.

Strock analyzes former U.S. President Ronald Reagan's political career and approach to leadership using Reagan's own writings and speeches and examples from his acting career, governorship, and presidency. The book's first section addresses Reagan's philosophy of leadership, including chapters on vision, decisiveness, negotiating from strength, and learning from failure. The second section describes Reagan's approach to management. The third focuses on his communication skills, with chapters on focusing on your audience and being a good speechwriter. The final section shows how Reagan viewed leadership as a way of life, and describes how his courage, competence, grace, and empathy formed his leadership style. Each chapter ends with a list of "Reagan on Leadership" points of advice for readers. Includes bibliographical references and index.

Subject(s): Biography: Reagan, R.; U.S. presidents: Reagan, R.

Terrill, R. (1980). *Mao: A biography.* New York: Harper & Row.

Terrill's biography of the late Chinese leader is imbued with his familiarity with and respect for Chinese culture. He shows how Mao identified his own suppression as a boy under an unrelenting, dictatorial father with the suppression of the peasants and consequently forged strength and lessons useful in his complex future. Includes bibliographical references and index.

Subject(s): Biography: Mao Tse-tung; Chinese leadership

Washington, J. M. (1986). *I have a dream: Writings and speeches that changed the world.* San Francisco: HarperCollins.

This is a collection of Martin Luther King, Jr.'s most famous speeches and critiques. It includes: *I Have a Dream, Letter from a Birmingham Jail, The Drum Major Instinct,* and *Pilgrimage to Nonviolence.* Washington provides a chronology of King's life and has arranged the speeches in sequence with an introduction on the time period and significance.
Subject(s): Historical speeches

New

Wegemer, G. B. (1996). *Thomas More on statesmanship.* Washington, DC: Catholic University Press.

Thomas More (1478-1535) was an English statesman and author who served in Parliament and under Henry VII, and is probably best known for writing *Utopia.* In this book Wegemer uses More's writings to assess his beliefs about leadership and governing, addressing three aspects of More's work: his political theory, his literature, and his political experience. First, Wegemer describes More's view of the role of the statesman and compares More's work to that of St. Augustine and Cicero. Several chapters then apply this analysis of More's views specifically to *Utopia.* Finally, the book details some of the issues More encountered in his own career, such as the role of religion in government. Includes bibliographical references and index.
Subject(s): Biography: More, T.

Wills, G. (1994). *Certain trumpets: The call of leaders.* New York: Simon & Schuster.

Wills, the Pulitzer Prize-winning author of *Lincoln at Gettysburg: The Words That Remade America* (Touchstone Books, 1992), reexamines the nature of the leader-follower partnership in this book. He claims that leadership is the reciprocal engagement of two wills, "one leading (often in disguised ways), the other following (often while resisting)." Through biographical sketches of 16 leaders and 16 antileaders Wills paints a portrait of leadership through history and across the range of human experience. Representing politics is a discussion of Franklin D. Roosevelt as an elected leader and Adlai Stevenson as an antitype. Other portraits include: religious leader, King David and antitype, Solomon; military leader, Napoleon and antitype, George McClellan; business leader, Ross Perot and antitype, Roger Smith; artistic leader, Martha Graham and antitype, Madonna. Includes bibliographical references and index.
Subject(s): Leaders in history

LEADERSHIP COMPETENCIES

Aberbach, D. (1996). *Charisma in politics, religion and the media: Private trauma, public ideals.* Washington Square: New York University Press.

This book describes the public images, often created by the media, of famous people who have or had charismatic appeal. The author draws surprising parallels in the lives of individuals who have nothing in common except their charismatic personalities. Among the people studied are: Adolf Hitler; Marilyn Monroe; Charlie Chaplin; John Lennon; Indian religious leader, Krishnamurti; German philosopher and author, Martin Buber; and Hebrew poet, Chaim Nachman Bialik. Includes a bibliography, name index, and subject index.
Subject(s): Charisma, media influence

New
Ackoff, R. L. (1999). **Transformational leadership.** *Strategy & Leadership*, *27*(1), 20-25.

Ackoff defines a transformational leader as "a person with the ability to create or facilitate the creation of an organizational vision of an idealized state." Because leadership is an aesthetic activity, it naturally transforms. It pursues truth, plenty, goodness, beauty, and fun. Followers naturally gravitate to an idealized vision that contains those elements yet is just out of reach. Ackoff explains how four types of organizational systems—deterministic, animated, social, and ecological—may be transformed by mobilizing idealized visions. Includes bibliographical references.
Subject(s): Transformational leadership, vision

Agor, W. H. (Ed.). (1989). *Intuition in organizations: Leading and managing productively.* Newbury Park, CA: Sage.

Intuition is not magical or paranormal. It is a brain skill integrating physical, emotional, mental, and spiritual functions. Executives use intuition to create visions, make decisions, predict trends, and solve problems. The *Agor Intuitive Management Survey* evaluates individual intuition level. Charts compare national norms by management level, sex, ethnic group, and occupation. There are case studies, practical guidelines for developing intuitive skills, and an agenda for future research. Includes bibliographical references and index.
Subject(s): Intuition

New
Amabile, T. M. (1998). **How to kill creativity.** *Harvard Business Review*, *76*(5), 77-87.

Creativity in the arts involves an original idea. In business a creative idea must also be useful and feasible. Expertise, creative-thinking skills, and motivation are the keys to useful and feasible creativity at work. Amabile suggests that managers can enhance creativity by challenging employees, by granting autonomy in work processes, and by providing resources and encouragement. She explains how managers

can turn creativity-killing situations into creativity-supporting opportunities.
Subject(s): Creativity

New
Anderson, C. (1997). **Values-based management.** *Academy of Management Executive*, *11*(4), 25-46.

The most difficult decisions for managers to make involve choices that will not benefit everyone and may in fact contribute to harm of some. Downsizing is one current situation exemplifying this dilemma. The environmental effects of a business's actions are another. This article serves to increase managerial understanding of the complexities involved in making value choices. The author differentiates between value choices and ethical dilemmas by emphasizing that ethical principles are the building blocks for moral reasoning, and are static. He states that value choices are made based upon one's ethical principles. The dilemmas that result from these value choices and their resolutions define the value and performance of an organization. The article defines the four goals of an organization and presents dilemmas inherent in these goals. These are followed by three factors affecting the decision-making process, and finally, several resolutions and recommendations are listed. Includes two figures, bibliographical references, and an appendix.
Subject(s): Values

New
Anderson, T. (1998). *Transforming leadership: Equipping yourself and coaching others to build the leadership organization* (2nd ed.). Boca Raton, FL: St. Lucie Press.

"Transforming leaders," according to Anderson, build their companies into creative, learning organizations using skills from five distinct areas: self-management, interpersonal communication, problem management, consultative skills, and role- and style-shifting skills. This book is designed to help individuals develop their skill sets, first offering readers the *Leadership Skills Inventory* self-assessment and then describing ways to improve the 56 specific skills identified. Worksheets, development plans, and sample dialogues are provided. Includes index.
Subject(s): Competencies overview

New
Argyris, C. (1998). **Empowerment: The emperor's new clothes.** *Harvard Business Review*, *76*(3), 98-105.

Argyris suggests that the concept of empowerment is like the emperor's new clothes. We praise it in public but privately wonder why we can't see it. This article ponders the illusive concept, its potential for producing highly motivated employees, and its challenge to become a reality. One key is the internal commitment of employees who define their own tasks, goals, and behaviors. There is a strong temptation for

managers to define these elements as well as visions, strategies, and work processes. When that happens employees lose faith in the program and empowerment can't exist.
Subject(s): Empowerment

Armstrong, D. M. (1992). *Managing by storying around.* New York: Doubleday.

At Armstrong International, Inc., management by storytelling has been used with success for five years. Armstrong shares his philosophy for this simple, fun, and memorable way to pass along corporate traditions, train new employees, recognize special efforts, recruit, and sell. He shares many of his favorite stories, including the morals of each story, to prove that there are valuable lessons to be learned from this method of management.
Subject(s): Storytelling

New
Avolio, B. J., Howell, J. M., & Sosik, J. J. (1999). **A funny thing happened on the way to the bottom line: Humor as a moderator of leadership style effects.** *Academy of Management Journal, 42*(2), 219-227.

The authors compare the use of humor in three styles of leadership—transformational, contingent-reward, and laissez-faire. A study of 115 managers and their followers in a Canadian finance firm confirmed their hypotheses. Results indicate that humor used by transformational leaders positively impacts the leader's performance appraisal and unit performance. The same is true for humor used by contingent-reward leaders. Humor used by laissez-faire leaders has a negative impact in both areas. Includes bibliographical references.
Subject(s): Communication, humor

New
Badaracco, J. L., Jr. (1998). **The discipline of building character.** *Harvard Business Review, 76*(2), 115-124.

When professional responsibilities conflict with one's deepest values, a leader faces a defining moment. The author isn't referring to ethical dilemmas in which there is a clearly right, albeit difficult, solution. He refers to even tougher situations in which there are two equally right yet incompatible choices. At the personal level this may represent the delicate balance between work and family. Managers of work groups may be challenged to bring consensus and form processes that support organizational values. Executives face defining moments when their organizational vision is challenged. The author recommends drawing on one's reserves of shrewdness, expediency, creativity, and tenacity to build character from life's defining moments.
Subject(s): Character

Baker, D. B. (1992). *Power quotes: 4,000 trenchant soundbites on leadership and liberty, treason and triumph, sacrifice and scandal, risk and rebellion, weakness and war, and other affaires politiques.* Detroit: Visible Ink Press.

Historical to contemporary quotes on leadership, ethics, and power are arranged by category, then chronologically. An authors' index aids the reader's search for a favorite pundit and includes very brief biographical information. From humor to inspiration, the quotes are reported to be originals or best translated versions. Includes index.
Subject(s): Power, ethics, quotations

New
Barrie, J., & Pace, W. (1998). **Learning for organizational effectiveness: Philosophy of education and human resource development.** *Human Resource Development Quarterly, 9*(1), 39-54.

HRD can be considered either an element of personnel practice and human resource management or part of a larger discourse on adult education and learning. The educational perspective is based on the premises that learning is normatively good, is related to cognitive development, and entails a process. Organizational learning is a broader, more cooperative concept than organizational performance, which consists of the demonstration of specific behaviors and is based on behavior control. The authors say that since well-educated people can bring more value to a business than simply well-trained people, it would be wise for organizations and HRD professionals to focus on organizational learning, and not simply on training for improved performance. Includes bibliographical references.
Subject(s): Learning competency, organizational learning

New
Barth, T. J., & Bartenstein, J. (1998). **Fostering a learning, innovative government: The role of academic/practitioner collaboration.** *The Public Manager, 27*(1), 21-26.

The "reinventing government" movement that began in the early 1990s sparked an interest in making public agencies into learning organizations. This article describes how academic research and "real world" practitioners can work together to create a "learning and innovative government." The authors say that while academics can provide practitioners with a fresh perspective on their work, practitioners offer academics an opportunity to do reality-based research. Collaborative study that addresses current issues will be needed if public agencies hope to foster continuous learning and innovation. Includes bibliographical references.
Subject(s): Learning competency, organizational learning

New
Bass, B. M., & Steidlmeier, P. (1999). **Ethics, character, and authentic transformational leadership behavior.** *Leadership Quarterly: Special Issue, Part I: Charismatic and Transformational Leadership: Taking Stock of the Present and Future, 10*(2), 181-217.

This article states that authentic transformational leadership is grounded in moral foundations. This style of leadership is based on idealized influence, inspirational motivation, intellectual stimulation, and individualized consideration.

These elements are subjected to a moral analysis that considers a leader's developmental level of conscience, degree of freedom, and intention. The analysis also considers the ends sought, the means employed, and the consequences of a leader's actions. It is determined that transformational leadership is authentic when founded on moral character, concern for others, congruence of ethical values, and moral action. When the focus is on deception and exploitation of followers the leadership is pseudotransformational. Includes bibliographical references.
Subject(s): Charismatic leadership, transformational leadership, values

Belasco, J. A., & Stayer, R. C. (1993). *Flight of the buffalo: Soaring to excellence, learning to let employees lead.* New York: Warner Books.

Belasco, author of the management best-seller *Teaching the Elephant to Dance* (1990), and Stayer, the Johnsonville Foods CEO featured in Tom Peters' video *The Leadership Alliance* (1988), share their insights on leadership. Having been autocratic leaders in their own organizations, they each felt like a head buffalo followed blindly by a herd of employees. Using the buffalo herd metaphor, they share the learning processes that allowed them to change their own behaviors. Using another metaphor they explain how they transferred ownership to employees who now resemble flocks of geese flying in V-formation with every goose responsible for its own flight.
Subject(s): Participation

New
Belasco, J. A., & Stead, J. (1999). *Soaring with the Phoenix: Renewing the vision, reviving the spirit, and re-creating the success of your company.* New York: Warner.

Belasco and Steed say that a successful future cannot be based on incremental changes to today, but depends on leaders radically recreating their organizations to deal with tomorrow's challenges. This book uses the metaphor of the phoenix, a bird that continually renews itself, to describe a method of "revivolutionary" self-renewal based on five principles: 1) renew yourself, 2) plug into your connections, 3) create success for all your connections, 4) learn more in order to contribute to others' success, and 5) take ownership of your company and your life. Each chapter includes a "Phoenix Workshop" providing exercises leaders can do to evaluate and improve their organizations.
Subject(s): Innovation

New
Bell, C. R., & Shea, H. (1998). *Dance lessons: Six steps to great partnerships in business and life.* San Francisco: Berrett-Koehler.

This book uses the metaphor of dance to explain how to create and maintain partnerships in business, both on an organizational and an individual level. Partnership is described as a six-step process: 1) preparing, 2) picking great partners, 3) getting the partnership in shape, 4) keeping the magic in motion, 5) managing the pain, and 6) calling it curtains. Each chapter contains drills and activities to help readers master the partnership steps. Quotes from business leaders and dancers are used to illustrate important concepts. Includes bibliographical references and index.
Subject(s): Partnerships

New
Bennebroek Gravenhorst, K. M., & Boonstra, J. J. (1998). **The use of influence tactics in constructive change processes.** *European Journal of Work and Organizational Psychology, 7*(2), 179-196.

The authors surveyed 479 Dutch workers to determine what influence tactics were most commonly used in constructive change processes and how those tactics were affected by job position and direction of influence. They used the Dutch version of Yukl's *Influence Behavior Questionnaire* to measure the frequency with which workers used nine influence tactics—rational persuasion, inspirational appeals, consultation, ingratiation, personal appeals, exchange, coalition tactics, legitimating tactics, and pressure. Analysis showed that the most common tactics used in change processes were rational persuasion, inspirational appeals, and consultation, and that line managers, staff specialists, and consultants each use these tactics differently. The study also determined that the use of influence tactics differs depending on whether the influence is aimed upward, downward, or laterally. Includes bibliographical references.
Subject(s): Change process

Bennis, W. G. (1989). *Why leaders can't lead: The unconscious conspiracy continues.* San Francisco: Jossey-Bass.

What prevents leaders from taking charge and making changes? Bennis writes here about the dark side of leadership, especially the problems a leader encounters in attempting to take charge of an organization. He believes we are presently lacking any true leaders. By the author's definition true leaders embody six important virtues: integrity, dedication, magnanimity, humility, openness, and creativity. Includes index.
Subject(s): Competencies overview, negative views of leadership

New
Beyer, J. M. (1999). **Taming and promoting charisma to change organizations.** *Leadership Quarterly: Special Issue, Part I: Charismatic and Transformational Leadership: Taking Stock of the Present and Future, 10*(2), 307-330.

Beyer examines charisma from a sociological rather than a psychological perspective. She suggests that charisma is not about individual attributes and behaviors. It is "a social structure that emerges from complex interactions of multiple factors that cannot be separated neatly into causes, moderators, and effects." Beyer also suggests that Max Weber's early concept of charisma (*The Theory of Social and Eco-*

nomic Organization, 1947) has been diluted from a rare phenomenon to a current paradigm of common occurrence. Charisma has been romanticized, tamed, and proven to be evil in some situations. Beyer concludes that the concept of charismatic leadership is too narrow to be authenticated. Includes bibliographical references.
Subject(s): Charismatic leadership, transformational leadership

Bierma, L. L. (1996). **How executive women learn corporate culture.** *Human Resource Development Quarterly, 7*(2), 145-164.

Bierma interviewed and observed 11 female executives in Fortune 500 companies to determine how women learn organizational culture. She discovered that culture learning is a process that includes cognitive, experiential, and collaborative tactics. Cognitive learning experiences such as reading, adjunct teaching, and public speaking helped the women to build confidence and strengthen skills. Observation and reflection were useful experiential techniques for learning office politics. Collaborative tactics such as mentorships, peer support, and networking helped the women learn to function in male-dominated cultures and to develop influence.
Subject(s): Learning competency

Bigelow, J. (1992). **Developing managerial wisdom.** *Journal of Management Inquiry, 1*(2), 143-153.

Wisdom is an elusive concept, difficult to define and often not addressed in management development programs. As a management educator Bigelow strives to incorporate issues regarding wisdom into his courses. In this article he examines historical attitudes through quotations from high-achievers and classic literature. He examines personal growth from naiveté to wisdom and offers a model of wisdom development.
Subject(s): Wisdom

Black, J. S., & Gregersen, H. B. (1997). **Participative decision-making: An integration of multiple dimensions.** *Human Relations, 50*(7), 859-878.

Participative decision making (PDM) has several components, including the degree of employee involvement and the decision-making process itself. The decision process has five stages: identifying the problem, generating alternative solutions, selecting a solution, planning to implement the solution, and evaluating the implementation. This study of employees at a manufacturing company examined the differential impact of these two aspects of PDM. The authors found that employees with above-average involvement in the decision-making process reported higher levels of satisfaction and performance. Moreover, the more stages of the decision making employees were involved in, the higher their levels of satisfaction.
Subject(s): Shared decision making

Blake, R. B., & McCanse, A. A. (1991). *Leadership dilemmas: Grid solutions.* Houston: Gulf.

This book updates the Grid tool introduced in Blake and Mouton's *The Managerial Grid* (Gulf, 1964). Using the terms *leadership* and *management* interchangeably, the Grid is a framework for plotting an individual's approaches to performing tasks and relating with other people. The five styles on the original grid are: impoverished management (low task, low relationship); country club management (low task, high relationship); authority compliance (high task, low relationship); middle of the road (mid-task, mid-relationship); and team management (high task, high relationship). Added to the Grid in this edition are: paternalistic management (reward and punishment) and opportunistic management (what's in it for me?).
Subject(s): Relationship building, *The Managerial Grid*

Blank, W. (1995). *The nine natural laws of leadership.* New York: AMACOM.

By applying quantum mechanics to the business world, Blank has developed a new paradigm that he calls *quantum leadership*, based on the premise that "at the deepest levels, reality is a field, an interaction that cannot be understood in terms of separate parts." Central to this paradigm are the "nine natural laws of leadership," which include: a leader has willing followers, leaders use influence beyond formal authority, and leadership involves risk and uncertainty. Based on these laws Blank offers over 150 "Action Ideas," practical suggestions on how to use quantum leadership in everyday situations. Includes bibliographical references and index.
Subject(s): Chaos

New
Bloch, D. P., & Richmond, L. J. (1998). *Soul work: Finding the work you love, loving the work you have.* Palo Alto, CA: Davies-Black.

The authors identify seven spiritual themes—change, balance, energy, community, harmony, calling, and unity—and use them to examine the concept of career. Each theme is addressed in a chapter with four sections: a story about a person facing a career dilemma, a list of career issues they faced, a set of reflections on that chapter's theme, and a series of exercises that helps readers apply these themes to their lives. Includes bibliographical references.
Subject(s): Spirit

Block, P. (1993). *Stewardship: Choosing service over self-interest.* San Francisco: Berrett-Koehler.

Stewardship replaces top-down control with partnership and choice at all levels. Individuals within an organization take responsibility and hold themselves accountable. Block presents models of stewardship for organizations and for individuals. He states that organizations that practice stewardship will succeed by choosing service over self-interest and by integrating the best of the human spirit with the demands of the marketplace. Includes an index.
Subject(s): Empowerment

Bolman, L. G., & Deal, T. E. (1994). *Leading with soul: An uncommon journey of spirit.* San Francisco: Jossey-Bass.

As social scientists the authors pursued an uncommon journey of their own to link leadership with spirituality—reclaiming the human capacity that gives lives passion and purpose. Using the ancient literary style of conversations between a troubled leader and a wise guide (in this case, a Japanese guide), this book reveals the process of finding, believing, sharing, and leading with soul. Includes bibliographical references.

Subject(s): Spirit

New

Boonstra, J. J., & Bennebroek Gravenhorst, K. M. (1998). **Power dynamics and organizational change: A comparison of perspectives.** *European Journal of Work and Organizational Psychology, 7*(2), 97-120.

In the introduction to this special issue on power and organizational change the editors describe how change processes, power, and the agents involved in change interact. They describe five perspectives for understanding this relationship: the power model, which focuses on position power and domination; the expert model, based on personal power and influence; the negotiation model, which uses structural power and exchange; the sales model, focusing on cultural power and management of meaning; and the developmental model, which uses power dynamics and dialogue. Different types of research that use these perspectives are addressed, and the article concludes with a description of the research that appears in the issue. Includes bibliographical references.

Subject(s): Power, organizational change

New

Booth, E. (1997). *The everyday work of art: How artistic experience can transform your life.* Naperville, IL: Sourcebooks.

Booth claims that artistic experiences awaken one's dormant skills and reveal the answers to life's challenges. He explains that all people create works of art in their everyday lives and can learn to be more purposeful about this creativity. There are three basic actions: 1) making things with meaning, 2) exploring things that others have made, and 3) maintaining a work-of-art attitude. This book guides readers through a series of experiments and suggestions for utilizing artistic sources and tools such as yearning, intentional noticing, imagining, making metaphors, and reading the world. Includes bibliographical references and index.

Subject(s): Creativity

New

Bouwen, R. (1998). **Relational construction of meaning in emerging organizational contexts.** *European Journal of Work and Organizational Psychology, 7*(3), 299-319.

Although individuals and organizations are generally considered separate entities, Bouwen says that in change

processes the interaction between the two is so important that they must be studied together. This article uses a case study from an oil refinery to show the benefits of using a relational approach to organizational change. Bouwen says that language, dialogue, co-ownership of the change process, and participation by the workers are all key factors in the success of a change effort. Includes bibliographical references.

Subject(s): Change process

New

Bradford, D. L., & Cohen, A. R. (1998). *Power up: Transforming organizations through shared leadership.* New York: Wiley.

According to Bradford and Cohen, organizations used to function under heroic leadership wherein employees looked to a manager for the definitive solution. Moving away from that philosophy into participatory and worker-empowered management has not proved to be effective, therefore this source presents a model for a new approach to post-heroic leadership. The first few chapters present the groundwork for this change, beginning with a description of the current leadership trap and then moving to a discussion of participatory management, with comparisons of the two. Chapter four presents a case study to assist in application of the new ideals. This actual example profiles an executive with Applico who made the transition from heroic to shared leadership. The second portion of the book expands on the new model with three essential elements of shared leadership: shared-responsibility team, tangible vision, and mutual influence. The final part of this source delves extensively into a case study of the Pharmco company and its transition.

Subject(s): Shared leadership

New

Bradshaw, P. (1998). **Power as dynamic tension and its implications for radical organizational change.** *European Journal of Work and Organizational Psychology, 7*(2), 121-143.

Bradshaw argues that there are two major tensions in the conceptualization of power: manifest/surface power versus latent/deep power, and individual versus collective power. These two polarities can be combined to create a framework of power consisting of four concepts: surface structural power, surface personal power, deep personal power, and deep cultural power. Bradshaw uses this framework to suggest four "paths to change," or ways organizations can create transformation by addressing the complexities of power. These paths are restructuring, personal action, deconstruction, and resistance. A case study of an eight-week strike by professors at York University in Toronto illustrates how the different tensions and levels of power interact. Includes bibliographical references.

Subject(s): Power, organizational change

New

Branden, N. (1998). *Self-esteem at work: How confident people make powerful companies.* San Francisco: Jossey-Bass.

Branden says that in today's economy self-esteem is "an urgent economic need" because workers with good self-esteem are able to achieve high performance. This book describes the historical changes that have made self-esteem so important in business and identifies the six practices most essential to building self-esteem: 1) living consciously, 2) self-acceptance, 3) self-responsibility, 4) self-assertiveness, 5) living purposefully, and 6) personal integrity. Branden then describes how leaders can develop their own self-esteem and use it to manage change, create a culture of accountability, support innovation, and treat work as a vehicle for personal growth. An appendix includes activities for a 21-week program of personal growth.
Subject(s): Confidence

Briskin, A. (1996). *The stirring of soul in the workplace.* San Francisco: Jossey-Bass.

Briskin calls his book "a reality check on management and the workplace: where we are, where we have been, and where we may be going." He uses historical background and real-life stories to develop a theory of the role the soul plays in the workplace, and the role it should play. Chapters address issues including the legacy of efficiency, managing emotions, taking up organizational roles, and how to affirm your experience at work. Includes bibliographical references and index.
Subject(s): Spirit

New

Brophy, D. R. (1998). **Understanding, measuring, and enhancing collective creative problem-solving efforts.** *Creativity Research Journal, 11*(3), 199-229.

In this review of the existing research, creative problem solving (CPS) is defined as "seeking original ways to reach a goal when the means to do so are not apparent." Brophy first concludes that individuals are generally better at CPS than groups and then describes way groups can improve their CPS skills. These include allowing members to use their knowledge and experience, encouraging positive and tolerant attitudes, and motivating members to contribute what they can. Ways that organizations can encourage CPS are then listed. They include using leaders who support CPS efforts, providing material and technical support, and diversifying assignments and tasks. Brophy proposes integrating these findings using a tri-level matching theory that advocates matching individuals, groups, and organizations with certain attributes to the types of problems they are best suited to solving. Includes bibliographical references.
Subject(s): Creative problem solving

New

Brophy, D. R. (1998). **Understanding, measuring, and enhancing individual creative problem-solving efforts.** *Creativity Research Journal, 11*(2), 123-150.

In this review of the literature, creative problem solving (CPS) is defined as "seeking original ways to reach goals when the means to do so are not readily apparent." Brophy says that a complete CPS process requires practitioners to have several sets of skills: the ability to think both divergently and convergently, to formulate a problem and a solution, and to alternate between innovation and adaptation. Most people, however, show an inclination for one skill in each set and tend to use only one way of thinking rather than both. But Brophy argues that most people can be trained to appreciate other inclinations and perform all parts of CPS better. He also says that such a wide variation exists in the types of problems and solutions found in CPS that the best strategy may be to match problems with the individuals best suited to solve them. Includes bibliographical references.
Subject(s): Creative problem solving

Bryner, A., & Markova, D. (1996). *An unused intelligence: Physical thinking for 21st century leadership.* Berkeley, CA: Conari Press.

Physical thinking integrates mind and body to create a natural source of vitality. It allows one to deliver and receive messages through verbal communication and body language. The authors explain how to understand physical thinking in learning organizations, job stress, trust, respect of other people's limits, vision, and collaborative leadership. Physical practice exercises with instructions and photographs accompany each chapter. There is a chart that helps readers relate theory to practice. Includes bibliographical references, an index, and an appendix explaining the five disciplines of a learning organization.
Subject(s): Creative thinking, organizational learning

New

Burkan, W. (1998). **Developing your wide-angle vision.** *Futurist, 32*(2), 35-38.

When organizations use forecasting they limit their options by committing to a certain set of beliefs. But when organizations practice anticipation they prepare themselves for many possible futures and increase their options. For this article Burkan interviewed people for whom anticipation is a life-or-death matter—including Secret Service agents, Marine snipers, and fighter pilots—and identified four key anticipation skills. First, these professionals use "splatter vision" or "taking in everything as a whole, focusing on nothing." Second, they develop explicit, detailed mental models. Third, these workers are skilled at reading the signs in front of them, and fourth, they have an early-warning system in place.
Subject(s): Vision

Calvert, G. (1993). *Highwire management: Risk-taking tactics for leaders, innovators, and trailblazers.* San Francisco: Jossey-Bass.

Risk management has taken on new meaning as organizations face productivity challenges with reduced resources, shorter cycles, and increased workloads. Calvert shares his views on risk-taking as a management strategy to help others learn how to welcome risk as a positive force. Three self-assessments, *Risk Attitudes Inventory, Risk-taking Control Scale,* and *Risk Success Quiz,* provide a foundation for knowing one's strengths and weaknesses. Managers from a variety of industries share their risk-taking experiences, successful tactics, skills and attitudes, and ways to avoid emotional stress and unnecessary costs. Includes bibliographical references and index.
Subject(s): Risk-taking

New
Cameron, J. (1996). *The vein of gold: A journey to your creative heart.* New York: Jeremy P. Tarcher/Putnam.

This companion to *The Artist's Way* (Cameron, 1992) leads readers on a journey—a treasure hunt—in search of the pot of gold deep within themselves. Cameron believes that everyone has a creative child inside waiting to be rediscovered. This source outlines tasks for learning and practicing creative processes. To achieve a state of artful living, readers visit and conquer challenges in seven kingdoms: 1) story—where language shapes self-image, 2) sight—where we receive information holistically, 3) sound—where there is harmony and a melodic flow of life, 4) attitude—where life's difficulties become lessons and opportunities, 5) relationship—where we develop relationships with those we trust, 6) spirituality—where there is a connection to a higher power, and 7) possibility—where the artful life is achieved with passion. Includes creative cluster guidelines, glossary, discography, bibliographical references, and index.
Subject(s): Creativity

Campbell, D. (1993). **Good leaders are credible leaders.** *Research Technology Management, 36*(5), 29-31.

Credibility is defined as being believable and worthy of trust and is considered the most significant determination of good leadership. A study of 55 R&D managers, using self- and other *Campbell Leadership Index* assessments, indicates that R&D managers are more credible than average managers. But in some cases a considerable gap exists between self- and other ratings. Adjectives describing credible managers are: *considerate, cooperative, optimistic, resilient,* and *well-adjusted.* Adjectives describing those with low credibility are: *cynical, depressed, moody, sarcastic,* and *self-centered.*
Subject(s): Credibility

Chaleff, I. (1995). *The courageous follower: Standing up to and for our leaders.* San Francisco: Berrett-Koehler.

Chaleff introduces the psychological dynamics of the leader-follower dyad. In the worst-case scenarios such as Nazi

Germany, followers blindly accept a leader's behavior and are afraid to challenge. In the best-case scenarios, followers are proactive, take responsibility, challenge unethical behavior, and champion change. Being a courageous follower means knowing when to separate from a leader whose purpose or behavior no longer warrants support. Includes bibliographical references and index.
Subject(s): Followership, courage

New
Chibber, M. L. (1995). *Sai Baba's mahavakya on leadership: Book for youth, parents, and teachers.* Faber, VA: Leela Press.

The concepts in this book were introduced in a leadership course at the Sri Sathya Sai Institute of Higher Learning near New Delhi, India. One concept claims that leadership is an ancient capability with evidence dating back 5,000 years. Another suggests that leadership must be holistic, encompassing one's body (action), mind (cognition), and entire being. There are suggestions for knowing oneself, dealing with others, and strengthening one's leadership potential. An appendix lists 108 people who inspire. Includes bibliographical references.
Subject(s): Spirit; Indian leadership; cultural context: Indian

New
Church, A. H., & Waclawski, J. (1999). **Influence behaviors and managerial effectiveness in lateral relations.** *Human Resource Development Quarterly, 10*(1), 3-41.

Influencing a peer to do something is significantly different from ordering a subordinate to perform a task, and these influence skills are becoming more important as firms move to flatter organizational structures. This study used an instrument that measures influence tactics to determine what factors predicted whether employees would use informal influence effectively. Over 200 workers in nonmanagerial positions, their peers, and their supervisors were surveyed and the results were analyzed using multiple regression. The authors identify managerial self-awareness as a significant factor in influence effectiveness, particularly in cross-departmental relationships. An invited commentary by James L. Farr praises the study's methodology but questions the theoretical development of the concepts of influence and self-awareness. Includes bibliographical references.
Subject(s): Influence

New
Ciampa, D., & Watkins, M. (1999). *Right from the start: Taking charge in a new leadership role.* Boston: Harvard Business School.

A leader's first six months in a new organization are critical. If momentum and personal credibility are not established during this period, achieving long-term success may be impossible. This book offers an action plan leaders can use to establish authority and gain support in their new roles from the beginning. The authors identify three core tasks leaders should concentrate on: creating momentum; mastering the enabling technologies of learning, visioning, and coalition building; and managing oneself. Self-assessment tests and exercises are provided for each task. Includes index.

Subject(s): Competencies overview

New

Ciulla, J. B. (Ed.). (1998). *Ethics, the heart of leadership.* Westport, CT: Praeger.

This book grew out of the Kellogg Leadership Studies Project in which most of the contributors were members of a focus group on leadership and ethics. It is based on the premise that leadership is "a complex moral relationship between people, based on trust, obligation, commitment, emotion, and a shared vision of the good." Joanne Ciulla, Al Gini, and Robert Solomon provide philosophical discussions on the link between *good* as in competent and *good* as in moral. Edwin Hollander and Bernard Bass provide a psychological perspective with essays on leader-follower relationships. Management scholar Michael Keeley and historian Thomas Wren argue James Madison's leadership and ethical struggle to meet the needs of many factions while building unity in a newly formed republic. Foreword by James MacGregor Burns. Includes bibliographical references and index.

Subject(s): Ethics

Clemens, D. S. (1992). *Leadership literacy: The solution to our present crisis.* Englewood, CO: Leadership America.

Clemens explores the importance and benefits of a leadership-literate society and identifies particular leadership traits by examining the characteristics of Susan B. Anthony, Harry S. Truman, John F. Kennedy, Lee Iacocca, and Martin Luther King, Jr. He points out that all were goal-oriented, looked to themselves to make things happen, believed in the need to break from the status quo, and believed an integral part of human nature is an inherent desire for self-improvement. Includes an index.

Subject(s): Competencies overview

New

Coad, A. F., & Berry, A. J. (1998). **Transformational leadership and learning orientation.** *Leadership & Organization Development Journal, 19*(3), 164-172.

The authors propose that transformational leadership is the leadership style most conducive to employees' learning competency. More than 200 British accountants responded to a survey about their performance goals—based on the desire for positive evaluations—and their learning goals—based on the desire to improve competence. They then responded to questions about their superiors' leadership styles. The authors found a positive correlation between employee learning factors and their superiors' transformational leadership factors. Contingent reward factors also correlated with learning factors. The management-by-exception style correlated to

employee performance but not learning. Includes bibliographical references.

Subject(s): Learning competency

Cohen, S. G., Chang, L., & Ledford, G. E., Jr. (1997). **A hierarchical construct of self-management leadership and its relationship to quality of work life and perceived work group effectiveness.** *Personnel Psychology, 50*(2), 275-308.

Self-management as defined by Manz and Sims' *Self-Management Leadership Questionnaire* (1987, *Administrative Science Quarterly, 32,* 106-138) is characterized by self-observation, self-goal setting, incentive modification, rehearsal, and self-expectation. The authors used the *SMLQ* to compare self-managed and traditionally managed employees in a large telephone company. They affirmed the validity of the *SMLQ* and found that self-managing work teams were more effective. The study also showed that when leaders of both kinds of work groups exhibit self-managing behaviors, the quality of work life and effectiveness of the group increased.

Subject(s): Self-leadership

New

Confessore, S. J., & Kops, W. J. (1998). **Self-directed learning and the learning organization: Examining the connection between the individual and the learning environment.** *Human Resource Development Quarterly, 9*(4), 365-375.

Do self-directed learners have a place in learning organizations? After conducting a review of the literature the authors contend that they do. They say that individuals in learning organizations must take responsibility for their own learning while connecting their work to organizational goals, and that organizations must develop a culture and environment that supports independent learning and experimentation. HRD professionals should be aware of the learning/organization relationship so that they can offer appropriate support to employees who are directing their own learning. Includes bibliographical references.

Subject(s): Learning competency, organizational learning

Conger, J. A. (1991). **Inspiring others: The language of leadership.** *Academy of Management Executive, 5*(1), 31-45.

There's a critical link between a leader's vision and his or her ability to powerfully communicate its essence. To motivate and inspire, a leader must be a rhetorician. Conger recommends that executives learn basic rhetorical skills. Framing is the process of defining the purpose of an organization in a meaningful way. Rhetorical crafting is the skill of using symbolic language to give power to a message. Using stories, metaphors, and rhythm generates excitement.

Subject(s): Communication

New

Conger, J. A. (1998). ***Winning 'em over: A new model for managing in the age of persuasion***. New York: Simon & Schuster.

Conger argues that the traditional approach of management by command authority no longer applies to today's business world, and instead managers must lead through persuasion and teamwork. He describes four components of effective management by persuasion: building credibility, finding common ground, finding compelling positions and evidence, and connecting emotionally with co-workers. Appendices describe "The Passing Age of Command" and "The New Age of Persuasion." Includes index.

Subject(s): Persuasion

New

Conger, J. A. (1999). **Charismatic and transformational leadership in organizations: An insider's perspective on these developing streams of research.** *Leadership Quarterly: Special Issue, Part I: Charismatic and Transformational Leadership: Taking Stock of the Present and Future, 10*(2), 145-179.

Conger suggests that the evolution of charismatic and transformational leadership has been shaped by simultaneous forces from the academic and business worlds. In the mid- to late-1980s a new concept was needed to explain the complex style of leadership in a rapidly changing, globally competitive environment. The sibling concepts, charismatic and transformational leadership, evolved together to meet this need. Conger details the progress of these concepts in the areas of: 1) leader behaviors and their effects, 2) followership, 3) leadership contexts, 4) succession, and 5) liabilities. Includes bibliographical references.

Subject(s): Charismatic leadership, transformational leadership

Conger, J. A., & Associates. (1994). ***Spirit at work: Discovering the spirituality in leadership.*** San Francisco: Jossey-Bass.

With the collapse of traditional sources of support and connectedness (family, church, and community) the workplace has become the primary community for many people. Conger claims that the workplace can and should offer a link to spirituality through leadership practices of integrity, prudence, justice, and fortitude. Chapters cover such issues as the differences between spirituality and religion, dealing with paradoxes of private self and public service, and creating spiritual connectedness through storytelling. Includes bibliographical references and index.

Subject(s): Spirit

New

Conger, J. A., & Hunt, J. G. (1999). **Overview: Charismatic and transformational leadership: Taking stock of the present and future (part I).** *Leadership Quarterly: Special Issue, Part I: Charismatic and Transformational Leadership: Taking Stock of the Present and Future, 10*(2), 121-127.

Guest editors Conger and Hunt introduce this special issue on the paradigm that finds compatibility between charismatic and transformational leadership. Part I contains essays that review recent literature and assess the current state of the paradigm. Part II, which follows in *Leadership Quarterly, 10*(3), discusses empirical studies of the paradigm. Scholars who contribute to the special issue include Bernard Bass and Gary Yukl. Includes bibliographical references.

Subject(s): Charismatic leadership, transformational leadership

Conger, J. A., Kanungo, R. N., & Associates. (1988). ***Charismatic leadership: The elusive factor in organizational effectiveness.*** San Francisco: Jossey-Bass.

This work is a gathering of thoughts and research by experts from various fields: organizational development, management, psychology, and sociology. The rationale: to provide a broad analysis of the concept of charismatic leadership. The contributors attempt to bring clarity to the problems and differences in understanding the meaning of charismatic leadership. What is it? How does it develop? How might it be cultivated? The authors argue that charismatic leadership can be trained. They offer training approaches and provide a questionnaire that can be used to identify individuals, in any setting, with the potential for charismatic leadership. Includes bibliographies and index.

Subject(s): Charismatic leadership

New

Conger, J. A., Spreitzer, G. M., & Lawler, E. E., III. (1999). ***The leader's change handbook: An essential guide to setting direction and taking action.*** San Francisco: Jossey-Bass.

How can leaders create leaner organizations and empower their workers at the same time? This collection attempts to answer that question with essays by John Kotter, David Nadler, Ronald Heifetz, Susan Albers Mohrman, and others. Chapters include a case study of Lucent Technologies, a description of culture change at Whirlpool, advice on leading corporate spinoffs, and a discussion of leadership and collaboration. Includes index.

Subject(s): Change, organizational learning

New

Cooper, R. K., & Sawaf, A. (1997). ***Executive EQ: Emotional intelligence in leadership and organizations.*** New York: Grosset/Putnam.

In an attempt to intensify the competition among the business world, daily emotions have been stifled or compromised. Cooper and Sawaf promote the importance of an emotional IQ. This source is intended as a tool to aid in the acknowledgment and exploration of the value of feelings in organizations. The authors introduce the readers to a Four Cornerstone Model, which "moves emotional intelligence out of the realm of psychological analysis and philosophical theories and into the realm of direct knowing, exploration, and application." The introduction shows the map of this model and the remainder of the book is divided into four sections for each cornerstone: Emotional Literacy is the corner of self-awareness; Emotional Fitness builds strength and flexibility in the heart; Emotional Depth is the place of character, integrity, and purpose; and Emotional Alchemy combines the sensing of opportunities with intuition and innovation to create the future. Includes *EQ* questionnaire, bibliographical references, and index.

Subject(s): Emotional intelligence

Couto, R. A. (1993). **Narrative, free space, and political leadership in social movements.** *Journal of Politics*, *55*(1), 57-79.

Interviews were conducted with 50 Civil Rights leaders to determine the power of narratives in political communication. It was determined that stories of evil oppression circulating through a community can fuel social movement. Stories of wisdom and virtue lend credibility to leaders of social movements.

Subject(s): Storytelling

New

Craig, S. B., & Gustafson, S. B. (1998). *Perceived Leader Integrity Scale*: **An instrument for assessing employee perceptions of leader integrity.** *Leadership Quarterly*, *9*(2), 127-145.

The authors introduce the *Perceived Leader Integrity Scale*, an instrument that identifies the leader behaviors associated with moral and ethical integrity. Subordinates respond to a list of unethical workplace behaviors and attitudes as they pertain to immediate supervisors. Thirty-one items fall into seven behavioral domains: 1) training and development, 2) resource and workload allocation, 3) truth-telling, 4) unlawful discrimination, 5) compliance with policies and procedures, 6) maliciousness, and 7) self-protection. Includes bibliographical references.

Subject(s): Integrity, assessment

Crawford, C. B. (1994). **Theory and implications regarding the utilization of strategic humor by leaders.** *Journal of Leadership Studies*, *1*(4), 53-68.

Of all the communication tools that leaders use, humor is one of the most promising and one of the least understood. Humor can be used to contrast two incongruent ideas or to release tension. It can increase the popularity or influence of a speaker. It links people together in a positive environment and communicates organizational culture. On the darker side, humor may be employed to suggest superiority or to disparage others. Crawford's research examines the purpose and appropriateness of humor in the context of leadership.

Subject(s): Communication, humor

Crawford, C. B., & Strohkirch, C. S. (1997). **Influence methods and innovators: Technocrats and champions.** *Journal of Leadership Studies*, *4*(2), 43-54.

This article reports on research of 238 students at a midwestern university who responded to two surveys, *Acceptance of Technological Innovation* and *Survey of Influence Behavior*. The purpose of the research was to study the relationship between technological innovation and methods of influence. The authors tested four hypotheses: 1) innovators would be more likely to use team influence methods than the majority and laggard adopters; 2) innovators would be more likely to use charismatic influence behaviors; 3) innovators would be more likely to use reward/punishment/manipulation influence behaviors; and 4) charisma, reward/punishment, and team influence behaviors predict innovativeness. The findings suggest that innovators will use coercive methods to achieve results and that these innovators do not have any more charisma or team influence than the majority.

Subject(s): Technical leadership

New

Daft, R. L., & Lengel, R. H. (1998). *Fusion leadership: Unlocking the subtle forces that change people and organizations.* San Francisco: Berrett-Koehler.

Daft and Lengel describe organizational leadership using the concept of "fusion," or bringing together, rather than "fission," or splitting apart. They argue that traditional hierarchy has suppressed individuals' creativity and spirit, but that when these forces are brought together they can transform organizations. This book describes both personal fusion, which occurs in the interior self, and organizational fusion and its related actions, such as dialogues and future searches. Six forces that affect organizational performance are also identified: 1) mindfulness, 2) vision, 3) heart, 4) communication, 5) courage, and 6) integrity. Includes index.

Subject(s): Competencies overview

Daily, C. M., & Johnson, J. L. (1997). **Source of CEO power and firm financial performance: A longitudinal assessment.** *Journal of Management*, *23*(2), 97-117.

This article examines the correlation between the power of a CEO and a company's financial performance. The authors measured four kinds of power—structural, ownership, prestige, and expert power—held by CEOs at 100 randomly selected Fortune 500 firms from 1987 through 1990. Three measures of firm financial performance were considered—return on equity; return on investment; and a risk-adjusted, market-based measure of performance. When correlated the authors concluded that this issue is complex and there are too many variables to draw simple conclusions. One apparent conclusion was that CEOs who serve on other boards wield greater power and run more successful companies. Includes bibliographical references.

Subject(s): CEOs

Daudelin, M. W. (1996). **Learning from experience through reflection.** *Organizational Dynamics, 24*(3), 36-48.

This article discusses the ancient learning process of reflection as a leadership development tool. It suggests that organizations create formal reflection practices for managers to stop amid their usual frantic pace to consider what has been learned from experience and what are new possibilities. Individual reflection may take the form of spontaneous thinking during routine activities, journal writing, or assessment instruments. Helper or peer-group reflection activities include performance appraisals, mentoring, and feedback discussions. Daudelin reports on her research study that introduced reflective activities to managers and the actions they took following reflection. The managers reported that individual and helper reflection activities significantly improved their management actions. Peer group reflection activities did not affect managers' subsequent actions. Includes bibliographical references.
Subject(s): Learning experiences

Davis, B. L., Hellervik, L. W., Skube, C. J., Gebelin, S. H., & Sheard, J. L. (1996). *Successful manager's handbook: Development suggestions for today's managers* (1996 ed.). Minneapolis: Personnel Decisions International.

This book contains suggestions for developing competencies in nine areas: administrative skills, communication, interpersonal skills, leadership, motivation, organizational knowledge, organizational strategy, self-management, and thinking skills. The leadership competencies include: providing direction, influence, fostering teamwork, coaching, and championing change. The book is organized around PDI's Wheel of Managerial Success so that it may be used alone or in conjunction with their *Profilor®* 360-degree instrument. Each of the nine sections offers tips for good practice, actions to take in current positions or stretch assignments, recommended readings, and suggested seminars. A section on international resources describes one U.S. seminar with a global focus and 35 management seminars in Canada, Europe, Australia, and Mexico.
Subject(s): Competencies overview

De Ciantis, C. (1996). **What does drawing my hand have to do with leadership? A look at the process of leaders becoming artists.** *Journal of Aesthetic Education: Special Issue: The Aesthetic Face of Leadership, 30*(4), 87-97.

Teaching leaders the process of making art enlarges their perceptual universe and enhances their competency to thrive in a chaotic world. De Ciantis describes how art and leadership are linked in the touchstone exercise, part of the LeaderLab® program at the Center for Creative Leadership. Participants use found materials to create three-dimensional artworks to represent their most deeply rooted sense of purpose. They keep their artwork in a place where, in the chaos of their daily lives, they can see it and be reminded of what is most important. De Ciantis also describes the methods for teaching art-making in the Center's Leading

Creatively program. Includes bibliographical references.
Subject(s): Leader as artist

De Jouvenal, B. (1949). *On power: Its nature and the history of its growth.* New York: Viking.

This is a classic work on the origins of power and the history of its development. Divided into what the author terms as *books*, each section delves into a particular aspect of the use and meaning of power. Book I examines the origins of civil obedience as well as the growth of sovereignty as a divine and political right. Subsequent sections study the notions of the power of command in time of warfare and explore the use of power in controlling social order. Later sections discuss how power may appear to change through revolution and new government when in fact its essential nature remains constant. The issue of limited versus unlimited power, as in the choice between liberty or security, is discussed. Includes bibliographical references in notes.
Subject(s): Power

De Pree, M. (1989). *Leadership is an art.* New York: Doubleday.

In the artistic industry of furniture design and manufacturing, Max De Pree leads his company, Herman Miller, to success through several measures. Practicing the art of leadership, De Pree supports the ideas of all employees, from designers to workers on the line. As a result Herman Miller has won awards for innovative designs including the Eames chair, which is in the permanent collections of New York's Museum of Modern Art and the Louvre. Herman Miller is consistently chosen as one the best companies to work for in America, cited for its Scanlon Plan, which rewards employees for their suggestions to improve productivity, quality, and customer service. It ranks among the top ten companies in return to investors and investment in R&D.
Subject(s): Art as metaphor for leadership

De Pree, M. (1992). *Leadership jazz.* New York: Currency/ Doubleday.

In a surprising look at the tough challenges facing today's leaders De Pree identifies two difficult concepts successful leaders must perfect: voice, the ability to express one's beliefs; and touch, the ability to demonstrate competence and resolve. These concepts, mastered in jazz, have never before been acknowledged in business. De Pree urges leaders to find their own voices and reconsider every assumption they hold on leadership. He compares leadership to an inspired jazz performance, dependent on environment, fellow players and their need for individual expression as it benefits the group, and the absolute dependence on the leader for guidance.
Subject(s): Leader as musician, jazz music as metaphor for leadership

New

De Vries, R. E., Roe, R. A., & Tallieu, T. C. B. (1999). **On charisma and need for leadership.** *European Journal of Work and Organizational Psychology, 8*(1), 109-133.

Charisma has traditionally been characterized by exceptional personal traits possessed by a leader. In this study the authors examined the relationship between charisma and the need for leadership, an asset possessed by followers. Over 900 Dutch workers were given a survey measuring the transformational/charismatic leadership qualities of their supervisors, their own need for leadership, and four outcome measures—job satisfaction, organizational commitment, work stress, and role conflict. In the past, charismatic leadership has been considered related to these outcomes, but analysis of these data showed that the need for leadership moderated those relationships. The data also showed a positive relationship between charisma and a need for leadership, leading the authors to conclude that "subordinates are more, instead of less, dependent when a charismatic leader is present." Includes bibliographical references. Commentary by James G. Hunt follows the article.

Subject(s): Charisma

Deal, T. E., & Jenkins, W. A. (1994). *Managing the hidden organization: Strategies for empowering your behind-the-scenes employees.* New York: Warner Books.

Deal and Jenkins use a theater metaphor to illustrate the value of employees who work quietly backstage to support the star employees who are in the limelight. They suggest strategies for casting the best talent and for giving ovations for outstanding performances. As management/leadership educators and consultants, the authors base their empowerment premise on their consulting work with 500 organizations, several in-depth case studies, interviews, and a study of the literature. Includes bibliographical references.

Subject(s): Performing art as metaphor for leadership

New

Denton, D. K. (1998). **Viewpoint: Blueprint for the adaptive organisation.** *Creativity and Innovation Management, 7*(2), 83-91.

Complex systems are constantly changing, and trying to control the future is futile. Instead of trying to keep their environment stable, organizations should learn to adapt to constant change. This article describes how the chaos theory can offer a model for adaptive leaders and organizations. Denton says that organizations should be based on a few simple rules developed from the bottom up, such as "do simple things first," and that leaders should keep a broad perspective of the future and not get bogged down in details. Xerox is offered as an example of an adaptive organization that was able to coordinate its efforts around key environmental forces. Includes bibliographical references.

Subject(s): Chaos, organizational change

New

Dooley, R. S., & Fryxell, G. E. (1999). **Attaining decision quality and commitment from dissent: The moderating effects of loyalty and competence in strategic decision-making teams.** *Academy of Management Journal, 42*(4), 389-402.

In a survey of 86 strategic decision-making teams, the authors find that two factors—loyalty and competence—have a significant impact on the quality of team decisions and the level of member commitment to team decisions. Diversity among team members is necessary to challenge assumptions, increase information, and avoid groupthink. However, diversity can enhance or deteriorate group process. The level of trust among members dictates whether dissent among diverse views will have a positive or negative impact on decisions. This study finds that a high level of trust encourages open communication and exploration of ideas, thus, team loyalty and a positive form of dissent. Likewise, when team members perceive competence in their teammates there is more pride and stronger commitment to group decisions. Includes bibliographical references.

Subject(s): Decision making

New

Douglas, E. F. (1998). *Straight talk: Turning communication upside down for strategic results at work.* Palo Alto, CA: Davies-Black.

Douglas describes the principles of effective communication and exercises for building communication skills. Intended for practical workplace application, there are suggestions for identifying others' communication styles, running meetings, resolving conflicts, planning marketing strategies, achieving group consensus, and understanding organizational culture. The increasingly important functions of interpersonal communication via teleconferencing and e-mail are also addressed. Includes bibliographical references and index.

Subject(s): Communication

New

Downs, A. (1998). *Seven miracles of management.* Paramus, NJ: Prentice Hall.

This book speaks of the basic truths we know as children—emotion and meaning—and the temptation to twist or deny them in the competitive situations of adulthood. These truths have a tremendous power to propel individuals and, thus, their organizations and society. Downs asserts that recalling these basic truths during daily routines helps to keep one on track toward personal fulfillment and business success. He explains how the practice of these seven miracles—Manifestation, Reciprocity, Honesty, Forgiveness, Passion, Esteem, and Transcending the Past—can have tremendous effect on us as individuals, bringing authenticity to our lives both personally and professionally. Includes bibliographical references and index.

Subject(s): Values

Downton, J. V., Jr. (1973). *Rebel leadership: Commitment and charisma in the revolutionary process.* New York: Free Press.

Downton explains leadership in social systems in this early work about followers searching for identity through transactional relations with charismatic leaders. Rebel leaders who influence mass movements gain authority from the commitment and trust of their followers. Downton compares his theory with Weber's theory of charismatic heroes described in Gerth and Mills, *From Max Weber: Essays in Sociology* (Oxford, 1946). Includes a bibliography.
Subject(s): Charisma, rebel leadership

Drath, W. H. (1993). *Why managers have trouble empowering: A theoretical perspective based on concepts of adult development.* Greensboro, NC: Center for Creative Leadership.

This report, based on eight years of research with high-level managers, considers the character factors that enable managers to empower subordinates. Drath argues that the authoritative character factors that help managers achieve their positions are the same ones that cause them to have difficulty sharing authority. The lifelong process of creating personal meaning conflicts with the demands of leadership. The solution lies in creating a balance between these two worlds. Drath defines the strengths and weaknesses of managers who have difficulty empowering subordinates and those who have developed into participative managers. Organizational support plays a key role in this development. Includes bibliographical references.
Subject(s): Empowerment, adult development

New
Drazin, R., Glynn, M. A., & Kazanjian, R. K. (1999). **Multilevel theorizing about creativity in organizations: A sensemaking perspective.** *Academy of Management, 24*(2), 286-307.

This article introduces a multilevel model of creativity through the lens of sense-making in organizations. In this model creativity begins at an individual level where one develops a cause-and-effect map, puts oneself into the map, and takes action accordingly. The next level involves various stakeholders on a creative project team. Technical staff work from a frame of reference that includes experimentation and technical creativity. Administrative staff focus more on cost, schedule, functionality, and manager creativity. Long-term creative project teams work to build collective frameworks through shifting balance of power, crises, reframing, and the evolution of new belief structures. Includes bibliographical references.
Subject(s): Creativity, sense-making

Dreher, D. (1996). *The Tao of personal leadership.* New York: HarperBusiness.

Dreher observes that leaders in all fields are informed by ancient principles such as those written two thousand years ago in the *Tao Te Ching* by Lao Tzu. The 81 poems in the *Tao* reveal the wisdom of living systems—in nature, in

people, and in relationships. This book draws leadership lessons from the *Tao*, as well as from Buddhism and the martial art of aikido. In part one, "The Yin of Inner Leadership," Dreher concentrates on the personal elements of leadership and self-development. In part two, "The Yang of Leadership in Action," she focuses on the relationships and responsibilities of leadership. Includes bibliographical references and index.
Subject(s): Spirit, Eastern philosophy

New
Drummond, H. (1998). **Go and say, "We're shutting": Ju jutsu as a metaphor for analyzing resistance.** *Human Relations, 51*(6), 741-759.

Ju jutsu is a martial arts philosophy that teaches practitioners how to use defensive skills to resist a physically stronger opponent. This article uses three forms of ju jutsu—judo, aikido, and atemi jutsu—as metaphors for how employees can resist managerial impositions. Tactics individuals can use when resisting a larger opponent include redirecting their opponent's energy, disturbing their opponent's balance, and striking at weak points. A case study describes how one British worker was able to use these techniques to mobilize his community and stop the closing of a historic swimming pool. Includes bibliographical references.
Subject(s): Resisting power

New
Ekvall, G., & Ryhammar, L. (1998). **Leadership style, social climate, and organizational outcomes.** *Creativity and Innovation Management, 7*(3), 126-130.

The authors surveyed 130 professors at a Swedish university to determine whether leadership style affected the organization's climate or its creativity/productivity. Statistical analysis of the data showed that while leadership style had only a minimal effect on creativity outcomes, it did influence climate. This may indicate that leadership style has an indirect effect on outcomes, since organizational climate directly influences creativity and productivity. The authors acknowledge, however, that formal, hierarchical leadership is typically less important in universities than in other organizations, so these results may not be useful in other settings. Includes bibliographical references.
Subject(s): Organizational climate

Fagen, R. R. (1965). **Charismatic authority and the leadership of Fidel Castro.** *Western Political Quarterly, 18*, 275-284.

Fagen notes that the appellation of *charismatic* has been applied quite freely to various leaders with a variety of meanings. His purpose in this article is to take a first step toward rational explication of the concept of charisma and to show, using Fidel Castro as an example, how the concept might be used in empirical inquiry.
Subject(s): Negative views of charisma

Fairholm, G. W. (1993). *Organizational power politics: Tactics in organizational leadership.* Westport, CT: Praeger.

In a power situation two or more parties compete for materials, space, or energy. Using power tactics leads to action that will meet the goals of one party. Fairholm identifies 22 power tactics, including: using ambiguity, displaying charisma, legitimizing control, rationalization, and ritualism. He compares ethics, frequency of use, and effectiveness in varying relationships and varying bases of power. Includes bibliographical references and index.
Subject(s): Power, organizational politics

Fairholm, G. W. (1994). *Leadership and the culture of trust.* Westport, CT: Praeger.

Fairholm describes leadership as "a process of building a trust environment within which the leader and follower feel free to participate toward accomplishment of mutually valued goals using agreed-upon processes." This book teaches how to build organizations in which work is done collectively and all parties contribute to an ever-changing culture that responds to organizational needs. Chapters include: "Defining Culture," "The Process of Developing Trust," "Shared Governance," and "Integrating Quality." Includes bibliographical references and index.
Subject(s): Trust

Fairholm, G. W. (1997). *Capturing the heart of leadership: Spirituality and community in the new American workplace.* Westport, CT: Praeger.

Fairholm observes that leaders must bring to their tasks "their whole selves, their knowledge of the spiritual dimension of life that, perhaps, more powerfully than any other force, guides daily action." In this book he takes a creative approach to building a framework for understanding the spiritual nature of leadership and its potential manifestation in the workplace. Some examples are: spirituality helps leaders understand self and others better, spirituality is a holistic approach that considers the needs of employees and the goals of the organization, spiritual leaders help others reach their highest potential, and spiritual leaders live out their deeply held personal values. Includes bibliographical references and index.
Subject(s): Spirit, organizational culture

Fairhurst, G. T., & Sarr, R. A. (1996). *The art of framing: Managing the language of leadership.* San Francisco: Jossey-Bass.

Framing is about the leadership opportunities that exist in the many conversations of everyday work situations. Leaders use communication tools such as metaphors, jargon, contrast, spin, and stories to clarify and influence. Selecting the proper tool for each situation is called framing. To determine the extent that framing is used and that opportunities for framing are lost the authors conducted communication research. In a successful company 200 work-related conversations lasting 30 minutes each were taped and analyzed. They concluded that leadership situations are often spontaneous and cannot be

scripted in advance, but leaders can learn to send thoughtful messages by framing.
Subject(s): Communication

Felton, K. S. (1995). *Warriors' words: A consideration of language and leadership.* Westport, CT: Praeger.

Felton examines the public discourse of history's great communicators to examine their rhetoric, impact on listeners, and influence on society. Featured are Gandhi's "doctrine of the sword," Clarence Darrow's defense summation in a murder trial, Winston Churchill's speeches to Parliament, Franklin D. Roosevelt's fireside chats, Martin Luther King, Jr.'s Nobel Prize acceptance speech, and others. Felton also acknowledges the negative impact of persuasive speech from demagogues such as Adolf Hitler and Joseph McCarthy. Includes bibliographical references and index.
Subject(s): Communication

Fiedler, F. E. (1992). **Time-based measures of leadership experience and organizational performance: A review of research and a preliminary model.** *Leadership Quarterly: Special Issue: Individual Differences and Leadership: II, 3*(1), 5-23.

Work experience is comprised of time in service, time in a leadership position, time in a work unit, diversity of experience, relevant experience, and overlearned behavior. Leadership experience alone does not correlate to performance. Research indicates that intellectual abilities and effort must correlate to experience for high performance, particularly in times of stress or uncertainty.
Subject(s): Experience

Fiedler, F. E. (1995). **Cognitive resources and leadership performance.** *Applied Psychology, 44*(1), 5-28.

Selection and promotion are typically based on one's intelligence, experience, and expertise. Fiedler examines the relationship of these three characteristics with leadership performance. He reviews studies of U.S. Army infantry leaders, fire fighters, U.S. Coast Guard personnel, and ROTC cadets to support the Cognitive Resource Theory and its implications for work environment and training.
Subject(s): Experience, intelligence

Fisher, R., Ury, W., & Patton, B. (1991). *Getting to yes: Negotiating agreement without giving in* (2nd ed.). Boston: Houghton Mifflin.

This book is about the method of principled negotiation. It describes the problems that arise in using standard strategies of positional bargaining and explains the four principles of this method of negotiation: 1) separate people from the problem; 2) focus on interests, not positions; 3) invent options for mutual gain; and 4) insist on using objective criteria. The second edition remains unchanged except for minor updates and a new section with questions frequently asked of the authors and their answers.
Subject(s): Negotiation

New

Flauto, F. J. (1999). **Walking the talk: The relationship between leadership and communication competence.** *Journal of Leadership Studies, 6*(1/2), 86-111.

This paper reports on a study of the link between communication and leadership. Several factors were considered: a cognitive perspective of communication, which focuses on ability and potential; a behavioral perspective of communication; and leadership style. More than 150 employees in nine organizations responded to a survey about their perceptions of their bosses in these areas. Results indicate that a transformational leadership style has the highest positive correlation to communication ability and behavior. The author believes that this is because several elements of transformational leadership—charisma, individual consideration, and intellectual stimulation—are communication based. Includes bibliographical references.
Subject(s): Communication

Flin, R. (1996). *Sitting in the hot seat: Leaders and teams for critical incident management.* New York: Wiley.

This book is for and about leaders in life-threatening crisis situations. There are three scenarios: 1) leaders have prior warning as in the cases of riots or storms; 2) they are on-site when the crisis occurs as in ship and plane accidents or industrial disasters; or 3) leaders are called to the scene as in the cases of fires, hostage situations, or explosions. In all cases, Flin claims that leadership training is as important as the planning of mobilization procedures. Military models of command-and-control are most often used, but Flin recommends that crisis leaders understand and employ other styles such as consultative, coaching, situational, and team leadership. Flin describes some leadership training techniques in the military, aeronautical, fire, police, offshore oil, and nuclear power industries. Includes bibliographical references and index.
Subject(s): Crisis leadership

New

Forster, N., Cebis, M., Majteles, S., Mathur, A., Morgan, R., Preuss, J., Tiwari, V., & Wilkinson, D. (1999). **The role of story-telling in organizational leadership.** *Leadership & Organization Development Journal, 20*(1), 11-17.

Technology has improved the choices and convenience for communicating in a chaotic, global society. However, the authors state that face-to-face dialogue remains the most powerful form of communication. This article explains the power of storytelling as part of the human experience and its application in a corporate setting. Storytelling is a tool for communicating a vision, explaining organizational culture, and inspiring employees during difficult times. Stories that put a human face on organizational performance have greater motivational impact than productivity goals and statistics. Examples from Hewlett-Packard, The Body Shop, and Ford Motor Company illustrate the effectiveness of corporate storytelling. Includes bibliographical references.
Subject(s): Storytelling

New

Freeman, R. B., & Rogers, J. (1999). *What workers want.* Ithaca, NY: Cornell University Press.

The Commission on the Future of Worker-Management Relations is a national body appointed by the Clinton administration to examine labor law. From 1994 to 1995 the Commission conducted the Worker Representation and Participation Study, a series of focus groups, phone interviews, and mail surveys, that analyzed attitudes of American workers toward workplace relations and power. This book reports the findings of that study. The authors say that the main finding was that most workers wanted more participation and say in the management of their workplace, and that they supported existing unions and the formation of new ones. Appendices provide methodological details, copies of the phone and mail surveys used, and other materials. Includes bibliographical references and index.
Subject(s): Empowerment

New

Friedman, B., Hatch, J., & Walker, D. (1998). *Delivering on the promise: How to attract, manage, and retain human capital.* New York: Free Press.

This book is intended to assist chief executives, human resource executives, and managers in recognizing and developing the value of their people. The first part reviews the concept of *human capital*, profiles the current status, and provides an outlook for the near future in Asia, Europe, and North America. The remainder of the book presents the *Human Capital Appraisal* method to "measure and increase the returns on companies' investments in people." The five stages of this process—clarification, assessment, design, implementation, and monitoring—are presented in the following chapters. In addition, Friedman, Hatch, and Walker provide a discussion of assessing human capital fit, cost, and value. Finally, the book concludes with case studies of human capital in such companies as Mobil Oil, IBM, *The Chicago Tribune*, and Hyatt Hotels. Includes bibliographical references.
Subject(s): Human capital

New

Friedman, L., & Gyr, H. (1998). *The dynamic enterprise: Tools for turning chaos into strategy and strategy into action.* San Francisco: Jossey-Bass.

A *Dynamic Enterprise* is defined as an organization with the ability to advance and thrive under the impacts of continuous change. The authors propose "an integrated set of tools to guide the creation of the *Dynamic Enterprise.*" The intended audience consists of organizational leaders, stakeholders, and change agents who are the key motivators for "leading and implementing strategic multidimensional change." As readers are led through the *STEP* enterprise development process they are given strategies to assist in viewing their organization as a whole and ways to organize their thinking in order to move toward a shared vision for the future. The authors emphasize the role of leaders in modeling and developing strategies during times of change. The conclusion implements the *Enterprise Development Workplan* and is followed by an epilogue concerning the future. Includes bibliographical references and index.

Subject(s): Chaos, strategic leadership

Fritz, S. M., Brown, F. W., Lunde, J. P., & Banset, E. A. (Eds.). (1996). *Interpersonal skills for leadership.* Needham Heights, MA: Simon & Schuster Custom.

This book is compiled by the faculty of the Department of Agricultural Leadership, Education, and Community at the University of Nebraska–Lincoln. The authors share ideas for conceptual and experiential learning with others who teach courses in agriculture and food science. There are ideas for teaching active listening skills, goal setting, and conflict management. Other lessons help students understand the nature of self-esteem, power, perception, and values. One chapter focuses on servant leadership and another suggests journaling as a learning experience. Each chapter contains a case study, discussion starters, activities, and references for further reading.

Subject(s): Competencies overview

New

Frost, P., & Robinson, S. (1999). **The toxic handler: Organizational hero—and casualty.** *Harvard Business Review*, 77(4), 96-106.

Toxic handlers are the corporate managers who "voluntarily shoulder the sadness, frustration, bitterness, and anger that are endemic to organizational life." Frost and Robinson interviewed and observed 70 such toxic handlers to understand what they do, why they do it, and how organizations can support their efforts. Five key behaviors are identified. Toxic handlers listen empathetically, suggest solutions, work behind the scenes to prevent pain, carry the confidences of others, and reframe difficult messages. Those who assume such a role have a natural tendency to be peacemakers—to be calm, trustworthy, and nonjudgmental. They understand that easing employees' pain helps performance and the achievement of organizational goals. To prevent burnout, organizations need to recognize and support their toxic handlers by acknowledging that the dynamic exists, arranging for networks and emotional support, reassigning toxic handlers to safe zones when necessary, and encouraging all employees to follow the model set by toxic handlers.

Subject(s): Leader as peacemaker

Frost, T. F., & Moussavi, F. (1992). **The relationship between leader power base and influence: The moderating role of trust.** *Journal of Applied Business Research*, 8(4), 9-14.

Trust and its effects on a leader's power base and ability to influence subordinates is examined. Frost and Moussavi offer two models differentiating organizational and individual bases of power. Expert, referent, and information power bases have a positive effect on trust. Legitimate, coercive, and reward power bases have a negative effect on trust.

Subject(s): Power bases, trust

Gabriel, Y. (1997). **Meeting God: When organizational members come face to face with the supreme leader.** *Human Relations*, 50(4), 315-342.

This article focuses on the religious or literary theme of meeting God and relates that theme to the experience of an organizational member who meets the organization's top leader. From a psychoanalytic view Gabriel describes the primal fantasies that organizational members project onto their leaders. He finds four core fantasies: 1) the leader cares for his or her followers, 2) the leader is accessible, 3) the leader is omnipotent and omniscient, and 4) the leader has a legitimate claim to lead others. Includes bibliographical references.

Subject(s): Charisma

Galpin, T. J. (1996). *The human side of change: A practical guide to organizational redesign.* San Francisco: Jossey-Bass.

Galpin asserts that organizational change is not new. Organizations have merged, downsized, and restructured with a focus on technical and financial issues. Many of these changes have resulted in lost talent and bad relations. He states that a new kind of change is in order—one that combines the technical with the human side—to create a lasting transformation. This nonacademic, non-theoretical book is written for working leaders who seek a framework and the techniques to achieve such a change. A nine-step change-management process is designed to be achieved in 13 to 20 months. Galpin bases his framework and techniques on his experience as an organizational development consultant who has helped government and commercial organizations plan and achieve positive change. In the appendices two toolkits help the reader apply the chapter lessons to real-life situations: a strategic toolkit for executives and an implementation toolkit for supervisors and mid-level managers. Includes a glossary, bibliographical references, and index.

Subject(s): Organizational change

New

Gardner, H. (1997). *Extraordinary minds: Portraits of four exceptional individuals and an examination of our own extraordinariness.* New York: Basic Books.

In this book Gardner, best known for his work on multiple intelligences, examines extraordinary individuals. He profiles four people who illustrate different forms of extraordinariness: Gandhi, the Influencer; Mozart, the Master; Freud, the Maker; and Virginia Woolf, the Introspector. Gardner found that three characteristics were common to these and other extraordinary individuals: the ability to analyze the events of their lives, a skill for identifying and using their strengths, and the ability to turn setbacks into successes. Includes bibliographical references and index.

Subject(s): Intelligence

New

Gardner, W. L., & Avolio, B. J. (1998). **The charismatic relationship: A dramaturgical perspective.** *Academy of Management Review*, *23*(1), 30-58.

This article considers the strategies employed to create and sustain the image of charismatic leadership. This image building is described in a dramaturgical sense that compares leaders to actors who use script, performance, and setting to define their identity for their audience (followers). A Dramaturgical Model of the Charismatic Relationship illustrates this dynamic, reciprocal, and iterative relationship. Its components include: the self-esteem of both actors and audience, the alignment of their values to an idealized vision, and the identity images attributed to actors and desired by the audience. The authors explain how this type of relationship can lead to positive organizational outcomes. Includes bibliographical references.

Subject(s): Charismatic leadership

Gastil, J. (1994). **A definition and illustration of democratic leadership.** *Human Relations*, *47*(8), 953-975.

Previous definitions of democratic leadership identify three primary functions: 1) distribution of responsibility, 2) empowering the membership, and 3) participatory decision making. Gastil presents a decision-tree model that promotes shared authority and good group relations. This model is intended for groups of all sizes, from small work teams to large societies. To illustrate the model he describes the Kettering Foundation's National Issues Forum, a case study in democratic leadership.

Subject(s): Democratic leadership

New

Goldberg, R. A. (1998). **A new lens on mission and vision.** *Leadership in Action*, *18*(3), 6-12.

Goldberg sees mission statements as the *what* and visions as the *how* of organizations. Creating a mission statement is a future-oriented activity that names strategic objectives, tactical goals, and action plans. Visioning identifies and reinforces organizational values. Several organizations that have struggled to align their mission and vision, their ideal future and their fundamental values, are described. Although this is a deceptively difficult process, Goldberg believes that it is key to successful organizational leadership.

Subject(s): Vision

New

Goleman, D. (1998). *Working with emotional intelligence.* New York: Bantam.

Goleman coined the term EQ in his 1995 book *Emotional Intelligence*. The concept is based on self-awareness and self-confidence, commitment and integrity, communication and influence, and the ability to initiate or accept change. In this book Goleman applies those competencies to the workplace. He explains how people at any stage in their careers may develop social radar, increase their EQ, and become stars at

work. Appendices summarize the original book, define the EQ competencies of stars, explain the relevance of EQ to gender and minority issues, and discuss training concerns. Includes bibliographical references and index.

Subject(s): Emotional intelligence

Greenleaf, R. K. (1977). *Servant leadership: A journey into the nature of legitimate power and greatness.* New York: Paulist Press.

This book is a constructive and critical examination of leadership and the perversions of leadership in major spheres of American life, including the crucial sphere of the responsibility (and irresponsibility) of boards of trustees. It develops the concept of the servant leader and deals with the structure and mode of government that will favor optimal performance of our many institutions as servants of society. It also gives biographical models of two great servant leaders. Includes index.

Subject(s): Servant leadership

New

Greenleaf, R. K., Frick, D. M. (Ed.), & Spears, L. C. (Ed.). (1996). *On becoming a servant leader.* San Francisco: Jossey-Bass.

This collection of previously unpublished writings by Robert Greenleaf includes the text of his manuscript *The Ethic of Strength*; transcripts of a series of lectures on Leadership and the Individual that he gave at Dartmouth in 1969; and essays on power, management, and organizations. Includes a foreword by Peter Drucker and an index.

Subject(s): Servant leadership

New

Greenleaf, R. K., & Spears, L. C. (Ed.). (1998). *The power of servant leadership.* San Francisco: Berrett-Koehler.

This collection of eight essays by Robert Greenleaf, the founder of the concept of *servant leadership*, includes a foreword by Peter Vaill and an introduction by Larry Spears, current CEO of The Greenleaf Center for Servant-Leadership. The essays include "The Leadership Crisis," "The Servant as Religious Leader," and "My Debt to E. B. White." Includes index.

Subject(s): Servant leadership

New

Gryskiewicz, S. S. (1998). **Leading renewal: The value of positive turbulence.** *Leadership in Action*, *18*(5), 1-7.

Positive turbulence in an organization is the harnessing of external change and converting it into internal creativity and innovation. Leaders who can read the turbulence in information, the competitive environment, and organizational structure can select which forces to harness. This article describes informational turbulence in which new information is significantly different and arrives at a rapid pace. Gryskiewicz explains how a leader's creativity style, tolerance for ambiguity, and ability to make remote associa-

tions enhance the ability to get a good reading and respond with positive action. There are recommendations for seeking turbulence at the individual, team, and organizational levels.
Subject(s): Renewal, change as turbulence

New
Gryskiewicz, S. S. (1999). *Positive turbulence: Developing climates for creativity, innovation, and renewal.* San Francisco: Jossey-Bass.

This book explains how to build organizational structures that turn the energy of rapid change into a positive force for harnessing creativity. There are four key elements: 1) difference —breaking out of the status quo, 2) multiple perspectives— inviting divergent viewpoints and nontraditional interpretations, 3) intensity—keeping turbulence at an optimal level for change, and 4) receptivity—creating an environment that encourages positive turbulence. Organizations can embrace positive turbulence by opening their boundaries, allowing new ideas to penetrate, and encouraging employees to watch the periphery. Gryskiewicz offers suggestions for developing and managing positive turbulence and for tearing down the barriers that hinder it. Examples from Norfolk Southern, Hallmark, and 3M illustrate positive turbulence at work. An appendix suggests credible fringe business publications. Another explains the technique of targeted innovation. Includes bibliographical references and index.
Subject(s): Renewal, change as turbulence

New
Guntern, G. (Ed.). (1997). *The challenges of creative leadership.* London: Shepheard-Walwyn Ltd.

Guntern sees an overwhelming state of mediocrity in society and claims that creative leadership is the antidote. It is "the weaver at the enchanted loom able to weave the patterns of unique, well functioning, beautiful forms of high value for society." Nine creative leaders contribute essays about their personal creative experiences, obstacles overcome, and goals reached. Among them are: writer and poet, Maya Angelou; Nobel Prize-winning medical doctor and scientist, Gerald M. Edelman; author and ethologist, Jane Goodall; and Nobel Prize-winning poet and playwright, Wole Soyinka. Guntern is the founder of the International Foundation for Creativity and Leadership in Martigny, Switzerland.
Subject(s): Creative leadership, social perspective

Hackman, M. Z., & Johnson, C. E. (1996). *Leadership: A communication perspective* (2nd ed.). Prospect Heights, IL: Waveland.

This textbook assumes that "leadership is best understood as a product of symbolic communication." Leaders use symbols, both in words and actions, to create visions, build trust, and influence others. The first section of the book introduces the fundamentals of leadership and its link to communication. The second section discusses leadership in different contexts: teams, organizations, politics, diversity, creativity, and ethics. Chapters contain theoretical background, cases, and exercises

to illustrate the practical application of each lesson. Contains bibliographical references and index.
Subject(s): Communication, textbook

Hagberg, J. O. (1994). *Real power: Stages of personal power in organizations* (Rev. ed.). Salem, WI: Sheffield Publishing.

Personal power is derived from external sources (expertise, titles, degrees, authority) and from internal sources (introspection, personal struggles, accepting and valuing self). Hagberg presents a model of the six stages of personal power: powerlessness, power by association, power by symbols, power by reflection, power by purpose, and power by gestalt. Each stage is demonstrated with applications to life and work situations. Summary pages may be photocopied. Questionnaires allow the reader to evaluate personal stages. This revised edition contains a new introduction, a new chapter called "Beyond Ego and Gender: Leading from Your Soul," and revised surveys. Includes a bibliography.
Subject(s): Power bases

Hale, G. A. (1996). *The leader's edge: Mastering the five skills of breakthrough thinking.* New York: Irwin.

Hale recommends five critical-thinking skills for leaders: 1) situation review, 2) cause analysis, 3) decision making, 4) plan analysis, and 5) innovation. In this practical guide he explains through anecdotes and hypothetical situations how to master the skills well enough to teach them to others. There are also suggestions for using critical-thinking skills to advocate for new ideas and to solve people problems. Includes an index.
Subject(s): Critical thinking

New
Hambrick, D. C., Nadler, D. A., & Tushman, M. L. (1998). *Navigating change: How CEOs, top teams, and boards steer transformation.* Boston: Harvard Business School Press.

The articles in this collection address five factors in organizational transformation: CEOs, top management teams, boards of directors, discontinuous change, and integration. In Part I, chapters describe the psychological factors of CEOs and their interaction with their environment. Part II, on top management teams, includes articles on conflict within teams and how CEOs deal with teams. Part III describes how boards of directors act as change agents, how to increase board creativity, and offers a framework for board/CEO relationships. Part IV includes case studies of discontinuous change in major companies and highlights the roles of technology and the senior team. Finally, Part V integrates these themes, emphasizing how successful corporate transformation requires the cooperation of the CEO, the top management team, and the board. Includes index.
Subject(s): Change, CEOs, corporate boards, executive teams

New

Hamson, N. (1998). ***After Atlantis: Working, managing, and leading in turbulent times.*** Boston: Butterworth-Heinemann.

Hamson edited this collection of writings addressing how organizations can become sustainable in today's environment of constant change. Part I, titled "After Atlantis," addresses flow and adaptability in organizations, shared learning, and creating productive organizational architectures. Part II, which describes additional tools and approaches, includes writings on total quality, discontinuous improvement, and decision making.
Subject(s): Change as turbulence

New

Hanpachern, C., Morgan, G. A., & Griego, O. V. (1998). **An extension of the theory of margin: A framework for assessing readiness for change.** *Human Resource Development Quarterly*, *9*(4), 339-350.

The margin in life (MIL) scale measures the load of burdens and responsibilities people face in relation to the power that they have to handle them. This article applies MIL to the field of organization development, using this measure to identify workers' readiness to change. The authors surveyed employees of a manufacturing company about work and personal factors to determine whether workers would participate in, promote, or resist organizational change efforts. Analysis shows that when workers have positive MIL for their job demands, organizational culture, job skills, and management-leadership relations, they are likely to be ready for change. The authors suggest that organizations use these findings to create interventions to support change efforts. Includes bibliographical references.
Subject(s): Change readiness

New

Hardy, C., & Leiba-O'Sullivan, S. (1998). **The power behind empowerment: Implications for research and practice.** *Human Relations*, *51*(4), 451-483.

The authors say that empowerment programs often fail because managers do not consider how their efforts are affected by power. This article describes power using a four-dimension model that takes into account resources used to influence decision-making processes, access to those processes, the hegemonic legitimation of power, and the limits of power. These dimensions of power affect empowerment practices because they impact the interaction between individuals within an organization. The implications of this model on critical, mainstream, and Foucauldian management research are also discussed. Includes bibliographical references.
Subject(s): Empowerment

Harrison, F. C. (Ed.). (1989). ***Spirit of leadership: Inspiring quotations for leaders.*** Germantown, TN: Leadership Education and Development.

Poets, presidents, and philosophers are but a few of the many individuals represented in this collection of quotations that address the multifaceted nature of leadership. Includes an index.
Subject(s): Spirit, quotations

Harvey, J. B. (1988). ***The Abilene paradox and other meditations on management.*** Lexington, MA: Lexington Books.

Here, through a series of essays, Harvey contemplates the organizational behaviors in business life that unintentionally set up obstacles to success, growth, and innovation. The title essay, "The Abilene Paradox," illustrates how people in organizations take part in projects or assignments in which there is unspoken agreement that an idea won't work, and yet they proceed to pour valuable time, effort, and money into it. Harvey's parables about human behavior in organizations are insightful and engaging. Includes a bibliography.
Subject(s): Communication breakdown, groupthink

New

Hayes, J., & Allinson, C. W. (1998). **Cognitive style and theory and practice of individual and collective learning in organizations.** *Human Relations*, *51*(7), 847-871.

Cognitive style is an individual's "preferred way of gathering, processing, and evaluating information," and it largely determines how individuals learn. While organizations do not have cognitive styles the authors say that collective groups do develop mental models that determine how members organize and interpret experiences. Understanding these mental models can help managers improve both individual and collective learning in their organizations. The article describes three categories of interventions that can facilitate learning and performance: improving individual-job fit, improving the effectiveness of training interventions, and managing group composition to promote effective learning. Includes bibliographical references.
Subject(s): Learning competency

New

Heenan, D. A., & Bennis, W. (1999). ***Co-leaders: The power of great partnerships.*** New York: John Wiley & Sons.

As organizational structures change, more corporations depend on co-leaders—people who are responsible for the work in an organization but remain out of the limelight—rather than one CEO. This book describes a dozen co-leaders who achieved success. Biographical information explains how these co-leaders became dynamic duos. The stories include the Chrysler Corporation leadership, the technological twosome of Intel and Microsoft, Anne Sullivan Macy and Helen Keller, sports heroes, presidents and their vice presidents, the literary figures of Holmes and Watson, and the forces behind the People's Republic of China. Includes bibliographical references and index.
Subject(s): Shared leadership

Heider, J. (1985). *The Tao of leadership.* Atlanta, GA: Humanics New Age.

Primarily an adaptation of the Chinese classic tome of wisdom *Tao Te Ching* by Lao Tzu, Heider has found a new application for this work. As a teacher and trainer of group leaders Heider has taken the principles set down in the *Tao* and applied them to the leadership process. Based upon the same structure as the *Tao*, each page is the author's version of the meaning of Lao Tzu's own words. This text is meant to provide inspiration and a path to the higher intentions of leadership for those who lead, in whatever context, whether family or group, church or school, business or military, political or administrative. Includes a bibliography.
Subject(s): Spirit, Eastern philosophy

Heifetz, R. A., & Laurie, D. L. (1997). **The work of leadership.** *Harvard Business Review, 75*(1), 124-134.

Heifetz, Director of Harvard University's Leadership Education Project, and Laurie address leadership in situations of *adaptive change*—how to mobilize people throughout an organization to develop new strategies and learn new ways of operating. They identify "six principles for leading adaptive work: 'getting on the balcony,' identifying the adaptive challenge, regulating distress, maintaining disciplined attentions, giving the work back to people, and protecting voices of leadership from below." Recent changes at KPMG Netherlands illustrate the concepts.
Subject(s): Adaptive change

New
Heller, F. (1998). **Influence at work: A 25-year program of research.** *Human Relations, 51*(12), 1425-1456.

Heller draws on extensive longitudinal and comparative research conducted over the last 25 years to describe and analyze influence within organizations. He argues that despite extensive research and writing on worker empowerment and participation, most organizations do not practice influence sharing but keep power firmly entrenched in their top levels. Four possible explanations are offered: 1) expectations have been unrealistic; 2) necessary antecedents to power sharing, such as laws and skills, have been ignored; 3) managers have unreasonably expected influence sharing to work in all situations; and 4) most participation efforts have been socially constructed, isolated events, rather than comprehensive systems. Includes bibliographical references.
Subject(s): Influence

Hesse, H. (1956). *The journey to the East.* New York: Farrar, Straus & Giroux.

This classic work of fiction was the inspiration for much of Robert Greenleaf's work with servant leadership. The story follows a group of leaders from different cultures and backgrounds, called the League. They embark on a highly successful expedition until their humble servant disappears. Unable to settle on a common path or pursuit, the league breaks up and the leaders go in their own directions.
Subject(s): Servant leadership, parables, Eastern philosophy

New
Hey, K. R., & Moore, P. D. (1998). *The caterpillar doesn't know: How personal change is creating organizational change.* New York: Free Press.

This book argues that any organizational restructuring must take into account the revolution in personal values and attitudes about work that has occurred in American society since World War II. Developing sustainable relationships with employees and customers is the only way to ensure business success in the new American environment. This can be done through brand development and social contracts, but firms must also recognize the importance of communities. Each chapter ends with a recap of that section's "critical insight." Includes bibliographical references and index.
Subject(s): Change

New
Hiam, A. (1998). **Nine obstacles to creativity—and how you can remove them.** *Futurist, 32*(7), 30-34.

Hiam, a business consultant, says that organizations and individuals often block creativity by failing to: 1) ask questions, 2) record ideas, 3) revisit ideas, 4) express ideas, 5) think in new ways, 6) wish for more, 7) be creative, 8) keep trying, and 9) tolerate creative behavior.
Subject(s): Creativity

New
Hirshberg, J. (1998). *The creative priority: Driving innovative business in the real world.* New York: HarperBusiness.

Hirshberg, the founding director of Nissan Design International, Inc., uses stories from his years in the automotive industry to describe how organizations can encourage innovation. Businesses can use the 11 strategies described here to make creativity their fundamental organizing principle. The strategies are organized around four ideas: polarity, unprecedented thinking, beyond the edges, and synthesis. Using the idea of polarity, organizations should encourage creative abrasion, hire in divergent pairs, and not be afraid to "embrace the dragon." Unprecedented thinking allows organizations to develop creative questions before creative answers; step back from the canvas on occasion; and accept failure, cheating, and play. Firms that look beyond the edges blur disciplinary boundaries, value intercultural creativity, and "drink from diverse wells." Finally, synthesis allows organizations to use "informed intuition" and "porous planning." Includes bibliography and index.
Subject(s): Innovation, intuition, planning

Hitt, W. D. (1996). *A global ethic: The leadership challenge.* Columbus, OH: Battelle Press.

Hitt examines the need for a global set of core values. Leaders are challenged to: 1) find the common ground by being a citizen of the world, 2) strive to become a fully functioning person, 3) live a life of total dedication to the truth, 4) be truly committed to the good life, and 5) enlist others to be citizens of the world. To live the good life, Hitt

believes one should live a life of compassion, contribution, integrity, communication, and cooperation. The book has exercises to help one understand why there is a need for a global ethic and how to live the good life in a global community. Includes bibliographical references and index.
Subject(s): Values, global leadership

Hogan, R., Raskin, R., & Fazzini, D. (1990). **How charisma cloaks incompetence.** *Personnel Journal, 69*(5), 73-76.

Employees promoted into management positions or applicants who interview well share common personality traits. Intelligence, confidence, charm, energy, and assertiveness are apparent. The authors describe three types of ineffective managers with personality traits that are not so easily apparent. The *betrayer* uses negative information against associates. The *high likability floater* has no agenda and accomplishes little. The *narcissist* is motivated by a need for recognition, not achievement.
Subject(s): Charisma

New
Holman, P., & Devane, T. (Eds.). (1999). *The change handbook: Group methods for shaping the future.* San Francisco: Berrett-Koehler.

This book compiles examples of 18 change methods that leaders can use to create dramatic, sustainable change in their organizations and communities. The authors group the change methods into three categories based on their primary application—planning, structuring, and adapting—and address how to apply each method to real-life issues. Each change method is described in a chapter that includes a historical story about its use, a review of its theoretical basis, advice on getting started and sustaining the results, and a discussion of the impact of the method on power and authority. Appendices offer a comparative matrix of the methods and a list of further readings and related organizations. Includes bibliographical references and index.
Subject(s): Change

Hooijberg, R. (1996). **A multidirectional approach toward leadership: An extension of the concept of behavioral complexity.** *Human Relations, 49*(7), 917-946.

This is a report of a study done on 534 middle managers in a large manufacturing firm and in the public utility industry. Peers, subordinates, and superiors responded to a questionnaire about each manager's behavior repertoire and leadership effectiveness. The behavior repertoire includes four functions: people leadership, adaptive leadership, stability leadership, and task leadership. Data imply that effective leaders need to have a broad repertoire of leadership functions and the ability to vary their behavior depending on their various interactions.
Subject(s): Competencies overview

Hosmer, L. T. (1994). *Moral leadership in business.* Boston: Irwin.

This is a textbook for students of leadership ethics. The author defines moral problems, reasoning, and principles and applies those concepts to organizational issues and managerial responsibilities. There are numerous case studies and assignments in each chapter. The leveraged buyout of RJR Nabisco, the wreck of the Exxon Valdez, and Ford versus Greenpeace are among the cases used to illustrate ethical problems in business. Includes bibliographical references and index.
Subject(s): Ethics, textbook

House, R. J., & Howell, J. M. (1992). **Personality and charismatic leadership.** *Leadership Quarterly: Special Issue: Individual Differences and Leadership: III, 3*(2), 81-108.

Personalized charisma is self-aggrandized, non-egalitarian, and exploitive. Socialized charisma is collectively oriented, egalitarian, and non-exploitive. Machiavellian, narcissistic, and authoritarian personalities seek power for personal motives at the expense of others. Self-confident, nurturing, sensitive, and considerate personalities can transform followers' needs and aspirations from self to the greater good of the whole.
Subject(s): Negative views of charisma

Howard, A., & Wellins, R. S. (1994). *High-involvement leadership: Changing roles for changing times.* Pittsburgh, PA: Development Dimensions International; Tenafly, NJ: Leadership Research Institute.

High-involvement leadership occurs when "organizations empower their employees by pushing down decision-making responsibility to those close to internal and external customers." This study examined the response of over 1,300 workers, from senior managers to associates, to high-involvement leadership. It found that although this leadership style had widespread benefits, many barriers to its implementation still exist, and senior managers often view it "through rose-colored glasses." Based on these results the authors offer their recommendations for implementing high-involvement leadership, including involving high-level managers in organizational transformation, establishing rewards for employees, and identifying individuals' specific developmental needs.
Subject(s): Participation

Howard, V. A. (1996). **The aesthetic face of leadership.** *Journal of Aesthetic Education: Special Issue: The Aesthetic Face of Leadership, 30*(4), 21-37.

Howard claims that artistry and leadership are complex subjects about which much has been written but little is agreed. He finds that books written by historians, journalists, and biographers, not by social scientists, reveal the "emotionalized thinking" that link artistry and leadership, the aesthetic face of leadership. This emotionalized thinking is represented by the sensitivity, judgment, persuasiveness, imagination, and timing exemplified in the actions, decisions, rhetoric, and public presence of great leaders. He argues that while some leadership skills can be taught, leadership itself can only be achieved through painful refinement of one's sensibilities. Includes bibliographical references.

Subject(s): Art as metaphor for leadership

New

Hughes, R. L. (1998). **Strategic leadership.** *Leadership in Action, 18*(4), 1-8.

Hughes offers a three-part framework for understanding strategic leadership: 1) an individual's experiences, motivation, personality, and behaviors; 2) the competitive environment that includes technology, culture, and economic factors; and 3) an organization's systems, climate, and work processes. Any two perspectives may interface. For example, the individual and competitive environment perspectives together illuminate the uncertainty and complexity of leadership roles and one's ability to deal with them. When all three perspectives interface, a strategic leader is armed with a holistic view and the relationships necessary to guide an organization's long-term vision. Includes bibliographical references.

Subject(s): Strategic leadership

New

Hughes, R. L., Ginnett, R. C., & Curphy, G. J. (1999). *Leadership: Enhancing the lessons of experience* (3rd ed.). New York: Irwin/McGraw-Hill.

Based on a framework describing the relationships between leaders, followers, and situations, this book serves as a guide for interpreting leadership theory and research. The authors say that leadership is not a position but a process, and they discuss how leadership is developed through education and experiences, how it is assessed, and various theoretical models including charismatic and transformational leadership. The third edition provides expanded information on women's leadership and cultural diversity and includes a continuing focus across the book on three global leaders— Colin Powell, Madeleine Albright, and Konosuke Matsushita. Each chapter includes key terms, discussion questions, and leadership quotes. The book's final section describes basic and advanced leadership skills. Includes bibliographical references and index.

Subject(s): Learning experiences

New

Hultman, K. (1998). *Making change irresistible: Overcoming resistance to change in your organization.* Palo Alto, CA: Davies-Black.

Any organizational change effort will face resistance from employees. In this book Hultman offers advice on how to overcome this resistance and involve workers in change efforts. Part I addresses human behavior, identifying the conditions under which people support change, how to promote high morale, and describing the motivational cycle. Part II describes how to diagnose resistance to change and how leaders can build the trust needed to overcome that

resistance. Includes bibliographical references and index.

Subject(s): Resistance to change

New

Hunt, J. G. (1999). **Transformational/charismatic leadership's transformation of the field: An historical essay.** *Leadership Quarterly: Special Issue, Part I: Charismatic and Transformational Leadership: Taking Stock of the Present and Future, 10*(2), 129-144.

Hunt's historical overview points out that in the 1980s leadership literature suffered from a plethora of boring work that asked inconsequential questions and provided static answers. He calls this the gloom and doom period that could have caused the death of leadership as a serious academic interest. However, the introduction of a new leadership style characterized as transformational, charismatic, visionary, and change-oriented created a paradigm shift that inspired new scholarship. Hunt follows the evolution of leadership theories through time and the links to multiple leadership approaches. He claims that the field has emerged from the introduction and elaboration stage into the concept evaluation stage. He predicts that in the future the field will enter into a concept-consolidation stage. Includes bibliographical references.

Subject(s): Charismatic leadership, transformational leadership

New

Hunt, M. (1998). *DreamMakers: Putting vision and values to work.* Palo Alto, CA: Davies-Black.

Hunt says that DreamMakers are visionary leaders who "have the unique ability to tap into the seeming chaos of our lives and find the common yearnings for something better." This book profiles 12 DreamMakers from organizations including America Online, the U.S. Customs Service, and the Holocaust Museum who have made their dreams a reality. Each story is told in a first person narrative, and after each profile Hunt identifies the characteristics these leaders share. For example, DreamMakers express vision and values, nurture interpersonal relationships, focus on education and continuous learning, follow a moral compass, and demonstrate responsibility to a larger community. Hunt's own story concludes the book. Includes further suggested readings.

Subject(s): Vision, values

Hurst, V. (1996). **The nomenclature of leadership.** *Journal of Leadership Studies, 3*(1), 123-129.

Hurst believes that to make a change in an organization, institution, or society there needs to be collaboration instead of leadership. Collaborative relations allow people to have a social mind-set that is concerned with common welfare. According to Hurst the words leadership and collaboration have different meanings. Leadership describes position and unequal influence. Collaboration promotes mutuality and equality. Hurst feels that leadership will always have a place in society but that it is collaboration that will ultimately make the monumental changes.

Subject(s): Collaboration

Janis, I. L. (1982). *Groupthink: Psychological studies of policy decisions and fiascoes* (2nd ed.). Boston, MA: Houghton Mifflin.

The author examines five events from World War II to Watergate that turned into major fiascoes for five American presidents: Franklin Roosevelt being unprepared for the attack on Pearl Harbor; Harry Truman and the invasion of North Korea; John Kennedy and the Bay of Pigs invasion; Lyndon Johnson's escalation of the Vietnam War; and Richard Nixon's role in the Watergate cover-up. By a close examination of the group process that led to the course of action taken for each of these events, Janis seeks to answer the question: "How could such bright, shrewd leaders and their advisors arrive at such poor decisions?" The author has developed a convincing and controversial set of dynamics to explain group decision-making strategies and how they can fail. Includes bibliography and index.
Subject(s): Groupthink, negative views of leadership

New
Jenkins, W. A., & Oliver, R. W. (1997). *The eagle and the monk: The seven principles of successful change*. Norwalk, CT: Gates & Bridges.

This fable about a Japanese man who turns into a monk and an American man who becomes an eagle illustrates the seven principles of successful change: 1) accept your worth, acknowledge others' worth; 2) generate trust; 3) learn by empathy; 4) embrace change; 5) unleash the synergy; 6) discover champions, depend on masters, find a sage; and 7) liberate decision making. Includes discussion questions for each principle.
Subject(s): Change

Johnson, D. P. (1979). **Dilemmas of charismatic leadership: The case of the People's Temple.** *Sociological Analysis*, *40*, 315-323.

A proposed model of charismatic leadership is used to interpret the power of Jim Jones's People's Temple, which ended in a mass suicide in Jonestown, Guyana. Charismatic leaders are continually seeking ways in which to reinforce their power.
Subject(s): Negative views of charisma

New
Judge, W. Q. (1999). *The leader's shadow: Exploring and developing executive character*. Thousand Oaks, CA: Sage.

Judge believes that the majority of executive development programs focus more on what leaders do rather than who they are. This book is intended for executive coaches and trainers as well as students of leadership. It promotes the idea that exhibiting potential as an executive is dependent upon personal character. Judge adopts a term from Carl Jung called *shadow*, which is explored and related to leadership. This source discusses surveyed CEOs and examines the values, personality, and spirituality of executive leaders. Judge also delves into the creation of a vision of the future, strategic

priorities, and organizational trust. The concluding chapters examine the interrelationships of character and creative fruits. Includes bibliographical references and index.
Subject(s): Values, character

Kahai, S. S., Sosik, J. J., & Avolio, B. J. (1997). **Effects of leadership style and problem structure on work group processes and outcomes in an electronic meeting system environment.** *Personnel Psychology*, *50*(1), 121-146.

This article reports on a laboratory study of participative versus directive leadership styles and their effects on problem solving through the use of an electronic meeting system (EMS), also called group decision support systems (GDSS). The anonymity of members using this system enhances participative leadership and group potency when solving unstructured or moderately structured problems. Includes bibliographical references. A similar study is reported in Sosik, Avolio, and Kahai (1997), "Effects of leadership style and anonymity on group potency and effectiveness in a group decision support system environment," *Journal of Applied Psychology*, *82*(1), 89-103.
Subject(s): Decision making and technology

New
Kakabadse, A., Notier, F., & Abramovici, N. (1998). *Success in sight: Visioning*. London: International Thomson Business Press.

It is essential for organizations to have a shared vision supported by a specific purpose, mission, and values. This collection of edited papers presents an overview of the visioning process and uses the history and philosophy of leadership to apply this process, allowing for different organizational cultures. One particular approach to visioning is discussed, and the subsequent chapters exemplify the success of two organizations using the visioning process. The final chapter cautions some of the possible pitfalls encountered with visioning and concludes by redefining visioning in a philosophical context. Includes bibliographical references, index, tables, and figures.
Subject(s): Vision

New
Kamoche, K., & Mueller, F. (1998). **Human resource management and the appropriation-learning perspective.** *Human Relations*, *51*(8), 1033-1060.

Academic and practitioner-oriented literature usually address human resource management from a financial perspective, but this article is based on the concept of appropriation. The authors say that appropriation, or "the securing of individuals' efforts" for the benefit of the organization, is the goal of most HRM practices. This article uses both traditional HRM theories and innovation management research to develop an appropriation-learning perspective, integrating the ideas of learning and knowledge into the practice of managing people. The authors apply this perspective to the four key appropriation structures: training and development, the internal labor market, commitment, and organizational culture. Includes bibliographical references.

Subject(s): Learning competency, organizational learning

Kanungo, R. N., & Mendonca, M. (1996). *Ethical dimensions of leadership.* Thousand Oaks, CA: Sage.

The authors believe that the actions of a leader "are effective only to the extent that they are imbued with sound ethical principles." This book provides both a conceptual framework for ethical leadership and strategies for its practical applications. The first sections analyze the different approaches to leadership, the motivations of a leader, the relationship between leaders and followers, and the nature of altruism as a motivational construct and an ethical justification for a leader's actions. Later chapters focus on how leaders can prepare themselves to function ethically, dismissing standard methods of teaching ethics as an intellectual exercise and focusing instead on spirituality and how individuals develop their moral character. Includes references and an index.

Subject(s): Ethics

New

Kao, J. (1996). *Jamming: The art and discipline of business creativity.* New York: HarperCollins.

Kao believes that, like a jazz ensemble, every organization needs creativity if it is to survive and thrive. This book serves as a guide for managers to foster creativity in their organizations. Kao begins by answering questions grounded in the necessity for creativity. Conducting an audit of the existing amounts of creativity in the organization is the next step, and the following chapter defines Kao's use of *Jamming* as it relates to creativity and management. The next portion of the book sets the stage for enhanced creativity by preparing the mind for creative thoughts, finding comfortable spaces for thought, and eliminating interfering beliefs. The remainder of the book delves into the creative organization and its role in technology. Includes an epilogue containing tips for implementing *Jamming.*

Subject(s): Leader as musician, jazz music as metaphor for leadership

Kaplan, R. E. (1996). *Forceful leadership and enabling leadership: You can do both.* Greensboro, NC: Center for Creative Leadership.

Kaplan's previous research on expansive executives and ongoing consultation with executives has led him to an appreciation for versatility. This report explains his new theory on the opposing virtues of forceful leadership and enabling leadership. Kaplan explains how executives who are forceful, who assert themselves and push others to perform, can avoid becoming tyrannical. And executives who are enabling, who bring out the capabilities in others, can avoid self-effacement. Kaplan has developed the *Executive Roles Questionnaire,* a 360-degree-feedback instrument, to identify the forceful and enabling dimensions of an executive's leadership style. Once identified, an executive may learn to

de-emphasize one dimension and develop another. Includes bibliographical references.

Subject(s): Power

New

Kaplan, R. E. (1999). *Internalizing strengths: An overlooked way of overcoming weaknesses in managers.* Greensboro, NC: Center for Creative Leadership.

While executives who want to improve their performances generally focus on their weaknesses, this report describes how recognizing strengths can also improve performance. Kaplan uses examples from his one-on-one work with executives to describe how managers often underestimate their strengths, including intelligence. Five principles for executives hoping to improve or managers responsible for developing others are identified: don't take strengths for granted, engage in potent self-reflection, concentrate the message and distill the data, get personally involved, and stay involved.

Subject(s): Competencies overview

Katz, R. (Ed.). (1997). *The human side of managing technological innovation: A collection of readings.* New York: Oxford University Press.

The readings presented in this collection focus on "issues critical to the effective management of technical professionals and cross-functional teams through the innovation process." Articles are organized around six themes: the management and motivation of professional performance, managing innovative groups and project teams, the management and leadership of technical professionals, managing professionals within innovative organizations, the management of organizational processes, and managing technological innovation. Includes an index.

Subject(s): Innovation, technical leadership

Katzenbach, J. R., & the RCL Team. (1995). *Real change leaders: How you can create growth and high performance at your company.* New York: Random House, Inc.

According to the authors, in between the present and the future is a period of change called the *delta state.* They believe that "real change leaders (RCLs) learn how to survive and win in the delta state." Major change efforts that start at the top of companies often stall midway down, so Katzenbach and his team interviewed 150 mid-level managers they call "down-the-line leaders." These RCLs, from organizations including Compaq, Shell, and the New York City Transit Authority, are able to create change by visualizing what needs to be done and motivating the people around them. The book is aimed at both middle managers who want to develop RCL characteristics and executives who want to recognize the RCLs in their own companies. Includes bibliographical references and index.

Subject(s): Leader as change agent

New

Kaye, B., & Jacobson, B. (1999). **True tales and tall tales: The power of organizational storytelling.** *Training & Development, 53*(3), 44-50.

Storytelling can be a powerful tool for communicating vision and building leadership in organizations, and can be used in both spontaneous and deliberate settings to facilitate organizational learning. The storytelling process typically has three stages: first, someone tells a story and people listen, then both the listeners and the teller begin to understand something they knew only superficially before, and finally the group uses the shared meaning that has developed to gain a wider understanding. Leaders who want to use stories should look to their own personal histories and experiences for people or events that have patterns, consequences, lessons, utility, and vulnerability. Effective storytellers should also consider their audience carefully and allow time for debriefing.
Subject(s): Storytelling

Kelley, R. E. (1992). *The power of followership: How to create leaders people want to follow and followers who lead themselves.* New York: Currency/Doubleday.

"Leaders contribute on the average no more than 20% to the success of most organizations." Kelley's assertion begins a new look at the roles of leaders and followers in organizations. Breaking from the conventional definition of followers as sheep, Kelley defines them as people who know what to do without being told. He also asserts ambition is less and less a correlate of success; groups with many leaders can be chaotic, whereas groups with none can be very productive; and there are styles of followership, just as there are styles of leadership. Leaders are urged to understand and embrace shared responsibility and reward. Includes bibliographical references and index.
Subject(s): Followership

Kenney, R. A., Schwartz-Kenney, B. M., & Blascovich, J. (1996). **Implicit leadership theories: Defining leaders described as worthy of influence.** *Personality and Social Psychology Bulletin, 22*(11), 1128-1143.

The authors report on three studies of followers' expectations for leaders worthy of influence (LWI). In the first two, participants were asked to rank order the influence-rendering traits and behaviors of appointed leaders (study 1) and elected leaders (study 2). Both study groups were asked to judge all of the traits and behaviors to determine if they are most often exhibited by appointed leaders, elected leaders, or equally by both kinds of leaders. The authors were surprised to find a wide difference between followers' influence expectations of appointed and elected leaders. The third study tested participants' cognition of LWI prototypes. Results indicated that follower expectations are based on memory, context, and labels assigned by others. The authors call for additional research to be done on followers' perceptions and expectations of leaders who are worthy of influence. Includes bibliographical references.
Subject(s): Influence

New

Kerr, S. (Ed.). (1997). *Ultimate rewards: What really motivates people to achieve.* Boston: Harvard Business School Press.

This collection of *Harvard Business Review* articles and interviews focuses on individual and organizational motivation. Included are: "Asinine Attitudes Toward Motivation" by Harry Levinson; "What Business Can Learn From Nonprofits" by Peter Drucker; "Power Is the Great Motivator" by David McClelland and David Burnham; "The New Managerial Work" by Rosabeth Moss Kanter; and "The Work of Leadership" by Ron Heifetz and Donald Laurie. Kerr's introduction to the volume outlines a framework of key issues. He explains that rewards should increase equity and efficiency and that availability, eligibility, visibility, and reversibility should be considered up front. Kerr also revisits the issue of intrinsic rewards that help employees achieve self-actualization. Includes an index.
Subject(s): Motivation

Khan, S. (1997). **The key to being a *leader* company.** *Journal for Quality and Participation, 20*(1), 44-50.

To determine the state of employee empowerment in today's business world the author surveyed managers and quotes many of their answers here. Khan describes whether managers feel empowered or not, what actions they take to empower their employees, and then develops a definition of empowerment and a list of its benefits. The article includes a list of the risks of empowerment, reasons it can fail, steps companies can take to empower employees, and methods for inspiring employee trust in the empowerment process.
Subject(s): Empowerment

Kidder, R. M. (1995). *How good people make tough choices.* New York: William Morrow.

At the Institute for Global Ethics Kidder hears repeated concerns over the breakdown of morality. In executive ethics seminars for corporate, nonprofit, academic, and governmental clients he asks participants to bring to the table real ethical dilemmas they have encountered. In this book Kidder shares these dilemmas without revealing identities. Discussion of ethics paradigms and mental tools for solving dilemmas help the reader understand the decision-making process in situations of truth-versus-loyalty, individual-versus-community, and justice-versus-mercy. Includes bibliographical references and index.
Subject(s): Ethical decision making

Kim, W. C., & Mauborgne, R. A. (1992). **Parables of leadership.** *Harvard Business Review, 70*(4), 123-128.

The Oriental technique of using parables to teach the essential wisdom of life is employed here to teach the essential qualities of leadership. Five one-page parables tell of characters who learn to listen beyond spoken words and into the hearts of others, to remain humble, to commit to a purpose, to see truth from different viewpoints, and to trust in the strength of a team.

Subject(s): Competencies overview, parables

New

King, S. C. (1998). **Creativity and problem solving: The challenge for HRD professionals.** *Human Resource Development Quarterly*, 9(2), 187-191.

HRD professionals trying to facilitate creativity and problem solving in their organizations should ask themselves three questions: Who can solve problems? What is creativity? How can we develop an environment conducive to creative problem solving? King says that everyone is capable of creative problem solving, which occurs when knowledge from one domain is applied to another in a "fundamental shift or movement of the mind." HRD can create an environment that supports this process by promoting job rotation, mentoring, diverse groups, and collective learning. Includes bibliographical references.

Subject(s): Creative problem solving

Kirkpatrick, S. A., & Locke, E. A. (1996). **Direct and indirect effects of three core charismatic leadership components on performance and attitudes.** *Journal of Applied Psychology*, 81(1), 36-51.

This article reports on a laboratory simulation designed to determine if charismatic leadership positively affects follower outcomes. The authors studied seven theories of transformational and charismatic leadership to identify three core competencies: vision, vision implementation through task cues, and communication style. Two actors portrayed leaders—one as a charismatic leader and one without vision, task cues, or charismatic communication style. University students participated as followers of both leaders. The most significant finding is a leader's vision strongly affects a follower's intellectual stimulation, inspiration, congruence with a leader's values, trust in a leader, and perception of a leader as charismatic. Includes bibliographical references.

Subject(s): Charismatic leadership

New

Klein, G. (1998). *Sources of power: How people make decisions.* Cambridge, MA: MIT Press.

Rather than using laboratory experiments to study decision making, Klein observed how professionals including fire fighters, critical-care nurses, and nuclear power plant operators make life-and-death decisions in an instant. From his fieldwork he developed a model of "naturalistic decision-making," in which people use different "sources of power" to identify patterns and make choices. These sources of power include intuition, mental stimulation, stories, metaphors, and rational analysis. Includes bibliography and index.

Subject(s): Decision making, power bases, intuition, storytelling

New

Komaki, J. L. (1998). *Leadership from an operant perspective.* New York: Routledge.

Komaki emphasizes that much of management difficulties are inherent in ensuring that employees are maintaining quality work. This source serves as a tool for effective leadership using a model with its basis in B. F. Skinner's *Operant Conditioning Theory.* The model presented here, *The Operant Model of Effective Supervision,* stems from research studies in North America, Europe, and Australia. The model consists of leaders' behaviors, supervisory effectiveness, the interaction process, and boundaries. The author defines what leaders do and follows with the model research and implications for use. Importance is placed on the two managerial behaviors of performance monitoring and communication. Includes notes, bibliographical references, and indices.

Subject(s): Competencies overview

Kotter, J. P. (1978). **Power, success, and organizational effectiveness.** *Organizational Dynamics,* 6(3), 26-40.

Kotter describes power in organizations: how people acquire and manage power, why success in some jobs depends on power-oriented behavior but in other jobs does not, and how and why successful power-oriented behavior can work for or against the overall interests of the organization.

Subject(s): Power

Kotter, J. P. (1996). *Leading change.* Boston: Harvard Business School Press.

This book is an extension of Kotter's previous works on change (Leading change: Why transformation efforts fail, *Harvard Business Review,* 1995; *A Force for Change: How Leadership Differs from Management,* 1990; *Corporate Culture and Performance,* 1992; *The New Rules: How to Succeed in Today's Post-Corporate World,* 1995). The previous works cite empirical evidence and examples of change efforts in real organizations. This book is more personal. It's an analysis formed during Kotter's years as a professor of leadership at Harvard and a scholar of organizational change. He outlines an eight-stage change process. He also forecasts an increasingly important capacity for organizations to continually change and for their leaders to continually learn.

Subject(s): Change

New

Kouzes, J. (1998). **Voice lessons.** *The Journal for Quality and Participation,* 21(1), 64.

This article presents a metaphorical insight to leadership. Kouzes compares leaders to artists in search of their unique style. Many leaders demonstrate a style that they have learned verbatim but have not internalized. Kouzes advocates practicing what one is preaching and being true to oneself. The process by which this may occur is depicted in its three stages. The first is the recitation of learned material, the

second is self-realization and the need for something more, and finally, the discovery of the true self.
Subject(s): Art as metaphor for leadership

Kouzes, J. M., & Posner, B. Z. (1993). *Credibility: How leaders gain and lose it, why people demand it.* San Francisco: Jossey-Bass.

Based on surveys of more than 15,000 people, 400 case studies, and 40 in-depth interviews, this book explains why leader credibility is the cornerstone of corporate performance and global competitiveness. Built on the relationship between leader and constituents, credibility results from honesty, boldness of vision, courage of conviction, understanding, respect, and energetic involvement. Six disciplines help a leader achieve credibility: self-discovery, appreciating others' differences, shared values, competence, purpose, and hope. Includes bibliographical references and indexes.
Subject(s): Credibility

New
Kraut, A. I., & Korman, A. K. (1999). *Evolving practices in human resource management: Responses to a changing world of work.* San Francisco: Jossey-Bass.

This collection of articles explores how the nature of human resources management has been affected by changes in the business world. The articles in Part One describe the signs and causes of these changes, which have affected HR practices such as motivation and commitment. Part Two describes specific HR functions, including recruitment, performance management, diversity, and managing teams. Finally, Part Three looks at perspectives on the future and offers chapters on organizational change and organizational surveys. Includes bibliographical references and index.
Subject(s): Competencies overview

New
Krisco, K. H. (1997). *Leadership and the art of conversation: Conversation as a management tool.* Rocklin, CA: Prima.

Krisco, an executive coach, offers guidance for new leaders who want to increase their communication skills. There are eight basic principles: 1) be aware of how you listen and speak, 2) don't dwell on past conversations, 3) manage background conversations—assumptions and unwritten rules, 4) shift from past to present to future, 5) be proactive, 6) distinguish between substance and language, 7) shape your image, and 8) go for a breakthrough—results beyond expectations. Includes excerpts from Krisco's coaching sessions and an index.
Subject(s): Communication

Kritek, P. B. (1994). *Negotiating at an uneven table: A practical approach to working with difference and diversity.* San Francisco: Jossey-Bass.

Kritek, a nurse and professor of nursing, examines the process of resolving conflict in which unacknowledged inequality influences the situation and its outcome. She compares traditional approaches to an uneven table with more constructive approaches and offers ten "ways of being" that can positively affect inequality and diversity. These include: be a truth teller, honor your integrity, find a place for compassion, draw a line in the sand without cruelty, know what you do and do not know, and know when and how to leave the table. Exercises and personal stories from Kritek's nursing experience accompany each chapter. Includes bibliographical references and index.
Subject(s): Negotiation

Kuczmarski, S. S., & Kuczmarski, T. D. (1995). *Values-based leadership.* Englewood Cliffs, NJ: Prentice Hall.

The authors write about their concern over the apparent lack of values in corporate America. They believe the foundation lies in a value-less society of disintegrating families and is reflected in the decreasing productivity of American workers. Interviews with employees from banks, law firms, nonprofit organizations, and restaurants uncovered a general feeling of "anomie," a lack of purpose or an apathetic attitude at work. The authors believe that awareness of this problem is the first step to combating it. They suggest ways for corporate leaders to develop value norms in themselves and their companies and to help employees gain meaning and self-satisfaction at work. Building personal relationships, showing passion, allowing conflict without blaming, encouraging personal success, and building teams are some of the ways to cement values and increase productivity. Includes an index.
Subject(s): Values

Kuczmarski, T. D. (1996). *Innovation: Leadership strategies for the competitive edge.* Lincolnwood, IL: NTC Business Books.

Kuczmarski lists four goals for this book: 1) convince CEOs of the power of innovation; 2) increase top management involvement in and commitment to innovation; 3) unleash the power of employees to think creatively and innovate; and 4) provide practical tools, techniques, and guidelines for making innovation work. Each chapter contains figures, self-assessment tests, lists of action steps, and an "innovation checklist." Chapters address kick-starting your organization, the role of shareholders, measuring innovation progress, and developing your personal commitment. Includes an index.
Subject(s): Innovation

Kunich, J. C., & Lester, R. I. (1996). **Leadership and the art of feedback: Feeding the hands that back us.** *Journal of Leadership Studies*, 3(4), 3-22.

This article focuses on leaders and their ability to provide and receive feedback, especially in a supervisor/subordinate relationship. Feedback from a supervisor to an employee helps to inform and motivate the employee. The word feedback can be used as an acronym that defines leadership: Frequent, Early, Evidence-based, Dialogue-oriented, Beneficial, Accurate, Clear, and Kind. For example, frequent means that an employee is not just receiving a yearly report card but, instead, is receiving feedback as needed. Discussion questions are provided.

Subject(s): Giving and receiving feedback

Land, G., & Jarman, B. (1992). *Breakpoint and beyond: Mastering the future—today.* New York: HarperBusiness.

All systems in nature, individuals as well as organizations, go through a process of change that can lead to renewal and transformation. Understanding nature's creative process can aid in the understanding and acceptance of change. *Breakpoint* is defined as a break with the past, a push to the edge of an era, and a leap into the unknown. Land and Jarman teach the reader how to recognize personal and organizational breakpoints, to embrace the process of change with creativity, and to build bridges into the future. Includes bibliographical references and index.

Subject(s): Renewal

Lawler, E. E., III. (1992). *The ultimate advantage.* San Francisco: Jossey-Bass.

High-involvement management practices—those that foster quick adaptation and change and satisfy work relationships—are not just a good idea; they are an economic necessity. Acknowledging that employees give more to their work when they have a say in how the company is run, Lawler outlines programs that go beyond the total-quality-management approach. Providing a competitive advantage is characterized by diversity, entrepreneurial behavior, and respect for the individual. Organizations encourage innovation, increase cost-effectiveness, deliver enhanced quality, customer service, and speed by setting up work teams. Includes bibliographical references and index.

Subject(s): Participation

Leavy, B. (1996). **On studying leadership in the strategy field.** *Leadership Quarterly, 7*(4), 435-454.

Is a strategy a plan or a past pattern of action? Leavy argues that it is both, a mixture of intended and emergent processes in which leadership is constantly changing with time and context. This article offers a three-part conceptual framework for viewing strategic leadership: the situational leadership challenge; the leader's personal ability and convictions; and the symbolism, image, and credibility inherent in the leader's role. These three factors determine an individual's leadership capacity, which will decide a group's performance and strategic impact over time. Political and business leaders from Margaret Thatcher to Anita Roddick, founder of The Body Shop, are used to illustrate the framework.

Subject(s): Strategic leadership

New

Ledeen, M. A. (1999). *Machiavelli on modern leadership: Why Machiavelli's iron rules are as timely and important today as five centuries ago.* New York: Truman Talley Books.

Niccolo Machiavelli's views on leadership still spark debate. Ledeen represents these views in this six-part source

depicting the negative connotations inherent in Machiavelli's leadership style. Ledeen takes readers into Machiavelli's thinking about human nature and humankind's aversion to peace, and the inherent evilness of man. The belief that proper leadership is the only way humans can be inspired to do good, and that man cannot be left to his own devices, is explored. In a chapter devoted to ruling, Ledeen describes the leadership of contemporary leaders and compares them to Machiavelli. The concluding chapter delves into the concept of freedom. Includes bibliographical references and index.

Subject(s): Abuse of power

New

Lencioni, P. (1998). *The five temptations of a CEO: A leadership fable.* San Francisco: Jossey-Bass.

Lencioni creatively presents five common pitfalls of top leaders in a fictional account of an executive in trouble. Each of these five temptations displayed by the fable's protagonist is depicted in the eleven chapters of the story. An afterword makes up the second portion of the book, modeling each of the five temptations followed by a self-evaluation. Lencioni attributes many executive failures to the common mistake of hiding these five temptations rather than enlisting help from subordinates, and embracing the self-examination that allows the pitfalls to be addressed and overcome. The first temptation of a CEO is to place personal career status ahead of the company's results. The desire for popularity among subordinates taking precedence over accountability is a second temptation. This can be displayed in the third temptation, which is based on the fear of making a wrong decision and therefore avoiding any decision. Temptation number four is the fear of disrupting harmony with conflict within the organization, and the final temptation is demonstrated as invulnerability or an inability to trust employees. Includes suggestions for action.

Subject(s): Competencies overview, fables

Leslie, J. B., & Van Velsor, E. (1996). *A look at derailment today: North America and Europe.* Greensboro, NC: Center for Creative Leadership.

The Center for Creative Leadership has been studying executive derailment for 12 years, first among U.S. executives and most recently among executives from the European Union. This book compares the factors that contribute to derailment and success over time and across cultures. Four enduring themes have emerged as predictors of derailment: 1) problems with interpersonal relationships, 2) failure to meet business objectives, 3) failure to build and lead teams, and 4) inability to change during times of transition. Includes bibliographical references.

Subject(s): Derailment

New
Lewicki, R. J., Saunders, D. M., & Minton, J. W. (1999). *Negotiation: Readings, exercises, and cases* (3rd ed.). New York: Irwin McGraw-Hill.

This textbook provides an introduction to all types of negotiation, from persuasion to conflict management to dispute resolution. Chapters describe dozens of negotiating tactics, advance planning, sources of power, ethical considerations, and cultural differences. There are 40 readings on negotiation issues reprinted from original sources. The book also includes 27 exercises, eight case studies, and four assessments for classroom use. Includes bibliographical references and author and title indexes.
Subject(s): Negotiation

Likert, R., & Likert, J. G. (1976). *New ways of managing conflict.* New York: McGraw-Hill.

The authors have written a highly detailed text on the methodology, principles, and step-by-step procedures for managing social conflict within organizations, referred to as "System 4." The basic strategy to the Likert method is to change the "win-lose" approach to a "win-win" philosophy. The text provides administrators in business, government, education, and community groups a clearly detailed presentation on how to reduce internal and external conflict. This book has special relevance for social-science educators and students. Includes bibliography and index.
Subject(s): Conflict management

Lindholm, C. L. (1990). *Charisma.* Cambridge, MA: Basil Blackwell.

Adolph Hitler, Charles Manson, and Jim Jones. These three were able to transform the lives of their followers and to change the course of history. What power was present in all three that allowed them to lead others past the fundamental laws of self-preservation? Lindholm uses the theories of Hume, Mill, Weber, Durkheim, and Freud to explore the depths of the human agency and social change. He argues that there is a deep human desire to escape from the limits of self and that charismatic leaders provide the avenue required. The question becomes how to harness the positive, productive potential of this power to effect constructive change. Includes bibliographical references and index.
Subject(s): Negative views of charisma

Lindsey, E. H., Homes, V., & McCall, M. W., Jr. (1987). *Key events in executives' lives.* Greensboro, NC: Center for Creative Leadership.

This report is designed for those individuals who are concerned with the development of executive talent. Drawing on information gathered from over 191 successful executives from six major corporations, this book systematically examines the key events and pivotal experiences that have contributed to these individuals' "high potential" designation. Includes bibliographical references.
Subject(s): Learning experiences

New
Lippitt, L. L. (1998). *Preferred futuring: Envision the future you want and unleash the energy to get there.* San Francisco: Berrett-Koehler.

Lippitt describes a variation of a problem-solving technique called "preferred futuring." This technique takes a historical perspective and examines everything that is working as well as what is not working. It identifies values and scans the horizon for trends to determine a desired future. This vision of the future is then translated into action goals and a realistic plan is implemented. There are separate chapters to illustrate how the preferred futuring model works in organizations and communities. In the appendices are a *Reality Checklist*, a *Task Force Summary Report*, and sample agendas for preferred futuring events. Includes bibliographical references and index.
Subject(s): Problem solving, vision

New
Lippitt, M. (1999). **How to influence leaders.** *Training & Development, 53*(3), 18-22.

Leaders can be divided into six groups based on how they make decisions: inventors, catalysts, developers, performers, protectors, and challengers. Knowing what profile a leader fits can help managers influence that leader's decisions. This article presents two case studies in which managers were able to "lead up" and influence their supervisors' decisions on specific issues. Lippitt identifies five steps for becoming more influential: 1) identify your own profile, 2) identify your leader's profile, 3) develop some questions that would be of interest to the leader, 4) identify how to answer the questions to satisfy both your interest and the leader's, and 5) write a statement confirming the leader's priorities.
Subject(s): Influence

Lumsden, G., & Lumsden, D. (1997). *Communicating in groups and teams: Sharing leadership* (2nd ed.). Belmont, CA: Wadsworth.

This is a textbook for courses in communication and teamwork with a focus on shared leadership. It is written for the student, moving from personal experience to theories to practical applications. Most of the book suggests that all team members assume leadership responsibility, but one chapter focuses on the special skills needed by a designated leader. This new edition provides information on computer-assisted techniques—electronic meetings, also called GDSS or group decision support systems—that foster interaction and eliminate domination by any one member. Chapters include excerpts from articles, cases, assessments, learning activities, cartoons, models, writing exercises, and reflections. Appendices provide suggestions for doing team projects, planning meetings, and making presentations. Includes a glossary, bibliographical references, name index, and subject index.
Subject(s): Communication, shared leadership, textbook

Machiavelli, N. (c. 1513). *The prince.*

Machiavelli wrote this commentary on politics and statesmanship to demonstrate how a new prince, a usurper, could
carve out a new principality for himself. It is a lesson in
manipulative behavior and abuse of power. For instance one
lesson says that "men ought to be treated well or crushed,
because they can avenge themselves of lighter injuries." The
cruelty and unscrupulousness of his fictional prince shocked
even Machiavelli's contemporaries in 16th-century Italy. It is
suspected that Machiavelli wrote this book as political advice
for the Medici family who aspired to public office and for
whom Machiavelli secretly felt disdain. This leadership
classic is of value to everyone who is likely to work for a
manipulative leader or be tempted to become one.
Subject(s): Abuse of power

New
Maddock, R. C., & Fulton, R. L. (1998). *Motivation, emotions,
and leadership: The silent side of leadership.* Westport, CT:
Quorum Books.

The authors say that the substance of leadership is motivation and that effective leaders know how to manage the
emotions that motivate people to action. This book presents
an 11-level model of motivation ranging from weaker
motivators like play and circumstances to strong motivators
including personal orientation and passion. Strategies on how
leaders can use "vertical" and "lateral fixes" to guide their
employees' motivation are also offered. Includes bibliographical references and index.
Subject(s): Motivation

New
Mailick, S., Stumpf, S. A., Grant, S., Kfir, A., & Watson, M. A.
(1998). *Learning theory in the practice of management
development: Evolution and practice.* Westport, CT: Quorum
Books.

The authors say that the short-term goal of most management
development programs is to change behavior, and often the
long-term goal is to motivate managers to learn from their
experiences in a continuous learning process. This book
describes how different learning processes can help achieve
both objectives. The book's first section describes the nature
of management development and the passive learning
approaches and synthetic experiential approaches on which it
is traditionally based. The second section describes a natural,
work-based experiential learning approach, which the authors
recommend, and the third and final section examines the
theory and practice of management development in more
depth. Includes bibliographical references and index.
Subject(s): Learning competency

Marcic, D. (1997). *Managing with the wisdom of love:
Uncovering virtue in people and organizations.* San Francisco:
Jossey-Bass.

According to the author the root cause of problems in
American business today is "lack of love," and this book

attempts to operationalize spirituality and teach managers to
act with virtue. Quotes from the writings of different
religions are used throughout the book to show that spirituality can be inclusive of all, and examples from the business
world illustrate the concepts. Marcic includes checklists and
charts to help readers apply her theories in their own lives
and organizations.
Subject(s): Spirit

Masters, R. D. (1996). *Machiavelli, Leonardo, and the science
of power.* South Bend, IN: University of Notre Dame Press.

Masters wrote this book to suggest "a return to the naturalistic tradition of Western thought, in which a scientific study of
human life is directly related to questions of morality and
law." He believes that Niccolo Machiavelli, the 16th-century
Florentine politician and author, originated the scientific
study of human affairs. Analysis of Machiavelli's life and
writings cause Masters to suspect that Machiavelli was
strongly influenced by his friendship with artist, engineer,
and scientific innovator Leonardo da Vinci. This analysis
suggests that Machiavelli's use of power is often misunder-
stood as abuse of power. Masters examines the basic social
and political relationships of animals and humans to illustrate
the natural state of societies and governments defined by
Machiavelli. Nineteen pages of illustrations, primarily da
Vinci's paintings and technical drawings, support the integration of biology, psychology, philosophy, and human
ethology. Includes bibliographical references and index.
Subject(s): Power

New
McCall, M. W., Jr. (1998). *High flyers: Developing the next
generation of leaders.* Boston: Harvard Business School Press.

McCall challenges the idea that certain people are born with
"the right stuff" and argues instead that leaders are developed
through learning experiences. This book describes a strategy
senior managers can use to develop executives in their
organizations and link that development to business strategy.
Specific chapters address derailment, assessing potential, and
catalysts for development, and an appendix offers advice on
"Taking Charge of Your Development." Includes bibliographical references and index.
Subject(s): Learning experiences

McCall, M. W., Jr., Lombardo, M. M., & Morrison, A. M.
(1988). *The lessons of experience: How successful executives
develop on the job.* Lexington, MA: Lexington Books.

"Where do successful business leaders come from?" "How
do they learn the skills that propel them to the top of their
companies?" In pursuit of answers these authors sought out
top executives across the U.S. and asked them about the work
experiences that had the greatest influence on the direction of
their careers. By examining these career profiles and
evaluating them in a systematic manner against current
research in the fields of learning and human motivation, the
authors reveal surprising answers to what actually shapes the

managerial lives of individuals with executive leadership potential. Includes bibliography and index.
Subject(s): Learning experiences

McCormick, D. W. (1994). **Spirituality and management.** *Journal of Managerial Psychology, 9*(6), 5-8.

For many managers, incorporating spirituality into their work is a challenge but is necessary for their personal well-being. This article offers a working definition of spirituality and then explores five themes relevant to an individual leader's relationship with the sacred: compassion, right livelihood, selfless service, work as meditation, and problems with pluralism.
Subject(s): Spirit

New
McCosh, A. M., Smart, A. U., Barrar, P., & Lloyd, A. D. (1998). **Proven methods for innovation management: An executive wish list.** *Creativity and Innovation Management, 7*(4), 175-192.

In 1994 the Economic and Social Research Council, a British governmental research group, asked leaders from British companies what they wanted to know about innovation. This article attempts to answer six of the resulting questions by surveying the existing literature and describing current research. The questions addressed include how companies can spot a winning creative idea, how they can create competence for innovation, and how leaders can find useful academic work. A summary of current findings in the field are offered for each question, and an appendix provides a list of all 18 questions generated by the study. Includes bibliographical references.
Subject(s): Innovation

McCoy, B. H. (1983). **The parable of the sadhu.** *Harvard Business Review, 61*(5), 103-108.

McCoy shares his experience when faced with a real life-and-death moral dilemma while climbing in the Himalayas. The author and fellow climbers had a narrow window of opportunity to reach a particular summit and fulfill their mission when they discovered an Indian holy man close to death along the path. Each climber offered food, clothing, water, or brief transport toward a place of safety. Yet none of them forsook their own goals to carry the holy man down the mountain. McCoy examines the choices he and others made that day and the choices he makes today when confronted with moral dilemmas in his business.
Subject(s): Spirit, parables

New
McFadzean, E. (1998). **The creativity continuum: Towards a classification of creative problem solving.** *Creativity and Innovation Management, 7*(3), 131-139.

Many different techniques for enhancing creative thinking exist, but not every technique is appropriate for every individual or group. McFadzean proposes a way of classify-

ing creative problem-solving techniques into three groups: 1) paradigm-preserving techniques, such as brainstorming, that do not introduce new elements or relationships; 2) paradigm-stretching techniques, such as metaphors, that introduce either new elements or new relationships; and 3) paradigm-breaking techniques, such as guided fantasy, that introduce both new elements and new relationships. These techniques can be arranged on a "creativity continuum," in which inexperienced groups can start with preserving activities while well-trained groups can move down the continuum to paradigm-breaking exercises. Includes bibliographical references.
Subject(s): Creative problem solving

McLagan, P., & Nel, C. (1996). **A new leadership style for genuine total quality.** *Journal of Quality and Participation, 19*(3), 14-16.

According to the authors today's "new style of leadership" means that everyone in a company, not just upper management, has to practice leadership skills. They list six steps that can help managers who have traditionally been followers develop the new skills: 1) look deep within and transform yourself, 2) create direct relationships with employees, 3) help managers and front-line workers change, 4) see the leader as a focused visionary, 5) share information throughout the organization, and 6) support this new definition of leadership.
Subject(s): Participation, quality

McLagan, P. A., & Nel, C. (1995). *The age of participation: New governance for the workplace and the world.* San Francisco: Berrett-Koehler.

McLagan and Nel call for a fundamental shift toward participative governance in the workplace. Their four major challenges to leaders are: 1) let go of authoritarian perspectives and behaviors, 2) lead the emotional transition, 3) be accountable stewards of high performance and high involvement, and 4) give leadership away to every member of the organization. Self-management, broad business, understanding, knowledge of business finance and economics, critical-thinking skills, integrative communication skills, mutual learning skills, and flexible decision making are needed from everyone in an organization to achieve successful participative governance. A *Governance Assessment* is included to help organizations evaluate their distribution of authoritarian and participative governance. Includes bibliographical references and index.
Subject(s): Participation

McVey, R. S. (1995). **Critical thinking skills for leadership development.** *Journal for Leadership Studies, 2*(4), 86-97.
McVey reviews theories on thought process and its influence on behavior. He notes that vertical thinking has been a common practice of business managers who solve immediate problems at the expense of long-term planning. He asserts that lateral thinking better serves the business leader who

must create a vision, innovate new processes, and plan strategically. He urges teachers across the curriculum, from elementary school to college level, to develop their students' common sense and teach lateral, critical-thinking skills. He recommends the use of case methods, real or hypothetical, as effective teaching tools.
Subject(s): Critical thinking

Menke, M. M. (1997). **Essentials of R&D strategic excellence.** *Research Technology Management, 40*(5), 42-47.

This article reports on a benchmarking study of 45 best decision-making practices in 79 leading R&D organizations. Each organization responded to a questionnaire about the decision-making practices in use, number of new products, sales of new products, and return on R&D investment. The study revealed a top-ten list of best practices: 1) understand the drivers of industry change; 2) coordinate long-range business R&D plans; 3) focus on customer needs; 4) agree on clear, measurable project goals; 5) use a formal development process; 6) use cross-functional teams; 7) coordinate development with commercialization; 8) determine, understand, and measure end-customer needs; 9) refine projects with regular customer feedback; and 10) hire the best and maintain expertise. Includes bibliographical references.
Subject(s): Decision making, technical leaders

Merritt, S., & DeGraff, J. (1996). **The revisionary visionary: Leadership and the aesthetics of adaptability.** *Journal of Aesthetic Education: Special Issue: The Aesthetic Face of Leadership, 30*(4), 69-85.

The authors address the challenge of training leaders to create adaptable, if not predictable, visions in a discontinuous, chaotic world where very little is predictable. Merritt, founder of the Polaroid Creativity Lab, shares her insights on developing the aesthetic competencies of her company's leaders. She employs two frameworks: Parson's five stages of aesthetic development in *How We Understand Art* (Cambridge University Press, 1987) and Thompson's *Visionary Leadership Inventory* (Human Factors, 1994). A new model illustrates how leaders can identify where their aesthetic competencies are at a given point and where they can aim to achieve growth from self-awareness to an awareness of larger, transpersonal forces. Includes bibliographical references.
Subject(s): Vision, chaos, self-awareness

Messick, D. M., & Bazerman, M. H. (1996). **Ethical leadership and the psychology of decision making.** *Sloan Management Review, 37*(2), 9-22.

From a psychological perspective the authors explain weaknesses in the decision-making process. One can make errors in determining risks or use bias in seeking information to support one side of an issue. Unrealistic beliefs about the world, other people, and themselves can trap executives in ethical dilemmas. The authors explain how to recognize and avoid these traps and to make decisions that pass the sunshine test—decisions that stand up in the light of day and under public scrutiny.
Subject(s): Ethical decision making

New
Meyer, P. J., Houze, R., & Slechta, R. (1998). ***Bridging the leadership gap.*** Arlington, TX: Summit Publishing Group.

The methodology presented in this source is for bridging the leadership gap that can occur if a key element of an organization is neglected. Three values—stewardship, integrity, and a servant's heart—are the bedrock for this bridge, and predetermined goals are needed to begin the building of the bridge. Developing a mission or purpose for the organization is the first pillar, and a written plan of action pertaining to the goals is the second pillar. A passion for achievement turns a wish into a goal, and a mutual trust across the organization and ironclad commitment are essential to the support of this bridge. In addition to the five pillars of support, the bridge is dependent upon the organization's ability to embrace change as an opportunity. The final element is to cross the leadership bridge, which requires effective leadership strategies. Includes an appendix.
Subject(s): Values

New
Michalko, M. (1998). **Thinking like a genius: Eight strategies used by the super creative, from Aristotle and Leonardo to Einstein and Edison.** *Futurist, 32*(4), 21-25.

When faced with a problem, geniuses do not think reproductively, basing solutions on past experiences, but think productively, asking, "How many different ways can I solve it?" In this article Michalko describes eight strategies that can help readers think more productively: 1) look at problems many different ways, 2) make thoughts visible, 3) produce, 4) make novel combinations, 5) force relationships, 6) think in opposites, 7) think metaphorically, and 8) prepare for chance.
Subject(s): Creative problem solving

New
Miller, W. C. (1999). ***Flash of brilliance: Inspiring creativity where you work.*** Reading, MA: Perseus Books.

Miller says that creativity is not a genetic trait possessed by an eccentric minority. Instead he describes creativity as a skill that can be managed and says that everyone can learn to make more creative decisions. This book describes the creative process as a four-part journey, made up of the challenge, the focus, the creative solutions, and the completion. Miller explains how this process can be used to express individual creativity, to create a climate that promotes creativity in groups, to lead corporate-wide creative efforts, and to reconcile goals of high performance and social responsibility. Includes bibliographical references and index.
Subject(s): Creativity

Mintzberg, H. (1973). *The nature of managerial work.* New York: Harper & Row.

Mintzberg has sought to identify the whole range of relationships that constitute the manager's world in the contemporary organization, and as a result his conclusions have great worth in a world dependent on leadership skills. An identification of the behavioral skills combined with an overview of how managers manage is presented. Characteristics of managerial work, work roles, variation in work, science and the manager's job, and the future of managerial work are topics covered. Includes a bibliography.
Subject(s): Competencies overview

Mintzberg, H. (1994). *The rise and fall of strategic planning: Reconceiving roles for planning, plans, planners.* New York: Free Press.

The former president of the Strategic Management Society concludes that the term *strategic planning* is an oxymoron. Planning is an analytical process while strategy is more intuitive. Mintzberg reviews the origins of strategic planning and models that didn't work. He is convinced that planning can harm an organization by destroying commitment and encouraging politics. The alternative is to reconceive the process of creating strategy through informal learning and personal vision. Includes bibliographical references and index.
Subject(s): Strategic planning

New
Mitroff, I. I. (1998). *Smart thinking for crazy times: The art of solving the right problems.* San Francisco: Berrett-Koehler.

Mitroff says that decision-makers often commit what he calls a Type III error: solving the wrong problem precisely. There are five different ways to do this: 1) picking the wrong stakeholders, 2) selecting too narrow a set of options, 3) phrasing a problem incorrectly, 4) setting the boundaries too narrowly, and 5) failing to think systematically. This book describes strategies for avoiding these errors and formulating problems correctly, and emphasizes the development of critical-thinking skills. Each chapter ends with questions readers can use to apply these concepts in their organizations. Includes index.
Subject(s): Problem solving

New
Molinari, M. A. (1997). **The intuitive side of leadership.** *The Journal for Quality and Participation,* 20(4), 74-76.

Molinari advocates the need for leaders to tap into their intuitive side. Effective leadership is dependent upon the use of all capabilities including intuition and the five senses. This article offers suggestions for intuition development. To encourage empathy Molinari suggests listening to and feeling what others are saying and doing. The next step is to create an energy field to sense what others are thinking rather than what they are saying. Combining the reality of a situation to create a big picture is the next skill described. Having an

appropriate sense of timing is the final advice for developing intuition.
Subject(s): Intuition

Morgan, G. (1993). *Imaginization: The art of creative management.* Newbury Park: Sage.

Imaginization is a new way of thinking, organizing, and helping people develop their creative potential. It is a means for finding innovative solutions to difficult problems, and it empowers people to trust themselves in a world of constant change. Morgan demonstrates imaginization in action as an invitation to reimage ourselves and organizational management. Includes bibliographical references and index.
Subject(s): Imagination

Morgan, S., & Dennehy, R. F. (1997). **The power of organizational storytelling: A management development perspective.** *Journal of Management Development,* 16(7), 494-501.

Stories can be an effective way to teach skills and information as the research reviewed in this article shows. Using several stories as examples, including one about McDonald's founder Ray Kroc, the authors list the characteristics of a good story and describe the five-step framework that every learning story should contain: setting, build-up, crisis or climax, learning, and new behavior or awareness. Advice on how to become a better storyteller, such as telling stories in pairs and writing in a journal, is also offered. Includes bibliographical references.
Subject(s): Storytelling

New
Morris, T. V. (1997). *If Aristotle ran General Motors: The new soul of business.* New York: Henry Holt.

Written by a former philosophy professor, this book applies classical thinking to modern business problems. Morris identifies four virtues—Truth, Beauty, Goodness, and Unity—that structure human life, but which he says are lacking in today's corporate culture. Using examples from his teaching experience and from companies such as GE and Tom's of Maine, the author shows how these virtues can be applied to the business world. Throughout the book are quotes by thinkers including Cicero, Confucius, Longfellow, Emerson, and Churchill.
Subject(s): Spirit

New
Morrison, E. W., & Phelps, C. C. (1999). **Taking charge at work: Extrarole efforts to initiate workplace change.** *Academy of Management Journal,* 42(4), 403-419.

This article reports on a study of the extrarole behavior called *taking charge.* The focus is not on modest behaviors such as helping colleagues with their workload, or principle-based behaviors such as whistleblowing. It is on change-oriented behaviors that attempt to challenge the status quo and guide an organization toward improved performance. The authors find several factors that motivate employees to step outside their prescribed roles and take charge of organizational change. Taking charge is positively related to: 1) the perceived openness of top management, 2) work group norms that support change, 3) the employee's self-efficacy, 4) the employee's internalized sense of responsibility regarding change, and 5) the employee's level of expert power. Includes bibliographical references.

Subject(s): Participation

New

Moxley, R. S. (1999). **Leadership as partnership.** *Leadership in Action, 19*(3), 9-11.

Moxley suggests an alternative to individual leadership that is described as a partnership. The practice of leadership as a partnership requires that two or more people share power, share a common goal, share a sense of responsibility, and respect each other. Moxley describes real-world examples in which leadership as partnership is practiced at team and organizational levels to the benefit of all.

Subject(s): Partnerships

New

Moxley, R. S. (2000). *Leadership and spirit: Breathing new vitality and energy into individuals and organizations.* San Francisco: Jossey-Bass.

Moxley says that the practices of leadership too often suffocate the spirit of workers, sapping individuals and organizations of vitality and energy. This book first defines spirit and analyzes today's prevalent practices of leadership, showing why these two threads must be woven together. The second half of the book describes ways readers can develop new ways of leading that support the spirit. Moxley says that by developing the inner self and fostering community, individuals can learn new ways of being and doing and find new satisfaction in their work. Includes bibliographical references and index.

Subject(s): Spirit

Mumford, M. D., & Connelly, M. S. (1991). **Leaders as creators: Leader performance and problem solving in ill-defined domains.** *Leadership Quarterly: Special Issue: Individual Differences and Leadership: I, 2*(4), 289-315.

Problem solving relies on well-organized knowledge structure and the cognitive processes that contribute to effective solutions. Creative problem solving occurs when a problem is poorly defined, when novelty is needed, and when information structures are reorganized. Because leaders face varying and ever-changing problems, problem construction relates to leader performance more than does knowledge structure.

Subject(s): Creative problem solving

Mumford, M. D., Gessner, T. L., Connelly, M. S., O'Connor, J. A., & Clifton, T. C. (1993). **Leadership and destructive acts: Individual and situational influences.** *Leadership Quarterly, 4*(2), 115-147.

A leader's personality, values, and beliefs affect decision making, organizational goal setting, and long-term performance. Situational forces may exert a strong influence on destructive acts, but an individual chooses whether to act destructively. A study reveals characteristics that contribute to destructive behavior: low self-esteem, negative belief in humanity, lack of empathy, narcissism, self-aggrandizement, fear, dominant power motives, and social alienation.

Subject(s): Personality, negative views of leadership

New

Munduate, L., & Dorado, M. A. (1998). **Supervisor power bases, co-operative behavior, and organizational commitment.** *European Journal of Work and Organizational Psychology, 7*(2), 163-177.

The authors studied 78 Spanish workers to determine whether the type of power they believed their supervisors used affected the cooperative behavior and organizational commitment of the workers. Rahim's *Leader Power Inventory* was used to measure how the workers perceived their managers' coercive, reward, legitimate, expert, and referent power bases. Other instruments measured cooperation and commitment of workers. Statistical analysis showed that supervisors' reward and expert power bases were positively related to their referent power, and referent power did influence their subordinates' behavior. The authors conclude by suggesting that managers try to extend their power bases from position to personal ones. Includes bibliographical references.

Subject(s): Power bases

New

Nadler, D. A., & Nadler, M. B. (1998). *Champions of change: How CEOs and their companies are mastering the skills of radical change.* San Francisco: Jossey-Bass.

The Nadlers make a case for CEO involvement in successful change efforts, arguing that leaders must be involved in and committed to change for it to succeed. This book presents a strategy for designing organizational change, consisting of five phases: 1) recognizing the change imperative, 2) developing a shared direction, 3) implementing change, 4) consolidating change, and 5) sustaining change. Real-life change strategies at companies including Lucent Technologies, Sun Microsystems, Xerox Corporation, and 3M are described in examples and case studies. Includes bibliographical references and index.

Subject(s): Leader as change agent, CEOs

New

Nadler, D. A., & Tushman, M. L. (1999). **The organization of the future: Strategic imperatives and core competencies for the 21st century.** *Organizational Dynamics, 28*(1), 45-60.

This article suggests that the twin principles of integration and differentiation are required to strategically lead a complex modern organization. A series of figures illustrates the dynamics among environmental pressures, resources,

people, tasks, organizational culture, and organizational systems. To meet the challenges of more rapid strategic cycles, the authors recommend that leaders facilitate flexibility, enhance competitive innovation, design structural divergence, and promote organizational modularity. Includes bibliographical references.
Subject(s): Strategic leadership

Neck, C. P., & Milliman, J. F. (1994). **Thought self-leadership: Finding spiritual fulfillment in organizational life.** *Journal of Managerial Psychology*, 9(6), 9-16.

Although spirituality is rarely discussed in business the authors says that "work is intended to be one of the most profound ways of experiencing the divine presence in the world." This article defines what spirituality means in a corporate context and how it positively affects job performance. The authors then describe the thought self-leadership theory, which proposes that workers can lead themselves by using specific cognitive strategies, including mental imagery and directed thought patterns. A strategy that uses this theory to enhance spirituality on the job is also offered. Includes bibliographical references.
Subject(s): Spirit

New
Nicholson, N. (1998). **How hardwired is human behavior?** *Harvard Business Review*, 76(4), 135-147.

This is a discussion of evolutionary psychology and its roots in six areas of science: anthropology, behavioral genetics, comparative ethology, neuropsychology, paleontology, and social psychology. It examines the biogenetic origins of human culture and capacity to learn. Nicholson states that hardwired traits help managers trust their instincts and emotions over reason, build confidence, compete, and share information. Conversely, hardwired managers prefer to avoid risky situations and resist change. Evolutionary psychology disputes theories of leadership development that claim managers can learn to change their behaviors.
Subject(s): Competencies overview

New
Nystrom, H. (1998). **The dynamic marketing-entrepreneurial interface: A creative management approach.** *Creativity and Innovation Management*, 7(3), 122-125.

Marketing and entrepreneurship have become more and more connected in recent years. The management literature reflects this, but most of the existing research has used an economic management approach. Nystrom argues that the dynamic marketing-entrepreneurship interface can be better explained using a creative management approach, which extends the economic approach to consider radical change, experimentation, and possible multiple solutions to one problem. The creative approach allows the researcher to see the dynamic, convergent nature of the entrepreneur and to achieve a more balanced view of the entire process. Includes bibliographical references.
Subject(s): Entrepreneurship

O'Connor, H., Mumford, M. D., Clifton, T. C., Gessner, T. L., & Connelly, M. S. (1995). **Charismatic leaders and destructiveness: An histriometric study.** *Leadership Quarterly*, 6(4), 529-555.

A discussion of personalized versus socialized charisma and a sampling of real-world leaders identifies traits of destructive charismatic behavior: high need for power, object beliefs, negative life themes, outcome uncertainty, narcissism, and fear. Speeches of 82 national leaders were analyzed and compared to the subjects' psychological profiles of behavior and harm or influence on society. Examples of socialized leaders are: Andrew Carnegie, Sir Winston Churchill, Martin Luther King, Jr., and Joseph Pulitzer. Examples of personalized or destructive leaders are: Idi Amin, Jim Bakker, Fidel Castro, John DeLorean, Adolph Hitler, and Jimmy Hoffa.
Subject(s): Negative views of charisma

O'Toole, J. (1995). *Leading change: Overcoming the ideology of comfort and the tyranny of custom.* San Francisco: Jossey-Bass.

O'Toole uses an artistic metaphor to illustrate how a leader/artist can create order through design, composition, tension, balance, and harmony. James Ensor's painting "Christ's Entry in Brussels in 1889" depicts a community's self-absorption and disrespect for the leader-figure of Christ. After discussion of value-based leadership O'Toole observes harmony in Georges Seurat's painting "Sunday Afternoon on the Island of La Grande Jatte." Another artistic metaphor describes *Rushmorean* leadership based on the styles of the four U.S. presidents immortalized on Mt. Rushmore. O'Toole recommends four candidates who exhibit value-based leadership styles for a Corporate Mt. Rushmore. Includes bibliographical references and index.
Subject(s): Artist as leader, resistance to change

New
Owen, H. (1999). *The spirit of leadership: Liberating the leader in each of us.* San Francisco: Berrett-Koehler.

Owen, the author of *Open Space Technology*, says that the key to leadership is creating the space to allow Spirit to act in powerful and productive ways. This book describes how leaders can do that, including such strategies as open space technology, organization transformation, and storytelling. Owen also addresses such issues as supporting spirit with structure, leadership in informal organizations, and leadership lessons for the disenfranchised. Includes bibliographical references and index.
Subject(s): Spirit

Palus, C. J., & Horth, D. M. (1996). **Leading creatively: The art of making sense.** *Journal of Aesthetic Education: Special Issue: The Aesthetic Face of Leadership*, 30(4), 53-68.

The authors propose that the processes of leadership are fundamentally art-making. They argue that this art-making is an aesthetic competency that enhances other, more rational-

analytical competencies so often used to face the complex challenges in organizations. Through collaborative inquiry, or co-inquiry, individuals and communities come together to make meaning around what is real, important, and possible. The authors explain how the Leading Creatively program at the Center for Creative Leadership helps leaders to develop these aesthetic competencies: noticing; subtle representation; fluid perspective; right-brain mental processing; personalizing work; skeptical inquiry; shared meaning process; serious play; portraying paradoxes, conflicts, and the unknown; and facility with metaphors. Includes bibliographical references.
Subject(s): Art as metaphor for leadership, sense-making

New
Palus, C. J., & Horth, D. M. (1998). **Leading creatively.** *Leadership in Action, 18*(2), 1-8.

Creative leadership is defined as "the ability to work with people to create shared understanding of complex and rapidly changing situations and to generate possible responses." Creative leaders must develop two sets of competencies: 1) rational skills such as planning, analyzing, and decision making; and 2) aesthetic competencies such as noticing, sense-making, personalizing, legitimizing, intuition, collaborative inquiry, and serious play. This article describes the second set of competencies, their development, their interface, and their practicality in the workplace.
Subject(s): Creative leadership, sense-making

New
Pearman, R. R. (1998). *Hard-wired leadership: Unleashing the power of personality to become a new millennium leader.* Palo Alto, CA: Davies-Black.

Pearman discusses six habits of the mind—communication, problem management, learning, blind spots, team building, and values—and their importance to new millennium leaders. He suggests that we can all learn to adjust the hardwiring in our minds to improve our leadership effectiveness. Within the context of the *Myers-Briggs Type Indicator® (MBTI)* 16 personality types, Pearman introduces 16 mental function patterns. A chapter is devoted to each habit of the mind with charts for each *MBTI* type and suggestions for growth. Includes bibliographical references and index.
Subject(s): Competencies overview, self-knowledge, *Myers-Briggs Type Indicator*

Perreault, G. (1997). **Ethical followers: A link to ethical leadership.** *Journal of Leadership Studies, 4*(1), 78-89.

Perreault considers followers active participants in the leadership process, saying that followers have an ethical responsibility to do two things: "1) follow a leader whose goals and practices are ethical and 2) carry out the goals and practices in an ethical manner." She then lists four components of ethical decision making that followers must possess: the ethical sensitivity to interpret a situation, the ethical reasoning to figure out what one ought to do, the ethical motivation to decide what one intends to do, and the ability to

carry out that decision. Famous cases in which followers both did and did not act ethically, including Watergate, the release of the Pentagon Papers, and the Beech-Nut apple juice scandal, are used to illustrate this decision-making process. Ultimately Perreault argues that both leaders and followers must take ethical responsibility for their behavior. Includes references.
Subject(s): Ethics

Petrick, J. A., & Quinn, J. F. (1997). *Management ethics: Integrity at work.* Thousand Oaks, CA: Sage.

The authors combine a conceptual framework of management ethics with real-life cases to make this book both practical and theoretically sound. First, they identify four processes of management—ethical planning, organizing, leading, and controlling. They then describe seven management clusters: accounting/auditing, finance/investment, marketing/advertising, business management/human resources, technology/quality operations/organizational behavior, public/nonprofit/health care, and international/public policy. Twenty-eight mini-cases, from organizations including Sears, United Way, E.F. Hutton, and Dow Corning, are then used to apply the theories and tools to each process in each cluster. The appendices include six tools and assessment instruments. Also includes index and references.
Subject(s): Integrity

Pfeffer, J. (1992). *Managing with power: Politics and influence in organizations.* Boston: Harvard Business School Press.

A decision changes nothing unless it is implemented. But getting others to do something they wouldn't ordinarily do requires power. Examples from Lyndon Johnson and Henry Kissinger to Henry Ford show how strong leaders amass the support and resources they need to get things done. Pfeffer explores sources of power in organizations, outlines strategies for effectively using power (including timing, interpersonal influences, and symbolic actions), and shows how power is lost. Though power and influence are an organization's "last dirty secret," they provide the means to effect change and bring about innovation. Includes bibliographical references and index.
Subject(s): Power, organizational politics

New
Pickett, L. (1998). **Competencies and managerial effectiveness: Putting competencies to work.** *Public Personnel Management, 27*(1), 103-115.

Pickett, an Australian consultant, describes how organizations can use management competency programs to improve results and increase competitiveness. He says that managers should focus on helping their workers improve in a few key areas rather than overwhelming them with lists of competencies. Each individual competence should be related to workplace practices, expressed as an outcome, capable of assessment, complementary to performance criteria, sensible

to trainees, and transferable. Pickett also identifies the steps in implementing a competency program, including conducting executive briefings, obtaining input on competency outlines, communicating the program, and consolidating the information.
Subject(s): Competencies overview

Pillai, R. (1996). **Crisis and the emergence of charismatic leadership in groups: An experimental investigation.** *Journal of Applied Social Psychology*, *26*(6), 543-562.

Pillai claims that many theories of charismatic leadership focus too heavily on the personal attributes of the charismatic leader and not enough on the situation that fosters the leader's emergence. He believes that crisis situations are important to the emergence of charismatic leadership. This article reports on a laboratory study of 96 undergraduate university students. Sixteen groups of six members each participated in a simulated crisis situation to provide data on leader emergence and follower reactions. Pillai concluded that a crisis highlights the inferential and attributional process among followers. Includes bibliographical references.
Subject(s): Charismatic leadership, emergence of leadership

Plas, J. M. (1996). *Person-centered leadership: An American approach to participatory management.* Thousand Oaks, CA: Sage.

Despite this country's reverence for the individual, American business has traditionally neglected individuals, paying attention to problems, not people. Plas offers a model of person-centered leadership that "does not just focus on workers, it focuses on the *individual* worker." Plas uses companies including Southwest Airlines, Wal-Mart, and FedEx to illustrate her theory and offers readers a strategy for making their own organizations person-centered. Information boxes and pulled quotes highlight key concepts, and each chapter includes a list of references for further reading. Includes bibliographical references and index.
Subject(s): Participation

New
Poell, R. F., Van der Krogt, F. J., & Wildemeersch, D. (1999). **Strategies in organizing work-related learning projects.** *Human Resource Development Quarterly*, *10*(1), 43-61.

The network theory of learning in organizations identifies workers, managers, and HRD staff as actors who organize learning through their interactions. Research has identified four ideal types of learning networks—vertical, horizontal, external, and liberal—but few studies have addressed what strategies individual actors within the networks use. This study used comparative analysis of 16 learning network cases to determine which of the four strategies individual workers employ: direct representation, continuous adaptation, professional innovation, or individual negotiation. The authors found that the type of work being done influenced the strategies used and that different actors within a network

often employed different learning strategies. Includes bibliographical references.
Subject(s): Learning competency, organizational learning

Prince, F. A. (1993). *C and the box: A paradigm parable.* San Diego, CA: Pfeiffer.

This five-minute cartoon-illustrated book is intended to deliver a simple message. *C* goes through life as a conformist until it finds a coil that allows it to spring out of its box and begin a life filled with creativity. The message is to seek a new outlook and new ways to solve problems, overcome conformity and bureaucracy, and discover inner strength and motivation. Also available on video.
Subject(s): Creative problem solving

New
Proudlove, N. (1998). **'Search widely, choose wisely': A proposal for linking judgemental decision-making and creative problem-solving approaches.** *Creativity and Innovation Management*, *7*(2), 73-82.

Efforts to increase creativity often focus on divergent activities, like brainstorming, that create new options and possibilities. Equally important is convergence, or narrowing and selecting among options. In this article Proudlove describes a qualitative method of making convergent choices —criterion matrix—and a quantitative method—the Judgemental Analysis System. He says that while these methods are not comprehensive, both can help individuals and teams make decisions. Includes bibliographical references.
Subject(s): Creative decision making

Quigley, J. V. (1993). *Vision: How leaders develop it, share it, and sustain it.* New York: McGraw-Hill.

Quigley states that many corporations lack a vision that has broad-based commitment. In this book he outlines a plan for the formation of a new corporate vision, widespread communication techniques, stewardship, renewal, and sustaining strategy. He also addresses the basic human need for meaning and fulfillment in the workplace. "Rx for Leaders" throughout each chapter offer quick tips for easy reference. Examples of successful visions at work highlight the lessons. Includes an index.
Subject(s): Vision

Quinn, R. E. (1996). *Deep change: Discovering the leader within.* San Francisco: Jossey-Bass.

Quinn describes painful, yet rewarding, experiences of deep personal and organizational change. He argues that every person can be a change agent who demands excellence of self and who improves his or her surrounding systems. Each chapter contains a lesson on how to "walk naked into the land of uncertainty." Some of the leadership lessons are: lifelong learning, finding and maintaining vitality, acting with integrity, and building interdependent relationships. The reflection questions at the end of each chapter are organized into personal and organizational steps to achieve change.

Quinn recommends writing responses in a journal to capture key learning moments. Includes brief bibliographical references and index.
Subject(s): Personal change

Quinn, R. E., Faerman, S. R., Thompson, M. P., & McGrath, M. R. (1996). *Becoming a master manager: A competency framework* (2nd ed.). New York: Wiley.

This textbook is for business schools that want to teach more than technical competence. It helps to teach the paradoxical thinking that is required by managers in a rapidly changing world. The Competing Values Model illustrates the struggles between flexibility versus control and focus on internal versus external values. Each chapter describes a different managerial role—mentor, facilitator, monitor, coordinator, director, producer, broker, and innovator. There are activities for learning competencies in each role and for integrating two or more roles. Includes bibliographical references and index.
Subject(s): Competencies overview, values, textbook

New
Ramamoorthy, N., & Carroll, S. J. (1998). **Individualism/ collectivism orientations and reactions toward alternative human resource management practices.** *Human Relations*, *51*(5), 571-588.

In this study over 300 business students were given instruments measuring their individualism/collectivism (I/C) orientation, and were then given a scale that measured their reaction to different HR practices, including selection, appraisal, reward systems, and training. Analysis showed that an individual's I/C orientation was correlated with his or her response to certain HR practices. The authors suggest that HR professionals should be aware of how individuals may react to specific practices when hiring workers and implementing new policies. Includes bibliographical references and copies of the scales used.
Subject(s): Collectivism, individualism

Ready, D. A., Valentino, D. J., & Gouillart, F. J. (1994). *Champions of change: A global report on leading business transformation.* Lexington, MA: International Consortium for Executive Research and Gemini Consulting.

This is a report of the 1994 International Competitive Capabilities Project. More than 1,450 managers and executives from 12 global corporations responded to a survey about organizational effectiveness and leadership competencies. Researchers drew six conclusions: 1) transformation is not a program or a one-time event—it is a regenerative process; 2) sustainable competitive advantage depends on flexibility and on being close to the customer; 3) evidence suggests that we are not prepared for the future; 4) the new leadership challenge is to continually renew organizations; 5) for leaders to develop, they must have opportunity, organizational support, and self-determination; and 6) there is a large gap between the current global mind-set and the one we'll need in the future.
Subject(s): Change

New
Reiter-Palmon, R., Mumford, M. D., & Threlfall, K. V. (1998). **Solving everyday problems creatively: The role of problem construction and personality type.** *Creativity Research Journal*, *11*(3), 187-197.

How one defines a problem is often key to determining what the solution will be. This study attempted to measure whether problem construction and solution development are affected by an individual's personality. The authors asked students to complete instruments that identified personality types and problem construction ability, and then participate in a problem-solving task. They analyzed the data and found that there were connections between these factors: individuals who were able to construct a problem that fit their personality were more likely to find a successful solution. Includes bibliographical references.
Subject(s): Creative problem solving

Renesch, J. (Ed.). (1994). *Leadership in a new era: Visionary approaches to the biggest crisis of our time.* San Francisco: New Leaders Press.

Twenty-three leadership practitioners and scholars share their expectations for leaders of the near future. The issues new leaders will face are: dealing with challenging times, welcoming change, and seeking responsibility. Essays include: "Cinderella Can Be Tough, John Wayne Can Cry" by Barbara R. Hauser; "Diversity and Leadership Development" by Ann M. Morrison; "An Adventure in Enlightened Leadership" by Ed Oakley; "Leadership Challenges in Technical Organizations" by Peter K. Krembs; "Leading Change: The Leader as the Chief Transformation Officer" by Warren Bennis; "A Sacred Responsibility" by Barbara Shipka; "Servant-Leadership: Toward a New Era of Caring" by Larry C. Spears; "The Innocent Leader: Accepting Paradox" by E. Magaziner; "Leadership: The Values Game" by Carol McCall; "Attributes of Leadership: A Checklist" by Max DePree; and "Winning Trust" by Perry Pascarella.
Subject(s): Vision, values

Richardson, J. (1997). **Strategic leadership: From fragmented thinking to interdisciplinary perspectives.** *A Leadership Journal: Women in Leadership—Sharing the Vision*, *1*(2), 91-100.

According to Richardson, a community activist and professor of environmental studies, leaders today have "developed fragmented perspectives" and lack a "comprehensive understanding" of the problems they face. She uses examples from her experience in the environmental movement, including the debate over the management of Lake Champlain, to illustrate how destructive a fragmented approach can be. This article encourages leaders to use a holistic, strategic approach to solving problems and offers ten suggestions on how to do this, including know thyself, share knowledge with others, and know the local culture. Includes bibliographical references.
Subject(s): Strategic leadership, environmental leadership

New

Rijsman, J. B. (1999). **Role-playing and attitude change: How helping your boss can change the meaning of work.** *European Journal of Work and Organizational Psychology*, 8(10), 73-85.

Classic research on role-playing argues that when people take on a role their experience influences how they view that role. Rijsman, after examining the structural aspects of role play, says that this interpretation may not be accurate. He notes that in experimental situations, only subjects who have volunteered to play a role are studied. This automatically eliminates anyone who does not already want to collaborate in the activity. Rijsman concludes that role-playing actually demonstrates a follower's willingness to support a leader's work and that positive attitudes develop as a result of this co-ownership of the work. Includes bibliographical references.
Subject(s): Experience, role-playing

Ripley, R. E., & Ripley, M. J. (1993). **Empowerment: What to do with troubling employees?** *Journal of Managerial Psychology*, 8(3), 3-9.

Troubling employees are described as immature, demanding, blaming, incompetent, uncooperative, passive-aggressive, or psychologically unhealthy. In other words they are employees a manager would be afraid to empower. Ripley and Ripley discuss empowering solutions such as modeling from the top and concentrating on objective, nonthreatening training in the areas of quality and continuous improvement.
Subject(s): Empowerment

Robbins, S. P., & Hunsaker, P. L. (1996). *Training in interpersonal skills: TIPS for managing people at work* (2nd ed.). Upper Saddle River, NJ: Prentice Hall.

This textbook supports the notion that skills training supersedes theoretical understanding. The TIPS learning model contains ten actions: assess basic skill level, review key concepts, test knowledge, identify behaviors to learn, observe behaviors, practice behaviors, assess deficiencies, test understanding, do experiential learning exercises, and develop an action plan. These actions are applied to leadership skills in the chapters: "Self-awareness," "Providing Feedback," "Empowering," "Coaching," and "Building Teams."
Subject(s): Competencies overview, textbook

Rosen, R. H., & Brown, P. B. (1996). *Leading people: Transforming business from the inside out.* New York: Viking.

The authors contend that leading is hard work made possible by adopting eight principles: vision, trust, participation, learning, diversity, creativity, integrity, and community. In-depth interviews with 36 leaders and reviews of their organizations' documents, awards, speeches, and videos paint profiles of each leader's unique strengths. James DePreist, conductor and music director of the Oregon Symphony Orchestra, serves as an example of a visionary leader. Douglas G. Myers, executive director of the San Diego Zoo,

provides a lesson in trust. The story of Alan Mulally, senior vice president of Boeing's Airplane Development division, illustrates the value of participation and teamwork. The work of Shirley DeLibero, executive director of the New Jersey Transit Corporation, provides a lesson in building community. The remaining leaders each have a leadership lesson to teach based on one of the eight principles. Includes index.
Subject(s): Competencies overview

New

Rothwell, W. J. (1999). *The action learning guidebook: A real-time strategy for problem solving, training design, and employee development.* San Francisco: Jossey-Bass.

Action learning is a real-time learning experience that teaches an individual or group while at the same time meeting an organizational need. In this book Rothwell describes how to facilitate and evaluate action learning programs, including how to determine what activities are appropriate for action learning, how to incorporate it into training programs, and what the facilitator's role should be. Worksheets and questionnaires for planning action learning projects are provided, along with a computer disk that allows readers to customize worksheets. Includes bibliographical references, an index, and an assessment instrument for action learning facilitators.
Subject(s): Action learning

New

Runco, M. A., & Pritzker, S. R. (Eds.). (1999). *Encyclopedia of creativity.* San Diego, CA: Academic Press.

This two-volume reference set presents articles about the major topics in creativity, including theories, research methods, and common fields of study. Articles address issues such as birth order, education, design, serendipity, and conformity. Significant individuals, including Georgia O'Keeffe, Sylvia Plath, Sigmund Freud, and Vincent van Gogh, are also profiled. Each entry contains an outline, glossary, cross-references, and bibliography. Includes index.
Subject(s): Creativity

New

Ruscio, J., Whitney, D. M., & Amabile, T. M. (1998). **Looking inside the fishbowl of creativity: Verbal and behavioral predictors of creative performance.** *Creativity Research Journal*, 11(3), 243-263.

In order to determine how intrinsic motivation affects product creativity, the authors had 150 college students complete a motivational measure and then perform tasks in three different domains of creativity. Students completed a problem-solving activity, made a collage, and wrote an American haiku poem, and the creativity of their results was judged. Analysis showed that while intrinsic motivation (measured as "involvement in the task") did affect the creative product, it was only one component. Other influential factors included domain-relevant skills, such as assuredness, and creativity-relevant processes, including striving and using a wide focus. Includes bibliographical references.

Subject(s): Creativity

Sankowsky, D. (1995). **The charismatic leader as narcissist: Understanding the abuse of power.** *Organizational Dynamics*, *23*(4), 57-71.

Research on leadership today often focuses on the empowerment of followers, but here Sankowsky describes how leaders can misuse their power. This article concentrates on one form of power, symbolic status, in which leaders act as parent figures and guide the belief systems of their followers. Sankowsky defines symbolic status, explains how leaders use it to manipulate their followers, and describes typical follower response to these charismatic leaders. Examples of such leaders, from Steve Jobs at Apple to Michael Eisner at Disney, are used to illustrate the concepts. Includes bibliographical references.

Subject(s): Negative views of charisma, abuse of power

Sayles, L. R. (1993). *The working leader: The triumph of high performance over conventional management principles.* New York: Free Press.

Astute working leaders do not presume systems are designed efficiently, nor do they see "customer consciousness" or "quality consciousness" as compartmentalized activities. Through case studies Sayles shows that leaders who concentrate on work-flow relationships between jobs, functions, and departments can increase the sense of responsibility and motivation among subordinates. This effective management of work systems leads to high performance in quality, efficiency, and service. Includes bibliographical references and index.

Subject(s): Competencies overview

Sayles, L. R. (1996). *High performance leadership: Creating value in a world of change.* Portland, OR: Productivity Press.

This pocket-sized book imparts leadership advice in a one-hour read. It is an updated and synthesized version of Sayles's book *The Working Leader* (McGraw-Hill, 1993). The reader is reminded of commonsense "old style" leadership skills and introduced to new competencies for changing work environments. Includes brief bibliographical notes.

Subject(s): Competencies overview

New
Schaefer, C., & Voors, T. (1996). *Vision in action: Working with soul and spirit in small organizations* (2nd ed.). Hudson, NY: Lindisfarne Press.

Described as a "workbook for those involved in social creation," this British book describes how individuals can develop small, healthy organizations that will benefit society. Leadership is key in this process because leaders must actively "integrate" an organization, dividing tasks among workers while ensuring that everyone works toward a single goal and vision. Exercises and case studies address issues

including why initiatives fail, listening skills, funding start-up initiatives, and long-range planning. The final chapter, "Signs of Hope," offers descriptions of current social transformation initiatives, such as Waldorf schools, as role models.

Subject(s): Values

New
Scholtes, P. R. (1998). *The leader's handbook: Making things happen, getting things done.* New York: McGraw-Hill.

Scholtes says that in the past, effective leaders needed to be forceful, task oriented, and bottom-line driven, but that today's leaders need a different set of competencies to succeed. These new skills include understanding systems, using planning and problem solving, using different types of learning, and a knowledge of human behavior. This handbook offers practical advice on how to apply these new competencies to everyday work, using stories, exercises, graphs, and cartoons to illustrate concepts. Each chapter contains activities and recommended readings. Includes index.

Subject(s): Competencies overview

Schrage, M. (1997). **The Gary Burton Trio.** *Fast Company*, *1*(6), 110-113.

Schrage conducts an interview with Gary Burton, a jazz vibraphonist and educator. They discuss the similarities between jazz combos, known for their creativity and spontaneity, and management teams. Burton compares orchestra conductors to autocratic CEOs. Both jazz combos and management teams need strong leaders to carry the vision and to help musicians and managers learn new riffs or ways of work, discipline, and spontaneity. Burton explains that strong leaders can enable an active flow of creativity as long as the vision of the group is maintained.

Subject(s): Jazz music as metaphor for leadership

Schultz, M. C. (1992). **Leadership and the power circle.** *Human Systems Management*, *11*(4), 213-217.

An individual's power circle is comprised of position, expertise, and referent power. Awareness of one's power-base strengths and weaknesses maximizes effective leadership. Suggesting that power usage is determined by situations rather than preferred style, Schultz concludes that effectiveness is achieved through self-recognition and self-understanding. Strengthening power effectiveness in particular situations enhances one's future power potential in similar situations, leading to enhanced leadership abilities.

Subject(s): Power bases

New
Schuster, F. E. (1998). *Employee-centered management: A strategy for high commitment and involvement.* Westport, CT: Quorum Books.

Schuster describes the kind of organizational culture that promotes employee commitment, innovation, and high productivity. His seven-step Strategy A process for develop-

ing such a high-involvement culture is: 1) use a valid organizational culture survey to determine the company's baseline, 2) identify and act upon key opportunities for improvement, 3) use evaluation and reward practices for effective management of people as well as for productivity and profit, 4) remove artificial barriers such as executive dining rooms and parking spaces, 5) report to employees about changes already made and solicit their involvement in planning new changes, 6) conduct a new organizational culture survey to determine changes in attitudes, and 7) compare the survey data to measures of organizational performance. An appendix details this type of baseline study, intervention, and follow-up study at a Canadian company. Includes bibliographical references and index.
Subject(s): Participation

Schuster, F. E., Morden, D. L., Baker, T. E., McKay, I. S., Dunning, K. E., & Hagan, C. M. (1997). **Management practice, organization climate, and performance: An exploratory study.** *Journal of Applied Behavioral Science*, *33*(2), 209-226.

This article reports on a five-year experiment in a Canadian dairy-processing and distribution firm. To develop and sustain competitive advantage, the firm recognized the need for employee-centered management. Over five years the new structure was implemented in seven steps: 1) develop a baseline of employee participation, performance, and satisfaction; 2) initiate improvements in communication, rewards, and shared decision making; 3) change executive evaluation and reward practices to measure and compensate for human development as well as production; 4) remove barriers to participation; 5) involve employees in planning the changes; 6) measure the changes in participation, performance, and satisfaction; and 7) use criteria to reinforce or modify the strategies. The experiment resulted in a significant growth in operating income as well as significant improvements in employee morale and commitment. Includes bibliographical references.
Subject(s): Participation

New
Service, R. W., & Boockholdt, J. L. (1998). **Factors leading to innovation: A study of managers' perspectives.** *Creativity Research Journal*, *11*(4), 295-307.

The authors conducted a literature review to determine what gives an organization the ability to innovate, and they identify eight contributing factors: management, structure, human resources, innovation players, organizational culture, external environment, innovation characteristics, and marketing. They then conducted a survey of over 150 managers and their supervisors to determine what factors these groups believed influenced innovation. They found differences between what managers and their supervisors perceived as important factors, and from these findings developed a model in which factors affecting innovation are mediated by an organization's levels of commitment and

communication. Includes bibliographical references.
Subject(s): Innovation

New
Shamir, B., & Howell, J. (1999). **Organizational and contextual influences on the emergence and effectiveness of charismatic leadership.** *Leadership Quarterly: Special Issue, Part I: Charismatic and Transformational Leadership: Taking Stock of the Present and Future*, *10*(2), 257-283.

The authors argue that charismatic leadership emerges and is effective in 15 organizational situations. These include crises, psychologically weak situations such as ambiguity, dynamic situations that encourage innovation, adaptive organizational culture, and the entrepreneurial or renewal stages of organizational life. The authors warn that the 15 conditions identified in this article are not necessary or sufficient to nurture charismatic leadership on their own. The relationship between leader and follower characteristics, behaviors, and actions within a given context produces the phenomenon of charismatic leadership. Includes bibliographical references.
Subject(s): Charismatic leadership

Shaw, R. B. (1997). ***Trust in the balance: Building successful organizations on results, integrity, and concern.*** San Francisco: Jossey-Bass.

According to Shaw, trust is an organizational factor that must be integrated into the very structure of organizations. He addresses trust at four different organizational levels: individual credibility, one-to-one collaboration, team performance, and overall organizational vitality. Two assessment surveys —for organization and leadership—are included to help the reader fulfill the author's three key imperatives: achieving results, acting with integrity, and demonstrating concern. Includes bibliographical references and index.
Subject(s): Trust, integrity

Shelton, K. (1997). ***Beyond counterfeit leadership: How you can become a more authentic leader.*** Provo, UT: Executive Excellence.

Shelton claims that our society is abundant with counterfeit leaders—executives, politicians, and celebrities who have more visibility than credibility. Counterfeit leaders commit more acts of deceit than great accomplishments. He encourages readers to face their own counterfeit qualities— incapacitation, imitation, ignorance, indolence, irresponsibility, and insecurity—and become authentic leaders who get quality results and build strong relationships. A model of Shelton's leadership cycle shows readers how to enter at any stage of counterfeit leadership, understand the causes, find a cure, and achieve authentic leadership. Warren Bennis wrote the foreword to this book.
Subject(s): Credibility, authentic leadership

New

Shenkman, M. H. (1996). *The strategic heart: Using the new science to lead growing organizations.* Westport, CT: Praeger.

Shenkman says that the notion of businesses as rational, ruthless organizations that are best run like military units is false. Instead he advocates using the newly emerging theories of complexity and flow to understand how organizations work. The first half of the book describes how complexity can help leaders unleash the power of their organizations, and focuses specifically on values and mission. The second half explains how to use Csikszentmihalyi's concept of flow to develop high-performance individuals, and includes discussions of responsibility and vision. Used together these ideas can help leaders create a strategic organization, which Shenkman describes as having "the courage and the ability to aspire to . . . greatness." Includes index.

Subject(s): Strategic leadership, flow, complexity

Shipka, B. (1997). *Leadership in a challenging world: A sacred journey.* Boston: Butterworth-Heinemann.

Shipka calls her book "a walking stick to support your walk on the path of your life's work—the work of providing leadership in the business world during times of enormous change and transition." She describes eight powers—aliveness, passion, integrity, authenticity, relatedness, expression, perspective, and reverence—and how business leaders can harness these powers to make their work benefit humanity. Each chapter contains quotations, illustrations, and questions for reflection. Includes bibliographical references and index.

Subject(s): Values

New

Simmons, S., & Simmons, J. C. (1997). *Measuring emotional intelligence: The groundbreaking guide to applying the principles of emotional intelligence.* Arlington, TX: Summit Publishing Group.

The authors have three goals in this book: to describe all the facets of emotional intelligence, to demonstrate how to precisely measure these facets, and to show how to use this knowledge to build success. First, the 13 facets of character that make up emotional intelligence are identified: emotional energy, stress, optimism, self-esteem, commitment to work, attention to detail, desire for change, courage, self-direction, assertiveness, tolerance, consideration for others, and sociability. Each characteristic is addressed in a chapter that discusses how to measure it and offers specific advice on how to identify, modify, and manage people with different degrees of that characteristic. Special attention is given to the use of the *Simmons Personal Survey*, an instrument developed by the authors to measure emotional intelligence. The authors describe how to use this survey to hire employees and to develop relationships. Includes index and a list of survey providers.

Subject(s): Emotional intelligence

New

Simon, H. A. (1997). **Information tidal wave? Expert decision making and the managerial future.** *Monash Mt. Eliza Business Review, 1*(1), 30-37.

Simon, a Nobel Prize-winning economist, says that technological advances have the potential to change the way managers make decisions. In this article he first identifies two types of thinking involved in decision making, analytic and intuitive. He then describes how most individuals do not use completely rational decision-making processes but instead make decisions by choosing a solution that is as good as can be attained with reasonable effort. Simon says that the computer, and particularly communication networks like the World Wide Web, will allow organizations to rely more on computers' artificial intelligence and decentralize decision making.

Subject(s): Decision making

Sims, H. P., Jr., & Manz, C. C. (1996). *Company of heroes: Unleashing the power of self-leadership.* New York: Wiley.

The authors of *SuperLeadership* (Prentice Hall, 1989) revisit their theory of the enabling leader who teaches others to lead themselves. This book compares superleadership to other frameworks, especially visionary and heroic leadership. It suggests four steps to apply the superleadership theory and create an organization of self-leaders, a company of heroes. The four steps are: 1) leaders must practice self-leadership behavior, 2) encourage followers to practice self-leadership, 3) foster teamwork, and 4) build a company culture of self-leadership. Examples of superleaders are former U.S. President Jimmy Carter, whose hands-on role with Habitat for Humanity encouraged thousands of new volunteers, and Jack Welch, CEO of GE, whose town meeting-style Work Out sessions broke down barriers between workers and management and revitalized flagging productivity. Includes bibliographical references and index.

Subject(s): Self-leadership

New

Slye, J. M. (1998). **Orville Wright did not have a pilot's license.** *The Public Manager, 27*(2), 17-23.

Companies like 3M, DuPont, and Coca-Cola have long traditions of encouraging creativity and innovation. Slye argues that the federal government must also develop an environment that encourages creativity on a day-to-day basis. This article describes how departments in some federal agencies, including the Departments of Labor and Agriculture, have increased efficiency and effectiveness by encouraging creative problem solving. Suggestions on how to nurture creativity, such as allowing mistakes and dedicating time and space to play, are also provided.

Subject(s): Creative problem solving

New

Smith, P. M. (1998). *Rules and tools for leaders: A down-to-earth guide to effective managing.* Garden City Park, NY: Avery.

Smith intends this handbook as an everyday tool for leaders. This source contains 24 brief chapters delineating Smith's leadership advice on topics ranging from the organizational mission, decision making, time management, and staffing, and includes delicate issues such as communicating with media, leading in crises, and balancing the role of the leader's spouse. Smith also includes a brief description of 30 leadership fundamentals. The appendices to the source include quick reference checklists for many of the topics discussed within the chapters as well as case studies of challenging situations. Finally, the book lists additional sources and programs teaching leadership skills.
Subject(s): Leadership competencies

Smith, R. A. (1996). **Leadership as aesthetic process.** *Journal of Aesthetic Education: Special Issue: The Aesthetic Face of Leadership, 30*(4), 39-52.

The philosophy of aesthetics considers the nature of art, its interpretation and appreciation, its critical evaluation, and its cultural context. The process of leadership as defined by Drath and Palus in *Making Common Sense* (Center for Creative Leadership, 1994) considers the efforts of a community of practice to achieve a common understanding. Smith links the two concepts to explain leadership as an aesthetic process. The result is a creative process of continual learning and social responsibility. Includes bibliographical references.
Subject(s): Art as metaphor for leadership

Smither, R. D. (1991). **The return of the authoritarian manager.** *Training, 28*(11), 40-44.

The authoritarian style of management remains an effective alternative in many cases. Following are some situations where authoritarianism is likely to work well: when employees are poorly educated or do not want responsibility for decision making, when productivity is more important than employee satisfaction, and when short-term performance goals must be met. While *authoritarian management* is not a synonym for *oppressive* or *punitive management*, there is no evidence that teamwork or quality circles in themselves will result in improved productivity.
Subject(s): Authority

New

Solomon, R. C. (1999). *A better way to think about business: How personal integrity leads to corporate success.* New York: Oxford University Press.

This book aims to be a lesson in business ethics. It is about the values that constitute integrity, the ways to reinforce integrity, and the ways in which integrity is compromised. One section of the book defines 45 business virtues in encyclopedic form. Each virtue is explained in a mythologi-

cal and a business context, is considered for its usefulness to self and others, and is compared at the extremes of excess and deficiency. Includes bibliographical references and index.
Subject(s): Integrity

Sosik, J. J., Avolio, B. J., & Kahai, S. S. (1997). **Effects of leadership style and anonymity on group potency and effectiveness in a group decision support system environment.** *Journal of Applied Psychology, 82*(1), 89-103.

This article reports on a laboratory study of transactional versus transformational leadership style and their effects on group decision making when using a group decision support system (GDSS). The GDSS is an interactive network of computers used to generate solutions to unstructured problems. The anonymity of members using this system enhances transformational leadership and group potency. Includes bibliographical references. A similar study is reported in Kahai, Sosik, and Avolio (1997), "Effects of leadership style and problem structure on work group process and outcomes in an electronic meeting system environment," *Personnel Psychology, 50*(1), 121-146.
Subject(s): Decision making and technology

New

Sosik, J. J., & Dworakivsky, A. C. (1998). **Self-concept based aspects of the charismatic leader: More than meets the eye.** *Leadership Quarterly: Special Issue: 360-Degree Feedback in Leadership Research, 9*(4), 503-526.

The authors propose a model based on theories in the literature of leadership and emotional intelligence. The model represents the culmination of charismatic leadership by linking self-awareness to purpose in life and self-monitoring behavior. A sample of information technology managers and subordinates tested the model via a series of questionnaires. The results generally support the model and suggest that managers can improve leadership skills through awareness of their purpose in life and self-monitoring behavior. Includes bibliographical references.
Subject(s): Charismatic leadership

New

Sosik, J. J., Kahai, S. S., & Avolio, B. J. (1998). **Transformational leadership and dimensions of creativity: Motivating idea generation in computer-mediated groups.** *Creativity Research Journal, 11*(2), 111-121.

In this study the authors use group decision support system (GDSS) software to determine whether transformational leadership and anonymity affect a group's creativity in brainstorming exercises. Four measures—fluency, flexibility, originality, and elaboration—were used to analyze the creativity of 36 groups of students. The results showed that when a group's leader used transformational leadership techniques, such as individualized consideration and inspirational motivation, creativity in the exercise did increase slightly. Anonymity also had a slightly positive impact on

creativity. The authors suggest that organizations hoping to increase creativity should train GDSS facilitators in transformational leadership. Includes bibliographical references.
Subject(s): Creative problem solving, transformational leadership, decision making and technology

Spears, L. C. (1995). *Reflections on leadership: How Robert K. Greenleaf's theory of servant-leadership influenced today's top management thinkers.* New York: Wiley.

This collection of 27 essays on servant leadership begins with two essays written by Robert K. Greenleaf. *Life's Choices and Markers* describes the five significant influences in Greenleaf's life from which he evolved the philosophy of leadership through service. *Reflections from Experience* is published for the first time in this book. Over the past two decades the philosophy of servant leadership has been applied in business, trusteeship, community-leadership programs, leadership studies, and personal growth. Paying tribute to Greenleaf, the man, and servant leadership as an emerging leadership paradigm, are authors such as M. Scott Peck; Peter Senge; the Greenleaf Center's director, Larry Spears; and Robert Greenleaf's son, Newcomb Greenleaf. Includes bibliographical references and index.
Subject(s): Servant leadership

Spears, L. C. (Ed.). (1998). *Insights on leadership: Service, stewardship, spirit, and servant-leadership.* New York: Wiley.

Robert Greenleaf's theory of servant leadership has influenced many of today's prominent leadership thinkers. This sequel to Spears's *Reflections on Leadership* (Wiley, 1995) contains over 30 essays by respected thinkers in the field, including Stephen Covey, Peter Block, Margaret Wheatley, James Autry, and Ken Blanchard. Essays are organized around the themes of service, stewardship, spirit, and servant leadership. Includes index.
Subject(s): Servant leadership

New
Stolovitch, H. D., & Keeps, E. J. (Eds.). (1999). *Handbook of human performance technology: Improving individual and organizational performance worldwide* (2nd ed.). San Francisco: Jossey-Bass.

This reference guide offers both academic and practical information on Human Performance Technology (HPT), a field of study centered on "striving to improve human performance in the workplace." Sections describe the history and development of HPT, the field's central process model, particular ways of achieving performance results, meeting performance goals, and HPT applications in real-world settings. The second edition includes new information on international performance management, effective interventions, and performance-based training. Includes bibliographical references and name and subject indexes.
Subject(s): Competencies overview

New
Tan, G. (1998). **Managing creativity in organizations: A total system approach.** *Creativity and Innovation Management, 7*(1), 23-31.

Organizations often use a single approach to encourage creativity, but Tan argues that an integrated, total system approach is needed. This article provides a framework explaining how leaders can foster creativity in their organizations. Tan argues that organizations have four subsystems—culture, management, techno-structural subsystems, and people—that can create barriers to creativity. Leaders must use a combination of three types of interventions to overcome these barriers. These interventions are cultural, through training and team building; organizational, through redesigning systems; and training and development, directed at changing people's behavior. The interventions allow the three ingredients of creativity—foundations, competencies, and support—to flourish and lead to creative outcomes that will benefit the organization as a whole. Includes bibliographical references.
Subject(s): Creativity, systems in organizations

Tannen, D. (1994). *Talking from 9 to 5: How women's and men's conversational styles affect who gets heard, who gets credit, and what gets done at work.* New York: William Morrow.

This is the third book in Tannen's implicational hierarchy on communication (*That's Not What I Meant!: How Conversational Style Makes or Breaks Your Relations with Others*, 1986, and *You Just Don't Understand: Women and Men in Conversation*, 1991). For this book Tannen collected transcripts of business conversations, both one-on-one and in groups, to research how conversational style at work determines credibility. Discussion of conversational style remains focused on personal influences such as gender differences, geographic region, ethnicity, class, and age. Includes bibliographical references and index.
Subject(s): Communication

Theus, K. T. (1995). **Communication in a power vacuum: Sense-making and enactment during crisis-induced departures.** *Human Resource Management: Special Issue on Leadership Transitions, 34*(1), 27-49.

The case of American University President Richard Berendzen's 1990 resignation following his arrest for making obscene telephone calls is presented. That kind of sudden departure can have numerous disruptive influences on an organization, such as emotional instability, damaged reputation, and a power vacuum. Theus compares Berendzen's case to similar situations at Kodak and American Express to frame a model for leading effectively during times of transition.
Subject(s): Communication, sense-making

New

Thompson, J. L. (1997). *Strategic management: Awareness and change* (3rd ed.). Boston: International Thomson Business Press.

   This textbook helps managers and students learn how to be strategically aware of corporate position and opportunities for change, how changes actually happen, and how to effectively manage the change process. There are chapters that describe strategic leadership, decision making, culture, and values as the forces that drive organizational strategy. Chapters include learning objectives, key concepts, suggested readings, a variety of short and long case studies to illustrate a variety of strategies, quotations, and suggestions for research assignments. Includes author and subject indexes. A related website, www.itbp.com, offers case study updates, teaching notes, and links to other strategy websites.
   Subject(s): Strategic leadership, textbook

New

Thoms, P., & Greenberger, D. B. (1998). **A test of vision training and potential antecedents to leaders' visioning ability.** *Human Resource Development Quarterly*, 9(1), 3-24.

   Visioning is the ability to create a positive image of an organization in the future—an important step in an organization's strategic planning and leadership. For this study the authors surveyed managers before and after visioning training to determine whether structured training could improve an individual's visioning skills. They measured factors including future time perspective, positivism, learning ability, and reaction to training. Factor analysis of the data showed that training did improve individuals' visioning skills, especially in individuals with more positive outlooks. An invited reaction by James R. Meindl questions both the value of visionary leadership and the validity of the measurement criteria used in this study. Includes bibliographical references.
   Subject(s): Vision

Townsend, P. L., & Gebhardt, J. E. (1997). *Five-star leadership: The art and strategy of creating leaders at every level.* New York: Wiley.

   This book assumes that leadership is a behavior, not a position. It revisits old management theories, total quality management, and military leadership to build a case for the distribution of power, leadership, and development throughout an organization. The authors suggest skills to develop in self and others for empowering leaders at every level. Among the appendices are: the description of a new military philosophy called *Total Quality Leadership*; more than a dozen lists of leadership skills, principles, practices, and competencies drawn from the literature; and an article on love and leadership reprinted from the *Marine Corps Gazette* (1982). Includes a bibliography and index.
   Subject(s): Empowerment

New

Trollestad, C. (1998). **Leading by values.** *efmd FORUM*, 98(1), 45-49.

   Trollestad says that a slow but steady shift in cultural values is redefining work as a place where people find meaning and fulfillment. He interviewed managers for an exploratory study and found that while the majority held a traditional and instrumental view of management, a significant minority held a more "communicative and voluntaristic view" that emphasizes values in the workplace. In this new paradigm of leadership, managers who create a base of common organizational values and encourage open communication can create both a respect for the individual and increased productivity. However, Trollestad also warns against the danger of imposing totalitarian value systems from above, saying that leaders should draw these common values from the existing spirit of the organization.
   Subject(s): Values

New

Tropman, J. E. (1998). *The management of ideas in the creating organization.* Westport, CT: Quorum Books.

   Tropman introduces the concepts of IdeaManagement and IdeaLeadership to inspire organizational commitment toward the nurturing of new ideas. IdeaManagers are those in a position to offer support and resources for idea development. IdeaLeaders are those who think of new ideas and generate excitement about the possibilities. They are found throughout an organization, and most employees fill this leadership role at some point. Five C's support the concept: 1) Characteristics of the managers and leaders, 2) their Competencies, 3) Conditions within the organization, 4) Contexts dictated by the environment, and 5) development of positive Change. Includes bibliographical references and index.
   Subject(s): Innovation

Turner, J. R., Grude, K. V., & Thurloway, L. (Eds.). (1996). *The project manager as change agent: Leadership, influence and negotiation.* New York: McGraw-Hill.

   This textbook helps project managers learn to lead in three directions: downward—leading a team to complete a project on time and within budget; outward—influencing and winning support from peers; and upward—serving as project ambassador to win support from those in power. To do this project managers must understand the nature of change and the culture of projects. Chapters focus on organizational change, teams and team roles, internal marketing, and ethics. Case studies throughout illustrate project managers as change agents. There are tools for diagnosing change and determining the health of a project. Includes bibliographical references and indexes.
   Subject(s): Leader as change agent, project management, textbook

New

Ulrich, D., Zenger, J., & Smallwood, N. (1999). *Results-based leadership.* Boston: Harvard Business School Press.

The heart of the authors' argument is that "effective leaders get results." This book describes four areas in which leaders should deliver results, and the action needed to do that. To get employee results leaders must invest in human capital, for organization results they have to create capabilities, customer results require building firm equity, and to get investor results leaders must build shareholder value. Worksheets and surveys help readers apply these ideas to their organizations. Includes index.

Subject(s): Competencies overview

Van Velsor, E., & Hughes, M. W. (1990). *Gender differences in the development of managers: How women managers learn from experience.* Greensboro, NC: Center for Creative Leadership.

Based on studies of 189 male and 78 female managers, this report investigates gender differences in experiential learning. Experiences are categorized into 16 key events, such as assignments, hardships, and dealing with people. From these events 33 lessons are identified. Compared to men, women more frequently reported learning about their own personal limits and how to recognize and seize opportunities. Men more frequently reported learning technical skills and shouldering responsibility. Men reported more experience with turnaround and start-up assignments. Includes a bibliography.

Subject(s): Learning experiences, men as managers, women as managers

New

Vansina, L. (1999). **Leadership in strategic business unit management.** *European Journal of Work and Organizational Psychology, 8*(10), 87-108.

In the early 1980s Vansina studied successful general managers to determine what characteristics they shared. He found that these managers typically managed their whole companies, not just their boards; managed the identity of their company; operated from within the system; and exerted personal leadership. Ten years later Vansina conducted another study in which he examined in depth how a general manager handled a major organizational change. He interviewed and observed this manager at meetings and workshops and determined that although the business world has changed since his original study, the characteristics of a successful manager remain the same. Includes bibliographical references. Commentary by the general manager studied follows the article.

Subject(s): Strategic leadership

Volkema, R. J. (1997). **Managing the problem formulation process: Guidelines for team leaders and facilitators.** *Human Systems Management, 16*(1), 27-34.

Volkema suggests methods for team leaders to manage the problem formulation process and reduce Type III errors (solving the wrong problem). It is important to involve the right people and to not rush the process. Team leaders need to recognize the biases in human judgment that influence the process such as: personal experiences outweigh more valid data; first or most recent data are given undue importance; aversion to taking risks; and selective perception. When sufficient effort is devoted to formulating a problem the remainder of the decision-making process is improved. Includes bibliographical references.

Subject(s): Problem-solving process

Von Oech, R. (1986). *A kick in the seat of the pants: Using your explorer, artist, judge, and warrior to be more creative.* New York: Harper & Row.

Von Oech believes that to develop our creative process we must adopt four roles: explorer, artist, judge, and warrior. The explorer searches for new information and the artist turns resources into new ideas. A judge evaluates the merits of a new idea and the warrior carries the new ideas into action. When these roles are combined they form a creative team in the theater of your mind. Von Oech describes how one can expand into unfamiliar roles and be flexible in switching roles through exercises and anecdotes. Includes bibliography and index.

Subject(s): Creativity

Vroom, V. H. (1995). *Work and motivation.* San Francisco: Jossey-Bass.

This updated version of Vroom's 1964 *Work and Motivation* is part of the Jossey-Bass management series of classic works. The original work was an attempt to develop a theoretical structure for research in industrial and organizational psychology. Twenty-eight pages of preface and introduction explain the author's new perspectives on the subjects of job performance, work satisfaction, and occupational choice. If he were to rewrite his expectancy theory 30 years after the original, Vroom states that his own life experiences, changes in scientific reporting, and new research discoveries would alter the model. This book remains a classic for the student of organizational psychology. Includes bibliographical references and index.

Subject(s): Motivation

Vroom, V. H., & Yetton, P. W. (1975). *Leadership and decision making.* Pittsburgh, PA: University of Pittsburgh.

This book is written for scholars, researchers, managers, and administrators who share an interest in leadership, decision making, and organizational behavior. Central to all the research reported in this book is the role of situational differences as determinants of the choice of a decision process. A summary of the major findings and how they relate to other approaches in the study of leadership is provided. Includes a bibliography.

Subject(s): Decision making

Walberg, H. J., & Others. (1996). **Childhood traits and experiences of eminent women.** *Creativity Research Journal, 9*(1), 97-102.

This is a summary of research that examined the early traits, conditions, and experiences of 256 eminent women who influenced their times and achieved importance in their fields. Included are: skater Sonja Henie, blind and deaf educator Helen Keller, painter Grandma Moses, business-woman Helena Rubinstein, and political leader Eleanor Roosevelt. Historians and practitioners rated each woman on childhood factors such as: alert to novelty, hardworking, persevering, and well traveled. The most common factors were identified as: intelligence, perseverance, and stimulating social environments. The women were found to have been encouraged and stimulated by parents, teachers, and other adults, while living in environments that were receptive to different ideas.
Subject(s): Creativity, experience, women's leadership development

New
Waldman, D. A., & Yammarino, F. J. (1999). **CEO charismatic leadership: Levels-of-management and levels-of-analysis effects.** *Academy of Management Review, 24*(2), 266-285.

Many leadership models represent individual, dyadic, or small group behaviors, attributes, and interpersonal relationships. In this article the authors present a model for leadership on a larger scale. The Model of CEO Charismatic Leadership represents the effect of a powerful individual on close and distant relationships with a large number of people. When close followers trust and give voice to a CEO's vision there is a cascading effect throughout the organization. Those in the socially distant echelons then buy into the CEO's symbolic behaviors and ideology. The result is a significant impact on performance and organizational culture. Includes bibliographical references.
Subject(s): Charismatic leadership, CEOs

Walton, R. E. (1987). *Managing conflict: Interpersonal dialogue and third-party roles* (2nd ed.). Reading, MA: Addison-Wesley.

Conflict resolution is an important skill necessary at all levels of management. The author has developed an outline for diagnosing continuing conflicts, and offers several options for resolving them. Methods and concepts are presented here that can be applied to various types of conflict, including both interpersonal and inter-system. Topics span fundamental steps of managing conflict, skills for facilitating open dialogue, and third-party advantages of consultants. Examples of conflict resolution are provided through three case studies and through a presentation of an international workshop on the dialogue of conflict over border disputes. Includes bibliographies.
Subject(s): Conflict management

New
Watkins, K. E., Ellinger, A. D., & Valentine, T. (1999). **Understanding support for innovation in a large-scale change effort: The manager-as-instructor approach.** *Human Resource Development Quarterly, 10*(1), 63-77.

This study examined an organizational change initiative in a large automobile company to determine what factors predicted managerial support for the innovation. The cornerstone of the initiative was the Managers-as-Instructors concept in which senior and mid-level managers act as teachers for their subordinates. Surveys based on the Concerns-Based Adoption Model measured managers' responses to the innovation process and to their new roles as instructors. Analysis showed that the fit between organizational and individual values was important, but that many managers felt overwhelmed and ill-prepared for their teaching responsibilities. The authors suggest that when organizational change requires managers to take on new roles, HRD staff need to take extra steps to support the managers and effectively address early-stage concerns. Includes bibliographical references.
Subject(s): Organizational change

Weber, J. (1996). **Influences upon managerial moral decision making: Nature of the harm and magnitude of consequences.** *Human Relations, 49*(1), 1-22.

This article examines possible ethical dilemmas faced by managers and the moral considerations that affect their decision making. A sample of 259 managers enrolled in an MBA program completed the *Moral Judgment Interview* (Colby & Kohlberg, 1987) to determine how they perceived degrees of harm and consequence. Situations involving physical harm received top priority, followed by economic harm and psychological harm. Life-and-death issues were ranked of greatest consequence, followed by injury and job-termination issues. The results of this study have implications for further research and ethical decision-making models. The *Moral Judgment Interview* is in the appendix. Includes bibliographical references.
Subject(s): Decision making, ethics

Weed, F. J. (1993). **The MADD queen: Charisma and the founder of Mothers Against Drunk Driving.** *Leadership Quarterly, 4*(3/4), 329-346.

Candy Lightner, the charismatic founder of MADD, is featured in this examination of the pros and cons of charismatic leadership. Lightner's personal tragedy fueled the growth of an active and well-funded national organization. Lightner became a symbol of bereavement turned into moral mission. The same traits that helped her inspire others to build a large, complex organization are the traits that interfered with the routine management of that organization and caused Lightner's loss of influence and leadership position.
Subject(s): Charisma

New

Weisinger, H. (1998). ***Emotional intelligence at work: The untapped edge for success.*** San Francisco: Jossey-Bass.

Weisinger describes emotional intelligence as the ability to "intentionally make your emotions work for you by using them to help guide your behavior and thinking in ways that enhance your results." The first section of this book describes how to increase your emotional intelligence by developing self-awareness, managing your emotions, and motivating yourself. The second section offers advice on how to apply emotional intelligence to your relationships with others through communication skills, interpersonal expertise, and by helping others help themselves. Each chapter contains exercises and tips readers can use to increase their emotional intelligence, and an appendix offers an instrument for "developing your emotional intelligence." Includes bibliographical references.
Subject(s): Emotional intelligence

Whicker, M. L. (1996). ***Toxic leaders: When organizations go bad.*** Westport, CT: Quorum Books.

Whicker discusses the dark side of leadership in this book. She separates leaders into three categories: trustworthy, transitional, and toxic. Part I explains the need for trustworthy leadership and the characteristics that make a leader trustworthy. Part II contrasts trustworthy leaders with toxic and transitional leaders. Parts III and IV give examples of different types of transitional and toxic leaders including: absentee leader, busybody, controller, enforcer, street fighter, and bully. These snapshots of problem leaders include a thumbnail sketch, hallmark characteristics, likely sources of inadequacy, operational styles, impact on an organization, and ways to protect against them. Part V explains how toxic leaders influence organizational decline and how an organization can regain its health after a decline. Includes bibliographical references and index.
Subject(s): Negative views of leadership, abuse of power

Wills, G. (1992). ***Lincoln at Gettysburg: The words that remade America.*** New York: Touchstone.

The Civil War battle at Gettysburg, Pennsylvania, was a military disaster for both the North and South. Each side lost several thousand soldiers and suffered severe psychological defeat. Bodies were hastily buried in shallow, unsuitable graves. In time, proper arrangements were made for reburial in a new national cemetery. The dedication ceremony became a symbol of healing the pain of a war-torn country. President Abraham Lincoln's three-minute speech on that occasion convinced his listeners that America was founded on the principle that all men are created equal. His brief words had the power to bring the nation together. In this Pulitzer Prize-winning book Wills examines Lincoln's personal history and the speech itself to understand the power of communication. Includes bibliographical references and index.
Subject(s): Communication; U.S. presidents: Lincoln, A.

New

Wind, J. Y., & Main, J. (1998). ***Driving change: How the best companies are preparing for the 21st century.*** New York: Free Press.

This source presents a framework to assist leaders in driving the change of corporations. Wind and Main first delineate the drivers of change: information technology, increased competition, societal and customer expectations. The second part enlists real-life examples of customer focus, a new model of leadership, and treatment of employees. Part three analyzes examples in the use of information technology and innovation as well as increased speed and quality. The final portion surrounds organizations as a whole and the necessity for networking and globalization, continued organizational learning and restructuring, and meeting societal demands. Includes bibliographical references and index.
Subject(s): Corporate leadership

Wofford, J. C. (1994). **Getting inside the leader's head: A cognitive processes approach to leadership.** *SAM Advanced Management Journal*, *59*(3), 4-9.

Cognitive processes are important functions for managers, especially in performance appraisal, reward, discipline, communication, interpersonal conflict, and training. This case study follows a newly appointed manager of a spinning mill in India. His negotiations and policy development with union leaders are used to follow the cognitive processes of management.
Subject(s): Learning competence

New

Yagil, D. (1998). **Charismatic leadership and organizational hierarchy: Attribution of charisma to close and distant leaders.** *Leadership Quarterly*, *9*(2), 161-176.

This study is based on the premise that charisma is an attribute given to a leader by his or her followers. Yagil examines the attribution of charisma to socially close and distant leaders. More than 550 Israeli combat soldiers participated. Half responded to questions about their platoon commanders (socially close leaders). The other half responded to questions about their battalion commanders (socially distant leaders). Perceived charisma in close leaders was related to strong interpersonal relations, extraordinary traits, leader's confidence in subordinate's ability, and behavioral modeling. Perceived charisma in distant leaders was related to general impression, leader's confidence in group's ability, and acceptance of the leader's ideas. Includes bibliographical references.
Subject(s): Charismatic leadership, power distance

New

Yang, H. (1998). **The concept of trust and trust building.** *A Leadership Journal: Women in Leadership—Sharing the Vision*, *2*(2), 19-28.

Yang argues that trust is critical to both leadership and conflict resolution because it facilitates effective working

relationships. This article reviews the existing research on the concepts of "trust" and "trust building." Definitions of trust, essential factors in trust building, and contextual and cultural implications of trust are discussed. Includes bibliographical references.
Subject(s): Trust

New
Yukl, G. (1999). **An evaluation of conceptual weaknesses in transformational and charismatic leadership theories.** *Leadership Quarterly: Special Issue, Part I: Charismatic and Transformational Leadership: Taking Stock of the Present and Future, 10*(2), 285-305.

Yukl critically evaluates several theories of transformational and charismatic leadership. He identifies conceptual weaknesses such as ambiguous influence and behavior constructs, an overemphasis on dyads, and a bias toward heroic leadership. A comparison of transformational and charismatic leadership argues against merging the two theories into one. Yukl suggests that it may not be appropriate to apply vague definitions such as charismatic or transformational to individual leaders. Includes bibliographical references.
Subject(s): Charismatic Leadership Theory, Transformational Leadership Theory

Zaccaro, S. J., Gilbert, J. A., Thor, K. K., & Mumford, M. D. (1991). **Leadership and social intelligence: Linking social perspectives and behavioral flexibility to leader effectiveness.** *Leadership Quarterly: Special Issue: Individual Differences and Leadership: I, 2*(4), 317-342.

Successful leaders have two characteristics of social intelligence: social perceptiveness and behavioral flexibility. This

paper proposes that those who are considered successful leaders: 1) have increased knowledge structures regarding people and situations, 2) better understand and respond to the critical social elements of organizational problems, and 3) grasp more quickly the implications of social affordances inside and outside the organizational environment.
Subject(s): Social perspective, intelligence

Zand, D. E. (1997). *The leadership triad: Knowledge, trust, and power.* New York: Oxford University Press.

Triadic leadership combines the forces of knowledge, trust, and power in equal measure. When properly exercised triadic leadership is: having access to knowledge and putting it into action, giving loyalty and asking for commitment, and understanding when to use power and when to give it away. Cases and charts throughout the book illustrate a variety of situations in which leaders may integrate the triad. Includes index.
Subject(s): Competencies overview

New
Zuo, L. (1998). **Creativity and aesthetic sense.** *Creativity Research Journal, 11*(4), 309-313.

The need for aesthetic sensibility in the arts is well established, but Zuo argues that it is equally important in problem solving. Both problems and their solutions can be aesthetically pleasing, and striving for such a balance between problem and solution is an important aspect of creativity. Zuo cites examples from Kant to Darwin and advocates teaching creativity in the schools in order to refine students' aesthetic sense. Includes bibliographical references.
Subject(s): Creative problem solving

RESEARCH, THEORIES, AND MODELS

Aktouf, O. (1992). **Management and theories of organizations in the 1990s: Toward a critical radical humanism.** *Academy of Management Review, 17*(3), 407-431.

Theories developed over the past 20 years contribute to Aktouf's conclusion that a radical-humanistic position is the basis of successful management. This person-centered theory relies on developing an employee's desire to belong and encouraging the use of his or her intelligence. He recommends a neo-Marxist humanist ideology to foster creativity and productivity through the willing participation of all parties in a common endeavor.
Subject(s): Review of leadership theories, humanist perspective

Alvesson, M. (1996). **Leadership studies: From procedure and abstraction to reflexivity and situation.** *Leadership Quarterly, 7*(4), 455-485.

Conventional approaches to leadership research have used positivistic methods, often quantitative and hypothesis-based, that emphasize objectivity and procedure. Alvesson believes that these methods are so removed from everyday life that they are of little use, and criticizes mainstream research and its search for "objective reality." He advocates using a reflexive, situational approach that recognizes the biases of the researcher and opens up new ways of understanding. This style, according to the article, is more appropriate for studying something as subjective as leadership.
Subject(s): Qualitative research

Bass, B. M. (1998). *Transformational leadership: Industrial, military, and educational impact.* Mahwah, NJ: Lawrence Erlbaum.

Bass synthesizes research on transformational leadership to help the U.S. Army Research Institute develop a relevant military theory of leadership. He includes the findings from business, education, government, and health care organizations to create an overview of transformational leadership that inspires subordinate commitment, involvement, loyalty, and performance. Issues of importance to military leadership are: stress among followers; the contingencies of emergency, conflict, and crisis; organizational culture; gender differences; policy implications; predicting and developing leadership; and substitutes for leadership. Includes bibliographical references, author index, and subject index.
Subject(s): Transformational Leadership Theory

New
Bass, B. M. (1999). **Two decades of research and development in transformational leadership.** *European Journal of Work and Organizational Psychology, 8*(10), 9-32.

Bass reviews the past 20 years of literature on transformational leadership, comparing the range of transformational and transactional leadership and listing some of the issues involved in measuring these traits empirically. Related concepts and measures, such as leader-member exchange and directive and participative leadership, are described, and the research on training, education, and development of transactional leadership is also addressed. Bass notes that some studies have shown that women exhibit more transformational leadership than men, and he calls for further research in this area. Includes bibliographical references. Commentary by Christian Vandenberghe follows the article.
Subject(s): Transformational Leadership Theory

New
Boyd, N. G., & Taylor, R. R. (1998). **A developmental approach to the examination of friendship in leader-follower relationships.** *Leadership Quarterly, 9*(1), 1-25.

The authors examine social psychology literature on friendships and research on the leader-member exchange theory to determine how friendship develops in a leader-follower dyad and how such a friendship affects leadership effectiveness. A model depicts the similarities between the development of friendships and the development of high-level leader-follower relationships: similarity, proximity, richness of communication and social exchange, trust, respect, and mutual support. The authors conclude that leader-follower friendship positively affects leadership effectiveness within supportive organizational cultures and up to the point where the friendship becomes overly close or exploitive. Includes bibliographical references.
Subject(s): LMX Theory, friendship

Chemers, M. M. (1997). *An integrative theory of leadership.* Mahwah, NJ: Lawrence Erlbaum.

In this book Chemers attempts to review the literature on leadership and integrate and reconcile the existing theories and the empirical findings. He addresses transactional and exchange theories, the contingency model, and transformational leadership. There are also chapters on the influence of culture on leadership processes and women in leadership. Includes bibliographical references and indexes.
Subject(s): Review of leadership theories

Chen, C. C., & Van Velsor, E. (1996). **New directions for research and practice in diversity leadership.** *Leadership Quarterly: Special Issue: Leadership and Diversity (Part II), 7*(2), 285-302.

In this conclusion to the two-part special issue on Leadership and Diversity, Chen and Van Velsor examine the intersection between the two. First, they identify four areas for further study: the impact of social-group identities on organizations, the unconscious sociopsychological processes, the political aspects of leadership, and follower perspectives. Then they offer four leadership frameworks that can be further developed to address diversity: attribution theories of leadership

and followership, theories of leadership prototypes, the leader-member exchange model, and the behavioral complexity model. Finally, practical implications are addressed, including how to understand the unique strengths and needs of diverse leaders and how to develop global leaders.
Subject(s): New leadership frameworks, diversity

New
Choi, Y., & Mai-Dalton, R. R. (1998). **On the leadership function of self-sacrifice.** *Leadership Quarterly: Special Issue: 360-Degree Feedback in Leadership Research, 9*(4), 475-501.

This paper examines the concept of self-sacrifice, as opposed to self-interest, in organizational settings. Specifically it examines situations of self-sacrificial leadership and the effects on followers. A schematic model of self-sacrificial leadership demonstrates how followers are influenced by their perceptions of leaders' charisma, competence, and legitimacy; followers' intent to imitate self-sacrificing behavior; and organizational security. The authors hope that this model will encourage research about the phenomenon of self-sacrificial leadership. Includes bibliographical references.
Subject(s): New leadership frameworks, self-sacrifice

Conger, J., & Kanungo, R. (1994). **Charismatic leadership in organizations: Perceived behavioral attributes and their measurement.** *Journal of Organizational Behavior, 15*(5), 439-452.

This article reports on the development of a questionnaire intended to measure the perceived behavioral dimensions of the Conger and Kanungo charismatic leadership model (1987, 1988). Data were collected from 488 managers belonging to four organizations located in the U.S. and Canada. Analysis of the results and implications for future research and practice are discussed.
Subject(s): Charismatic Leadership Theory

New
Conger, J. A. (1998). **Qualitative research as the cornerstone methodology for understanding leadership.** *Leadership Quarterly, 9*(1), 107-121.

Conger supports the use of qualitative methods to study the complex topic of leadership. Qualitative methods offer insights into the context of relationships, longitudinal perspectives, and paradigm shifts that quantitative measures don't. Conger relates his experience using observation as a field research strategy, the yield of rich data, and the tedious task of organizing the resulting sea of information. He recommends that doctoral programs include seminars on qualitative research methods. Includes bibliographical references.
Subject(s): Qualitative research

Dansereau, F., Yammarino, F. J., & Markham, S. E. (1995). **Leadership: The multiple-level approaches.** *Leadership Quarterly: Special Issue: Leadership: The Multiple-level Approaches [Part I], 6*(2), 97-109.

This article introduces a series on classic and contemporary leadership theory in two special issues of *Leadership Quarterly (LQ)*. Part I, in *LQ 6*(2), includes essays on: the Ohio State approach, contingency, participative decision making, charismatic leadership, transformational leadership, and leader-member exchange. Part II, in *LQ 6*(3), contains essays on: information processing, substitutes for leadership, romance of leadership, self-leadership, multiple-linkage model, multilevel theory, and individualized leadership. The introduction compares the major theories to find various methods of analysis and various assumptions about leadership characteristics, situations, and relationships with followers.
Subject(s): Review of leadership theories

Drath, W. H., & Palus, C. J. (1994). *Making common sense: Leadership as meaning-making in a community of practice.* Greensboro, NC: Center for Creative Leadership.

A common way of viewing leadership has been to see it as a process of social influence. In this report the authors offer a new perspective—seeing it as a process in which people engaged in a common activity create shared knowledge and ways of knowing. Taking this perspective makes it possible to gain a new understanding of such concepts as influence, individual action, motivation, and the relationship between authority and leadership. The implications of this shift for the practice of leadership and leadership development are discussed. Includes bibliographical references.
Subject(s): New leadership frameworks, sense-making

New
Farling, M. L., Stone, A. G., & Winston, B. E. (1999). **Servant leadership: Setting the stage for empirical research.** *Journal of Leadership Studies, 6*(1/2), 49-72.

This paper offers a definition and model of servant leadership to provide a foundation for empirical research. Five variables —vision, influence, credibility, trust, and service—move through a sequential, upward spiral and then repeat the process. Servant leadership is compared to transformational leadership although based on a different foundation of universal principles. Servant leadership has a spiritual foundation and transformational leadership is based on justice and equality. Includes bibliographical references.
Subject(s): Servant leadership

Fernandez, C. F., & Vecchio, R. P. (1997). **Situational leadership theory revisited: A test of an across-jobs perspective.** *Leadership Quarterly, 8*(1), 67-84.

Hersey and Blanchard's situational leadership theory is based on the idea that leaders should use different levels of task and relationship behavior for different followers, depending on the followers' readiness/maturity levels. Though popular, the

theory is backed by little empirical evidence. This study criticizes the readiness/maturity factor for being imprecise, and asks whether job level could be used as a measure instead when testing the validity of the theory within a university. The authors found that "supervisor monitoring and considerateness may be differentially related to outcome variables as a function of job-level."
Subject(s): Situational Leadership Theory

Fiedler, F. (1967). *A theory of leadership effectiveness.* New York: McGraw-Hill.

This book presents a contingency theory of leadership effectiveness that takes account of the leader's personality as well as the situational factors in the leadership situation. This theory attempts to specify, in more precise terms, the conditions under which one leadership style or another will be more conducive to group effectiveness. The book summarizes the results of a 15-year program of research on leadership and a theory of leadership effectiveness, and integrates the findings. Includes bibliographical references and index.
Subject(s): Contingency Theory

Fitzgerald, C., & Kirby, L. K. (Eds.). (1997). *Developing leaders: Research and applications in psychological type and leadership development: Integrating reality and vision, mind and heart.* Palo Alto, CA: Davies-Black.

This edited book begins with an overview of the *Myers-Briggs Type Indicator® (MBTI)* for those not familiar with it. Mary McCaulley of the Center for Psychological Type explains the link between personality types and leadership development. John Fleenor and Ellen Van Velsor report on the Center for Creative Leadership's research of the *MBTI*'s use with group performance and 360-degree feedback. Paul Roush reports on the U.S. Naval Academy's research using *MBTI* data to effect behavior changes. Fitzgerald and Kirby describe the methods for applying *MBTI* dynamics to leadership development. Other researchers and practitioners write about the application of the *MBTI* in simulations, feedback instruments, organizational change, and strategic planning. Includes bibliographical references and indexes.
Subject(s): Review of leadership research, leadership development, personality, *Myers-Briggs Type Indicator*

Graen, G. B., & Uhl-Bien, M. (1995). **Relationship-based approach to leadership: Development of leader-member exchange (LMX) theory of leadership over 25 years: Applying a multi-level multi-domain perspective.** *Leadership Quarterly, 6*(2), 219-247.

LMX theory dictates that leaders exist only in relation to their followers. Without that relationship leadership doesn't exist. The LMX theory has evolved from a vertical leader-follower dyad to an analysis of relationships in groups and networks. The authors discuss the development of this theory as a comprehensive approach to leadership study. They examine issues of measurement and dimension and compare LMX, transformational, and transactional leadership theories.
Subject(s): LMX Theory, relationship building

Guastello, S. J. (1995). **Facilitative style, individual innovation, and emergent leadership in problem solving groups.** *Journal of Creative Behavior, 29*(4), 225-239.

After reviewing recent literature the authors determined that little research had been done on the leadership of creative groups. In this article they review what theories do exist on leading creative teams and then describe their study, in which a group of university security officers were observed playing the Island Commission game, an exercise in teamwork. The research asked whether facilitative leadership style and individual creative contribution were related to emergent leadership in a leaderless situation. Analysis of the guards' interaction and their responses afterwards show that both factors were positively related to perceptions of leadership.
Subject(s): Review of leadership theories, emergence of leadership, creative teams

Hollander, E. P. (1992). **Leadership, followership, self, and others.** *Leadership Quarterly: Special Issue: Individual Differences and Leadership: II, 3*(1), 43-54.

Rather than focus solely on leaders' attributes and effect on others, this paper focuses on followers' perceptions and expectations. Hollander refers to prior research and models to illustrate interpersonal relationships, mutual identification, bases of power, giving and taking credit for good and bad leadership behavior, and charisma. A perceptual/attributional perspective credits or blames the leader for group outcomes.
Subject(s): Review of leadership research, followership

Hunt, J. G. (1991). *Leadership: A new synthesis.* Newbury Park, CA: Sage.

Hunt suggests a new synthesis, an expanded framework for scholarly study of leadership-knowledge content and orientation. His multiple-level leadership model includes studies from high levels of management down through organizations and across time. Hunt investigates varying concepts of leadership as reality and as perception, assumptions, definitions, purposes, and measurements. Includes bibliographical references and indexes.
Subject(s): Review of leadership theories

Insch, G. S., Moore, J. E., & Murphy, L. D. (1997). **Content analysis in leadership research: Examples, procedures, and suggestions for future use.** *Leadership Quarterly, 8*(1), 1-25.

Content analysis, a method for analyzing contextual material, is not often used by organizational researchers. This article gives a brief background to the method and summarizes leadership studies that have used it. The authors believe that the main strength of content analysis is its ability to combine quantitative and qualitative techniques. An 11-step process for using content analysis is also provided, which includes: identifying texts, generating a coding system, assessing reliability, and assessing construct validity.
Subject(s): Research methods

Jung, D. I., Bass, B. M., & Sosik, J. J. (1995). **Bridging leadership and culture: A theoretical consideration of transformational leadership and collectivistic cultures.** *Journal of Leadership Studies, 2*(4), 3-18.

This paper reviews the four I's of transformational leadership: idealized influence (charisma), inspirational motivation, intellectual stimulation, and individualized consideration. These characteristics are considered in the context of collectivism, as in the cultures of Japan, China, or Israel, as opposed to the individualism predominant in American culture. Because collectivistic cultures have higher levels of group orientation and commitment to collective accomplishment, there appears to be a conceptual bridge between these cultures and transformational leadership. The authors present a theoretical intersection where the two concepts meet and recommend this as an area for future research.

Subject(s): Transformational Leadership Theory, cross-cultural context

New
Lord, R. G., Brown, D. J., & Freiberg, S. J. (1999). **Understanding the dynamics of leadership: The role of follower self-concepts in the leader/follower relationship.** *Organizational Behavior and Human Decision Processes, 78*(3), 167-203.

This paper introduces a framework that integrates the research on self-concept and leadership. It considers self-concept at three levels: 1) the individual level that defines one's uniqueness as a person, 2) the interpersonal level that defines one in terms of roles and relationships, and 3) the group level that identifies with the collective welfare of a work team or other group. A working self-concept (WSC) operates at all levels and includes current goals as well as broader, long-term standards called *possible selves*. The authors propose that leaders who understand the WSC of their followers have more influence on followers' self-regulation, positive goals, and positive relationships. Includes bibliographical references.

Subject(s): Research report, leader and follower relations

Loye, D. (1977). *The leadership passion.* San Francisco: Jossey-Bass.

This book surveys 180 years of thought and research bearing on the relationships between ideology in the individual, social leadership, and management styles. Variables receiving major attention include liberalism-conservatism, risk-taking, alienation, anomie, extremism, activism, Machiavellianism, locus of control, as well as leader-follower, parent-child, and age-generational relationships. Findings support new models of ideological functioning. Includes bibliography and index.

Subject(s): Review of leadership theories, social perspective

New
Lucius, R. H., & Kuhnert, K. (1999). **Adult development and transformational leader.** *Journal of Leadership Studies, 6*(1/2), 73-85.

This paper integrates the concept of transformational leadership and the constructive-development (CD) theory of adult development. The CD theory holds that adults view their worlds through unique and personal lenses. As adults develop, their meaning-making systems grow more complex until they understand and appreciate others' perspectives. To determine the correlation between the two concepts, the authors gathered data on 32 cadets at a military college. Data included peer ratings, subject/object interviews, and a survey on moral judgment. An initiative score was determined by the cadets' involvement and prestige in extracurricular activities. The results indicate that CD maturity correlates positively to perceptions of leadership, although further study is needed to determine if it is a transformational style of leadership. Includes bibliographical references.

Subject(s): Transformational leadership, adult development

New
Manzoni, J., & Barsoux, J. (1998). **The set-up-to-fail syndrome.** *Harvard Business Review, 76*(2), 101-113.

This is a report of two studies on the causal relationship between leadership style and subordinate performance. One study involved 50 boss-subordinate pairs in large manufacturing firms and the other surveyed about 850 executives attending development programs at INSEAD, an executive education institution in France. Findings from both studies indicate that bosses are often complicit in their employees' successes and failures. The dynamic that aids subordinate failure begins with early perceptions of an employee's underperformance. A mistake or personality clash may reduce the boss's trust and the subordinate's confidence. Further, breakdowns in communication and a directive leadership style serve to undervalue the subordinate's contribution. The authors suggest ways to avoid or undo this set-up-to-fail syndrome. Includes bibliographical references.

Subject(s): Research report, relationship building

Norris, W. R., & Vecchio, R. P. (1992). **Situational leadership theory: A replication.** *Group & Organization Management, 17*(3), 331-342.

Recent research studies on Hersey and Blanchard's situational leadership theory have attempted to measure optimal supervision and follower maturity. Norris and Vecchio studied 91 nurses and their supervisors in a three-way interaction involving structuring, consideration, and maturity. Followers with low maturity required high task-supervision and low relationship-supervision. Followers with high maturity required low task- and low relationship-supervision.

Subject(s): Situational Leadership Theory

Northouse, P. G. (1997). *Leadership: Theory and practice.* Thousand Oaks, CA: Sage.

This textbook is intended for students in graduate and advanced undergraduate leadership courses in business, communication, political science, and health services. It is divided into sections that describe leadership theories and their relative merits. Each section provides case studies, a bibliography, an instrument, and suggestions for applying each theory to practice. Sections and their accompanying instruments are: the trait approach with the *Leadership Trait Questionnaire (LTQ);* the style approach with the *Style Questionnaire;* the situational approach with *Situational Leadership: A Brief Questionnaire;* contingency theory with the *Least Preferred Co-worker (LPC) Measure;* path-goal theory with the *Path-Goal Leadership Questionnaire;* leader-member exchange theory with the *LMX 7 Questionnaire;* transformational leadership with the *Multifactor Leadership Questionnaire Form 6S;* team leadership theory with the *Team Effectiveness Questionnaire;* the psychodynamic approach with the *Psychodynamic Styles Checklist;* and women and leadership with the *Attitudes Toward Women as Managers (ATWAM) Scale.* Includes bibliographical references and indexes.
Subject(s): Review of leadership theories, textbook

New
Parry, K. W. (1998). **Grounded theory and social process: A new direction for leadership research.** *Leadership Quarterly,* 9(1), 85-105.

Parry argues for the use of grounded theory to study leadership as a process of social influence. Much previous leadership research has been conducted in the field of psychology using quantitative methodologies. Parry suggests that longitudinal, qualitative research is more appropriate to study the key themes repeated in the literature of leadership: change; influence; transformation based on persuasion, not coercion; and the existence of leadership within a social system. Grounded theory emerges from such social phenomena and is developed and verified through systematic data collection and analysis pertaining to those phenomena. The relationship between theory, data collection, and analysis is reciprocal. Includes bibliographical references.
Subject(s): Qualitative research, social perspective

Podsakoff, P. M., MacKenzie, S. B., Ahearne, M., & Bommer, W. H. (1995). **Searching for a needle in a haystack: Trying to identify the illusive moderators of leadership behaviors.** *Yearly Review of Management: A Special Issue of the Journal of Management,* 21(3), 423-470.

The authors review 25 years of leadership theory, specifically path-goal and substitutes-for-leadership theories. They identify many moderators of leadership behavior including subordinate characteristics, supervisor traits, tasks, role perceptions, and organizational characteristics. They also analyze research methods, the percentage of moderators actually identified, and the nature of the moderating effects.

Little support to validate a large amount of the research was found.
Subject(s): Substitutes-for-Leadership Theory, Path-goal Theory

Podsakoff, P. M., MacKenzie, S. B., & Bommer, W. H. (1996). **Transformational leader behaviors and substitutes for leadership as determinants of employee satisfaction, commitment, trust, and organizational citizenship behaviors.** *Journal of Management,* 22(2), 259-298.

In this study data were collected on over 1,500 employees from different industries and job levels to determine whether a connection exists between two theories of leadership—the transformational leadership theory and the "substitutes for leadership" theory. Extensive statistical analysis resulted in the authors' finding little support for the substitutes theory, but they advocate more research. Tables and graphic representations of the findings accompany the article.
Subject(s): Transformational Leadership Theory, Substitutes-for-Leadership Theory, organizational citizenship

Proehl, R. A., & Taylor, K. (1997). **Leadership, cognitive complexity, and gender.** *A Leadership Journal: Women in Leadership—Sharing the Vision,* 1(2), 39-48.

The authors combine two theories of adult development to create their own model of good leadership using gender as one factor. The first theory is introduced in R. Kegan (1982), *The Evolving Self: Problem and Process in Human Development,* Cambridge: Harvard University Press. The second theory comes from J. Rosener (November/December 1990), "Ways Women Lead," *Harvard Business Review,* pp. 119-125. In this theoretical work Kegan's thoughts on complexity of mind are blended with more recent work on women's capacity for a relational-based approach to knowing. The authors ultimately believe that cognitive complexity, not gender, is the basis for good leadership. Includes bibliographical references.
Subject(s): Adult development, women's leadership development, intelligence

Rejai, M., & Phillips, K. (1997). *Leaders and leadership: An appraisal of research and theory.* Westport, CT: Praeger.

This book briefly reviews leadership theories over time, including those that identify leadership skills, types of leaders, and functions of leadership. The authors recommend areas for future leadership research: gender issues, minority and Third World leadership, crisis leadership, and the tenure of leaders. Includes bibliographical references and index.
Subject(s): History of leadership theories

New
Sagie, A. (1997). **Leader direction and employee participation in decision making: Contradictory or compatible practices?** *Applied Psychology: An International Review,* 46(4), 387-452.

Sagie examines the conflicting values of directive leadership and participative decision making, also called a loose-tight

dilemma. He offers three interpretations for balancing "loose" and "tight": 1) employees make decisions and the leader provides direction for execution, 2) the leader plans strategy and employees decide on tactical issues, and 3) the leader provides a framework such as a problem and the employees decide how to solve it. A model of loose-tight leadership at the dyadic, group, organizational, and environmental levels indicates that such a leadership style affects employee attitudes and performance. Nine scholars follow with commentaries on the model and the effectiveness of loose-tight leadership. Includes bibliographical references.
Subject(s): Loose-tight leadership model, shared decision making

New
Scandura, T. A. (1999). **Rethinking leader-member exchange: An organizational justice perspective.** *Leadership Quarterly*, *10*(1), 25-40.

Scandura reviews the literature on leader-member exchange (LMX) from the perspective of organizational justice. In ideal LMX situations leaders treat members as part of an in-group, as trusted assistants. In ineffective situations leaders treat members as part of an out-group, as hired hands. Scandura identifies LMX in-group behaviors such as honesty, open exchange of information, feedback, shared decision making, and equitable treatment of all group members. Over time, such in-group behaviors lead to the perception of fair treatment and organizational justice. Includes bibliographical references.
Subject(s): LMX Theory

Schnake, M., Dumler, M. P., & Cochran, D. S. (1993). **The relationship between "traditional" leadership, "super" leadership, and organizational citizenship behavior.** *Group & Organization Management*, *18*(3), 352-365.

This article describes the five behaviors of organizational citizenship behavior (OCB). They are: 1) altruism—an employee helping another employee voluntarily, 2) conscientiousness—doing more than is necessary, 3) sportsmanship—refraining from complaining or causing annoyances, 4) courtesy—keeping others informed, and 5) civic virtue—keeping oneself informed and participating responsibly in decisions and meetings. The authors report on a study of these five behaviors measured against traditional leadership and superleadership in one organization. Contrary to their expectations the traditional leadership characteristics of initiating structure and consideration had higher correlation to OCB than did the superleadership characteristics of self-goal-setting, self-observation, and self-expectation.
Subject(s): Organizational citizenship

New
Schriesheim, C. A., Castro, S. L., & Cogliser, C. C. (1999). **Leader-member exchange (LMX) research: A comprehensive review of theory, measurement, and data-analytic practices.** *Leadership Quarterly*, *10*(1), 63-113.

The authors review the evolution of the leader-member exchange (LMX) theory over a period of 30 years. A helpful table documents the contributions of 147 works. Another table identifies the measures and analytic methods used in the 147 empirical studies. The authors conclude that scale development and validity are necessary to further the evolution of the LMX theory. Includes bibliographical references.
Subject(s): LMX Theory

New
Smith, J. A., & Foti, R. J. (1998). **A pattern approach to the study of leader emergence.** *Leadership Quarterly*, *9*(2), 147-160.

This article reports on a study to determine the presence of dominance, intelligence, and self-efficacy in emerging leaders. An all-male student population participated in the study. Three tests were administered: the *General Self-Efficacy Scale* (Sherer et al., 1982); the *Wonderlic Personnel Test* (Wonderlic, 1983), to measure general intelligence; and the *Personality Research Form* (Jackson, 1987), to assess dominance. Students were placed in small groups that included one member with high test scores in all areas, one member with three low scores, and two members with mixed scores. After participating in a manufacturing simulation, students ranked group leaders and took the *General Leadership Impression* (Lord et al., 1984). The results indicate a strong presence of dominance, intelligence, and self-efficacy in emerging leaders. Includes bibliographical references.
Subject(s): Emergence of leadership, intelligence, research report

New
Spreitzer, G. M., de Janasz, S. C., & Quinn, R. E. (1999). **Empowered to lead: The role of psychological empowerment in leadership.** *Journal of Organizational Behavior*, *20*(4), 511-526.

This paper examines the relationship between psychological empowerment and change-oriented leadership. Psychological empowerment involves four types of workplace cognition: meaning, competence, self-determination, and impact. A survey of mid-level supervisors found that psychological empowerment is positively related to two characteristics associated with change—being innovative and upward influence. Psychological empowerment was only moderately related to inspiration of subordinates and not related at all to a negative factor—maintaining the status quo by monitoring. Includes bibliographical references.
Subject(s): Empowerment, leader as change agent, research report

New

Waldman, D. A., Lituchy, T., Gopalakrishnan, M., Laframboise, K., Galperin, B., & Kaltsounakis, Z. (1998). **A qualitative analysis of leadership and quality improvement.** *Leadership Quarterly, 9*(2), 177-201.

This is a multiple case study that looks for links between transformational leadership and the process of quality improvement (QI). In three North American organizations—a manufacturing plant, a hospital, and a national police force—data were collected by interview and observation. Data were analyzed to determine: 1) the nature and extent of leadership involved in the QI process and 2) how successfully the organizations met QI guidelines as defined by the Malcolm Baldrige National Quality Award and the Canadian Awards for Excellence in Business. From the research the authors developed a theory and model for alternative paths of managerial leadership and commitment in a QI process. An appendix contains the leadership categories for coding from the two awards. Includes bibliographical references.
Subject(s): Qualitative research, transformational leadership

Wheelan, S. A., & Johnston, F. (1996). **The role of informal member leaders in a system containing formal leaders.** *Small Group Research, 27*(1), 33-55.

In this exploratory field study researchers observed attendees at a group relations conference to examine the emergence of informal leaders in a temporary group that already has formal leaders. The Group Development Observation System was used to analyze the verbal interaction patterns of subjects. Earlier research found that informal leaders typically behaved as extensions of formal leaders, but Wheelan and Johnston found that when member leaders emerged they often acted in opposition to formal leaders.
Subject(s): Research report, emergence of leadership

New

Wofford, J. C., Goodwin, V. L., & Whittington, J. L. (1998). **A field study of a cognitive approach to understanding transformational and transactional leadership.** *Leadership Quarterly, 9*(1), 55-84.

The authors propose a model that uses a cognitive perspective for understanding leader behavior. They administered the *Multifactor Leadership Questionnaire* (Bass & Avolio, 1990) to managers and subordinates in an engineering services firm to determine the managers' transformational or transactional leadership styles. They also solicited answers to open-ended questions to determine each leader's schemata—the formulation of memory, the way that information is stored and retrieved. Partial Least Squares analyses generally supported the model. It was determined that leaders with more experience have more complex and better organized schemata. Transformational leaders have more abstract and transactional leaders have more concrete schemata. Includes bibliographical references.
Subject(s): Transformational Leadership Theory

New

Yammarino, F. J., Dubinsky, A. J., & Spangler, W. D. (1998). **Transformational and contingent reward leadership: Individual, dyad, and group levels of analysis.** *Leadership Quarterly, 9*(1), 27-54.

Analysis of two leadership styles—transformational and contingent reward—is reported. The domestic sales force of a large medical products organization, 111 subordinates and their 34 superiors, participated. Subjective data were gathered from the *Multifactor Leadership Questionnaire* (Bass & Avolio, 1990) and objective data were gathered from sales records. Hypotheses were tested at individual, dyad, and group levels. Findings indicate that transformational leadership is positively related to subjective subordinate performance and contingent reward leadership is positively related to objective subordinate performance. All findings were indicated at the individual level and indicate differences among individuals. Includes bibliographical references.
Subject(s): Transformational Leadership Theory, Contingent Reward Theory

Yukl, G. (1989). **Managerial leadership: A review of theory and research.** *Journal of Management, 15*, 251-289.

This article is a review and evaluation of leadership theories and research findings. Major topics and controversies are: leadership versus management, leader traits and skills, leader behavior and activities, leader power and influence, situational determinants of leader behavior, situational-moderator variables, transformational leadership, importance of leadership for organizational effectiveness, and leadership as an attributional process. A notable emerging concept is leadership as a shared process.
Subject(s): Review of leadership theories

TRAINING AND DEVELOPMENT

New
The 2000 annual (34th ed.). (2000). San Francisco: Jossey-Bass/Pfeiffer.

This series, formerly called the *Annual Handbook for Group Facilitators*, has been issued each year since 1972. Now in two volumes, the set includes descriptions of more than 20 new experiential learning activities, six new assessment instruments, and 20 presentation resources for human resources development practitioners. All material is written by practicing trainers and consultants. *Volume I: Training* is intended for individual and group trainers. *Volume II: Consulting* is intended for organizational consultants. Each volume contains a subject index to the entire set since 1972.
Subject(s): Trainer resources

New
Abernathy, D. J. (1999). **Thinking outside the evaluation box.** *Training & Development, 53*(2), 18-23.

Evaluating workplace training is difficult since benefits are often not found in bottom-line numbers. In 1959 Kirk proposed a four-level model of training evaluation that measures trainee satisfaction, test scores, job improvement, and organizational improvement. While this model is still widely used, newer evaluation models are gaining support. This article describes some newer ways of evaluating training, including Kaplan and Norton's Balanced Scorecard, a model based on stakeholder expectations, and traditional ROI. Includes recommended readings, a list of the top ten reasons evaluation fails, and examples of "hard" and "soft" data that evaluations can measure.
Subject(s): Program evaluation

New
Adams, S. (1999). ***Don't step in the leadership: A Dilbert book.*** Kansas City, MO: Andrews McMeel.

Adams takes a humorous poke at corporate leadership. This collection of Dilbert cartoons provides a laugh at the many ways leadership can go awry. Among the un-leaders are: the pointy-haired boss from Hell; Ratbert, the simpleminded optimist; Mordac, the preventer of information services; Catbert, the evil human resources manager; Dogbert, the arrogant consultant; Asok, the politically naive intern; Alice, who will never be Superwoman; and Dilbert, the beleaguered employee in a cubicle.
Subject(s): Training resources

New
Albrecht, M. H. (1997). ***Cultural diversity: Exercises, cases, resources.*** Champaign, IL: Stipes Publishing.

Twenty exercises and six cases are designed to teach lessons on cultural diversity. Primarily intended for students, the topics include: group identity, discrimination, cultural differences, ethnocentrism, and integration. Questionnaires

test one's knowledge about religions of the world and negotiation. Writing exercises create new myths, break stereotypes, and compare values. A cultural diversity card game includes pullout cards, questions, and instructions for play. Includes bibliographical references and a video list.
Subject(s): Exercises

Astin, H. S., Astin, A. W., & Others. (1996). ***A Social Change Model of leadership development guidebook*** (Version III ed.). Los Angeles: UCLA Higher Education Research Institute.

The Social Change Model proposes that leadership is a process occurring at three levels: individual, group, and community. The model's seven critical values for leadership development are dubbed the 7 C's. At the individual level, they are: Consciousness of self, Congruence, and Commitment. Group values are: Collaboration, Common purpose, and Controversy with civility. The critical value at the community and society level is Citizenship. This guidebook shares ideas for applying this model to service-oriented leadership development programs, primarily on college and university campuses. The collaborative research effort to develop this model was funded by the Dwight D. Eisenhower Leadership Development Program and the U.S. Department of Education.
Subject(s): Program models, Social Change Model

New
Avolio, B. J. (1999). ***Full leadership development: Building the vital forces in organizations.*** Thousand Oaks, CA: Sage.

Avolio describes leadership as a system made up of people, timing, resources, and interactions, and says that when organizations develop effective leadership systems, they empower both the firm and the individuals within it. This book uses scholarly research and personal anecdotes to address issues, including whether leaders are born or made, transactional versus transformational leadership, shared leadership, and how leadership affects performance. Each chapter offers descriptions of relevant studies and concludes with a list of "Some Things Worth Repeating." Includes bibliographical references and index.
Subject(s): Systemic leadership development

New
Baldwin, T. T., Danielson, C., & Wiggerhorn, W. (1997). **The evolution of learning strategies in organizations: From employee development to business redefinition.** *Academy of Management Executive, 11*(4), 47-58.

In response to turbulent times in business corporations, the authors suggest an evolutionary model of organizational learning strategies. The first stage, Employee Development, is depicted as the method most frequently used in organizational development programs. This is limited to informing and enhancing known business practices and does not serve

to meet challenges of the unknown. The proposed model demonstrates the evolution from stage one to stage two, Imminent Business Needs, which utilizes new issues to promote the continuous improvement of the organization. The final stage of the model, Unknown Business Development, leads the organization beyond the known frames of reference in order to excel in times of rapid change. The remaining portion of the article presents this model in action with a case analysis of Motorola University. Includes bibliographical references.
Subject(s): Development in organizations

Barker, R. A. (1997). **How can we train leaders if we do not know what leadership is?** *Human Relations*, *50*(4), 343-362.

Barker analyzed the literature of leadership and conducted informal surveys on working leaders and students of organizational behavior. He found a broad range of definitions for leadership and many cases in which leadership was not defined at all. He suggests that leadership scholars and practitioners stop categorizing leadership as an ability, behavior, action, role, function, or experience. Leadership is a dynamic process that resembles a river, continuously flowing, forever changing in speed and strength. Leadership happens through mutual influence and community efforts to reach the greatest good. Based on these conclusions Barker recommends that leadership education focus more on self-awareness than on skills- or goal-orientation.
Subject(s): Leadership development

New
Bartlett, C., & Ghoshal, S. (1997). **Beyond strategy, structure, systems to purpose, process, people.** *Monash Mt. Eliza Business Review*, *1*(1), 54-61.

Over the last 50 years businesses have organized around the philosophy that "structure followed strategy and that systems support structure." However, the authors say that these organizations cannot function in today's ever-changing global business environment. After interviewing over 200 international managers Bartlett and Ghoshal have developed a new, more flexible model for organizations that focuses on building processes that create knowledge and treating people like assets. Their new "transnational organisation" has three central characteristics: 1) multidimensional perspectives; 2) distributed, interdependent capabilities; and 3) flexible, integrative processes. Includes bibliographical references.
Subject(s): Development in organizations

New
Bassi, L. J., & Van Buren, M. E. (1999). **Sharpening the leading edge.** *Training & Development*, *53*(1), 23-33.

This review of ASTD's 1998 Benchmarking Service of the training industry identifies 55 organizations on "the leading edge" in terms of the amount and types of training they provide. These leading organizations are compared to other firms in the survey on factors including training expenditures, percentage of employees trained, employees per trainer, and

use of learning technologies. Statistics show that the amount of money spent on training and the number of employees receiving training is growing, but the gap between average firms and "leading edge" organizations is widening. Graphs of the findings and a business sector overview are included.
Subject(s): Training industry

Bell, C. R. (1996). *Managers as mentors: Building partnerships for learning.* San Francisco: Berrett-Koehler.

Bell describes mentoring as the "power-free facilitation of learning . . . teaching through consultation and affection rather than constriction and assessment." In this book he identifies these keys to being an effective mentor: push employees to take risks, be known as a dramatic listener, be a model of your own values, and celebrate successes. Chapters also address feedback, remote learning, and mentoring around equipment, and a self-check scale is included so readers can evaluate their mentoring abilities. Includes bibliographical references and index.
Subject(s): Mentoring

Bellman, G. M. (1993). *Getting things done when you are not in charge.* San Francisco: Berrett-Koehler.

This sequel to *The Quest for Staff Leadership* is focused toward middle managers, advisors, functional experts, and support personnel. Chapters offer practical advice on handling office politics, effecting change, and earning the respect of top management. Bellman teaches those in supporting roles to empower themselves, increasing their contributions professionally while achieving satisfaction personally. Includes bibliographical references and index.
Subject(s): Self-development, middle managers

Bennis, W., & Goldsmith, J. (1994). *Learning to lead: A workbook on becoming a leader.* New York: Addison-Wesley.

This workbook walks the reader through the core competencies of life with discussion of basic principles, exercises for self-improvement, and assessment to measure your progress. Chapters address integrity, trust, goal setting and achievement, reflection, learning from failure, and commitment. The authors expect those readers who respond to activities and assessments with honest answers to become capable leaders of organizations that share a common vision, have empowered members at every level, and promote continuous learning. At the end of the book an annotated bibliography by A. Khoo and H. Im suggests 20 books for further leadership studies. These books were identified as favorites in a survey of top-level managers and academicians in the field of leadership research. Includes an index.
Subject(s): Self-development

Bigelow, J. (1995). **Teaching managerial skills: A critique and future directions.** *Journal of Management Education*, *19*(3), 305-325.

This article begins with a summary and grouping of the current practices in teaching managerial skills within the university setting. Bigelow concentrates this summary on the nine major managerial skills texts. In response to his findings the author identifies two key issues: 1) skill learning is not carrying over to later practice, and 2) skill practice is more complex and divergent than the current image of skills implies. The critique concludes with a proposal for changes in current university practices.

Subject(s): Management education

Bowen, D. D., Lewicki, R. J., Hall, F. S., & Hall, D. T. (1997). *Experiences in management and organizational behavior* (4th ed.). New York: Wiley.

This book contains 65 exercises for use in management education. Of particular interest are: The Henderson Account, a role play to develop communication and group decision-making skills; *Analysis of Personal Power*, a questionnaire; *The Culture Quiz Sweepstakes*, a quiz for teams; and Krunchian Aircraft Co., Ltd., a role play to explore cultural differences. Most exercises are complete with handouts. Some recommend reading materials to complete the experience. Includes bibliographical references.

Subject(s): Trainer resources

Bracken, D. W., Dalton, M. A., Jako, R. A., McCauley, C. D., & Pollman, V. A. (1997). *Should 360-degree feedback be used only for developmental purposes?* Greensboro, NC: Center for Creative Leadership.

This book presents papers from a debate at the 1996 annual meeting of the Society for Industrial and Organizational Psychology. Debate centered around the use of 360-degree feedback for development of high-potential employees or using it for making administrative decisions about promotions and pay. The hot issues included: confidentiality, quality of data, positive and negative halo effects, potential for abuse of feedback data, ways to maximize the use of feedback, its value to an organization, and its value to individuals.

Subject(s): 360-degree feedback

New
Bricker's international directory: University-based executive development programs (31st ed.). (2000). Princeton, NJ: Peterson's.

This directory is designed to help upper-level management and executives select management programs at leading universities worldwide. Most programs run four weeks or less, some are longer, and some are offered in split sessions with classes offered weeks or months apart. The programs are listed under subject headings such as General Management, Leadership, Business Environment and Global Concerns, Business Strategy, Technology Management, Government and Nonprofit Management, and Executive MBA Programs. Information includes program objectives, location, duration, profile of participants, methods of instruction, calendar of sessions, tuition, faculty, special features, and the name of the official contact person. Includes institution, geographic, and

subject indexes. An online version is also available through www.petersons.com.

Subject(s): Directory of programs, executive education

Brownfain, E., & Churgel, S. (1997). *EBTD directory: Experience-based training and development programs.* Boulder, CO: Association for Experiential Education.

This directory lists organizations that provide experience-based programs for human resource development and organizational change. Such organizations offer programs that create situations to help participants discover their own insights into challenging business situations. Many of the programs have been accredited by the Association for Experiential Education. Some organizations listed are: Breckenridge Outdoor Education Center in Breckenridge, Colorado; Corporate Adventure Training Institute in St. Catherines, Ontario; Project Adventure in Portland, Oregon; and Outward Bound with several locations. Includes a bibliography.

Subject(s): Directory of programs, management education

Brungardt, C. (1996). **The making of leaders: A review of the research in leadership development and education.** *Journal of Leadership Studies, 3*(3), 81-95.

Brungardt reviews 70 years of literature that debates the question, "Can leaders be made?" There is abundant theory and research to support the concepts of leadership development, education, and training. Brungardt defines leadership development as "a continuous learning process that spans an entire lifetime." Leadership education "includes learning activities and educational environments that . . . foster leadership abilities." Leadership training "refers to learning activities for a specific role or job." Brungardt examines the literature in two contexts: leadership development theory, which is development throughout a lifetime, and learning leadership theory, which is the role that education plays in leadership development.

Subject(s): Leadership development

Burack, E. H., Hochwarter, W., & Mathys, N. J. (1997). **The new management development paradigm.** *Human Resource Planning, 20*(1), 14-21.

Increased globalization and technological changes in the last 25 years have required American corporations to integrate business strategies and human resources practices in order to remain competitive. This article defines such integration as management development (MD) and identifies MD features common to world class organizations. The features include: "seamless" or layerless organizational structure, having a global and cross-cultural orientation, emphasizing individual learning, and recognizing core competencies. A model for defining competencies, which the authors believe is central to organizational effectiveness, is also developed.

Subject(s): Management development

New

Cacioppe, R. (1998). **An integrated model and approach for the design of effective leadership development programs.** *Leadership & Organization Development Journal, 19*(1), 44-53.

Cacioppe offers advice to human resources development (HRD) professionals who evaluate or design leadership development programs. He recommends starting with an examination of the organization's key strategic objectives and the leadership competencies vital to meeting those objectives. Next, a program should be designed with an integrated approach that includes: skill building, observing models of good leadership, immersing developing leaders into change efforts, focusing on global issues, networking, and participating in strategic decision making. Other important elements of an effective program are: 360-degree feedback, coaching, group feedback, health assessment, personality analysis, and learning journals. Crucial to the successful transfer of learning is follow-up after the program. Includes bibliographical references.

Subject(s): Program models, human resources development

Campbell, D. P. (1984). *If I'm in charge here, why is everybody laughing?* (2nd ed.). Greensboro, NC: Center for Creative Leadership.

This book examines a number of questions: How can leaders bring out the best in the people they work with? What are the best ways to overcome opposition? Why are friendships so special to people in charge? Campbell issues a call to take up the challenge of leadership, which can be demanding, enriching, and exhilarating. This is a book full of useful tips for people who are in charge, who make things happen, and who want to have an impact on their world.

Subject(s): Self-development

New

Carley, M. S. (1999). **Training goes to the movies.** *Training & Development, 53*(7), 15-18.

Carley describes the leadership lessons found in 12 feature films. *The Wizard of Oz* (1939) represents a feeling of disorientation found in situations of sudden change. However, Dorothy and friends reach their goals by overcoming every obstacle along their journey. In *The River Wild* (1994) Meryl Streep takes her family on a whitewater rafting trip and chaos ensues. *The Dirty Dozen* (1967) contains a lesson on building a successful team from an uncontrollable bunch of misfits. *The Commitments* (1991) demonstrates how interpersonal conflict in a talented band destroys their chance for success. Creative problem solving is portrayed in *Apollo 13* (1995), *Fly Away Home* (1996), and *Flight of the Phoenix* (1965). Diversity issues are highlighted in *Lone Star* (1996) and *Do the Right Thing* (1989). Leadership style and crisis management are dramatized in *Crimson Tide* (1995) and *Gettysburg* (1993).

Subject(s): Videos as training technique

Carol, L. (1997). **KIVA: A leadership initiative and technique.** *Journal of Leadership Studies, 4*(2), 116-118.

KIVA is a group management technique adopted from an ancient ceremonial tradition of the Pueblo tribe. It allows large groups to examine transcendent issues surrounding a concept, program, project, or problem, and it can be used to identify and refine leadership initiatives. Often used as a convening mechanism, it works best when: 1) group members have different levels of responsibility in a hierarchy, 2) members represent three institutional sectors, and 3) multiple members have private perspectives. Details are provided on how to arrange a KIVA and what is necessary for its success. For example, Carol recommends pre-selecting a topic and using a time frame.

Subject(s): Program models, Native American leadership

New

Cini, M. A., & Fritz, J. M. H. (1997). **Organizational leadership and professional communication: Dovetailing theory with praxis for adult learners.** *A Leadership Journal: Women in Leadership—Sharing the Vision, 2*(1), 133-138.

Duquesne University offers an accelerated, Saturday-only degree program in organizational leadership for adult students. In this article Cini and Fritz, professors in the program, argue that adult learners have unique instruction and assessment needs. They suggest that professors use small group activities, assign journals and papers instead of tests, and explain the difference between academic and lay writing and research. Includes bibliographical references.

Subject(s): Program descriptions

Clawson, J. G., & Doner, J. (1996). **Teaching leadership through aikido.** *Journal of Management Education, 20*(2), 182-205.

Clawson and Doner teach a two-hour aikido session in many of the leadership courses in the Darden School's executive education and MBA programs at the University of Virginia. Students come to class dressed in loose-fitting clothing, ready to learn the Eastern philosophy behind this defensive martial art. Through relaxation and breathing exercises, students become centered. They practice staying centered as classmates push them physically. To illustrate the concept of ki, the harmony of mind and body, students are asked to have positive thoughts, then negative thoughts, while being pushed. Inevitably the negative thoughts weaken students and they become vulnerable to the pushing. The next module teaches students to sense the energy of others. Finally, students realize how to harmonize with the energy of others. The authors report that participants find the physical metaphor of aikido a powerful tool to become centered around purpose and principles, clarify a vision, sense danger, and convert challenges into positive energy.

Subject(s): Program descriptions, Eastern philosophy

Clemens, J. K., & Albrecht, S. (1995). *The timeless leader.* Holbrook, MA: Adams Publishing.

Clemens and Albrecht share some of the leadership lessons developed at the Hartwick Humanities in Management Institute. Shakespeare's *Henry IV* and *Henry V* teach us about mentors and protégés, listening, trust, inspiration, and the language of leadership. Cleopatra is an example of a woman leading in a male-dominated society, collaboration, and intercultural understanding. Other lessons are derived from Plato's allegory of the cave, Captain Ahab's maniacal obsession with Moby Dick, Martin Luther King, Jr.'s dialogue that inspired change, Winston Churchill's persuasive rhetoric skills, and Mahatma Gandhi's example of ethics and humility.
Subject(s): Trainer resources, leadership lessons in literature

Cockrell, D. (Ed.). (1991). *The wilderness educator: The Wilderness Education Association curriculum guide.* Merrillville, IN: ICS Books.

Written as a textbook for W.E.A.'s National Standard Program for expedition leaders, this book outlines wilderness education theories and principles. Chapters written by practitioners include: judgment and decision making, group dynamics, environmental ethics, rations planning, adventure skills, and emergency procedures. How to prepare, market, administrate, and evaluate a wilderness expedition are discussed in depth. Includes an index.
Subject(s): Program models, adventure education

Cohen, N. H. (1995). *Mentoring adult learners: A guide for educators and trainers.* Malabar, FL: Krieger.

Cohen's purpose is to "provide pragmatic guidance to those who assume responsibility for the mentor role." The book includes two versions of a self-assessment instrument, *The Principles of Adult Mentoring Scale*, one for postsecondary education and one for business and government. Cohen wants to link knowledge from psychology and interpersonal communications to challenges facing mentors. His intended audience includes college faculty, administration and staff, professionals running intern training programs, and human-resource development specialists in business and government. Chapter subjects include: relationship emphasis, information emphasis, facilitative focus, confrontational focus, mentor model, and mentee vision. Includes bibliographical references and index.
Subject(s): Mentoring

Collins, S. (1995). *Our children are watching: Ten skills for leading the next generation to success.* Barrytown, NY: Barrytown, Ltd.

Drawing on her own life experiences and many that have been shared by the participants in her seminars, Collins concludes that parenting is the ultimate leadership experience. She tells compelling stories to teach parents, educators, business managers, and government officials how to progress from childlike following-behavior to adult leadership-

behavior. Her ten skills for success include: focusing on successes, imagining positive outcomes, and deleting mental obstacles.
Subject(s): Self-development

Conger, J. A. (1992). *Learning to lead: The art of transforming managers into leaders.* San Francisco: Jossey-Bass.

To fill the leadership void, are companies wasting millions of dollars of valuable assets on ineffectual leadership training? Conger looks at the tremendous emphasis on leadership training and reexamines the question of whether leaders are made or born, beginning with a look at leadership training in the time of Plato. Personal growth, conceptual, feedback, and skill-building approaches are examined for their effectiveness in developing leaders. Conger then goes "beyond Myers-Briggs" in defining his view of leadership training in the future. Includes bibliographical references and index.
Subject(s): Leadership development

New
Conger, J. A., & Benjamin, B. (1999). *Building leaders: How successful companies develop the next generation.* San Francisco: Jossey-Bass.

Conger and Benjamin identify three common approaches to leadership development: individual skill development, instilling organizational values promoting leadership, and strategic interventions. This book examines the strengths and weaknesses of each strategy, and uses case studies of companies such as Federal Express, National Australia Bank, and Ernst & Young to describe best practices in each leadership development approach. The authors also address the new format of action learning, which they say has great potential as a teaching method but has been hindered by program design flaws.
Subject(s): Leadership development

Consalvo, C. M. (1993). *Experiential training activities for outside and in.* Amherst, MA: HRD Press.

Thirty-six activities are intended to add fun to training sessions while helping participants change their awareness and behaviors. The Egyptian Mummy and King Tut exercises are used to practice trust. Bureaucratic Maze and Jigglers and Bursters are group juggling exercises that require teamwork and creative problem solving. Many of the exercises require physical strength, but there are also nonphysical roles for observers and coaches. Each exercise includes suggestions for debriefing and variations.
Subject(s): Exercises

New
Cook, J. E., & Young, M. V. (1999). **Preparing women leaders: The Astin Social Change Model in action.** *A Leadership Journal: Women in Leadership—Sharing the Vision, 3*(2), 93-97.

This article describes how Converse College's Institute for Leadership used the Astin Social Change Model to create a

holistic program for developing women's leadership. The program is a 21-credit curriculum consisting of three phases: developing leadership skills such as speaking in public and writing for an audience, familiarizing students with the history of women's leadership, and designing an interdisciplinary program of study focused on a specific societal problem and the leadership skills needed to solve it. The program also has a cocurricular component in which the students attend seminars, work in leadership teams, do service projects, and participate in field studies. The authors believe that this program prepares students to lead outside of the classroom by connecting in-class learning to real-world activities.
Subject(s): Program descriptions, Social Change Model, women's leadership development

Council for the Advancement of Standards. (1997). **Council for the Advancement of Standards in Higher Education— Student leadership programs: Standards and guidelines.** *Concepts & Connections: A Newsletter for Educators, 5*(2), 17-19.

Newly established standards and guidelines for designing and delivering leadership programs are presented. Two articles in the same issue provide background information. Dennis Roberts describes the evolution of teaching leadership throughout the history of higher education in "The Changing Look of Leadership Programs" (pp. 1, 3, 11-14). Ted Miller describes how and why CAS wrote the standards and how leadership educators should apply them in "Leadership Training Concepts and Techniques: Professional Standards for Student Leadership Programs" (pp. 7-9).
Subject(s): Program standards

Craig, R. L. (Ed.). (1996). *The ASTD training and development handbook: A guide to human resource development* (4th ed.). New York: McGraw-Hill.

Fifty-one human resource developers from major corporations contribute essays describing the best practices in the field. James DeVito of Johnson & Johnson writes about the learning organization. Robert Hayles explains The Pillsbury Company's diversity training and development program. Jeffrey Howell and Larry Silvey of Arthur Andersen Worldwide Organization describe interactive multimedia training systems. Donald Conover discusses AT&T's leadership development program. Edward Bales shares Motorola University's experience with business education partnerships. Includes bibliographical references and index.
Subject(s): Trainer resources

New
Crainer, S. (1997). *Which executive programme?: A critical guide to the world's best management development courses.* London: Economist Intelligence Unit.

Compiled by the Economist Intelligence Unit, this book serves as a guide to international management development courses. Part I describes global trends in management development, including corporate and personal imperatives,

the changing approaches of providers, and open versus custom programs. Part II is a directory of 90 providers divided into four geographical regions: North America, the United Kingdom and Ireland, Continental Europe, and the rest of the world. Each provider's entry includes contact information, type of teaching methods, descriptions of open and tailored programs, and comments by the author.
Subject(s): Directory of programs, executive education

Crotty, P. T., & Soule, A. J. (1997). **Executive education: Yesterday and today, with a look at tomorrow.** *Journal of Management Development, 16*(1), 4-21.

Executive education "yesterday" involved companies sending top-level managers to university-based executive MBA (EMBA) programs. "Today" companies partner with universities to customize executive training or structure their own in-house corporate universities. "Tomorrow" a global focus will drive executive education. To move across cultural boundaries and maximize potential markets executives will need to develop strong customer relationships and create winning strategies through organizational change. The authors predict that a variety of approaches will be used: university-based MBA and EMBA programs, in-house corporate universities, customized contract programs, distance learning, and technology-based training.
Subject(s): Executive education

New
Crozier, A. J. G. (1998). **Accreditation of management development: The process of European integration.** *efmd FORUM, 98*(3), 17-22.

The European Union has established a series of directives intended to ensure that EU nationals can study and work in all EU countries, and that professional diplomas and accreditation will be recognized throughout the EU. Crozier says that while in theory this system allows individuals to enjoy academic and professional mobility within the EU, in practice it is often a complicated, bureaucratic process. And because management is not a licensed profession, MBA and management development degrees often fall outside these guidelines altogether. This article advocates the development of standardized accreditation systems for all disciplines, including management education, to safeguard the professional mobility of EU citizens in the future.
Subject(s): Program accreditation

Czarniawska-Joerges, B., & Guillet de Monthoux, P. (Eds.). (1994). *Good novels, better management: Reading organizational realities in fiction.* Newark, NJ: Gordon & Breach.

Authors from ten countries contribute essays on the use of fiction to teach management, each describing a novel about business and society in the late 19th century. The stories tell of the tensions that occurred as industrialism brought conflict between big business and family-owned shops, between economics and humanitarianism, and between company loyalty and abuse of power. The editors believe that fiction

provides a mirror of the human condition and makes visible otherwise invisible thoughts and feelings. Some of the novels discussed are: Emile Zola's *The Ladies' Paradise*, H. G. Wells' *The History of Mr. Polly*, Miguel de Cervantes' *Don Quixote*, and Rosa Montero's *My Beloved Master*. Includes bibliographical references.
Subject(s): Leadership lessons in literature

Dalton, M. A., & Hollenbeck, G. P. (1996). *How to design an effective system for developing managers and executives.* Greensboro, NC: Center for Creative Leadership.

A model for executive development evolved from the Center for Creative Leadership's program, Tools for Developing Successful Executives, and the shared experience of 1,000 corporate partners. This six-step model can be used by human resource professionals to design a new program or evaluate an existing one. The steps are: 1) find and use organizational support for creating a process, 2) define the program purpose and the behaviors to be developed, 3) use feedback as the baseline for executive development, 4) define and communicate the critical role of the manager, 5) write the development plan, and 6) make the program accountable. Includes bibliographical references.
Subject(s): Program models, management education, executive education

Darnay, B. T. (Ed.). (1997). *Consultants and consulting organizations directory* (17th ed.). Detroit: Gale.

Over 23,000 independent consultants and consulting firms are briefly listed in this two-volume set. There are descriptive entries for firms involved in business management, human resources development, education, and personal development. Information includes the names of the principals, year founded, seminars, videos, publications, unique services, SIC codes, fax and toll-free numbers, e-mail and website addresses, and the ability to handle international clients. Volume 2 contains geographic, firm, and activities indexes with cross-references to main listings. All information is verified.
Subject(s): Trainer resources

Daugherty, R. A., & Williams, S. U. (1997). **The long-term impacts of leadership development: An assessment of a statewide program.** *Journal of Leadership Studies*, 4(2), 101-115.

This article assesses the long-term impact of a statewide community-based leadership development program. The Oklahoma Family Community Leadership Program (OFCLP) offers workshops to prepare adults for involvement in public-policy decision making. In 30 counties that sponsored the program for at least three years, program agents responded to a survey about: types of community leadership activity, types of OFCLP preparation (workshops, OFCLP materials, and handbooks), most valuable program components, willingness to expand activities, future needs, and long-term impacts. The study found that participants continued their leadership roles

beyond their program commitments and that the program's methodology worked well for emerging community issues.
Subject(s): Program evaluation

New
De Bono, E. (1999). *Six thinking hats* (Rev. ed.). Boston: Little, Brown.

De Bono describes a method for utilizing six types of thinking using colored hats as a mental hook. Individuals and groups practice white hat thinking when concerned with objective facts. Red hat thinking provides an emotional perspective. The black hat is cautious and points out weaknesses, yellow is optimistic, green is creative, and blue is organized. The hats provide a reminder to think from all perspectives and a tool to diffuse arguments. De Bono suggests more thinking tools in *Lateral Thinking* (1990). Another book, *Six Action Shoes* (1991), offers a framework for six modes of action: routine, crisis, investigation, leadership, pragmatism, and caring.
Subject(s): Exercises

De Ciantis, C. (1995). *Using an art technique to facilitate leadership development.* Greensboro, NC: Center for Creative Leadership.

This report is a description of the touchstone exercise, an activity in which leadership program participants create an artwork that represents their vision and purpose as leaders. De Ciantis describes how the exercise is conducted, provides examples of touchstones produced in programs at the Center for Creative Leadership, and considers the effectiveness of the activity as a means of defining ourselves as leaders. The appendix contains useful information on how anyone can conduct a touchstone exercise. Includes bibliographical references.
Subject(s): Art as training technique

New
Donathen, E. A., & Hines, C. A. (1998). **Growing our own future leaders: A case study in Texas leadership training.** *A Leadership Journal: Women in Leadership—Sharing the Vision, 2*(2), 93-106.

In 1994 the Texas A&M University system established the Center for Leadership in Higher Education to develop leaders, especially women and minorities, within the university. This article describes how the Center developed its program and selected core competencies to teach, and then presents the results of an independent evaluation. While revisions to this program continue, the authors believe that some sort of system-wide leadership development is necessary to ensure future leaders in higher education. Appendices include a sample curriculum and suggested periodical resources. Includes bibliographical references.
Subject(s): Program descriptions

New

Dotlich, D. L., & Cairo, P. C. (1999). *Action coaching: How to leverage individual performance for company success.* San Francisco: Jossey-Bass.

 The authors define action coaching as "a process that fosters self-awareness and leads to the motivation to change" by focusing on both individual growth and organizational performance. A successful manager can coach his employees through the four levels of coaching goals: self-awareness, performance improvement, performance breakthrough, and transformation. This book describes the different types of coaches—including managers, executives, peers, and external coaches—and offers checklists and activities to help readers develop the attributes they need to be successful action coaches. Includes index.
 Subject(s): Coaching

New

Dotlich, D. L., & Noel, J. L. (1998). *Action learning: How the world's top companies are re-creating their leaders and themselves.* San Francisco: Jossey-Bass.

 The authors describe an action learning program that integrates executive development with business strategy. Its roots are in 1980s strategic boot camps at Honeywell and GE that challenged executives to learn by doing and experiment with new attitudes. A framework for action learning includes 12 elements: a sponsor, strategic mandate, learning process, selection of participants, learning teams, coaching, orientation to issues, data gathering, data analysis, draft presentation, actual presentation, and reflection. Such programs can be customized around globalization, technology, customer satisfaction, business strategy, or other organizational issues. The authors share ideas for designing new programs and success stories of action learning in major companies. Appendices include diagrams and outlines of action learning programs. Includes bibliographical references and index.
 Subject(s): Program models, action learning, corporate leadership

New

Douglas, C. A. (1997). *Formal mentoring programs in organizations: An annotated bibliography.* Greensboro, NC: Center for Creative Leadership.

 Formal mentoring programs have become a popular means of management development, but investigating the track records of such programs and learning how to build them has been difficult. This bibliography summarizes 80 books and articles selected from the practical and academic literature, describing the experiences of individuals and organizations with formal mentoring programs. Also addressed are benefits and drawbacks, organizational objectives, and methods for building effective programs. Includes index.
 Subject(s): Mentoring

New

Drucker, P. F. (1999). **Managing oneself.** *Harvard Business Review*, 77(2), 64-74.

 Drucker's advice for success in the knowledge economy is to know oneself. To identify personal strengths, Drucker recommends seeking feedback analysis. Once strengths are identified a person can concentrate efforts where they'll have the most impact. One must also understand his or her personal style of learning and performing. For most people that style would be reading, listening, writing, or talking. The most important element in self-knowledge is living one's values—finding congruence between personal and organizational values. Understanding one's strengths, one's style of learning and performing, and one's values helps to answer the questions, Where do I belong? and What can I contribute?
 Subject(s): Self-knowledge

Edwards, M. R., & Ewen, A. J. (1996). *360-degree feedback: The powerful new model for employee assessment and performance improvement.* New York: AMACOM.

 The authors give a general overview of 360-degree feedback—assessment by self, supervisors, direct reports, peers, and customers—for those unfamiliar with the concept. They discuss the value of this kind of assessment, how to design a feedback project, and how to evaluate the process. The appendix provides more than 100 questions to use when designing a project. They are related to competencies in: organizational skills, organizational climate, communication skills, group effectiveness, coaching, teams, and leadership. The issue of instrument validity is briefly discussed. Includes bibliography and index.
 Subject(s): 360-degree feedback

Eichinger, R. W., & Lombardo, M. M. (1990). *Twenty-two ways to develop leadership in staff managers.* Greensboro, NC: Center for Creative Leadership.

 This report notes the gap in developmental opportunities between staff (human resources, engineering, R&D, PR) and line (sales, manufacturing, operations, management). Employees in line functions have authority to make final decisions and can measure their output by revenue. They are therefore exposed to the experiences that develop successful executives. Staff managers can gain developmental experience by taking challenging jobs such as start-ups, fix-its, or leaps in responsibility. Lessons can be learned from role models, coursework, and hardships that cause self-examination. A variety of experiences leads to success. A study of 250 executives' most significant learning experiences explains why a gap exists between staff and line development. Twenty-two recommendations are made for closing the gap. Includes a bibliography.
 Subject(s): Leadership development, managers

Eitington, J. E. (1996). *The winning trainer: Winning ways to involve people in learning* (3rd ed.). Houston: Gulf.

 Participative training methods such as icebreakers, small group exercises, role plays, simulations, puzzles, instruments, problem solving, in-basket, and team building are covered in this how-to manual for group-in-action trainers. Chapters include techniques for using each method, ideas for involving all participants, and samples of activities. There are also suggestions for training methods with less participant involvement: case studies, films, and lectures. A four-D model illustrates four steps of the training cycle: 1) determine need, 2) design programs, 3) deliver programs, and 4) discern differences (evaluation). The appendices contain 97 handouts and worksheets, which may be photocopied or made into overhead transparencies. Includes a glossary, bibliographical references, and index.

Subject(s): Trainer resources

Ellet, W., & Winig, L. (Eds.). (1996). *A critical guide to management training videos and selected multimedia, 1996.* Boston: Harvard Business Reference.

This book intends to lighten the costly and time-consuming process of selecting training videos. It objectively evaluates new releases using criteria suggested by trainers. Films are rated on a four-star basis according to: support of training objectives; quality of production, acting, and script; portrayal of women and minorities; support materials; and value for the money. There are films on change management, communication skills, diversity, innovation, leadership, team building, and more. A small sample of CD-ROM training products is included. Each review includes a brief description of the reviewer's background. Includes a source directory and an index.

Subject(s): Videos as training technique

Evans, P. (1997). **New horizons for management development.** *efmd FORUM, 97*(2), 22-25.

This article is based on a speech to the 1997 Global Forum on Management Education. Evans, a professor of organizational behavior at INSEAD, likens the dual responsibilities for human resource development to a split egg. The operational functions are the supportive bottom half of the egg. Development of strategies, new products, and emerging leaders are the visible and glamorous top half of the egg. To achieve operational goals a manager must push responsibility downward, thus empowering employees and making development happen. The ideal split egg creates a balance between providing challenges and managing risks.

Subject(s): Management development

New
Evarts, T. M. (1998). **Human resource development as a maturing field of study.** *Human Resource Development Quarterly, 9*(4), 385-389.

Human resource development (HRD) is a practice that draws from three disciplines: economics, general systems theory, and psychology. However, no cohesive theory unifying these concepts exists, largely because HRD is an applied field that has been more concerned with outputs than concepts. Evarts says that in order for HRD to be taken seriously as a field of

study and for the practice to evolve and grow, researchers must develop theories that will integrate current knowledge and create a framework for understanding future findings. Includes bibliographical references.

Subject(s): Human resources development

New
Facteau, C. L., Facteau, J. D., Schoel, L. C., Russell, J. E. A., & Poteet, M. L. (1998). **Reactions of leaders to 360-degree feedback from subordinates and peers.** *Leadership Quarterly: Special Issue: 360-Degree Feedback in Leadership Research, 9*(4), 427-448.

In this study 220 managers of a public utility company provided data about their reactions to feedback from peers and subordinates. Researchers aimed to learn if the managers accepted feedback as accurate or considered feedback useful for the development of leadership skills. Data were derived from pre- and post-training surveys, performance ratings, perceptions of organizational support, and perceptions of rater abilities. It was determined that overall ratings were related to acceptance of feedback. There were mixed results for usefulness of feedback. Includes bibliographical references.

Subject(s): 360-degree feedback

Fanning Leadership Center. (1996). *Youth leadership in action: A community focus: Program planning guide.* Athens: Fanning Leadership Center, University of Georgia. Phone: (706) 542-1108.

This guide is written for local organizers of the Fanning Leadership Center's Youth Leadership in Action program but would be helpful to any organizer of youth leadership programs. There is an outline of eight learning modules that focus primarily on skill building. The guide also contains a planning section with schedules, sample letters, and evaluation forms. Other helpful materials include icebreakers, mentoring strategies, suggestions for journal keeping, and case scenarios to spark group discussion. Separate *Participant Workbooks* may be purchased.

Subject(s): Program descriptions, youth leadership

Fanning Leadership Center. (1997). *Community leadership program: Planning guide* (1997-1998 series ed.). Athens: Fanning Leadership Center, University of Georgia. Phone: (706) 542-1108.

This guide is written for local coordinators of the Fanning Leadership Center's Community Leadership Program but would be helpful for anyone planning a grassroots leadership program. The role of program coordinator and descriptions of supporting committees are outlined with task lists and a timeline for completing tasks. An outline of the 12-module Community Leadership Program, sample letters, meeting agendas, and evaluation forms are included. Additional books are available for instructors and participants.

Subject(s): Program descriptions, community leadership

Feinberg, R. A. (1996). **Leadership education and the cinematic experience: Using film to teach leadership.** *Journal of Leadership Studies, 3*(4), 148-157.

Feinberg shares his favorite films for teaching leadership in the classroom. Fellini's *Orchestra Rehearsal* (1979), a film about an old orchestra rebelling against a new conductor, illustrates the relationship between leaders and followers. *Space Camp* (1986), a film about young misfits accidentally launched into space, enhances a lesson on teamwork. Feinberg uses Mel Gibson's version of *Mutiny on the Bounty* (*The Bounty,* 1984) to teach students about followers' dependency on a leader's positional power and ethics. Other favorites include: *Lord of the Flies* (1992), *Boyz N the Hood* (1991), *Dave* (1993), *Tommy Boy* (1995), *A League of Their Own* (1998), *Toy Story* (1995), and *Working Girl* (1988).
Subject(s): Leadership lessons in videos

Fenwick, W. E., & Steffy, B. E. (1997). **Using film to teach leadership in educational administration.** *Educational Administration Quarterly, 33*(1), 107-115.

The authors like to use film as a teaching tool because it presents a longitudinal view of leadership in context. It illustrates the consequences of a leader's decisions and behaviors. Students can observe and discuss the development of relationships. Fenwick and Steffy briefly describe ten films and the leadership lessons they contain: *Nixon* (1985), *Gandhi* (1982), *Joan of Arc* (1985), *Malcolm X* (1993), *The Last Emperor* (1987), *Patton* (1969), *Inherit the Wind* (1960), *Matewan* (1987), *Lawrence of Arabia* (1962), and *Viva Zapata!* (1952).
Subject(s): Leadership lessons in videos

New
Filipovic, N. (1998). **Education quality: Let the market be the judge.** *efmd FORUM, 98*(3), 23-28.

Filipovic says that far too often, especially in "countries in transition," business educators ignore the issues of quality improvement and customer satisfaction. Management education organizations need to avoid merely meeting mechanical output standards and focus instead on improving the quality of services delivered. The model used in determining European Quality Awards (EQA) offers one way of doing this, identifying five quality enablers: leadership, policy and strategy, people management, resources, and processes. The EQA also describes four results parameters, which include people satisfaction, customer satisfaction, impact on society, and business results. Following this model can help organizations measure their effectiveness and treat business education like a service industry.
Subject(s): Program evaluation, management education

Fleenor, J. W., McCauley, C. D., & Brutus, S. (1996). **Self-other rating agreement and leader effectiveness.** *Leadership Quarterly, 7*(4), 487-506.

Multi-perspective rating instruments, which solicit information on an individual's performance from various sources,

offer researchers the opportunity to compare the differences between self-ratings and the ratings of others. Past work created four categories for the levels of self-other agreement: over-estimators (who rated themselves higher than others rated them), under-estimators (who rated themselves lower than others rated them), in-agreement/good raters, and in-agreement/bad raters. In this study the authors asked whether adding more categories allowed for a more detailed analysis of self/other ratings. They found that adding the two further distinctions of over-estimators/good and under-estimators/poor helped compare agreement groups more effectively.
Subject(s): 360-degree feedback

Fleenor, J. W., & Prince, J. M. (1997). *Using 360-degree feedback in organizations: An annotated bibliography.* Greensboro, NC: Center for Creative Leadership.

This book serves as an introduction to the literature on multi-rater assessment tools. In addition to the 56 books and articles described, the authors answer frequently asked questions about 360-degree feedback: the development of the concept, the benefits to individuals and organizations, recommended uses, and future trends. The appendices contain the criteria for selection in this bibliography, related sources, and a glossary. Includes author and title indexes.
Subject(s): 360-degree feedback

Freedman, N., & Mitchell, A. (1997). **Leadership training in companies.** *efmd FORUM, 97*(2), 39-44.

This article reports on a meeting of senior management developers from 20 leading companies in the European Union. These training directors shared their program descriptions, benchmarks, models, and concerns. The highlights are featured in this article. Phillips Company employed a transformation program called Operation Centurion to survey employees' perspectives on company leadership, provide 360-degree feedback to managers, and teach a variety of leadership styles. The executives at the Swiss bank UBS served as faculty in leadership development programs for high-potential employees. Ericcson offered three-tiered leadership programs and partnered with business schools to deliver one of the tiers.
Subject(s): Program descriptions, management education

New
Friedman, E. H. (1990). *Friedman's fables.* New York: Guilford Press.

Rabbi Edwin Friedman conjures up a cast of characters to dramatize the paradoxes that can happen in interpersonal relationships. His fables aim to shatter the illusions that communication is intellectual rather than emotional, that insight will influence people who cannot be motivated to change, that resistance can be overcome by trying harder, and that seriousness yields better results than playfulness. An accompanying manual provides a tongue-in-cheek moral for each fable as well as ten leading questions to spark discussions.
Subject(s): Storytelling as training technique, fables

New

Friedman, S. D., DeGroot, J., & Christensen, P. M. (Eds.). (1998). *Integrating work and life: The Wharton resource guide.* San Francisco: Jossey-Bass/Pfeiffer.

This guide offers a research-based framework for balancing work and personal life. Three principles form the foundation: 1) clarify what's important, 2) recognize and support the whole person, and 3) continually experiment with the way goals are achieved. More than 30 activities focus on the individual actions and the support from managers and organizations that create balance. Most are presented as two- to three-hour modules that include a lecture, readings, discussion, and an activity—a case study, self-assessment, action plan, or role play. One example, Unifying Principles in Work/Life Satisfaction, helps participants identify their value systems and use them as a basis for decisions. Pedal to the Metal Versus a Balanced Life Experience includes a debate that highlights the trade-offs between career achievement and family satisfaction. Includes bibliographical references and tables that classify activities by type and audience.

Subject(s): Trainer resources, work and life balance

Frigon, N. L., Sr., & Jackson, H. K., Jr. (1996). *The leader: Developing the skills and personal qualities you need to lead effectively.* New York: AMACOM.

This workbook is designed for those beginning leadership positions in business, community, or personal situations. Its building blocks for learning to be a leader are: 1) leadership principles, which include integrity, consideration, and teamwork; 2) leadership traits, which include initiative, ethical behavior, and dependability; and 3) leadership skills, which include planning, decision making, communication, coaching, and knowledge. Diagrams and activities throughout the book guide the reader through each building block. In the appendices are a Leadership Self-Assessment to take at the beginning of the workbook and a Leadership Plan to complete after the book is read. Includes bibliographical references and index.

Subject(s): Self-development

Frohlich, N., & Oppenheimer, J. A. (1997). **Tests of leadership solutions to collective action problems.** *Simulation & Gaming, 28*(2), 181-197.

The best way to measure the effectiveness of leadership and the efficacy of leadership solutions has long been debated. This article examines that question in regard to a specific simulation of entrepreneurial leadership. The authors debate the effectiveness of simulations and experiments and discuss the results of a simulation on communication and collective goods. Includes bibliographical references.

Subject(s): Simulation as training technique

Fulmer, R. M. (1997). **The evolving paradigm of leadership development.** *Organizational Dynamics, 25*(4), 59-72.

Fulmer states that leadership programs are moving away from "management training" on a university campus to

customized "executive education" offered at schools, training centers, and at corporate facilities. He sees seven trends that will drive the future of leadership programs. Participants will grow from passive listeners to active learners. Development will evolve from one-time events to an ongoing process. The purpose of leadership development will change from knowledge to action. Study of cases and best practices will switch focus from past performance to the future. Those who plan, design, deliver, and select development programs will move from specialists in their field into partnerships that pool their expertise. Trainers will concentrate on substance more than style. Finally, leadership development will move from the "ivory tower to factory floor."

Subject(s): Leadership development programs, executive education

Fulmer, R. M., & Vicere, A. A. (1995). *Executive education and leadership development: The state of the practice.* University Park, PA: Penn State Institute for the Study of Organizational Effectiveness.

In a world of constant change the advantage goes to the organization that learns the fastest. To meet this challenge organizations are spending $12 billion annually on executive education and leadership development programs in-house, at universities, through consultants, and at nonuniversity training organizations. Based on a survey of education suppliers, interviews with executives, and a review of recent studies, this book summarizes key trends in the field. Includes bibliographical references. Appendices list intellectual resources (people and publications).

Subject(s): Leadership development programs, executive education

New

Furnham, A., & Stringfield, P. (1998). **Congruence in job-performance ratings: A study of 360-degree feedback examining self, manager, peers, and consultant ratings.** *Human Relations, 51*(4), 517-530.

This study examined the 360-degree feedback of 56 managers and 7 consultants who worked together in task-oriented teams. Data were analyzed to determine the congruence levels between the ratings of self, manager, peer, and consultant. The findings confirmed previous work in the field, which showed that subjects rank themselves higher than others rank them and that correlations between others are higher than correlations between self and others. Includes bibliographical references.

Subject(s): 360-degree feedback

New

Gass, M. A. (1995). *Book of metaphors: Volume II.* Dubuque, IA: Kendall/Hunt.

The Association for Experiential Education presents 57 learning activities contributed by their members. Each uses a metaphor to help participants discover changes they could make in their own behaviors. The activities are arranged by audience: therapeutic, corporate, school, and general populations. For the corporate audience, some activities are Computer Disinfectant (to practice team skills), and 2B or Knot 2B (to reinforce decision-making and problem-solving skills). A general audience activity is The Chocolate Game, which identifies competitive and cooperative behaviors. Volume I was distributed to the 45 authors who contributed to the first edition of this title and is available to anyone who contributes a metaphor activity for Volume III.

Subject(s): Exercises

New
Gelb, M. J. (1998). *How to think like Leonardo da Vinci: Seven steps to genius every day.* New York: Delacorte Press.

Gelb views Leonardo da Vinci as a genius, and this book proposes to assist readers in exploring their inner selves for true potential. Gelb begins by paralleling the Renaissance era with our current time before presenting biographical information pertaining to da Vinci. The second portion of the book introduces seven principles that Gelb discovered were inherent in da Vinci's life: a curious approach to life, a commitment to test knowledge, refinement of the senses, the ability to embrace uncertainty, whole-brain thinking, fitness and poise, and a systematic way of thinking. A chapter is devoted to each of these principles, including self-improvement exercises and samples of da Vinci's genius. The final chapter is an introductory drawing course. Includes additional reading list.

Subject(s): Self-development

Gilley, J. W., & Boughton, N. W. (1996). *Stop managing, start coaching! How performance coaching can enhance commitment and improve productivity.* Chicago: Irwin.

The authors claim that organizational failure is the result of managerial malpractice—the failure to develop healthy manager-employee relations. But when managers coach rather than control, they support an employee's personal growth and encourage commitment to the organization—and that leads to organizational success. There are four roles for a performance coach to assume. As a trainer the coach helps an employee build technical skills. A career coach supports an employee's personal goals and encourages growth. In the confronting role a coach identifies performance shortfalls and strategies for improvement. The mentor helps an employee to develop networks and to become politically savvy. The chapters in this book are devoted to practical suggestions for becoming a performance coach, including the important issue of rewards. Includes index.

Subject(s): Coaching

New
Gookin, J., Green, R., & Doran, M. (Eds.). (1998). *1998 NOLS leadership education toolbox.* Lander, WY: The National Outdoor Leadership School. Phone: (307) 332-8800. Website: www.nols.edu

This book explains the philosophy and curriculum for leadership development at the National Outdoor Leadership

School (NOLS). A recommended four-phase progression of skill building and experience includes: 1) orienting—setting goals and observing role models; 2) acquiring—learning about leadership roles and responsibilities; 3) developing—practicing, peer coaching, and increasing challenges; and 4) transitioning—leading, realizing limitations, and stepping back as others take the lead. Includes course readings, handouts, and exercises.

Subject(s): Program models, adventure education

Gredler, M. E. (1994). *Designing and evaluating games and simulations: A process approach.* Houston: Gulf.

This book provides a structure for analyzing games and simulations that have no right or wrong answers and no presumed values. The activities discussed here rely on interaction between the participants and situations, crises, and tasks, as well as interaction among the participants themselves. The types of activities discussed are academic and computer games and simulations of decision making, crisis management, and understanding social systems. Includes bibliographical references and index.

Subject(s): Simulation as training technique

New
Guthrie, V. A. (1999). *Coaching for action: A report on long-term advising in a program context.* Greensboro, NC: Center for Creative Leadership.

Process advisors provide long-term coaching and support that helps advisees understand and develop their goals. The Center for Creative Leadership uses process advisors in its LeaderLab® program, an action-learning program for managers that spans six months and guides participants through developing and implementing action plans. This report describes how CCL developed the role of process advisor, lessons learned about the process, and how to determine if process advising is right for your organization. Appendices include a description of the LeaderLab program, a process-advising case study, and examples of advisors in action. Includes bibliographical references.

Subject(s): Coaching

New
Hackman, M. Z., Olive, T. E., Guzman, N., & Brunson, D. (1999). **Ethical considerations in the development of the interdisciplinary leadership studies program.** *Journal of Leadership Studies, 6*(1/2), 36-48.

The authors insist that colleges and universities have an ethical imperative to provide courses that transform followers into leaders. Advanced courses should continue to be available for the small percentage of high-potential leaders identified at an early age. However, leadership responsibilities throughout organizations and communities require that a larger population receive instruction. Programs at the University of Colorado at Colorado Springs and the University of North Carolina at Wilmington meet this need. The authors describe the ethical sensitivity, reasoning, motivation,

and action that developed both programs. Includes biblio-graphical references.
Subject(s): Program descriptions

New
Hall, D. T., & Associates. (1996). **The career is dead—long live the career: A relational approach.** San Francisco: Jossey-Bass.

The traditional perception of the career as a series of steady upward moves with increasing power, income, and status no longer holds true. Today career security is the responsibility of the individual, and personal relationships are the most important element in career development. This book presents a collection of writings that explain this relational approach to careers. Chapters address issues including how to create developmental relationships outside of work, learning from experience, and career development for the older worker. Includes bibliographical references and index.
Subject(s): Career development

New
Harris, P. R. (1998). *New work culture: HRD transforma-tional management strategies* (2nd ed.). Amherst, MA: HRD Press.

This book is intended to be a reference guide for adult learners interested in improving their work environment in the wake of the global shift to an information and service economy. This second edition is divided into four sections that emphasize the people who work in organizations. The first section addresses HRD challenges in organizational transformation, including the effect of culture on organiza-tional behavior. The second unit describes new work culture perspectives and includes chapters on entrepreneurialism and the potential of robotics. Chapters in the third unit deal with the meta-industrial work environment. The final unit addresses new human resource leadership strategies and includes chapters on managing teams, managing by network-ing, and transformational management. Each chapter begins with an executive summary and ends with "Capsule Conclu-sions." Includes bibliographical references and glossary.
Subject(s): Human resources development

New
Holkeboer, R., & Hoeksema, T. (1998). *A casebook for student leaders.* New York: Houghton Mifflin.

Twenty-four cases are designed to sharpen communication, critical thinking, and team work skills. Cases about ethics, diversity, group dynamics, and individual rights are based on actual situations and rooted in academic culture. Each brief case is supplemented by activities to reinforce the lesson. There are brief instructions for students and facilitators. A separate facilitator's manual is available. Includes biblio-graphical references and recommended Internet resources.
Subject(s): Cases

Holsbrink-Engles, G. A. (1997). **Computer-based role-playing for interpersonal skills training.** *Simulation & Gaming, 28*(2), 164-180.

Role-playing is an important part of interpersonal skills training but is often too complex for beginners. Computer-based role-playing can simplify the process. In this study one group of students did a conventional role-playing exercise, while a second group did a computer-based role play and then a conventional one. The researchers measured the learning outcomes of the two groups and conclude that computer role plays can be a useful lead-in to traditional role plays, although not a replacement for them. Includes bibliographical references.
Subject(s): Role-playing as training technique

Howe, W., & Freeman, F. (1997). **Leadership education in American colleges and universities: An overview.** *Concepts & Connections: A Newsletter for Leadership Educators, 5*(2), 5-7.

The authors report on their 1996 survey intended to deter-mine the range and scope of leadership courses and programs on college and university campuses. About one-fourth are single academic courses and one-fourth are offered through student-affairs programs. Almost two-thirds are focused on undergraduates and two-thirds award academic credit. More than half teach a balance of theory and application. When compared to a similar survey conducted by the Center for Creative Leadership in 1986, it appears that leadership education has grown by 20% over ten years.
Subject(s): Leadership education survey

New
Hudson, F. M. (1999). *The handbook of coaching: A compre-hensive resource guide for managers, executives, consultants, and human resource professionals.* San Francisco: Jossey-Bass.

This basic resource guide for both new and experienced coaches begins with a thorough review of what coaches do and of coaching as a profession. Part II of the book describes the theoretical basis for coaching including psychological and social theories of adult development. Part III presents a conceptual model for coaching consisting of advice on coaching through life transitions, coaching for basic values, and coaching and visioning. The book concludes with specific advice on coaching young adults and older adults. Each chapter includes a "Basic Library for Coaches," an extensive reading list on that topic. Appendices provide lists of assessments, inventories, and training programs for coaches. Includes index.
Subject(s): Coaching

Jaworski, J., & Flowers, B. S. (Eds.). (1996). *Synchronicity: The inner path of leadership.* San Francisco: Berrett-Koehler.

Jaworski describes his early years, which were filled with dramatic peaks and valleys until a personal crisis alerted him that he was living an unfulfilled life. At that point he embarked on a journey to find his life's meaning and discovered synchronicity—the connectedness of people and events that enrich your life if you let go of control. He recommends that all leaders adopt a synchronistic mind-set to see the importance of relationships, commit to one's passion, and use the flow of energy that results. Jaworski teaches these lessons as founder of the American Leadership Forum, founder of the Centre for Generative Leadership, and member of MIT's Center for Organizational Learning. Peter Senge writes a moving introduction to this book. Includes index.

Subject(s): Self-development

Johnson, C. (1997). **A leadership journey to the East.** *Journal of Leadership Studies, 4*(2), 82-88.

Directed toward trainers and teachers, this article describes a Taoist perspective of leadership. A historical overview of this Eastern philosophy is presented with suggestions for introducing Taoist principles to students of leadership. Taoism prescribes that leadership should be minimal and that leaders should model their own behavior on principles found in nature. For example, leaders should be like uncarved blocks of wood, shapeless and simple. They should reject wealth, status, and cleverness. Johnson describes how he presents Taoism inductively in the classroom with a focus on nature.

Subject(s): Program models, Eastern philosophy

Jones, K. (1994). *Simulations: A handbook for teachers and trainers* (3rd ed.). New York: Nichols.

This book first introduces the reader to the basic processes and terminology of simulations. It covers the topics of simulation design, choosing a simulation, how to effectively use simulations, and issues in using simulations for assessment. There are examples to help teachers and trainers use this experiential learning mode to full advantage. Includes bibliography and index.

Subject(s): Simulations

Jones, K. (1997). *Icebreakers: A sourcebook of games, exercises, and simulations* (2nd ed.). Houston: Gulf.

This book includes advice on when and how to use icebreakers and 66 icebreaking activities in three categories: games in which participants have a duty to win, exercises dealing with problems, and simulations involving roles. Facilitator guidelines note the required time, materials, procedure, and debriefing instructions for each activity. Includes reproducible handouts and bibliographical references.

Subject(s): Exercises

Kaplan, R. E., Drath, W. H., & Kofodimos, J. R. (1991). *Beyond ambition: How driven managers can lead better and live better.* San Francisco: Jossey-Bass.

The authors' research with senior executives reveals that leadership development is based more on personal growth than on behavioral change. Executives were analyzed by themselves, co-workers, current families, and original

families to determine inner character. The authors explain the challenge of gaining self-awareness and how expansive character and elevated position can create executive-performance problems. Through stories of real people and three case studies, they describe how a process of character shift can result in more effective leadership and greater personal happiness. Includes bibliographical references and index.

Subject(s): Leadership development

Karp, H. B. (1996). *The change leader: Using a Gestalt approach with work groups.* San Diego, CA: Pfeiffer.

This workbook helps readers learn to be champions of change by using a Gestalt approach. This approach is based on a clinical theory that people can make better choices for themselves and take full responsibility for their choices. Nine chapters address awareness, negotiation, power, commitment, and resistance. Each chapter concludes with several change-leader activities.

Subject(s): Program models, leader as change agent

New

Kaufmann, S. W., Beale, R. L., Hollenshead, C. H., Callahan, M. R., & Thompson, H. J. (1997). **The Michigan Women's Leadership Project: Leadership for social change.** *A Leadership Journal: Women in Leadership—Sharing the Vision, 2*(1), 145-154.

The leaders of social change organizations serving women and girls are usually not prototypical corporate executives, but often come from direct-service jobs, and may have begun as service recipients. This article describes the Michigan Women's Leadership Project, a program designed to develop and deliver leadership training to these women, who are often too stretched for time and resources to develop their leadership skills. These programs, created by the University of Michigan Center for the Education of Women and the Michigan Women's Foundation, included experiential learning, customized consultation, and peer support. Information on how participants were recruited, sample course topics, and the results of a follow-up phone survey are provided. Includes bibliographical references.

Subject(s): Program descriptions, women's leadership development, social change

Kaye, B., & Jacobson, B. (1996). **Reframing mentoring.** *Training & Development, 50*(8), 44-47.

The authors challenge the traditional view of mentoring as a one-on-one process, developing instead a model in which groups of employees are taught by "learning leaders." Advice on how to be an effective learning leader is offered, including how to determine an employee's learning needs, how to lead group discussions, and how to give learning assignments.

Subject(s): Mentoring

New

Kaye, B. L. (1997). *Up is not the only way: A guide to developing workforce talent* (2nd ed.). Palo Alto, CA: Davies-Black.

As a consultant in human resources development Kaye recommends strategies for those who guide others' careers. Her six-stage process includes: 1) organizational analysis and planning, 2) identifying and testing employees, 3) exploring career options, 4) making strategic action plans for development, 5) acquiring new skills and knowledge, and 6) sustaining the process. Organizations that conscientiously develop employees are better able to retain a knowledge pool of trained and experienced workers. In addition to higher morale and productivity, organizations find a steady stream of information about talent for future promotions and about staffing problems. Includes bibliographical references and index.

Subject(s): Human resources development

New

Keirsey, D. (1998). *Please understand me II: Temperament, character, intelligence.* Del Mar, CA: Prometheus Nemesis Book Company.

As an update to the original edition, *Please Understand Me* (Keirsey, 1984), this later edition also aspires to help individuals accept rather than change one another. Keirsey begins with an updated inventory, *The Keirsey Temperament Sorter II*, and applies the results to the *Myers-Briggs Type Indicator*®. The second chapter presents the theory and history of the temperament and character studies. The following four chapters are devoted to the specific types: Artisans, Guardians, Idealists, and Rationals. Applicability to personal and working relationships is the focus of the next few chapters as the temperaments are exemplified in mate, parental, and leadership roles. Includes bibliographical references and notes pertaining to the first two chapters.

Subject(s): Self-development, personality, character, intelligence, *Myers-Briggs Type Indicator*

Kelly, J. M., & Grose, P. G., Jr. (1997). **Case teaching and why it works in leadership education.** *A Leadership Journal: Women in Leadership—Sharing the Vision, 1*(2), 21-30.

Dismissing "high-tech management education packages," the authors argue that case teaching, in which "class discussions approximate a single-subject meeting where one urgent problem is resolved," is the most effective way to teach leadership skills. In this article they describe the role of the teacher in the case method and give examples of programs where it has been used successfully. They then offer a sample case, a problem faced by a county administrator, complete with teaching notes and possible student solutions.

Subject(s): Leadership education

Keys, J. B. (1995). **Centres of excellence in management education.** *Journal of Management Development, 14*(5), 3-4.

Keys is guest editor of this special issue that focuses on organizations that provide innovative leadership and manage-

ment development programs. The featured organizations include: the School of Management Studies at Templeton College, Oxford University; MIT Organizational Learning Center; Inter Cultural Management headquartered in Paris; the Center for Creative Leadership; the Center for Leadership at the University of Tampa; and the College of Business Administration at the University of Hawaii. Keys is Director of the Center for Managerial Learning and Business Simulation at Georgia University. Each article describes one center's history, structure, focus, research, and plans for the future.

Subject(s): Program descriptions, management education

New

Keys, J. B., & Fulmer, R. M. (Eds.). (1998). *Executive development and organizational learning for global business.* New York: International Business Press.

In their introduction the editors identify seven imperatives for executive education and organizational learning in the global world: 1) think and act globally, 2) be a global learning organization, 3) focus on the whole global system, 4) develop global leadership skills, 5) empower teams, 6) make learning a core competence, and 7) reinvent yourself and your organization regularly. The writings that follow address three basic themes. The first section considers globalization and learning, including issues such as managing global workers and creating international teams. The second section addresses developing the global executive with chapters on scenarios, action learning, and several case studies. The final group of writings describes how to develop a learning organization and offers discussions of systems dynamics and microworlds. Includes index.

Subject(s): Executive education, organizational learning, global leadership

Keys, J. B., Fulmer, R. M., & Stumpf, S. A. (1996). **Microworlds and simuworlds: Practice fields for the learning organizations.** *Organizational Dynamics, 24*(4), 36-49.

According to the authors most organizations have "learning disabilities," barriers that prevent managers from learning, including horizontal and vertical fragmentation. But managers can use the risk-free environment of *simuworlds*, derived from competitive business games, and *microworlds*, which evolved from in-basket simulations, to achieve the "big picture learning" often missing in large companies. A number of specific simulations are profiled, and stories of individual companies and managers illustrate the concepts.

Subject(s): Simulation as training technique

New

Kirkpatrick, D. L. (1998). *Another look at evaluating training programs.* Alexandria, VA: American Society for Training and Development.

This collection contains 50 articles from *Training & Development* and *Technical Training* magazines that address evaluating training programs. The articles are divided into

sections on evaluation philosophies, reaction, learning, behavior, results, and return-on-investment. Includes bibliographical references.
Subject(s): Program evaluation

New
Kirkpatrick, D. L. (1998). *Evaluating training programs: The four levels.* San Francisco: Berrett-Koehler.

Kirkpatrick describes a model for evaluating training that examines the effects of a program on four levels: reaction, learning, behavior, and results. Each successive level is more difficult to define and measure but offers a deeper under-standing of a program's effects. Kirkpatrick says that while evaluations should progress from reaction to results, pro-grams should be planned in the reverse order. Thirteen case studies are used to show how this model is used to evaluate different kinds of programs, ranging from stress management classes to outdoor-based training. Includes index.
Subject(s): Program evaluation

New
Kouzes, J. M., & Posner, B. Z. (1999). *The leadership challenge planner: An action guide to achieving your personal best.* San Francisco: Jossey-Bass.

In *The Leadership Challenge* (1995) Kouzes and Posner identified five exemplary leadership practices: 1) challenging the process, 2) inspiring a shared vision, 3) enabling others to act, 4) modeling the way, and 5) encouraging the heart. This planner contains activities and worksheets designed to help readers implement these practices in their organizations. A planning section allows readers to set both long-term and weekly project goals, and a final chapter offers the opportu-nity for reflection on the leadership process.
Subject(s): Self-development

New
Kummerow, J. M., Barger, N. J., & Kirby, L. K. (1997). *Worktypes: Understand your work personality—how it helps you and holds you back, and what you can do to understand it.* New York: Warner Books.

The authors believe that readers can both improve their performance and better understand their co-workers by applying lessons from the *Myers-Briggs Type Indicator®* to their work. This book identifies eight common workplace issues—leadership, communication and conflict, time management, meetings, teamwork, balance, change, and stress—and shows how psychological type can explain individuals' reactions to these issues. Includes exercises for "making the most of your type at work."
Subject(s): Self-knowledge, personality, *Myers-Briggs Type Indicator*

New
Kunich, J. C., & Lester, R. I. (1999). **Leadership and the art of mentoring: Tool kit for the time machine.** *Journal of Leadership Studies, 6*(1/2), 17-35.

This introduction to mentoring explains the subject through the mnemonic: *M*odel *E*mpathize *N*urture *T*each *O*rganize *R*espond *I*nspire *N*etwork *G*oal-set. Descriptions of well-known mentors and protégés illustrate each point. One example is Jackie Robinson, who broke baseball's color barriers. He mentored younger African-American players Roy Campanella and Don Newcombe by serving as a model. Another example is Anne Sullivan, who personally overcame obstacles and mentored Helen Keller by empathizing with the enormity of her challenges. Includes bibliographical references.
Subject(s): Mentoring

New
Kur, E., & Bunning, R. (1996). **A three-track process for executive leadership development.** *Leadership & Organiza-tion Development Journal, 17*(4), 4-12.

Many executives feel that traditional multi-day or multi-week management development programs do not adequately prepare them for leadership roles. The authors of this article address that complaint by offering a "three-track leadership" program. Participants in this program, which stretches over 18 months, train in three different areas: business, leadership, and personal. A combination of off-site workshops, on-the-job assignments, and independent work allow managers to develop and apply their skills right away. The authors offer anecdotal evidence of the success of their three-track program, arguing that it affects organizational culture, individual development, and bottom-line revenue. Includes bibliographical references.
Subject(s): Program models, executive education

Lamond, D. A. (1995). **Using consulting projects in manage-ment education: The joys and jitters of serving two masters.** *Journal of Management Development, 14*(8), 60-72.

Lamond reports on an action-learning approach used in the MBA program at the Macquarie University Graduate School of Management, New South Wales, Australia. Students assume roles as consultants to the executives of client companies. Working in project teams, each student contrib-utes eight 40-hour weeks to perform industry analysis, organizational analysis, and problem solving. Many of the involved students are experienced managers sponsored in the MBA program by their employers. Their consulting projects usually benefit their own companies. Others are arranged in the local business community. Includes bibliographical references.
Subject(s): Program descriptions, management education

New
Landrum, G. N. (1999). *Eight keys to greatness: How to unlock your hidden potential.* Amherst, NY: Prometheus Books.

Contrary to popular belief, this author advocates traits other than high intelligence quotients as the key to genius, which is defined here as "someone who influences another for the

good or bad." The first eight chapters are dedicated to each of eight personality traits that Landrum argues are the keys to greatness. The first trait is based on charisma and effective communication and profiles such leaders as Hitler, Mother Teresa, Fred Smith, and Oprah Winfrey. The second key focuses on the need for competition and the desire to win. Confidence and self-esteem bordering on arrogance make up the third key to greatness as demonstrated by Picasso and Martin Luther King, Jr. Incredible energy and drive are characteristics descriptive of the fourth key, as exemplified by Napoleon and Catherine the Great. The next key depicts intuition through such visionaries as Darwin, Freud, Einstein, and Bill Gates. Rebellious renegades including Karl Marx and Walt Disney are the subject of the sixth key. Risk-taking and persistence are the final keys, with Amelia Earhart and Stephen King among the examples. Includes a self-assessment as well as bibliographical references and index.
Subject(s): Self-development

Lankford, D. (1997). **License to lead: Instilling decision making skills in our young people.** *Schools in the Middle,* 6(3), 32-33.

This brief article describes NASSP's *License to Lead* program designed for middle school students. The nine 30-minute segments present ethical dilemmas that may be easily understood by young people. There are no easy answers. The program's purpose is to teach adolescents how to make tough decisions and how to apply that process to leadership and to daily situations. *License to Lead* is available from NASSP. Phone: (800) 253-7746.
Subject(s): Program descriptions, youth leadership

Lawrence, H. V., & Wiswell, A. K. (1993). **Using the work group as a laboratory for learning: Increasing leadership and team effectiveness through feedback.** *Human Resource Development Quarterly,* 4(2), 135-148.

Managers from a municipal government participated in a field study to determine the effects of training on managers' interactions with work groups. *SYMLOG®* (System for the Multiple Level Observation of Groups) was used for pre- and post-test measurement of individual and group dominance versus submissiveness, friendliness versus unfriendliness, and accepting versus opposing task orientation of established authority. Feedback-skills training generated higher post-test scores in the areas of dominance and friendliness.
Subject(s): Program evaluation

New
Learning to lead: Technology is driving the demand for executive education—and creating lots of new options for companies. (1999, October 18). *Business Week,* pp. 76-80.

Business Week reports on a survey that ranks the top providers of executive education programs. More than 60 business school, private, and nonprofit institutions are considered in the areas of general management education, leadership, innovation, global business, information systems, and

customized programs. The survey reports that the top five leadership programs are at the Center for Creative Leadership, Harvard University, the University of Virginia, the University of Pennsylvania, and the University of Michigan. The top overall provider is Harvard University. Additional analysis on MBA programs, entrepreneurship, and electronic delivery follows on pages 85-94.
Subject(s): Program rankings

New
Lee, M., & Stead, V. (1998). **Human resource development in the United Kingdom.** *Human Resource Development Quarterly,* 9(3), 297-308.

Tracing the growth of HRD in the U.K. over the last 50 years, this article describes how social and political changes in the country from the post-war years to the present have affected HR. While the late 1940s saw a need for stability and security in management, the practice of HR management and development emerged during the economic growth of the 1950s and 1960s. During the 1970s and early 1980s corporations focused on the power of the market and how organizations could act like entrepreneurs. In recent years, especially following the rise of the new Labour government, HRD has become more strategic and the HR manager has come to be seen as a change agent, not simply a manager. Includes bibliographical references.
Subject(s): Human resources development

New
Lee, R. J., & King, S. N. (1999). **Executive effectiveness and fulfillment: A leadership factor.** *Leadership in Action, 19*(5), 1-7.

Lee and King demonstrate how leadership effectiveness grows through a process of self-examination at both the personal and professional levels. They recommend that leaders regularly assess their values and the integration of those values with their behaviors and aspirations. A values exercise and four probing questions help readers begin the examination process. Includes bibliographical references.
Subject(s): Leadership effectiveness, values, work and life balance, self-development

Lepsinger, R., & Lucia, A. D. (1997). *The art and science of 360 feedback.* San Diego, CA: Pfeiffer.

Written by feedback consultants, this book offers advice to leaders planning to implement such a 360-degree-feedback program in their organization. There are sections on choosing a feedback method, selling the idea in your organization, gathering and presenting feedback, and follow-up. Appendices include examples of 360 feedback, sample worksheets for feedback and interpretation, and a 360 feedback administration flowchart.
Subject(s): 360-degree feedback

New

Leslie, J. B., & Fleenor, J. W. (1998). *Feedback to managers: A review and comparison of multi-rater instruments for management development* (3rd ed.). Greensboro, NC: Center for Creative Leadership.

This report compares 24 multiple-perspective assessment instruments that are widely used for management and leadership development. The authors begin with a general discussion of test format, length, types of raters and response scales, scoring process, item development, psychometric properties, feedback display, cost, and support for trainers and participants. Each of the 24 examples is then analyzed in detail. The authors conclude that test development is an ongoing process and that reliable new tests will continually become available as the field of assessment for development continues to grow. The tests analyzed in this edition are: *Benchmarks®, Campbell Leadership Index®, COMPASS, Executive Success Profile, Survey of Executive Leadership, Leader Behavior Analysis II™, The Visionary Leader: Leader Behavior Questionnaire, Leadership Effectiveness Analysis, Acumen® Leadership Skills, Leadership/Impact™, Leadership Practices Inventory, Life Styles Inventory®, Manager View/360™, MATRIX: The Influence Behavior Questionnaire, Management Effectiveness Profile System, Multifactor Leadership Questionnaire, The PROFILOR®, PROSPECTOR™, Survey of Leadership Practices, The Survey of Management Practices, SYMLOG®, Types of Work Index, VOICES®,* and *Acumen® Leadership WorkStyles.* Includes bibliographical references for each test and 16 tables of comparisons.

Subject(s): 360-degree feedback

New

Liedtka, J. M., Weber, C., & Weber, J. (1999). **Creating a significant and sustainable executive education experience: A case study.** *Journal of Managerial Psychology, 14*(5), 404-420.

This article reports on the evaluation of a one-week executive education experience custom designed and delivered by the University of Virginia for a large financial firm. Almost 400 graduates responded to a survey about the application of their new learning after returning to the workplace. One surprising finding is that the most sustained learning occurred among participants who thanked direct reports for providing feedback and shared their new learning with direct reports. Support from human resources staff also increased sustainability. Another finding is the importance of a peer network among program graduates within each class and from class to class. This finding is unique in customized programs for a single company. Includes bibliographical references.

Subject(s): Program evaluation

New

Lombardo, M. M., & Eichinger, R. W. (1996). *For your improvement™: A development and coaching guide.* Minneapolis, MN: Lominger Limited.

This book for managers, coaches, and feedback-givers describes the 67 workplace competencies in Lominger's

Leadership Architect® Suite of leadership development programs and products. A sample of the competencies includes: action oriented, dealing with ambiguity, approachability, creativity, managing diversity, learning on the fly, perseverance, drive for results, and strategic agility. With each description of a competency are ten suggestions for making improvements. There are also descriptions of 19 career stallers and stoppers, with ten remedies for each. The appendices include tools for self-analysis and making action plans for improvement.

Subject(s): Training resources

New

Marcic, D. (1998). *Organizational behavior: Experiences and cases* (5th ed.). St. Paul, MN: West Publishing.

Marcic has compiled 90 exercises, instruments, and cases from a variety of sources. These tools support lessons in ethics, decision making, communication, group dynamics, influence, diversity, power, conflict management, learning organizations, and cross-cultural sensitivity. Some popular leadership exercises found in this book are: Tower Building, Prisoner's Dilemma, Ugli Orange, and Border Dispute. The fifth edition includes new exercises on stereotypes, stress, values, and listening skills. There are adapted versions of inventories to determine leadership style, level of empowerment, and style of conflict resolution. Cases focus on ethical issues, organizational design, diversity problems, and corporate culture.

Subject(s): Exercises, cases, textbook

Maxwell, J. C. (1995). *Developing the leaders around you.* Nashville, TN: Thomas Nelson Publishers.

Maxwell states the "truly successful leaders who are in the top 1% . . . know that acquiring and keeping good people is a leader's most important task." He argues that the key to great leadership is developing the good people around you into leaders who will contribute to your vision. The material in this book is taken from his sermons and lectures at the Skyline Wesleyan Church in San Diego and INJOY, a leadership development institute. The chapters include: "The Leader's Toughest Challenge: Creating a Climate for Potential Leaders," "The Leader's Primary Responsibility: Identifying Potential Leaders," and "The Leader's Greatest Joy: Coaching a Dream Team of Leaders."

Subject(s): Leadership development

New

McCauley, C. D., & Brutus, S. (1998). *Management development through job experiences: An annotated bibliography.* Greensboro, NC: Center for Creative Leadership.

A literature search reveals the importance of job assignments in the role of leadership development, and several common themes. Assignments that present new situations and responsibilities help managers broaden perspectives, learn to rely on others, and deal with ambiguity. New assignments that involve creating change and building relationships offer

lessons in responsibility and achieving cooperation. Negative experiences help managers identify their limitations, cope with stress, and take charge of their own careers. This report also examines the role of the individual in a developmental situation and organizational practices that support on-the-job development. Nearly 70 research-based and applied books and articles are annotated. Includes a bibliography of additional references and author and title indexes.
Subject(s): Leadership development, learning assignments

McCauley, C. D., Eastman, L. J., & Ohlott, P. J. (1995). **Linking management selection and development through stretch assignments.** *Human Resource Management: Special Issue on Leadership Transitions, 34*(1), 93-115.

Matching the right person to the right job depends on a candidate's competencies and on his or her ability to stretch to meet the job requirements. The authors discuss the organizational benefits of developing employees through stretch assignments. A factor analysis of the *Developmental Challenge Profile®* resulted in a framework with 15 developmental components that include: unfamiliar responsibilities, handling external pressure, managing diversity, influencing without authority, and dealing with a difficult boss.
Subject(s): Leadership development, learning assignments

McCauley, C. D., & Hughes-James, M. W. (1994). *An evaluation of the outcomes of a leadership development program.* Greensboro, NC: Center for Creative Leadership.

This research report describes an evaluation study of the Chief Executive Officer Leadership Development Program, which was designed for school superintendents. The program combines a six-day classroom experience, a follow-up year working on personal goals and learning projects, support from an executive facilitator, and reflective journal writing. Thirty-eight Florida superintendents participated in this study. Pre- and post-program assessments and end-of-program interviews provided evaluation data. In addition, five superintendents were studied more in depth. The participants' outcomes, the contributions of various portions of the program, and the variations among individual outcomes are analyzed. Includes bibliographical references and index.
Subject(s): Program evaluation

New
McCauley, C. D., Moxley, R. S., & Van Velsor, E. (Eds.). (1998). *The Center for Creative Leadership handbook of leadership development.* San Francisco: Jossey-Bass and Center for Creative Leadership.

Researchers and trainers explain the Center for Creative Leadership's unique perspective on developing leaders. They begin with basic assumptions that leadership development is about expanding an individual's capacities, that everyone can be more effective in their leadership roles and processes, and that we can all learn, grow, and change. A model of developmental experiences, the ability to learn, and organizational context provides a foundation for the book's lessons.

Chapters address 360-degree feedback and its use in training programs, skill-based training, job assignments, developmental relationships, learning from hardships, race and gender issues, cross-cultural issues, and global leadership. Process is discussed in chapters on systems, learning, and assessment. The final chapter considers the future of leadership development, particularly as a distributed process. Includes bibliographical references, name index, and subject index.
Subject(s): Leadership development

McDermott, L. (1996). **Wanted: Chief executive coach.** *Training & Development, 50*(5), 67-70.

Most senior executives do very little coaching, although the author considers it an essential part of leading an organization. This article details the reasons executives most often give for not practicing coaching and lists the qualities and behaviors of the ideal executive coach. Quotes and stories from famous coaches of sports teams, including Phil Jackson, Tommy Lasorda, and Don Shula, are used to illustrate how many different styles of coaching there are and how effective coaching can be.
Subject(s): Coaching

McEvoy, G. M. (1997). **Organizational change and outdoor management education.** *Human Resource Management, 36*(2), 235-250.

Outdoor management education, such as ropes courses, has become popular in recent years, but little empirical evidence exists to prove its effectiveness. This study examined two groups of employees from an information-processing company—one group that received outdoor training and one that did not—to determine whether the training affected learning and behavior. Tables, graphs, and quotes from employees all help illustrate the results, which show that the training did have some positive long-term effects. An appendix of sample questions from the measurement instrument and bibliographical references are included.
Subject(s): Management education, experiential education

McLean, J. (Ed.). (1994). *Training and development organizations directory* (6th ed.). Detroit, MI: Gale Research.

This directory lists 2,600 training and development organizations and 12,000 programs, seminars, and workshops. The reader may search by subject heading to find information on assessment instruments, citizen involvement, crisis management, and 2,000 other types of training activities. There are also indexes for geographical location, personal name, and company name.
Subject(s): Directory of training organizations

Meister, J. C. (1998). *Corporate universities: Lessons in building a world-class work force* (Rev. ed.). New York: McGraw-Hill.

Business organization structures are changing from pyramids (with thinkers on top and doers on the bottom) to flatter organizations. Employees at all levels are required to solve

problems and respond to customers with speed and efficiency. These employees are expected to have communication and collaboration skills, global business literacy, and cross-sectional skills in addition to the core skills of the older edition: interpersonal and creative thinking skills as well as basic education and technological competency. An increasing number of organizations provide continuous education in the form of corporate universities. Their programs have shifted from training based with instructor-led education to continuous learning and development programs using multiple formats. Meister provides an updated report on some of the 50 corporate universities including: First Union, Motorola, Dell Computers, General Electric, Saturn, Sun Microsystems, and Xerox. Smaller companies such as Verifone have also adopted the corporate university system with success. Includes bibliographical references, appendix, and index.
Subject(s): Program descriptions, corporate universities

New
Michalak, B., Fischer, S., & Meeker, L. (1994). *Experiential activities for high-performance teamwork.* Amherst, MA: HRD Press.

This book proposes that teams develop through experiences with effective communication, problem solving, diversity, trust, cooperation, effective teamwork, and team spirit. Chapters on these topics begin with a brief explanation of each concept, anecdotes to illustrate the concept, and several well-defined exercises. Many are old favorites such as Minefield, Trolleys, Spider Web, Trust Walk, and The Grid.
Subject(s): Exercises

New
Mitstifer, D. I. (1998). **Reflective human action.** *A Leadership Journal: Women in Leadership—Sharing the Vision, 2*(2), 45-53.

When the members of Kappa Omicron Nu Honor Society could not find a leadership program that fit their needs, they developed their own framework for a values-based comprehensive leadership theory called Reflective Human Action. This article presents the framework as an action wheel centered around the concepts of authenticity, ethical sensibility, and spirituality. Mitstifer describes how the Reflective Human Action model was used in workshops and leadership modules, and offers personal stories from participants who used this model in their work. Includes bibliographical references.
Subject(s): Program models, humanist perspective, Kappa Omicron Nu

Mohrman, S. A., & Mohrman, A. M., Jr. (1997). *Designing and leading team-based organizations: A workbook for organizational self-design.* San Francisco: Jossey-Bass.

This workbook for leaders who are establishing or refining team-based organizations is composed of nine modules—including designing team structures, designing management and leadership roles, building a decision-making framework,

and managing and improving performance—that give the reader a series of steps to follow. Each module includes charts, definitions, and exercises to complete. A leader's/facilitator's guide that accompanies the workbook is also available.
Subject(s): Training resources

New
Morgan, M. G., & Mackey, D. A. (1999). *The Corporate University guide to management seminars* (15th ed.). Point Richmond, CA: Corporate University Press.

This guide describes more than 1,400 university- and institution-based management programs, divided into 17 categories, including communication, entrepreneurship, finance, personal development, and marketing. Entries detail the program focus, subject matter, intended audience, cost, and location of each program. This guide serves as a supplement to the Corporate University's *The Evaluation Guide to Executive Programs,* which has more detailed descriptions of longer executive programs that are offered primarily by universities. All program information is also available on a web-based searchable database available from the Corporate University (www.corporate-u.com).
Subject(s): Directory of programs, management education

New
Moulton, H. W., & Morgan, M. G. (1999). *The Corporate University evaluation guide to executive programs* (15th ed.). Point Richmond, CA: Corporate University Press.

This guide evaluates 140 executive programs offered by universities and reputable private institutions. To meet criteria for inclusion, the programs must be at least one week in length; regularly scheduled; in existence for at least two years; and open to private, public, and nonprofit sectors. In addition to descriptive data, comments from human resource professionals and program participants are provided. A faculty strength grid indicates faculty's specialties. Appendices list executive MBA programs and index reviewed programs by starting date, cost, location, participants' geographical dispersion, and faculty strength. For an annual directory of 1,400 short programs check the annual *Corporate University Guide to Management Seminars.* All program evaluation information is also available on a web-based searchable database available from the Corporate University Press (www.corporate-u.com).
Subject(s): Directory of programs, executive education

New
Mullen, E. J. (1998). **Vocational and psychosocial mentoring functions: Identifying mentors who serve both.** *Human Resource Development Quarterly, 9*(4), 319-331.

Mentors can perform both vocational functions, which assist their protégés' career development, and psychosocial functions, which help a protégé develop self-concepts such as competence and identity. Relationships in which the mentor serves both functions are generally stronger and more beneficial for the protégé. This study analyzed survey data, examining characteristics of both the mentor and the relationship, to determine what variables predict whether mentors will play both roles. Analysis showed that older mentors who perceive their protégés as competent and who initiate the relationship are more likely to perform both functions. Mullen suggests that organizations use these findings to restructure formal mentoring programs, allowing participants to initiate contact and guide the relationship. Includes bibliographical references.

Subject(s): Mentoring

New

Myers, I. B., McCaulley, M. H., Quenk, N. L., & Hammer, A. L. (1998). *MBTI manual: A guide to the development and use of the Myers-Briggs Type Indicator.* Palo Alto, CA: Consulting Psychologists Press.

The updated version of this guide reinforces the relationship of the *MBTI* to its grounding in Jung's psychological types. The book begins with an overview of the *MBTI*, the 16 personality types, and eight characteristics. Part two discusses the theory of type according to Carl Jung. The third part of this source prepares administrators of the inventory by covering the who, what, and how of administration. Research pertaining to reliability, validity, and test construction is presented in the following section. Part five discusses the use of this indicator in educational, psychological, and career areas. Includes bibliographical references and an extensive glossary.

Subject(s): Leadership development, personality, *Myers-Briggs Type Indicator*

Napolitano, C. S., & Henderson, L. J. (1998). *The leadership odyssey: A self-development guide to new skills for new times.* San Francisco: Jossey-Bass.

The authors say that their book is "designed to be used as well as read," and they begin by dividing leadership into three domains—self-leadership, people leadership, organizational leadership—and describing specific skills and attributes within each area, such as having focus, engaging in dialogue, facilitating learning, and promoting a corporate culture. Readers can then evaluate their own skills using the included skills-assessment kit, which includes forms, directions, and instructions on how to analyze the data. The book's final section contains developmental exercises readers can use to address skills deficits and enhance their existing strengths. Includes bibliographical references.

Subject(s): Self-development

Nemerowicz, G., & Rosi, E. (1997). *Education for leadership and social responsibility.* Washington, DC: Falmer Press.

The authors present a new leadership paradigm that they call *inclusive leadership.* It's based on their experimental Women's Leadership Institute at Wells College. The institute grew from a traditional program serving only the school's undergraduate students to a larger nontraditional program

serving community and business leaders, alumnae, teenagers, and young children. The authors' research is based on interviews with children and with artists and a content analysis of *Fortune* magazine. From their experience and research emerged a framework for teaching leadership at all levels, beginning with very young children and continuing through all arenas of one's life. This inclusive leadership is a process in which all citizens have a right and a responsibility to participate. Includes bibliographical references and index.

Subject(s): Program descriptions, women's leadership development, social responsibility

New

Newell, T. (1999). **Leadership education for a democratic society: FEI's core program turns 30.** *The Public Manager, 28*(1), 13-18.

This article is the centerpiece of a miniforum on the Federal Executive Institute, an agency within the Office of Personnel Management that provides leadership training for senior government officials. FEI's programs focus on four curricula themes: personal leadership, fostering organizational change, understanding policy and the political environment, and operating on a global scale. Here Newell describes Leadership for a Democratic Society, FEI's core program, which is a four-week course that focuses on values in leadership and constitutional governance. Other articles in the miniforum include commentaries by the past and present directors of FEI, a description of the FEI Alumni Association, and a discussion of FEI's custom programs.

Subject(s): Program descriptions, public service leadership

New

Newstrom, J., & Scannell, E. (1998). *The big book of team building games: Trust-building activities, team spirit exercises, and other fun things to do.* New York: McGraw-Hill.

The 70 activities and games described here address creating team identity, setting team goals, communication and cooperation, energizing meetings, problem solving, building self-esteem, and coping with change. Listed for each game are objectives, materials required, procedures, discussion questions, further activities, and tips for trainers.

Subject(s): Exercises, teams

Newstrom, J. W., & Scannell, E. E. (1980). *Games trainers play: Experiential learning exercises.* New York: McGraw-Hill.

Trainers manage the content, process, and environment of learning situations. Exercises, illustrations, and activities are among the games trainers use to present learning situations. In this collection the format outlines each game's objective, procedure, or method of instruction, discussion questions, approximate time, and materials required. Supporting materials may be photocopied for handouts or made into overhead transparencies. For more games see Scannell and Newstrom's *More Games Trainers Play* (1983), *Still More Games Trainers Play* (1991), and *Even More Games*

Trainers Play (1994). Each book in the series contains about 100 different games to be used in lessons on problem solving, communication, leadership, and team building.
Subject(s): Exercises

New
Nilson, C. (Ed.). (1998). ***Training and development yearbook 1998*** (9th ed.). Paramus, NJ: Prentice Hall.

This collection is intended as an annual ready reference tool comprising article abstracts and reprints, book reviews, case studies, research summaries, and a trainer's almanac, all based on current best practices in the organizational learning field. Each of the seven sections contains information pertinent to the major training functions. A management section discusses downsizing and intellectual capital as well as the changing global markets. Needs analysis for equal opportunity, new competencies, and empowerment is the focus of the second section, followed by case studies delineating instructional design and delivery using technologies and new possibilities. The standards for training evaluation are addressed as the last function, which precedes the final portions of the book, containing a detailed trainer's almanac and an extensive index.
Subject(s): Training resources

Nilson, C. D. (1993). ***Team games for trainers***. New York: McGraw-Hill.

Nilson argues that games support learning, and presents 100 games that trainers can use to enhance group learning. The games are divided into three sections: team building, team function, and team maintenance. Each game is described in a structured format that lists the objectives, procedures, materials, and approximate time needed for each activity. This makes it easy to target where a particular group needs to work—communication, conflict resolution, or building a vision. There are also discussion questions and tips for team training. Includes an index.
Subject(s): Exercises, teams

Oberst, G. F., & Wanke, J. (1997). **Women are citizen leaders: The citizen leadership training program.** *A Leadership Journal: Women in Leadership—Sharing the Vision, 1*(2), 81-89.

In 1993 Florida's Gulf Coast Community College founded the Citizen Leadership Institute, designed to build community by developing and strengthening the leadership skills of community members. This article discusses how the Institute's programs have been adapted to address leadership skills and roles for women. The authors describe the gender-specific needs of women and how programs are modified around them, offer examples of historic female community leaders including Rosa Parks, and describe women who have gone through CLI's programs and the community work they do. Includes bibliographical references.
Subject(s): Program descriptions, women's leadership development

Odenwald, S. B., & Matheny, W. G. (1996). ***Global impact: Award winning performance programs from around the world.*** Chicago: Irwin.

The authors identify results-oriented HRD training programs around the world. The case studies include: Glaxo Wellcome Inc.'s adoption of corporate values (Canada); SmithKline Beecham's Information Resources Competency Development (U.S.); Amil's virtual university program for learning managers (Brazil); ISS's action-learning program for executives (Denmark); Teva Pharmaceutical Industries, Ltd's Passage program for young professionals (Israel); ISCOR, Ltd's diversity training program (South Africa); Samsung's cross-cultural training programs (Korea); and Omron Corporation's international training system (Japan).
Subject(s): Program descriptions, global leadership

New
O'Neill, M., & Fletcher, K. (Eds.). (1998). ***Nonprofit management education: U.S. and world perspectives***. Westport, CT: Praeger.

This source depicts the efforts toward nonprofit management education programs in the U.S. as well as Australia, Ireland, and England. The introduction notes several issues facing nonprofit management education, as well as future dilemmas. Due to constraints of these programs it is not possible to fulfill all of the demands and requirements, therefore, the second part of the book discusses a case study presenting prioritized recommendations according to three stakeholder groups. Their findings relate to curricula of the programs and budgetary and faculty concerns. An additional survey was conducted to determine the amount of higher education offered in the area of volunteer administration. The issue of cooperation among management support organizations and academic centers providing nonprofit education is addressed through personal interviews. Finally, the authors address theoretical issues related to the future of nonprofit education. Includes bibliographical references and index.
Subject(s): Management education, nonprofit leadership

Palus, C., & Drath, W. (1995). ***Evolving leaders: A model for promoting leadership development in programs.*** Greensboro, NC: Center for Creative Leadership.

Palus and Drath focus on a problem that many leadership educators encounter. Because the importance of leadership development is largely implied and not specified, it is difficult to design and evaluate programs that seek to promote it. The model presented in this report specifies how programs can influence a key aspect of leadership development—the psychological development of the individual. Includes bibliographical references.
Subject(s): Leadership development

New

Pearson, C. S. (1998). *The hero within: Six archetypes we live by* (3rd ed.). San Francisco: HarperCollins.

Pearson applies the six Jungian archetypes—orphan, innocent, magician, wanderer, warrior, and altruist—to everyday life, arguing that developing the strengths of each type can help individuals take charge of their lives. The first section of the book describes the "heroic journey" and the role the archetypes play in actions such as surviving difficulty and achieving happiness. The book's second section offers a "guidebook" for the journey, describing how the archetypes can act as a compass and code for people who recognize their effects. Appendices include a self-test for readers to measure the archetypes in their own personalities and advice on forming a "heroic journey group."
Subject(s): Self-development

New

Peterson, D. B., & Hicks, M. D. (1996). *Leader as coach: Strategies for coaching and developing others.* Minneapolis: Personnel Decisions International.

Peterson and Hicks present this second book in a series for leaders developing their people. Five particular strategies are discussed in this source for the purpose of making coaching manageable. Once the meaning of coaching has been communicated, the five strategies are then introduced and discussed. The first strategy is to set a foundation by forging partnerships and building trust. The second strategy is the means by which a coach inspires the natural motivation in people. The next step is to help people grow their skills. This entails first determining areas in need, followed by the appropriate methods to aid those areas. Promoting persistence and shaping the environment are the final two strategies for coaching. This final strategy is centered around building organizational support starting with the CEO as a role model. Includes bibliographical references.
Subject(s): Coaching

Pfeiffer, J. W., & Ballew, A. C. (1988-1989). *UA training technologies.* San Diego, CA: University Associates.

This set consists of seven volumes covering the following topics for use in human resources development: structured experiences; instruments; lecturettes, theories, and models; role plays; case studies, simulations, and games; design skills; and skills for presentation and evaluation. An index to all volumes is included.
Subject(s): Training resources

Pfeiffer, J. W., & Jones, J. E. (Eds.). (1985). *Handbook of structured experiences for human relations training.* San Diego, CA: University Associates.

A complementary series to the annuals, this series now contains ten volumes, with the last volume published in 1985. Each contains structured experiences designed to promote varied learning experiences and to be useful in a variety of settings. Includes bibliographies.
Subject(s): Exercises

Pfeiffer, J. W., & Nolde, C. (Eds.). (1991). *The encyclopedia of team-building activities.* San Diego, CA: Pfeiffer.

This book contains 55 activities to help HRD professionals teach team building as opposed to team development. Exercises include Images: Envisioning the Ideal Team; The Car: Feedback on Team-Membership Styles; The Gold Watch: Balancing Personal and Professional Values; Nominations: Analyzing Trust Within a Team; Kaleidoscope: Team Building Through Role Expansion; Control or Surrender: Altering Approaches to Problem-Solving; and Project Colossus: Examining Group Dynamics. Most exercises can be done in one to two hours and require no special materials except a flip chart and the handouts provided in the book. Includes bibliographical references.
Subject(s): Exercises, team building

Phi Theta Kappa. (1993). *Leadership development program.* Jackson, MS: Phi Theta Kappa.

Phi Theta Kappa, the international honor society of two-year colleges, created this extensive program and certifies faculty from community, technical, and junior colleges to teach it on their campuses. Fifteen modules address leadership skills and issues through a learn-by-doing philosophy. Classic leadership case studies, debates, exercises, role plays, simulations, films, and surveys are included in each module. Sample titles are: Your Personal Leadership Philosophy, Conceiving and Articulating a Vision, and Using Logic and Creativity in Decision Making. Includes bibliographical references.
Subject(s): Program descriptions

Phillips, J. J. (1996). **Meeting the ROI challenge: A practical approach to measuring the return on investment in training and development.** *efmd FORUM, 96*(3), 24-28.

For years executives assumed that the results of training could not be measured. But growing training budgets and an emphasis on accountability across organizations have increased interest in measuring the return on investment (ROI). Phillips offers an ROI process model that includes: methods for collecting post-program data, how to isolate the effects of training, converting the data to monetary value, how to identify intangible benefits, and a simple formula for calculating the ROI.
Subject(s): Return on investment

Posner, B., & Kouzes J. (1996). **Ten lessons for leaders and leadership developers.** *Journal of Leadership Studies, 3*(3), 3-10.

The authors of *The Leadership Challenge* and *Credibility* discuss ten lessons in leadership for individuals and organizations. Based on a personal-best leadership study, the conclusions of the lessons reveal not only that leadership is an observable, learnable set of practices, but also that the belief that leadership can't be learned is a far more powerful deterrent to development than is the nature of the leadership process itself.
Subject(s): Leadership development

Reed, T. K. (1997). **Developing an introductory course for the study of leadership: A sample syllabus.** *A Leadership Journal: Women in Leadership—Sharing the Vision*, *1*(2), 129-136.

Based on an introductory course on leadership from Columbia College in South Carolina, this article stems from a theoretical model of how to teach students about leadership. The model is made up of four quadrants—a knowledge base, knowledge about self, interactive skills, and practical applications. A sample syllabus for a leadership studies course—including course objectives, sample journal entries and learning contracts, and suggested books and articles—is also given.
Subject(s): Program descriptions

Robinson, J. (1996). *Coach to coach: Business lessons from the locker room.* San Diego, CA: Pfeiffer.

John Robinson, former football coach of the University of Southern California and the Los Angeles Rams, compares his coaching experiences to corporate coaching. He pays homage to his early mentors from whom he learned about challenge, persistence, authority, and winning. In football and in business Robinson recommends that a successful coach have vision, love what he or she does—the process, not just the result—and build a cohesive team. Robinson's 18-year coaching record includes five conference championships, six college bowl wins, four players who won the Heisman Trophy, and several conference and national Coach of the Year awards. This book is part of the Warren Bennis Executive Briefing Series.
Subject(s): Coaching

New
Rohnke, K., & Butler, S. (1995). *Quicksilver: Adventure games, initiative problems, trust activities, and a guide to effective leadership.* Dubuque, IA: Kendall/Hunt Publishing.

This book describes: 1) the four elements of adventure training—trust, communication, cooperation, and fun; and 2) the five steps to adventure leading—assessment, planning, preparation, leading, and evaluation. Section one of the book explains the leader's role, core leadership functions, and developing one's own style. Section two describes more than 100 adventure-leading activities. More activities are available in Rohke's other books: *Funn Stuff* (1995), *The Bottomless Bag Again* (1994), *Cowstails and Cobras* (1989), and *Silver Bullets* (1984).
Subject(s): Exercises

Rohs, F. R., & Langone, C. A. (1997). **Increased accuracy in measuring leadership impacts.** *Journal of Leadership Studies*, *4*(1), 150-158.

While instructional programs in leadership development are becoming more and more common, little research exists on how to measure the impact of these programs. This study surveyed Georgia community leaders before and after they completed a 12-week leadership development program to determine the best way to measure the impact of the experience. The results showed that a then/posttest method was more effective than a traditional pretest/posttest model because it accounted for the response shift that occurred as the subjects' understanding of leadership changed. Includes bibliographical references and tables of the study results.
Subject(s): Program evaluation, community leadership

Rollins, P. C. (1997). **Hollywood takes on the White House.** *The World & I*, *12*(7), 56-65.

Rollins reviews five films that depict real and fictional U.S. chief executives and their presidential character. *Wilson* (1944) shows Woodrow Wilson as a paragon of integrity, self-sacrifice, and family values. In *Dr. Strangelove; or How I Learned to Stop Worrying and Love the Bomb* (1964) President Merkin Muffley is an ineffective intellectual who cannot control his military advisors and nuclear weapons. *Nixon* (1995) portrays Richard Nixon as a tragic leader and complex personality with both base and noble qualities. *The American President* (1995) takes a delightful peek at the personal side of President Shepherd's romantic interests. More dramatically, this president faces ugly opposition with strength of character. The handsome, young President Whitmore in *Independence Day* (1996) demonstrates integrity, collaboration with his constituents, and courage—characteristics that help him to save the world from annihilation.
Subject(s): Leadership lessons in videos, U.S. presidents

Rothwell, W. J. (1994). *Effective succession planning: Ensuring leadership continuity and building talent from within.* New York: AMACOM.

For any organization to survive it must have competent, continuous leadership. In this book Rothwell presents a seven-step plan for ensuring systematic succession: 1) make the case for change, 2) get started, 3) refine the program, 4) appraise the short-term needs, 5) project long-term needs, 6) build from inside, and 7) build from outside. A case study from a major insurance company, recommended book and software lists, and over 60 worksheets, graphs, and forms are included to make this book a practical guide for companies planning to create their own leadership-succession program. An index is also included.
Subject(s): Succession planning

Ruderman, M. N., & Ohlott, P. J. (1990). *Traps and pitfalls in the judgment of executive potential.* Greensboro, NC: Center for Creative Leadership.

Ruderman and Ohlott report on the process of identifying high-potential employees. Organizations can profit from early identification by offering these employees enhanced developmental opportunities. Supervisors' personal values or employees' personal traits are among common biases that lead to misidentification. Suggested are objective criteria for identification such as job-behavior categories, internal talent scouts, multiple data, and appropriate framing of screening

questions. Includes a bibliography.
Subject(s): Leadership development, assessment

Ruderman, M. N., & Ohlott, P. J. (1994). *The realities of management promotion.* Greensboro, NC: Center for Creative Leadership.

This report describes a study of how 64 management promotions were made at three Fortune 500 companies. Interviewers asked questions of the person promoted, the immediate boss, the approving boss, and a human resource representative. What they learned was that there is no such thing as a typical promotion. Managers typically rationalized a promotion based on a candidate's personal attributes. The study suggests that promotions actually result from a mix of personal attributes, organizational needs, and a candidate's proximity to the decision-maker. Includes bibliographical references.
Subject(s): Selection

New
Rylatt, A., & Lohan, K. (1997). *Creating training miracles.* San Francisco: Pfeiffer.

The purpose of this source is to guide the workplace trainer in the improvement of promoting discovery and learning. Rylatt and Lohan offer strategies and techniques to accomplish this. Based on real-life experiences each chapter presents frameworks, models, and advice for understanding the concepts presented here. Topics covered in this source include global trends in training, strategies to gain support for workplace training, the principles and benefits of competency based and self-directed training, and accelerative learning. Other beneficial topics surround communication, energizing, and icebreaking techniques. The final portion highlights five ingredients for a successful training miracle. Includes three appendices with program activities.
Subject(s): Training resources

New
Sadler, P. (Ed.). (1997). *International Executive Development Programmes* (2nd ed.). London: Kogan Page.

Sadler edits this guide to international management education programs and trends of thought. This updated version presents an editorial on current innovations in business schools and includes programs for cross-cultural management, consortia, partnerships, executive education, multimedia, and computer technologies. It also describes the Hong Kong program of flexible management development. Following this section is a profile of educational programs available in Europe, Africa, Australia, and the Americas. The third portion of this guide lists contact information for reference purposes and includes areas of specialization. The final section includes an index of program specialization and an index of institutions.
Subject(s): Directory of programs, management education

New
Salopek. J. J. (1999). **Stop playing games.** *Training & Development,* 53(2), 28-38.

Trainers can prepare to use a game or exercise by asking themselves the traditional reporter's questions: Who is playing? What kind of game is it? When in the training program is the game used? Where will the game be played? How can it be best facilitated? And why is the game used and what is its purpose? This article examines these questions in depth, specifically addressing what to do when games don't work, how to provide closure, and how to connect lessons learned in games with the real world. Includes information on icebreakers and a list of 26 types of games, such as case studies, experiential learning, interactive lectures, role plays, and television games.
Subject(s): Exercises as training technique

Santora, J. C. (1996). **Looking Glass, Inc.: A classroom experience.** *Journal of Leadership Studies,* 3(1), 158-165.

Santora describes his experience with the in-basket business simulation Looking Glass, Inc.® (LGI; Center for Creative Leadership, 1989). He explains the division of roles and the logistics of space, equipment, and time. His students found the simulation very relevant to their classroom learning although it was difficult to accomplish in several classes ranging from 45 minutes to two-and-a-half hours. The frenetic pace and observational demands on the facilitator were the biggest problems. Santora recommends using LGI at the end of a semester, videotaping the simulation to provide feedback later, and investing the necessary time on logistics.
Subject(s): Program evaluation

Schatz, M., & Currie, D. M. (1995). **The bricks, mortar, and architecture of the MBA program: Dealing with the issue of leadership.** *Journal of Leadership Studies,* 2(3), 42-67.

The authors state that MBA programs were the educational darlings of the 1980s, turning out experts in mergers, acquisitions, and takeovers. Ten years later business needs have changed. Businesses are now seeking leaders who can respond to diminishing authority and global competition. In response they recommend a redesign of MBA program curricula. To hold together MBA bricks (basic business principles) they apply mortar (learning experiences such as a leadership laboratory, international exchange projects, assessments, teamwork, simulations, and case studies). For easy reference they lay out the integrated curriculum in chart form.
Subject(s): Program models

Schwartz, M. K., Axtman, K. M., & Freeman, F. H. (1998). *Leadership education: A source book of courses and programs* (7th ed.). Greensboro, NC: Center for Creative Leadership.

The 7th edition contains more than 200 examples of leadership majors and minors, academic leadership courses, and cocurricular programs. Course syllabi are from departments

of education, business, agriculture, nursing, physical education, political science, and others. Cocurricular courses include campus programs for women, a portfolio program, citizen leadership training, and youth programs. Nonacademic examples are also included to provide a lens for viewing the continuation from leadership studies to lifelong learning. Programs for professionals and for grassroots leaders provide this focus.
Subject(s): Program descriptions

New
Seelye, H. N. (Ed.). (1996). *Experiential activities for intercultural learning: Volume 1.* Yarmouth, ME: Intercultural Press.
The essay "Creating a Context: Methodologies in Intercultural Teaching and Training," by Sheila Ramsey, offers trainers and teachers an introduction to theory and practice in the field of cross-cultural communication. The essay is followed by 32 practical activities to help adults and adolescents develop sensitivity and skills useful in expatriate situations or any contacts that cross cultural boundaries. Proverbs, visual imagery, stereotypes, cultural values, self-testing, case studies, and exploration of unfamiliar situations are applied to learning experiences.
Subject(s): Exercises, multicultural diversity, cross-cultural communication

Segal, M. (1997). *Points of influence: A guide to using personality theory at work.* San Francisco: Jossey-Bass.
Segal profiles the work of nine personality theorists, including Freud, Jung, Skinner, and Bowen, with a specific emphasis on how understanding these theories can help managers influence behavior and effect change in the workplace. Each profile includes examples of work situations in which that theory would apply and real-life stories of how leaders have benefited from understanding a particular behavior and its motivations. The conclusion helps integrate these nine theories into a cohesive picture of how the organizational implications of personality theory can help leaders understand their followers, take action, and increase their own self-awareness.
Subject(s): Self-development, personality

Sharma, B., & Roy, J. A. (1996). **Aspects of the internationalization of management education.** *Journal of Management Development*, *15*(1), 5-13.
This paper examines the expansion in number and content of management programs with a global focus. The authors report on efforts to internationalize curricula, course contents, modes of delivery, and research. Some examples of successful efforts are: international internships and faculty exchanges, multicultural case studies and simulations, and partnerships between business schools in different countries.
Subject(s): Management education

New
Shen, J., Cooley, V. E., Ruhl-Smith, C. D., & Keiser, N. M. (1999). **Quality and impact of educational leadership programs: A national study.** *Journal of Leadership Studies*, *6*(1/2), 3-16.
This article reports on a survey of undergraduate and graduate students enrolled in educational administrator leadership programs. The students responded to questions about their perceptions of school leadership before and during the program. Findings indicate that the further students progress through their programs, the more complex is their understanding of school leadership. At the highest level they understand that educational institutions serve an important social function in improving society. Also, students favor skill-based courses over theoretical courses, desire field-based internships, and believe that experience is the best way to develop leadership.
Subject(s): Program evaluation

New
Shenton, G. (1998). **EQUIS: The quality standard for European business education.** *efmd FORUM*, *98*(3), 10-16.
EQUIS, the European Quality Improvement System, was developed by the European Forum for Management Development (efmd) to be an international strategic audit and accreditation system for business education. Intended to address both academic and corporate needs, EQUIS was designed to meet the needs of all European countries while not being historically linked to any particular one. This article describes the "Dynamic Model" of ten quality criteria used to judge programs, and details the rigorous audit and review process that schools must go through to receive EQUIS accreditation. A statement summarizing the core values of an EQUIS school is included.
Subject(s): Program accreditation

New
Shenton, G., & Conraths, B. (1999). **The strengths and weaknesses of European management education.** *efmd FORUM*, *99*(1), 20-25.
This article reports on the pioneering phase of EQUIS, the European Quality Improvement System, that set a standard for management education in undergraduate through executive-level programs. One key element is internationalism. Institutions receive high rankings for hiring faculty and attracting students and participants from outside national boundaries. Another key element is a focus on soft skills (cross-disciplinary courses that tackle current business problems, leadership behavior, change management, personal development, and learning as a skill). EQUIS also benchmarks institutional research, corporate partnerships, the use of technology, and faculty credentials.
Subject(s): Program accreditation

Sikes, S. (1995). *Feeding the zircon gorilla: And other team-building activities.* Tulsa, OK: Learning Unlimited.

This book contains 38 activities for small to large groups of any age—children through adults. The learnings range from simple to sophisticated. Don't Touch Me sets up a shifting paradigm as participants switch places without bumping into others. In The Group Leader a sighted leader guides a blindfolded team though a physical task. Oogly is a cornstarch batter that replicates change. When pounded forcefully it offers resistance. Provide too much energy and it fractures; provide too little energy and it drools. Handouts in the book may be photocopied.
Subject(s): Exercises

New
Silberman, M. (Ed.). (1999). *The 1999 training and performance sourcebook.* New York: McGraw-Hill.

Seasoned trainers share their favorite ideas for human resources development (HRD). There are 40 essays and reproducible activities to help design new HRD programs, hone training skills, and support individual development inside and outside the classroom. Removing the Blinders is an activity that demonstrates the value of asking for feedback. *POINTS: Power and Influence Tactics Scale* is an instrument to aid program planning. Essays include guidelines for determining the value of intellectual capital and creating effective learning environments. Other items are related to career planning, sales, sexual harassment, and other HRD issues.
Subject(s): Training resources

New
Simmons, A. (1999). **Using art in training.** *Training & Development, 53*(6), 32-36.

Simmons says that when training participants are asked to draw pictures of their organizations they often reveal problems or express feelings that don't come across in words. This article describes how to integrate art into training programs, and includes examples of four participant drawings and analyses of what they represent. Simmons also offers suggestions for using art in programs, encouraging trainers to create trust, preempt blame and defensiveness, give everyone a turn, instill confidence, and let the art do its own work.
Subject(s): Art as training technique

Smitter, R. (1995). **Criteria for selecting case studies of leadership.** *Journal of Leadership Studies, 2*(2), 146-152.

The use of case studies in business and leadership classrooms is popular because it gives students a chance to grapple with real-life leadership problems. Smitter's criteria for selecting cases include the following questions: Does it portray leadership as a position or relationship? Does it cast leadership as a transaction or transformation? Does it define leadership as a process or single event? Does it raise issues of ethics, vision, or diversity? Does it suggest change? What forms of power are available? How are followers portrayed?
Subject(s): Cases as training technique

New
Stone, F. M. (1999). *Coaching, counseling, mentoring: How to choose and use the right technique to boost employee performance.* New York: AMACOM.

Coaching, counseling, and mentoring are three separate techniques that require different skills. Coaching involves continually developing employees to perform their jobs better, and coaching skills include hiring the best, clarifying responsibilities, and providing feedback. Counseling is a nonpunitive disciplinary process involving one-on-one meetings between a manager and employee and consists of four stages: verbal counseling, written warnings, demotion or transfer, and termination. In mentoring, leaders do more than simply train their employees to do better jobs; they share their experience and wisdom. This book uses sample situations in the workplace to illustrate the different techniques and the steps, actions, and pitfalls in each. Includes index.
Subject(s): Coaching, mentoring

Stumpf, S. A. (1995). **Applying new science theories in leadership development.** *Journal of Management Development, 14*(5), 39-49.

Stumpf is cofounder of the nonprofit MSP Institute, Inc., which creates simulations for teaching organizational management. The institute's approach to leadership development is consistent with "new science" (Wheatley, 1992) theories for learning to lead complex organizations in turbulent environments. Stumpf explains how the institute applies quantum mechanics, self-organizing systems, and chaos theory to activity-based leadership lessons. One example of this application is the LOMA Middle Management Workshop on Leadership, a five-day program for mid-level managers in the life insurance industry.
Subject(s): Program descriptions

Stumpf, S. A., & Mullen, T. P. (1992). *Taking charge: Strategic leadership in the middle game.* Englewood Cliffs, NJ: Prentice Hall.

This guide is intended for middle managers who wish to develop their strategic leadership skills. Identification of vision, mission, goals, and objectives is illustrated by real examples from actual companies. Assessment of one's personal preference for communication, decision making, and creativity provides a starting point for learning alternative behaviors. The authors suggest ways to create opportunities to practice and refine new leadership skills.
Subject(s): Self-development, middle managers

Stumpf, S. S., Dunbar, R. L. M., & Mullen, T. P. (1991). **Developing entrepreneurial skills through the use of behavioral simulations.** *Journal of Management Development, 10*(5), 32-45.

The authors discuss the use of simulations to teach the sense-making and opportunity-seeking processes of entrepreneurship. This paper outlines typical simulation goals and objectives, setup, facilitation, and feedback. A research study

identified several entrepreneurial behaviors: identifying constraints, creating vision, innovation, resiliency, and tolerance.
Subject(s): Simulation as training technique, sense-making

Tetrault, L. A., Schriesheim, C. A., & Neider, L. L. (1988).
Leadership training interventions: A review. *Organization Development Journal, 6*(3), 77-83.

This article is a review of the five major leadership models used in leadership training interventions: Blake and Mouton's (1978) Managerial Grid; Hersey and Blanchard's (1977) Situational Leadership model; Leader Match concept by Fiedler, Chemers, and Mahar (1976); Graen's (1975) Leader-Member Exchange; and Vroom and Yetton's (1973) Contingency model. The authors discuss the degree of effectiveness these individual programs offer as well as the drawbacks associated with these specific models. The larger question regarding the effectiveness of leadership training in general is addressed.
Subject(s): Program models

New
Thach, L., & Heinselman, T. (1999). **Executive coaching defined.** *Training & Development, 53*(3), 34-39.

There are three kinds of executive coaching: feedback, in-depth development, and content coaching. Companies must identify the type of coaching their executives need and how it fits into their organizational strategy before initiating any coaching program. This article provides real-life examples of each kind of coaching, sample coaching scenarios, and a list of coaching providers. It also lists the characteristics of an effective coach, which include accountability, top management modeling, integration with other organizational systems, and confidentiality.
Subject(s): Coaching

Thiagarajan, S., & Thiagarajan, R. (1995). *Diversity simulation games: Exploring and celebrating differences.* Amherst, MA: HRD Press.

This book contains instructions for five simulations that focus on cross-cultural differences. They are brief—30 minutes total time for instruction, play, and debriefing. Brief Encounters simulates the misinterpretations that occur during a first-contact experience with another culture. Chatter teaches students to accept differences in conversation and behavior during cross-cultural communication. Exclude allows students to experience the frustration of being the one left out of a group activity. Reincarnation examines the differences among people that contribute to their triumphs and traumas. Same Difference helps students identify their commonalities with people in several groups.
Subject(s): Exercises

New
Tornow, W. W., London, M., & CCL Associates. (1998). *Maximizing the value of 360-degree feedback: A process for successful individual and organizational development.* San Francisco: Jossey-Bass and Center for Creative Leadership.

This book is based on the Center for Creative Leadership philosophy that feedback from multiple perspectives is key to leadership development. The authors contend that feedback may be a useful tool for performance appraisal but offers maximum benefit when used as an ongoing process that includes assessment, developmental experiences, personal responsibility, and organizational support. They discuss the details of feedback standards, quality of ratings, information processing, behavioral outcomes, customer input, learning organizations, and multicultural influences. Includes bibliographical references and index.
Subject(s): 360-degree feedback

New
Ukens, L. L. (1999). *All together now! A seriously fun collection of training games and activities.* San Francisco: Jossey-Bass.

Ukens introduces this book of 60 games with a discussion of the experiential learning cycle and the facilitator's role. She suggests how to select appropriate activities and conduct debriefing sessions that help participants reach their own conclusions. Among the leadership-related games are Perfect Square, Tower of Power, and Runway. Other games highlight team dynamics, creativity, conflict management, decision making, problem solving, and communication skills.
Subject(s): Exercises

Ulmer, W. F. (1994). **Missing links in the education of senior leaders.** *The Public Manager, 23*(2), 9-12.

In order for managerial performance to create organizational rejuvenation, the education of senior leaders should be examined. Development programs for executives should include three critical elements that are rarely given serious attention: 1) the role of personality and self-awareness; 2) an enlargement of the conceptual model of leader behavior; and 3) an improved approach to the evaluation of individuals, teams, and organizations. Ulmer is the retired president and CEO of the Center for Creative Leadership.
Subject(s): Executive education

New
Useem, M. (1998). *The leadership moment: Nine true stories of triumph and disaster and their lessons for us all.* New York: Times Business/Random House.

Useem considers leadership to be the act of making a difference—employing a strategic vision, making an active choice, mobilizing others to get the job done, and getting tangible results. Here he focuses on exceptionally difficult decisions with extraordinary stakes and profound outcomes. Nine examples of leaders facing critical moments provide lessons for those who wish to develop as leaders. Included are: Roy Vagelos of Merck & Company, whose humanitarian investment cured river blindness in Africa; Eugene Kranz of NASA Mission Control, who masterminded a long-distance repair that saved Apollo 13 from disaster; and Alfredo Cristiani, the President of El Salvador, who negotiated an end

to his country's civil war. Includes bibliographical references and index.
Subject(s): Self-development

New
Valkeavaara, T. (1998). **Exploring the nature of human resource developers' expertise.** *European Journal of Psychological Assessment, 7*(4), 533-548.

Human resource developers are organizational practitioners who focus on training, career development, and organizational development. In order to study these managers' expertise the author surveyed members of Finnish HRD associations to learn about their work roles, needed competencies, and developmental interests. Analytical and coaching skills were found to be important, and the author asserts that HR developers must use these skills to communicate their expertise to others. Results also showed that contextual factors often determine specific work areas, and that HR developers cannot depend on established job descriptions but must build their own roles in their organizations. Includes bibliographical references. Commentary by Jim Dukes follows the article.
Subject(s): Human resources development

Van Maurik, J. (1994). *Discovering the leader in you.* New York: McGraw-Hill.

This book is based on the premise that leadership is emotional, not logical—an attitude, not a position. Van Maurik defines leadership as "something you choose to do through a process of action and self-discovery." He presents classic management theories and definitions of leadership to highlight skills and behaviors to practice when learning leadership. At the end of each chapter are a summary and a quiz, making this book suitable for individual use or a classroom text. Includes bibliographical references and index.
Subject(s): Self-development

Van Velsor, E., Leslie, J. B., & Fleenor, J. W. (1997). *Choosing 360: A guide to evaluating multi-rater feedback instruments for management development.* Greensboro, NC: Center for Creative Leadership.

An increasingly popular vehicle for getting feedback from one's boss, peers, and subordinates is the multiple-perspective, or 360-degree, feedback instrument. This book, which updates *Feedback to Managers, Volume 1* (1991), presents a step-by-step process that shows how to evaluate multiple-feedback instruments intended for management development. Issues addressed include instrument development, validity and reliability, feedback display, scoring strategies, and cost. Includes bibliographical references.
Subject(s): 360-degree feedback

Van Wart, M. (1993). **Providing a base for executive development at the state level.** *Public Personnel Management, 22*(2), 269-282.

Four levels of training and development—employee, supervisory, management, and executive—have different needs,

commitment issues, design concerns, and evaluation problems. Management development programs must be sophisticated, integrating theory and practical examples. Executive development programs are often expensive and handicapped by time pressures. Both levels of programming need to focus on interpersonal and conceptual skills. Existing state programs for managers and executives are briefly described with emphasis on their relationship to the overall human-resource-development system.
Subject(s): Program models, public service leadership

Vicere, A. A. (1992). **The strategic leadership imperative for executive development.** *Human Resource Planning, 15*(1), 15-31.

The strategic leadership model indicates an organizational time/life cycle from emergence, growth, and maturity to decline and decay. Organizations move through stages of innovation and creativity, organizing structure, opportunity and growth, control, and adaptation to survive competition. Some organizations reach a crisis stage of reaction that usually leads to bureaucracy. The model depicts the challenges of dealing with the aftermath of an organization's growth and success.
Subject(s): Executive education, strategic leadership, organizational life cycles

Vicere, A. A. (1996). **Executive education: The leading edge.** *Organizational Dynamics, 25*(2), 67-81.

To illustrate the importance of innovative, hands-on executive education the author profiles three different training programs: the Center for Creative Leadership's LeaderLab®, AT&T's Leadership Development Program, and ARAMARK's Executive Leadership Institute. The content and impact of these programs are discussed as well as their implications for other executive education initiatives.
Subject(s): Executive education, program descriptions

New
Vicere, A. A. (1997). *Changes in practices, changes in perspectives: The 1997 international study of executive development trends.* University Park, PA: The Penn State Institute for the Study of Organizational Effectiveness. Phone: (814) 865-3435.

Every five years Penn State's Institute for the Study of Organizational Effectiveness surveys businesses to learn how they conduct executive development. This report summarizes the findings of the 1997 survey. The results show a continuation of some trends identified in earlier reports, including the development of an increasingly competitive marketplace of executive development providers and a trend toward more customized, strategic programs. Four new trends were also identified: an increase in the role of technology and distance delivery, a shift away from programs and toward experience-based methodologies, increased importance of performance feedback, and a shift in perspective toward leadership competencies highlighting adaptability and flexibility.
Subject(s): Executive education

New

Vicere, A. A., & Fulmer, R. M. (1998). *Leadership by design.* Boston: Harvard Business School Press.

To effectively compete in a rapidly changing, global economy, organizations must simultaneously develop in two areas: 1) leadership and 2) organizational structures and processes. Rather than view these as separate challenges, the authors present the concept of a joint developmental focus called *strategic leadership development.* It blends traditional executive education with new ideas for training partnerships and real-time learning laboratories in organizations. Several systemic models demonstrate how leadership development relates to human resources practices, strategic imperatives, and organizational life cycles. Several case studies argue the benefits and drawbacks of external and internal training programs. There are suggestions for designing the appropriate mix of initiatives for your organization and six examples of new paradigm approaches to strategic leadership development: the Center for Creative Leadership's LeaderLab® program, AT&T's Leadership Program for Middle Managers, ARAMARK's Executive Leadership Institute, the World Bank's Executive Development program, new initiatives at Johnson & Johnson, and MIT's Center for Organizational Learning. Includes bibliographical references and index.
Subject(s): Leadership development, strategic leadership, human resources development

Vincent, A., & Seymour, J. (1995). **Profile of women mentors: A national survey.** *SAM Advanced Management Journal,* *60*(2), 4-10.

The results of a national survey on mentoring are discussed. The survey addressed gender, race, education, salary, experience, and age factors within a mentoring-protégé relationship. Among the findings were: 1) women are as willing to mentor as men, 2) previous mentors or protégés are more willing to enter subsequent mentoring relationships, and 3) female mentors have primarily female protégés while male mentors have both female and male protégés. Other findings and the population for the survey are also discussed.
Subject(s): Women as mentors

New

Waldman, D. A., Atwater, L.E., & Antonioni, D. (1998). **Has 360-degree feedback gone amok?** *Academy of Management Executive,* *12*(2), 86-94.

A recent trend in management development programs is the use of the 360-degree-feedback model in helping managers to understand their strengths and weaknesses. The authors' purpose in this article is to increase awareness of the pitfalls associated with 360-degree feedback. One concern deals with imitation. Many organizations may not be well informed about the model, but will plunge into use of of it because their key competitors are doing so. A second concern with the 360-degree rush is its use for evaluation rather than development. Certain organizations use the ratings to determine a manager's future. Political gain is the third motivation experienced from the 360-degree model. The

authors recommend the use of certain precursors to the costly commitment of this system, including a test pilot program or focus group. A case study of one company illustrates these principles, and the article concludes with a general review. Includes bibliographical references.
Subject(s): 360-degree feedback

Waldroop, J., & Butler, T. (1996). **The executive as coach.** *Harvard Business Review,* *74*(6), 111-117.

Coaching requires finding the correct "balance between carrot and stick." This article offers executives advice on how they can best help their managers change negative behavior. Readers are told how to tell when a manager needs coaching—for example, how to decide whether a behavior is changeable or if it is a character trait. Waldroop and Butler also identify what skills are needed in a coach, such as the ability to be a teacher, not a judge. Finally, they offer suggestions on what coaching techniques work best, including setting microgoals and using script-writing and role plays.
Subject(s): Coaching, executives

Walter, G. M. (1997). *Corporate practices in management development.* New York: Conference Board.

This is a Conference Board report of a survey and interviews conducted to determine the training and development practices in large organizations. Findings indicate that the future of management development will: link development efforts to organizational strategy, focus heavily on experience-based development, involve university-and-business partnerships, provide high-potential managers with risks as well as challenges, institutionalize systems of management development, and invest in pre- and post-training efforts.
Subject(s): Management development, best practices

New

Warech, M. A., Smither, J. W., Reilly, R. R., Millsap, R. E., & Reilly, S. P. (1998). **Self-monitoring and 360-degree ratings.** *Leadership Quarterly: Special Issue: 360-Degree Feedback in Leadership Research,* *9*(4), 449-473.

This paper asks if a personality variable influences 360-degree-feedback ratings. The variable is self-monitoring (SM), one's sensitivity and responsiveness to social and interpersonal cues about behavior. To determine the answer 191 telecommunications managers participated in an assessment center study. Data were gathered from 360-degree-feedback reports, assessor ratings, and self-monitoring assessments following the assessment center experience. SM ability was positively related to some ratings of interpersonal effectiveness and negatively related to some ratings of business competence. Overall, SM ability was not significantly related to feedback ratings. Includes bibliographical references.
Subject(s): 360-degree feedback

Witherspoon, R., & White, R. P. (1997). *Four essential ways that coaching can help executives.* Greensboro, NC: Center for Creative Leadership.

This report elaborates on the coaching relationship between consultants and their clients: chief executives, board members, and senior managers of organizations. As a coach the consultant's role is to provide focused learning regarding a client's specific task, his or her present job, a future job, or the client's long-range goals. These learnings are categorized into four executive coaching roles: coaching for skills, coaching for performance, coaching for development, and coaching for the executive's agenda. As the authors describe each role they also provide an example that includes a situation, a process, and results. Includes bibliographical references.
Subject(s): Coaching, executives

New
Witzel, M. (1998). **Re-designing management development in the new Europe.** *efmd FORUM, 98*(1), 6-12.

This article summarizes a report by the Torino Group of the European Training Foundation, which describes how the information revolution, downsizings, and globalization have changed the nature of management development and executive training. In the new business environment, training must focus on results-based development, measuring the value added, establishing partnerships, and using technology. The report offers eight recommendations for improving the practice of management development: 1) know yourself, 2) develop and pursue a vision, 3) aim to be a learning organization, 4) reshape the external providers, 5) draw benefits from networking, 6) pursue quality, 7) mobilize public and societal support, and 8) have the courage to innovate.
Subject(s): Program models, management education

New
Wognum, I. (1998). **HRD policymaking in companies: An interpretation of the differences.** *Human Resource Development Quarterly, 9*(3), 255-269.

Wognum says that the HRD policy-making process is critical to a company's success because these policies determine whether employees have the competencies they need. In this study HRD representatives of over 100 Dutch companies with more than 500 employees were surveyed to measure how HRD policy-making was impacted by three factors: company characteristics, the situation that served as a starting point for policy development, and characteristics of the HRD department. Analysis showed that both company characteristics and strategic starting points affected HRD policies, and that most companies emphasized tactical and operational training. Wognum says that to be most effective, HRD policy-making must be strategic and linked to the organization's wider objectives. Includes bibliographical references.
Subject(s): Human resources development

New
Woodall, J., & Winstanley, D. (1998). *Management development: Strategy and practice.* Oxford, England: Blackwell Business.

This book analyzes management and leadership development from the perspective of both the organization and the individual manager. The authors begin by explaining the purpose of management development and then discuss how to identify developmental needs, including managerial competencies and individual needs. The third section describes management development interventions, including off-the-job development and work-based methods. The book concludes by addressing how to determine different individuals' development needs, including the unique needs of women, international managers, and senior executives. Learning objectives and exercises are provided for each chapter. Includes bibliographical references and index.
Subject(s): Leadership development

Woyach, R. B. (1993). *Preparing for leadership: A young adult's guide to leadership skills in a global age.* Westport, CT: Greenwood Press.

High school and college students who serve in leadership positions can learn how to work more effectively in their current positions and prepare themselves for future leadership roles. Woyach explains that leadership is not a position of power; it is a relationship among people. A leader creates and shares a vision, builds consensus among members, resolves conflicts, and ensures that the group has all it needs to achieve success. The steps to achieve these skills are effectively defined in text, flowcharts, graphs, and cartoons. Includes bibliographical references and index.
Subject(s): Self-development, youth leadership

Woyach, R. B. (1997). **Portfolios as means for promoting continuity in leadership development.** *Journal of Leadership Studies, 4*(2), 144-158.

Woyach describes a portfolio program that has been implemented in three high schools in Oakland County, Michigan. This portfolio program is intended to enhance student leadership abilities and display students' progress in learning the skills and competencies of civic leadership. This article describes the learning objectives and the components of the portfolios. Some examples of learning objectives are active listening, time management, envisioning, and willingness to take responsibility. Examples of components include a cover letter, table of contents, and section introductions. Woyach gives tips for designing portfolio assessments and advising students.
Subject(s): Program descriptions, portfolios as training technique, youth leadership

Wren, J. T. (1994). **Teaching leadership: The art of the possible.** *Journal of Leadership Studies, 1*(2), 73-93.

Wren shares the most recent version of his introductory leadership course at the University of Richmond's Jepson

School of Leadership Studies. This Foundations course is a prerequisite for the curriculum, which pursues leadership from a liberal arts perspective. The article is a discussion of course structure and student competencies and does not include a syllabus.

Subject(s): Program descriptions

Yammarino, F. J., & Atwater, L. E. (1997). **Do managers see themselves as others see them? Implications of self-other rating agreement for human resources management.** *Organizational Dynamics*, 25(4), 35-44.

The authors estimate that 10% to 15% of today's organizations use multi-rater feedback instruments for performance evaluations or to plan their managers' developmental learning. In this article Yammarino and Atwater discuss the rationale for gathering 360-degree feedback from a manager, peers, subordinates, and superiors. The important data are found in the agreement between the self-rating and the feedback from others. A manager who overestimates his or her abilities has a high need for development. This person is a candidate for derailment. One who gets negative feedback from self and others may be a poor performer who has a high need for development. A manager who underestimates his or her talents may need to set higher aspiration levels and has only a moderate developmental need. The manager who gets favorable feedback and has a positive self-image is a high performer with the lowest need for development.

Subject(s): 360-degree feedback

Young, D. P., & Dixon, N. M. (1996). **Helping leaders take effective action: A program evaluation.** Greensboro, NC: Center for Creative Leadership.

This is an evaluation of the Center for Creative Leadership's LeaderLab® program. Conducted over a six-month period LeaderLab guides self-awareness of one's behaviors, encourages change, and supports action plans for change. To evaluate LeaderLab, researchers collected quantitative data from the *Impact Questionnaire* administered before and after the program and qualitative data from telephone interviews with participants, co-workers, and LeaderLab process advisors. Results indicate that a long-term, action-oriented program does help participants to improve their leadership effectiveness. The most significant changes appeared in the areas of: interpersonal relations, organizational systems, coping with emotional disequilibrium, listening, vision, and balancing work and family responsibilities. Includes bibliographical references and index.

Subject(s): Program evaluation

SOCIAL, GLOBAL, AND DIVERSITY ISSUES

New

Aaltio-Marjosola, I., & Lehtinen, J. (1998). **Male managers as fathers? Contrasting management, fatherhood, and masculinity.** *Human Relations, 51*(2), 121-136.

Managers' gender inevitably affects their professional behavior. Most research on this issue has addressed female managers, but this article examines the impact of fatherhood on male managers. While the authors do not advocate managers' developing a paternalistic relationship with their subordinates, they do hope that male managers can apply some lessons learned as parents to their professional lives. An analysis of the movie *Hook*, a variation of the Peter Pan story, illustrates how the management style of the main character changed as he developed as a father. Includes bibliographical references.

Subject(s): Men's leadership

Abramms, B., & Simons, G. F. (Eds.). (1996). *Cultural diversity sourcebook.* Amherst, MA: HRD Press.

Barbara Ehrenreich, Robert Fulghum, bell hooks, Maya Angelou, George Bush, and Elie Wiesel are among the contributors to this anthology of writings, speeches, poems, magazine articles, and short stories addressing diversity. Abramms and Simons take the unusual step of structuring their book around the issue of class, although some chapters also address race, gender, diversity under fire, applications, spirit, alternative models and visions, and affirmative action.

Subject(s): Diversity overview

Adler, N. J. (1996). **Global women political leaders: An invisible history, an increasingly important future.** *Leadership Quarterly: Special Issue: Leadership and Diversity (Part I), 7*(1), 133-161.

Adler draws a historic pattern of women's global leadership with a list of 25 women who have led modern governments. She compares their paths to power, high visibility, and inconsistent support to find similarities across time and cultures. When compared to the experiences of men in global leadership positions a pattern emerges. Among the women on her list are: Indira Gandhi, former Prime Minister of India; Golda Meir, former Prime Minister of Israel; Aung San Suu Kyi, Opposition Leader in Burma; Margaret Thatcher, former Prime Minister of Great Britain; and Isabel Perón, former President of Argentina.

Subject(s): Women as global leaders, women as political leaders

Adler, N. J. (1997). *International dimensions of organizational behavior* (3rd ed.). Cincinnati, OH: South-Western College Publishing.

This textbook is based on the premise that "global complexity is neither unpredictable nor random. Variations across cultures and their impacts on organizations follow systematic, predictable patterns." A learning module is included in each chapter. Some examples of chapters are: "Creating Cultural Synergy," "Multicultural Teams," and "Global Leadership, Motivation, and Decision Making." Each includes charts, exercises, questions for reflection, cases, and bibliographical references. Adler describes three videos that she produced to supplement lessons in the study of work beyond national boundaries. The most relevant to leadership is the two-part series that follows the development of a multinational team on a project in Africa. *It's a Jungle Out There* and *The Survival Guide* document the team's experience and analyze their problems with cross-cultural communication and decision making. Includes index.

Subject(s): Global leadership, textbook

Ali, A. J. (1996). **Organizational development in the Arab world.** *Journal of Management Development, 15*(5), 4-21.

Ali is guest editor of this special issue on management development in the Middle East. His article analyzes the various Islamic schools of thought on such OD applications as: change, self-development, training, and conflict. Other articles in this special issue are: A. Reichel, "Management Development in Israel: Current and Future Challenges"; H. S. Atiyyah, "Expatriate Acculturation in Arab Gulf Countries"; D. M. Hunt and M. I. At-Twaijri, "Values and the Saudi Manager: An Empirical Investigation"; and A. Al-Meer, "A Comparison of the Need Importance Structure Between Saudis and Westerners: An Exploratory Study."

Subject(s): Cultural context: Middle East

New

Ardichvili, A., Cardozo, R. N., & Gasparishvili, A. (1998). **Leadership styles and management practices of Russian entrepreneurs: Implications for transferability of Western HRD interventions.** *Human Resource Development Quarterly, 9*(2), 145-155.

In 1994 interviews were conducted with over 200 Russian entrepreneurs to determine whether Western HRD interventions could be used effectively in Russian firms. The researchers specifically examined decision making, leadership styles, and the entrepreneurs' degree of involvement in HRD processes. Analysis showed that the Russian managers had strong collectivist tendencies, which clashed with the individualistic premise of many American HRD interventions. The authors suggest that HR professionals wishing to work in Russia should recognize Russians' collectivist nature, concentrate on traditional management techniques, and be aware of Russians' sensitivity to power and status differences. Includes bibliographical references.

Subject(s): Cultural context: Russia

Astin, H. S., & Leland, C. (1991). ***Women of influence, women of vision: A cross-generational study of leaders and social change.*** San Francisco: Jossey-Bass.

Astin and Leland profile 77 women in education who provided leadership in the modern women's movement of the 1960s through the 1980s. This book documents key experiences, formative influences, role models, perspectives, and accomplishments of the women who initiated and sustained a major social movement. The intent of this book is to provide a conceptual model for future studies of leadership and social change. Practical strategies are offered for emerging leaders to overcome discouragement, avoid burnout, and find time for personal lives. Includes bibliographical references and index.
Subject(s): Women as leaders of social movements

New
Becker, C. E. (1997). **Women's leadership: Why the debate is important.** *A Leadership Journal: Women in Leadership— Sharing the Vision, 2*(1), 27-37.

Becker says that to understand women's leadership in the church, four factors have to be considered: how women describe their leadership, how women use their power, how church systems respond, and how societal attitudes influence women's leadership. She says that while women can clearly identify their own leadership styles, societal and church structures are still not comfortable with women in power and continue to hold them back. Includes bibliographical references.
Subject(s): Women as religious leaders

Bennis, W., Parikh, J., & Lessem, R. (1996). ***Beyond leadership: Balancing economics, ethics and ecology*** (Rev. ed.). Cambridge, MA: Blackwell Business.

Written for practitioners and students of leadership this revised edition focuses on a global approach to management with a concern for a balance of ethical, economic, and ecological managerial skills. The American, Asian, and Afro-European roots of the authors are reflected in a marriage of Eastern and Western philosophies in this book. The authors present an ethical paradigm with four elements: personal development, group synergy, organizational learning, and sustainable development. The philosophy behind the paradigm is that organizations are living systems where every individual depends on the whole and the whole depends on every individual. Includes index.
Subject(s): Multicultural context

Berdahl, J. L. (1996). **Gender and leadership in work groups: Six alternative models.** *Leadership Quarterly: Special Issue: Leadership and Diversity (Part I), 7*(1), 21-40.

Berdahl compares six models to determine the emergence of task oriented (masculine) or social (feminine) leadership. The first model, No Sex Differences, assumes that personal differences in abilities or behavior have no connection to one's gender. The second model, Stereotypical Sex Differ-

ences, asserts that social differences have biological origins. The third model, Gender Schema, claims that gender role identity is a psychological choice. The fourth model, Status Roles, relates to expected competence or dominance in group interaction. The fifth model, Social Roles, emphasizes the social expectations of men and women. Finally, the Multicultural Model suggests that cultural and experiential differences, more than sex differences, account for individual task- or social-leadership behaviors. Berdahl recommends that gender/leadership researchers study groups over time and use a variety of models.
Subject(s): Women as corporate leaders, men as corporate leaders

New
Bond, M. A., & Pyle, J. L. (1998). **The ecology of diversity in organizational settings: Lessons from a case study.** *Human Relations, 51*(5), 589-623.

Bond and Pyle used surveys, group meetings, and in-depth interviews to conduct a case study of a large chemical company's efforts to support workplace diversity. From this research they identified four lessons about diversity based on a social ecological perspective: 1) organizational history and tradition affect diversity; 2) employees' experiences of events may differ; 3) informal organizational processes are powerful; and 4) connections exist between the individual, the organization, and broader cultural values. The authors conclude that to support diversity, organizations must address three components: representation, interaction, and culture. Includes bibliographical references.
Subject(s): Diversity in workplace

Bonilla-Santiago, G. (1992). ***Breaking ground and barriers: Hispanic women developing effective leadership.*** San Diego, CA: Marin Publications.

This book reports on the Hispanic Women Leaders' Project, a collection of oral histories from 99 Hispanic women who have made significant contributions despite the challenges they faced in a racist and sexist society. Their stories reveal common attitudes toward family values, education, challenges, aspirations, authority, and leadership style. Seventeen stories are shared in detail. Among them are: Miriam Colon, Artistic Director and Founder of the Puerto Rican Traveling Theater in New York; Polly Baca, former Colorado State Senator; Patricia Diaz-Dennis, former Federal Communications Commissioner; Esther Novak, Director of Urban Affairs at AT&T; Lena Guerrero, former Texas Commissioner of Railroads and Transportation and legislator in the Texas State House of Representatives; Nelly Galan, Manager of WNJU TV in New York; and Iliana Ros-Lehtinen, U.S. Congresswoman.
Subject(s): Hispanic leadership, women's leadership

New

Bowen, W. G., Bok, D., & Burkhart, G. (1999). **A report card on diversity: Lessons for business from higher education.** *Harvard Business Review, 77*(1), 139-149.

This is a report on race-sensitive university admissions policies and their implications for corporate America. Research sponsored by the Mellon Foundation developed a college-and-beyond database by tracking students who entered 28 selective colleges and universities in the fall terms of 1976 and 1989. Findings are published in the authors' book *The Shape of the River* (Princeton University Press, 1998). As former presidents of Princeton University and Harvard University respectively, Bowen and Bok present well-informed analysis about the benefits of diversity and the importance of free choice. They encourage employers to take a more sophisticated approach to building diverse pools of talent for the corporate leaders of tomorrow.
Subject(s): Ethnic diversity in higher education

Brake, T. (1997). *The global leader: Critical factors for creating the world class organization.* Chicago: Irwin.

To understand global leadership one must consider environment, key competencies, and organizational support. Global environment is comprised of those who buy (the ten largest emerging markets are China, Indonesia, India, South Korea, Turkey, South Africa, Poland, Argentina, Brazil, and Mexico) and the companies with goods and services to market. Key competencies—business acumen, relationship management, and personal effectiveness—form the model Global Leadership Triad. Organizational support builds onto the triad adding strategy, architecture, culture, education, and performance systems. Brake reports on his interviews with leading global companies such as Avon, Colgate-Palmolive, and NYNEX. Includes bibliographical references and index.
Subject(s): Global leadership

New

Brinkerhoff, D. W., & Coston, J. M. (1999). **International development management in a globalized world.** *Public Administration Review, 59*(4), 346-361.

Development management is the "theory and practice that concentrates upon organizational and managerial problems, issues, and practices" in developing nations in Africa, Asia, Latin America, and Eastern Europe. This article examines the current state of development management, first describing the societal trends that have affected the field and then offering a brief history of how it evolved after World War II. Development management today can be seen in four ways: as a toolkit of management techniques, as a means to foreign assistance programs, as a process intervention, and as a system of values. Public administrators must connect theory and practice in all four aspects of development management in order to help the citizens of developing countries. Includes bibliographical references.
Subject(s): Global leadership

New

Burns, M. J. (1999). **Women as international leaders: How gender and culture affect international leadership training outcomes for women from North America, Latin America, and Brazil.** *A Leadership Journal: Women in Leadership—Sharing the Vision, 3*(2), 5-15.

Although research has been done on female international leaders, particularly on political leaders and female expatriates, the author says that little is known about how international women develop leadership skills. In this study American, Latin American, and Brazilian participants in a two-year international leadership training program sponsored by the Kellogg Foundation were surveyed. Results showed that the women used what they learned in training more than the men in the study did, and that leaders from developing nations used the training more than American participants did. Tables display statistical results. Includes bibliographical references.
Subject(s): Women as global leaders

Carnevale, A. P., & Stone, S. C. (1995). *The American mosaic: An in-depth report on the future of diversity at work.* New York: McGraw-Hill.

Research sponsored by the U.S. Department of Labor, the American Society for Training and Development, and the Joyce Foundation is reported in this volume of data and description. The authors analyze the cultural implications, wage issues, and demographic trends for racial and ethnic groups, men and women workers, disabled persons, gay and lesbian workers, and older workers. Historical references, the current debate over affirmative action, and projections for the future are presented. Includes bibliographical references and index.
Subject(s): Diversity in workplace

Catalyst. (1996). *Women in corporate leadership: Progress and prospects.* New York: Author.

In 1995 Catalyst surveyed 461 female executives about their career paths and strategies. They found that successful women's career paths were spread across industries and functions. Their critical career strategies were: 1) exceed performance expectations, 2) develop a style with which male managers are comfortable, 3) seek difficult assignments, and 4) have an influential mentor. In related research Catalyst surveyed 325 CEOs of Fortune 1000 companies on the subject of female executives. The CEOs cited lack of experience as the primary reason why so few women achieve top-level positions. They considered appropriate efforts to support female leadership development: 1) giving women high visibility assignments, 2) ensuring that diverse candidates are considered in succession plans, and 3) mentoring programs.
Subject(s): Women as corporate leaders

New

Catalyst. (1998). *Advancing women in business—the Catalyst guide: Best practices from the corporate leaders.* San Francisco: Jossey-Bass.

Gender issues remain a barrier to females in management and executive positions. Catalyst, a national nonprofit consulting organization, supports and motivates women to maximize their leadership potential. This source is a tool for companies and individuals wishing to diversify leadership roles in their corporations. It combines research reports, case histories, and reported best practices for effective methods in the advancement of women. This three-part book begins with a framework for establishing change supported by real-life examples of successful initiatives. The second part uses benchmarking activities to profile some of the best practices fostered by Catalyst. The final portion details the accomplishments of Catalyst award-winning companies. Includes four indexes.
Subject(s): Women as corporate leaders

New

Catalyst. (1999). *Creating women's networks: A how-to guide for women and companies.* San Francisco: Jossey-Bass.

Women's networks are formal or informal groups of women that form in organizations to act as resources for both the members and the company. These groups are typically formed to address three problems women in corporations face: existing biased assumptions, isolation in the social structure, and exclusion from established career paths. This book offers advice on how to develop a women's network in an organization, including how to determine if one is needed, what the network's role should be, how to build company-wide support, and dealing with potential problems. Case studies of women's networks at companies including Kodak, Kimberly-Clark, and Bausch & Lomb are provided. Includes index.
Subject(s): Women as corporate leaders

New

Catalyst. (1999). *Women of color in corporate management: Opportunities and barriers.* New York: Author.

Catalyst conducted a three-year, multiphase study to determine the status of women of color in corporate management and to find out how the women themselves perceive the challenges and opportunities they face. The study included a literature review, a statistical analysis of census data, a mail survey, focus groups, and interviews with managers. This report includes information on how women of color in management view their work environment, diversity initiatives, their managers, and their organizations. It also describes differences in the experiences of African American, Asian American, and Hispanic women managers. A 1997 report, *Women of Color in Management: A Statistical Picture*, details the study's statistical findings, while *Women of Color in Corporate Management: Dynamics of Career Advancement* (1998) offers results from the mail survey.
Subject(s): Women as managers

New

Ch'ng, D. (1997). **Managing the relationship factor in East Asia.** *Monash Mt. Eliza Business Review*, *1*(1), 62-73.

The Confucian values that dominate most Asian countries make building and maintaining relationships crucial to doing business. This article describes the basic types of Confucian relationships and some of the problems that can occur between Western and Eastern management styles, such as the individualism/familiarism and contacts/contracts conflicts. Western managers can facilitate the development of relationships by promoting empathy, sincerity, trust, the exchange of gifts, sharing benefits, reciprocity, arbitration, and allowing others to save face. Mediators can also help facilitate relationships, but whether Western managers choose to use intermediaries or not, they must learn to build relationships in order to succeed in the Asian market. Includes bibliographical references.
Subject(s): Cultural context: East Asia

New

Clegg, S. R., Ibarra-Colado, E., & Bueno-Rodriquez, L. (Eds.). (1999). *Global management: Universal theories and local realities.* London: Sage.

The editors argue that many resources for management "how to" are not necessarily applicable to universal situations. Until recently these resources failed to depict the effects of global issues and trends on international business. Several chapters are devoted to issues of organizational restructuring and universal strategies of anti-poverty programs. Entrepreneurship in post-Soviet Russia, the Asia-Pacific region, and Japanese-based management practices are the focus of the second section of the book. The following section presents a critical view of such global management theories as total quality management in the United Kingdom, intelligent organizations, and Mexican self-regulating systems. The source concludes with a focus on values and new practices for global management. Includes bibliographical references and index.
Subject(s): Global leadership

Cleveland, H. (1993). *Birth of a new world: An open moment for international leadership.* San Francisco: Jossey-Bass.

As a political scientist and public executive, Cleveland has formed an extensive alliance with leaders of international peacekeeping organizations. From 1986 to 1989 this alliance, informally called The Group and formally titled the International Governance Project, met to discuss the requirements for international cooperation through the prisms of scientific discovery, technological innovation, and the rapid delivery of information. In this book Cleveland reports on The Group's conclusions for shared responsibility, lessons learned from history, the success of democracy, the necessity of private enterprise, and the roles of the United States and the United Nations. Includes bibliographical references and index.
Subject(s): Global leadership, social responsibility

Cox, T., Jr. (1993). *Cultural diversity in organizations: Theory, research, and practice.* San Francisco: Berrett-Koehler.

Cox defines cultural diversity as the "representation, in one social system, of people with distinctly different group affiliations of cultural significance." He argues that managers who maximize the advantages of diversity will profit from innovation and improved communication. A model for planning organizational change contains five parts: 1) leadership must commit to change and map a strategy for communication; 2) there should be assessment of organizational culture, experiences, and attitudes; 3) educational programs should increase awareness and build communication skills; 4) human resource departments should recruit, develop, compensate, and promote without bias; and 5) accountability and evaluation of the change efforts should be ongoing. Concepts covered in this book include: group identities, prejudice, stereotyping, ethnocentrism, organizational culture, acculturation, and informal integration. These concepts are summarized in proposition statements that may be used by teachers and trainers to frame class discussions or exam questions. Includes bibliographical references and index.
Subject(s): Cultural diversity

Cox, T., Jr., & Beale, R. L. (1997). *Developing competency to manage diversity: Readings, cases & activities.* San Francisco: Berrett-Koehler.

Cox calls this book the "action" sequel to his original "theory book," *Cultural Diversity in Organizations: Theory, Research and Practice* (1993). He and Beale provide managers with the tools they need to successfully manage a diverse workforce, including 31 activities, 23 readings, and six case studies. The tools are divided into three categories—those that will provide a foundation for competency in diversity, tools that develop individual competency, and tools that develop organizational competency. Includes bibliographical references and index.
Subject(s): Diversity overview

New
Crosby, B. C. (1999). *Leadership for global citizenship: Building transnational community.* Thousand Oaks, CA: Sage.

Crosby claims that society is being pulled toward a global community but people have no idea how to be global citizens. In this book she explains the rights and responsibilities of global citizenship. The focus is not on heads of state or leaders of multinational businesses. It is on leaders in the *global commons* who are crossing national boundaries to build worldwide organizations that support the common good. Within this framework Crosby describes the fluid nature of leading and following as the context demands. Chapters are devoted to personal, team, and organizational leadership as well as vision, ethics, and change cycles. Case studies of Amnesty International and the International Women's Rights Action Watch support the framework for

global citizenship. Includes bibliographical references and index.
Subject(s): Global leadership

Dell, T. (1996). *The corporate environmental leader: Five steps to a new ethic.* Menlo Park, CA: Crisp.

Written by the president of an environmental research firm, this book describes five steps that corporate leaders can take to make their business environmentally friendly: ground yourself in nature's principles, respect the tide of history, expand the vision, emulate the principles, and neutralize negatives with positives. Chapters include an extensive environmental timeline; checklists of the positive steps both companies and individuals can take and their results; and an appendix that gives environmental case studies of 30 major corporations, including Coca-Cola, Procter & Gamble, and Wal-Mart. Includes bibliographical references.
Subject(s): Environmental leadership

New
Den Hartog, D. N., House, R. J., Hanges, P. J., Ruiz-Quintanilla, S. A., Dorfman, P. W., & Associates. (1999). **Culture specific and cross-culturally generalizable implicit leadership theories: Are the attributes of charismatic/transformational leadership universally endorsed?** *Leadership Quarterly: Special Issue, Part I: Charismatic and Transformational Leadership: Taking Stock of the Present and Future, 10*(2), 219-256.

This article describes the Global Leadership and Organizational Behavior Effectiveness (GLOBE) research program. About 170 researchers from 62 cultures united to test culturally endorsed implicit theories of leadership. One hypothesis is that "charismatic/transformational leadership is universally endorsed as contributing to outstanding leadership." Findings across the cultures support this universal endorsement. Also in the article are leader attributes that are universally endorsed, those that impede leadership, and those with cultural implications. Includes bibliographical references.
Subject(s): Multicultural context, charismatic leadership, transformational leadership

DiTomaso, N., & Hooijberg, R. (1996). **Diversity and the demands of leadership.** *Leadership Quarterly: Special Issue: Leadership and Diversity (Part II), 7*(2), 163-187.

In the past, diversity literature and leadership literature have been connected only minimally, and studies of diversity have considered leaders "the targets of influence rather than the agents of change." This introduction to Part II of the special Leadership and Diversity issue argues that diversity and leadership must be connected on multiple levels and in multiple dimensions. The authors begin making these connections by dividing the existing diversity literature into four parts: interpersonal and intergroup interaction, the impact of organizational transformation on diversity, social science studies of inequality, and the morality and ethics of diversity and multiculturalism.
Subject(s): Diversity overview

Dobbs, M. F. (1996). **Managing diversity: Lessons from the private sector.** *Public Personnel Management, 25*(3), 351-367.

Dobbs describes successful diversity programs at three major companies, including the Xerox Corporation, and identifies the qualities that make them successful. These include having top management commitment, employee support, a variety of interventions, and a supportive corporate culture. These programs are then compared with the city of San Diego's diversity program. Dobbs describes a new framework modeled on corporate diversity programs that public agencies can use. Advice on integrating diversity into organizational practice, dealing directly with resistance, and using evaluations is included.
Subject(s): Diversity in workplace

Dorfman, P. W., Howell, J. P., Hibino, S., Lee, J. K., Tate, U., & Bautista, A. (1997). **Leadership in Western and Asian countries: Commonalities and differences in effective leadership processes across cultures.** *Leadership Quarterly: Special Issue: International and Cross-Cultural Leadership Research (Part I), 8*(3), 233-274.

Can the effectiveness of specific leadership behaviors be generalized across cultures? This study surveyed over 1,500 managers and professionals in five countries—Japan, South Korea, Taiwan, Mexico, and the United States—to determine the effectiveness of six leadership behaviors: directive leadership, leader-contingent rewards, leader-contingent punishment, supportive leadership, participative leadership, and charismatic leadership. Visual models of the results and theoretical descriptions of leadership in each country are given. Overall the study found that three behaviors (supportive, contingent reward, and charismatic) were culturally universal, while the effectiveness of the other behaviors was culturally specific. Includes bibliographical references.
Subject(s): Cross-cultural context

Eagly, A. H., Karau, S. J., & Makhijani, M. G. (1995). **Gender and the effectiveness of leaders: A meta-analysis.** *Psychological Bulletin, 117*(1), 125-145.

The authors aggregated the results of 76 laboratory and organizational studies on gender and leader effectiveness. Although some differences in behavior were reported, no difference was found in the general tendency of men and women leaders. Conditions that favored one gender over another were the type of organization, the level of leadership, and the prejudicial attitudes about specific leadership roles. Leaders received higher ratings in roles that were congruent with masculine/feminine expectations. Male leaders were rated higher in task-related roles, while women received higher ratings in relationship roles.
Subject(s): Women's leadership, men's leadership

Earley, P. C., & Erez, M. (Eds.). (1997). *New perspectives on international industrial/organizational psychology.* San Francisco: New Lexington Press.

Do national differences in people's values and beliefs affect their work behavior? This compendium addresses that question by examining recent developments in cross-cultural industrial/organizational psychology around the themes of theory, motivation and values across cultures, working across cultural borders, and power relationships. The chapters, often written by colleagues from different cultures working together, address specific issues that include: organizational justice, decision making, cross-cultural leadership, communication difficulties, and individual-union-organization relationships. Includes bibliographical references and index.
Subject(s): Cross-cultural context

New
Elenkov, D. S. (1998). **Can American management concepts work in Russia?** *California Management Review, 40*(4), 133-156.

The author surveyed over 300 Russian and American managers using six measures that identify cultural differences in managerial values: power distance, individualism as opposed to collectivism, competitive orientation, uncertainty avoidance, political-influence orientation, and dogmatism. The results showed that the Russian managers were less individualistic than their American counterparts and employed a greater power distance and uncertainty avoidance. These cross-national differences affect what management style will be most effective with Russian workers, and Elenkov describes the implications for leadership style, motivational approaches, performance appraisal systems, strategic planning systems, and organizational configurations. Includes bibliographical references.
Subject(s): Cultural context: Russia

Enkelis, L., Olsen, K., & Lewenstein, M. (1995). *On our own terms: Portraits of women business leaders.* San Francisco: Berrett-Koehler.

The authors highlight the careers and personal development of 14 women, including: Ruth Owades, President of Calyx & Corolla, a florist catalog company; Wilma Mankiller, Principal Chief of the Cherokee Nation; Elaine Chao, President and CEO of United Way of America; Marjorie Silver, President of Pinsly Railroad Company; and Carol Bartz, President, CEO, and Chairman of the Board of Autodesk, Inc., a computer software company. In their own words each woman documents her climb to a position of power, sharing her experience to serve as a model and source of advice. The authors fill in appropriate details such as company history and revenues. Photographs help complete the portrait of each woman at work and home.
Subject(s): Women as corporate leaders

Etzioni, A. (1993). *The spirit of community: Rights, responsibilities, and the Communitarian agenda.* New York: Crown.

A Communitarian movement founded by Etzioni (a former White House Fellow) proposes that Americans strive to balance the rights of individuals with social responsibilities. He presents a case for a new moral order without government oppression, law and order without a police state, and free

speech without hate and hostility. In a Communitarian society the institutions of families, schools, and neighborhoods are strengthened, while special-interest groups and politics are checked. Includes bibliographical references and index.
Subject(s): Social responsibility

Etzioni, A. (1996). *The new golden rule: Community and morality in a democratic society.* New York: BasicBooks.

What makes a good society? According to Etzioni, founder of the Communitarian Network, it requires a balance between individual rights and social responsibilities. Contrary to Western beliefs, freedom and morality do not have to conflict but can reinforce each other. In this "positive doctrine" of communitarianism Etzioni addresses the two founding principles of a good society, social order and autonomy, how they interact, and how they have emerged in Western society. The concept of society is examined from both a historical and sociological perspective, and each chapter includes "implications for practice and policy." Includes bibliographical references and index.
Subject(s): Social responsibility

Ferdman, B. M. (Ed.). (1994). *A resource guide for teaching and research on diversity.* St. Louis, MO: American Assembly of Collegiate Schools of Business.

This guide is designed for faculty and program directors who plan and teach courses on diversity. Educators and researchers share perspectives on the definition of diversity, course content and philosophy, pedagogical approaches, and management theory. Syllabi of 27 courses focus on diversity in undergraduate, master's level, and doctoral programs. Eight more syllabi illustrate how diversity can be integrated into other courses. Reading lists and two additional bibliographies suggest books, articles, and films to supplement coursework. A list of 193 teachers, researchers, and consultants working on diversity includes name, address, phone number, area of expertise, current projects, and publications for each. Includes bibliographical references and index.
Subject(s): Diversity overview

New
Fox, R. L., & Schuhmann, R. A. (1999). **Gender and local government: A comparison of women and men city managers.** *Public Administration Review, 59*(3), 231-242.

The authors surveyed 875 male and female city managers to determine whether female managers behaved or led differently from their male counterparts. The survey asked questions about motivation for being in city government, decision making, and responsibilities. Statistical analysis of the data revealed that women were more likely to incorporate citizen input, facilitate communication, and encourage citizen involvement in the decision-making process. The authors suggest that these differences allow women to provide a distinct voice in city government. Includes bibliographical references.

Subject(s): Women as public service leaders, men as public service leaders

New
Funakawa, A. (1997). *Transcultural management: A new approach for global organizations.* San Francisco: Jossey-Bass.

Funakawa uses American and Japanese relations to illustrate the importance of successful cross-cultural management. He identifies five core competencies essential to managing in a transcultural environment: strategic focus, geocentric mindset, cross-cultural communication skills, culturally sensitive management practices, and synergy learning systems. Subsequent chapters offer specific advice on how to conquer language barriers, cross-cultural alliance management, and dealing with foreign workers. Includes index.
Subject(s): Cultural context: U.S.; cultural context: Japan

Gaines, K. K. (1996). *Uplifting the race: Black leadership, politics, and culture in the twentieth century.* Chapel Hill, NC: University of North Carolina Press.

The author describes American society in the late 20th century as subtly racist. Post-civil rights neoliberal goals have fallen short of a color-blind society with equal justice and equal opportunities. This book explains how that happened through a historical perspective of what it means to be black or white in America. Discourses on racist and anti-racist theories are compared. The ideology of racial uplift is discussed in terms of the black middle class who align with conservative mores and of the blacks trapped in poverty who embrace optimistic liberal ideals. Writings of black social scientists throughout the century document the struggles and the leadership that made progress toward civil rights and racial uplift. Includes bibliographical references and index.
Subject(s): Ethnic diversity in society

Gentile, M.C. (1994). *Differences that work: Organizational excellence through diversity.* Boston: Harvard Business School Press.

Gentile has brought together 16 articles on diversity from the *Harvard Business Review.* Together they present the idea that new growth, learning, and innovation can come from taking another perspective on the differences among people in the workforce. The book begins with a historical look at discrimination and the demographics of those who work. It then focuses on the issues of harassment and the limitations in job advancement faced by minorities. Other topics discussed are AIDS, aging, and family life and their relationship to the workplace. Gentile stresses that differences among people can enhance success because they channel new learning both in individuals and in organizations. Includes bibliographical references and index.
Subject(s): Diversity in workplace

Gibson, C. B. (1995). **An investigation of gender differences in leadership across four countries.** *Journal of International Business Studies, 26*(2), 255-279.

Over 200 male and female managers in Norway, Sweden, Australia, and the U.S. were surveyed about leadership styles and behaviors to determine gender and cultural differences. In all four countries results showed that males placed the strongest emphasis on goal-setting behavior and females emphasized interpersonal-facilitation behavior. One significant difference in style preference emerged from the Australian subjects who preferred a directive style of leadership, whereas all others preferred a nondirective style. The authors suggest that their findings serve as a base for further research on global and gender differences.
Subject(s): Cultural context: men's leadership; cultural context: women's leadership

Glaser, C., & Smalley, B. S. (1995). *Swim with the dolphins: How women can succeed in corporate America on their own terms.* New York: Warner Books.

Being female is an advantage in today's workplace. The desired behaviors for today's managers are: empowering, nurturing, and consensus building—behaviors that come naturally to many women. This book presents a balanced management style, the style of a dolphin manager—decisive, flexible, confident, and caring. Today's manager won't get far behaving as a shark—commanding and controlling—or as a guppy—powerless and ineffective. Thirteen dolphin-women who swam to positions of power share their stories. Not only women can be dolphins, though. The authors include tips for men who are seeking a balanced management style. Includes bibliographical references and index.
Subject(s): Women as corporate leaders

New
Gordon, J. R., & Whelan, K. S. (1998). **Successful professional women in midlife: How organizations can more effectively understand and respond to the challenges.** *Academy of Management, 12*(1), 8-27.

Women in midcareer and midlife, ages 35 to 54, bring maturity and experience to their jobs as well as a need for continuing challenge and achievement. This article reports on a study of 36 women who have made successful transitions into the midcareer stage. One finding is a cognitive shift that helps women set limits and develop their personal definitions of success. Midcareer women also make tradeoffs and learn to deal with political realities. This study also indicates that organizational support and developmental opportunities often favor this group's two counterparts—younger women and midlife men. The authors make suggestions for organizations that want to leverage the talent of midcareer women. Representatives from Allstate Insurance, Procter & Gamble, and the University of Southern California add commentary. Includes bibliographical references.
Subject(s): Women as corporate leaders

New
Granrose, C. S. (Ed.). (1997). *The careers of business managers in East Asia.* Westport, CT: Quorum Books.

Exporting management strategies into a cross-cultural situation can be complicated and ineffective. The majority of information available to aid in such an endeavor has been limited to North American and European experiences; however, those techniques are not universal. Granrose intends this source to expand the available options. The management careers of people in three East Asian countries are profiled in addition to reviewed information regarding Euro-American experiences. Granrose presents a framework for career analysis and applies it in this volume. The subsequent three chapters are devoted to a closer look at the careers of managers in Hong Kong, Taiwan, and Japan. The final chapter makes a comparison across the cultures. Includes appendix and index.
Subject(s): Cultural context: East Asia

Grobler, P. A. (1996). **In search of excellence: Leadership challenges facing companies in the new South Africa.** *SAM Advanced Management Journal, 61*(2), 22-34.

Major political transitions in South Africa have also thrown the country's business community into turmoil. In the past many South African corporations were "overmanaged and underled . . . floating in an ocean of authoritarianism and bureaucratic hierarchies." Grobler maintains that South Africa's greatest weakness is its lack of human capital and emphasizes the importance of developing more leaders with new leadership styles. He advocates a form of transformational leadership in which leaders challenge their subordinates to learn new skills. A number of visual aids and graphs are used to illustrate the concepts.
Subject(s): Cultural context: South Africa

Hackel, S. W. (1997). **The staff of leadership: Indian authority in the missions of Alta California.** *William and Mary Quarterly*, 3rd Series, *54*(2), 347-376.

Hackel examines a period in the history of California. To protect the Spanish interest in the new world, 18th-century Spanish authorities established Franciscan missions from San Diego to San Francisco. Native Americans who converted were given homes and work inside the missions. Within their ranks leaders emerged to run the communities of 500 to 1,000 residents. Scholars have long argued whether the missions and their Indian leaders were protective or committing cultural genocide. Hackel's essay doesn't moralize. Instead it describes the selection of Indian leaders and their responsibilities as well as the Spanish influence of leadership style and its adaptation to native culture. He identifies patterns of leadership that eventually led to a successful rebellion against the Franciscans.
Subject(s): Native American leadership

Harris, P. R., & Moran, R. T. (1996). *Managing cultural differences* (4th ed.). Houston: Gulf.

As part of a series on managing cultural differences, this book serves as a resource for both practitioners and students on how to develop cross-cultural expertise in a global market. Unit I focuses on the worldwide influences impacting leaders and management efforts. Topics include the globalization of economies, challenges in global communications, and creating synergistic relationships amid cultural differences. Unit II focuses on how leaders can understand, analyze, cope with, and become more sensitive to cultural differences while improving interactions in a global market. Unit III offers cultural specifics for doing business in North America, Latin America, Asia, Europe, the Middle East, and Africa. Backgrounds, customs, negotiating strategies, and business courtesies for each region are provided. The authors stress that cultural differences can and should be seen as a resource, not an impediment. An accompanying *Instructor's Guide* for both professors and human resource development professionals is available. Includes index.
Subject(s): Cultural diversity

Harvey, S. (1996). **Two models to sovereignty: A comparative history of the Mashantucket Pequot Tribal Nation and the Navajo Nation.** *American Indian Culture and Research Journal, 20*(1), 147-194.

Harvey presents two sides to the issue of gaming as a means to economic independence and self-sufficiency for Indian nations. About one-third of the 500 tribes in the U.S. currently offer some form of gaming, casinos or bingo parlors, as a form of economic enterprise, resulting in several billion dollars of profit. The small Pequot tribe of Connecticut owns the largest casino in the Western hemisphere and uses its profits to rebuild the tribe. The larger Navajo tribe of New Mexico resists the lure of gaming money, preferring to build the tribe through traditional means—at home and school. Harvey examines each tribe's style of leadership, culture, and pursuit of sovereignty. Includes bibliographical references in notes.
Subject(s): Native American leadership

New
Hayes, A. (1999). **The new presence of women leaders.** *Journal of Leadership Studies, 6*(1/2), 112-121.

Hayes remarks on the increasing numbers of female leaders in business, politics, higher education, and communities around the world. An examination of economic and social factors explains how this increase occurred. Hayes also examines the unique behaviors of female leaders and their relevance to current leadership roles. She concludes that today's leadership requires the talents of men and women who: lead with vision, focus energy, foster cooperation, assure high tech and high touch, accept accountability, and promote individual development. Includes bibliographical references.
Subject(s): Women as leaders

Heifetz, R. A. (1994). *Leadership without easy answers.* Cambridge, MA: Belknap Press.

As the Director of the Leadership Education Project at the Kennedy School of Government, Harvard University, Heifetz reflects on teaching leadership. His experience includes teaching undergraduate, for-credit, noncredit, master's level, midcareer, executive, and military leadership courses. From this varied background Heifetz draws conclusions about the role of leadership in a complex society. It has become common to blame leaders for the ills of society and to expect leaders to solve our problems. Heifetz suggests that it's time to redefine citizenship and let everyone, those with and without authority, take leadership roles to strengthen our democratic society. Includes bibliographical references and index.
Subject(s): Social responsibility

Helgesen, S. (1990). *The female advantage: Women's ways of leadership.* New York: Doubleday.

This book is not about what women can learn from business but what business can learn from women. Contemporary organizations are eliminating pyramids and trimming bureaucratic structures at the same time that women are increasingly pressed into the workforce for economic reasons. Women constitute 45% of the total workforce. Eighty percent of female college graduates work. One-third of all new businesses are started by women. Helgesen reports on her diary studies of female executives in four organizations: Girl Scouts of U.S.A., Western Industrial Contractors, Ford Motor Company, and Brunson Communications. Includes bibliographical references.
Subject(s): Women's leadership

New
Helgesen, S. (1998). *Everyday revolutionaries: Working women and the transformation of American life.* New York: Doubleday.

Helgesen offers this book as a modern variation of William Whyte's 1956 book *The Organization Man*, which portrayed the prototypical American as a middle-class man working for a large organization, adapting to organizational values, and influencing organizations and society with middle-class male values. Helgesen's research on working women reveals a new prototype. Within the past 30 years women entering the workforce and assuming positions of power have revolutionized postindustrial American business, home and family responsibilities, consumerism, and public policy. A study of contemporary women in the Chicago suburb of Naperville, Illinois, illustrates the new American prototype and her many spheres of influence. Includes bibliographical references and index.
Subject(s): Women as leaders of social movements

New
Hesselbein, F., Goldsmith, M., Beckhard, R., & Schubert, R. F. (Eds.). (1998). *The community of the future.* San Francisco: Jossey-Bass.

This is a collection of essays about our social selves and new ways of forming communities. Some authors debate the power of strong economies and the responsibility of strong societies. Others suggest that global communities cause a disappointing blending of cultures that were once rich in their uniqueness. Nevertheless, new relationships in cyberspace, workplace, and global communities are built on shared values rather than on proximity. Other issues addressed are the impact of the baby-boomer generation, intellectual capital, leadership of nonprofit organizations, and humankind's social responsibility to each other and to the environment. The foreword and afterword are written by Peter Drucker and Elie Wiesel respectively. Includes index.
Subject(s): Social responsibility

Hofstede, G. (1980). *Culture's consequences: International differences in work-related values.* Beverly Hills, CA: Sage.

This book explores the differences in thinking and behavior in 40 countries. Surveys of 116,000 employees of multinational companies and studies of children's literature in each society identify four dimensions of personal values and collective cultures. Power distance is defined as dominance and the distance between worker and boss. Uncertainty avoidance deals with rule orientation, anxiety, security, and dependence. Individualism is the relationship between individual and society or between personal time and work commitment. Masculinity addresses the duality of the sexes, assertiveness versus nurturing qualities, and their value in a society. There are implications for policy-making and research, but this is also a valuable tool for those studying global business concerns.
Subject(s): Multicultural context

Hofstede, G. (1980). **Motivation, leadership, and organizations: Do American theories apply abroad?** *Organizational Dynamics, 9*(1), 42-63.

It is important to remember that management theories developed and studied in one country may be of little use in other countries due to differences in culture. National culture has been divided into four dimensions: power distance, uncertainty avoidance, individualism-collectivism, and masculinity-femininity. Differences in employee motivation, attitudes, management styles, and organizational structures between countries can be traced to differences in mental programming. Includes bibliography and index.
Subject(s): Cross-cultural context

New
Hofstede, G. (1999). **Problems remain, but theories will change: The universal and the specific in 21st-century global management.** *Organizational Dynamics, 28*(1), 34-44.

In this special *Organizational Dynamics* issue on management in the 21st century, Hofstede predicts that our understanding of leadership will not change. He provides examples from the Book of Genesis, the French Revolution, and American history to illustrate that time doesn't affect our

understanding of leadership but cultural values do. However, the convergence of three ancient philosophies may offer hope for a universal understanding of leadership. The principle of moderation found in the 5th-century B.C. writings of Buddha, Confucious, and Socrates works as a universal value for global leaders. Includes bibliographical references.
Subject(s): Cultural context

New
Holden, N., Cooper, C., & Carr, J. (1998). *Dealing with the new Russia: Management cultures in collision.* Chichester, UK: Wiley.

Westerners working in the former Soviet Union often find that communication barriers and cultural differences make doing business in this new market difficult. This book advises managers and entrepreneurs specializing in the Russian/CIS market on how to build relationships—a critical element in Russian business. The first part of the book puts Russian business into historical and cultural context. This section includes chapters on 20th-century Russian history, management practices in the Soviet Union, perestroika, the challenges facing Russian managers in today's economy, and the troubled relationships between Russian and Western business partners. The book's second section addresses interpersonal communication. It contains basic information on the Russian language, a chapter on transferring management terms and concepts into Russian, and advice on the social side of doing business in Russia. Includes bibliographical references and index.
Subject(s): Cultural context: Russia

Hooijberg, R., & DiTomaso, N. (1996). **Leadership in and of demographically diverse organizations.** *Leadership Quarterly: Special Issue: Leadership and Diversity (Part I), 7*(1), 1-19.

This article introduces a special issue on leadership and demographically diverse organizations. The authors review current knowledge of male/female, white/nonwhite, and U.S./non-U.S. differences and their relevance to leadership. They propose six areas for further research: 1) use a leader-member exchange model to examine racially mixed dyads; 2) explore various ethnocentric views; 3) learn the effect that a leader from one demographic group has on all members of a team; 4) study the impact of integrated leadership at the top of an organization; 5) explore the characteristics of masculine, feminine, and androgynous behaviors and the indication of leadership emergence; and 6) study influence tactics.
Subject(s): Diversity overview

Hunt, J. G., & Peterson, M. F. (1997). **Overview: International and cross-cultural leadership research.** *Leadership Quarterly: Special Issue: International and Cross-Cultural Leadership Research (Part I), 8*(3), 201-202.

This introduction to the first part of a special issue on international leadership poses the questions the authors hope the issue can answer. Does "leadership" have meaning

outside the English language? How can leadership theories with an American bias apply to other countries? Is international leadership an oxymoron? Hunt and Peterson also provide a brief overview of the articles that follow, which address how to adapt American leadership measures to other countries, the problems of a culturally diverse workforce, influence, and motivation.
Subject(s): Cultural context: U.S.

Jackson, S. E., & Ruderman, M. N. (Eds.). (1995). *Diversity in work teams: Research paradigms for a changing workplace.* Washington, DC: American Psychological Association.

The editors see a need for understanding diversity in work teams, based on two significant changes in the American workforce at the end of the 20th century. First, the face of the workforce is changing. Women and people of color represent a source of growth. At the same time corporate globalization brings together colleagues from various cultures. The second change is a structural reorganization from hierarchical to flatter, more flexible organizations that rely on teamwork. In response to these changes social scientists are seeking and substantiating new theories that integrate organizational demography, social identity, psychological distance, inter-group competition, and negotiation. The term *diversity* is used broadly to include demographic differences (gender, ethnicity, age), psychological differences (knowledge, values), and organizational differences (tenure, level). J. E. McGrath, J. L. Berdahl, and H. Arrow present a map of this concept and describe four theoretical approaches for under-standing work team diversity. G. B. Northcraft, J. T. Polzer, M. A. Neale, and R. M. Kramer examine the interpersonal dynamics of multidisciplinary teams through social identity theory and the principles of negotiation. A. S. Tsui, K. R. Xin, and T. D. Egan study age, tenure, educational, and social differences between employees and their supervisors. D. J. Armstrong and P. Cole use social distance theory to analyze the difficulties that arise from geographically dispersed work teams. Includes bibliographical references and index.
Subject(s): Diversity in workplace

James, J. (1997). *Transcending the talented tenth: Black leaders and American intellectuals.* New York: Routledge.

The ongoing presumption in American politics, according to the author, is that "there are leaders, and then there are black leaders." This book examines how historically "leadership has been articulated in and for black communities" and how those communities approach leadership today. First, James shows how women and radicals have been erased from the history of black leadership. Then she addresses contemporary crises, including racial violence, intellectual elitism in the black community, and the intertwined oppressors of race, class, and gender. Extensively researched, the book includes quotes and poems from W.E.B. Du Bois, James Baldwin, and Audre Lorde. Includes bibliographical references and index.
Subject(s): African American leadership

New
Joplin, J. R. W., & Daus, S. (1997). **Challenges of leading a diverse workforce.** *Academy of Management Executive, 11*(3), 32-47.

Employee reactions to the demographical changes within a company can determine the success of today's leaders and their organizations. These reactions have produced six predominant challenges facing leaders of diverse organizations. The dilemmas of power shifting, differing opinions, absence of empathy, tokenism, participation, and overcoming inertia are presented in progression from intolerance to tolerance/acceptance, and finally to the goal of appreciation among the growing diverse members of organizations. Included in the discussion of the challenges are appropriate strategies for leaders in propelling the organization toward acceptance. The conclusion warns that leaders must recognize the current level of diversity tolerance when conducting activities to promote diversity acceptance. Includes bibliographical references and appendix.
Subject(s): Diversity in workplace

Jules, F. (1988). **Native Indian leadership.** *Canadian Journal of Native Education, 15*(3), 3-23.

Jules examines the relevant features of leadership in Native American context. A review of the literature and interviews with three Native American leaders reveal dissatisfaction with the quality of education for Native American children. Jules applies a model of Native American leadership to educational administration. Native American groups have linguistic and geographic differences but common values and spiritual identity. Knowledge of Native American culture, group decision making, respect for elders, wisdom, integrity, and humility are essential for educational leadership in a Native American context.
Subject(s): Native American leadership

New
Jung, D. I., & Avolio, B. J. (1999). **Effects of leadership style and followers' cultural orientation on performance in group and individual task conditions.** *Academy of Management Journal, 42*(2), 208-218.

This article reports on a crossed two-by-two experiment involving Caucasian and Asian university students. Each group was divided into two groups—one in which students worked individually and one in which they worked together. Students were tested for their preference to work individually or collectively. Then they worked on brainstorming tasks, some with a transactional-style group leader and some with a transformational-style group leader. Results indicate that the most new ideas were generated by students with a collective orientation working with a transformational leader and by individualists working with a transactional leader. The results do not generalize across cultural differences. Includes bibliographical references.
Subject(s): Cross-cultural context

New
Keiser, R. A. (1997). *Subordination or empowerment? African-American leadership and the struggle for urban political power.* New York: Oxford University Press.

In this source black political subordination is compared to minority empowerment. The subordination concept in this case refers to minority groups in political participation without significant influence. The contrast of empowerment involves a reallocation of political power to minority leaders. This book's purpose is to analyze the struggle for elimination of political inequality, and a struggle of empowerment among minority groups, namely black leaders. Chapters two through five discuss case histories of this struggle in four U.S. cities. Keiser depicts the political subordination demonstrated in Chicago and Gary, the biracial political cooperation in Philadelphia, and the black empowerment in Atlanta. Includes bibliographical references, notes, and index.
Subject(s): African American leadership, political leadership

New
Kiuchi, T. (1998). **Business lessons from the rain forest.** *Futurist, 32*(1), 50-53.

This article uses knowledge about the environment, particularly rain forests, to develop five lessons for global business leaders: 1) watch where you are going; 2) use the environment as an opportunity; 3) true profit comes from design, not materials; 4) use the design principles of the rain forest, including using feedback, adapting to change, and differentiating; and 5) the mission of business is to develop the human ecosystem, sustainably.
Subject(s): Environmental leadership

Klenke, K. (1996). *Women and leadership: A contextual perspective.* New York: Springer.

In Chapter 1 Klenke uses a metaphor of lenses or prisms for the interactions of leadership, gender, context, and culture. In Chapter 2 she suggests that leadership in history has been shaped by contexts such as religion or politics. Portraits of women such as Joan of Arc, Mary Baker Eddy, Elizabeth I, Harriet Tubman, and Alice Paul reinforce Klenke's belief in contexts as shaping. Chapter 3 is a discussion of several leadership theories such as the trait approach, followed by applications using Margaret Thatcher, Debbie Fields, and Candy Lightner as examples. In Chapter 4 the difference and need for balance between management and leadership is discussed. Janet Reno is Klenke's example of a woman manager and Mary Kay Ash is her example of a woman leader. Portrayals and coverage of women leaders in the media are analyzed in Chapter 5. In Chapter 6 gender differences in leadership are debunked, as are barriers to women's development. Chapter 7 examines the visible and not-so-visible barriers to women's leadership. In Chapter 8 Klenke examines women leaders in the contexts of sports, religion, and politics. Cross-cultural differences in worldwide context are examined in Chapter 9. European leaders include: Mary Robinson of Ireland; Tansu Ciller of Turkey; Aung San

Suu Kyi, Burmese dissident; Eva Perón of Argentina; and Isabel Perón, also of Argentina. The final chapter is on leadership education and new programs. Includes bibliographical references and index.
Subject(s): Women's leadership

Kossek, E. E., & Lobel, S. A. (Eds.). (1996). *Managing diversity: Human resource strategies for transforming the workplace.* Cambridge, MA: Blackwell Business.

Scholars in human resource management contribute essays on the subject of diversity at work. They acknowledge the complexities of designing HR practices for nonhomogenous groups which include persons of different genders, ethnicity, functions, nationality, language, ability, religion, lifestyle, or tenure. Increased diversity in the workforce combined with the turbulence caused by downsizing and rapidly changing technology together increase the importance of developmental relationships and activities. The authors recommend strategies for recruiting and selection, mentoring, and training. Includes bibliographical references and index.
Subject(s): Diversity in workplace

New
Landis, D., & Bhagat, R. S. (Eds.). (1996). *Handbook of intercultural training* (2nd ed.). Thousand Oaks, CA: Sage.

This handbook examines the theoretical and methodological issues inherent to management training within intercultural contexts. Contributors from the U.S., Israel, Russia, Canada, Hong Kong, the U.K., and Australia write of their training experience and cultural research around the globe. The editors propose a new model of intercultural behavior and training. Other essays include: "Ethics in Intercultural Training," "Intercultural Trainer Competencies," "The Intercultural Sensitizer," "Developing Expatriate Managers for Southeast Asia," and "A Framework for Understanding Latin American and Latino/Hispanic Cultural Patterns." Includes bibliographical references and name and subject indexes.
Subject(s): Multicultural context

New
Lane, D., & Ross, C. (1999). *The transition from communism to capitalism: Ruling elites from Gorbachev to Yeltsin.* New York: St. Martin's Press.

A critical issue that emerged as a result of the demise of state socialism in the USSR dealt with the leadership of Mikhail Gorbachev, the rise of Boris Yeltsin, and the transformation to a capitalist state. In an attempt to understand the elite rulers of Russia and to gauge the transition process, Lane and Ross present this two-part book. Section one describes the leadership structure during the later part of socialism under Gorbachev, and the second delves into questions concerning the post-soviet governing elites with a focus on Yeltsin. Includes bibliographical references, index, and appendices.
Subject(s): Cultural context: Russia

Lauterbach, K. E., & Weiner, B. J. (1996). **Dynamics of upward influence: How male and female managers get their way.** *Leadership Quarterly: Special Issue: Leadership and Diversity (Part I), 7*(1), 87-108.

Do male and female managers use different strategies to influence their superiors? Based on Nancy Chodorow's theory of gender formation Lauterbach and Weiner hypothesized that female managers' influence processes would be characterized by interdependence and social connection while men's processes would be based on independence and autonomy. Their study, consisting of interviews and surveys of male and female managers in a Fortune 100 company, supported this hypothesis. Women were more likely than men to act out of organizational interest, not self-interest; to involve others in planning; and to consider others' viewpoints and feelings.
Subject(s): Women as managers, men as managers, influence

New
Leslie, J. B., & Van Velsor, E. (1998). *A cross-national comparison of effective leadership and teamwork: Toward a global workforce.* Greensboro, NC: Center for Creative Leadership.

The Center for Creative Leadership and the SYMLOG Consulting Group conducted a joint study to identify similarities and differences in the perceptions of effective leadership and teamwork across national boundaries. Almost 2,000 mid- to upper-level managers from six countries of the European Union and the U.S. participated by responding to the English-language *SYMLOG Individual and Organizational Values Rating Form*. Report findings may be used by cross-national teams to understand others' dominance or submissiveness, acceptance of authority, task orientation, and desire for friendliness and cooperation. Appendices include the rating form and tables of comparison. Includes bibliographical references.
Subject(s): Cross-cultural context: U.S. and European Union; teamwork; research report

Lewis, R. D. (1996). *When cultures collide: Managing successfully across cultures.* London: Nicholas Brealey.

Lewis addresses both the theoretical and practical aspects of cultural diversity. The first section of his book examines how people are culturally conditioned at an early age and the interrelatedness between language and thought, and later chapters address specific cultural differences and how to handle them. Lewis divides the world's cultures into three rough categories: linear-actives (including Germans and Swiss), multi-actives (including Italians and Latin Americans), and reactives (including Chinese and Finns). A final section offers specific cultural information on more than 20 countries, including Spain, Russia, Italy, Sweden, China, and France. Includes index.
Subject(s): Cross-cultural context

New
Lindahl, G. (1998). **Globalising leadership: Tapping the creative potential of cultural diversity.** *Monash Mt. Eliza Business Review, 1*(3), 24-29.

Creativity is essential in a business environment characterized by constant change and decentralization, and cultural diversity can help foster creativity. This article describes how ABB, a global group of engineering companies, uses its diversity to help the organization adapt to changing circumstances and new challenges. Globalizing an organization consists of three stages: 1) globalization of the business by building sales and marketing around the world, 2) using technology to transfer experience into new markets, and 3) globalizing leadership by recruiting and developing international executives.
Subject(s): Cultural diversity

Lipman-Blumen, J. (1996). *The connective edge: Leading in an interdependent world.* San Francisco: Jossey-Bass.

Today's leaders face two opposing forces, interdependence and diversity, that are making old forms of leadership obsolete. Lipman-Blumen proposes a new model of *connective leadership* based on the idea that since physical and political boundaries no longer restrict us, connections between people are tightening. She identifies three types of connective leadership—direct, relational, and instrumental—and then applies her model to research on managers and executives and to women in leadership positions. Includes bibliographical references and index.
Subject(s): Social perspective

New
Livers, A. (1999). **Leading together: An African American perspective.** *Leadership in Action, 19*(2), 7-12.

Livers presents a frank discussion on racial tension in the workplace. Two mock dialogues, drawn on personal experience and the stories of participants in The African-American Leadership Program at the Center for Creative Leadership, typify workplace dialogues between black and white managers. Livers explains how such dialogues and their inferred attitudes assume stereotypes, betray trust, and discount competence. When white managers practice such behavior, whether subliminally or blatantly, black managers may enter a protective mode rather than the fully functioning mode that they prefer. Livers suggests that blacks and whites take responsibility for their own portions of the problem, honestly checking their assumptions and working to build interpersonal trust.
Subject(s): African American leadership, ethnic diversity in workplace

New
Lubatkin, M., & Powell, G. (1998). **Exploring the influence of gender on managerial work in a transitional, Eastern European nation.** *Human Relations, 51*(8), 1007-1031.

Most research on gender differences in managers has been conducted in Western, industrialized countries, but this study

examines how the gender of Hungarian managers affects their work. Telephone surveys of nearly 200 managers measured their beliefs about what managers do, their managerial values, and their attitudes about person-employment fit. Analysis found little difference in the work-related beliefs, values, or attitudes of male and female managers, but the authors suggest that this may be because female managers often conform to traditionally male behavior in order to succeed in the male-dominated professional world. Includes bibliographical references.
Subject(s): Cultural context: Hungary; cultural context: women's leadership; cultural context: men's leadership

Luke, J. S. (1998). *Catalytic leadership: Strategies for an interconnected world.* San Francisco: Jossey-Bass.

In today's complex world an effective public leader is not a hierarchical authority figure but an individual who can bring together "diverse individuals from multiple agencies to address interconnected public problems and work together towards solutions." Luke develops a framework for this new style of leadership, dividing his book into three sections— challenges facing leaders, the catalytic tasks of public leaders, and foundational skills for public leaders. An appendix offers advice on establishing criteria based on desired outcomes, which Luke says reduces political bargaining and improves group decision making. Includes bibliographical references and index.
Subject(s): Social perspective

New
Lumpkin, J. L. (1998). **Leadership challenges for women modeling physical activity.** *A Leadership Journal: Women in Leadership—Sharing the Vision, 2*(2), 55-66.

Although physical activity has been shown to have positive effects on women's achievement, emotional well-being, and physical health, the author describes a number of cultural barriers that discourage girls and women from being physically active. These include the myth of female fragility and the idea that women are not psychologically equipped for athletic competition. Lumpkin says that to overcome these barriers women must act as role models for young girls and advocate physical activity. She also offers a list of ways that women can encourage girls to be active at both the family and community levels. Includes bibliographical references.
Subject(s): Cultural context: women's leadership; fitness and leadership

Lusane, C. (1994). *African Americans at the crossroads: The restructuring of Black leadership and the 1992 elections.* Boston: South End.

Lusane frames the concept of black leadership within the political, social, and economic context of American society from 1965 through 1992. The growth of conservative intolerance, end of the Cold War, escalating national debt, health care crisis, and increase in crime have all affected the black community. A variety of leadership responses have emerged ranging from grassroots activism to presidential campaigning. Lusane describes former Los Angeles gang members who have stepped into leadership positions in an effort to negotiate peace treaties between warring gangs. In addition to these and other grassroots leadership efforts he discusses the Congressional Black Caucus, Nation of Islam Minister Louis Farrakhan, Supreme Court Justice Henry Thomas, and the Reverend Jesse Jackson. He closes his book with a call to the black community to exhibit and demand leadership actions. Includes bibliographical references and index.
Subject(s): African American leadership

New
Maggio, R. (Ed.). (1998). *An impulse to soar: Quotations by women on leadership.* Paramus, NJ: Prentice Hall.

This little book contains more than 500 quotations by women on leadership. Represented are contemporary scholars, executives, politicians, authors, and celebrities, as well as voices from the past. Quotations are organized by subjects such as power, team building, change, risks, and intuition. The title was inspired by Helen Keller, who said, "One can never consent to creep when one feels the impulse to soar."
Subject(s): Women's leadership, quotations

Martinez-Cosio, M. (1996). **Leadership in communities of color: Elements and sensitivities of a universal model.** *Journal of Leadership Studies, 3*(1), 65-77.

This article considers the definition of leadership presented in Rost's *Leadership for the Twenty-first Century* (Praeger, 1993) and applies that definition to communities of color. Rost says that leadership is "an influence relationship among leaders and followers who intend real changes that reflect their mutual purposes." Martinez-Cosio believes that this definition provides a framework for people of various ethnic and cultural backgrounds to participate fully in the dominant society while maintaining their cultural differences. She describes many examples of Hispanic leaders whose work supports this definition. Includes bibliographical references.
Subject(s): Ethnic diversity in society

Mead, R. (1994). *International management: Cross cultural dimensions.* Cambridge, MA: Blackwell.

This textbook was written for MBA students or others wanting to learn interpersonal skills for managing across national borders. Chapters address analysis of cultural differences, structures for decision making, patronage relationships, cross-cultural communication, motivation, dispute and negotiation, expatriate staff assignments, and planning change. Each chapter contains a discussion of theory and exercises to practice new learnings. Includes bibliographical references and index.
Subject(s): Global leadership, textbook

Miller, D. I. (1978). **Native American women: Leadership images.** *Integrated Education, 6*(1), 37-39.

Miller contrasts the role of female leaders played out in Native American culture with that found in the majority culture. She notes that although there are wide differences in Native American societies, certain central value themes typify most Native American people, including cooperation, cohesiveness, concern for others, and "scorn toward egotistical or self-seeking behavior on the part of one as against the group." The difficulties of modern Native American women, who must straddle two cultures and who also have to deal with the distorted images that whites have of Native Americans, are addressed.
Subject(s): Native American leadership, women's leadership

New
Miller, F. A. (1998). **Strategic culture change: The door to achieving high performance and inclusion.** *Public Personnel Management, 27*(2), 151-160.

Miller says that while diversity has become a significant force in business today, organizations should really be striving for inclusion, in which all members of the group are able to participate and contribute. He argues that inclusive organizations are more able to compete and achieve strategic goals than exclusive firms and that differences should be seen as assets rather than barriers. This article offers strategies for overcoming exclusive organizational practices and describes the role that HR professionals can play in establishing a culture that values inclusion. An appendix outlines the differences between affirmative action, diversity, inclusion, and EEO.
Subject(s): Diversity in workplace

New
Miller, W., Kerr, B., & Reid, M. (1999). **A national study of gender-based occupational segregation in municipal bureaucracies: Persistence of glass walls?** *Public Administration Review, 59*(3), 218-229.

The authors used data from the U.S. Equal Opportunity Commission to study the gender-based employment patterns in municipal governments from 1985 to 1993. They hypothesized that the type of policy an agency dealt with would affect its personnel practices, including its employment of women. Analysis of the data showed that while women were well represented in agencies with redistributive functions, they were severely underrepresented in distributive and regulatory agencies. Redistributive agencies address what are perceived as women's issues, such as welfare, health, and social justice, but they also typically have lower salaries, resulting in gender-based pay inequities. Includes bibliographical references.
Subject(s): Women as public service leaders

Millner, S. Y. (1996). **Recasting civil rights leadership: Gloria Richardson and the Cambridge Movement.** *Journal of Black Studies, 26*(6), 668-687.

This article documents the emergence and leadership style of Gloria Richardson, who was one of only a few women to transform the civil rights movement. Richardson was a middle-aged mother and member of an elite African American family when she responded to recruiters from the Student Nonviolent Coordinating Committee. Within a year Richardson was co-chair of the Cambridge branch and a nationally recognized spokesperson. Much of the media attention she received focused on her class status and her gender, discounting her message in sexist, racist, and paternalistic tones. In this article Millner sifts through the language to identify the leadership characteristics that enabled Richardson to assume power easily, take risks readily, and have enough impact to move the civil rights movement north of the Mason-Dixon line. Includes bibliographical references.
Subject(s): Women as leaders of social movements, African American leadership, civil rights movement

Moen, J. K. (1995). **Women in leadership: The Norwegian example.** *Journal of Leadership Studies, 2*(3), 3-19.

Norwegian women hold a large number of political leadership positions including prime minister, cabinet members, and 40% of the parliament. Moen conducted interviews with 15 of these women to gain insight into social and political conditions, leadership styles, and the difficulties they face. Cultural and geographic factors unique to Norway that contribute to a national sense of equality are identified. Pertinent to women everywhere, Moen finds the recurring themes of leadership based on strong interpersonal relationships, team-building skills, and advocacy for human rights.
Subject(s): Cultural context: Norway; women as political leaders

New
Moore, D. P., & Buttner, E. H. (1997). *Women entrepreneurs: Moving beyond the glass ceiling.* Thousand Oaks, CA: Sage.

The authors used interviews, surveys, and focus groups to study 129 female entrepreneurs from 13 cities. This book presents their results, beginning by describing the corporate environment from which most of the entrepreneurs launched their careers. A distinction is made between women who enter corporate jobs planning to leave to become entrepreneurs and those who never intended to start their own businesses. The authors then describe some initial problems these women faced, how they use entrepreneurial networking, and some of their successful strategies. Appendices describe the methodology and provide a copy of the research questionnaire. Includes bibliography and index.
Subject(s): Women as entrepreneurs

Moore, P. (1994). **Voices on change: Hard choices for the environmental movement.** *Leadership Quarterly: Special Issue: Leadership for Environmental and Social Change, 5*(3/4), 247-252.

One of the founders of the Greenpeace movement describes the differences between confrontation and acceptance at the

policy-making table. For over 20 years Moore has moved from the role of alarmist to that of collaborator between governments, corporations, public institutions, and environmentalists. His efforts at sustained development and collaboration are viewed as treasonous by some ecoextremists who favor antidevelopment and zero-tolerance attitudes.
Subject(s): Environmental leadership

New
Morrison, A., Gregersen, H., & Black, S. (1998). **The importance of savvy in global leaders.** *Monash Mt. Eliza Business Review*, *1*(2), 46-53.

Business leaders typically embrace the values of their culture —American leaders are generally decisive and aggressive while Japanese leaders favor teamwork and quality. So how do leaders cope in today's global business environment? The authors used survey data and interviews to determine the necessary competencies for a new global leader. This article focuses on one of those competencies, savvy, which the authors say has three dimensions: 1) substantive and factual knowledge, 2) theory or paradigms for structuring observations, and 3) tacit knowledge or skills associated with action. Leaders must have both the business savvy to identify opportunities and the organizational savvy to effectively manage resources. The authors also identify the "four T's" needed to develop global leaders: travel, teams, training, and transfer. Includes a profile of Ta-Tung Wang, a vice president of Kentucky Fried Chicken who used savvy to establish KFC in China.
Subject(s): Global leadership, multicultural context

Morrison, A. M., Schreiber, C. T., & Price, K. F. (1995). *A glass ceiling survey: Benchmarking barriers and practices.* Greensboro, NC: Center for Creative Leadership.

This report presents the results of a survey conducted by the Human Resource Planning Society and the Center for Creative Leadership involving more than 300 human resource managers. They were asked: 1) What barriers exist today that prevent women and people of color from reaching senior management? 2) What key practices does your organization use to overcome these barriers? Results include the most prevalent, critical, and effective practices. Includes bibliographical references.
Subject(s): Diversity in workplace

Morrison, A. M., White, R. P., Van Velsor, E., & the Center for Creative Leadership. (1992). *Breaking the glass ceiling: Can women reach the top of America's largest corporations?* (Updated ed.). New York: Addison-Wesley.

Since 1987, when the first edition of this book was published, the term *glass ceiling* has become a symbol of inequality for women, and recently for people of color. In this updated edition much of the original text is kept intact. New research, based on interviews with 100 executives, provides a look at progress over five years and implications for further strides. A new chapter describes techniques organizations are using

to remove barriers that prevent women and other nontraditional managers from advancing. Includes bibliographical references and index.
Subject(s): Women as corporate leaders

Moya Ah Chong, L., & Thomas, D. C. (1997). **Leadership perceptions in cross-cultural context: Pakeha and Pacific Islanders in New Zealand.** *Leadership Quarterly: Special Issue: International and Cross-Cultural Leadership Research (Part I)*, *8*(3), 275-293.

In New Zealand citizens of European heritage, mainly descendants of British immigrants, are called Pakeha. This study surveyed Pakeha and Pacific Islander supervisors and employees of major public organizations to determine whether the two ethnic groups view leadership differently. The results support the researchers' hypotheses: leader and follower ethnicity interact to affect follower satisfaction, and leadership prototypes held by members of the two groups seem to have culturally based differences. Includes bibliographical references.
Subject(s): Cultural context: New Zealand

Naisbitt, J. (1996). *Megatrends Asia: Eight Asian megatrends that are reshaping our world.* New York: Simon & Schuster.

Futurist John Naisbitt predicts a shift of power from the Western world to the Pacific Rim. The World Bank declares that the emergence of Asian business is an economic miracle. Naisbitt agrees that there's a miracle occurring in the East but believes it's more than economic growth—it's a miracle of human spirit. He predicts an Asian renaissance during which Asia will dominate the world economically, politically, and culturally. Very briefly Naisbitt discusses the new breed of leaders emerging in Asia. Includes bibliographical references and index.
Subject(s): Cultural context: Asia

New
Nicholls, C. E., Lane, H. W., & Brechu, M. B. (1999). **Taking self-managed teams to Mexico.** *Academy of Management Executive*, *13*(3), 15-25.

While training in Mexico the authors surveyed 243 executives about self-managed teams. Considering cultural values, Mexican workers place higher value on collectivism than individualism, have a low tolerance for risk and ambiguity, and accept a hierarchical tradition of power distance. Together these cultural values are antithetical to the bottom-up participation and decision making in teams. To develop new behaviors for new roles, the Mexican executives recommend changes in four areas. Top leadership must model delegation and distribution of authority. Training must be provided for employees. Motivation must be established through rewards, incentives, and performance evaluations. There must be value congruence between top management and work teams. In this article the authors make practical suggestions for implementing these changes. Includes bibliographical references.
Subject(s): Cultural context: Mexico; self-managed teams

Nichols, N. A. (Ed.). (1994). *Reach for the top: Women and the changing facts of work life.* Boston: Harvard Business School Press.

This book is a collection and examination of *Harvard Business Review*'s most controversial articles on women in the workplace. The 12 articles present analyses of women's issues, including job opportunities and limitations, balancing work and motherhood, sexual harassment, and the undermining of women's managerial skills. Nichols states that there are no swift solutions to solve these problems but, rather, a variety of alternatives: fighting discrimination, becoming an entrepreneur, or turning a deaf ear. She encourages women to "reach for the top" to fulfill themselves, contribute to the well-being of their families and their employers, and to reap financial rewards that have previously eluded women. The book closes with three stories of women who each made a difference in a male-dominated workplace by reaching for the top. They are: Rosemarie B. Greco, President, CEO, and Director of CoreStates First Pennsylvania Bank; Kye Anderson, President, CEO, and Chairman of Medical Graphics Corporation; and Lore Harp, the CEO of Vector Graphic Design Inc. Includes bibliographical references and index.
Subject(s): Women as corporate leaders

Odenwald, S. B. (1996). *GlobalSolutions for teams: Moving from collision to collaboration.* Chicago: Irwin.

Multinational corporations have become a mainstay of today's global economy, and this book is a reference for such corporations and their leaders, offering resources and advice. Chapters address issues such as multinational corporate culture, competencies for global teams, and transformation; and a practical model for global teams is presented. Case studies from companies including Ford, Apple, National Semiconductor, and Motorola follow each chapter. A reference list of assessments, books, videos, and games on international business is included, along with an index.
Subject(s): Multicultural context

New
Ohlott, P. M. (1999). **Change and leadership development: The experience of executive women.** *Leadership in Action,* *19*(5), 8-12.

Ohlott reports on a study of the Center for Creative Leadership's Women's Leadership Program. Sixty executive women provided data at the beginning and end of the program and again at two weeks, six months, and one year after completing the program. One focus of the study is on change desired and change achieved inside and outside the workplace. Findings indicate that as participants reflect on their goals and practice new behaviors, they achieve significant and purposeful changes in their jobs, relationships, health, and personal growth. The depth and clarity of goals set during the program enhance participants' abilities to achieve their desired changes.
Subject(s): Women's leadership

New
Overton-Adkins, B. J. (1997). **Beyond managing and celebrating diversity: Implications for women's leadership.** *A Leadership Journal: Women in Leadership—Sharing the Vision, 2*(1), 19-25.

This article addresses three questions: How has our society attempted to deal with diversity? Are there new strategies to consider? Do women have inherent characteristics that make them more effective at leading diverse organizations? The author says that women may be better than men at developing "cultural dexterity," or "an empathetic connection to cultures and groups other than one's own," which is an essential skill for leading in a diverse society. Includes bibliographical references.
Subject(s): Women's leadership

Parker, P. S., & ogilvie, d. t. (1996). **Gender, culture, and leadership: Toward a culturally distinct model of African-American women executives' leadership strategies.** *Leadership Quarterly: Special Issue: Leadership and Diversity (Part II), 7*(2), 189-214.

According to the authors, current literature describes two distinct models of leadership—the Anglo-American male hierarchical model and the "distinctly female" model. But these models do not apply to African American women executives (AAWE) who face the interactive effects of sexism and racism. The authors propose a third model of leadership that takes into account the unique social location of AAWEs within the dominant culture organizations. In this model simultaneous race and gender oppression force AAWEs to create their own leadership strategies, which include risk-taking, campaigning, networking/mentoring, and maintaining a sense of biculturalism.
Subject(s): Women's leadership, African American leadership

Peterson, M. F., & Hunt, J. G. (1997). **International perspectives on international leadership.** *Leadership Quarterly: Special Issue: International and Cross-Cultural Leadership Research (Part I), 8*(3), 203-231.

Peterson and Hunt begin by saying that they hope to offer a context for the work in this special issue on international leadership. They then address four basic questions: Is leadership a global idea? Why study leadership internationally? Why study leadership "scientifically"? Does leadership have a technological/modern U.S. bias? After discussing the existing theories around these themes the article offers a brief history of the study of leadership from the 19th century through the current status of the discipline, specifically focusing on international studies and international management. Includes bibliographical references.
Subject(s): Multicultural context

New

Petrick, J. A., Scherer, R. F., Brodzinski, J. D., Quinn, J. F., & Ainina, M. F. (1999). **Global leadership skills and reputational capital: Intangible resources for sustainable competitive advantage.** *Academy of Management Executive, 13*(1), 58-69.

This article argues for the competitive edge that is enjoyed by organizations with good reputations in the global marketplace. A good reputation is based on delivery of the "highest quality goods and services at the lowest cost, in a timely responsible manner, while simultaneously stimulating workforce morale and building collective learning capacities." Companies earn this reputation when individual and collective leadership balance four competing forces: 1) profitability and productivity, 2) continuity and efficiency, 3) commitment and morale, and 4) adaptability and innovation. Achieving such balance increases reputational capital. Serving as responsible stewards of human and natural resources also increases reputational capital. There are examples of companies that have achieved and leveraged good reputations. Includes bibliographical references.
Subject(s): Global leadership

Plato. (c. 387 B.C.). *Republic.*

The ancient Greek philosopher Plato wrote his most enduring work, the *Republic,* sometime around 387 B.C. The main character, Socrates, who was Plato's teacher and mentor, shares his philosophy on the nature of justice and his vision of an ideal society. In the story Socrates argues with the citizens of Athens about the issue of restructuring society so that each man has the opportunity to achieve his highest potential.
Subject(s): Social responsibility, justice

Portugal, E., & Yukl, G. (1994). **Voices on change: Perspectives on environmental leadership.** *Leadership Quarterly: Special Issue: Leadership for Environmental and Social Change, 5*(3/4), 271-276.

Growing environmental concerns affect organizational policies, programs, and budgets. How do individual and organizational leaders influence a broad assortment of stakeholders to consider the complex issues of environmental responsibility? The authors address this concern with a two-dimensional framework for environmental leadership process. This transformational style of leadership involves visioning, consensus-building, sense-making, and symbolic action.
Subject(s): Environmental leadership

New

Prasad, P., Mills, A. J., Elmes, M., & Prasad, A. (Eds.). (1997). *Managing the organizational melting pot: Dilemmas of workplace diversity.* Thousand Oaks, CA: Sage.

This collection of articles describes the serious dimensions of difference that gender creates in organizations and how these organizations and their leaders have handled these differences. The book's first section theorizes the dilemmas of workplace diversity and includes chapters on nonhierarchical

organizations, the Protestant work ethic, the reality of intergroup relations, and class discipline. Articles in the second section address more practical dilemmas in diversity management, including women in academia, how corporate masculinity contributed to the Challenger explosion, immigrant women of color in the labor force, and gender and colonization. Includes bibliographical references and index.
Subject(s): Diversity in the workplace

New

Prescott, J. (1997). **Management challenges for Australia in the Asian century.** *Monash Mt. Eliza Business Review, 1*(1), 38-45.

Australia's European heritage has often distanced the country from its Asian neighbors, but Asia's rising economic and political power makes a more global view necessary. This article first identifies the major challenges confronting Australia, including an aging population, the shift from a commodities market to a service market, and the growing importance of technology and communication. Prescott then describes four strategies Australia can use to engage the Asian market: redefine its national identity, develop an economic framework, formulate a set of common goals, and build an intellectual infrastructure. Finally, cultural issues, human resources, technology, and competition are listed as the major management challenges facing the country. Includes bibliographical references.
Subject(s): Cultural context: Australia

Rao, A., Hashimoto, K., & Rao, A. (1997). **Universal and culturally specific aspects of managerial influence: A study of Japanese managers.** *Leadership Quarterly: Special Issue: International and Cross-Cultural Leadership Research (Part I), 8*(3), 295-312.

Noting that most measures of managerial influence have been developed in the U.S., the authors developed their own instrument to survey managers in a large Japanese corporation. Their research found that Japanese managers use some culturally specific influence tactics, including sanctions, appeals to higher authority, and socializing, that are not found in American measures. The implications of these findings are also discussed, including the possibility that Japanese managers may have difficulty influencing subordinates from other cultures. Includes bibliographical references.
Subject(s): Cultural context: Japan

Reed, T. K. (1997). **Leadership to match a new era: Democratizing society through emancipatory learning.** *Journal of Leadership Studies, 4*(1), 58-77.

Changes in American society are transforming the qualities that make an effective leader. In this article Reed first describes seven of these changes, including the rise of the information age, an increased awareness of diversity, growing ecological concerns, and changing demographics. She then outlines a transformational-learning model of leadership in which leaders create "learning collaboratories" with their followers where team members learn about themselves. An appendix lists the four stages of transformational learning: 1) beliefs are unveiled and come into conflict with others' beliefs, 2) discomfort arises from this conflict, 3) old ways of thinking are released and new insights are developed, and 4) the learners accept themselves and their new insights. Includes bibliographical references and four graphic figures that illustrate this learning process.

Subject(s): Social responsibility, learning competency

Reichel, A. (1996). **Management development in Israel: Current and future challenges.** *Journal of Management Development, 15*(5), 22-36.

Reichel reports on a study of 217 top-level Israeli executives. His research examines executive training and development needs relative to Israel's size and location. These executives are also affected by Israeli-Arab relations, military activity, immigration, technology, and tourism. Reichel concludes that Israeli executives need training programs that focus on service, entrepreneurial skills, research and development, and a combination of nationalism and multiculturalism.

Subject(s): Cultural context: Israel

Ruderman, M. N., Ohlott, P. J., & Kram, K. E. (1996). *Managerial promotion: The dynamics for men and women.* Greensboro, NC: Center for Creative Leadership.

The authors interviewed men and women who had been promoted within a Fortune 500 company in order to analyze the gender differences in promotion dynamics. Reasons for promotion, such as a record of success and good interpersonal skills, are identified, and ways the promotion process can undermine women's advancement are discussed. The authors also outline strategies companies can use to make more balanced promotion decisions. Includes references and an appendix of interview questions.

Subject(s): Women as corporate leaders, men as corporate leaders

New
Ruderman, M. N., Ohlott, P. J., Panzer, K., & King, S. N. (1999). **How managers view success: Perspectives of high-achieving women.** *Leadership in Action, 18*(6), 6-10.

The authors report on a study of women executives and their definitions of success. Alumnae of The Women's Leadership Program at the Center for Creative Leadership participated in a one-year study conducted by survey and a series of interviews. The executives reported that success encompassed all areas of their lives, from achievement at work to strong personal relationships, financial security, and contribution to their communities. They also revealed a perceived discrepancy between their own definitions of success and their organizations'. Many of the women perceived that organizational definitions of success were more narrowly focused on productivity measures and time commitments. The authors suggest actions to help women executives cope with this dichotomy. Includes bibliographical references.

Subject(s): Women as corporate leaders

Rusaw, A. C. (1996). **All God's children: Leading diversity in churches as organizations.** *Leadership Quarterly: Special Issue: Leadership and Diversity (Part II), 7*(2), 229-241.

How do pastors, as leaders without formal authority, inspire their congregations to support diversity and integration? Rusaw conducted a case-study analysis of pastors at three urban churches to discover how they created follower commitment to desegregation. Four leadership strategies pastors use in response to diversity issues are identified: raising awareness and support for subgroups within the organization, modulating change in small group settings, giving voice to different stories, and mediating transcendent vision and experiences.

Subject(s): Diversity in churches, religious leadership

New
Safty, A. (1999). **A view on global leadership.** *Leadership in Action, 19*(1), 1-5.

Safty, former director of the United Nations University International Leadership Academy in Amman, Jordan, shares his observations on global leadership. Much of what is written about this subject pertains to leadership of corporations that span national boundaries. Safty's perspective integrates corporate and political leadership with the efforts of international organizations who support universally shared human values. His image of true global leadership recognizes economic interests but is driven by human interests. It is forward looking and border crossing. It exists in public- and private-sector activities that are committed to advancing global concerns such as peace, human rights, and a harmony of cultures.

Subject(s): Global leadership

Sai, Y. (1995). *The eight core values of the Japanese businessman: Toward an understanding of Japanese management.* New York: International Business Press.

Based on a literature review and interviews, Sai's book attempts to explain the complicated values of Japanese business people. The eight core values that are most commonly shared by Japanese in the business world are: group orientation, diligence, aesthetics and perfectionism, curiosity and emphasis on innovation, respect for form, a mind for competition and emphasis on innovation, the importance of silence, and perceptions of time. Each broad value is discussed in more specific terms and illustrated with examples. Includes bibliographical references and index.

Subject(s): Cultural context: Japan

Santellanes, D. (1989). **Leadership in the Hispanic community: The importance of context.** *Community Education Journal, 16*(4), 12-13.

Community educators succeed in direct relation to their training. This article suggests a new training design for Hispanic-community educators, one that is sensitive to social, economic, and cultural factors. Conceptual skills would familiarize educators with Hispanic values, cultural mores,

and the extended-family support system. Technical skills would include unobtrusive needs assessments. Human skills would stress the importance of verbal communication, particularly listening.
Subject(s): Hispanic leadership

Scandura, T. A., & Lankau, M. J. (1996). **Developing diverse leaders: A leader-member exchange approach.** *Leadership Quarterly: Special Issue: Leadership and Diversity (Part II)*, *7*(2), 243-263.

The leader-member exchange theory, a much-studied approach to leadership, focuses on the working relationship between leaders and followers. However, LMX literature has not addressed the role that diversity due to race or gender may play in these relationships. This article attempts to integrate the existing LMX and diversity literature to show how diversity affects the stages of the leader-follower relationship, including the role-taking, role-making, and role-routinization stages. The authors believe that understanding how differences affect the success of leader-member relationships will greatly enhance the promise of the LMX model.
Subject(s): Diversity in workplace, LMX Theory

New
Scarborough, J. (1998). *The origins of cultural differences and their impact on management.* Westport, CT: Quorum Books.

Scarborough argues that the beliefs that individuals derive from their culture determine how they communicate, negotiate, process information, and make decisions. When people from different cultures work together, these cross-cultural differences can have serious managerial implications. This book first describes how culture affects beliefs about societal role, human nature, time, communication, power, status, and gender roles. Scarborough then addresses how the cultures of specific countries—including Japan, China, Mexico, Russia, Germany, and India—help determine how their citizens act and interact. Includes bibliographical references and index.
Subject(s): Multicultural context

New
Shaw, J. B., & Barrett-Power, E. (1998). **The effects of diversity on small work group processes and performance.** *Human Relations*, *51*(10), 1307-1325.

The authors use a model of group development to describe how diversity affects interaction and performance in small groups. The model describes four sets of activities that groups participate in—forming, storming, norming, and performing. The authors then identify a number of moderating factors that determine how diversity will impact these activities. The moderating factors include readily detectable personal attributes, underlying personal attributes, cognitive costs and rewards, diversity management skills, and cognitive performance resources. The authors conclude that a group's diversity determines its overall behavior and performance,

and that diversity can positively affect group performance and attitudes by increasing a group's task-related cognitive resources. Includes bibliographical references.
Subject(s): Diversity in workplace

New
Shenkar, O., Ronen, S., Shefy, E., & Hau-siu Chow, I. (1998). **The role structure of Chinese managers.** *Human Relations*, *51*(1), 51-72.

Since the 1950s Western scholars have attempted to describe the work managers do by describing the different roles in managerial work. But these models rarely take a manager's culture into account, and the authors believe that the environment can significantly affect how a manager works. This study analyzed survey data collected from 93 managers in China's Henan province to see if Western managers and Chinese managers formulated their roles differently. The authors then conducted in-depth interviews with several Chinese managers to interpret the differences they found. These managers and the authors conclude that the role of the Chinese manager is evolving as Chinese society is affected by Western culture. Includes bibliographical references.
Subject(s): Cultural context: China

Shrivastava, P. (1994). **Ecocentric leadership in the 21st century.** *Leadership Quarterly: Special Issue: Leadership for Environmental and Social Change*, *5*(3/4), 223-226.

The world is facing ecological crises at a rapidly increasing rate. The depletion of the ozone layer, species extinction, air pollution, acid rain, and toxic waste threaten the world's resources for future generations. Economic development, public policy, and individual behavior are all responsible for the problem and the solution. As the engineers of economic development, the corporate sector holds the largest share of responsibility and the greatest promise for resolution. The author warns corporate leaders to not tack ecological concerns onto their decisions as afterthoughts. He encourages decision-makers to promote sustainable economic development and the quality of life for all the world's inhabitants at the center of corporate planning.
Subject(s): Environmental leadership

New
Sinha, J. B. P. (1995). *The cultural context of leadership and power.* Thousand Oaks, CA: Sage.

This book provides an Indian perspective on the research of leadership and power, which are primarily of Western origin. The evolution of leadership theories from the *great man* theory to trait, situational, interactional, and transformational leadership are illustrated with examples from Indian politics and business. Sinha explains the traditional Indian concept of power, describes characteristics of Indian subordinates, and compares Indian and Japanese business managers. There is also discussion of organizational culture embedded within sociocultural environments and a leader's responsibility for building organizational culture. An appendix contains a

Leader's Style Scale for personal assessment. Includes bibliographical references and index.
Subject(s): Cultural context: India

Slack, J. D., Myers, N., Nelson, L., & Sirk, K. (1996). **Women, research, and mentorship in public administration.** *Public Administration Review, 56*(5), 453-458.

This study examined the rate at which women's research was published in *Public Administration Review* and found that female researchers publish at lower rates than men and tend to enter into fewer joint research ventures than men do. One reason offered for this is that few women have mentors in the field because men occupy most of the senior positions in public administration and tend to offer their advice and support to other men. The study did show that the number of women publishing in the field seems to be increasing in the 1990s.
Subject(s): Women as mentors, women as public service leaders

Slowinski, G., Chatterji, D., Tshudy, J. A., & Fridley, D. L. (1997). **Are you a leader in environmental R&D?** *Research-Technology Management, 40*(3), 47-54.

Industrial R&D leaders can be pivotal in determining their organizations' environmental awareness and policies. This article offers a self-assessment questionnaire for R&D directors to use to evaluate the environmental policies of their organizations. R&D factors measured include environmental policies, strategic planning, the organizational approach, environmental training, and management processes. This questionnaire was previously given to 30 major companies, and the authors list the five that scored highest, including Dow Chemical and Clorox, and identify management characteristics that these companies share.
Subject(s): Environmental leadership

New

Smith, D. (1998). **The business case for diversity.** *Monash Mt. Eliza Business Review, 1*(3), 72-81.

Smith defines diversity as "the quality of being different and unique at an individual or group level" and says that having good diversity practices can improve an organization's bottom line. This article first describes four different layers of diversity: personality, internal, external, and organizational. Then, preconditions of effective diversity management are identified, including a well-articulated and understood mission and a culture that values openness. Smith next describes a seven-stage process for managing diversity that includes scanning the environment, analyzing data, creating interventions, and checking progress. Finally, reasons organizations resist change through diversity, such as insufficient leadership and a desire to avoid risk, are listed. Includes bibliographical references.
Subject(s): Diversity in workplace

Smith, E. (1997). **Leader or manager: The minority department chair of the majority department.** *Journal of Leadership Studies, 3*(1), 79-94.

This article asks whether minorities can lead or manage, or do both, as department chairs of colleges and universities. Smith suggests that chairpersons are managers who make a department function, and they are also leaders who establish a vision for their departments. Actions to increase the inclusiveness of minorities are: allowing a three-month training period before one assumes the chair position, and training for gender equity and diversity.
Subject(s): Ethnic diversity in higher education

Taormina, T. (1996). *Virtual leadership and the ISO9000 imperative.* Upper Saddle River, NJ: Prentice Hall.

ISO9000 is a quality management system that was developed in the 1970s in cooperation with the European Community. It transcends language and cultural barriers and establishes a global accreditation system for companies doing international business that is now used in over 80 countries. Taormina explains the fundamentals of ISO9000, details what it means for companies, and describes the leadership necessary to move American companies to this global mind-set. Along with reader-friendly graphs and boxes, this book offers companies a practical strategic implementation plan, sample quality manuals, an internal auditor training course, and an audit checklist. Includes bibliographical references and index.
Subject(s): Global leadership

Thackray, C., & McCall, M. (1997). **Women evolving as leaders.** *Journal of Leadership Studies, 4*(2), 18-26.

Thackray and McCall researched leadership from women's perspective to see if women were evolving through time as leaders. They studied ten women—five from the pre–Civil War era and five from the 20th century. Women in the first group included Frances Wright, the first woman to deliver a publicly recorded speech, and Elizabeth Stanton, the first woman to publicly call for the elective franchise. They were found to be more action oriented and to use greater emotion than 20th-century women. Women leaders of the 20th century included Barbara Jordan, the first black woman to serve on the Texas State Senate, and Geraldine Ferraro, the first female vice-presidential nominee. The findings suggested that women as leaders were evolving through time, although there were not significant differences among the women studied.
Subject(s): Women's leadership development

Thomas, D. A., & Ely, R. J. (1996). **Making differences matter: A new paradigm for managing diversity.** *Harvard Business Review, 74*(5), 79-90.

In the past, companies have viewed diversity two ways, through either the discrimination-and-fairness paradigm or the access-and-legitimacy paradigm. In these two frameworks, say Thomas and Ely, people often feel exploited, and while the staff get diversified the work does not. They

advocate a third paradigm, in which diversity is connected to work perspectives, so that "we are all on the same team, *with* our differences—not *despite* them." After researching organizations across the country the authors have defined the preconditions and actions necessary for companies to transform their vision of a diversified workplace.
Subject(s): Diversity in workplace

New
Thomas, D. A., & Gabarro, J. J. (1999). *Breaking through: The making of minority executives in corporate America.* Boston: Harvard Business School Press.

This study used interviews to trace the careers of minority and white executives at three large companies, analyzing how each individual's childhood, education, and professional achievements affected their work experiences. The profiles of these executives show that the paths minorities followed to the executive ranks are very different from those of white executives. The authors say that most minority executives experienced a point of "breaking through" their firm's invisible barriers, and describe some strategies companies use to enable minority advancement and create points of break-through. The book concludes with lessons for the next generation of minority executives, including: build a network of developmental relationships, the organization matters, and take charge of your own career. Interview responses illustrate the findings. Includes bibliographical references and index.
Subject(s): Ethnic diversity in workplace, executives

New
Thorp, L., & Townsend, C. (1998). **Rethinking leadership education: Giving women a fighting chance.** *A Leadership Journal: Women in Leadership—Sharing the Vision, 2*(2), 81-92.

The authors studied students in Texas A&M's academic leadership courses in order to answer three questions: 1) were there differences in the self-perceived leadership skills of men and women, 2) was there a connection between women's self-perceived leadership skills and their past leadership experiences, and 3) were the self-perceived leadership skills different for women in coeducational and all-female settings? Both quantitative and qualitative data were collected using the *Leadership Skills Inventory*, reflective journals, course evaluations, personal-vision papers, and transcipts from small group discussions. Based on their findings the authors recommend adding all-female lab sections to leadership courses. Includes bibliographical references.
Subject(s): Women's leadership development

New
Valian, V. (1998). *Why so slow?: The advancement of women.* Cambridge, MA: MIT Press.

Valian uses observational and experimental data as well as statistical information to describe the position of women in society today. She draws from the fields of psychology,

sociology, economics, and biology to explain why women lag behind men in professional advancement. After establishing how men and women develop a "gender schema" that determines differences in behavior and perception, Valian addresses achievement discrepancies in business and academia, affirmative action, interpreting success and failure, and the effects of gender schemas on the self. The book concludes with a chapter of "remedies" that suggest ways to prevent gender schemas from limiting women's advancement. Includes bibliographical references and index.
Subject(s): Women's leadership

Valikangas, L., & Okumura, A. (1997). **Why do people follow leaders? A study of a U.S. and a Japanese change program.** *Leadership Quarterly: Special Issue: International and Cross-Cultural Leadership Research (Part I), 8*(3), 313-337.

What motivates people to follow a leader? The authors argue that this answer differs across cultures. This article examines major change initiatives in two companies, GE in the U.S. and Japanese pharmaceutical manufacturer Eisai, and determines that the two CEOs used very different methods to motivate their employees. The American leader emphasized the consequences of the changes for employees and appealed to the shared values of all employees, and the Japanese leader focused on developing a corporate identity that would inspire followers to change in order to remain a part of their social group. Appendices describe the two companies, their histories, and their change plans in detail. Includes bibliographical references.
Subject(s): Cross-cultural context: U.S. and Japan

Van Belle, D. A. (1996). **Leadership and collective action: The case of revolution.** *International Studies Quarterly, 40*(1), 107-132.

In a collective action, such as a revolution, there are the activists who pay a high price, the free riders who reap benefits without paying the price, and the leaders who do both—pay the price and receive the benefits. Van Belle explains that individuals enter collective action with the intent of assuming leadership and reaping the greatest rewards. He presents formulas and models that illustrate the rational choice, success threshold, and relative deprivation in a revolutionary situation. Strategies employed by the revolutionary leader include altering the value of the status quo and creating safety buffers. Van Belle hopes that this examination of leadership in the context of revolution will aid the understanding of leadership in all collective action. Includes bibliographical references.
Subject(s): Social movements

New
Waiguchu, J. M., Tiagha, E., & Mwaura, M. (Eds.). (1999). *Management of organizations in Africa: A handbook and reference.* Westport, CT: Quorum Books.

Although there are national and regional orientations to management in Africa, this textbook provides a continental

focus. The editors characterize the general state of African management of public organizations as bureaucratic and inept, sometimes corrupt. They view the management of private enterprise to be more efficient but resembling 19th-century authoritarianism more than a modern style of management. By exposing problems as a commonality the authors suggest that common solutions may be adapted from local successes. Chapters review basic management and leadership theories and illustrate how successful practices in Nigeria, Kenya, Zimbabwe, Ghana, and other locales can serve as examples from which students and practicing managers may learn. Includes bibliographical references and index.
Subject(s): Cultural context: Africa; textbook

New
Weaver, G. R. (1998). *Culture, communication and conflict: Readings in intercultural relations* (2nd ed.). Needham Heights, MA: Simon & Schuster.

This anthology of readings is intended for professionals in the field of intercultural relations—cultural diversity managers, consultants and trainers, managers in multinational companies, or others who must communicate across cultures. Although most of the expertise in this field is developed through experience, the editor submits that the conceptual frameworks in this book enhance the body of knowledge in this emerging field. Contributors represent many cultures and multiple disciplines. Some essays are: "On Gemeinschaft and Gesellschaft," "The Chinese Practice of Guanxi," and "Adopting Japanese Management: Some Cultural Stumbling Blocks." Includes bibliographical references and name and subject indexes.
Subject(s): Multicultural context

New
Weeks, J. R. (1997). **Styles of success: The thinking and management styles of women and men entrepreneurs.** *A Leadership Journal: Women in Leadership—Sharing the Vision, 2*(1), 109-132.

In 1994 the National Foundation for Women Business Leaders conducted a study using the assessment instrument *Success Style Profile* to determine whether male and female entrepreneurs have different thinking and management styles. This article summarizes the findings, providing charts and tables of data and sample questions from the instrument. While the study found many similarities in the entrepreneurs' thinking styles, the data also showed that men tend to emphasize logical thinking styles while women use more intuitive methods. Includes bibliographical references.
Subject(s): Women as entrepreneurs, men as entrepreneurs

Weisbord, M. R. (1992). *Discovering common ground: How future search conferences bring people together to achieve breakthrough innovation, empowerment, shared vision, and collaborative action.* San Francisco: Berrett-Koehler.

Based on his chapter "Inventing the Future" in *Productive Workplaces* (Jossey-Bass, 1987), Weisbord shares his

visionary concept of future-search conferences, a shift from expert problem solving to shared responsibility for our world's problems. Business, government, education, and all sectors of society meet for three-day conferences to discover common ground, imagine ideal futures, expand horizons, and build democratic social values. He describes successful conferences, potential pitfalls, and planning advice for practitioners. Includes bibliographical references and index.
Subject(s): Social responsibility

New
Wentling, R. M. (1997). **Women in management: A longitudinal study of their career development and aspirations.** *A Leadership Journal: Women in Leadership—Sharing the Vision, 2*(1), 93-107.

Begun in 1989 this longitudinal study uses case studies of 30 women in midlevel management positions to analyze the career progress of female managers. The study identified factors that helped and hindered women's career development and found that the majority of women felt that they were not progressing as rapidly as they should. Most women in the study still believed that they could reach top-level management positions, but the authors, citing the barriers to women's advancement, question the reality of those beliefs. Includes bibliographical references.
Subject(s): Women as managers

New
Wentling, R. M., & Palma-Rivas, N. (1998). **Current status and future trends of diversity initiatives in the workplace: Diversity experts' perspective.** *Human Resource Development Quarterly, 9*(3), 235-253.

The authors conducted telephone interviews with 12 experts in the field of diversity management, asking questions about six major research areas: barriers to diverse groups in the workplace, factors that influence diversity initiatives, the importance of managing diversity, strategies for managing diversity, diversity training programs, and future trends. Content analysis of the responses showed that while there are major benefits to managing diversity in organizations, including improved productivity and competitiveness, there remain major barriers to overcome. The findings suggest that in the future diversity training will be incorporated with other training, requiring all corporate trainers to understand and teach diversity issues. Includes bibliographical references.
Subject(s): Diversity in workplace

New
Wilson, M. S., & Dalton, M. A. (1998). *International success: Selecting, developing, and supporting expatriate managers.* Greensboro, NC: Center for Creative Leadership.

Expatriate managers in an ever-changing global economy may be faced with insurmountable challenges due to a lack of proper preparation for foreign country assignments. The authors address this dilemma through a Selection, Development, and Support (SDS) framework. They begin with statistics of the high failure rate of expatriate assignments in organizations without a systematic approach to expatriation and repatriation. Although the definition of expatriate effectiveness is subjective, the authors present a figure of developed criteria to explain this concept. The SDS framework is utilized to present information relevant to human resource managers when developing expatriate assignments. Includes bibliographical references, and appendices with research overviews and interview protocols.

Subject(s): Multicultural context, expatriate managers

New
Wilson, M. S., & Dalton, M. A. (1999). **What every leader should know about expatriate effectiveness.** *Leadership in Action, 19*(3), 1-8.

In studies with 89 expatriate managers the authors learned that there are three keys to successful expatriate assignments—selection, development, and support (SDS). This article proposes an SDS framework to facilitate managing the expatriate-repatriate system. Short-term selection factors include personality measures and consideration of early-life experiences. A long-term view is necessary to determine family readiness. Short-term development factors include language and cultural training. Long-term development involves on-the-job training. Support factors in the short term are the facilitation of a smooth job transition and family adjustment. Support over the long term involves equitable compensation and a plan for repatriation. Includes bibliographical references.

Subject(s): Multicultural context, expatriate managers

Wilson, M. S., Hoppe, M. H., & Sayles, L. R. (1996). *Managing across cultures: A learning framework.* Greensboro, NC: Center for Creative Leadership.

The multicultural team of authors combine their education, research, and experience to design a framework for U.S. managers who are confronted with cross-cultural business interactions. The framework is comprised of seven dimensions that describe workplace dilemmas experienced in every culture: identity, goals, authority, ambiguity, knowledge acquisition, time, and outlook on life. Each chapter discusses one dilemma in the form of a continuum with two opposing choices. First, the authors provide a description of values for each pole. Then, examples from the workplace reveal how those values affect specific situations. Finally, the authors present four steps to apply the framework and improve cross-cultural understanding: observe your own and others' behavior, construct a provisional hypothesis or stereotype for behaviors in other cultures, constantly revise your hypothesis based on your experiences, and challenge yourself to grow. Includes bibliographical references.

Subject(s): Multicultural context

Xin, K. R. (1997). **Asian American managers: An impression gap?** *Journal of Applied Behavioral Science, 33*(3), 335-355.

Why are there so few Asian Americans in leadership positions? Xin hypothesizes that this is partly due to differences in Asian Americans' impression management style, or the way they present themselves to their superiors. She surveyed a group of Asian American managers and their supervisors, and a group of European American managers and their supervisors, and found that both the managers and supervisors viewed the impression management behavior of Asian Americans and European Americans differently—with Asian Americans losing out in the process. The article also includes background on the theory of impression management and how Asian cultural roots may affect this.

Subject(s): Asian American leadership

Xin, K. R., & Tsui, A. S. (1996). **Different strokes for different folks? Influence tactics by Asian-American and Caucasian-American managers.** *Leadership Quarterly: Special Issue: Leadership and Diversity (Part I), 7*(1), 109-132.

This article reports on a survey of 141 Caucasian American and 196 Asian American managers who live and work in Southern California, their superiors, and their direct reports. All participants were asked about the managers' behaviors when exerting influence. The study finds almost no cultural differences between the two groups of managers, although the authors suggest that may be because they live and work in the same culture. Both groups used different tactics when influencing upward (with their superiors) and downward (with their direct reports). Also in both groups, raters' perceptions differed from managers' perceptions in terms of rationality, ingratiation, and upward appeal. The authors suggest that diversity issues may be more relevant to position than to ethnicity.

Subject(s): Asian American leadership, multicultural context

New
Yammarino, F. J., & Jung, D. I. (1998). **Asian Americans and leadership: A levels of analysis perspective.** *Journal of Applied Behavioral Science, 34*(1), 47-67.

A levels-of-analysis approach is applied to hypotheses comparing the leadership styles of Asian Americans and Caucasian Americans. The authors propose that Asian Americans link to a person-group model while Caucasian Americans link to a balanced dyadic model. Cultural values explain the differences. Asian culture is based on the Confucian principles of collectivism, emphasizing the importance of the group over self. Significant distance between leader and followers emphasizes a leader's status and power. Group-based rewards reflect the importance of group work and performance. There is discussion of culturally homogeneous and heterogeneous groups, the acculturation process, and company location. Commentary by Clayton Alderfer follows on pages 68-75. Yammarino and Jung respond to Alderfer's comments on pages 76-81. Includes bibliographical references.

Subject(s): Asian American leadership

Yoshimura, N., & Anderson, P. (1997). *Inside the Kaisha: Demystifying Japanese business behavior.* Boston: Harvard Business School Press.

A Japanese middle manager and an American professor collaborate in this effort to describe the internal workings of large Japanese companies (*kaishas*). Based on interviews with Japanese salarymen, the book challenges the idea that Japanese business practices are based on traditional cultural values. Rather, Yoshimura and Anderson argue that Japanese businesses have developed "organizational mechanisms" that dictate behavior. They use these mechanisms to explain six apparent contradictions that exist in Japanese companies; for example, harmony is emphasized, yet workers are fiercely competitive. Includes bibliographical references and index.

Subject(s): Cultural context: Japan

TEAM LEADERSHIP

New

Aranda, E. K., Aranda, L., & Conlon, K. (1998). ***Teams: Structures, process, culture, and politics.*** Upper Saddle River, NJ: Prentice Hall.

Effective teams have to address four issues: defining the team structure, developing consistent processes, creating a team culture, and advancing team renewal. This workbook contains exercises and discussion questions that guide the reader through these four issues, and also addresses specific questions about establishing ground rules, decision making, rituals, and internal and external politics. An appendix offers a step-by-step guide to designing an individual team charter. Includes index.

Subject(s): Teams

Bennis, W., & Biederman, P. W. (1997). ***Organizing genius: The secrets of creative collaboration.*** Reading, MA: Addison-Wesley.

Successful groups aren't just trying to fix a problem, they're trying to "put a dent in the universe." Bennis, an expert in leadership issues, collaborates with writer Biederman to explain why certain teams are able to produce greatness and why "none of us is as smart as all of us." After describing seven "Great Groups" from the Manhattan Project to the 1992 Clinton campaign the book offers "take-home lessons" on the characteristics of a successful team. These include that Great Groups think they are on a mission from God; they see themselves as winning underdogs; and they are optimistic, not realistic. Includes bibliographical references and index.

Subject(s): Team characteristics

Cannella, A. A., Jr., & Rowe, W. G. (1995). **Leader capabilities, success, and competitive context: A study of professional baseball teams.** *Leadership Quarterly, 6*(1), 69-88.

To study leadership succession in a situational context the authors studied baseball field managers. Characteristics of this group are: high visibility during the decision-making process, their function as targets for criticism, high compensation, competitive intensity, and the perceived value of their experience. All major league teams from 1951 to 1980 were analyzed for performance, manager ability, rivalry, reorganization, and player turnover. The implications for business are discussed.

Subject(s): Sports leadership

Carley, M. S. (1996). **Teambuilding: Lessons from the theatre.** *Training & Development, 50*(8), 41-43.

The author, a trainer and veteran stage director, describes how a great theatrical production is a model of teamwork, using his experience directing the show *Noises Off* as an example. The article includes a list of the qualities that both a successful team and stage production need, including a clear focus on task, mutual trust, well-defined roles, flexible

leadership, innovation and improvisation, and closure.

Subject(s): Team characteristics, team building

Daniels, D. (1996). **Leadership lessons from championship basketball.** *Journal for Quality and Participation, 19*(3), 36-48.

Daniels calls basketball "a metaphor for today's marketplace and society. It is characterized by constant movement . . . and winning demands teamwork." He parallels the positions on a basketball team and the roles in organizations: the human resources group is like a point guard, production is like a power forward, and senior management is comparable to a center. The importance of transition and how companies can create transition and proactive behavior in their workers is also discussed. Examples from recent Chicago Bulls teams and companies including FedEx and Motorola illustrate Daniels' ideas.

Subject(s): Sports leadership

New

Dew, J. R. (1998). ***Managing in a team environment.*** Westport, CT: Quorum Books.

Dew developed team environments at several companies and won an *Industry Week* magazine award for his team initiative at Lockheed Martin. In this book he describes the conceptual differences between traditional management and team management and shares examples of his practical applications. He recommends that teams begin with a charter that defines their mission, roles, structure, and membership. Chapters address more team issues such as goal setting, performance measurement, conflict resolution, strategic planning, creativity, and the development of team leadership. An appendix contains a *Team Health Survey*. Includes bibliographical references and index.

Subject(s): Team leadership

Donnellon, A. (1996). ***Team talk: The power of language in team dynamics.*** Boston: Harvard Business School Press.

Donnellon calls this a "sociolinguistic look at teams" because she analyzes not just the actions of teams but their conversation, stories, and jargon and uses this information to differentiate between real teams and teams in name only. Teams from four Fortune 200 companies are analyzed in depth and form the basis for chapters on hierarchy, leadership, and personal commitment. Donnellon also offers "Advice to Teams" and "Advice to Managers," and a "team talk audit" is included so readers can analyze their own teams' conversation and exchanges. Includes index and appendices that describe Donnellon's research methods.

Subject(s): Group dynamics, team communication

New

Duarte, D. L., & Snyder, N. T. (1999). *Mastering virtual teams: Strategies, tools, and techniques that succeed.* San Francisco: Jossey-Bass.

This book provides a series of checklists, exercises, and assessments that managers of virtual teams can use to ensure their teams' success. The authors address team member roles and competencies, building trust, overcoming cultural and technological boundaries, and virtual team meetings. They also identify six major steps in developing a virtual team: 1) identify team sponsors, 2) develop a team charter, 3) select team members, 4) contact team members, 5) conduct an orientation session, and 6) develop team processes. Includes index.

Subject(s): Geographically dispersed teams

Fisher, B., & Thomas, B. (1996). *Real dream teams: Seven practices used by world class leaders to achieve extraordinary results.* Delray Beach, FL: St. Lucie Press.

To discover how real "dream teams" are created Fisher and Thomas identified 12 "world-class team leaders": coaches Lou Holtz, John Wooden, Jody Conradt; business leaders Don Tyson and Donald Petersen; author Norman Vincent Peale; scientist Gertrude Elion; university dean Sybil Mobley; Major General Patrick Henry Brady; mountain climber Lou Whittaker; musician Carl Schiebler; and pilot Steve Trent. Based on interviews with these leaders the authors define seven practices essential to effective teams: 1) commitment to a clear mission; 2) mutual support, respect, and encouragement; 3) clearly defined and accepted roles; 4) win-win cooperation; 5) individual competency; 6) empowering communication; and 7) a winning attitude. Each practice is illustrated by quotes from the leaders, graphs, and figures. Includes references.

Subject(s): Team characteristics

New

Forrester, R., & Drexler, A. B. (1999). **A model for team-based organization performance.** *Academy of Management Executive, 13*(3), 36-49.

The authors draw on their consulting experiences to form a model of team-based organization performance. Seven elements contribute to the process: formation, dependability, focus, buy-in, coordination, impact, and vitality. The model illustrates the benefits of mastering each element, key steps to achieving mastery, and offkeys—the problems that could arise if the element is not mastered. Examples of the elements in real work situations further explain the process. Includes bibliographical references.

Subject(s): Team-based performance

New

Ginnett, R. C. (1999). **The essentials of leading a high-performance team.** *Leadership in Action, 18*(6), 1-5.

Ginnett compares team performance to automobile performance. If one wants the superb drive and handling of a

Mercedes, it is available, but at a substantial cost. One cannot take a Yugo, invest in a new suspension or steering system, and expect to get Mercedes performance at a fraction of the cost. The structure for high performance isn't there. Similarly in organizations, if structure supports individualism and competition, teams can't achieve optimal performance. Ginnett offers a model of direction, design, and development that builds a solid structure for team effectiveness. Includes bibliographical references.

Subject(s): Team-based performance

Hallam, G. L. (1996). *The adventures of Team Fantastic: A practical guide for team leaders and members.* Greensboro, NC: Center for Creative Leadership.

At CCL Hallam has researched and trained hundreds of teams and has coauthored instruments for developing teams and team leaders. In this book he introduces Team Fantastic, a virtual team that travels through time and space. Each adventure presents a new challenge and suggested actions for team success. When Team Fantastic lands on the moon, they manage their time carefully to finish assignments before running out of oxygen. In New York City empowered team members operate equipment and direct traffic to repair a water main before rush hour. They practice feedback skills before their opening performance of a Shakespearean play. This fantastic team travels through 15 more scenarios to demonstrate commitment, organizational support, conflict management, and innovation.

Subject(s): Team leadership

Harrington-Mackin, D. (1994). *The team-building tool kit: Tips, tactics, and rules for effective workplace teams.* New York: AMACOM.

This resource is intended for start-up and existing teams that are developing their own set of rules. Chapters include starting up, meetings, team behavior, how to handle team members' fear and control, decision making, problem solving, evaluation, performance rewards, and training. Real team scenarios emphasize each rule in each chapter. Questions most frequently asked by teams in progress are listed at the end of each chapter to reinforce the text. Includes bibliographical references and index.

Subject(s): Team building

New

Harshman, C. L., & Phillips, S. L. (1994). *Teaming up: Achieving organizational transformation.* San Diego, CA: Pfeiffer.

This book is intended for practitioners who deal with organizational change and development at all levels. The authors propose a team-based change strategy that contains three elements: 1) understanding where an organization is now, 2) defining where it wants to be, and 3) planning how to get there. Brief explanations of organizational theory and change tactics are combined with step-by-step guidance for collecting data, identifying barriers, determining level of team participation, developing leadership teams, developing communication systems, and solving problems. Appendices compare change processes in public versus private organizations and describe the unique elements of change in unionized workplaces. Includes bibliographical references and index.

Subject(s): Team-based performance

New

Haywood, M. (1998). *Managing virtual teams: Practical techniques for high-technology project managers*. Boston: Artech House.

A virtual, or distributed, team is one in which "one or more of the team members is geographically separated from the other members." This book offers advice on six key factors in managing distributed teams: solving communication problems, building teams, developing remote management skills, organizing the team's work, using networking technology, and implementing a telecommuting program. Appendices include assessment checklists for team members, a guide to the tax consequences of home offices, and a questionnaire measuring return on investment for virtual teams. Includes references and index.

Subject(s): Geographically dispersed teams

New

Jassawalla, A. R., & Sashittal, H. C. (1999). **Building collaborative cross-functional new product teams.** *Academy of Management Executive*, *13*(3), 50-63.

The authors report on their study of cross-functional teams in high-technology firms. Formed to facilitate faster and smoother development of new products, these teams are expected to collaborate. A newly formed team of compartmentalized functional members begins with low collaboration. Through increasingly complex behaviors and processes, a team reaches developmental milestones: information sharing, cooperation around decisions, joint planning, coordination of activities, equitable sharing of power, transparent boundaries, trust, and synergy. This article suggests how to develop teams in this way. Includes bibliographical references.

Subject(s): Cross-functional teams, team building, new product development

Johnson, D. W., & Johnson, F. P. (1997). *Joining together: Group theory and group skills* (6th ed.). Boston: Allyn and Bacon.

This is a textbook for students of group theory. Chapters are on group dynamics, experiential learning, group goals and social interdependence, communication within groups, leadership, decision making, controversy and creativity, conflict of interests, the use of power, dealing with diversity, leading learning and discussion groups, leading growth and counseling groups, and team development and training. In this new edition the authors work to further bridge the gap between theory and practice by combining empirical

knowledge with practical exercises and simulations that apply to any area of life involving group dynamics. Coordinator instructions are detailed for over 80 exercises. Includes bibliographical references, a glossary of terms, and index.

Subject(s): Group dynamics, textbook

New

Katzenbach, J. R. (1998). *Teams at the top: Unleashing the potential of both teams and individual leaders*. Boston: Harvard Business School Press.

Katzenbach says that a company's executives must be able to work both as a team and as single leaders because different situations require different strategies. Executive teams are most common and most effective in unexpected crises, in which the whole organization works toward one goal. This book describes how to identify when teamwork is needed and how executive groups can switch between the two methods of working. It also describes how CEOs can help integrate the discipline and skills needed for team and nonteam leadership and play multiple roles within the organization. Appendices offer a glossary of team terms and a diagnostic guide. Includes bibliographical references and index.

Subject(s): Executive teams

Laiken, M. E. (1994). **The myth of the self-managing team.** *Organization Development Journal*, *12*(2), 29-34.

Laiken reports on two studies of team management in large organizations. In the first, three scenarios were observed. Traditional, highly directive team leaders had dependent and angry team members. Team leaders who assumed no management role had chaotic and dysfunctional team members. Facilitative team leaders who adapted their behavior to the teams' stage of development had high-performing and satisfied team members. In the second study team leaders received training to anticipate role changes and all teams reported satisfaction. Laiken concludes that conflict resolution is the toughest challenge facing team management and that a trained, facilitative leader is a necessary element for team success.

Subject(s): Self-managing teams

New

Lembke, S., & Wilson, M. G. (1998). **Putting the "team" into teamwork: Alternative theoretical contributions for contemporary management practices.** *Human Relations*, *51*(7), 927-944.

This article uses the social identity theory to understand teamwork, examining teams as units rather than collections of individuals. The theory explains that members become a part of the team by adopting an identity governed by the team and its social context. In order for this to occur, members must recognize the team as a unit and perceive a benefit to being a part of it. Includes bibliographical references.

Subject(s): Team characteristics

Manion, J., Lorimer, W. L., & Leander, W. J. (1996). *Team-based health care organizations: Blueprint for success.* Gaithersburg, MD: Aspen.

This book for health care administrators promotes a transformation of the health care system through the use of teams and shared leadership. The authors build a strong case for the cost benefits, work performance, individual commitment, and job satisfaction that exist in team-based organizations. Chapters explain the planning process, stages for implementing teams, perils and pitfalls, leading change, and lessons from teamwork in the corporate sector. Teamwork among health care providers raises special issues. Cross-functional teams of specialists have different levels of skill and responsibility yet must coordinate among themselves and with other cross-functional teams to provide continuity of care for patients. Tips, techniques, and case studies illustrate how it can be done. Includes bibliographical references and index.
Subject(s): Team-based performance, health care organizations

Mankin, D., Cohen, S. G., & Bikson, T. K. (1996). *Teams and technology: Fulfilling the promise of the new organization.* Boston: Harvard Business School Press.

This book introduces a framework called mutual design and implementation. MDI links teams and the information systems they need to enhance knowledge and improve performance. This framework makes it possible to pool knowledge quickly around complex issues. MDI's basic principles are: using conflict creatively, flexible planning that allows for serendipity, inviting cross-functional and multi-level involvement, and creating learning systems. The authors fit the framework to five kinds of teams: work teams, project teams, parallel teams, management teams, and ad hoc networks. In each case the team composition, leadership, external connections, information resources, and suggested training programs are described. Includes bibliographical references and index.
Subject(s): Team-based performance, technical leadership

New
McClure, B. A. (1998). *Putting a new spin on groups: The science of chaos.* Mahwah, NJ: Lawrence Erlbaum.

This book challenges how we think about small group dynamics. It covers the integration of standard small group dynamic theory with chaos theory, the importance of conflict in group development and growth, and how groups change, evolve, and mature. Specific chapters include case studies of dysfunctional groups, ethical concerns in teaching about groups, and the specific leadership skills required in group activities. Includes bibliographical references and index.
Subject(s): Group dynamics, chaos

New
McDermott, L., Waite, B., & Brawley, N. (1999). **Putting together a world-class team.** *Training & Development, 53*(1), 46-51.

The key to creating a successful world-class or globally dispersed teams is to establish goals and measure achievements from the start. The authors describe a Team Goal Development and Alignment process consisting of four steps: 1) establish the team's driving goal, 2) identify critical success factors, 3) set no more than ten priority goals, and 4) create a team accountability matrix. Measures of success should be established so that the team can judge its progress, and teams should convene regularly for "Team Learning Stops" to assess their progress and celebrate successes.
Subject(s): Geographically dispersed teams

New
McIntyre, M. G. (1998). *The management team handbook: Five key strategies for maximizing group performance.* San Francisco: Jossey-Bass.

Although the term *management teams* has been used for some time to describe groups of managers, the results of these teams have generally not met the potential. McIntyre presents a practical guide for department heads and other managing groups as well as for students of management to realize their potential. The book begins with seven objectives including defining success factors and challenge points, assessment tools, solutions and suggestions for selection and transition. Five success factors are defined and incorporated into the *team model* preceding an extensive chapter for each of the five. The second part of the handbook focuses on maintaining the team's production with new member selection, managing transitions, and solving team troubles. The conclusion delineates 12 guidance principles to assist in higher management team performance. Includes bibliographical references.
Subject(s): Team-based performance

New
Moxnes, P. (1998). **Fantasies and fairy tales in groups and organizations: Bion's basic assumptions and the deep roles.** *European Journal of Work and Organizational Psychology, 7*(3), 283-298.

Group psychologist Wilfred Bion theorized that in group interactions members unconsciously adopt one of the archetypal "deep roles" found in fairy tales: King, Queen, Witch, Clown, Wise Man, or Whore. Groups also develop collective fantasies that shape their actions. These fantasies can include a dependency on a parental leader, creating an enemy to fight, or hoping for messianic deliverance. The author thoroughly reviews Bion's theories and then describes how his own observations of work groups support them. Though little quantitative research has been done on Bion's work to date, the author says that Bion's explanations of group behavior may have practical applications in the business world. Includes bibliographical references.
Subject(s): Group dynamics

New

Nadler, D. A., Spencer, J. L., & Associates of Delta Consulting Group. (1998). *Executive teams*. San Francisco: Jossey-Bass.

CEOs and senior executives, whose work is increasingly more complex, find it useful, if not necessary, to establish corporate-level leadership teams. From their work with more than 60 CEOs who lead teams the writers identify the requirements for and the nature of executive team leadership. Part One, "A New Leadership Model," details the purpose and organization of executive teams. Part Two, "Managing the Executive Team," addresses team chemistry, trust, management of poor performance, and the manifestation and resolution of conflict. Part Three, "Leading the Organization: The Work of Executive Teams," examines the value-added functions of corporate governance, development and implementation of strategy, and change in organizational culture. Primarily most beneficial to the CEO charged with the responsibility of designing and deploying the executive team, this book also enlightens team members looking for better understanding of their roles, the environment in which they work, and how, as individuals, they contribute to the team's chemistry and performance. Includes bibliographical references and index.
Subject(s): Executive teams

Nurick, A. J. (1993). **Facilitating effective work teams.** *SAM Advanced Management Journal, 58*(1), 22-27.

Effective project teams are characterized by task factors such as timely performance, staying within budget, and achievement of quality, and by relationship factors such as conflict resolution, trust, and communication. Group dynamics that can derail a team are: different points of view, role conflict, implicit power struggles, and groupthink. A strategy for development of effective teams is selecting team members with good interpersonal skills and offering additional communication skills training.
Subject(s): Team-based performance, project management

Odenwald, S. (1996). **Global work teams.** *Training & Development, 50*(2), 54-57.

Leading global teams requires a unique combination of skills. In this article team leaders from international companies list the competencies they believe are necessary, including physical stamina; a sense of humor; excellent interpersonal skills; a tolerance for ambiguity; and loyalty to family, country, and organization. The author uses examples from Egypt and China to further describe the challenges of global teams and discusses the role of HR in forming and maintaining these teams.
Subject(s): Geographically dispersed teams

New

Sessa, V. I., Hansen, M. C., Prestridge, S., & Kossler, M. E. (1999). *Geographically dispersed teams: An annotated bibliography.* Greensboro, NC: Center for Creative Leadership.

Geographically dispersed teams are work groups whose members are separated by time and distance. This bibliography summarizes what the current literature has to say about how these teams should be formed, developed, and led. A discussion of the key themes in the literature is followed by over 80 annotations of books, journals, and World Wide Web resources. Includes title and author indexes.
Subject(s): Geographically dispersed teams

New

Stewart, G. L., Manz, C. C., & Sims, H. P. (1999). *Team work and group dynamics.* New York: John Wiley.

This book uses an input-process-output framework to understand teams, arguing that successful teams must be effective at each level. A team's input is its design, including its leadership, goals, and composition. Processes include development, socialization, conflict, and continuing leadership behaviors. Finally, output concerns the effectiveness of a team, which can be defined in a number of ways: productivity, member satisfaction, or team viability. An organization must decide how to determine team effectiveness and what a team's potential is before it can try to improve team performance. Nine case studies are used to illustrate these concepts. Includes index.
Subject(s): Teamwork, group dynamics

Torres, C. (1994). *The Tao of teams: A guide to team success.* San Diego, CA: Pfeiffer.

The *Tao Te Ching*, an ancient Chinese philosophy, inspired this collection of poetic images. Applied to teamwork this philosophy teaches self-knowledge and respect for others. Aligning with forces of the universe, the negative yin and the positive yang, allows teams to accept change as a natural event. Eighty-one passages reinforce lessons on trust, flexibility, diversity, intuition, power, and conflict resolution. Includes bibliographical references.
Subject(s): Team characteristics, Eastern philosophy

Wilson, J. M., George, J., Wellins, R. S., & Byham, W. C. (1994). *Leadership trapeze: Strategies for leadership in team-based organizations.* San Francisco: Jossey-Bass.

The authors, who all work for the human resources trainer Development Dimensions International, acknowledge that leading teams can be as scary as flying on a trapeze. Part One of this book describes how the roles of leaders are changing as more companies shift to a team system, and includes case studies and flow charts to illustrate the new model. Part Two is prescriptive, detailing a course of action, complete with discussion plans and self-checks, for managers in team situations and for organizations hoping to support their team leaders.
Subject(s): Team-based performance

ORGANIZATIONAL LEADERSHIP

New

Argyris, C., & Schon, D. A. (1996). *Organizational learning II: Theory, method, and practice.* Reading, MA: Addison-Wesley.

Organizational learning literature tends to be either practical, prescriptive, and uncritical or scholarly and distant from practice. These two branches of study are typically isolated from each other, but Argyris and Schon identify four key questions about organizational learning that cross the boundaries: 1) why is an organization a good learning venue; 2) in what ways are real-world organizations capable of learning; 3) among the kinds of organizational learning, which ones are desirable; and 4) how can organizations develop their capacity for learning? This book attempts to answer these questions for both branches of study by addressing defensive reasoning, interventions, and consultation. Includes references and indexes.
Subject(s): Organizational learning

New

Bain, A. (1998). Social defenses against organizational learning. *Human Relations, 51*(3), 413-429.

All organizations have defenses, or unconsciously created ideas and rituals that protect the organization and the people in it from anxiety created by carrying out the organization's purpose. But while protective, these defenses can also prevent organizational learning from occurring. The author of this study examined three organizations—a British computer firm, a British nursery school, and an Australian prison—and identified five factors that can overcome defenses and lead to organizational learning: 1) a primary task; 2) project ownership; 3) leadership, authority, and roles; 4) individual, group, and organizational interdependence; and 5) reflection and learning spaces. Includes bibliographical references.
Subject(s): Organizational learning

Bass, B. M., & Avolio, B. J. (Eds.). (1994). *Improving organizational effectiveness through transformational leadership.* Thousand Oaks, CA: Sage.

In 1985 Bernard Bass presented a theory of transformational leadership that employed four behaviors: idealized influence, inspirational motivation, intellectual stimulation, and individualized consideration. In this book, ten years later, leadership theorists discuss the application of the transformational theory in real organizations. They address the issues of delegation, culture, teams, decision making, quality, and human resources practices. Includes bibliographical references and index.
Subject(s): Organizational leadership, transformational leadership

New

Beugre, C. D. (1998). *Managing fairness in organizations.* Westport, CT: Quorum Books.

Beugre defines organizational justice as "perceptions of fair treatment within organizations." This subjective term is an important aspect of employee performance within organizations and affects the sense of community. This source begins by discussing theories of distributive justice, or the "perceived fairness of the distribution of outcomes." Several models and theories of procedural justice relating to distribution of rewards in an organization are detailed in the second chapter. Chapter Three compares interactional justice with procedural justice, and variables influencing perceptions of justice are analyzed in Chapters Four and Five. Chapter Six depicts the reactions of employees to organizational justice, and the conclusion offers suggestions for creating fair organizations. Includes bibliographical references and index.
Subject(s): Organizational justice

Bolman, L. G., & Deal, T. E. (1997). *Reframing organizations: Artistry, choice, and leadership* (2nd ed.). San Francisco: Jossey-Bass.

The authors of *Modern Approaches to Understanding and Managing Organizations* (1984) have written again about enriched managerial thinking. From a large and complex body of leadership theory they present a simple four-frame model for understanding organizations. The structural frame is a factory with a task-oriented structure, rules, and goals. The human resource frame is a family in which relationships are most important. The political frame is a jungle where power and conflict reign supreme. The symbolic frame is a temple filled with culture, rituals, heroes, and inspiration. Learning to look through multiple lenses, or reframing, allows managers to broaden their repertoire. New to the second edition are: discussions of organizational structure in response to technology and the global economy; a new chapter on the relationship among ethics, soul, and spirit in organizations; and a new case that explores the reframing process in action. Includes bibliographical references and index.
Subject(s): Organizational leadership

Brion, J. M. (1996). *Leadership of organizations: The executive's complete handbook.* Greenwich, CT: JAI Press.

This three-volume set may be used by practitioners or students who want to learn about leadership, executive ability, and organizational behavior. Volume 1 contains information on the social aspects: the human factor, learning, behavior, values, motivation, appraisal, and management by objectives. Volume 2 covers technical issues: power, communication, participation, decision making, planning, structure, and the human resources department. Volume 3 is about integrating the first two: change, leadership roles and responsibilities, leadership training and development, managing conflict, justice, and problem solving. All subjects are treated with overviews of major theories as well as practical suggestions for implementation. Charts and models throughout support the text. Appendices include summaries and questions to clarify the lessons in each volume. An extensive bibliography, a name index, and a subject index are in Volume 3.

Subject(s): Organizational leadership, textbook

New
Bruce, R., & Wyman, S. (1998). *Changing organizations: Practicing action training and research.* Thousand Oaks, CA: Sage.

> Bruce and Wyman apply the work of Neely Gardner, an organization development pioneer, to the current state of changing organizations. Gardner devised a model to develop changing organizations in the late 1960s. This methodology is termed *action training and research* and was created for the purpose of allowing each employee to be a trainer and change agent in a changing organization. Part one presents the history behind action training and research. The remainder of the book devotes one chapter to each of the 12 stages in this model. The strategic, decision-making research phase consists of the first half of the cycle, including: orientation, contract setting, reconnaissance/exploring the issue, identifying problems and opportunities, aspirations, and action options. The change-implementation action phase of this model consists of experimentation, experiment results analysis, program design, implementation, program evaluation, and recycling. Includes bibliographical references.

Subject(s): Organizational change

New
Buchanan, D., & Badham, R. (1999). **Politics and organizational change: The lived experience.** *Human Relations, 52*(5), 609-629.

> Most literature on organizational change tends to ignore political behavior or discount its legitimacy, but political activity is an integral and inevitable part of organizational life. This article analyzes interviews with five British managers from business and educational organizations to determine how change agents use politics in their everyday interactions. The authors conclude that political behavior is an accepted part of change efforts; that it can serve organizational as well as personal goals; and that even if specific behaviors seem unacceptable, political actions are usually defensible in context. Includes bibliographical references.

Subject(s): Organizational change

Carlopio, J. R. (1994). **Holism: A philosophy of organizational leadership for the future.** *Leadership Quarterly: Special Issue: Leadership for Environmental and Social Change, 5*(3/4), 297-307.

> As organizations struggle to adapt to an increasingly chaotic, globally interdependent society, traditional leadership

philosophies are being rewritten. Carlopio suggests that the time is right for a holistic approach to leadership. This approach gives equal credence to whole organizations and the individuals within. Like the yin and the yang, holistic leadership depends on the balance of seemingly diverse yet actually connected forces: making a profit and serving the community, leaders who are really supporters, and employees who are empowered decision-makers. The Body Shop is described as an example of a holistic organization.

Subject(s): Holistic leadership

New
Casey, C. (1999). **"Come, join our family": Discipline and integration in corporate organizational culture.** *Human Relations, 52*(2), 155-178.

> Organizations increasingly try to integrate employees into a corporate culture that formulates the organization as a team or family. This is typically seen as a reaction against the controlling, bureaucratic organizations of the past, but Casey says that enforcing a team or family culture is simply another way of controlling employees. She conducted field research at a large multinational corporation and describes the anxiety and ambivalence that the team culture created among employees. Ultimately, Casey argues that this new corporate culture allows management to achieve integration, compliance, and control, while making it difficult for workers to rebel against a system that seems to empower them. Includes bibliographical references.

Subject(s): Organizational culture

New
Clegg, S. R., Hardy, C., & Nord, W. R. (Eds.). (1999). *Managing organizations: Current issues.* London: Sage.

> The 1996 *Handbook of Organization Studies* offered a comprehensive look at organizations with a primary audience of researchers. In 1999 the book was split into two paperback volumes to better address the needs of practicing managers. Volume I, *Studying Organizations*, focuses on theoretical issues, while this volume contains writings on more practical management problems. Karl Weick contributes a chapter on organizational learning, and other issues addressed include decision making in organizations, communication and groups, technology and structuring, and innovation. Includes bibliographical references and index.

Subject(s): Organizational leadership

New
Conner, D. R. (1998). *Leading at the edge of chaos: How to create the nimble organization.* New York: Wiley.

> A nimble organization is one that views change not as a one-time event but as an ongoing process. These organizations succeed by implementing organizational change more effectively and efficiently than their competitors, and success often depends on an organization's leadership. Leaders in all organizations respond to change with one of six different leadership styles: 1) anti-change, 2) rational, 3) panacea,

4) bolt-on, 5) integrated, and 6) continuous. While none of these styles is wrong, nimble leaders should be aware of which style their organization needs and apply that method for the best results. Whatever the style, leading "nimbly" always requires resilience and flexibility. Conner also emphasizes the importance of "human due diligence," or paying careful attention to the needs of people during organizational change. Appendices describe the adaptation mechanism and "the people side of realignment initiatives" in depth. Includes bibliography and index.
Subject(s): Organizational change, chaos

New
Crossan, M. M., Lane, H. W., & White, R. E. (1999). **An organizational learning framework: From intuition to institution.** *Academy of Management Review, 24*(3), 522-537.

This article presents a framework for organizational learning as a dynamic process. The framework includes four I's in the learning process: intuiting, interpreting, integrating, and institutionalizing. The I's create a tension and dynamic movement among three levels: individual, group, and organizational. Feeding forward begins at the individual level. This process of learning through intuition and interpretation is deemed to be learning by exploration. Feeding back begins at the organizational level. Such learning by institutionalization is called learning by exploitation. When the process begins at the group level—learning by integration—the dynamic feeds forward and back simultaneously. The authors suggest that this framework provides a holistic approach to organizational learning. Includes bibliographical references.
Subject(s): Organizational learning, intuition

New
Deal, T. E., & Kennedy, A. A. (1999). *The new corporate cultures: Revitalizing the workplace after downsizing, mergers, and reengineering.* Reading, MA: Perseus Books.

The American workplace has changed since Deal and Kennedy began writing about corporate culture 20 years ago. Downsizing, outsourcing, and mergers have created a corporate environment of fear and cynicism. The authors say that people in organizations still naturally form communities that establish identity and meaning, but that the new corporate culture consists of smaller subcultures that develop away from formal organizational structures. Managers in today's workplace must use "cultural leadership" to unite these informal identity groups and motivate workers. Exercising cultural leadership involves eliminating fear in an organization, creating a code of conduct based on ethical beliefs, and connecting an organization's formal institutions to its existing informal subcultures. Includes bibliographical references and index.
Subject(s): Organizational culture

New
Deal, T. E., & Key, M. K. (1998). *Corporate celebration: Play, purpose, and profit at work.* San Francisco: Berrett-Koehler.

Ritual and ceremony create a shared sense of significance among people. This book examines that principle at work in organizations. Celebrating triumphs and marking milestones link people to the meaning and joy in their work. Rituals provide comfort during times of hardship. Succession rites bring closure and ease transitions. All forms of corporate celebration help to mold a corporate culture and reinforce corporate values. And best of all, the authors state, a sense of play energizes employees to take pride in doing good work, which benefits the workforce, the customers, the bottom line, and the stockholders. Includes bibliographical references and index.
Subject(s): Organizational culture

New
DiBella, A. J., & Nevis, E. C. (1997). *How organizations learn: An integrated strategy for building learning capability.* San Francisco: Jossey-Bass.

DiBella and Nevis researched seven companies, including Motorola and Fiat Auto, and used their findings to develop tools that help organizations build learning capacity. This book describes those tools, beginning with a review of the literature on learning organizations and then describing ten Facilitating Factors, practices or conditions that must be present for organizational learning to occur. These include a concern for measurement, organizational curiosity, continuous education, and involved leadership. The authors also describe how firms can conduct an "organizational learning profile" and use the results to improve their learning capacity. Includes references and index.
Subject(s): Organizational learning

New
Eggert, N. J. (1998). *Contemplative leadership for entrepreneurial organizations: Paradigms, metaphors, and wicked problems.* Westport, CT: Quorum Books.

"Wicked problems" in organizations are those recurring, insidious tangles of contradictions that are so difficult to solve—balancing family pressures and work demands, meeting customers' future needs and focusing on past successes, assimilating technological change and maintaining core values. Eggert suggests a mindshift to deal with these problems. She employs the medieval German mystic Meister Eckhart as a guide to the contemplative process. Meister's alternative ways of thinking, perceiving, inquiring, valuing, and acting suggest a new style of leadership. Contemplative leaders are: 1) lucid—facing all situations without illusion; 2) attentive—radically aware, sensitive, and mindful; 3) vulnerable—open to life's challenges; and 4) disciplined—maintaining an environment of freedom and openness. Includes bibliographical references and index.
Subject(s): Organizational leadership

New
Finstad, N. (1998). **The rhetoric of organizational change.** *Human Relations, 51*(6), 717-740.

Although organizational change is generally viewed as a rational/functional process, Finstad says that it is often rhetoric and symbolism that define a change process. Case studies of four Norwegian municipal service offices illustrate four kinds of rhetoric that can induce change: monocratic, opportunistic, anarchical, and professional. Finstad says that organizations that take advantage of both the formal, planned aspects of change and its informal, rhetorical systems in their change efforts will have the most success. Includes bibliographical references.
Subject(s): Organizational change

New
Friedman, S. D., Christensen, P., & DeGroot, J. (1998). **Work and life: The end of the zero-sum game.** *Harvard Business Review, 76*(6), 119-129.

The authors draw on their expertise in work and life balance at the University of Philadelphia Wharton School's Work/Life Project and Roundtable and in human resources strategy at Merck & Company. They explain the three principles that create an organizational culture that is win-win for employees and employers. First, both parties must clarify their priorities. Second, employers must see and support their employees as whole people, celebrating their lives outside the office. Third, employers must be flexible about work processes, valuing productivity over face time.
Subject(s): Organizational culture

New
Fritz, R. (1999). *The path of least resistance for managers: Designing organizations to succeed.* San Francisco: Berrett-Koehler.

Fritz bases his arguments on how to restructure organizations on three principles: 1) energy moves along the path of least resistance, 2) the underlying structure of anything determines this path, and 3) we can change the path of least resistance by creating new structures. This follow-up to Fritz's *The Path of Least Resistance* describes how leaders can design their organizations to avoid oscillation, how to use structural tension to progress, and how to create checklists to measure advancement. Includes a foreword by Peter Senge and an index.
Subject(s): Organizational leadership

New
Goffee, R., & Jones, G. (1998). *The character of a corporation: How your company's culture can make or break your business.* New York: HarperCollins.

This book presents a framework for understanding corporate culture at the team, departmental, and organizational levels. The Double S Cube plots the concepts of sociability and solidarity around four basic cultural forms: networked, mercenary, fragmented, and communal. Each option is a positive or negative force, depending on the competitive environment and the life cycle of the organization. Because several cultures may coexist in any organization, the authors explain how to maximize the strengths of each type and purposely move from one to another. There are several tests for determining culture type and suggestions for making changes. Includes bibliographical references and index.
Subject(s): Organizational culture

Greenberg, J. (1996). *Managing behavior in organizations: Science in service to practice.* Upper Saddle River, NJ: Prentice Hall.

This is a textbook for undergraduate, MBA, and executive students of organizational behavior. Greenberg reviews organizational behavior theories and their relevance to actual organizational practices. The 12 chapters cover: historical background, psychology and social perception, motivation, job satisfaction, organizational culture, communication and influence, group dynamics, leadership, decision making, organizational structure, change, and today's challenges. Each contains explanations of major theories and their application, an example of best practice in a major company, a brief self-assessment, a group exercise, and a case study. Personal name, company name, and subject indexes are included.
Subject(s): Organizational leadership, textbook

Guns, B. (1996). *The faster learning organization: Gain and sustain the competitive edge.* San Diego, CA: Pfeiffer.

Guns has developed a model for a faster learning organization (FLO), specifically one that learns more quickly than its competitors. He describes how an organization can become a FLO by simultaneously implementing three strategies: "surge learning" around a few key points, cultivating human resources, and transforming the organizational environment into one that challenges and supports faster learning. Examples from Xerox, Toyota, and NASA, as well as charts, pictures, and cartoons, illustrate the concepts. This book is part of the Warren Bennis Executive Briefing Series.
Subject(s): Organizational learning

New
Haeckel, S. H. (1999). *Adaptive enterprise: Creating and leading sense-and-respond organizations.* Boston: Harvard Business School Press.

In the postindustrial business environment successful organizations sense incoming information and respond rapidly. Their adaptability to unpredictable, discontinuous change is purposeful. This sense-and-respond style is based on theories of systems and complexity with a recognition of the human element in organizations. Haeckel explains the role of organizational leadership in developing such adaptive social systems. IBM's Advanced Business Institute is presented as a case study. Appendices describe more examples of sense-and-respond organizations at work. Includes bibliographical references and index.
Subject(s): Organizational change

New
Halal, W. E. (Ed.). (1998). *The infinite resource: Creating and leading the knowledge enterprise.* San Francisco: Jossey-Bass.

The editor of this source equates the current information revolution with the long-ago industrial revolution. Halal presents various viewpoints of consultants, academics, and executives to "make a clearer path through today's economic jungle." These views are presented in this three-part book complete with an overview written by Halal. Part One is titled "Creating the Internal Enterprise System." This section depicts the change of organizational design from hierarchy to internal enterprises and includes case studies to exemplify the authors' views. "Network of Cooperative Alliances" is the focus of the second section. The ideal presented here is the strategic combination of cooperation and dynamic enterprise. The final section, "Leveraging Knowledge with an Intelligent Infrastructure," recommends a high level of organizational intelligence to "manage this infinite power of revolutionary knowledge." Halal concludes with a table summarizing the importance of cooperation, enterprise, and knowledge to assist in this rapidly changing age of information. Includes bibliographical references and index.
Subject(s): Organizational leadership, knowledge management

Handy, C. (1995). *Gods of management: The changing work of organizations.* New York: Oxford University Press.

This is an updated version of Handy's 1978 classic management book of the same name. The author describes four organizational cultures as represented by four gods from Greek mythology. An organization led by Zeus has a club culture, one that is defined by functions or products. An organization led by Apollo has a culture of rules and order. Athena is task oriented and manages through the continuous and successful solution of problems. Dionysus rules the existential organization where cooperation and consensus prevail. Handy suggests that managers understand the four cultures for two reasons. First, to be most effective they should work in organizations that match their personal preferences. Second, the work of management requires a full battery of styles to apply in different situations. Includes bibliographical references and index.
Subject(s): Organizational culture

New
Hendry, J. (1999). **Cultural theory and contemporary management organization.** *Human Relations, 52*(5), 557-577.

This article applies Mary Douglas's theory of culture to business organizations in order to show how conflicts within corporate cultures affect business operations. Douglas argued that a matrix of grid and group control created three distinct cultural types: hierarchical societies, market societies, and sects. Most corporations began as hierarchical organizations, but the downsizings, delayerings, and outsourcings of the 1980s and 1990s have shifted many firms to a more market-based culture. A cognitive conflict exists between these two

cultures, and the author says that business leaders run into problems when they use hierarchical management methods on a workforce operating in a market society. One possible solution is for organizations to actively encourage the group loyalty and vision common in sects, and to integrate those elements into the newly developing market culture. Includes bibliographical references.
Subject(s): Organizational culture

New
Herman, R. E., & Gioia, J. L. (1998). **Making work meaningful: Secrets of the future-focused corporation.** *Futurist, 32*(9), 24-38.

Today's workers want "meaning in their work and balance in their lives," and companies hoping to succeed in the new marketplace must develop a meaningful corporate culture. To do this companies must first create meaningful work in which employees make an impact, are responsible for outcomes, and get meaningful rewards. At the same time companies must also create meaningful organizations that help employees balance work and family, allow for both personal and professional growth, and display corporate social responsibility. The article also lists "seven skills for meaningful workers": technical and technological skills, visionary skills, numbers and measurement, ability to organize, persuasive skills, communication skills, and ability to learn.
Subject(s): Organizational culture

Hersey, P., Blanchard, K. H., & Johnson, D. E. (1996). *Management of organizational behavior: Utilizing human resources* (7th ed.). Upper Saddle River, NJ: Prentice Hall.

Almost 30 years ago this book was introduced to help managers, parents, teachers, human resource professionals, and students to understand behavioral science. Each chapter has been revised for this new edition and there is increased focus on the issues of quality and the international dimension of management. Chapters discuss theories in management, motivation, group dynamics, and leadership with heavy emphasis on situational leadership. Blanchard's concept of the one-minute manager is recapped. Charts throughout each chapter compare different theories as well as simplify and summarize the lessons. Includes bibliographical references and index.
Subject(s): Organizational leadership

Hesselbein, F., Goldsmith, M., & Beckhard, R. (Eds.). (1997). *The organization of the future.* San Francisco: Jossey-Bass.

Thirty-eight leadership and organization scholars and practitioners share their thoughts on the future of American business organizations. Chapters include: "How Generational Shifts Will Transform Organizational Life" by Jay Conger; "Will the Organization of the Future Make the Mistakes of the Past?" by Jeffrey Pfeffer; "The Circular Organization" by Frances Hesselbein; "The Mondragon Model: A New Pathway for the Twenty-first Century" by Joel Barker; "Restoring People to the Heart of the Organization of the

Future" by Rosabeth Moss Kanter; "Competitiveness and Civic Character" by Philip Kotler; "Creating Sustainable Learning Communities for the Twenty-first Century" by Stephanie Pace Marshall; "Self-Esteem in the Information Age" by Nathaniel Branden; "Leading Across Cultures: Five Vital Capabilities" by John Alexander and Meena Wilson; and "The Next Challenge" by Chris Argyris. Includes index.
Subject(s): Organizational leadership

New
Hickman, G. R. (Ed.). (1998). *Leading organizations: Perspectives for a new era.* Thousand Oaks, CA: Sage.

Organizational leadership can be conceptualized as a framework in which external changes in the environment are analyzed and incorporated into the organizational context. Leaders in this framework must help organizational participants create a vision that will help the organization move toward its mission and contribute to society. In this book Hickman has collected writings by leading scholars that address elements of this framework, such as leadership authenticity in organizational culture, structure, social responsibility, and leader-participant relationships. Contributors include Warren Bennis, Larraine Matusak, Jay Conger, Robert Greenleaf, Max DePree, and John Kotter. Includes bibliographical references and index.
Subject(s): Organizational leadership

Hirschhorn, L. (1997). *Reworking authority: Leading and following in the post-modern organization.* Cambridge, MA: MIT Press.

Hirschhorn uses the term "post-industrial" to signify an era of technological and economic change and the term "post-modern" to signify recent changes in organizational climates and work relationships. Individuals are relying more on personal authority than hierarchical authority. The benefit is that individuals bring more ideas, feelings, and values to their jobs. The problem is that individuals lack respect for those in positional power. Hirschhorn recommends building a culture of openness to encourage risk-taking, forgive failures, stimulate creativity, and establish a sense of community. Includes bibliographical references and index.
Subject(s): Organizational leadership

New
Huber, G. P. (1998). **Synergies between organizational learning and creativity and innovation.** *Creativity and Innovation Management, 7*(1), 3-8.

Huber says that "an organization learns when, through its processing of information, it increases the probability that its future actions will lead to its improved performance." This learning can occur through three modes: sensing, experiential learning, and vicarious organizational learning. Huber also argues that creativity is a critical part of organizational learning that leaders must encourage in order to reap the full benefits of innovation in the organization. Information-rich environments contribute to both learning and creativity,

making communication and information-sharing key factors in any organizational learning effort. Includes bibliographical references.
Subject(s): Organizational learning, creativity

New
Hurst, D. K. (1995). *Crisis and renewal: Meeting the challenge of organizational change.* Boston: Harvard Business School Press.

This book is for leaders of mature organizations that face instability, crisis, or decay. It explains how to renew the founding values and emotional commitment that created and grew an organization in its early years. The Bushman hunters of the Kalahari Desert provide an example of organizational evolution. Leaving their nomadic hunting society behind for a more settled farming society led to breakdowns in communication, bureaucracy, and near extinction. The desertion of their core values mirrors changes that are taking place in modern organizations. Ecological examples illustrate a similar type of decay in nature followed by rebirth. This natural evolutionary process forms a model of organizational ecocycle. Stories of real-world corporate crises and renewal support the model. Includes bibliographical references and index.
Subject(s): Renewal

New
Hutchens, D., & Gombert, B. (Illustrator). (1998). *Outlearning the wolves: Surviving and thriving in a learning organization.* Waltham, MA: Pegasus Communications.

This illustrated fable follows a flock of sheep with a powerful vision. They dream of a life without threat from wolves. However, if they maintain the status quo, wolf attacks will be inevitable. Their only chance to achieve their dream is to learn how to learn together as an organization. After challenging their existing beliefs, communicating innovative ideas, and sharing knowledge, the sheep develop a new awareness of their situation and new capabilities to deal with it. Only then are they able to outsmart the wolves and enjoy their dream come true. Includes a discussion guide to help readers apply the organizational learning concept to the workplace.
Subject(s): Organizational learning, fables

New
Hutchens, D., & Gombert, B. (Illustrator). (1999). *Shadows of the Neanderthal: Illuminating the beliefs that limit our organization.* Waltham, MA: Pegasus Communications.

Loosely based on "The Allegory of the Cave" (Plato, c. 387 B.C.), this illustrated fable follows Boogie, the caveman, as he questions his old mental model and explores a new world. Boogie marvels at the colors of the landscape, the diversity of life forms, the food, and the fun to be found outside the security of his old familiar cave. A seer of truth introduces the concept of many truths and mental models, which starts Boogie on the road to evolution. A discussion guide helps

readers apply the fable's lessons in creative ability and organizational learning to the workplace.
Subject(s): Organizational learning, fables

Kets de Vries, M. F. R. (1995). *Life and death in the executive fast lane: Essays on irrational organizations and their leaders.* San Francisco: Jossey-Bass.

Organizational leaders have two roles to fill—the charismatic role that envisions, empowers, and energizes, and the instrumental role that structures the organization and rewards followers. Each leader brings with him his past, his inner needs, conflicts, and dreams. Kets de Vries explains how leaders influence corporate culture with their distinctive personal styles. CEO succession, downsizing, mergers, international assignments, gender issues, family businesses, and bad bosses all add to the complexity of leadership style and its effect on corporate culture. Includes bibliographical references and index.
Subject(s): Organizational leadership, negative views of leadership

New
Kirkman, B. L., Lowe, K. B., & Young, D. P. (1999). *High-performance work organizations: Definitions, practices, and an annotated bibliography.* Greensboro, NC: Center for Creative Leadership.

This annotated bibliography serves two purposes for readers. First is the task of defining high-performance work organizations, which have received much attention but lack a concrete definition. The authors combine existing concepts into the dimensions of self-managing work teams, employee participation, total quality management, integrated production technologies, and the learning organization. Following a discussion of these dimensions are 168 annotated citations representing available literature on the high-performance work organization and, more specifically, the five dimensions mentioned above. Includes author and title indexes.
Subject(s): Organizational leadership

Lawler, E. E. (1996). *From the ground up: Six principles for building the new logic corporation.* San Francisco: Jossey-Bass.

Lawler uses examples from major companies, including Procter & Gamble, United Airlines, and IBM, to illustrate his belief that organizations should be based on six principles: 1) organization is the ultimate competitive advantage, 2) involvement is the most effective source of control, 3) all employees must add significant value, 4) lateral processes are the key to organizational effectiveness, 5) organizations should be designed around products and customers, and 6) effective leadership is the key to organizational effectiveness. Chapters address the issues of teams, rewards, communication and measurement, and human resources. Includes bibliographical references and index.
Subject(s): Organizational leadership

New
Longanbach, P. (1998). **Results management: Learning can do it.** *The Public Manager, 27*(2), 25-28.

As the demand for government accountability grows, more public leaders are turning to management-for-performance, which links individual performance to organizational goals. The balanced scorecard is one technique managers can use to encourage learning and improve performance. This article explains how to apply the balanced scorecard to government agencies, and describes how the Department of Transportation used this method to measure its procurement functions and human resource management. Includes bibliographical references.
Subject(s): Organizational learning, balanced scorecard

New
Making it happen: Stories from inside the new workplace. (1999). Waltham, MA: Pegasus Communications.

This is a collection of 16 articles from *The Systems Thinker* newsletter. In each is the story of one learning organization's efforts to implement large-scale change. Their experiences include successes, failures, and lessons learned. They describe tools and methods such as causal loop diagrams, systems archetypes, stock and flow diagrams, simulation modeling, Human Dynamics, and dialogue. One story is about Ford Motor Company's Leadership Process Office and Organizational Learning Team. Their efforts built important new formal and informal networks internally and externally, encouraged employee participation in planning, and fostered commitment rather than compliance.
Subject(s): Learning organizations, storytelling

New
Miles, R. E., Snow, C. C., Mathews, J. A., Miles, G., & Coleman, H. J. (1997). **Organizing in the knowledge age: Anticipating the cellular form.** *Academy of Management Executive, 11*(4), 7-24.

This article explains organizational eras and their typical forms. The Era of Standardization, seen in early functional organizations, is based on hierarchies and mass production. The Era of Early Customization represents divisional and diversified companies. The authors assign the term Matrix Organization to explain the organizational form used in those two eras. More recently, a Network Organization form has emerged in response to an increased demand for service and knowledge. The authors claim that the immediate future will bring the Era of Innovation and the Cellular Organizational form. This article details the characteristics of the new form and describes two organizations that already demonstrate Cellular characteristics. Includes bibliographical references and an executive commentary.
Subject(s): Organizational leadership

Morgan, G. (1997). *Images of organization* (2nd ed.). Thousand Oaks, CA: Sage.

Morgan visualizes organizations as metaphors and uses these characterizations to understand organizations' structures, how they identify problems, and how they implement solutions. Metaphors are used to describe organizations as machines, organisms, cultures, political systems, instruments of domination, and psychic prisons. The second edition includes an expanded section on the implications for practice and how readers can use "metaphor to negotiate the demands of a paradoxical world." Includes bibliographical references and index.

Subject(s): Organizational systems

Nadler, D. A., Shaw, R. B., Walton, A. E., & Associates. (1995). *Discontinuous change: Leading organizational transformation.* San Francisco: Jossey-Bass.

Over a ten-year period the authors have noted increased efforts at organizational change and shifts in the type of change desired. They share their experiences and observations for the benefit of executives who are responsible for large-scale changes, consultants who work with these executives, and students of change theory and practice. This book provides a framework for recognizing the need for change before a crisis erupts, the types of change and action strategies to deal with them, and the methods to build the leadership capability for a change-capable organization. Includes bibliographical references and index.

Subject(s): Organizational change

Natemeyer, W. E. (1978). *Classics of organizational behavior.* Oak Park, IL: Moore.

As stated in the title, this volume is a classic. From Maslow on motivation to Hersey and Blanchard on the life-cycle theory, this book is a foundational presentation of organizational behavior. The 32 individual essays and articles are some of those we see over and over again. It is nice to have them all in one volume. Includes bibliographical references.

Subject(s): Organizational leadership

New
The new workplace: Transforming the character and culture of our organizations. (1998). Waltham, MA: Pegasus Communications.

Compiled from *The Systems Thinker* newsletter, the articles in this anthology describe how traditional, hierarchical organizations can be transformed into learning communities that benefit the individual, the organization, and the larger society. The writings address three themes: rethinking the purpose of work, creating new concepts in leadership, and envisioning and building learning communities. Contributors include Arie de Geus, Peter Senge, and Edgar Schein. Includes bibliographical references.

Subject(s): Organizational learning, systems in organizations

Nirenberg, J. (1997). *Power tools: A leader's guide to the latest management thinking.* New York: Prentice Hall.

Nirenberg wrote this book for managers who are tired of quick fixes that promise to solve organizational problems but don't. In an overview of management fads and common

wisdom he synthesizes management thinking into a few basic principles. He describes, in depth, seven management techniques and tools that evolved from customized solutions for unique problems: self-managing work teams, systems thinking, quality, reengineering, authentic communication, a Japanese management model, and a new business paradigm influenced by technology and changing work roles. Nirenberg provides a framework to help the reader determine the most appropriate tool or technique for his or her own organization. At the end of the book an annotated compendium describes more than 100 tools and techniques. Includes bibliographical references and index.

Subject(s): Management theories

New
O'Reilly, K. W. (Ed.). (1995). *Managing the rapids: Stories from the forefront of the learning organization.* Cambridge, MA: Pegasus Communications.

Originally published in *The Systems Thinker* newsletter, the articles in this collection describe innovators who have created "a new paradigm of business based on systems thinking and the other emerging disciplines of the learning organization." Eleven organizations are profiled including Ford, Digital Equipment Corporation, Georgia Power Company, and the San Jose Medical Center. The profiles focus on three aspects of innovation: surfacing mental models and shifting assumptions, creating large-scale change, and scenario planning and policy testing. Includes bibliographical references.

Subject(s): Organizational learning

New
Organizational learning at work: Embracing the challenges of the new workplace. (1998). Waltham, MA: Pegasus Communications.

These articles from *The Systems Thinker* newsletter represent theory and practice in the field of organizational learning. Daniel Kim's article argues that systemic theory lays a foundation for practical matters such as achieving organizational success. In a traditional flat model key factors combine to yield success. However, Kim's loop perspective illustrates the dynamics that create positive changes and reinforce success. Other articles describe the benefit of opposing values, the importance of processes, and the implementation of best practices. Includes bibliographical references.

Subject(s): Learning organizations, systems theory

New
Ostroff, F. (1999). *The horizontal organization: What the organization of the future looks like and how it delivers value to customers.* New York: Oxford University Press.

Organizations have traditionally been structured as a vertical hierarchy, which too often results in overspecialization, turf wars, and top-down management. Ostroff offers an alternative to the vertical structure, saying that horizontal organizations are "capable of responding to today's diverse

challenges." These organizations focus on core processes, make the teams the central work unit, integrate with customers, encourage multiskilling, and use information technology intensively. This book describes horizontal organizations and how they work, and then identifies the three stages in building one: setting direction, formulating design, and institutionalizing the approach. Includes index.
Subject(s): Organizational leadership

New
Pasternack, B. A., & Viscio, A. J. (1998). *The centerless corporation: A new model for transforming your organization for growth and prosperity.* New York: Fireside.

The authors describe a new strategy for managing organizations in turbulent times, in which accountability and responsibility are decentralized, knowledge management is key, and the "people power" of employees is considered a prime resource. In this model the organization coheres around a core of knowledge and leadership, which allows for more flexibility and faster change than the hierarchical central management setup of traditional organizations can provide. The final chapter offers specific steps leaders can take to change the content of their work, change the structure of the organization, develop a shared vision, and prepare employees for change. Includes bibliographical references and index.
Subject(s): Organizational leadership

New
Purser, R. E., & Cabana, S. (1998). *The self managing organization: How leading companies are transforming the work of teams for real impact.* New York: Free Press.

Organizations still entrenched in bureaucratic beliefs need to change their design systems in order to compete in the current society. Purser and Cabana argue this point in their book and promote an entirely self-managed organization. Written particularly for executives and managers to implement fundamental change, this source is intended as a toolbox to assist in building a foundation of self-managing work groups. The two parts of the book approach self-managing organizations from both the concepts and the implementation. In part one the self-managing organization is exemplified and differentiated from traditional models. Also, the participative design method is discussed. Part two delineates the methods and techniques needed to successfully redesign an organization. Case studies are presented to demonstrate the two methods of participative design and search conference. Finally, Purser and Cabana discuss the changing role of management in this new organizational system. Includes bibliographical references.
Subject(s): Organizational leadership

New
Rajan, A. (1998). **Awakening the knack for knowledge creation and exchange.** *efmd FORUM, 98*(3), 44-50.

Rajan says that knowledge management is "leveraging existing knowledge inside an organisation and creating new knowledge in the process," or the process of turning individual knowledge into organizational knowledge. Preserving an organization's wisdom is becoming more and more important as companies continue to lose corporate memory because of delayering and downsizing. This article identifies key elements of knowledge management systems, including enabling technology, performance management, and people practices. Rajan then describes the values and behaviors needed to develop an effective system, which include tolerance, trust, reciprocity, role models, and direction.
Subject(s): Organizational leadership, knowledge management

Redding, J. (1997). **Hardwiring the learning organization.** *Training & Development, 51*(8), 61-67.

Redding describes the use of instruments to measure an organization's potential for learning. He advises on the steps of the assessment process: defining the reason for assessment, selecting the right tool, administering the instrument, developing an organizational strategy to building learning capabilities, and planning learning initiatives. A chart provides brief information on 21 instruments, their learning focus, administration, and source information. The article includes references to several books that describe learning initiatives already in place in companies and government agencies.
Subject(s): Organizational learning

Ritti, R. R. (1998). *The ropes to skip and the ropes to know: Studies in organizational behavior* (5th ed.). New York: Wiley.

This book is useful to organizational newcomers. Its 55 allegorical stories and cautionary tales demonstrate in a narrative fashion the "real" things that happen to managers and employees in organizations. Ritti offers insights about the unwritten protocols that exist in all organizations. These protocols about how people behave are never found in staff procedures manuals or company histories. Ritti sees survival and success in any organization as being dependent upon the ability of a person to read the invisible definitions to which the organization subscribes. Includes bibliographical references.
Subject(s): Organizational culture, fables

New
Rollins, T., & Roberts, D. (1998). *Work culture, organizational performance, and business success: Measurement and management.* Westport, CT: Quorum Books.

Although there are conflicting definitions of work culture, Rollins and Roberts advocate it as a combination of behavior, shared assumptions, and values among people in organizations. This source presents findings supporting the notion that work culture influences organizational performance, and serves to evaluate methods of measuring and managing work cultures. The first portion of the book links work culture with a successful business. Chapter Three contains HayGroup's

four cultural models: 1) functional, 2) process driven, 3) time based, and 4) network. The following three chapters present a literature review of employee surveys and measurement data including case studies. The final chapter discusses the implications of work cultures, organizational change, and work culture measurements. Includes bibliographical references and appendices.
Subject(s): Organizational culture

New
Rosinski, P. (1998). **Constructive politics: Essential to leadership.** *Leadership in Action*, *18*(3), 1-5.

Rosinski defines constructive organizational politics as building and exercising one's power in order to achieve meaningful goals in service to an organization. Leaders fall into four political types: 1) the individual achiever—low power and low service, 2) the prince—high power and low service, 3) the idealist—low power and high service, and 4) the builder—high power and high service. To build power one needs an external network, internal allies, and a source of knowledge. To develop a service orientation one must listen, share, care, and build trust and respect. Includes bibliographical references.
Subject(s): Organizational politics

Schein, E. H. (1992). *Organizational culture and leadership* (2nd ed.). San Francisco: Jossey-Bass.

This updated version deletes some original chapters, expands others, and includes new materials on the culture concept. There is increased emphasis on the leadership-culture relationship. New chapters explore subgroup culture, the role of the founder, and the impact of information technology. Schein discusses organizations in midlife and turnaround periods of changing culture. This volume is intended to be a supplement to, not a replacement of, the original. Includes bibliographical references and index.
Subject(s): Organizational culture

Schein, E. H. (1996). **Three cultures of management: The key to organizational learning.** *Sloan Management Review*, *38*(1), 9-20.

While many people have talked about the importance of organizational culture, Schein argues that every organization contains three distinct cultures—the community of executives, of engineers, and of day-to-day operators. Schein believes that most organizations cannot effectively learn and move forward because these cultures work against, not with, each other. This article describes each culture and its assumptions, and the implications of these differences. Schein also briefly outlines a plan for creating dialogue and cooperation across an organization's cultures. Includes bibliographical references.
Subject(s): Organizational culture, organizational learning

New
Schruijer, S. G. L., & Vansina, L. S. (1999). **Leadership and organizational change: An introduction.** *European Journal of Work and Organizational Psychology*, *8*(10), 1-8.

Schruijer and Vansina say that the purpose of this special issue is to review current and new research developments on the theme of leadership and organizational change. They cite two major reasons for the increased interest in leadership over the past two decades: increased turbulence in society and the need of individuals to define their identities as leaders or followers. The articles in this issue address some important issues developing in this field, including when transformational leaders are wanted, the context an individual leader operates in, and dependency versus empowerment. Includes bibliographical references.
Subject(s): Organizational change

New
Senge, P., Kleiner, A., Roberts, C., Ross, R., Roth, G., & Smith, B. (1999). *The dance of change: The challenges of sustaining momentum in learning organizations.* New York: Doubleday/Currency.

This resource book, which complements *The Fifth Discipline* (1990), identifies four challenges in organizational change: getting started, initiating change, sustaining transformation, and redesigning and rethinking. The authors describe how managers can overcome such common problems as not having enough time, fear and anxiety about change, and assessing and measuring change. Solo and team exercises as well as recommended books and websites accompany the discussion of each challenge. Includes index.
Subject(s): Organizational learning, change

Senge, P. M. (1990). *The fifth discipline: The art and practice of the learning organization.* New York: Doubleday/Currency.

Successful organizations tap people's commitment and capacity to learn at all levels. Senge teaches the theory and techniques of team learning. A team using interactive dialogue can achieve greater results than any one individual effort. At the same time, each individual on the team learns and grows beyond his or her ability to do so alone. Senge also teaches the theory and technique of systems thinking, and the ability to see a vision and to implement the forces necessary to get there. A learning organization fosters reciprocal commitment between individual and organization. Includes bibliographical references and index.
Subject(s): Organizational learning

Senge, P. M., Roberts, C., Ross, R. B., Smith, B. J., & Kleiner, A. (1993). *The fifth discipline fieldbook: Strategies and tools for building a learning organization.* New York: Currency/Doubleday.

Senge, Director of the Center for Organizational Learning at the MIT Sloan Business School of Management, first introduced his theory of learning organizations in *The Fifth Discipline* (1990). Based on that theory Senge, his coauthors, and 67 contributors have organized a collection of tools, methods, stories, ideas, exercises, and resources into a fieldbook for businesses, schools, community agencies, or any organizations wishing to overcome their learning disabilities. This fieldbook is intended to be written in during meetings, conflicts, or whenever ideas occur. Cross-references, margin icons, and an index help the reader easily access topics of current interest.

Subject(s): Organizational learning

New
Shamir, B. (1999). **Leadership in boundaryless organizations: Disposable or indispensable?** *European Journal of Work and Organizational Psychology*, *8*(10), 49-71.

How does the emergence of boundaryless, "post-bureaucratic" organizations affect the role of leadership in organizations? Shamir describes a number of weak leadership scenarios, such as collective leadership or teleleadership, but he says that leadership in boundaryless organizations should be expanded, not weakened. He says that the new challenge for leaders is to act as both agents of change and centers of gravity in continuously changing organizations, and that a form of identity-based leadership may best achieve this. Includes bibliographical references.

Subject(s): Organizational leadership

New
Snyder, W. M., & Cummings, T. G. (1998). **Organization learning disorders: Conceptual model and intervention hypothesis.** *Human Relations*, *51*(7), 873-895.

The authors identify four stages of organizational learning—discovery, invention, production, and generalization—but say that most organizations have "learning disorders" that block these processes. They identify a number of specific disorders, including blindness, simplemindedness, paralysis, superstition, and amnesia, and describe how they affect organizational knowledge. The article concludes with hypotheses about how various interventions can resolve organizational learning disorders. Includes bibliographical references.

Subject(s): Organizational learning

Stacey, R. D. (1996). *Complexity and creativity in organizations.* San Francisco: Berrett-Koehler.

Complexity, a field of study that has developed from the chaos theory, describes systems that "operate in an intermediate phase between stability and instability." Stacey believes that this also describes human organizations, and he has developed a new complex model of organizational behavior, which he compares to the traditional model. His book describes the science of complexity in depth, shows how complexity can be "mapped onto" organizations, and discusses the implications that the complexity theory may have for organizations. Examples from the European Technology Transfer Committee and companies including British chemical company Enigma illustrate the complex

ideas. Includes references, index, and a glossary of terms.

Subject(s): Organizational leadership, complexity, creativity, chaos

New
Strati, A. (1998). **Organizational symbolism as a social construction: A perspective from the sociology of knowledge.** *Human Relations*, *51*(11), 1379-1402.

Strati says that organizational symbolism, unlike other management research, is not based in practice or meant to produce real-world management strategies. Instead it is an "emergent and fluctuating" academic field that examines the "construction of organizational reality through the negotiation of symbolic universes." Specifically, Strati describes how these universes are constructed; the importance of planning in symbolism; and the power of myths, beliefs, and language. Organizational symbolism is described as "pluri-disciplinary," using a variety of approaches to develop a new way of studying organizations. Includes bibliographical references.

Subject(s): Organizational culture, sociological perspective

New
Tomer, J. F. (1998). **Organizational capital and joining-up: Linking the individual to the organization and to society.** *Human Relations*, *51*(6), 825-846.

Because the interests of individual employees often differ from those of their organizations, many employees act in ways that are suboptimal to the organization. Tomer combines economic and organizational behavior theories to suggest that organizations can optimize employees' performances by improving the "joining-up" process. Joining up occurs when the worker and company form a relationship, and employees who are both psychologically and financially committed to an organization will be more likely to display "organizationally responsible behavior." The ideal joining-up process links the individual not only to the company but to society as a whole. Includes bibliographical references.

Subject(s): Organizational leadership

New
Van der Krogt, F. J. (1998). **Learning network theory: The tension between learning systems and work systems in organizations.** *Human Resource Development Quarterly*, *9*(2), 157-177.

Although many organizations today are turning away from traditional training and toward the concept of learning, little theory on the structure of learning systems exists. This article offers the learning network theory, which conceives of an organization as "a network of actors who interact" and shape the organization's approach to "learning problems and the organization of learning processes." Learning networks typically focus on both the development of human potential and the development of the work process, sometimes leading to a tension between the organization's needs for humanity

and work relevance. The author suggests four themes for future research in this field: actors, action theories, and tactics; the quality of learning systems; problem diagnosis by actors; and comparative research in network participation. Includes bibliographical references.
Subject(s): Organizational learning

New
Webber, A. M. (1999). **Learning for a change.** *Fast Company*, *24*, 178-188.

In this interview Peter Senge discusses "what we've learned about learning" in the ten years since *The Fifth Discipline* was published and talks about his new book, *The Dance of Change*. Senge describes why organizational change has proved so difficult and how companies can successfully implement change initiatives. The article includes a timeline of the development of learning-organization concepts and Senge's list of the ten "challenges of change."
Subject(s): Organizational learning

Weick, K. E. (1995). *Sensemaking in organizations.* Thousand Oaks, CA: Sage.

Weick describes sense-making as "a developing set of ideas with explanatory possibilities," rather than a body of established knowledge, to understand the complexities and ambiguities of life. Weick draws heavily on the research of organizational theorists to introduce the concept of sense-making in organizations. Analysis of scholarly discussion reveals the concept's seven distinguishing characteristics. Sense-making is: 1) grounded in identity construction, 2) retrospective, 3) enactive of sensible environments, 4) social, 5) ongoing, 6) focused on and extracted by cues, and 7) driven by plausibility rather than accuracy. Understanding the framework of sense-making can enable leaders to deal with complexity, ambiguity, surprise, discrepancy, emergency, or excess information. Includes bibliographical references, author index, and subject index.
Subject(s): Organizational leadership, sense-making

Wheatley, M. J., & Kellner-Rogers, M. (1996). *A simpler way.* San Francisco: Berrett-Koehler.

The authors, who research nature and human nature and their influence on organizational development, share their unique philosophy about life-giving organizational forms. "There is

a simpler way to organize human endeavor. It requires a new way of being in the world. . . Being in the world with play and creativity. . . Being willing to learn and to be surprised." They believe that leadership evolves from how people agree to be together and behavior is rooted in these agreements. Photographs and poetry supplement the message in this optimistic book. Includes bibliographical references and index.
Subject(s): Organizational leadership

Yukl, G. A. (1998). *Leadership in organizations* (4th ed.). Upper Saddle River, NJ: Prentice Hall.

The focus of this textbook is managerial leadership of formal organizations. A balanced presentation of application and theory helps leaders deal with their immediate challenges and understand the concepts behind the methods. This new edition emphasizes leadership effectiveness and highlights guidelines for improving effectiveness throughout. There are new and expanded chapters on team leadership, change, strategic leadership, followership, distributed leadership, influence process, and developing leadership. Thirty-three cases of actual and modified business situations support the lessons. Includes extensive bibliographical references and author and subject indexes.
Subject(s): Organizational leadership, textbook

New
Zohar, D. (1997). *Rewiring the corporate brain: Using the new science to rethink how we structure and lead organizations.* San Francisco: Berrett-Koehler.

Zohar applies her expertise in physics and philosophy to business life for those who "manage at the edge." The first lesson is that organizations must nurture three kinds of intelligence: mental, emotional, and spiritual. The second lesson contrasts eight principles of old science—Newtonian assumptions of order and predictability—with eight principles of new science—quantum mechanics, relativity, chaos, and complexity theories. The result is a new model for organizational structure, leadership, and learning that thrives on uncertainty and releases the potential of all members. Working models in several European companies demonstrate the power of new science applied to organizational leadership. Includes bibliographical references and index.
Subject(s): Organizational leadership, complexity, chaos

JOURNALS AND NEWSLETTERS

The leadership journals and newsletters described in this section are frequently browsed for articles included in the bibliography. They range from scholarly journals that report cutting-edge research to magazines that are a source of book synopses and conference notices. This list is intended to help educators build a leadership library and to help authors identify appropriate publishers for new articles. Following each description is information about:

• frequency of publication
• sponsoring organization
• subscription address
• phone, fax, e-mail, and website
• subject

New
THE ACADEMY OF MANAGEMENT EXECUTIVE

This journal seeks to stimulate new ways of thinking about managing and leading. In collaboration with the *European Management Journal*, the column *Crosstalk* engages scholars from around the world in a dialogue on management research and practice. Also includes articles, book reviews, and research summaries. AoM also publishes *The Academy of Management Review* with articles on theory development and *The Academy of Management Journal* with articles that reflect the research and application interests of AoM members.

Frequency: Quarterly
Sponsoring Organization: Academy of Management
Subscription Address: Pace University, P.O. Box 3020, 235 Elm Road, Briarcliff Manor, NY 10510-2256
Phone: (914) 923-2607
Fax: (914) 923-2615
E-mail: academy@aom.pace.edu
Website: www.aom.pace.edu
Subject(s): Corporate leadership

ACROSS THE BOARD

This magazine supports the Conference Board's goal to improve the business enterprise system and to enhance the contribution of business to society. It includes book reviews and a Manager's Tool Kit section that introduces new books and technology.

Frequency: Ten times a year
Sponsoring Organization: The Conference Board
Subscription Address: 845 Third Avenue, New York, NY 10022-6679
Phone: (212) 759-0900
Fax: (212) 980-7014
E-mail: atb@conference-board.org
Website: www.conference-board.org
Subject(s): Corporate leadership

ADMINISTRATIVE SCIENCE QUARTERLY

Dissertation research and other fresh scholarly views in organization studies are published in this peer-reviewed journal, which also sponsors the ASQ Award for Scholarly Contribution. Includes book reviews and annual author and title indexes.

Frequency: Quarterly
Sponsoring Organization: Johnson Graduate School of Management at Cornell University
Subscription Address: 20 Thornwood Drive, Suite 100, Ithaca, NY 14850-1265
Phone: (607) 254-7143
Fax: (607) 254-7100
E-mail: asq_journal@cornell.edu
Website: www.johnson.cornell.edu/ASQ/asq.html
Subject(s): Organizational leadership

CALIFORNIA MANAGEMENT REVIEW

This journal aims to serve as a bridge between those who study management and those who practice it. Each year, the Andersen Consulting Award is given to the author(s) of the article judged to have made the most important contribution to improving the practice of management.

Frequency: Quarterly
Sponsoring Organization: Haas School of Business at the University of California
Subscription Address: S549 Haas School #1900, Berkeley, CA 94720-1900
Phone: (510) 642-7159
Fax: (510) 642-1318
E-mail: cmr@haas.berkeley.edu
Website: www.haas.berkeley.edu/cmr
Subject(s): Corporate leadership

CONCEPTS AND CONNECTIONS

Each issue of this thematic newsletter spotlights a successful campus leadership course or program. Leadership education as a discipline is examined through surveys of practice, historical context, standards and guidelines, updates on new research, funding ideas, conference notices, and book reviews.

Frequency: Several times per year
Sponsoring Organization: National Clearinghouse for Leadership Programs
Subscription Address: 1135 Stamp Student Union, University of Maryland, College Park, MD 20472-7174
Phone: (301) 405-0799
Fax: (301) 314-9634
E-mail: nclp@union.umd.edu
Website: www.inform.umd.edu/OCP/NCLP
Subject(s): Leadership education

New
CREATIVITY AND INNOVATION MANAGEMENT

This peer-reviewed journal aims to examine practical experiences against an emerging body of theory in the field of creativity and innovation. The contributors are primarily members of the European Association for Creativity and Innovation, but a global approach and multicultural issues are encouraged.

Frequency: Quarterly
Subscription Address: Blackwell Publishers, Inc., 350 Main Street, Malden, MA 02148
Phone: (781) 388-8200
Fax: (781) 388-8210
E-mail: jnlinfo@blackwellpublishers.co.uk
Website: www.blackwellpublishers.co.uk
Subject(s): Creativity

THE DIVERSITY FACTOR

New ideas about diversity in organizations are presented in this journal, which offers case studies, best practices, and articles on current societal issues. Includes book reviews and information about other training resources.

Frequency: Quarterly
Subscription Address: P.O. Box 3188, Teaneck, NJ 07666-9104
Phone: (201) 833-0011
Fax: (201) 833-4184
E-mail: sdlevitt@aol.com
Website: www.diversitymetrics.com/tdf
Subject(s): Diversity

EDUCATIONAL LEADERSHIP

This magazine is intended for leaders in K through 12 education but may be helpful to all who are interested in curriculum development and supervision in schools. Includes book and website reviews, announcements, and Portfolio—a showcase of images that inspire, amuse, or provoke.

Frequency: Eight times per year
Sponsoring Organization: Association for Supervision and Curriculum Development
Subscription Address: 1703 North Beauregard Street, Alexandria, VA 22311-1714
Phone: (800) 933-2723 x2 or (703) 578-9600
Fax: (703) 575-5400
E-mail: el@ascd.org
Website: www.ascd.org
Subject(s): Educational leadership

New
EUROPEAN JOURNAL OF WORK AND ORGANIZATIONAL PSYCHOLOGY

Each issue of this journal examines a specific concern for practicing organizational psychologists. A combination of professional and academic responses assures practical and theoretical coverage of each topic. Includes book reviews and professional news.

Frequency: Quarterly
Sponsoring Organization: European Association of Work and Organizational Psychology
Subscription Address: Psychology Press, Ltd., 27 Church Road, Hove, East Sussex, BN3 2FA UK
Phone: 44(0)1273 207411
Fax: 44(0)1273 205612
E-mail: information@psypress.co.uk
Website: www.psypress.co.uk
Subject(s): Corporate leadership

EXECUTIVE EXCELLENCE

Executive Excellence promotes personal and organizational leadership based on constructive values, sound ethics, and timeless principles. Leading authors contribute brief articles that are often summaries of newly released books. Includes additional brief book reviews.

Frequency: Monthly
Subscription Address: Executive Excellence Publishing, 1344 East 1120 South, Provo, UT 84606-6379
Phone: (800) 300-3454
Fax: (801) 356-8213
E-mail: custserv@eep.com
Website: www.eep.com
Subject(s): Corporate leadership, self-development

FAST COMPANY

Geared to a new generation of business people, the articles in *Fast Company* have a fresh focus on social justice and workplace democracy. Topics include leadership, personal success, change, and learning.

Frequency: Ten times per year
Subscription Address: Subscriptions, P.O. Box 52760, Boulder, CO 80328-2760
Phone: (800) 688-1545 or (303) 604-1465
E-mail: subscriptions@fastcompany.com
Website: www.fastcompany.com
Subject(s): Corporate leadership, social responsibility

New
GROUP & ORGANIZATION MANAGEMENT

This peer-reviewed journal presents new concepts and reviews of existing literature with recommendations for future research. Topics include leadership, strategic management, group process, communication, and organizational development.

Frequency: Quarterly
Sponsoring Organization: Eastern Academy of Management
Subscription Address: Sage Publications, Inc., 2455 Teller Road, Thousand Oaks, CA 91320-2234
Phone: (805) 499-0721
Fax: (805) 499-0871
E-mail: order@sagepub.com
Website: www.sagepub.com
Subject(s): Team leadership, organizational leadership

HARVARD BUSINESS REVIEW

HBR is written for professional managers. In addition to essays on improving business functions, there are stories on the human side of management. Includes book reviews, cartoons, case studies, and an annual index. Comprehensive indexes are published periodically.

Frequency: Bimonthly
Sponsoring Organization: Harvard Business School
Subscription Address: Harvard Business School Publishing, 60 Harvard Way, Boston, MA 02163-1000
Phone: (800) 274-3214 or (617) 783-7410
Fax: (617) 783-7493

E-mail: hbr_editorial@hbsp.harvard.edu
Website: www.hbsp.harvard.edu
Subject(s): Corporate leadership

HRMAGAZINE

This magazine aims to support the work of the human resource management profession. A regular feature is HR Pulse, a call-in survey on a hot topic and results of the previous month's survey. The website adds new material each month to supplement the topics covered in the printed issue.

Frequency: Monthly
Sponsoring Organization: Society for Human Resource Management
Subscription Address: 1800 Duke Street, Alexandria, VA 22314-3499
Phone: (703) 548-3440
Fax: (703) 535-6490
E-mail: hrmag@shrm.org
Website: www.shrm.org/hrmagazine
Subject(s): Human resources managers

HUMAN RELATIONS

This peer-reviewed journal is based on the belief that social scientists in all fields should integrate their work in order to understand the complexities of human problems. Papers are on theoretical developments, qualitative and quantitative data, presentation of new methods, empirical research, and book reviews. Includes an annual index.

Frequency: Monthly
Sponsoring Organization: The Tavistock Institute
Subscription Address: Sage Publications, Inc., 2455 Teller Road, Thousand Oaks, CA 91320-2234
Phone: (805) 499-0721
Fax: (805) 499-0871
E-mail: order@sagepub.com
Website: www.sagepub.com
Subject(s): Social perspective

HUMAN RESOURCE DEVELOPMENT QUARTERLY (HRDQ)

HRDQ is a peer-reviewed journal of the American Society for Training and Development and the Academy of Human Resource Development. It links HRD theory and application from the fields of economics, education, management, and psychology. Includes book reviews and an annual index.

Frequency: Quarterly
Sponsoring Organization: American Society for Training and Development (ASTD) and Academy of Human Resource Development
Subscription Address: Jossey-Bass Inc., Publishers, 350 Sansome Street, San Francisco, CA 94104-1342
Phone: (800) 956-7739 or (415) 433-1740
Fax: (800) 605-2665 or (415) 433-0499
E-mail: subinfo@jbp.com

Website: www.jbp.com/journals.html
Subject(s): Human resources development

New
HUMAN RESOURCE MANAGEMENT

This peer-reviewed journal aims to advance the field of human resources with articles that build theory and improve practice through research. Each issue focuses on a theme such as work and family, 360-degree feedback, global leadership, and exemplary practices. Includes interviews, book reviews, and annual index.

Frequency: Quarterly
Subscription Address: Wiley Interscience, 605 Third Avenue, New York, NY 10158-0012
Phone: (212) 850-6645
Fax: (212) 850-6021
E-mail: subinfo@wiley.com
Website: www.interscience.wiley.com
Subject(s): Human resources development

New
THE INDUSTRIAL-ORGANIZATIONAL PSYCHOLOGIST (TIP)

TIP is the publication of the Society for Industrial and Organizational Psychology, Inc., a division of the American Psychological Association. Included are articles, conference announcements, calls for papers, and job listings. The October 1999 issue reports on the annual SIOP member survey on the future of the field.

Frequency: Quarterly
Sponsoring Organization: Society for Industrial and Organizational Psychology, Inc. (SIOP)
Subscription Address: 745 Haskins Road, Suite D, P.O. Box 87, Bowling Green, OH 43402-0087
Phone: (419) 353-0032
Fax: (419) 352-2645
E-mail: lhakel@siop.bgsu.edu
Website: www.siop.org
Subject(s): Psychology of leadership

New
INTERNATIONAL JOURNAL OF INTERCULTURAL RELATIONS

This peer-reviewed journal is dedicated to advancing theory, practice, and research in intergroup relations. Articles cover such topics as field-based evaluations of training techniques, discussions of cultural diversity, and discussions of new training approaches. Includes an annual index.

Frequency: Quarterly
Sponsoring Organization: Academy for International Research
Subscription Address: Elsevier Science, P.O. Box 945, New York, NY 10159-0945
Phone: (888) 437-4636 or (212) 633-3730
Fax: (212) 633-3680

E-mail: usinfo-f@elsevier.com
Website: www.elsevier.com
Subject(s): Multicultural diversity

New
JOURNAL OF BUSINESS AND PSYCHOLOGY

This peer-reviewed journal publishes articles, case studies, and reports of empirical research about psychological concepts in business. Topics include personnel selection and training and organizational assessment and development.

Frequency: Quarterly
Sponsoring Organization: Business Psychology Research Institute
Subscription Address: Kluwer Academic/Human Sciences Press, Inc., 233 Spring Street, New York, NY 10013-1578
Phone: (800) 221-9369 or (212) 620-8468
Fax: (212) 807-1047
E-mail: kluwer@wkap.com
Website: www.wkap.nl/journalhome.htm/0889-3268
Subject(s): Psychology of leadership

New
THE JOURNAL OF CREATIVE BEHAVIOR

The diversity in creativity studies is reflected in this journal. There are case studies of people who exhibit extraordinary creative ability and ordinary people who apply creativity to solving everyday problems. Other articles present research reports and philosophical frameworks on the manifestation of creativity in business, education, science, and society.

Frequency: Quarterly
Sponsoring Organization: The Creative Education Foundation
Subscription Address: 1050 Union Road, Buffalo, NY 14224-3402
Phone: (716) 675-3181
Fax: (716) 675-3209
E-mail: cefhq@cef-cpsi.org
Website: www.cef-cpsi.org
Subject(s): Creativity

New
JOURNAL OF CROSS-CULTURAL PSYCHOLOGY

This journal features articles on the interrelationships between culture and psychological processes. Research reports compare the thinking and behavior of individuals of different ethnicities, from various nations, and across Eastern and Western cultures. Includes an annual index.

Frequency: Bimonthly
Sponsoring Organizations: Center for Cross-Cultural Research, Department of Psychology, Western Washington University, and the International Association for Cross-Cultural Psychology
Subscription Address: Sage Publications, Inc., 2455 Teller Road, Thousand Oaks, CA 91320-2234
Phone: (805) 499-0721

Fax: (805) 499-0871
E-mail: order@sagepub.com
Website: www.sagepub.com
Subject(s): Multicultural diversity

THE JOURNAL OF LEADERSHIP STUDIES

Aimed at those who teach, study, or practice leadership, this peer-reviewed journal includes examples of curriculum, teaching techniques, suggestions for evaluation, and articles on trends in leadership education. Includes book reviews and annual author, title, and subject indexes.

Frequency: Quarterly
Sponsoring Organization: Baker College Center for Graduate Studies
Subscription Address: 1050 West Bristol Road, Flint, MI 48507-5508
Phone: (810) 766-4105
Fax: (810) 766-4399
E-mail: Journal@Baker.edu
Website: www.baker.edu/departments/leadership/jls-main.htm
Subject(s): Leadership education

New
JOURNAL OF SCHOOL LEADERSHIP

This journal examines educational administration from theoretical and practical perspectives. Articles are on topics such as staff development, innovative programs, partnerships, and research applications.

Frequency: Bimonthly
Subscription Address: Scarecrow Press, Inc., 4720 Boston Way, Lanham, MD 27076
Phone: (800) 462-6420 or (717) 794-3800
Fax: (800) 338-4551 or (717) 794-3803
Website: www.scarecrowpress.com
Subject(s): Educational leadership

New
JOURNAL OF STAFF DEVELOPMENT

This magazine supports NSDC's mission to support professional learning opportunities for teachers, principals, and school administrators. Concise articles report on effective development programs and practices. Every issue focuses on a subject, such as program design, teacher leadership, assessment and measurement, and school standards.

Frequency: Quarterly
Sponsoring Organization: National Staff Development Council (NSDC)
Subscription Address: P.O. Box 240, Oxford, OH 45056
Phone: (800) 727-7288 or (513) 523-6029
Fax: (513) 523-0638
E-mail: nsdcoffice@aol.com
Website: www.nsdc.org
Subject(s): Educational leadership

LEADER TO LEADER

This publication from the Peter F. Drucker Foundation focuses on leadership development and organizational change. Peter Drucker and Frances Hesselbein contribute to most issues. Other articles are written by prominent authors, often summarizing newly released books. Includes annual author and subject indexes.

Frequency: Quarterly
Sponsoring Organization: Peter F. Drucker Foundation
Subscription Address: Jossey-Bass Inc., Publishers, 350 Sansome Street, San Francisco, CA 94104-1342
Phone: (800) 956-7739 or (415) 433-1740
Fax: (800) 605-2665 or (415) 433-0499
E-mail: subinfo@jbp.com
Website: www.jbp.com/journals.html
Subject(s): Leadership development, organizational change

LEADERSHIP IN ACTION

This newsletter aims to help practicing leaders and those who train and develop practicing leaders. It provides them with insights gained from the Center for Creative Leadership's educational and research activities. It is also a forum for the exchange of ideas between practitioners and CCL staff and associates.

Frequency: Bimonthly
Sponsoring Organization: Center for Creative Leadership (CCL)
Subscription Address: Jossey-Bass Inc., Publishers, 350 Sansome Street, San Francisco, CA 94104-1342
Phone: (800) 956-7739 or (415) 433-1740
Fax: (800) 605-2665 or (415) 433-0499
E-mail: subinfo@jbp.com
Website: www.jbp.com/journals.html
Subject(s): Leadership development

LEADERSHIP INSIGHTS

This newsletter is for community leaders in Georgia and across the nation. Articles discuss leadership issues in general and Georgia-based leadership programs specifically. There are ideas for civic groups, extension programs, and youth leadership.

Frequency: Three times per year
Sponsoring Organization: J. W. Fanning Institute for Leadership at the University of Georgia
Subscription Address: 1234 South Lumpkin Street, Athens, GA 30602-3552
Phone: (706) 542-1108
Fax: (706) 542-7007
E-mail: information@fanning.uga.edu
Website: www.fanning.uga.edu
Subject(s): Community leadership

A LEADERSHIP JOURNAL: WOMEN IN LEADERSHIP —SHARING THE VISION

This peer-reviewed journal contains articles on practical applications for, and current research of interest to, women leaders. Contributing authors are from the academic, corporate, and government sectors around the world. Includes book reviews.

Frequency: Twice per year
Sponsoring Organization: The Leadership Institute at Columbia College
Subscription Address: P.O. Box 3815, 1301 Columbia College Drive, Columbia, SC 29230-3815
Phone: (803) 786-3729
Fax: (803) 786-3806
Website: www.colacoll.edu/leadinst/journal.html
Subject(s): Women's leadership

LEADERSHIP QUARTERLY: AN INTERNATIONAL JOURNAL OF POLITICAL, SOCIAL AND BEHAVIORAL SCIENCE

This peer-reviewed journal is dedicated to advancing theory, research, and applications concerning leadership. Contributors are from many disciplines, and each issue offers diverse perspectives or comparative studies. Includes an annual index.

Frequency: Quarterly
Sponsoring Organization: Institute for Leadership Research
Subscription Address: Elsevier Science, Inc., P.O. Box 945, New York, NY 10010-0945
Phone: (888) 437-4636 or (212) 633-3730
Fax: (212) 633-3680
E-mail: usinfo-f@elsevier.com
Website: www.ilr.ba.ttu.edu/lq.htm
Subject(s): Leadership research

New

MANAGEMENT LEARNING: THE JOURNAL FOR MANAGERIAL AND ORGANIZATIONAL LEARNING

This peer-reviewed journal focuses on four themes: the nature of management learning and learning organizations, the learning process, learning outcomes, and the cultural and ethical issues of learning. Includes in-depth book reviews and an annual index.

Frequency: Quarterly
Subscription Address: Sage Publications, Inc., 2455 Teller Road, Thousand Oaks, CA 91320-2234
Phone: (805) 499-0721
Fax: (805) 499-0871
E-mail: order@sagepub.com
Website: www.sagepub.com
Subject(s): Learning competency, organizational learning

New
MONASH MT. ELIZA BUSINESS REVIEW

This journal for managers in the Asian Pacific region is published by the faculty at Monash Mt. Eliza Business School, and includes articles from thought leaders from around the world. Its focus is on innovations in global leadership. Each issue includes articles, case studies, and book reviews.

Frequency: Several times per year
Sponsoring Organization: Monash Mt. Eliza Business School
Subscription Address: P.O. Box 2224, Caulfield Junction, Victoria 3161 Australia
Phone: 61 3 9215 1177
Fax: 61 3 9572 3691
E-mail: klindsey@monashmteliza.edu.au
Website: www.monashmteliza.edu.au/services/publications/index.html
Subject(s): Global leadership

NONPROFIT MANAGEMENT & LEADERSHIP

This peer-reviewed journal is sponsored by the Mandel Center for Nonprofit Organizations at Case Western Reserve University and the Centre for Voluntary Organisation at the London School of Economics and Political Science. The papers emphasize human resources, resource development, financial management, change, and organizational effectiveness. Winter and summer issues feature case studies of ethical and strategic dilemmas.

Frequency: Quarterly
Sponsoring Organizations: Mandel Center for Nonprofit Organizations at Case Western Reserve University and the Centre for Voluntary Organisation at the London School of Economics and Political Science
Subscription Address: Jossey-Bass Inc., Publishers, 350 Sansome Street, San Francisco, CA 94104-1342
Phone: (800) 956-7739 or (415) 433-1740
Fax: (800) 605-2665 or (415) 433-0499
E-mail: subinfo@jbp.com
Website: www.jbp.com/journals.html
Subject(s): Nonprofit leadership

NONPROFIT WORLD: THE NATIONAL NONPROFIT LEADERSHIP AND MANAGEMENT JOURNAL

This journal is dedicated to building a strong network of professionals in the nonprofit world. The articles discuss funding, legal issues, staff development, and governance. A catalog lists books, videos, and software.

Frequency: Bimonthly
Sponsoring Organization: The Society for Nonprofit Organizations
Subscription Address: 6314 Odana Road, Suite 1, Madison, WI 53719-1141
Phone: (800) 424-7367 or (608) 274-9777
Fax: (608) 274-9978

E-mail: snpo@danenet.wicip.org
Website: danenet.wicip.org/snpo
Subject(s): Nonprofit leadership

NSEE QUARTERLY

This newsletter seeks to advance the understanding of experiential education theory and practice. Contributing authors are from all educational levels as well as from business, government, and nonprofit sectors. There is a calendar of opportunities for professional development.

Frequency: Quarterly
Sponsoring Organization: National Society for Experiential Education (NSEE)
Subscription Address: 1703 North Beauregard Street, Alexandria, VA 22311-1714
Phone: (703) 933-0017
Fax: (603) 250-5852
E-mail: info@nsee.org
Website: www.nsee.org/quarter.htm
Subject(s): Experiential education

ORGANIZATIONAL DYNAMICS: A QUARTERLY REVIEW OF ORGANIZATIONAL BEHAVIOR FOR PROFESSIONAL MANAGERS

Leading-edge thought and research in the fields of organizational behavior and organization development are examined in this peer-reviewed journal. Each issue features a case study describing a company in the process of change and a field report that presents new research. Includes book reviews.

Frequency: Quarterly
Sponsoring Organization: American Management Association International
Subscription Address: P.O. Box 319, Saranac Lake, NY 12983-0319
Phone: (800) 313-8650 or (518) 891-5510
Fax: (518) 891-0368
E-mail: cust_serv@amanet.org
Website: www.amanet.org/periodicals/od
Subject(s): Organizational leadership

PHI DELTA KAPPAN

This periodical contains articles concerned with educational research, service, and leadership. Regular features address federal and state education policies, legal issues, and new technology.

Frequency: Ten times per year
Sponsoring Organization: Phi Delta Kappan International, Inc.
Subscription Address: P.O. Box 789, 408 North Union, Bloomington, IN 47402-0789
Phone: (800) 766-1156 or (812) 339-1156
Fax: (812) 339-0018
E-mail: kappan@kiva.net

Website: www.pdkintl.org/kappan/kappan.htm
Subject(s): Educational leadership

PUBLIC ADMINISTRATION REVIEW

This journal features articles on public administration from local to global levels. Many articles are concerned with ethical issues, diversity, reform, and leadership. Includes book reviews and annual author and subject indexes.

Frequency: Bimonthly
Sponsoring Organization: American Society for Public Administration
Subscription Address: 1120 G Street, N.W., Suite 700, Washington, DC 20005-3885
Phone: (202) 393-7878
Fax: (202) 638-4952
E-mail: info@aspanet.org
Website: www.aspanet.org
Subject(s): Public service leadership

New
REFLECTIONS: THE SOL JOURNAL ON KNOWLEDGE, LEARNING, AND CHANGE

Reflections is focused on the interdisciplinary field of organizational learning. Research reports, learning histories, reflection pieces, and case studies in each issue examine knowledge and skills—how they are generated, disseminated, and utilized.

Frequency: Quarterly
Sponsoring Organization: The Society for Organizational Learning (SOL)
Subscription Address: MIT Press Journals, Five Cambridge Center, Cambridge, MA 02142-1407
Phone: (617) 253-2889
Fax: (617) 577-1545
E-mail: journals-orders@mit.edu
Website: http://mitpress.mit.edu/SOL
Subject(s): Organizational learning

RESEARCH TECHNOLOGY MANAGEMENT

This journal discusses management issues for technical industries such as aerospace, automotive, chemical, computer, and electronics. Articles are on standards, innovation, business issues, government policy, and global cooperation. Includes book reviews. Some articles are available on audiotape.

Frequency: Six times per year
Sponsoring Organization: Industrial Research Institute, Inc.
Subscription Address: Sheridan Press, P.O. Box 465, Hanover, PA 17331-0465
Phone: (202) 296-8811
Fax: (202) 776-0756
E-mail: vallarta@iriinc.org
Website: www.iriinc.org/RTM.htm
Subject(s): Technical leaders

THE SERVANT LEADER

This newsletter focuses on the Greenleaf Center's work in servant leadership. Articles describe how companies apply the philosophy to practice and improve their bottom lines. Educators share ideas for teaching servant leadership. Includes book reviews, conference notices, and other learning resources.

Frequency: Twice per year
Sponsoring Organization: The Robert K. Greenleaf Center for Servant Leadership
Subscription Address: 921 East 86th Street, Suite 200, Indianapolis, IN 46240
Phone: (317) 259-1241
Fax: (317) 259-0560
E-mail: greenleaf@iquest.net
Website: www.greenleaf.org
Subject(s): Servant leadership

SIMULATION & GAMING: AN INTERNATIONAL JOURNAL OF THEORY, PRACTICE, AND RESEARCH

This journal publishes original activities and reviews of board games, computer simulations, role plays, and other active learning products. There are research-based, empirical, and conceptual essays on the use of simulation and gaming in the classroom—often for the business classroom. Includes an annual index.

Frequency: Quarterly
Sponsoring Organizations: Association for Business Simulation and Experiential Learning (ABSEL), International Simulation and Gaming Association (ISAGA), Japan Association of Simulation and Gaming (JASAG), and North American Simulation and Gaming Association (NASAGA)
Subscription Address: Sage Publications, Inc., 2455 Teller Road, Thousand Oaks, CA 91320-2234
Phone: (805) 499-0721
Fax: (805) 499-0871
E-mail: order@sagepub.com
Website: www.sagepub.com
Subject(s): Simulation as a training technique

New
STRATEGY & LEADERSHIP

Articles in *Strategy & Leadership* offer practical information on strategy development and implementation.

Frequency: Bimonthly
Sponsoring Organization: Strategic Leadership Forum
Subscription Address: 435 North Michigan Avenue, Suite 1700, Chicago, IL 60611-4008
Phone: (800) 873-5995 or (312) 644-0829
Fax: (312) 644-8557
E-mail: cclark@bostrom.com
Website: www.slfnet.org
Subject(s): Strategic leadership

STUDENT LEADER

This magazine helps campus leaders prepare to serve in student government, Greek organizations, and clubs. Featured are articles on ethical solutions for common problems, tips for public relations, national polls, and stories of successful student leadership.

Frequency: Three times per year
Subscription Address: Oxendine Publishing, P.O. Box 14081, Gainesville, FL 32604-2081
Phone: (888) 547-6310 or (352) 373-6907
Fax: (352) 373-8120
E-mail: info@studentleader.com
Website: www.studentleader.com
Subject(s): Student leadership

New
THIAGI GAME LETTER

This newsletter is for trainers and consultants who facilitate exercises, simulations, and games for managers. Each issue contains new exercises designed by Sivasailam Thiagarajan and his colleagues as well as suggested methods for using exercises to improve managers' performance.

Frequency: Ten times per year
Subscription Address: Jossey-Bass Inc., Publishers, 350 Sansome Street, San Francisco, CA 94104-1342
Phone: (800) 956-7739 or (415) 433-1740
Fax: (800) 605-2665 or (415) 433-0499
E-mail: subinfo@jbp.com
Website: www.jbp.com/journals.html
Subject(s): Simulation as a training technique

TRAINING

Training features articles for and by corporate training consultants. There are book reviews, many training tools advertised, and an annual index. The January issue contains a four-year conference-planning calendar.

Frequency: Monthly
Subscription Address: Lakewood Publications, Inc., Lakewood Building, 50 South Ninth Street, Suite 400, Minneapolis, MN 55402-3165
Phone: (800) 707-7749 or (612) 333-0471
Fax: (612) 333-6526
E-mail: edit@trainingmag.com
Website: www.trainingsupersite.com
Subject(s): Trainer resources

TRAINING & DEVELOPMENT

Training & Development addresses training concerns from multicultural issues to career development. Regular features include a trends update, information about new technology, Training 101 essays, tips for building a consulting business, and book reviews. The Marketplace is a directory of tools, seminars, and job ads.

Frequency: Monthly
Sponsoring Organization: American Society for Training & Development (ASTD)
Subscription Address: 1640 King Street, Box 1443, Alexandria, VA 22313-2043
Phone: (800) 628-2783 or (703) 683-8100
Fax: (703) 683-8103
E-mail: info@astd.org
Website: www.astd.org
Subject(s): Trainer resources

INSTRUMENTS

The items in this section measure a variety of leadership skills and styles. Some are brief, self-scored tests that may be used to introduce concepts in a training module. Others are administered by certified facilitators and accompanied by detailed, computer-generated profiles and action plans. An increasing number are 360-degree instruments that provide feedback from one's peers, direct reports, and superiors. Whenever possible, the descriptions include reference to critical reviews and support materials such as leader's guides or articles that describe using an instrument for development. Each entry, as applicable, includes:

- the instrument's purpose and scales to be measured
- administration
- psychometric properties—we list what data are reported and where
- author and publication date
- cost
- time necessary to administer the instrument
- number of items
- intended audience
- subject
- source

We include primarily instruments that are supported by technical data—reports on the development of the scales and questions, validity and reliability studies, and norm groups. The editors recommend that facilitators gather detailed information about the psychometric properties of any instrument used for development purposes. An excellent guide to understanding psychometric properties is E. Van Velsor, J. B. Leslie, & J. W. Fleenor (1997), *Choosing 360: A Guide to Evaluating Multi-rater Feedback Instruments for Management Development.* Greensboro, NC: Center for Creative Leadership.

New
BARON EMOTIONAL QUOTIENT INVENTORY™ (EQ-I)

The *EQ-i* measures emotional intelligence—one's ability to deal with daily challenges in life and at work. Scales and subscales include emotional self-awareness, self-regard, independence, social responsibility, flexibility, optimism, and empathy. This test may be used for individual development or to determine the emotional skills that are most effective in an organization.

Administration: Qualified facilitators may administer this test in computer-based or paper-and-pencil versions. Computer scoring generates detailed individual and organizational reports.

Psychometric Properties: Test development, validity, and reliability are described in the *Technical Manual*. Norms are based on 20,000 individuals.

Author(s): Reuven Bar-On
Publication Date: 1997
Cost: Ten paper tests: $18; 25 computer tests: $200; *Technical Manual*: $47; *User's Manual*: $30; 25 computer reports: $450
Time: 30 minutes
Number of Items: 133
Audience: General
Subject(s): Emotional intelligence
Source: Psychological Assessment Resources, Inc. (PAR). Odessa, FL. (800) 331-8378. www.parinc.com

BENCHMARKS®

This 360-degree-feedback instrument measures a wide spectrum of management behaviors. The authors note that "it was developed from studying how managers develop rather than what they do." It is designed to assess the strengths in a manager, and to help find potential trouble spots that may lead to derailment. Results are presented in two sections: 1) 16 skills and perspectives that are important for success, and 2) five derailment scales. The test is available in multiple languages to allow English-speaking managers to get feedback from international raters. For a comprehensive review of the 1994 edition of this instrument, refer to J. B. Leslie & J. W. Fleenor (1998), *Feedback to Managers: A Review and Comparison of Multi-rater Instruments for Management Development* (3rd ed.). Greensboro, NC: Center for Creative Leadership.

Administration: The surveys may be administered on paper or online. Scoring is done by CCL. Feedback facilitators must be certified. They give participants detailed feedback information and a development guide for using the feedback to create a development plan. Two-day certification workshops are offered periodically.

Psychometric Properties: Test development, validity, and reliability are reported in the *Trainer's Manual*. Norm groups include middle- and upper-level management as well

as public and private sectors; some data are available for specific countries.

Author(s): Michael M. Lombardo & Cynthia D. McCauley
Publication Date: 1988, 1990, 1993, 1994, 2000
Cost: $275—includes one self-test, 11 observer tests, scoring, and development guide
Time: 30 to 40 minutes
Number of Items: 179 (8 are for research purposes only)
Audience: Executives, managers
Subject(s): Leadership development
Source: Center for Creative Leadership (CCL). Greensboro, NC. (336) 286-4480. www.ccl.org

THE BIRKMAN METHOD®

Participants respond to 125 statements about how they see most people and the same 125 statements about how they see themselves. They then respond to 48 possible career choices. The results are intended to link one's basic perceptions and values to career potential. There are ten scales attributed to the relative influence of social desirability: empathy, thought, esteem, change, authority, advantage, acceptance, activity, structure, and freedom. One report, the *Leadership Style Grid*, indicates a participant's style of leadership goals (direct or indirect involvement, task- or relationship-orientation), leadership styles (objective or subjective), environmental needs (objective or subjective), and leadership style when under stress.

Administration: Facilitators must complete Birkman Certification Training. The test may be administered by paper and pencil with computer scoring or administered and scored via Windows-based software, *Birkman 2000*℠.

Psychometric Properties: Test development, validity, and reliability are reported in *The Birkman Method: Reliabilities and Validities Supplement*. Large cultural, gender, and ethnic norms are provided.

Author(s): Roger W. Birkman
Publication Date: 1950-2000
Cost: Questionnaire: $2.25; individual reports: $27.50 to $175; group reports are also available
Time: 60 to 90 minutes
Number of Items: 298
Audience: Managers
Subject(s): Personality
Source: Birkman International, Inc. Houston, TX. (713) 623-2760. www.birkman.com

CAMPBELL-HALLAM TEAM DEVELOPMENT SURVEY™ (TDS™)

Team members, team leaders, and outside observers respond by agreement or disagreement with statements related to interaction of team members, the guidance and direction of the team leader, and the team's ability to perform. Key strengths and weaknesses are assessed including: mission clarity, innovation, satisfaction, shared responsibility, communication, and unity. Individual and team profiles are generated by computer scoring. A separate instrument, the *Campbell-Hallam*™ *Team Leader Profile* provides feedback on team leadership skills and behaviors.

Administration: Instruments are computer scored at NCS. Teams regroup for distribution of feedback, discussion, and action planning. A *Facilitator's Guide* offers detailed guidance for providing feedback and discussing results.

Psychometric Properties: Test development, validity, reliability, and norms are described in the *TDS* manual.

Author(s): David Campbell & Glenn Hallam
Publication Date: 1994
Cost: $15 per team member; $60 per team report
Time: 25 minutes
Number of Items: 166
Audience: Intact work groups
Subject(s): Teams
Source: NCS Workforce Development. Rosemont, IL. (800) 221-8378. www.ncs.com

CAMPBELL LEADERSHIP INDEX™ (CLI®)

This is a self-other 100-adjective checklist. Respondents are asked to indicate on a six-point scale how descriptive each adjective is of them or of the leader they are rating. The individual's self-evaluation of leadership characteristics is compared with the evaluations of others, thus allowing the individual to see patterns of leadership strengths and possible weaknesses. The *CLI* profile presents 22 standardized scoring measures within five orientations: leadership, energy, affability, dependability, and resilience. For a comprehensive review of this instrument, refer to J. B. Leslie & J. W. Fleenor (1998), *Feedback to Managers: A Review and Comparison of Multi-rater Instruments for Management Development* (3rd ed.). Greensboro, NC: Center for Creative Leadership.

Administration: Scoring is performed by NCS using optically scanned answer sheets. Before purchasing the *CLI,* users must complete a qualification form or attend an NCS certification workshop. Participants receive a lengthy feedback report including graphs that display both self-report and observer ratings on orientations, scales, and items. An enhanced report displays results by observer type.

Psychometric Properties: Test development, validity, reliability, and norms are reported in the *Manual for the CLI*.

Author(s): David Campbell
Publication Date: 1988, 1991, 1998
Cost: $195—includes one self-test, eight observer tests, standard report, and development planning guide; enhanced report: add $30; *Technical Manual*: $51; *User's Guide*: $35
Time: 20 to 30 minutes
Number of Items: 100
Audience: General
Subject(s): Leadership effectiveness
Source: NCS Workforce Development. Rosemont, IL. (800) 221-8378. www.ncs.com

CHANGE STYLE INDICATOR (CSI)

The *CSI* is designed to capture an individual's preferences in approaching change. Results place the respondent on a continuum that ranges from a *conserver* orientation to an *originator* orientation. Conservers prefer a gradual but continuous approach to change, whereas originators prefer a quicker and more radical approach. Stronger scores at either end of the continuum represent strength of preference, not degree of effectiveness or proficiency. The *CSI* can assist in understanding one's response to new situations and to changes in existing situations.

Administration: The *Facilitator's Guide* contains scoring software, instructions for reporting, and a PowerPoint presentation on the rationale and use of the instrument.

Psychometric Properties: Test development, validity, and reliability are reported in the *Facilitator's Guide*. Updated norm data is reported on the Discovery Learning website.

Author(s): W. Christopher Musselwhite & Robyn P. Ingram
Publication Date: 1995
Cost: $12.95—includes test and *Style Guide*; *Facilitator's Guide*: $125
Time: 15 minutes
Number of Items: 22
Audience: General
Subject(s): Change
Source: Discovery Learning. Greensboro, NC. (336) 272-9530. www.discoverync.com

THE CHOICES ARCHITECT™ TALENT MANAGEMENT TOOL

This questionnaire measures learning agility—the ability to learn and benefit from experience. The authors identify four factors that correlate learning agility to high performance: 1) people agility—knowing oneself and remaining cool under pressure; 2) results agility—getting results in first-time or difficult situations; 3) mental agility—being comfortable with complexity, ambiguity, and explaining one's thinking to others; and 4) change agility—being curious, creative, and interested in building new skills. This test is part of The Leadership Architect® Suite, a set of tools for training needs analysis and succession planning.

Administration: A certified facilitator oversees the administration and interpretation. Certification training is available from Lominger. *Choices* is available in a paper-and-pencil version or as a computerized test accompanied by sort cards.

Psychometric Properties: Information about test development, validity, and reliability is available from Lominger. Limited norms are provided for gender, age ranges, and level of management.

Author(s): Michael M. Lombardo & Robert W. Eichinger
Publication Date: 1997
Cost: $25—includes test and *User's Manual*
Time: 30 minutes
Number of Items: 81

Audience: High-potential managers
Subject(s): Learning
Source: Lominger Limited, Inc. Minneapolis, MN. (952) 542-1466. www.lominger.com

COACHING SKILLS INVENTORY

This test is designed as a two-step process. Prior to training, participants take Part A to identify their strengths and weaknesses. Following training, participants take Part B to assess new coaching skills. In both parts, there are 18 coaching scenarios with four alternative actions. Participants choose the actions they would be most likely to take when opening a coaching meeting, getting agreement, exploring alternatives, getting a commitment to act, handling excuses, and closing the meeting.

Administration: The tests are self-scored. Interpretation and guidelines for improving coaching skills are provided in the test booklets.

Psychometric Properties: The *Facilitator's Guide* describes scale development and reliability data. There is no information about validity. Limited sample norms are provided.

Author(s): Kenneth R. Phillips
Publication Date: 1987, 1991
Cost: Five tests (A or B): $36; *Facilitator Guide*: $25
Time: 30 minutes—each part
Number of Items: 18—each part
Audience: General
Subject(s): Coaching
Source: HRDQ. King of Prussia, PA. (800) 633-4533. www.hrdq.com

COMPASS: THE MANAGERIAL PRACTICES SURVEY

This instrument is designed to provide managers with information about their current behaviors on the job and to help them identify their strengths and expand their repertoire of effective management practices. Based on a 15-year research program, *COMPASS* measures 14 categories of management and leadership behaviors. These are: informing, clarifying, monitoring, planning, problem solving, consulting, delegating, inspiring, recognizing, rewarding, supporting, mentoring, networking, and team building. An electronic version is available from Jossey-Bass. For a comprehensive review of this instrument, refer to J. B. Leslie & J. W. Fleenor (1998), *Feedback to Managers: A Review and Comparison of Multi-rater Instruments for Management Development* (3rd ed.). Greensboro, NC: Center for Creative Leadership.

Administration: Facilitators must be certified at a certification workshop provided by Manus. *COMPASS* is computer scored by the vendor. A manual provides interpretive assistance and instrument background. Development and planning guides help participants understand feedback and make action plans for improvement.

Psychometric Properties: Test development, validity, reliability, and norms are reported in G. Yukl, S. Wall, & R. Lepsinger (1990), Preliminary report on validation of The Managerial Practices Survey, in K. E. Clark & M. B. Clark (Eds.), *Measures of Leadership* (pp. 223-237). The norm group is a sample of 1,025 managers.

Author(s): Gary Yukl
Publication Date: 1984, 1988, 1990, 1995
Cost: $185 to $295 per participant
Time: 30 minutes
Number of Items: 94
Audience: Managers
Subject(s): Leadership development
Source: Right Manus. Stamford, CT. (800) 445-0942. www.rightmanus.com

THE COMPREHENSIVE LEADER: A NEW VIEW OF VISIONARY LEADERSHIP

The authors' premise is that at the heart of leadership is knowledge—about oneself, others, one's organization, and the world. Visionary leadership develops comprehensive knowledge and builds a future based on that knowledge. These two behaviors and four levels of knowledge are assessed in this 360-degree inventory. Participants respond to how well their behaviors match 40 statements of knowledge-based behavior. Others provide feedback on the same 40 items to create a comprehensive leadership profile.

Administration: This instrument may be self-administered and self-scored, but HRDQ recommends that a facilitator assist with interpretation and follow-up training. Training suggestions and transparency masters are included in the *Facilitator's Guide*.

Psychometric Properties: A *Technical Development Update* contains brief information about test development, reliability, and limited norms. No validity data are reported.

Author(s): Eileen Russo & Laurie Ribble Libove
Publication Date: 1996
Cost: Five participant booklets: $45; five feedback forms: $18; *Facilitator Guide*: $45
Time: 90 minutes
Number of Items: 40
Audience: Executives, managers, teams
Subject(s): Vision
Source: HRDQ. King of Prussia, PA. (800) 633-4533. www.hrdq.com

CONFLICT MANAGEMENT SURVEY (CMS)

The *CMS* assesses one's interpretation of conflict and subsequent handling of it. The survey contains 60 alternative sets of attitudes to be ranked on a 10-point scale. In the scoring and interpretation section of the test booklet, concern for personal goals and concern for relationships are applied to a grid format. After participants complete their grid, they learn their one dominant and four back-up styles of conflict management. Associates may respond to the feedback companion survey, *Conflict Management Appraisal,* which is available separately.

Administration: This paper-and-pencil test may be self-administered and self-scored.

Psychometric Properties: The author briefly describes test development and reliability. A single norm group of mixed populations is provided.

Author(s): Jay Hall
Publication Date: 1969, 1973, 1986, 1996
Cost: $8.95
Time: 30 to 45 minutes
Number of Items: 60
Audience: General
Subject(s): Conflict management
Source: Teleometrics International. The Woodlands, TX. (800) 527-0406. www.teleometrics.com

New
CORPORATE COMMUNICATION ASSESSMENT

This survey measures several dimensions of communication within an organization and their effect on job satisfaction. Respondents rank the first 37 statements according to their satisfaction or dissatisfaction with the quantity of information. Specifically, they address receiving and conveying information, sources of information, and channels of communication. The next 37 statements address the quality of communication. Respondents rank how often they perceive quality practices in oral and written communication, multicultural communication, electronic communication, teamwork, and job satisfaction. The final question asks for open-ended comments about improving workplace communications.

Administration: Paper-and-pencil surveys may be given to all organizational members or a random sample. When completed, they are sent to HRD Press for computer scoring and reporting. A *Survey Administrator's Guide* contains "quick start" instructions for a designated company facilitator to administer the survey and conduct action planning meetings based on the results.

Psychometric Properties: The *Administrator's Guide* briefly mentions test development, validity, and reliability, but no data are reported.

Author(s): Thomas R. Watson
Publication Date: 1997
Cost: $495
Time: 30 minutes
Number of Items: 75
Audience: Organizational members
Subject(s): Communication
Source: HRD Press. Amherst, MA. (800) 822-2801. www.hrdpress.com

CREE QUESTIONNAIRE

This is a psychological test that measures an individual's creative-innovative potential. It has been used with a variety of populations, including managers and professionals. It provides scores on the following dimensions: social orientation—dominance and independence; work orientation—unstructured and under pressure; internal functioning—high energy, spontaneous, ideational; and interests—theoretical, artistic, and mechanical.

Administration: This paper-and-pencil instrument is hand scored. Facilitators must have completed appropriate coursework in psychology or education and have some technical knowledge of instrument construction and use.

Psychometric Properties: The *Interpretation and Research Manual* describes the test development, validity, and reliability. Norms are available for various levels of management.

Author(s): T. G. Thurstone & John Mellinger
Publication Date: 1996
Cost: 25 test booklets: $47; scoring sheets: $39; *Interpretation and Research Manual*: $24
Time: 20 minutes
Number of Items: 145
Audience: Executives, line managers, technical managers
Subject(s): Creativity
Source: NCS Workforce Development. Rosemont, IL. (800) 221-8378. www.ncs.com

DENISON LEADERSHIP DEVELOPMENT SURVEY

This 360-degree instrument is based on the Denison Model, which is built on four traits of organizational culture and 12 leadership skills that impact organizational performance. Participants indicate how accurately 96 statements reflect their leadership effectiveness. Peers, direct reports, and superiors respond to the same statements to identify areas of strength and weakness.

Administration: Send self- and observer surveys to Discovery Learning for scoring. Receive a summary feedback report and guide for planning actions for development. The *Facilitator's Guide* includes instructions for delivering feedback, a PowerPoint presentation, and prescriptive guidelines for individual improvement.

Psychometric Properties: The development of the Denison Model, upon which this instrument is based, is described in the *Facilitator's Guide*. Validity and reliability are also discussed.

Author(s): Daniel R. Denison & William S. Neale
Publication Date: 1996
Cost: $175—includes one self-survey, ten surveys for others, report, and action planning guide; *Facilitator's Guide*: $125
Time: 20 minutes
Number of Items: 96
Audience: Managers

Subject(s): Leadership effectiveness
Source: Discovery Learning. Greensboro, NC. (336) 272-9530. www.discoverync.com

DENISON ORGANIZATIONAL CULTURE SURVEY

This instrument measures the underlying beliefs, values, and assumptions held by members of an organization. Participants indicate how accurately 60 statements reflect their organization's culture in four areas: 1) involvement—teamwork, empowerment, and development; 2) consistency—agreement, core values, and integration; 3) adaptability—customer focus, change, and learning; and 4) mission—vision, goals, and strategy. This instrument may be used to benchmark an organization's culture to high- and low-performing organizations, to examine subcultures, to determine steps for performance improvement, or to manage transition during mergers or acquisitions.

Administration: Send surveys to Discovery Learning for scoring. Receive a summary feedback report for a group or the entire organization. The *Facilitator's Guide* includes instructions for delivering feedback, a PowerPoint presentation, and prescriptive guidelines for improving organizational performance.

Psychometric Properties: The development of the Denison Model, upon which this instrument is based, is described in the *Facilitator's Guide* and in D. R. Denison & A. K. Mishra (1995), "Toward a Theory of Organizational Culture and Effectiveness," *Organization Science*, 6(2), 204-223. Validity is also described but reliability is not. No norms are reported.

Author(s): Daniel R. Denison & William S. Neale
Publication Date: 1994
Cost: Test booklet and scoring: $13.95; report: $50; *Facilitator's Guide*: $125
Time: 15 minutes
Number of Items: 60
Audience: Intact work groups, organizational members
Subject(s): Organizational culture
Source: Discovery Learning. Greensboro, NC. (336) 272-9530. www.discoverync.com

DIMENSIONS OF LEADERSHIP PROFILE®

This instrument assesses leadership characteristics from two points of view—personal and situational. Participants rank the importance of five statements in 12 sets. Their scores are then plotted on a Leadership Wheel to learn their strengths in four areas: 1) character—enthusiasm, integrity, and self-renewal; 2) analysis—fortitude, perceiving, and judgment; 3) accomplishment—performing, boldness, and team building; and 4) interaction—collaborating, inspiring, and serving others.

Administration: This paper-and-pencil test may be self-administered and self-scored.

Psychometric Properties: Brief information about test development, validity, and reliability is provided in a

research report. Limited gender, age, educational level, and occupational norms are available.

Author(s): Miriam E. Kragness
Publication Date: 1994
Cost: $12
Time: 15 to 30 minutes
Number of Items: 60
Audience: General
Subject(s): Leadership styles
Source: Carlson Learning Company. Minneapolis, MN. (800) 777-9897. www.carlsonlearning.com

ENTREPRENEURIAL QUOTIENT (EQ)

The *EQ* identifies and measures an individual's ability to embrace change, innovation, improvement, and reform. Managerial traits measured are: risk tolerance, creativity, strategic thinking, and goal orientation. Personality traits measured are: extraversion, intuition, thinking, and perceiving. When the above traits are charted with an individual's ability to adapt, an entrepreneurial tendency may be identified and strengthened.

Administration: The diskette provided uses a Windows-based program to score the instrument and produces an *EQ Guide*, a 16- to 20-page narrative report. Scoring by fax or mail is also available.

Psychometric Properties: Test development, validity, and reliability are reported in the *User's Manual*. Subgroup standardized scores are presented.

Author(s): Wonderlic Personnel Test, Inc.
Publication Date: 1994
Cost: $175—includes five tests, user's manual, and scoring software
Time: 25 to 35 minutes
Number of Items: 100
Audience: General
Subject(s): Entrepreneurial leadership
Source: Wonderlic, Inc. Libertyville, IL. (800) 963-7542. www.wonderlic.com

New
EXECUTIVE SUCCESS PROFILE (ESP)

ESP is a developmental 360-degree-feedback instrument for executives. The first 140 questions ask how well developed the executive is in 22 competencies such as seasoned judgment, visionary thinking, global perspective, driving execution, and mature confidence. The next 22 questions rank the importance of each competency to success in the participant's current role. For a comprehensive review of this instrument, refer to J. B. Leslie & J. W. Fleenor (1998), *Feedback to Managers: A Review and Comparison of Multi-rater Instruments for Management Development* (3rd ed.). Greensboro, NC: Center for Creative Leadership.

Administration: Scoring is done by PDI. Feedback may be provided by PDI or by feedback-givers trained and certified by PDI.

Psychometric Properties: *The Executive Success Profile Technical Summary* and other PDI reports contain information about test development, validity, reliability, and norms.

Author(s): Personnel Decisions International (PDI)
Publication Date: 1987, 1993
Cost: $400—includes one self- and ten other-rater forms, scoring, feedback report, and development guide
Time: 30 minutes
Number of Items: 162
Audience: Executives, high-potential managers
Subject(s): Leadership development
Source: Personnel Decisions International. Minneapolis, MN. (800) 633-4410. www.pdi-corp.com

New
FUNDAMENTAL INTERPERSONAL RELATIONS ORIENTATION-BEHAVIOR (FIRO-B)™

The *FIRO-B* is based on a model of three interpersonal needs. The first need, inclusion, is reflected in the formation of new relationships, participation in groups, and desire for recognition. The second need, control, is indicated by the way one views power, seeks responsibility, and exerts influence. The third need, affection, relates to one's warmth and empathy. The test measures how much one expresses or wants these characteristics and the pattern of fulfilling each need. Results may be used to reveal leadership behaviors, team effectiveness, and organizational culture.

Administration: Scannable forms are returned to CPP for scoring and report generation. A qualified facilitator interprets the reports and provides feedback. Participants who take both the *FIRO-B* and *MBTI*® may get a Leadership Report for an additional $39.

Psychometric Properties: Test development, validity, reliability, and norms are described in *Psychometric Properties of the FIRO-B: A Guide to Research.*

Author(s): Eugene R. Schnell & Allen Hammer
Publication Date: 1993, 1996
Cost: Ten tests: $35; *Scales Manual*: $26; *Introduction to FIRO-B*: $8
Time: 15 minutes
Number of Items: 54
Audience: General
Subject(s): Interpersonal relationships
Source: Consulting Psychologists Press, Inc. (CPP). Palo Alto, CA. (800) 624-1765. www.cpp-db.com

New
THE INFLUENCE STYLES INVENTORY (ISI)

In this forced-choice test, participants must choose between two alternative actions in 24 scenarios of workplace influence. Responses are charted in the areas of passive, assertive, and aggressive styles of behavior. When participants become aware of dominant styles, they can learn and practice new influence tactics such as bargaining, reason, and upward appeal.

Administration: This pencil-and-paper test may be self-administered, self-scored, and self-interpreted. A *Trainer Guide* offers more detailed interpretation and suggestions for a skill-building workshop.

Psychometric Properties: Test development and validity are briefly mentioned in the *Trainer Guide*. No reliability or norm data are mentioned.

Author(s): Marshall Sashkin
Publication Date: 1997
Cost: Tests: $6.50; *Trainer's Guide*: $24.95
Time: 10 minutes
Number of Items: 24
Audience: General
Subject(s): Influence
Source: HRD Press. Amherst, MA. (800) 822-2801. www.hrdpress.com

INSIGHT INVENTORY®

Participants respond to 32 adjectives to describe their behavior at work and again to describe their behavior outside work. The scores reveal a profile of how individuals get their own way (direct or indirect), respond to people (reserved or outgoing), pace activities (urgent or steady), and deal with details (unstructured or precise).

Administration: This paper-and-pencil test may be self-administered and self-scored.

Psychometric Properties: A *Technical Manual* describes test development, validity, and reliability. Norms are reported by age and gender.

Author(s): Patrick G. Handley
Publication Date: 1988, 1990, 1991, 1995
Cost: Test A (with interpretive guide): $11.95; Test B (abbreviated version): $6.50; training manual and 45-minute video: $250
Time: 15 minutes
Number of Items: 64
Audience: General
Subject(s): Self-development
Source: HRD Press. Amherst, MA. (800) 822-2801. www.hrdpress.com

INSTRUCTIONAL LEADERSHIP EVALUATION AND DEVELOPMENT PROGRAM (ILEAD)

ILEAD is a set of instruments used by school administrators, teachers, and students. It is designed to identify and measure school climate and leadership practices that are associated with measurable improvements in student achievement. Scales reported include instructional leadership, commitment, personal values, motivational factors, and school district culture.

Administration: Completed answer sheets must be sent to MetriTech for scoring. Schools are then sent interpretive reports.

Psychometric Properties: Instrument development as well as reliability and validity studies are reported in journal articles. The norm group is from schools in the Midwest.

Author(s): Larry A. Braskamp & Martin L. Maehr
Publication Date: 1985, 1988
Cost: Contact the publisher
Time: Varies with each instrument
Number of Items: Varies with each instrument
Audience: Students, teachers, educational administrators
Subject(s): Educational leadership
Source: MetriTech, Inc. Champaign, IL. (800) 747-4868. www.metritech.com

INTERPERSONAL INFLUENCE INVENTORY (III)

This inventory helps individuals determine their interpersonal influence style by assessing the behaviors they use when they attempt to influence others. Inventory items are based on a behavior model that suggests a mix of open and candid behavior coupled with consideration of others. Four influence patterns are derived: assertive, passive, openly aggressive, and concealed aggressive. The author suggests that awareness of influence style has become increasingly important as organizations shift from being hierarchical to more collaborative.

Administration: This is a self-scored instrument. A *Facilitator Guide* discusses its background, provides guidelines for administration and interpretation, and offers suggestions for using it in training.

Psychometric Properties: The *Facilitator Guide* briefly discusses test development and reliability. No validity data are reported. Limited sample norms are provided.

Author(s): Rollin Glaser
Publication Date: 1983, 1986, 1990, 1993, 1995
Cost: Five tests: $32; *Facilitator Guide*: $30
Time: 60 to 90 minutes
Number of Items: 40
Audience: General
Subject(s): Influence
Source: HRDQ. King of Prussia, PA. (800) 633-4533. www.hrdq.com

New
INTUITIVE DECISION MAKING PROFILE

This instrument examines the use of intuition in work-related decision making. Participants decide to what extent they practice behaviors such as seeking patterns or tapping the experience of others. Scores determine their strengths and weaknesses in the areas of: knowledge or experience, reflection, emotional or cognitive biases, recognizing patterns or physical cues, and stress or time pressures and techniques to manage them. A model of intuitive processing is introduced in the test booklet to help the participants practice new skills and increase intuitive decision making.

Administration: This instrument is self-administered, self-scored, and self-interpreted. A *Facilitator Guide* contains an outline and materials for a one-hour training session.

Psychometric Properties: Test development and norms are briefly mentioned in the *Facilitator Guide*. Validity and reliability data are not included.

Author(s): James G. Andrews
Publication Date: 1999
Cost: Five tests: $45; *Facilitator Guide*: $40
Time: 15 to 20 minutes
Number of Items: 40
Audience: Managers
Subject(s): Intuition, decision making
Source: HRDQ. King of Prussia, PA. (800) 633-4533. www.hrdq.com

New
JOB CHALLENGE PROFILE (JCP)

This questionnaire aims to help managers use the challenges in their current jobs as growth opportunities. Ten job components are included: unfamiliar responsibilities, new directions, inherited problems, problems with employees, high stakes, job scope, external pressures, influence without authority, cross-cultural work, and work group diversity. The test booklet contains suggestions for taking advantage of these challenges. More in-depth guidance is in the *Facilitator's Guide*. Formerly titled *Developmental Challenge Profile®*.

Administration: This paper-and-pencil test is self-administered, self-scored, and self-interpreted. The *Participant's Workbook* contains an action planning guide. The *Facilitator's Guide* contains lessons for a half-day workshop.

Psychometric Properties: Test development, validity, reliability, and norms are described in the *Facilitator's Guide*.

Author(s): Cynthia D. McCauley, Patricia J. Ohlott, & Marian N. Ruderman
Publication Date: 1999
Cost: Participant workbook: $12.95; *Facilitator's Guide*: $24.95
Time: 15 minutes
Number of Items: 50
Audience: General
Subject(s): Learning assignments
Source: Jossey-Bass/Pfeiffer. San Francisco, CA. (800) 274-4434. www.pfeiffer.com

New
KEYS®: ASSESSING THE CLIMATE FOR CREATIVITY

KEYS identifies factors in the work environment that influence creativity and innovation. Stimulating factors include freedom, sufficient resources, and challenging work.

Obstacles include lack of trust, poor communication, and workload pressure. Test outcomes may be compared to other organizations or to the participating organization's desired level of creativity and innovation.

Administration: Scannable survey forms are returned to CCL for computer scoring and report generation. A separate *User's Manual* contains facilitator guidelines for interpreting the results, giving feedback, and conducting training.

Psychometric Properties: Survey development, validity, reliability, and norms are described in the *User's Manual*.

Author(s): Teresa M. Amabile & the Center for Creative Leadership
Publication Date: 1987, 1990, 1995
Cost: $20
Time: 20 minutes
Number of Items: 78
Audience: Intact work groups, organizations
Subject(s): Creativity
Source: Center for Creative Leadership (CCL). Greensboro, NC. (336) 286-4480. www.ccl.org

LEAD—LEADER EFFECTIVENESS AND ADAPTABILITY DESCRIPTION

The purpose of this inventory is to evaluate an individual's leadership style in terms of flexibility and adaptability. It describes this style in terms of telling, selling, participating, or delegating, and indicates whether the style is appropriate in various situations. *LEAD Self* provides self-perception and feedback. *LEAD Other*, completed by the leader's associates, provides a group profile of the leader's style.

Administration: *LEAD* is a short self-scoring instrument. Software is available for in-house administration, scoring, and profiles.

Psychometric Properties: Reliability and validity are briefly reported in a data sheet.

Author(s): Paul Hersey & Kenneth H. Blanchard
Publication Date: 1989, 1993
Cost: Tests: $8; 360-degree profile: $3
Time: 10 minutes
Number of Items: 12
Audience: Managers
Subject(s): Flexibility
Source: HRD Press. Amherst, MA. (800) 822-2801. www.hrdpress.com

LEADER BEHAVIOR ANALYSIS II™ (LBAII)

The *LBAII* is based on the situational leadership model of Hersey and Blanchard. It provides leaders with information about their own and others' perceptions of their leadership styles. Items are presented in the form of typical job situations in which the leader and staff member would be involved together. Respondents select one of four leader decisions that would best describe the target leader's behavior in that situation. There are four leadership-style

scales and two scales that measure flexibility and effectiveness. A related instrument, the *Supervisor Behavior Analysis II*, changes item wording slightly to reflect the level of supervisory responsibility. For a comprehensive review of this instrument, refer to J. B. Leslie & J. W. Fleenor (1998), *Feedback to Managers: A Review and Comparison of Multirater Instruments for Management Development* (3rd ed.). Greensboro, NC: Center for Creative Leadership.

Administration: The instrument is self-scored.

Psychometric Properties: A Blanchard report, *Research on the LBAII*, provides information on development, reliability, and validity. No norms are reported.

Author(s): Kenneth H. Blanchard, Ronald K. Hambleton, Drea Zigarmi, & Douglas Forsyth
Publication Date: 1985, 1991
Cost: Self-test: $9; observer test: $5; profile: $5
Time: 20 minutes
Number of Items: 20
Audience: Managers
Subject(s): Leadership styles
Source: Jossey-Bass/Pfeiffer. San Francisco, CA. (800) 274-4434. www.pfeiffer.com

LEADER REWARD AND PUNISHMENT QUESTIONNAIRE (LRPQ)

This questionnaire is designed to measure four leader-behavior variables related to the leader's use of reward and punishment. The four factors are: 1) performance-contingent reward behavior (the leader rewards high performance), 2) performance-contingent punishment (the leader punishes low performance), 3) noncontingent punishment (the leader's punishments are unrelated to performance), and 4) noncontingent reward (the leader's rewards are unrelated to performance).

Administration: This paper-and-pencil test is administered by a facilitator.

Psychometric Properties: The test is in an article that describes test development, validity, and reliability.

Author(s): Philip M. Podsakoff, William D. Todor, & Richard Skov
Publication Date: 1982, 1984
Cost: Contact the authors for availability and research use
Time: 10 minutes
Number of Items: 23
Audience: General
Subject(s): Leadership effectiveness
Source: P. M. Podsakoff, W. D. Todor, R. A. Grover, & V. L. Huber (1984), "Situational Moderators of Leader Reward and Punishment Behaviors: Fact or Fiction?" *Organizational Behavior and Human Performance, 34*, 21-63. Contact Philip Podsakoff, Department of Management, Kelley School of Business, Indiana University, Bloomington, IN 47405. (812) 855-2747. podsakof@indiana.edu

New
LEADERSHIP EFFECTIVENESS ANALYSIS (LEA)

The *LEA* is designed as a selection and development tool used in MRG's Strategic Leadership Development Program for individuals, for those who coach developing leaders, and for organizational audits. The test provides 360-degree feedback on 22 behaviors in six broad areas: creating a vision, implementing a vision, developing followership, team playing, following through, and achieving results. For a comprehensive review of this instrument, refer to J. B. Leslie & J. W. Fleenor (1998), *Feedback to Managers: A Review and Comparison of Multi-rater Instruments for Management Development* (3rd ed.). Greensboro, NC: Center for Creative Leadership.

Administration: Participants may take *LEA* on paper or online. MRG scores and prepares reports to be delivered by certified facilitators. Certification workshops are offered periodically.

Psychometric Properties: Test development, validity, reliability, and norms are described in reports from MRG.

Author(s): Management Research Group® (MRG)
Publication Date: 1987, 1993
Cost: Varies—from $105 to $300
Time: 30 minutes
Number of Items: 84
Audience: Managers
Subject(s): Leadership effectiveness
Source: Management Research Group. Portland, ME. (207) 775-2173. www.mrg.com

New
LEADERSHIP/IMPACT™ (L/I)

L/I indicates the techniques that a leader uses to motivate others. There are questions about prescriptive and restrictive strategies such as positive or negative role modeling and reinforcing by rewards or punishment. Other questions focus on types of impact such as constructive, passive, aggressive, or defensive impact. One more set of questions considers the leader's organizational effectiveness, personal effectiveness, and balance. Each leader's test results are compared to the leader's ideal, which provides the basis for a development plan. For a comprehensive review of this instrument, refer to J. B. Leslie & J. W. Fleenor (1998), *Feedback to Managers: A Review and Comparison of Multi-rater Instruments for Management Development* (3rd ed.). Greensboro, NC: Center for Creative Leadership.

Administration: Tests are sent to Human Synergistics for scoring and report generation.

Psychometric Properties: Information about test development, validity, reliability, and norms is available from Human Synergistics.

Author(s): Robert A. Cooke & Human Synergistics/Center for Applied Research
Publication Date: 1996

Cost: $175—includes one self-test, eight observer tests, scoring, and report
Time: 20 to 25 minutes
Number of Items: 156
Audience: Executives, managers
Subject(s): Leadership effectiveness
Source: Human Synergistics International/Center for Applied Research. Plymouth, MI. (800) 622-7584. www.humansyn.com

LEADERSHIP OPINION QUESTIONNAIRE (LOQ)

This instrument measures consideration and structure, two factors that evolved from the Ohio State leadership studies. It is a self-report format in which respondents indicate how frequently they feel they should do what is described in each item. A high score on the consideration scale suggests an emphasis on the group-process and human-relations aspects of managing, while a high structure score reflects a need to actively direct and structure tasks and activities. The *Examiner's Manual* suggests that the *LOQ*, which is completed by the supervisor, may be used in conjunction with a companion instrument, the *Supervisory Behavior Description Questionnaire*, which is completed by subordinates on how their managers behave. Users should be aware that these are separate instruments, not different versions of the same instrument.

Administration: Facilitators must have completed appropriate coursework in psychology or education and have some technical knowledge of instrument construction and use. The instrument may be scored by hand or computer.

Psychometric Properties: An *Examiner's Manual* (1989) provides a description of the *LOQ* and information on usage, development, reliability, and validity.

Author(s): Edwin A. Fleishman
Publication Date: 1960-1969, 1989
Cost: Package of 25 test booklets: $46; *Examiner's Manual*: $24; scoring software: $129
Time: 10 to 15 minutes
Number of Items: 40
Audience: Managers, supervisors
Subject(s): Interpersonal relations
Source: NCS Workforce Development. Rosemont, IL. (800) 221-8378. www.ncs.com

LEADERSHIP PRACTICES INVENTORY (LPI)

This instrument is based on the premise that leadership is an observable, learnable set of practices and that those with the desire and persistence to lead can improve their leadership skills. The five practices measured are: challenging the process, inspiring a shared vision, enabling others to act, modeling the way, and encouraging others. According to the authors, "The *LPI* helps you discover to what extent you have incorporated these five practices into your everyday behavioral repertoire." For a comprehensive review of this instrument, refer to J. B. Leslie & J. W. Fleenor (1998),

Feedback to Managers: A Review and Comparison of Multi-rater Instruments for Management Development (3rd ed.). Greensboro, NC: Center for Creative Leadership. Variations of this instrument include: *LPI–Delta* to assess changes in leadership practices, *Team LPI* to measure behaviors common to high-performing teams, *LPI–Individual Contributor* for self-development, and *LPI–Student* for college students.

Administration: The *LPI* can be self-scored or computer scored. The computer scoring generates a feedback printout. A facilitator's manual provides interpretive and background information, and a development guide helps individuals use the feedback provided.

Psychometric Properties: A report from the vendor, *Psychometric Properties of the LPI,* describes test development, validity, and reliability. Norms have been developed for several populations.

Author(s): Barry Z. Posner & James M. Kouzes
Publication Date: 1988, 1993, 1997
Cost: Self-test: $13; observer test: $4; *Facilitator's Guide*: $50—includes scoring software
Time: 10 minutes
Number of Items: 30
Audience: Managers
Subject(s): Leadership skills
Source: Jossey-Bass/Pfeiffer. San Francisco, CA. (800) 274-4434. www.pfeiffer.com

LEADERSHIP SKILLS

This multi-rater feedback instrument evaluates 16 competencies in four categories: task management, team development, business values, and leadership. The instrument's open architecture allows customers to customize items, demographics, score areas, graphics layout, report narratives, and company-specific norms. Feedback indicates management strengths, opportunities for development, skills that co-workers believe are most important for managers, and suggested activities for action planning. A personalized report delivers both graphic profiles and detailed, plain-English narratives that provide individualized feedback. For a comprehensive review of this instrument, refer to J. B. Leslie & J. W. Fleenor (1998), *Feedback to Managers: A Review and Comparison of Multi-rater Instruments for Management Development* (3rd ed.). Greensboro, NC: Center for Creative Leadership. This instrument was formerly titled *PRAXIS® for Managers.*

Administration: Available in paper-and-pencil, computer-based, and web-based formats. Acumen provides quarterly train-the-trainer sessions to certify qualified professionals.

Psychometric Properties: The *Technical Report on Methods and Validity* (1995) provides detailed development, reliability, and validity data. Norms are updated every two years.

Author(s): Christopher W. Guest, Peter D. Gratzinger, Ronald A. Warren, & Acumen International

Publication Date: 1990, 1993, 1996, 1998
Cost: $200 per participant for full service or software for in-house use: $7,500
Time: 20 minutes
Number of Items: 116
Audience: Executives, managers
Subject(s): Leadership skills
Source: Acumen International, Inc. San Rafael, CA. (415) 492-9190. www.acumen.com

New
LEADERSHIP WORK*STYLES*™

This multi-rater feedback instrument identifies 12 attitudes that reflect a leader's thinking styles: humanistic, affiliation, approval, conventional, dependence, apprehension, oppositional, power, competition, perfectionism, achievement, and self-actualization. The instrument's open architecture allows clients to customize demographics, items, score areas, graphics layout, report narratives, and company-specific norms. For a comprehensive review of this instrument, refer to J. B. Leslie & J. W. Fleenor (1998), *Feedback to Managers: A Review and Comparison of Multi-rater Instruments for Management Development* (3rd ed.). Greensboro, NC: Center for Creative Leadership. A variation for teams, *Team WorkStyles*, is also available.

Administration: Available in paper-and-pencil, computer-based, and web-based formats. Acumen provides quarterly train-the-trainer sessions to certify qualified professionals.

Psychometric Properties: Test development, validity, reliability, and norms are available in technical reports from Acumen.

Author(s): Ronald A. Warren, Peter D. Gratzinger, & Acumen International
Publication Date: 1987, 1992, 1998
Cost: $200 per participant for full service or software for in-house use: $7,500
Time: 15 minutes
Number of Items: 96
Audience: Executives, managers, teams
Subject(s): Thinking
Source: Acumen International, Inc. San Rafael, CA. (415) 492-9190. www.acumen.com

LEARNING STYLES QUESTIONNAIRE

This questionnaire helps individuals learn about their preferences for four learning styles. *Activists* are dominated by immediate experiences, get excited by new challenges, and are bored with implementation. *Reflectors* collect data, analyze experiences, and are cautious to act on new learnings. *Theorists* prefer logical, complex, integrated learning based on sound principles and systems thinking. *Pragmatists* seek out new ideas to put into practice.

Administration: This instrument is self-administered and self-scored. Interpretive and usage guidelines are in the test booklet. The *Facilitator Guide* contains suggestions for training.

Psychometric Properties: The *Facilitator Guide* briefly discusses test development and reliability. Construct validity has not been established. A wide variety of occupational norms are reported, as are cultural and gender norms.

Author(s): Peter Honey & Alan Mumford
Publication Date: 1986, 1989, 1995
Cost: Five tests: $32; five workbooks: $36; *Facilitator Guide*: $35
Time: 90 minutes
Number of Items: 80
Audience: General
Subject(s): Learning
Source: HRDQ. King of Prussia, PA. (800) 633-4533. www.hrdq.com

New
LEARNING TACTICS INVENTORY (LTI)

LTI is based on a model of four learning behaviors: action, thinking, feeling, and accessing others. In challenging situations, some learners rely on all four tactics. Others may overuse or underuse any one of the tactics causing behaviors such as procrastination or reinventing the wheel. This test aims to help participants identify their current learning behaviors and make a development plan for enhanced learning tactics.

Administration: This paper-and-pencil test is self-administered, self-scored, and self-interpreted. The *Participant's Workbook* contains an action planning guide. The *Facilitator's Guide* contains lessons for a half-day workshop.

Psychometric Properties: Test development, validity, reliability, and norms are described in the *Facilitator's Guide*.

Author(s): Maxine Dalton
Publication Date: 1999
Cost: Participant workbook: $12.95; *Facilitator's Guide*: $24.95
Time: 10 minutes
Number of Items: 32
Audience: General
Subject(s): Learning competence
Source: Jossey-Bass/Pfeiffer. San Francisco, CA. (800) 274-4434. www.pfeiffer.com

New
MANAGEMENT DEVELOPMENT QUESTIONNAIRE (MDQ)

This self-test is based on the MDQ Competency Model of five scales and 20 competencies: 1) managing change—initiative, risk-taking, innovation, and flexibility; 2) planning and organizing—analytical thinking, decision making, planning, and quality focus; 3) interpersonal skills—oral

communication, sensitivity, relationships, and teamwork; 4) results orientation—achievement, customer focus, business awareness, and learning orientation; and 5) leadership—authority, motivating others, developing people, and resilience. Participants indicate how strongly they agree that each of the 160 statements pertains to themselves and their competencies.

Administration: This paper-and-pencil test may be self-administered, self-scored, and self-interpreted. The test booklet includes guidelines for interpretation and activities for improving competencies.

Psychometric Properties: The test booklet contains a norm conversion table, but no psychometric data is available.

Author(s): A. P. Cameron & The Test Agency
Publication Date: 1997
Cost: Tests: $9.95 (paper) or $14.95 (computer); *User's Manual*: $24.95
Time: 35 minutes
Number of Items: 160
Audience: Managers
Subject(s): Self-development
Source: HRD Press. Amherst, MA. (800) 822-2801. www.hrdpress.com

New
MANAGING BY MOTIVATION (3RD ED.)

This test identifies the forces of personal motivation at work. Participants respond to 20 statements about their attitudes and feelings on work life such as "Being part of a close-knit group is very important to me" and "Chasing after dreams is a waste of time." Scores indicate the personal importance of four motivational forces: security, a sense of belonging, self-esteem, and self-actualization.

Administration: This paper-and-pencil test is self-administered and self-scored. The test booklet contains an interpretive guide. The trainer guide provides background information on Maslow's Need Hierarchy and Herzberg's Motivation-Hygiene Theory as well as a syllabus for a three-hour lesson on motivation.

Psychometric Properties: Test development, validity, and reliability are briefly described in the *Trainer Guide,* but no data are reported. No norms are available.

Author(s): Marshall Sashkin
Publication Date: 1986, 1990, 1996
Cost: Tests: $5.95; trainer guide: $24.95
Time: 15 minutes
Number of Items: 20
Audience: General
Subject(s): Motivation
Source: HRD Press. Amherst, MA. (800) 822-2801. www.hrdpress.com

New
MANCHESTER PERSONALITY QUESTIONNAIRE (MPQ)

This test focuses on personality traits that support creativity and the capacity to be an innovative manager. The most extensive version of the test measures 14 dimensions of personality: originality, openness to change, social confidence, communicativeness, role conscientiousness, decisiveness, rationality, assertiveness, empathy, independence, competitiveness, perfectionism, and apprehension. Also available are a seven-factor version and a "Big-Five" version that analyzes resilience, extraversion, achievement, agreeableness, and creativity.

Administration: This test is available in paper-and-pencil and online versions. Scoring and reporting are done by a qualified facilitator.

Psychometric Properties: The *Technical and User Manual* contains information about test development, validity, reliability, and norms.

Author(s): A. P. Cameron
Publication Date: 1996
Cost: Tests: $10 (paper) or $25 (computer); *Technical and User Manual*: $30
Time: 20 minutes
Number of Items: 120
Audience: General
Subject(s): Personality
Source: HRD Press. Amherst, MA. (800) 822-2801. www.hrdpress.com

MATRIX: THE INFLUENCE BEHAVIOR QUESTIONNAIRE

This instrument measures nine influence tactics: rational persuasion, inspirational appeal, consultation, ingratiation, personal appeal, exchange, coalition, pressure, and legitimation. Self-reported scores are compared to feedback from others to create an influence-behavior profile. A companion workbook contains interpretive information and dozens of exercises to help participants learn about types of power and appropriate times to use each influence tactic. For a comprehensive review of this instrument, refer to J. B. Leslie & J. W. Fleenor (1998), *Feedback to Managers: A Review and Comparison of Multi-rater Instruments for Management Development* (3rd ed.). Greensboro, NC: Center for Creative Leadership.

Administration: Facilitators must be certified at a certification workshop provided by Manus. *Matrix* is computer scored by the vendor. A manual provides interpretive assistance and instrument background. A workbook helps participants understand their feedback and plan actions for improvement.

Psychometric Properties: A Right Manus report describes test development, validity, and reliability.

Author(s): Gary Yukl, Rick Lepsinger, & Toni Lucia
Publication Date: 1997

Cost: $300 to $365 per participant
Time: 20 minutes
Number of Items: 45
Audience: Executives, managers, supervisors
Subject(s): Influence
Source: Right Manus. Stamford, CT. (800) 445-0942. www.rightmanus.com

MULTIFACTOR LEADERSHIP QUESTIONNAIRE (MLQ)

The *MLQ* measures transformational and transactional leadership skills as developed and defined by James MacGregor Burns, Bernard Bass, and others. Five scales reflect transformational leadership and three reflect transactional leadership. Additionally, there is a "non-transactional leadership" scale and three organizational-outcome scales. The transformational scales are idealized influence (attributions), idealized influence (behaviors), inspirational motivation, intellectual stimulation, and individualized consideration. The transactional scales are contingent reward, active management-by-exception, and passive management-by-exception. The three organizational-outcome scales are extra effort, effectiveness, and satisfaction. For a comprehensive review of this instrument, refer to J. B. Leslie & J. W. Fleenor (1998), *Feedback to Managers: A Review and Comparison of Multi-rater Instruments for Management Development* (3rd ed.). Greensboro, NC: Center for Creative Leadership. A *Team MLQ* is also available for assessing the leadership style of a work team.

Administration: This instrument is completed by a manager and a full range of raters (higher organizational level, same organizational level, lower organizational level, and don't want organizational level to be known). Vendor scoring provides an extensive, tailored interpretive report, including graphics and suggestions for improving leadership. Contact Mind Garden about using the *MLQ* as a research instrument.

Psychometric Properties: The *MLQ* is based on many studies of managers in varied kinds of organizations. The feedback scales were developed through factor analysis. Reliability studies include test-retest, internal consistency, and interrater. A number of validity studies are reported. Over 75 academic research studies have been completed and others are underway. Cross-national validity of the *MLQ* is discussed in B. M. Bass (1997), "Does the Transactional-Transformational Leadership Paradigm Transcend Organizational and National Boundaries?" *American Psychologist, 52*(2), 130-139.

Author(s): Bernard M. Bass & Bruce J. Avolio
Publication Date: 1985, 1989, 1990, 1995
Cost: $125—includes self-test, six feedback tests, computer scoring, and interpretive report
Time: 10 minutes
Number of Items: 45
Audience: Executives, managers, supervisors
Subject(s): Transformational leadership

Source: Mind Garden, Inc. Redwood City, CA. (650) 261-3500. www.mindgarden.com

MYERS-BRIGGS TYPE INDICATOR® STEP II (MBTI)

This instrument is used in some organizations for leadership development purposes. It is based on Jung's theory of types, measuring four bipolar aspects of personality: Extraversion-Introversion, Sensing-Intuition, Thinking-Feeling, and Judging-Perceiving. Combining these four dimensions yields 16 possible types. Each of the four personality dimensions is further examined by five component parts, which, when analyzed, suggest one's styles of communication, problem solving, decision making, change management, and conflict management.

Administration: Facilitators must meet educational requirements or attend a certification workshop. Completed tests are returned to CPP for computer scoring and generation of profile reports. Software for in-house scoring and reporting is available. Participants who take both the *MBTI* and the *FIRO-B*™ may receive a separate Leadership Report for an additional $39.

Psychometric Properties: Test development, validity, reliability, and norms are described in Myers, McCaulley, Quenk, & Hammer (1998), *MBTI Manual: A Guide to the Development and Use of the Myers-Briggs Type Indicator* (3rd ed.).

Author(s): Isabel Briggs Myers & Katherine C. Briggs
Publication Date: 1991
Cost: $29; *MBTI Applications*: $58
Time: 30 to 40 minutes
Number of Items: 131
Audience: General
Subject(s): Personality
Source: Consulting Psychologists Press, Inc. (CPP). Palo Alto, CA. (800) 624-1765. www.cpp-db.com

NEGOTIATING STYLE PROFILE (NSP)

NSP measures an individual's preferred style of negotiating. Participants learn about five styles: defeating the other party at any cost, collaborating for a win-win outcome, accommodating the other party's needs, withdrawal from the negotiation, and meeting the other party halfway. Feedback is available when using the optional *NSP-Other* test.

Administration: HRDQ recommends using this tool as a learning exercise before a training session on conflict management.

Psychometric Properties: Test development and reliability are reported in the *Facilitator Guide*. No validity studies are reported. Norms are provided for individuals in a variety of service and manufacturing industries.

Author(s): Rollin Glaser & Christine Glaser
Publication Date: 1983, 1986, 1989, 1991, 1996
Cost: Five tests: $36; five feedback booklets: $18; *Facilitator Guide*: $30

Time: 15 to 25 minutes
Number of Items: 30
Audience: General
Subject(s): Negotiation
Source: HRDQ. King of Prussia, PA. (800) 633-4533. www.hrdq.com

New
ORGANIZATIONAL BELIEFS QUESTIONNAIRE (OBQ)

Based on the work of Peters and Waterman in the book *In Search of Excellence* (1982) and Collins and Porras in *Built to Last* (1994), Sashkin has identified ten cultural values that are linked to organizational excellence: 1) work can be as much fun as play, 2) seek constant improvement, 3) accept specific and difficult goals, 4) accept responsibility for your actions, 5) care about one another, 6) quality is crucially important, 7) work together to get the job done, 8) measure success, 9) hands-on management, and 10) strong shared values guide actions. The test contains 50 statements related to these cultural values and participants rate their experiences and perceptions of each within their organizational context.

Administration: Paper-and-pencil surveys may be given to all organizational members or a random sample. When completed, they are sent to HRD Press for computer scoring and reporting. A *Survey Administrator's Guide* contains instructions for a designated company facilitator to administer the survey, interpret the results, and conduct a lecturette on values.

Psychometric Properties: The *Technical Manual* describes test development, validity, and norms. No reliability data are reported.

Author(s): Marshall Sashkin
Publication Date: 1984, 1988, 1991, 1997
Cost: $495
Time: 20 minutes
Number of Items: 50
Audience: Organizational members
Subject(s): Organizational culture
Source: HRD Press. Amherst, MA. (800) 822-2801. www.hrdpress.com

New
PENGUIN INDEX

This instrument, based on the authors' book, *A Peacock in the Land of Penguins* (1995, 1997), is designed to measure an organization's support of a diverse workforce. The items evaluate an organization's human resources and management practices in five areas: 1) pluralism—hiring a diverse workforce and valuing the differences among people; 2) openness—informing employees of opportunities and problems; 3) participation—employees are encouraged to develop ideas and make decisions; 4) support—employees receive all the training, information, equipment, and authority they need to do their jobs; and 5) fairness—recognition, rewards, and promotion are based on talent, skill, and contribution. Two companion instruments, the *Peacock Profile* and *Birds of Different Feathers*, measure individual uniqueness, work style, and organizational fit.

Administration: This instrument is self-scored and self-interpreted. The *Facilitator Guide* contains resources for four diversity workshops. A variety of books and training videos support the diversity lessons.

Psychometric Properties: Technical data about test development, validity, reliability, and norms are not available.

Author(s): Warren H. Schmidt & Barbara "BJ" Hately
Publication Date: 1995
Cost: $7.25; *Facilitator Guide*: $99
Time: 10 minutes
Number of Items: 25
Audience: Managers
Subject(s): Diversity
Source: Consulting Psychologists Press, Inc. (CPP). Palo Alto, CA. (800) 624-1765. www.cpp-db.com

New
PERCEIVED LEADER INTEGRITY SCALE (PLIS)

PLIS identifies the behaviors that contribute to impressions of a leader's integrity. Subordinates respond to a list of unethical behaviors and attitudes in an organizational setting as they pertain to immediate supervisors. Items fall within seven behavioral domains: 1) training and development, 2) resource and workload allocation, 3) truth telling, 4) unlawful discrimination, 5) compliance with policies and procedures, 6) maliciousness, and 7) self-protection. Response choices for each item are: not at all, somewhat, very much, and exactly. There is no safe middle choice that allows participants to avoid sensitive issues. A low score indicates the perception of a high level of ethical and moral integrity.

Administration: There are no scoring or interpretation guidelines available at this time.

Psychometric Properties: The article describes test development, validity, and reliability. No norms are reported.

Author(s): S. Bartholomew Craig & Sigrid B. Gustafson
Publication Date: 1998
Time: 10 minutes
Number of Items: 31
Audience: Supervisors
Subject(s): Integrity
Source: S. B. Craig & S. B. Gustafson (1998), "Perceived Leader Integrity Scale: An instrument for assessing employee perceptions of leader integrity," *Leadership Quarterly*, 9(2), 127-145. Bart Craig may be contacted at Discovery Learning. Greensboro, NC. (336) 272-9530.

POWER BASE INVENTORY

This instrument measures the following managerial power styles: information giving, expertise, goodwill, authority, reward, and discipline. Power is defined as the ability to influence people, either by personal power or position power. Individuals select whichever of two statements is more descriptive of the reasons why subordinates might comply with their wishes or beliefs.

Administration: The *Power Base Inventory* is self-scored and graphed on a chart in the test booklet. Eleven pages of interpretation and usage guidelines are also provided in the booklet.

Psychometric Properties: This instrument uses a forced-choice format and is based upon B. H. Raven's studies of power bases. Internal consistency and test-retest reliability coefficients are reported. Convergent validity and preliminary external validity data are also reported.

Author(s): Kenneth W. Thomas & Gail Fann Thomas
Publication Date: 1985, 1991
Cost: $6.75
Time: 30 minutes
Number of Items: 30
Audience: General
Subject(s): Power
Source: Consulting Psychologists Press, Inc. (CPP). Palo Alto, CA. (800) 624-1765. www.cpp-db.com

POWER MANAGEMENT INVENTORY (PMI)

This forced-choice instrument was developed from the three power styles identified by McClelland and Burnham. It was designed to assess both power motivation as well as power practices. For instance, when using power, a manager may be motivated by a need to control employees, a desire to benefit the organization, or a desire to be liked by others. That same manager may employ a power style that is autocratic, collaborative, or weak. This instrument is designed for managers to rate their own motives and styles and to compare their self-scores to those of their employees. The feedback companion instrument, *Power Management Profile,* is available separately.

Administration: Both instruments are self-administered. Scoring and interpretation are done by the manager or a third party.

Psychometric Properties: Reliability and validity data are discussed briefly in the test booklet and at greater length in a 1981 report available from the publisher. Norms for managerial populations in technology, manufacturing, sales, finance, human service, government, and law enforcement are available.

Author(s): Jay Hall & James Hawker
Publication Date: 1981, 1988, 1995
Cost: $8.95
Time: 15 to 30 minutes
Number of Items: 70
Audience: Managers

Subject(s): Power
Source: Teleometrics International. The Woodlands, TX.
(800) 527-0406. www.teleometrics.com

THE PROFILOR®

A customizable multi-rater feedback instrument, *The PROFILOR* measures 24 management skills, including analyzing issues, building relationships, and leading courageously. The authors state that they have "developed a new skills model based on the manager's current role, which requires such skills as fostering teamwork, participative management, championing change, and displaying organizational savvy." The three-part feedback consists of a summary, detailed information, and a development plan. Optional skill areas that may be included at the organization's request are: recognize global implications, value diversity, leverage networks, and innovate. *The PROFILOR for Individual Contributors* is recommended for professionals who do not have direct responsibility for managing people. For a comprehensive review of this instrument, refer to J. B. Leslie & J. W. Fleenor (1998), *Feedback to Managers: A Review and Comparison of Multi-rater Instruments for Management Development* (3rd ed.). Greensboro, NC: Center for Creative Leadership.

Administration: Scoring is done by PDI. Feedback may be provided by PDI or by feedback-givers trained and certified by PDI.

Psychometric Properties: This test grew out of PDI's model of management performance and an earlier instrument, the *Management Skills Profile*. Validity, reliability, and norms are presented in *The PROFILOR Technical Summary*.

Author(s): Personnel Decisions International (PDI)
Publication Date: 1991
Cost: $275—includes one self- and ten other-rater forms, feedback report, development guide, development plan, and scoring
Time: 30 to 45 minutes
Number of Items: 135
Audience: Managers
Subject(s): Leadership skills
Source: Personnel Decisions International. Minneapolis, MN. (800) 633-4410. www.pdi-corp.com

PROSPECTOR™

This multi-rater questionnaire is designed to measure an individual's ability to learn and take advantage of the growth experiences that facilitate leadership development. There are 11 dimensions: seeks opportunities to learn, acts with integrity, adapts to cultural differences, is committed to making a difference, seeks broad business knowledge, brings out the best in people, is insightful, has courage to take risks, seeks and uses feedback, learns from mistakes, and is open to criticism. For a comprehensive review of this instrument, refer to J. B. Leslie & J. W. Fleenor (1998), *Feedback to*

Managers: A Review and Comparison of Multi-rater Instruments for Management Development (3rd ed.). Greensboro, NC: Center for Creative Leadership.

Administration: Facilitators must meet qualification requirements. The *User's Guide* includes suggestions for giving feedback and planning development. Return completed tests to CCL for computer scoring and computer-generated report.

Psychometric Properties: Test development, validity, and reliability are described in the *User's Guide*. Norms are based on 2,500 managers from more than 100 national and multinational companies.

Author(s): Morgan W. McCall, Jr., Gretchen M. Spreitzer, & John Mahoney
Publication Date: 1994, 1995
Cost: $195; *User's Guide*: $30
Time: 10 minutes
Number of Items: 48
Audience: Managers
Subject(s): Learning
Source: Center for Creative Leadership (CCL). Greensboro, NC. (336) 286-4480. www.ccl.org

SKILLSCOPE®

This 360-degree-feedback instrument assesses managerial strengths and development needs. Results are summarized in 15 clusters of management skills, presented in a display that indicates whether the skill is a strength, development need, or neither. Some of the skill clusters are: informational, decision making, interpersonal, use of resources, and self-management.

Administration: Qualified facilitators administer the test, send scannable forms to CCL for scoring, and deliver feedback based on detailed reports. A *Trainer's Guide* provides guidelines for interpreting results and conducting training.

Psychometric Properties: Test-retest and internal-consistency reliability studies are reported in the *Trainer's Guide*. Validity was assessed using an independent measure of manager effectiveness.

Author(s): Robert E. Kaplan
Publication Date: 1988, 1996, 1997
Cost: $155—includes one self- and nine observer forms, scoring, report, and development planning guide; *Trainer's Guide*: $20
Time: 20 to 30 minutes
Number of Items: 98
Audience: Executives, managers, supervisors
Subject(s): Leadership skills
Source: Center for Creative Leadership (CCL). Greensboro, NC. (336) 286-4480. www.ccl.org

SOCIAL SKILLS INVENTORY (SSI)

Social communication is divided into sending skills (expressivity), receiving skills (sensitivity), and controlling skills. Nonverbal communication is classified as emotional, whereas verbal communication is classified as social. Use of these influence strategies is identified: rapport, mirroring, and deception. The author suggests that the *SSI* could be a useful tool in leadership development workshops. He also reports research that suggests high scorers on the *SSI* may be seen as charismatic.

Administration: This paper-and-pencil instrument should be administered by professionals who have a background in psychological testing.

Psychometric Properties: Test development, validity, and reliability are reported in the *SSI Manual*. Norms are based on a college student population.

Author(s): Ronald E. Riggio
Publication Date: 1989
Cost: 25 test booklets: $55; 25 answer sheets: $55; scoring key and manual: $41
Time: 30 to 45 minutes
Number of Items: 90
Audience: General
Subject(s): Communication
Source: Consulting Psychologists Press, Inc. (CPP). Palo Alto, CA. (800) 624-1765. www.cpp-db.com

STRENGTH DEPLOYMENT INVENTORY® (SDI)

This inventory measures an individual's self-reported style of relating to others under two conditions: when things are going well, and when things are not going well and the respondent is in conflict with others. Scores are plotted on an Interpersonal Interaction Triangle and graphically illustrate the individual's strength of motivation toward four polarities: altruistic-nurturing, assertive-directing, analytic-autonomizing, and flexible-cohering. The 1997 edition also reports on three blends: assertive-nurturing, judicious-competing, and cautious-supporting. The *Feedback Edition* collects data from co-workers. The *Personal Values Inventory* is a simplified version for young people or others who use colloquial English.

Administration: The *SDI* is self-administered. The self-contained form provides instructions for plotting scores as well as text and graphs for understanding and interpreting the results. A *Manual of Administration and Interpretation* provides facilitators and trainers with technical background and other administrative information. There is no special certification required to use and administer the *SDI*.

Psychometric Properties: Test development, validity, reliability, and norms are reported in the administration manual and in a separate *Reliability and Validity* brochure. External validity was tested by examining scores of groups.

Author(s): Elias H. Porter
Publication Date: 1973, 1989, 1992, 1997

Cost: Test: $9; premier test booklet with exercises: $20; feedback test: $4; administration manual: $30
Time: 20 minutes
Number of Items: 20
Audience: General
Subject(s): Interpersonal relations
Source: Personal Strengths Publishing®. Carlsbad, CA. (800) 624-7347. www.personalstrengths.com

THE STUDENT LEADERSHIP INVENTORY (SLI)

This is the student version of *The Visionary Leader: Leader Behavior Questionnaire* in which items have been rewritten with the assumption that the respondent is not yet in a position of leadership. Students and their peers respond to statements about ability, fairness, communication, credibility, respect, courage, confidence, influence, vision, and principles to determine if the participants exhibit a transactional or a transformational leadership style.

Administration: Answer sheets are returned to Dr. Rosenbach for scoring. Students receive separate reports for their self-test scores and for their observers' scores. A guidebook provides instructions for interpreting the reports.

Psychometric Properties: Development, reliability, and validity data are available on the instrument from which the *SLI* was derived, *The Visionary Leader: Leader Behavior Questionnaire*.

Author(s): Marshall Sashkin & William E. Rosenbach
Publication Date: 1995
Cost: $3—includes test, scoring, and report; minimum order of $100
Time: 30 minutes
Number of Items: 50
Audience: Students
Subject(s): Vision
Source: Available from Dr. William Rosenbach, Department of Management, Gettysburg College, Box 395, Gettysburg, PA 17325. (717) 337-6648. william.e.rosenbach@gettysburg.edu

SUBSTITUTES FOR LEADERSHIP SCALE—REVISED

This instrument is a considerably revised version based on one originally developed in 1978 by S. Kerr & J. M. Jermier ("Substitutes for Leadership: Their Meaning and Measurement," *Organizational Behavior and Human Performance*, 22(3), 375-403). It was designed to further test Kerr and Jermier's premise that in certain situations "certain individual, task, and organizational variables act as 'substitutes for leadership,' negating the hierarchical superior's ability to exert either positive or negative influence over subordinate attitudes and effectiveness." The *SLS-R* contains 13 subscales, each reflecting some aspect of the subordinate, task, or organization that may substitute for leader influence.

Administration: This paper-and-pencil test may be administered, scored, and interpreted with information in the article.

Psychometric Properties: Test development, validity, and reliability data are discussed in P. M. Podsakoff & S. B. MacKenzie (1994), "An Examination of the Psychometric Properties and Nomological Validity of Some Revised and Reduced Substitutes for Leadership Scales," *Journal of Applied Psychology, 79*(5), 702-713.

Author(s): Philip M. Podsakoff, Brian P. Niehoff, Scott B. MacKenzie, & Margaret L. Williams

Publication Date: 1993

Cost: Contact the authors for availability and research use

Time: 20 minutes

Number of Items: 74

Audience: General

Subject(s): Substitutes for Leadership Theory

Source: Philip M. Podsakoff, Brian P. Niehoff, Scott B. MacKenzie, & Margaret L. Williams (1993), "Do Substitutes for Leadership Really Substitute for Leadership? An Empirical Examination of Kerr and Jermier's Situational Leadership Model," *Organizational Behavior and Human Decision Processes, 54*(1), 1-44. Contact Philip Podsakoff, Department of Management, Kelley School of Business, Indiana University, Bloomington, IN 47405. (812) 855-2747. podsakof@indiana.edu

SUCCESS STYLE PROFILE® (SSP)

The *SSP* is based on the premise that the behaviors we associate with personality are influenced by a person's thinking style. This cognitive-styles inventory asks participants to state their preferences in pairs of situations related to leadership and stretch assignments. It also raises awareness of the operating-style differences among people and groups. Output about style information is presented as eight modes of thinking, each resulting from a different configuration of three basic dimensions: perception-conception, logic-feel, and external-internal focus of attention.

Administration: There are two alternatives for using the *SSP*: 1) Facilitators who interpret scores must attend a five-day certification workshop. Performance Support Systems provides computer scoring and individual reports that chart the results. A booklet and a summary chart of leadership modes are available to assist individuals in interpreting their results. An administrator's handbook and a facilitator's guide are available. 2) The second alternative is self-orientation. Individuals may purchase a set of Signature rank-order cards representing the eight modes to learn about their own leadership style. No data are generated. Facilitators may use the Signature cards for programs based on self-orientation without attending the certification workshop.

Psychometric Properties: A report from the author describes test development, validity, and reliability.

Author(s): Dennis E. Coates

Publication Date: 1988, 1992

Cost: $55—includes question booklet, scoring, analysis, and cards

Time: 30 to 45 minutes

Number of Items: 96

Audience: General

Subject(s): Leadership styles

Source: Performance Support Systems. Newport News, VA. (800) 488-6463. www.2020insight.net

SURVEY OF LEADERSHIP PRACTICES (SLP)

This survey measures leadership effectiveness. It is based on Wilson's model, the Leadership Task Cycle, which includes six competencies: 1) entrepreneurial vision—imagination and risk-taking; 2) leadership for change—organizational sensitivity, encouraging participation; 3) gaining commitment—empowering and persuasiveness; 4) monitoring personal impact—feedback; 5) drive—standards of performance, energy, perseverance, and push; and 6) recognizing performance—sharing credit. When there is a balance of high competency across the model, there are two consequences apparent in the test results—residual impact and power. The *Survey of Management Practices* is a similar instrument used to measure management skills such as goal setting and problem solving. The *Survey of Executive Leadership* measures the combined management and leadership skills needed to achieve organizational growth. *Our Team* and *My Team Mates* surveys apply the Task Cycle model to team processes. For a comprehensive review of *SLP* and *SMP*, refer to J. B. Leslie & J. W. Fleenor (1998), *Feedback to Managers: A Review and Comparison of Multi-rater Instruments for Management Development* (3rd ed.). Greensboro, NC: Center for Creative Leadership.

Administration: Facilitators may be required to attend a qualification workshop. *SLP* is computer scored. Feedback consists of narrative and graphs, and a personal-planning guide is available. A trainer's guide provides administration, background, and feedback information.

Psychometric Properties: Information about test development, validity, and reliability is available from the vendor.

Author(s): Paul M. Connolly & Clark L. Wilson

Publication Date: 1987, 1989, 1995, 1997

Cost: $21 to $28

Time: 30 minutes

Number of Items: 88

Audience: Managers, project leaders

Subject(s): Leadership skills

Source: Clark Wilson Group, Inc. Boulder, CO. (800) 537-7249. www.cwginc.com

SYMLOG®

This multi-rater instrument measures one's adherence to individual and organizational values. Based on the work of Robert F. Bales, it produces scores on three dimensions that have emerged repeatedly in research as critical in understanding individual and group behavior: friendliness versus unfriendliness, dominance versus submissiveness, and accepting versus opposing established authority. For a comprehensive review of this instrument, refer to J. B. Leslie & J. W. Fleenor (1998), *Feedback to Managers: A*

Review and Comparison of Multi-rater Instruments for Management Development (3rd ed.). Greensboro, NC: Center for Creative Leadership.

Administration: This instrument may be used for analysis at the individual, group, or organizational level. Facilitators must be certified. SYMLOG offers certification workshops.

Psychometric Properties: Numerous books and articles by Robert F. Bales describe the test development, validity, and reliability. There is a large norm group that is an aggregate of a number of samples.

Author(s): SYMLOG Consulting Group
Publication Date: 1983, 1984, 1986, 1990, 1991, 1997
Cost: Contact the publisher
Time: 20 to 30 minutes
Number of Items: 26 (repeated four times)
Audience: Executives, managers, teams
Subject(s): Values
Source: SYMLOG Consulting Group. San Diego, CA. (858) 673-2098. www.symlog.com

TEAM LEADER SURVEY

In this survey, team leaders rank how well they currently interact with team members. Team members, peers, and managers provide feedback to obtain a team leader effectiveness profile in six skill areas: communication, thinking, administration, influence, interpersonal skills, and change management. Worksheets help participants identify skills they wish to develop and make action plans for development.

Administration: The *Facilitator Guide* contains instructions for scoring, interpreting, and delivering feedback. It also includes an agenda for training, suggested actions for developing each of the six skills, and transparency masters. HRDQ also offers a scoring and feedback service.

Psychometric Properties: The *Facilitator's Guide* discusses test development and reliability. No validity data are reported. Limited norms are reported.

Author(s): Ann Burress
Publication Date: 1994, 1995
Cost: Five participant booklets: $32; five feedback booklets: $18; *Facilitator Guide*: $30
Time: 2 hours
Number of Items: 36
Audience: Teams
Subject(s): Teams
Source: HRDQ. King of Prussia, PA. (800) 633-4533. www.hrdq.com

TEAM PERFORMANCE QUESTIONNAIRE (TPQ)

The purpose of the *TPQ* is to provide team leaders and members with information about their work group characteristics and to identify opportunities for improvement. It is based on Riechmann's Team Performance Model, which describes six characteristics of high-performing teams:

leadership, goals and results, collaboration and involvement, competencies, communication processes, and emotional climate.

Administration: Team members complete the questionnaire prior to a three-hour team meeting. An administrator scores the anonymous tests and brings results to the team meeting. At the meeting, team members learn the summary scores and use the workbook to discuss the team's strengths and weaknesses and to plan team goals for improvement.

Psychometric Properties: The *Facilitator's Guide* briefly describes test development, validity, reliability, and norms.

Author(s): Donna Riechmann
Publication Date: 1997
Cost: Test and workbook: $12.95; *Facilitator's Guide*: $24.95
Time: 10 minutes
Number of Items: 32
Audience: Teams
Subject(s): Teams
Source: Jossey-Bass/Pfeiffer. San Francisco, CA. (800) 274-4434. www.pfeiffer.com

TEAMVIEW/360: EVALUATING TEAM PERFORMANCE

This is a computerized assessment system for intact work teams that generates both individual and team profiles. It is based on the *Individual Behavior Questionnaire (IBQ),* which assesses perceptions of individual behavioral effectiveness, ranging from cognitive to interpersonal. "Based on *a priori* conceptual schema, the 31 behaviors are grouped into seven categories." These categories are: problem solving, planning, controlling, managing self, managing relationships, leading, and communicating.

Administration: Each team member completes an *Individual Behavior Questionnaire* (which can be printed out by the software) to rate his or her own effectiveness, then uses equivalent Other Rating forms to assess each of the remaining team members. All rating data are then entered into a PC (presumably by a trusted person who is not part of the team) using the software program provided. The software can generate a number of charts, including a team profile and individual profiles, both of which compare self-ratings to ratings by others.

Psychometric Properties: A report from the author describes test development, validity, and reliability. No norms are reported.

Author(s): Michael R. Perrault, Kenneth R. Brousseau, Richard F. Gilmore, Max Mindel, & Marlene A. Benz
Publication Date: 1994
Cost: $30—includes software and one set of Team-Member profiles; additional Team-Member profiles: $30
Time: 15 minutes
Number of Items: 31
Audience: Intact work groups
Subject(s): Teams

ANG

Source: Jossey-Bass/Pfeiffer. San Francisco, CA. (800) 274-4434. www.pfeiffer.com

TEAMWORK-KSA TEST

This psychological test provides information about an individual's ability to work in a team setting. Participants respond to multiple-choice questions about hypothetical team situations to determine knowledge, skills, and abilities in five areas: conflict resolution, collaborative problem solving, communication, goal setting, and planning. Scores in each area identify training needs.

Administration: This test may be administered and scored by hand or on computer. Facilitators must have completed appropriate coursework in psychology or education and have some technical knowledge of instrument construction and use.

Psychometric Properties: The *Information Guide* discusses test development, validity, and reliability. Limited norms are reported by race, gender, and educational level.

Author(s): Michael J. Stevens & Michael A. Campion
Publication Date: 1994
Cost: 10 test booklets: $110; *Examiner's Manual*: $24; scoring software: $129
Time: 30 to 40 minutes
Number of Items: 35
Audience: Teams
Subject(s): Teams
Source: NCS Workforce Development. Rosemont, IL. (800) 221-8378. www.ncs.com

THOMAS-KILMANN CONFLICT MODE INSTRUMENT (TKI)

This instrument assesses an individual's self-reported behavior in conflict situations. It increases awareness of one's current style and alternative styles that one might practice. Styles of handling conflict include competing, collaborating, compromising, avoiding, and accommodating. A companion *Facilitator's Guide* provides three workshop formats, three group exercises, and case studies that may be used in conjunction with this instrument.

Administration: The instrument is self-scored and graphed on a chart in the test booklet. Seven pages of interpretation and usage guidelines are also provided in the booklet. A *Facilitator's Guide* includes three workshop formats, group exercises, case studies, and the instrument validity study.

Psychometric Properties: Validity and reliability data are reported in R. H. Kilmann & K. W. Thomas (1977), "Developing a Forced-choice Measure of Conflict-handling Behavior: The MODE instrument," *Educational and Psychological Measurement, 37*(2), 309-325.

Author(s): Kenneth W. Thomas & Ralph H. Kilmann
Publication Date: 1974
Cost: Test: $7; *Facilitator's Guide*: $103
Time: 15 minutes

Number of Items: 30
Audience: General
Subject(s): Conflict management
Source: Consulting Psychologists Press, Inc. (CPP). Palo Alto, CA. (800) 624-1765. www.cpp-db.com

THE VISIONARY LEADER: LEADER BEHAVIOR QUESTIONNAIRE (LBQ)

This questionnaire is completed by the leader and by the leader's associates. Each item describes a certain leadership behavior, characteristic, or effect a leader might have on the organization. Behavior patterns measured (scales) include clear leadership, communicative leadership, consistent leadership, caring leadership, creative leadership, confident leadership, empowered leadership, visionary leadership, and visionary culture building. Respondents are asked to indicate how true the statement is of the person they are rating. Scores provide information on the extent to which the person rated is a visionary leader, can elicit this response from others, and performs normal leadership functions. For a comprehensive review of this instrument, refer to J. B. Leslie & J. W. Fleenor (1998), *Feedback to Managers: A Review and Comparison of Multi-rater Instruments for Management Development* (3rd ed.). Greensboro, NC: Center for Creative Leadership.

Administration: The instrument is self-scored and results are plotted on a triangular grid. No certification is required to administer it.

Psychometric Properties: The *Trainer's Guide* contains information about test development, validity, reliability, and norms.

Author(s): Marshall Sashkin
Publication Date: 1984, 1985, 1988, 1990, 1995, 1998
Cost: $14.95—includes one self-test and three feedback tests; *Trainer Guide*: $24.95
Time: 20 minutes
Number of Items: 50
Audience: Managers
Subject(s): Vision
Source: HRD Press. Amherst, MA. (800) 822-2801. www.hrdpress.com

VOICES™

Voices is an electronic 360-degree assessment tool that is customized to fit individual learners. Data can be gathered on 67 core leadership competencies and 19 career stallers to provide continuous feedback from an unlimited number of raters over time. Participants design their own feedback reports to learn about their blind spots, hidden strengths, and relative importance of rated competencies. This tool is part of The Leadership Architect® Suite, an integrated set of tools that supports training needs analysis and succession planning. For a comprehensive review of this instrument, refer to J. B. Leslie & J. W. Fleenor (1998), *Feedback to Managers: A Review and Comparison of Multi-rater*

Instruments for Management Development (3rd ed.). Greensboro, NC: Center for Creative Leadership.

Administration: A certified facilitator oversees the administration and interpretation. Certification training is available from Lominger.

Psychometric Properties: Information about test development, validity, and reliability is available from Lominger.

Author(s): Michael M. Lombardo & Robert W. Eichinger
Publication Date: 1994, 1997
Cost: Administrative program: $1,000; report writer: $250; tests (self and other): $20 each use; contact Lominger for minimum purchase requirements and quantity discounts
Time: 60 minutes
Number of Items: 86—varies when customized
Audience: Executives, managers
Subject(s): Leadership development
Source: Lominger Limited, Inc. Minneapolis, MN. (952) 542-1466. www.lominger.com

New
THE YALE ASSESSMENT OF THINKING (YAT)

In an initial study of CEOs and subsequent surveys of a broader population, the authors identified three thinking domains common among successful leaders. These domains—reasoning, insight, and self-knowledge—make up a competency that the authors call *power thinking*. The *YAT* asks participants about behaviors that reflect their strong or weak performance in each domain. Brief suggestions in the test booklet and detailed guidelines in the authors' 2000 book, *Power Thinking for Leaders*, aim to strengthen this competency.

Administration: Paper-and-pencil test is self-administered and self-scored. Interpretation guidelines are in the test booklet.

Psychometric Properties: Test development, validity, and reliability are briefly reported in the test booklet. Norm data are discussed but not reported.

Author(s): John N. Mangieri & Cathy D. Block
Publication Date: 1999
Cost: Test: $14.95; book: $18.95
Time: 20 minutes
Number of Items: 54
Audience: General
Subject(s): Thinking, self-knowledge
Source: Teleometrics International. The Woodlands, TX. (800) 527-0406. www.teleometrics.com

EXERCISES

This section contains annotations of simulations, training devices, and experiential lessons in leadership development. An educator may use this active learning strategy to introduce a new concept, spark discussion, or change the pace in a classroom—inside or outside. Some items are brief ice-breakers, while others are complex experiences that evolve over several days. Most of those that require physical ability are adaptable to meet the needs of participants with physical limitations. Whenever possible, the descriptions include reference to support materials such as leader's guides or articles that describe using an exercise in the classroom. Each entry, as applicable, includes:

• author and publication date
• preparation tasks
• space and equipment needs
• cost
• number of participants
• time necessary to run the exercise
• intended audience
• subject
• source

New
2B OR KNOT 2B

Five different-colored ropes are tied into separate loops and a sixth one is looped through the others to join them together. All the ropes are tangled to disguise their pattern. The facilitator introduces the metaphor of a tangled economic problem in a small country and asks participants to determine the major factor controlling the other parts of the problem. Small groups must observe and discuss, without touching the tangle of ropes, to reach consensus on which rope holds the others together. The debriefing covers individual problem-solving techniques, the process of elimination, methods used to achieve consensus, and the relationship of the ropes to the problem metaphor.

Author: Jim Cain
Publication Date: 1995
Preparation: Tie knots
Space or Equipment Needs: Six ten-foot ropes of various colors
Number of Participants: Small groups
Time: 30 minutes
Audience: General
Subject(s): Decision making, problem solving, group consensus
Source: J. Cain in M. Gass (1995), *Book of Metaphors: Volume II* (pp. 164-166). Dubuque, IA: Kendall/Hunt. (800) 228-0810. www.kendallhunt.com

New
ADVENTURE IN THE AMAZON

This survival simulation is set in the Amazon rain forest of Brazil. While on an expedition to study tropical flora, a small plane makes an emergency landing and leaves the participants stranded in the wild. Participants must decide individually and then as a group which of 15 items are most crucial to their survival. Then as a group they decide on their best course of action. Rationale for recommended answers and scoring tables are included. This activity doesn't require a trained facilitator. Any member of the group may lead the activity.

Author: Lorraine L. Ukens
Publication Date: 1998
Cost: $6.95; *Leader's Guide*: $17.95
Number of Participants: 4 to 9
Time: 1-1/2 hours
Audience: General
Subject(s): Decision making, group consensus, teams
Source: Jossey-Bass/Pfeiffer. San Francisco, CA. (800) 274-4434. www.pfeiffer.com

AFTER NAFTA: A CROSS-CULTURAL NEGOTIATION EXERCISE

This exercise illustrates two styles of negotiating that are effective in cross-cultural situations: 1) logrolling, in which both sides lose a little to gain a lot, and 2) bridging, in which both sides must refocus on their most desirable outcomes. Participants assume roles as the mayors of towns on two sides of the U.S.-Mexico border. Each wants to entice the Japanese Kokishi Company to locate its chemical plant where his voters will benefit from new jobs and tax income. The mayors have strong cultural differences in the areas of individualism versus collectivism, power distance, and uncertainty avoidance. To achieve a win-win outcome the mayors must overcome cross-cultural miscommunication, must share information, and must learn to trust each other. For more explanation on logrolling and bridging negotiating styles, see J. K. Butler, Jr. (1996), Two integrative win-win negotiating strategies, *Simulation & Gaming, 27*(3), 387-392.

Author: John K. Butler, Jr.
Publication Date: 1996
Preparation: Photocopy role-player handouts
Space or Equipment Needs: Two rooms—one for activity and one for giving private instructions to observers
Number of Participants: Groups of 2 or 3
Time: 1 hour
Audience: General
Subject(s): Multicultural diversity, negotiation
Source: J. K. Butler, Jr. (1996), AFTER NAFTA: A cross-cultural negotiation exercise, *Simulation & Gaming, 27*(4), 507-516. Sage Publications, Inc. Thousand Oaks, CA. (805) 499-9774. www.sagepub.com

New
AHA

This board and card game teaches creative thinking. The cards are dealt to correspond with the six stages of the creative process: initialize, investigate, specify, ideate, integrate, and implement. Each player receives ten cards and picks one to match a specific stage. Other players may object and debate the appropriateness of the selection. A *Feedback Table* provides official answers. Players move around the board according to their correct plays and objections. Chance cards and die add challenge to the game. Includes a *Facilitator Guide*.

Author: Sivasailam Thiagarajan & Raja Thiagarajan
Publication Date: 1999
Cost: $89
Number of Participants: 2 to 16
Time: 30 to 45 minutes
Audience: General
Subject(s): Creativity
Source: Workshops by Thiagi, Inc. Bloomington, IN. (800) 996-7725. www.thiagi.com

New
AN ALIEN AMONG US

Participants in this game select six cultural ambassadors for a visit to the planet Bora-X5. There are 12 candidates with different attributes and backgrounds (sex, age, religion, disability, nationality, and reason for going). The selection process reveals that judgments are often biased and based on stereotypes. The debriefing emphasizes that differences enrich group efforts. Two facilitators are needed to run this game. The scenario may be adapted to real-life situations that involve multicultural work groups.

Author: Richard B. Powers
Publication Date: 1999
Cost: $19.95
Number of Participants: 9 to 12
Time: 1-1/2 hours
Audience: Managers
Subject(s): Diversity
Source: Intercultural Press. Yarmouth, ME. (800) 370-2665. www.interculturalpress.com

New
ALL ABOARD

This activity involves the teamwork necessary to accomplish a seemingly impossible task. A group of eight to twelve participants climbs onto a four-foot-square platform. Their assignment is to squeeze and balance until the entire group is safely on board. Once this is accomplished the team learns that they need to repeat the process on a three-foot platform. Planning and cooperation are required to succeed. Then the team is instructed to board a two-foot platform. This appears to be impossible but can be accomplished with creative planning, consideration of participants' diverse sizes and strengths, and cooperative teamwork.

Author: Beth Michalak, Steve Fischer, & Larry Meeker
Publication Date: 1994
Preparation: Construct three wooden platforms and anchor them into the ground
Space or Equipment Needs: Two sheets of plywood, 36 feet of 2"x4" lumber
Number of Participants: 8 to 12
Time: 15 to 25 minutes
Audience: Teams
Subject(s): Teams, diversity
Source: B. Michalak, S. Fischer, & L. Meeker (1994), *Experiential Activities for High-performance Teamwork* (pp. 55-57). Amherst, MA: HRD Press. (800) 822-2801. www.hrdpress.com

New
ALLIED CIRCUITS: AN EMPOWERMENT ROLE PLAY

This exercise is based on an actual workplace scenario in which all parties shared the same mission but differed in their ideas on how to accomplish the mission. In small groups participants assume the roles of Allied Circuits executives: marketing vice president, international relations manager, communication specialist, public relations manager, marketing manager, and company trainer. Handouts specify that the executives are charged with the task of creating a new global image for the company and provide a diverse set of personal opinions, aspirations, and agendas for each executive. Within this framework the company trainers

lead small group discussions on the meaning of empowerment. Observers note attitudes toward hierarchical structure and different definitions of empowerment. Following the exercise participants drop their roles for a debriefing.

Author: Barbara Pate Glacel & Emile A. Robert, Jr.
Publication Date: 1998
Preparation: Copy handouts
Space or Equipment Needs: Flip charts, markers, tape, and pencils
Number of Participants: 30 to 40
Time: 1 to 1-1/2 hours
Audience: General
Subject(s): Empowerment
Source: B. P. Glacel & E. A. Robert, Jr., in J. W. Pfeiffer, *The 1998 Annual: Volume 2, Consulting* (pp. 39-51). San Francisco: Jossey-Bass/Pfeiffer. (800) 274-4434. www.pfeiffer.com

ALPHA/BETA: EXPLORING CULTURAL DIVERSITY IN WORK TEAMS

This simulation explores the problems that arise when members of two cultures with significantly different social norms must work together productively. Through the exercise and subsequent discussion participants develop an understanding of the complexities of working in culturally diverse work teams. The two cultures are fictitious, which allows participants to more easily break away from their preconceived notions of appropriate behavior.

Author: Steven R. Phillips
Publication Date: 1994
Preparation: Photocopy handouts, make name tags, and print signs
Space or Equipment Needs: Pencils, paper, and clipboards for each observer; large supply of blank paper, 14 magazines, 14 pairs of scissors, glue, tape, and name tags; one large workroom and seven smaller rooms or workstations
Number of Participants: 35
Time: 2 hours
Audience: General
Subject(s): Multicultural diversity, teams
Source: S. R. Phillips in J. W. Pfeiffer, *The 1994 Annual: Developing Human Resources* (pp. 37-46). San Diego, CA: Pfeiffer & Company (Jossey-Bass/Pfeiffer). (800) 274-4434. www.pfeiffer.com

ALPHATEC: A NEGOTIATION EXERCISE WITH LOGROLLING AND BRIDGING POTENTIAL

Students assume the roles of negotiators who are buying and selling integrated circuits. A third student serves as an observer. The negotiators must deal with the issues of trust, information sharing, and a satisfactory outcome for both parties. Because personal promotions are at stake there is a tendency for negotiators to first seek win-lose situations. The exercise teaches negotiators to use a logrolling technique in which both sides give a little to gain a lot. It also teaches a bridging technique in which both negotiators must overcome initial positions, reveal information, and refocus on the most important issues at stake. Both techniques enable win-win outcomes. Detailed explanation of the two techniques is available in J. K. Butler, Jr. (1996), Two integrative win-win negotiating strategies, *Simulation & Gaming, 27*(3), 387-392.

Author: John K. Butler, Jr.
Publication Date: 1996
Preparation: Photocopy handouts
Number of Participants: Groups of 2 or 3
Time: 1 hour
Audience: General
Subject(s): Negotiation
Source: J. K. Butler, Jr. (1996), ALPHATEC: A negotiation exercise with logrolling and bridging potential, *Simulation & Gaming, 27*(3), 393-408. Sage Publications, Inc. Thousand Oaks, CA. (805) 499-9774. www.sagepub.com

New
ARCTIC EXPEDITION

In this survival simulation participants are caught in a snowstorm near Resolute, Canada, inside the Arctic Circle. They have traveled two hours from civilization on an all-terrain vehicle whose battery has died. To survive they must hike back to civilization and select individually and then as a group which of 12 items are most critical to their survival. Rationale for recommended answers and scoring tables are included. This consensus-building activity doesn't require a trained facilitator. Any member of the group may lead the activity.

Author: Lorraine L. Ukens
Publication Date: 1998
Cost: $6.95; *Leader's Guide*: $17.95
Number of Participants: 4 to 9
Time: 1-1/2 hours
Audience: Intact work groups
Subject(s): Decision making, group consensus, teams
Source: Jossey-Bass/Pfeiffer. San Francisco, CA. (800) 274-4434. www.pfeiffer.com

New
THE ART OF NEGOTIATING

This exercise involves learners in an abstract experience of creativity, teamwork, and ongoing relationships necessary for successful negotiations. Participants are divided into pairs of groups for negotiating an art project. Groups get opposing instructions and then have eight minutes to create their pictures and hang them on the wall. Each picture is scored by the opposing group, requiring negotiation for every point. A debriefing rewards the groups who considered the other team's needs, stated their own desires, and formed creative partnerships.

Author: Don McDonald
Publication Date: 1998
Preparation: Photocopy handouts
Space or Equipment Needs: Separate tables, colored paper, glue, tape, and scissors for each pair of groups

Number of Participants: 8 to 50
Time: 30 minutes
Audience: General
Subject(s): Negotiation
Source: D. McDonald (1998), The art of negotiating, *Simulation & Gaming, 29*(4), 475-479. Sage Publications, Inc. Thousand Oaks, CA. (805) 499-9774. www.sagepub.com

AWAKA: AN EXPLORATION IN DIVERSITY

The Richlanders, who are economically and technologically superior, plan a trip to aid the Awakians with a project. Their cultures are very different. This provides opportunity for miscommunication and conflict that simulates what naturally occurs when individuals work across cultural boundaries. The simulation's objectives are to: 1) experience issues involved with working across cultural and ethnic boundaries, 2) explore assumptions made about unfamiliar people, and 3) develop an effective process for entering a working relationship with people who are culturally different.

Author: W. Christopher Musselwhite
Publication Date: 1993
Preparation: Facilitator must have experience running a simulation and managing a debrief
Cost: Contact Discovery Learning for licensing or in-house delivery
Number of Participants: Small groups
Time: 2 hours
Audience: Managers
Subject(s): Multicultural diversity, communication
Source: Discovery Learning. Greensboro, NC. (336) 272-9530. www.discoverync.com

BAFÁ BAFÁ

This is one of the classic cross-culture simulations. Participants live and cope in a "foreign" culture and then discuss and analyze the experience. Bafá Bafá allows participants to explore the social, cognitive, and affective dimensions of interacting with culturally different others. They learn that what seems logical and reasonable to a member of one culture may seem irrational and unimportant to an outsider. In the discussion following the simulation the "mysteries" of each of the cultures are revealed and participants can see how stereotypes are formed and perpetuated. A variation of this simulation, Rafá Rafá, is designed for students in the 5th through 8th grades.

Author: Garry Shirts
Publication Date: 1977, 1999
Space or Equipment Needs: Two cassette players and a newsprint pad
Cost: $70 per participant; director's kit: $350
Number of Participants: 10 to 40
Time: 3 to 6 hours
Audience: General
Subject(s): Multicultural diversity
Source: Simulation Training Systems. Del Mar, CA. (800) 942-2900. www.stsintl.com

BASES OF POWER: DEVELOPING THE GROUP'S POTENTIAL

This exercise is based on the premise that without power, leadership is impossible. Using preliminary readings, discussion, self-analysis, and information sharing, participants are helped to identify their power bases (from among seven possibilities) and discover how they use power. The exercise also points out to group members the different power bases within the group. To wind up the experience each participant creates an action plan for enhancing his or her power bases.

Author: Mary H. Kitzmiller
Publication Date: 1991
Number of Participants: All members of an intact work group
Time: 3 hours
Audience: Intact work groups
Subject(s): Power
Source: M. H. Kitzmiller in J. W. Pfeiffer, *The 1991 Annual: Developing Human Resources* (pp. 43-50). San Diego, CA: University Associates (Jossey-Bass/Pfeiffer). (800) 274-4434. www.pfeiffer.com

New
THE BEAM

This exercise requires that team members consider their differences and develop solutions to accommodate those differences. Participants step onto the beams in no particular order. When they feel comfortable and stable they are instructed to rearrange themselves according to various criteria. Without stepping off the beam, participants must line up according to shoe size, birthday, height, alphabetically by name, or other criteria. The debrief helps participants reflect on the team advantages of individual differences such as varying size, strength, and agility.

Author: Beth Michalak, Steve Fischer, & Larry Meeker
Publication Date: 1994
Space or Equipment Needs: Two 8-foot beams of 6"x6" lumber
Number of Participants: 8 to 16
Time: 15 to 20 minutes
Audience: Teams
Subject(s): Teams, diversity
Source: B. Michalak, S. Fischer, & L. Meeker (1994), *Experiential Activities for High-performance Teamwork* (pp. 51-54). Amherst, MA: HRD Press. (800) 822-2801. www.hrdpress.com

New
BEYOND THE VALLEY OF THE KINGS

This is an intermediate- to advanced-level exercise in the Team Adventure Series™ of survival simulations. The scenario is a tour through Egypt, courtesy of 30 color slides, ending with a hot-air balloon ride over the Valley of the Kings—site of Tutankhamen's tomb and 61 others. Disaster strikes, the balloon crashes, and the group must make a plan to survive in the hostile desert environment. Participants rank the importance of ten supplies and six action alternatives. Then the group must reach consensus in both areas. Egyptologist Hisham Abdullah provides the expert rankings as a basis for comparison. Upon completion, teams plot their scores to understand their achievement in the seven-step process that leads to team synergy. The *Facilitator Guide* provides background information, rationale for rankings, and guidelines for a debriefing on team judgment.

Author: Rollin Glaser & Christine Glaser
Publication Date: 1994
Space or Equipment Needs: Pens, projector (optional)
Cost: Five participant booklets: $30; *Facilitator Guide*: $30; optional color slides: $32
Number of Participants: Groups of 4 to 6
Time: 2-1/2 hours
Audience: Intact work groups
Subject(s): Group consensus, decision making, teams
Source: HRDQ. King of Prussia, PA. (800) 633-4533. www.hrdq.com

New
BIG PICTURE

In this systems simulation the group must enlarge a famous painting from an eight-inch by ten-inch format to a four-foot by five-foot format. Sixteen artists (or teams) are each given one small section to replicate with watercolor paints. Each section must integrate nicely with the others to produce an appealing reproduction. Other players act as managers and customers who impose competing demands for exactness, originality, and completion on time and under budget. A debriefing midway through the exercise analyzes the difficulties of coordination among so many groups and the pressures of time, budget, and customer satisfaction. The group generalizes the systems lessons revealed by that analysis and decides on process improvements. When they return to work on the picture the group applies their new learnings and has a better experience, which yields better results. A final debriefing relates the lessons to the workplace. Separate versions are available for larger groups.

Author: Catalyst Learning
Publication Date: 1996
Space or Equipment Needs: Large room with work space for 16 artists and other players
Cost: $1,495
Number of Participants: 20 to 30
Time: 4 hours
Audience: Executives, managers
Subject(s): Systems thinking
Source: The Resources Connection. North Tonawanda, NY. (800) 295-0957. www.resourcesconnect.com

New
BLACK BEAR

This is an intermediate- to advanced-level exercise in the Team Adventure Series™ of survival simulations. A slide show sets the scene along the Appalachian Trail. The group is backpacking through the Great Smoky Mountains section of the trail in North Carolina when a black bear attacks the group leader. To save the leader's life participants must select one strategy and rank the importance of ten items. Buck Tilton, director of the Wilderness Medicine Institute, Inc., determined the expert rankings that provide a basis for comparison. Teams then plot their scores to understand their achievement in the seven-step process that leads to team synergy. The *Facilitator Guide* provides background information, rationale for rankings, and a guideline for a debriefing on group decision making in a crisis situation.

Author: Bradford Glaser
Publication Date: 1993, 1994
Space or Equipment Needs: Slide projector is optional
Cost: Five participant booklets: $30; *Facilitator Guide*: $30; optional color slides: $32
Number of Participants: Groups of 4 to 6
Time: 1-1/2 hours
Audience: Intact work groups
Subject(s): Group consensus, decision making, teams
Source: HRDQ. King of Prussia, PA. (800) 633-4533. www.hrdq.com

New
BLIND AND MUTE GEOMETRY

This exercise helps participants practice communication within and between teams. While blindfolded, two teams are instructed to form concentric squares from lengths of rope. Occasionally the facilitator taps one member on the shoulder to allow temporary sight. However, that member loses speech until the sight/speech switch is tapped again. When the squares are completed the pattern is laid to the ground and teams remove blindfolds. Participants rank the pattern on a scale of one to ten. If most participants think the pattern is well done and assign a score of eight or above, the team has practiced successful communication. The debrief considers how to communicate among team members with different perspectives and across team boundaries.

Author: Carmine M. Consalvo
Publication Date: 1996
Preparation: Cut rope into unequal parts
Space or Equipment Needs: 120 feet of rope
Number of Participants: 10 to 14
Time: 35 minutes to 1 hour
Audience: General
Subject(s): Teams, communication, quality
Source: C. M. Consalvo (1996), *Changing Pace: Outdoor Games for Experiential Learning* (pp. 143-144). Amherst, MA: HRD Press. (800) 822-2801. www.hrdpress.com

BLIND LEADERSHIP

As described by the authors, Blind Leadership "emphasizes the importance of leadership vision to the successful accomplishment of group tasks. In this exercise, a sighted group leader instructs blindfolded subordinates in putting together a Tinkertoy structure." Group leaders are given a picture of a completed Tinkertoy structure and told they may do whatever they wish (except remove blindfolds or touch the Tinkertoys) to get their subordinates to build the structure depicted. The authors note that the groups who finish first are usually the ones in which the leader communicated a "vision" of the final structure to the subordinates.

Author: Cindy P. Lindsay & Cathy A. Enz
Publication Date: 1991
Space or Equipment Needs: Blindfold for each participant, five sets of Tinkertoys, five pictures of the completed Tinkertoy structure
Number of Participants: 20 to 30
Time: 45 minutes to 1 hour
Audience: General
Subject(s): Communication
Source: C. P. Lindsay & C. A. Enz (1991), Resource control and visionary leadership: Two exercises, *Journal of Management Education, 15*(1), 127-135. Sage Publications, Inc. Thousand Oaks, CA. (805) 499-9774. www.sagepub.com

New
THE BLIND POLYGON

A small group surrounds a rope circle and discusses the types of polygons that might be made with the rope. After choosing one shape, the group learns that they will be blindfolded for the activity and their task is more complex than anticipated. Communication, group decision making, and cooperation are necessary to model the shape and place it on the ground. To simplify the activity the facilitator may assign simple shapes such as triangles or rectangles.

Author: Beth Michalak, Steve Fischer, & Larry Meeker
Publication Date: 1994
Preparation: Tie rope ends to form circle
Space or Equipment Needs: Blindfolds, 15-foot rope
Number of Participants: Small groups
Time: 15 to 20 minutes
Audience: Teams
Subject(s): Teams, problem solving, communication
Source: B. Michalak, S. Fischer, & L. Meeker (1994), *Experiential Activities for High-performance Teamwork* (pp. 31-34). Amherst, MA: HRD Press. (800) 822-2801. www.hrdpress.com

New
BOMB SQUAD

This is an advanced game that includes the possibilities of danger and an unsuccessful conclusion. However, it may be used by a skilled facilitator at the end of a training program to demonstrate the importance and difficulty of team learning. The scenario sends a bomb squad on a mission to neutralize terrorist bombs (water balloons). Participants face an element of chance (casting die) to get to the reactor room. Then there is a complex set of rules for disarming the bombs. When all water balloon bombs are disarmed they're tossed into a steel barrel (along with a cherry bomb) for destruction. The successful team learns that all members must understand the entire system and that each member has equal responsibility. Overvaluing or scapegoating any team member leads to failure.

Author: Carmine M. Consalvo
Publication Date: 1996
Space or Equipment Needs: Ten filled water balloons, fireplace gloves, shopping bag, ten-sided die, ten large tin cans, a length of rope, steel barrel, newspapers, matches, cherry bomb (optional)
Number of Participants: 9 or 10
Time: 35 minutes to 1 hour
Audience: Teams
Subject(s): Teams, learning, risk-taking, problem solving
Source: C. M. Consalvo (1996), *Changing Pace: Outdoor Games for Experiential Learning* (pp. 53-57). Amherst, MA: HRD Press. (800) 822-2801. www.hrdpress.com

BORDER DISPUTE

Border Dispute teaches students the appropriate use of competitive and collaborative behaviors and about the dynamics within and between groups. Half the students assume roles as negotiators from the developing country of Arak. The other half are negotiators from the neighboring country of Barkan. Because the neighbors have been squabbling over rights to resources and political jurisdiction, they need to negotiate a treaty before war breaks out. Students pair up to strike the most favorable and honorable deals possible in 30 minutes. The quality of each agreement is measured to determine each student's influence and collaboration skills. A debriefing session helps students understand the benefits of taking risks, the need for flexibility, and the stress caused by time limitations.

Author: Gary Whitney
Publication Date: 1992
Preparation: Photocopy handouts
Number of Participants: Any number of pairs
Time: 50 minutes to 1-1/2 hours
Audience: General
Subject(s): Negotiation
Source: G. Whitney in D. Marcic & J. Seltzer (1998), *Organizational Behavior: Experiences and Cases* (5th ed., pp. 193-194+). Cincinnati, OH: South-Western College Publishing. www.swcollege.com

BRIEF ENCOUNTERS

Brief Encounters is based on the science fiction theme of first contact with alien beings. Participants are divided into two groups to separately learn the behavior norms of the fictional Pandya and Chola cultures. The groups interact at a brief party organized to exchange cultural values. Cross-cultural differences create difficulties and illuminate the tendency to become ethnocentric. A debriefing session helps participants learn the difference between first impressions and reality. The author suggests varying the cultural norms to fit groups that are diverse in gender or age.

Author: Sivasailam Thiagarajan
Publication Date: 1995
Preparation: Photocopy handouts
Space or Equipment Needs: Timer and whistle
Number of Participants: 20 or more
Time: 20 minutes
Audience: General
Subject(s): Multicultural diversity
Source: S. Thiagarajan (1995), *Diversity Simulation Games* (pp. 13-21). Amherst, MA: HRD Press. (800) 822-2801. www.hrdpress.com

New
BUILDING TRUST IN PAIRS: AN OBSTACLE COURSE

Blindfolded "travelers" must perform five tasks along an obstacle course: hurdle boxes, walk a plank, step around jacks, spin six times, find the center of the room, and pass through a door. Each traveler has a "guide" to offer verbal or physical assistance and to ensure safety and successful completion of the obstacle course. The exercise includes suggestions for a debriefing discussion on trust.

Author: Valerie C. Nellen & Susan B. Wilkes
Publication Date: 1999
Preparation: Photocopy handouts, make a wall sign
Space or Equipment Needs: Blindfolds, five-foot board, large boxes, and several sets of jacks
Number of Participants: Any number of pairs
Time: 1 to 1-1/2 hours
Audience: General
Subject(s): Trust
Source: V. C. Nellen & S. B. Wilkes in J. W. Pfeiffer, *The 1999 Annual: Volume 1, Training* (pp. 53-57). San Francisco: Jossey-Bass/Pfeiffer. (800) 274-4434. www.pfeiffer.com

BUREAUCRATIC MAZE

Bureaucratic Maze is a group juggling exercise that demands creative problem solving and teamwork. Participants form a circle and toss a soft object to someone across the circle. A facilitator slowly adds one more object, then another object, until there are objects for everyone to juggle at once. The goal is to continue juggling without dropping any objects. Because that is impossible, the group must find creative solutions to sustain the juggling for three minutes. The author suggests numerous solutions for group juggling and for follow-up discussions on creativity. A variation of this exercise is Jigglers and Bursters, which is played with water balloons (pp. 305-310).

Author: Carmine M. Consalvo
Publication Date: 1993

Preparation: Photocopy handouts
Space or Equipment Needs: Stopwatch, soft objects for throwing—one for each participant, and a bag to hold all the objects
Number of Participants: 6 to 20
Time: 1-1/2 hours
Audience: General
Subject(s): Problem solving, teams
Source: C. M. Consalvo (1993), *Experiential Training Activities for Outside and In* (pp. 219-227). Amherst, MA: HRD Press. (800) 822-2801. www.hrdpress.com

BUSINESS SCRUPLES

In this role-playing game, participants confront and resolve workplace ethical dilemmas. Each participant takes a turn playing each of three roles: employer, employee, or member of society at large. A special scoring system allows participants to compare the ethical standards of these three groups. The objectives of Business Scruples are to enable participants to: 1) recognize ethical dilemmas in the workplace, 2) learn how to handle and resolve such dilemmas, and 3) compare individual values to group values.

Author: Rajib N. Sanyal & Joao S. Neves
Publication Date: 1993
Preparation: Prepare several business dilemmas on index cards (examples are provided in the article)
Number of Participants: 15 to 30
Time: 30 minutes to 1 hour
Audience: General
Subject(s): Ethics
Source: R. N. Sanyal & J. S. Neves (1993), Business Scruples: Confronting ethical issues in the workplace, *Simulation & Gaming, 24*(2), 240-247. Sage Publications, Inc. Thousand Oaks, CA. (805) 499-9774. www.sagepub.com

CALLOWAY POWER STATION: ASSESSING TEAM-LEADER EFFECTIVENESS

This case study exercise provides a forum for participants to evaluate a team leader's effectiveness on several dimensions and to discuss various aspects of team leadership. Participants also have the opportunity "to share their individual views about team leadership and how it affects team functioning." The case centers around a team leader who has been a supervisor for four years. The author suggests that this exercise is best used as part of a leadership development program.

Author: William N. Parker
Publication Date: 1996
Number of Participants: 12 to 30
Time: 1 hour
Audience: Teams
Subject(s): Teams
Source: W. N. Parker in J. W. Pfeiffer, *The 1996 Annual: Volume 2, Consulting* (pp. 57-66). San Diego, CA: Pfeiffer & Company (Jossey-Bass/Pfeiffer). (800) 274-4434. www.pfeiffer.com

New
THE CHANGE CYCLE GAME™

Participants move through six sequential and predictable stages of change in this card and board game. They identify the thoughts, feelings, and behaviors associated with loss, doubt, discomfort, discovery, understanding, and integration. The fast pace of the game aims to mimic the rapid pace of change in organizational settings. The game may be adapted for individual or team play. Includes a facilitator guide.

Author: Interchange International Inc. & QED Consulting
Publication Date: 1997
Cost: $149
Number of Participants: 1 or more
Time: 2 hours
Audience: General
Subject(s): Change
Source: Interchange International Inc. Washington, DC. (800) 878-8422. www.changecycle.com

New
THE CHANGE GAME

This board and card game explores organizational change. The cards are dealt to correspond with the five stages of the change process: awareness, self-interest, evaluation, tryout, and use (implementation). Each player receives ten cards and picks one to match a specific stage. Other players may object and debate the appropriateness of the selection. A *Feedback Table* provides official answers. Players move around the board according to their correct plays and objections. Chance cards and die add challenge to the game. Includes a *Facilitator Guide*.

Author: Sivasailam Thiagarajan, Raja Thiagarajan, & Diane Dormant
Publication Date: 1997, 1999
Cost: $89
Number of Participants: 2 to 16
Time: 30 to 45 minutes
Audience: General
Subject(s): Change
Source: Workshops by Thiagi, Inc. Bloomington, IN. (800) 996-7725. www.thiagi.com

New
THE CHOCOLATE GAME

The author recommends repeating this activity over a course of several days to emphasize the change in collaborative behavior and the improved results. Each participant receives a numbered blue poker chip and red poker chip and a copy of the M&M payout matrix. Placing a blue chip in the Choose sack yields a high individual payout for some players. Placing a red chip in the Choose bag represents personal sacrifice. The group payoff is on a sliding scale with the highest payoff occurring when team members make personal sacrifices and collaborate toward the team goal.

Author: Anthony Richards
Publication Date: 1995
Preparation: Number the poker chips, photocopy handouts
Space or Equipment Needs: Red and blue poker chips, two small sacks, M&Ms
Number of Participants: Small groups
Time: 30 minutes to 1 hour
Audience: General
Subject(s): Collaboration
Source: A. Richards in M. Gass (1995), *Book of Metaphors: Volume II* (pp. 225-229). Dubuque, IA: Kendall/Hunt. (800) 228-0810. www.kendallhunt.com

CHOOSING A LEADERSHIP STYLE: APPLYING THE VROOM AND YETTON MODEL

This exercise is designed to help participants learn how to diagnose leadership situations and then choose the most appropriate decision-making process for that situation (based on the Vroom and Yetton model). Participants analyze case studies in a group setting and arrive at a consensual decision on the appropriate leadership style. The styles range from making the decision yourself without any additional input to sharing the problem with your subordinates and coming to a consensus.

Author: Roy J. Lewicki, Donald D. Bowen, Douglas T. Hall, & Francine S. Hall
Publication Date: 1988
Preparation: Participants must read an article that describes the Vroom and Yetton model
Number of Participants: Groups of 3 to 5
Time: 50 minutes
Audience: General
Subject(s): Leadership styles
Source: R. J. Lewicki, D. D. Bowen, D. T. Hall, & F. S. Hall (1988), *Experiences in Management and Organizational Behavior* (3rd ed., pp. 121-131). New York: Wiley. (800) 225-5945. www.wiley.com

New
CITIUS 2002

Participants in this simulation are charged to make new plans for the Salt Lake City Olympic Committee in preparation for the 2002 Winter Olympic Games. Macro analyses as well as specific strategies are needed to ensure the spirit of the Games, create an artful flow, and protect the future viability of the Games. In small groups participants work on a PC to design a new Olympic Village and Tower within the constraints of location, transportation, environmental protection, and earthquake risks. On floor grids they plan a new core transportation network. Finally they build a one-person bobsled, which they test in real practice runs. Throughout their work on the multiple tasks groups face budget challenges and demands from multiple stakeholders. Facilitators may administer this simulation for one group or multiple groups simultaneously.

Author: John Schmidt
Publication Date: 1996
Space or Equipment Needs: PC for each group
Cost: This is a proprietary simulation; contact Executive Expeditions for information
Number of Participants: 8 to 250
Time: 3 to 4 hours
Audience: Executives, managers, intact work groups
Subject(s): Cross-functional teams
Source: Executive Expeditions. Roswell, GA. (678) 461-8880. www.executive-expeditions.com

New
C.O.A.C.H.

This board and card game explores the coaching process. The cards are dealt to correspond with the five stages of coaching: connecting, observing, assessing, coaching (conducting the conversation), and honing. Each player receives ten cards and picks one to match a specific stage. Other players may object and debate the appropriateness of the selection. A *Feedback Table* provides official answers. Players move around the board according to their correct plays and objections. Chance cards and die add challenge to the game. Includes a *Facilitator Guide*.

Author: Andy Kimball, Sivasailam Thiagarajan, Lynne Parode, & Raja Thiagarajan
Publication Date: 1999
Cost: $89
Number of Participants: 2 to 16
Time: 30 to 45 minutes
Audience: General
Subject(s): Coaching
Source: Workshops by Thiagi, Inc. Bloomington, IN. (800) 996-7725. www.thiagi.com

New
COMICS COUNSELING

Participants working in small groups identify a comic strip character who is facing a dilemma. Each group is given 15 minutes to state the character's problem, list a variety of solutions, and choose the best one. Then each group presents a report on its process and the facilitator leads a discussion on creative problem solving.

Author: Lorraine L. Ukens
Publication Date: 1999
Preparation: Prepare handouts
Space or Equipment Needs: Newspaper comics, pencils, clock or timer
Number of Participants: 5 to 30
Time: 30 minutes
Audience: General
Subject(s): Problem solving
Source: L. L. Ukens (1999), *All Together Now! A Seriously Fun Collection of Training Games and Activities* (pp. 41-43). San Francisco: Jossey-Bass/Pfeiffer. (800) 274-4434. www.pfeiffer.com

COMMON CURRENCY: THE COOPERATIVE-COMPETITION GAME

Common Currency is designed to teach teams and individuals that competition can create positive energy, even in collaborative situations. Participants are divided into eight teams, each representing a fictional country. The countries learn that their eight currencies will soon be unified, and each one attempts to maximize its wealth. No country knows the value of all the coins, so teams must negotiate, exchanging information and coins, to achieve success. As currency values become apparent teams employ strategic planning to get bonus points for collecting special combinations. In the debrief participants discuss the cooperative and competitive tasks and processes within and between teams. They identify the people who have assumed leadership roles. A variation of the game adds the element of change midway to challenge strategic planning and relationship skills.

Author: Lorraine Ukens
Publication Date: 1995, 1996
Preparation: The facilitator needs about two hours to read instructions, select debriefing questions, photocopy feedback forms, fill envelopes with coins, assemble flags, and arrange tables
Space or Equipment Needs: Paper, pencils, two flip charts, markers, calculator
Cost: $195
Number of Participants: 16 to 48
Time: 1-1/2 to 3 hours
Audience: Intact work groups
Subject(s): Collaboration
Source: HRDQ. King of Prussia, PA. (800) 633-4533. www.hrdq.com

New
COMMUNICATION DERAILED

The three modules in this exercise are designed to improve communication in three problem areas in contemporary organizations: in teams, in lateral communications, and during organizational stress. In each module groups of participants use flexible foam pieces to build a toy following instructions that make communication difficult. After a debrief the groups continue their task, this time practicing effective communication. In the teams module, individuals are given different interpretations of their task and different communication styles, while the lateral module establishes conflicting teams within each group. In the module on organizational stress, groups have to complete a poorly defined task under extreme time pressure. Each module concludes with discussion questions and action planning. This structure demonstrates the impact of poor communication and helps participants practice sharing information and giving and receiving feedback.

Author: Eileen M. Russo & Chris Bayley Giblin
Publication Date: 1996
Preparation: Photocopy handouts, print transparencies
Cost: $395

Number of Participants: 12 to 24
Time: 2 to 3 hours per module
Audience: General
Subject(s): Communication
Source: HRDQ. King of Prussia, PA. (800) 633-4533. www.hrdq.com

New
COUNCILS TO THE PRESIDENT: ACHIEVING CONSENSUS ON COMPLEX ISSUES

Small groups debate the possibility and desirability of eradicating violence and creating world peace. A handout suggests discussion topics such as: the defense of human rights, justice, the consequences of atomic warfare, the spiritual development of human beings, and a universally accepted world ethic. Within 35 minutes groups must come to a consensus and present their decisions to the larger group. A facilitator leads a debriefing discussion that asks if all members shared opinions and if all opinions were considered fairly in the final decision. An online version of this exercise is described.

Author: Michele Stimac
Publication Date: 1998
Preparation: Photocopy handouts
Space or Equipment Needs: Large meeting room and three to five breakout rooms; paper and pencil for each participant
Number of Participants: 15 to 30
Time: 1-1/2 to 2 hours
Audience: General
Subject(s): Decision making
Source: M. Stimac in J. W. Pfeiffer, *The 1998 Annual: Volume 2, Consulting* (pp. 9-17). San Francisco: Jossey-Bass/Pfeiffer. (800) 274-4434. www.pfeiffer.com

New
CRIME-FIGHTING TASK FORCE: UNDERSTANDING POLITICAL TACTICS IN GROUPS

Six participants play roles in a task force assigned to allocate grant money toward a crime-fighting initiative in a fictional city. Task force members are: retired Army officer, guidance counselor, farmer, retail store manager, office-supply store owner, and chairperson. Each member enters the planning process with a hidden agenda. Other participants actively observe the planning process to identify the use of political tactics, behaviors that help role players stay on task or derail, and effective methods for reaching consensus. During a debriefing session observers report on their findings and a facilitator leads a discussion on political behavior in groups.

Author: R. Bruce McAfee & Robert A. Herring III
Publication Date: 1999
Preparation: Photocopy handouts
Space or Equipment Needs: Name tags, clipboards, and pencils
Number of Participants: 15 or more
Time: 1-1/4 hours
Audience: General

Subject(s): Group dynamics
Source: R. B. McAfee & R. A. Herring III in J. W. Pfeiffer, *The 1999 Annual: Volume 1, Training* (pp. 35-48). San Francisco: Jossey-Bass/Pfeiffer. (800) 274-4434. www.pfeiffer.com

THE CRISIS GAME

This game is designed to have participants experience the dynamics of decision making in crisis conditions. A crisis condition is characterized by surprise, threat to vital interests, and incomplete information. The author says that within these conditions, the game director can tailor The Crisis Game by selecting a specific current crisis that fits the group. The game steps include: an announcement of a crisis condition, distributing a briefing package, group work on policy recommendations, random announcements of both relevant and irrelevant new information, further compression of an already short time frame, presentation of policy recommendations, and game debriefing. The sample briefing package included in this article is based on an international-relations incident, the Panamanian situation in early 1988, but as noted above, a crisis situation can be chosen and developed to correspond to any specific setting or group.

Author: H. Richard Friman
Publication Date: 1991
Preparation: Select and prepare a crisis briefing
Number of Participants: 5 to 60
Time: 1 to 2 hours
Audience: General
Subject(s): Decision making, crisis management
Source: H. R. Friman (1991), The Crisis Game, *Simulation & Gaming*, 22(3), 382-388. Sage Publications, Inc. Thousand Oaks, CA. (805) 499-9774. www.sagepub.com

CULTURE CLASH: AN ETHICAL INTERCULTURAL SIMULATION

This intercultural ethical simulation is based on a real case of Inuit seal hunters, economic development activists, and animal rights activists. Each group has a sympathetic base for its beliefs. The Inuits' culture and livelihood are threatened. The economic development activists rally for sustainable development while the animal rights activists fight to protect animals from suffering and death. The conflict among the three groups must be resolved through negotiation. Culture Clash provides each group with a briefing on its goals, values, and negotiating style. Through several rounds of negotiation, the groups move from seeing only their differences to a search for common ground.

Author: Linda Groff & Paul Smoker
Publication Date: 1995
Space or Equipment Needs: Props, such as fur coats, are optional
Cost: Contact Global Options for information
Number of Participants: 9 to 18
Time: 3 hours
Audience: Managers, civic leaders, students

Subject(s): Multicultural diversity, ethics, negotiation
Source: Global Options. Playa del Rey, CA. (310) 821-1864.

DECISIVE DECISION MAKING: AN EXERCISE USING ETHICAL FRAMEWORKS

This exercise enlightens students about five different ethical frameworks: utilitarianism, self-interest, categorical imperative, legality, and light of day. Each student assumes the role of a seismologist who calculates an 80 percent chance that a devastating earthquake will hit a major metropolitan area within 48 hours. There are five scenarios that describe the scientist's reaction: confirming the accuracy of the event, informing the media so that evacuation can begin, conforming with company policy, evaluating the cost of destruction versus the cost of chaos, or protecting one's personal interests. Students make individual choices about the most ethical reaction, then form groups to reach consensus. Intragroup and intergroup discussions highlight the values and limitations of each framework.

Author: Mark Mallinger
Publication Date: 1996
Preparation: Photocopy handouts
Number of Participants: 8 to 30
Time: 1 hour
Audience: Students
Subject(s): Decision making, ethics, group consensus
Source: M. Mallinger (1996), Decisive Decision Making: An exercise using ethical frameworks. *Journal of Management Education, 21*(3), 411-417. Sage Publications, Inc. Thousand Oaks, CA. (805) 499-9774. www.sagepub.com

DELEGATION: USING TIME AND RESOURCES EFFECTIVELY

This exercise is designed to assist participants in identifying the barriers to delegation, the benefits to delegation, and which kinds of tasks are suitable for delegating. A systematic method of delegating is presented, and each participant has an opportunity to apply this method to those tasks or projects that could be delegated but currently are not. Upon completion of the exercise participants have action plans for delegating tasks within their own jobs.

Author: Michael N. O'Malley & Catherine M. T. Lombardozzi
Publication Date: 1988
Space or Equipment Needs: Paper, pencils, newsprint, markers, and masking tape
Number of Participants: 15 to 30
Time: 2-1/4 hours
Audience: Executives, managers
Subject(s): Communication
Source: M. N. O'Malley & C. M. T. Lombardozzi in J. W. Pfeiffer, *The 1988 Annual: Developing Human Resources* (pp. 81-87). San Diego, CA: University Associates (Jossey-Bass/Pfeiffer). (800) 274-4434. www.pfeiffer.com

New
DESCRIBING CULTURES THROUGH THEIR PROVERBS

Proverbs are defined as pithy, epigrammatic statements that set forth well-known truths and contain messages about the values of a people. In this activity five proverbs are provided for analysis of cultural assumptions. Participants choose familiar phrases that approximate the meaning of each proverb. They seek clues about the values behind each proverb and try to identify the cultures from which they originated. At the end of the exercise the facilitator reveals that all proverbs are taken from folk literature of the African American slave. The debrief is a discussion on the inherent values of that culture.

Author: Sandra Tjitendero
Publication Date: 1996
Preparation: Prepare handouts
Space or Equipment Needs: Paper and pencils
Number of Participants: Any number
Time: Varies
Audience: General
Subject(s): Multicultural diversity, cross-cultural communication
Source: S. Tjitendero in H. N. Seelye (Ed.) (1996), *Experiential Activities for Intercultural Learning: Volume 1* (pp. 75-77). Yarmouth, ME: Intercultural Press. (800) 370-2665. www.interculturalpress.com

DESERT I SURVIVAL SITUATION

This exercise uses the scenario of a plane crash in the desert to teach group-consensus problem solving. Team members work individually and then as a group to assess the survival value of 15 items. Solutions are compared with those of a desert survival expert to initiate discussion of the methods and benefits of team decision making. An optional scene-setting video is available to enhance the exercise. An extended version of this, Desert II Survival Situation (1988, 1995), is designed for those who may have already experienced a shorter simulation, and it encourages more detailed discussion.

Author: Human Synergistics
Publication Date: 1987, 1996
Space or Equipment Needs: VCR and viewing screen
Cost: Participant booklet: $4.25; *Leader's Guide*: $25; *Observer's Guide*: $5; enhancement video: $125
Number of Participants: Small groups
Time: 1-1/2 to 2-1/2 hours
Audience: General
Subject(s): Group consensus, decision making, teams
Source: Human Synergistics International. Plymouth, MI. (800) 622-7584. www.humansyn.com

New
DIVERSITY BINGO

This variation of bingo is about culture and ethnicity. The boxes on each card contain descriptors such as "a person who is a grandparent" or "a person who is a naturalized citizen." When a participant finds a group member who fits the description the box is signed. When a card has a complete row of signatures across, down, or diagonally bingo is won. The game itself takes 15 minutes. The one-hour debriefing reveals the assumptions that participants have made about others and assumptions that others have made about them. Includes 50 bingo cards, a trainer's manual, and handouts and overhead transparencies to facilitate the debriefing.

Author: Advancement Strategies
Publication Date: 1992
Space or Equipment Needs: Pens
Cost: $99.95; extra cards: $49.95
Number of Participants: 15 to 50
Time: 1-1/4 hours
Audience: General
Subject(s): Diversity
Source: Jossey-Bass/Pfeiffer. San Francisco, CA. (800) 274-4434. www.pfeiffer.com

DIVERSOPHY™

Players roll dice and move around a game board, trying to avoid four diversity traps (Ethnocentricity, Stereotypes, Bias, and Assimilation). Players collect diversiCOINS for correct answers to question cards. There are four categories of questions: SMARTS (facts and statistics), CHOICE (business situations that require skilled decision making), SHARE (where players must relate personal diversity experience), and RISK (where chance determines play). Cards address general diversity issues as well as the values and customs of specific ethnic and cultural groups.

Author: George Simons International & Multus, Inc.
Publication Date: 1992, 1996
Cost: $199
Number of Participants: 4 to 6
Time: 1-1/4 to 1-1/2 hours
Audience: Managers
Subject(s): Multicultural diversity
Source: HR Press. Fredonia, NY. (800) 444-7139. www.hrpress-diversity.com

New
DO YOUR BEST

This set of 19 activities teaches lessons on direction setting in general and on mission, vision, and goal setting specifically. In each activity participants use small acrylic blocks to build a wall or sculpture as the facilitator instructs. Each lesson demonstrates one principle, such as clear direction, timebound goals, and positive reinforcement. For instance, in the Long/Short activity two teams have conflicting missions but must work together to build the proper wall providing a lesson in alignment. The individual exercises can stand alone or be combined to help participants create their own mission, vision, or set of goals. Discussion questions and a description of the learning principle follow each activity.

Author: R. Glaser, E. Russo, & M. Eckler
Publication Date: 1995
Preparation: Photocopy handouts, print transparencies
Cost: $195
Number of Participants: 4 to 6
Time: 10 to 15 minutes each
Audience: Managers, executives, teams
Subject(s): Mission, vision, goal setting
Source: HRDQ. King of Prussia, PA. (800) 633-4533. www.hrdq.com

New
EARTHQUAKE

This survival exercise develops decision-making skills and teamwork by asking groups to determine a course of action after an earthquake has trapped them in a basement. Participants are given a list of 12 action steps to either take or avoid, such as shutting off all utilities, lighting candles, and purifying the water source. Each individual ranks the steps and then the group uses consensus to develop a team ranking. These rankings are measured against an expert score and team and individual rankings are compared to determine the group's synergy and effectiveness. An optional video can help facilitators by presenting the situation dramatically and providing a debriefing.

Author: D. Joseph Fisher & D. Dawn Peters
Publication Date: 1990, 1992
Cost: Participant book: $4.95; facilitator guide: $20; overheads: $60; video: $125
Number of Participants: Small groups
Time: 27 minutes
Audience: General
Subject(s): Group consensus, teams, decision making
Source: Organizational Learning Tools, Inc. Novi, MI. (800) 684-1190.

New
EARTHQUAKE SURVIVAL

There are three activities in this survival simulation: the Earthquake Survival Situations Quiz, Things to Have to Prepare for an Earthquake, and Things to Do During and Immediately After an Earthquake. In each activity participants individually and in groups decide on the items or actions that are most important for survival. Expert solutions are provided for comparison. Scoring and debriefing reveal the consensus-building skills applied during the exercise. A *Leader's Guide* suggests variations and lecturettes.

Author: Arlette C. Ballew & Marian K. Prokop
Publication Date: 1994

Cost: $6.95; *Leader's Guide*: $17.95
Number of Participants: 4 to 9
Time: 1-1/2 hours
Audience: General
Subject(s): Group consensus, decision making
Source: Jossey-Bass/Pfeiffer. San Francisco, CA. (800) 274-4434. www.pfeiffer.com

ECO-CYCLIX

This exercise uses both indoor and outdoor components to simulate a worldwide manufacturing operation. It utilizes a matrix organizational structure, financial performance, and a "live market" to focus on key elements for competitive success. Through an accelerated time frame the simulation offers opportunities to assess the impact of organizational dynamics on strategies, decision making, and actual results. Eco-Cyclix can be tailored to meet specific client situations, including alternative use of outdoor features.

Author: John Schmidt
Publication Date: 1992
Cost: This is a proprietary simulation; contact Executive Expeditions for information
Number of Participants: 10 to 50
Time: 5 to 8 hours
Audience: Executives, managers, intact work groups
Subject(s): Decision making, cross-functional teams
Source: Executive Expeditions. Roswell, GA. (678) 461-8880. www.executive-expeditions.com

ECOTONOS

Ecotonos is a multicultural problem-solving simulation. Participants are divided into three groups and assigned different cultural norms. To reinforce cultural identity each group writes a historical myth. Participants are then mixed into multicultural groups to solve a problem. They make process maps to reflect their group's dynamics and problem-solving strategies. During the large group debriefing session all participants gain insights from their own and others' cross-cultural communication skills. Facilitators should have prior experience as participants or observers of this simulation.

Author: Nipporica Associates & Dianne Hofner Saphiere
Publication Date: 1993, 1997
Space or Equipment Needs: Flip chart, markers, masking tape, paper, and pencils for each group
Cost: $160
Number of Participants: 12 to 50
Time: 3 hours
Audience: General
Subject(s): Multicultural diversity, problem solving
Source: Intercultural Press, Inc. Yarmouth, ME. (800) 370-2665. www.interculturalpress.com

EDGEWORK®

EdgeWork is a business simulation designed to be imbedded in executive training programs that focus on group development, communication, and collaboration. Participants are divided into two groups that run the fictional companies Cheeta Xpress and TELEq. Participants assume the roles of managers, directors, and vice presidents who deal with a buyer-supplier relationship, make long-range plans, make routine decisions, and handle emergencies. During the simulation participants recognize the need for and learn new skills for communicating across internal and external boundaries. Facilitators must have the background to deliver the product and interpret the results and a knowledge of group dynamics. Certification is required.

Author: Center for Creative Leadership
Publication Date: 1997
Preparation: Participants must read three books that provide background information; the facilitator must read the same three books, become familiar with the simulation materials, and set up the rooms
Space or Equipment Needs: One large and five small conference rooms with tables, chairs, and flip charts; overhead projector is optional
Cost: $2,300 for the first kit; $1,800 for additional kits
Number of Participants: 8 to 20
Time: This one-day simulation is often imbedded in a multiple-day program
Audience: Executives, MBA students, intact work groups
Subject(s): Communication, teams
Source: Discovery Learning. Greensboro, NC. (336) 272-9530. www.discoverync.com

New
AN "EEE" EXERCISE IN CREATIVITY

This EEE exercise represents an "Easy, Effortless, and Enjoyable" way to enhance creative ability and understand the creative process. Small groups work together to generate ideas for products or services using the raw materials they're given. They select one idea to develop further and then create its identity, a slogan, and a video advertisement. During the process they experience four stages of creativity: preparation, incubation, illumination, and verification.

Author: Ann Armstrong
Publication Date: 1999
Preparation: Participants may read chapter on creative problem solving in D. A. Whetten & K. S. Cameron (1995), *Developing Management Skills* (3rd ed.); facilitator photocopies handouts
Space or Equipment Needs: Raw materials such as egg cartons, plastic straws, or styrofoam balls; video cameras and players (optional)
Cost: Cost of materials
Number of Participants: 16 to 50
Time: 2 hours
Audience: Students
Subject(s): Creativity
Source: A. Armstrong (1999), Teaching creativity: An "EEE" experiential exercise, *Journal of Management*

Education, 23(2), 174-179. Sage Publications, Inc. Thousand Oaks, CA. (805) 499-9774. www.sagepub.com

EFFECTIVE DELEGATION

The action in this role-play exercise centers around a renovation project that involves construction of access ramps for the handicapped. Participants, playing the roles of those who must manage and implement the project, are exposed to the elements of effective delegation. It is designed to help them develop effective delegation skills from both a manager's and subordinate's perspective. It also offers a chance to practice feedback skills.

Author: Roy J. Lewicki, Donald D. Bowen, Douglas T. Hall, & Francine S. Hall
Publication Date: 1988
Preparation: Read introductory material
Number of Participants: Groups of 3
Time: 1 hour
Audience: Managers
Subject(s): Communication
Source: R. J. Lewicki, D. D. Bowen, D. T. Hall, & F. S. Hall (1988), *Experiences in Management and Organizational Behavior* (3rd ed., pp. 142-148). New York: Wiley. (800) 225-5945. www.wiley.com

THE EGYPTIAN MUMMY TRUST PROGRESSION

Three Egyptian mummy exercises teach trust but are also used to teach spotting techniques for other activities in the same book. The first exercise is the Trust Fall. Participants are paired with other students of the same approximate size. One assumes a stiff-bodied mummy position and the other crouches behind to spot or safely catch the faller. Trust is learned through the careful communication between faller and spotter. In the Trust Circle a mummy participant is passed upright around a tight circle of spotters. This exercise increases the need for communication and cooperation from a pair to a group. The third exercise is King Tut's Rebirth, in which a mummy is lifted to shoulder height. Because this exercise presents the greatest risk, a group leader emerges to coordinate the effort. It is important to follow the recommended progression and build spotting skills for safety's sake. One trainer is needed for each 12 participants.

Author: Carmine M. Consalvo
Publication Date: 1993
Space or Equipment Needs: An open, level activity area; camera or videorecorder are optional
Number of Participants: Trust Fall: pairs; Trust Circle and King Tut's Rebirth: 7 to 13
Time: 1 to 1-1/2 hours
Audience: General
Subject(s): Trust
Source: C. M. Consalvo (1993), *Experiential Training Activities for Outside and In* (pp. 41-64). Amherst, MA: HRD Press. (800) 822-2801. www.hrdpress.com

ELECTRIC MAZE®

The Electric Maze is a pressure-sensitive carpet grid with visible and audible alarms. It can be programmed for various action-learning environments to teach communication and teamwork. In the Team Dynamics module two groups have 20 minutes to get each member safely across the maze without stepping on the hot squares that trigger alarms. Each team is offered $20 million in prize money with deductions taken for time spent—$1 million per minute—and for penalties. For example, crossing the maze in ten minutes wins the team $10 million. Teams learn that hitting hot spots provides necessary information to find the safe path and trying to avoid hot spots wastes valuable time and money. Individuals who break from the team plan and hit hot spots already identified also waste time and money. Other modules teach coaching and systems thinking skills. A variation of this simulation is The Sentinel, a three-dimensional maze built from eight columns that have electric eyes.

Space or Equipment Needs: 12-foot by 15-foot activity area, markers, flip chart
Cost: $3,680
Number of Participants: 4 to 24
Time: 1-1/2 hours
Audience: General
Subject(s): Communication, teams
Source: Interel, Inc. San Francisco, CA. (415) 566-0554.

New
THE EMPEROR'S POT

Eastern and Western cultures are simulated in this exercise. The scenario involves an urn with great spiritual significance for the East. Although it is considered priceless, parties from the West wish to purchase it for a museum. Participants assume various roles to participate in planning and negotiation. As the groups exchange delegates, participants pattern their role behavior on 19 cultural values described in their respective handouts. These values include individualism, social conformity, activism, moral superiority, and attitudes toward time and money. Additional handouts guide the stages of negotiation. This activity requires two facilitators.

Author: Donald Batchelder
Publication Date: 1996
Preparation: Prepare handouts
Space or Equipment Needs: Large pot, flip charts and markers, two rooms
Number of Participants: 16 to 50
Time: 1-1/2 to 2 hours
Audience: General
Subject(s): Multicultural diversity, cross-cultural communication
Source: D. Batchelder in H. N. Seelye (Ed.) (1996), *Experiential Activities for Intercultural Learning: Volume 1* (pp. 85-99). Yarmouth, ME: Intercultural Press. (800) 370-2665. www.interculturalpress.com

New
THE EMPOWERMENT EXERCISE

This in-basket exercise is organized for two outcomes. One set of instructions empowers the role-player and is accompanied by in-basket messages with helpful information and a sense of trust and responsibility. The other set of instructions and messages has the opposite effect. Participants receive one set or the other at random. After working on in-baskets for 25 minutes, students complete the *Affect Questionnaire* in Appendix B. Small and large group discussions and a worksheet for individual reflection reinforce the lesson. Appendix A suggests in-basket messages, Appendix C contains discussion topics, and Appendix D is a worksheet.

Author: Dafna Eylon & Susan Herman
Publication Date: 1999
Preparation: Photocopy handouts
Space or Equipment Needs: Blank paper and paper clips
Number of Participants: Any number
Time: 3 hours
Audience: General
Subject(s): Empowerment, information sharing
Source: D. Eylon & S. Herman (1999), Exploring empowerment: One method for the classroom, *Journal of Management Education, 23*(1), 80-94. Sage Publications, Inc. Thousand Oaks, CA. (805) 499-9774. www.sagepub.com

ERA

ERA is a simulation designed to teach leaders in flat organizations how to think strategically, turn strategy into action, and influence others to do the same. Participants assume roles as the top managers of ERA, Inc., a chain of specialty clothing stores. The CEO, CFO, and vice presidents of sourcing, strategic planning, distribution, and advertising must study new opportunities and make decisions that support the corporate vision as well as their own departments. As ERA executives, the participants attend virtual meetings and serve on task forces to practice their skills in gaining commitment for projects and goals. To succeed, the leaders must employ cross-functional cooperation. Following three hours of tactical work a debrief provides feedback on each leader's consistency of action and contribution to the process. A variation of this simulation is Academy Electronics and Equipment, which is geared to leaders in the field of technology.

Author: Bill Jockoe, Bernard Rosenbaum, & Shannon Rye Wall
Publication Date: 1996
Preparation: The facilitator must be certified by Manus; certification training is available
Cost: Contact Manus for information
Number of Participants: Groups of 4 to 6
Time: This one-day simulation is often imbedded in a multiple-day program
Audience: Managers, intact work groups
Subject(s): Decision making, influence

Source: Right Manus. Stamford, CT. (800) 445-0942. www.rightmanus.com

New
ETHICS IN ACTION: ALIGNING DECISIONS WITH ORGANIZATIONAL VALUES

Small groups identify the values expressed in organizational mission and vision statements as well as unwritten values that characterize the organization's culture. A facilitator leads a large group discussion that generates a short list of organizational values agreed upon by all participants. Small groups then work on three ethical problem-solving tasks. They recommend three solutions for each problem and highlight the one that most closely aligns with organizational values. In a debriefing session participants share their surprises, dilemmas, and actual experiences.

Author: Jean G. Lamkin
Publication Date: 1998
Preparation: Photocopy handouts
Space or Equipment Needs: Organizational mission and vision statements, flip charts and markers, tape, pencils
Number of Participants: 8 to 30
Time: 1-1/2 to 2 hours
Audience: Intact work groups
Subject(s): Values
Source: J. G. Lamkin in J. W. Pfeiffer, *The 1998 Annual: Volume 2, Consulting* (pp. 75-80). San Francisco: Jossey-Bass/Pfeiffer. (800) 274-4434. www.pfeiffer.com

New
EXPERIENCING INFLUENCE STYLES

This is a role play in which two supervisors try to influence two subordinates to wear safety goggles. Two people assume the same supervisor role, but the two subordinate roles have separate instructions. This mix allows for comparison of influence styles between the two supervisors personally and situationally. A handout introduces influence tactics and appropriate uses of each.

Author: Joseph Seltzer
Publication Date: 1998
Number of Participants: Groups of 4
Time: 50 minutes
Audience: General
Subject(s): Influence
Source: J. Seltzer in D. Marcic & J. Seltzer (1998), *Organizational Behavior: Experiences and Cases* (5th ed., pp. 137-138+). Cincinnati, OH: South-Western College Publishing. www.swcollege.com

FAR SIDE EXERCISE

This communication exercise uses cartoons from Gary Larson's *The Far Side*. The goal is for participants to uncover what the cartoon is communicating to the viewer. A combination of individual work, group consensus, and intergroup debate results in some interesting learnings,

according to Gilson. He notes that "the exercise begins with an apparent *shared* perception of humor. Very quickly, however, the exercise exposes divergent and distinct patterns of thought and judgment that sensitizes the students to some of the fundamental barriers to effective interpersonal communication."

Author: C. H. J. Gilson
Publication Date: 1991
Number of Participants: Any number
Time: 1 hour
Audience: General
Subject(s): Communication
Source: C. H. J. Gilson (1991), Teaching communications: Take a walk on "The Far Side." *Journal of Management Education*, *15*(1), 121-123. Sage Publications, Inc. Thousand Oaks, CA. (805) 499-9774. www.sagepub.com

FEEDBACK AWARENESS: SKILL BUILDING FOR SUPERVISORS

The purpose of this exercise is to enhance participants' awareness of the impact of feedback, to offer feedback guidelines and practice time, and to provide participants an opportunity to discuss and identify feedback characteristics and techniques. Participants record their perceptions of a partner's communication style during a brainstorming/discussion period. The perceptions are exchanged during a feedback session and later shared with the entire group.

Author: Robert W. Lucas
Publication Date: 1992
Preparation: Make posters
Space or Equipment Needs: Newsprint posters, clipboards for each participant, paper, pencils
Number of Participants: 16 to 24
Time: 2-1/4 hours
Audience: Managers, supervisors
Subject(s): Communication
Source: R. W. Lucas in J. W. Pfeiffer, *The 1992 Annual: Developing Human Resources* (pp. 29-36). San Diego, CA: Pfeiffer & Company (Jossey-Bass/Pfeiffer). (800) 274-4434. www.pfeiffer.com

FLYING STARSHIP®

The Flying Starship simulation teaches employees that overcoming one's resistance to change can improve work processes and deliver quality results. During the first factory run participants make paper stars in a routine assembly line of cutting, folding, and painting. Performance and profitability numbers are computed. Participants then redesign the factory to increase access to information, minimize critical specifications, and form cross-functional work teams. The second factory run usually produces better quality starships and higher profitability. The simulation can be adapted for groups working on team building and process improvement.

Author: William O. Lytle
Publication Date: 1983, 1998

Space or Equipment Needs: Four flip charts, markers, masking tape, calculator, timer, six tables, a chair for each participant
Cost: $70 per participant; *Leader's Guide*: $250
Number of Participants: Groups of 15 to 30
Time: 6 to 12 hours
Audience: Managers, intact work groups
Subject(s): Change
Source: Block Petrella Weisbord. Clark, NJ. (800) 296-1279. www.bpwconsulting.com

FOLLOW THE LEADER: AN INTRODUCTION TO SITUATIONAL LEADERSHIP

Situational leadership theory offers a method for managing people whereby a supervisor can adjust his or her leadership style according to what an individual subordinate needs in order to complete a specific task at a specific time. This exercise is designed to allow the participants to experience each of the four basic styles through a task using puzzle pieces. When finished the participants explore the ways in which leadership styles, tasks, and work groups affect one another.

Author: Karen S. Brown & Donald M. Loppnow
Publication Date: 1984
Number of Participants: 16 to 24
Time: 2-1/2 hours
Audience: General
Subject(s): Situational leadership
Source: K. S. Brown & D. M. Loppnow in J. W. Pfeiffer, *The 1984 Annual: Developing Human Resources* (pp. 38-43). San Diego, CA: University Associates (Jossey-Bass/Pfeiffer). (800) 274-4434. www.pfeiffer.com

FOUR FACTORS: THE INFLUENCE OF LEADER BEHAVIOR

R. Rosenthal and L. Jacobson's *Pygmalion in the Classroom* (Holt, Rinehart and Winston, 1968) is the source of the four leadership influence factors that are the basis of this exercise. The goals of the exercise are to acquaint participants with this theory and to "give the participants an opportunity to analyze case studies showing how particular leader approaches to Rosenthal and Jacobson's four factors (climate, feedback, input, and output) can positively or negatively affect followers." Participants analyze the cases separately, discuss them in small groups, then discuss them with the entire group.

Author: William N. Parker
Publication Date: 1989
Number of Participants: 16 to 24
Time: 1-3/4 hours
Audience: General
Subject(s): Influence
Source: W. N. Parker in J. W. Pfeiffer, *The 1989 Annual: Developing Human Resources* (pp. 39-46). San Diego, CA: University Associates (Jossey-Bass/Pfeiffer). (800) 274-4434. www.pfeiffer.com

FOURTEEN DIMENSIONS OF DIVERSITY: UNDERSTANDING AND APPRECIATING DIFFERENCES IN THE WORK PLACE

The goal of this exercise is threefold: to help participants understand that diversity is multidimensional and applies to everyone, to assist participants in exploring which of the dimensions of diversity have special relevance to their own identities, and to stimulate appreciation of the value of diversity in the workplace. Using a "diversity diagram" overhead for reference, the facilitator introduces the exercise by explaining that there are certain primary dimensions of diversity (race, age, gender, etc.) that affect the judgments people make about us, as well as secondary dimensions that are not necessarily part of our "core identity." Participants then fill in a blank diagram indicating which diversity dimensions are part of their core identity, how the importance of the dimensions have changed over time, and what special contributions they bring to the workplace because of their own diversity.

Author: Sunny Bradford
Publication Date: 1996
Number of Participants: 15 to 30
Time: 1-1/4 to 1-1/2 hours
Audience: General
Subject(s): Multicultural diversity
Source: S. Bradford in J. W. Pfeiffer, *The 1996 Annual: Volume 2, Consulting* (pp. 9-17). San Diego, CA: Pfeiffer & Company (Jossey-Bass/Pfeiffer). (800) 274-4434. www.pfeiffer.com

New
FRIDAY NIGHT AT THE ER®

This board game teaches the principles of systems thinking and the value of managing across boundaries. Players act as managers of four patient-care units—emergency, surgery, critical care, and step down. During play each manager makes decisions about managing resources and achieving good performance. An evaluation measures the quality of service and financial performance. Players have a tendency to become occupied with their own departments and to ignore the system as a whole. As time passes it becomes apparent that the units are interdependent and that their success depends on high-level collaboration. This game requires an experienced facilitator to administer and debrief. Includes a facilitator's guide, training video, and overhead transparency masters. Extra game boards may be added to facilitate larger groups.

Author: Breakthrough Learning Inc.
Publication Date: 1991, 1992
Preparation: Make transparencies and set up game boards
Space or Equipment Needs: Three tables and 12 chairs
Cost: $1,360
Number of Participants: 12
Time: 4 hours
Audience: Executives, managers, intact work groups
Subject(s): Systems thinking

Source: The Resources Connection. North Tonawanda, NY. (800) 295-0957. www.resourcesconnect.com

New
GLOBAL BEADS™

Colored beads represent the different ethnicities of the world. Participants use the beads to answer questions about people who have impacted their lives and social development. They also answer broader questions about community, organization, country, and world populations. The unique focus of this exercise is on one's personal experience and readiness to live and work in a global society rather than on a hypothetical situation. Includes a facilitator guide, participant workbooks, beads, and visual aids. This exercise must be facilitated by an experienced trainer. One-day facilitator training and certification is available for $1,500.

Author: Vincent R. Brown & Janet B. Reid
Publication Date: 1997
Cost: $749
Number of Participants: 25
Time: 30 to 45 minutes
Audience: Executives, managers
Subject(s): Diversity
Source: Global Lead Management Consulting. Cincinnati, OH. (800) 762-0882. www.globallead.com

GLOBAL DIVERSITY GAME

This is a board game intended for use in cross-cultural training programs. Each team moves a game piece to land on a category space and answer a multiple-choice question about global issues. The Demographics category questions are about population, gender, language, and ethnicity. The Jobs category questions relate to workforce trends, management issues, and industry. The Legislation category asks about policies and economic agreements. The Society category poses questions about culture, religion, education, and health care. When teams answer correctly they receive a colored chip. Teams who collect chips for all four categories travel to the inner circle to win. A facilitator's guide includes suggestions for debriefing. The Diversity Game©, a variation with a focus on general diversity issues, is also available.

Author: Quality Education Development, Inc.
Publication Date: 1993, 1998
Cost: $395
Number of Participants: 8 to 16
Time: 1-1/2 hours
Audience: General
Subject(s): Multicultural diversity
Source: QED Consulting. New York, NY. (800) 724-2215. www.qedconsulting.com

GLOBAL SERVICE PROVIDER: MANAGING CHANGE

In this exercise participants struggle with the ethical dilemmas that arise when the fictional company, Global Service Provider, makes a significant organizational change.

Participants form three groups and assume identities as the corporate human resource, operations, and communications departments. Each department is responsible for part of the downsizing and relocating process. Decisions must be made about eliminating jobs, meeting customer needs during the transition period, and the flow of information. This exercise gives participants the opportunity to reflect on their own personal and professional values as they struggle to meet organizational goals.

Author: Veronica P. Garza, Jeanette Guardia, Joe B. Rodgers, Charlene A. Ross, & Judith F. Vogt
Publication Date: 1997
Preparation: Photocopy handouts
Space or Equipment Needs: Masking tape, flip charts, and markers for each group
Number of Participants: 15 to 21
Time: 2 hours
Audience: General
Subject(s): Change, ethics
Source: V. P. Garza, J. Guardia, J. B. Rodgers, C. A. Ross, & J. F. Vogt in J. W. Pfeiffer, *The 1997 Annual: Volume 2, Consulting* (pp. 101-109). San Francisco: Pfeiffer (Jossey-Bass/Pfeiffer). (800) 274-4434. www.pfeiffer.com

GLOBALIZATION

This exercise helps participants understand and manage the paradigm of globalization and the tension it creates. Participants are divided into five groups and tagged according to a facet of life affected by globalization: societal, economic, political, technological, or environmental. Groups list the positive and negative forces that globalization has on their facets of life. The participants mix into new groups that include members representing each interest and they explore new perspectives. As they reach understanding of their interconnectedness they identify two new values and two new behaviors that would benefit themselves as well as others with diverse backgrounds.

Author: Bonnie Jameson
Publication Date: 1997
Preparation: Photocopy handouts
Space or Equipment Needs: Newsprint, flip charts, markers, and masking tape for the facilitator and each group; name tags, paper, pencils, and clipboards for each participant
Number of Participants: 25 to 30
Time: 2-1/2 hours
Audience: General
Subject(s): Values
Source: B. Jameson in J. W. Pfeiffer, *The 1997 Annual: Volume 1, Training* (pp. 19-31). San Francisco: Pfeiffer (Jossey-Bass/Pfeiffer). (800) 274-4434. www.pfeiffer.com

THE GOLD WATCH

The Gold Watch helps students examine their personal and professional values as they encounter business associates from other cultures who have different values. Participants are divided into groups to read and discuss a scenario involving a potential large sales order and a bribe with a gold watch. Each group ranks the ethical behavior of the six people involved. Intra- and intergroup discussions reinforce the lesson that values differ among persons and between cultures.

Author: Michael R. Lavery
Publication Date: 1974
Preparation: Photocopy handouts
Space or Equipment Needs: Newsprint, markers, masking tape, a clipboard for each group, a pencil for each participant
Number of Participants: 12 to 30
Time: 2 hours
Audience: General
Subject(s): Multicultural diversity, ethics
Source: M. R. Lavery in J. W. Pfeiffer & J. E. Jones (1974), *A Handbook of Structured Experiences for Human Relations Training, Volume X* (pp. 142-147). San Diego, CA: University Associates (Jossey-Bass/Pfeiffer). (800) 274-4434. www.pfeiffer.com

New
THE GRAND CANYON ADVENTURES

Three interrelated activities put participants into leadership and team-building scenarios while rafting down the Colorado River through the Grand Canyon. An 18-minute video sets the mood. In the first activity, Overboard in the Roaring River, participants must prioritize nine action steps to create a crisis management plan. Hiking Out of Lava Falls leads the group through a creative problem-solving process to plan a safe escape out of the Canyon. Up Deer Creek without a Boatman puts two competitive teams in a situation that requires collaboration. In all activities participants rate their own success before hearing the expert solutions provided by Grand Canyon and Colorado River experts. A *Facilitator's Guide* and ten participant workbooks contain training and debriefing guidelines.

Author: Carmine M. Consalvo
Publication Date: 1998
Preparation: Prepare handouts
Space or Equipment Needs: VCR, pencils, flip charts, and markers
Cost: $199.95
Number of Participants: Any number
Time: 1 to 1-1/2 hours each
Audience: Executives, managers, intact work groups
Subject(s): Creativity, collaboration, group consensus
Source: HRD Press. Amherst, MA. (800) 822-2801. www.hrdpress.com

New
GROWING A TEAM

This board game asks questions about the four stages of team development—forming, storming, norming, and performing—as described by Bruce Tuckman (1965, *Psychology Bulletin, 63*). Because answers can be challenged, team behavior during the game simulates the emotional and social interaction, communication, and competition that is typical to team development in general. This behavior throughout the game provides the background for debriefing and reflection. Includes a *Facilitator Guide*.

Author: Sivasailam Thiagarajan, Raja Thiagarajan, & Diane Dormant
Publication Date: 1997, 1999
Cost: $89
Number of Participants: 2 to 16
Time: 30 to 45 minutes
Audience: General
Subject(s): Team development
Source: Workshops by Thiagi, Inc. Bloomington, IN. (800) 996-7725. www.thiagi.com

New
THE HARWOOD DILEMMA

This case describes employee resistance to changes at the fictional Harwood Manufacturing Corporation. Participants select from 25 strategic actions to manage the change. Then in small groups they reach consensus about the best strategies and plan a solution. Scores are plotted to determine which strategies reflect the participants' beliefs about Theory X and Theory Y management styles. Hall recommends that facilitators and participants read more about this style introduced by Douglas McGregor in *The Human Side of Enterprise* (McGraw-Hill, 1960).

Author: Jay Hall
Publication Date: 1970, 1996
Cost: Participant booklets: $9.95; *Leader's Guide*: $24.95
Number of Participants: Small groups
Time: 2 hours
Audience: Managers
Subject(s): Theory X and Theory Y
Source: Teleometrics. The Woodlands, TX. (800) 527-0406. www.teleometrics.com

HATS "R" US: LEARNING ABOUT ORGANIZATIONAL CULTURES

Participants in this exercise are assigned to one of four groups, each representing a general type of organizational culture (as identified by T. E. Deal and A. A. Kennedy in *Corporate Cultures: The Rites and Rituals of Corporate Life*, Addison-Wesley, 1982). Each group is briefed on its culture type. Keeping its type in mind the group must: 1) design a hat that they think their culture would produce, 2) decide on marketing goals, and 3) devise a marketing action plan. If it is desired, a manager may be designated for each group and asked to function in the way that a manager from that culture would. In subsequent discussions and debriefing participants explore their learnings about the four culture types and their reactions to the type they were assigned (for example, whether they felt aligned or mis-aligned with their culture).

Author: Catherine J. Nagy
Publication Date: 1994

Number of Participants: 16 to 24
Time: 2-1/2 hours
Audience: General
Subject(s): Organizational culture
Source: C. J. Nagy in J. W. Pfeiffer, *The 1994 Annual: Developing Human Resources* (pp. 93-106). San Diego, CA: Pfeiffer & Company (Jossey-Bass/Pfeiffer). (800) 274-4434. www.pfeiffer.com

HOLLOW SQUARE: A COMMUNICATIONS EXPERIMENT

Hollow Square is a useful communication exercise for illustrating the importance of intergroup communication to complete a task. A planning group has access to information regarding the assembly of a puzzle. They are to instruct the implementing team on how to assemble the puzzle. A third group serves as observers of the process. Typically members of each team make unnecessary and limiting assumptions about the task. The debrief can be very rich with discussion about the planning process, authority relations, and outcomes and communication strategies within and between groups.

Author: Arthur Shedlin & Warren H. Schmidt
Publication Date: 1974
Preparation: Trace and cut puzzle pieces and divide into envelopes
Space or Equipment Needs: Envelopes and cardboard for puzzle pieces
Cost: Cost of materials
Number of Participants: Any number
Time: 1 to 2 hours
Audience: General
Subject(s): Communication, teams
Source: A. Shedlin & W. Schmidt in J. W. Pfeiffer & J. E. Jones (1974), *A Handbook of Structured Experiences for Human Relations Training, Volume II* (pp. 32-40). San Diego, CA: University Associates (Jossey-Bass/Pfeiffer). (800) 274-4434. www.pfeiffer.com

New
HPT 101

This board and card game is based on the human performance technology (HPT) process. Each deal of the game corresponds to one of five flexible HPT steps: analysis, design, installation, evaluation, and management. Players move around the board according to how well they can match card statements to each step. A *Feedback Table* provides official answers. Chance cards and die add challenge to the game. Includes a *Facilitator Guide*.

Author: Sivasailam Thiagarajan & Raja Thiagarajan
Publication Date: 1999
Cost: $89
Number of Participants: 2 to 16
Time: 30 to 45 minutes
Audience: General
Subject(s): Performance

Source: Workshops by Thiagi, Inc. Bloomington, IN. (800) 996-7725. www.thiagi.com

New
IN-BASKET PRACTICE TEST FOR SUPERVISORS

This in-basket exercise is intended for new supervisors or those seeking supervisory positions. The notes, letters, and memos in the fictional supervisor's in-box simulate communications in a financial services company. Participant responses are self-scored using a protocol sheet that details appropriate responses. The skills and behaviors identified are: support of management policies, difficulty with transition, vertical communication, anticipation of problems, willingness to take action, sensitivity, tolerance, and diplomacy. A version designed especially for government agencies is also available.

Author: James E. Larsen
Publication Date: 1999
Preparation: Photocopy blank memo sheets
Space or Equipment Needs: Pens, paper clips
Cost: $35
Number of Participants: 1 or more
Time: 1 to 2 hours
Audience: Supervisors
Subject(s): Leadership behaviors, communication
Source: Management Resources, 1100 Galloway, Lincoln, NE 68512. (402) 423-8960.

New
INFERNAL TOWER

Team members take turns leading in this exercise. The "leader" coaches a blindfolded "builder" to add a sugar cube to the team tower. When that is accomplished the builder becomes the leader who guides the next team member to add another cube, and so on. After planning, practicing, and the first round of building, teams may reorganize. Following the second round of building, a facilitator debriefs the teams on leadership in a flat organization where participants must shift between leader and follower roles rapidly.

Author: Steven I. Meisel & David S. Fearon
Publication Date: 1999
Preparation: Photocopy handouts
Space or Equipment Needs: Sugar cubes
Cost: Cost of materials
Number of Participants: Groups of 4 to 8
Time: 1-1/2 hours
Audience: Intact work groups
Subject(s): Shared leadership
Source: S. I. Meisel & D. S. Fearon (1999), The new leadership construct: What happens when a flat organization builds a tall tower?, *Journal of Management Education, 23*(2), 180-189. Sage Publications, Inc. Thousand Oaks, CA. (805) 499-9774. www.sagepub.com

New
INNOVATION STYLES®

This board and card game is based on a framework of innovation styles introduced by William Miller (*The Creative Edge,* 1987). Each deal of the game corresponds to one of four innovation styles: experimenting, exploring, modifying, and visioning. Players move around the board according to how well they can match card statements to each style. A *Feedback Table* provides official answers. Chance cards and die add challenge to the game. Includes a *Facilitator Guide.*

Author: William C. Miller, Alain Rostain, Sivasailam Thiagarajan, & Raja Thiagarajan
Publication Date: 1999
Cost: $89
Number of Participants: 2 to 16
Time: 30 to 45 minutes
Audience: General
Subject(s): Innovation
Source: Workshops by Thiagi, Inc. Bloomington, IN. (800) 996-7725. www.thiagi.com

ISLAND COMMISSION

In this exercise a team practices long-range planning and discovers emergent leadership. A planning commission is simulated when eight persons assume eight different roles: city planner, community action director, chamber of commerce director, corporate manager, organization development consultant, farmer, dentist, and lawyer. This newly organized commission must plan the expenditure of a multimillion dollar, multiyear grant. Their planning is complicated by economic, transportation, educational, housing, employment, and ethical issues. Reaching consensus requires the team to explore their communication, problem-solving, and decision-making skills. One group's experience with Island Commission is reported in S. J. Guastello (1995), Facilitative style, individual innovation, and emergent leadership in problem solving groups, *The Journal of Creative Behavior*, 29(4), 225-239.

Author: Peter G. Gillan
Publication Date: 1974
Preparation: Photocopy handouts
Space or Equipment Needs: Place card and pencil for each participant; newsprint and marker for each group
Number of Participants: Groups of 8
Time: 2 to 2-1/2 hours
Audience: Civic leaders, intact work groups
Subject(s): Teams
Source: P. G. Gillan in J. W. Pfeiffer & J. E. Jones (1974), *A Handbook of Structured Experiences for Human Relations Training, Volume VII* (pp. 99-104). San Diego, CA: University Associates (Jossey-Bass/Pfeiffer). (800) 274-4434. www.pfeiffer.com

JEFFERSON COMPANY EXERCISE

This exercise exposes students to some of the complexity encountered when attempting to implement change in an organization. "It is a role-play exercise, with four characters, designed to show how both employee and management resistance to change can hinder the implementation of an organizational change effort." The setting is a printing company that has recently been sold in a leveraged buyout. The four roles are: CEO, sales manager, shop foreman, and union steward.

Author: Anne H. Reilly
Publication Date: 1992
Number of Participants: Groups of 4 or 5
Time: 1-1/2 to 2 hours
Audience: MBA students
Subject(s): Change
Source: A. H. Reilly (1992), Understanding resistance to change: The Jefferson Company Exercise, *Journal of Management Education*, 16, 314-326. Sage Publications, Inc. Thousand Oaks, CA. (805) 499-9774. www.sagepub.com

New
JET FORMATION

This is an exercise in team problem solving as participants emulate a team of jet pilots flying in formation like a flock of geese. First they are instructed to reverse direction by moving the minimum number of jets. Next, in the advanced version, participants are told to fly in a formation that seems to require twice as many pilots as available. The ten pilots are instructed to form five rows of four. If planning time is allowed, it's easier for teams to find the solutions. Without planning, communication and cooperation are key elements.

Author: Carmine M. Consalvo
Publication Date: 1996
Number of Participants: 10
Time: 30 minutes to 1 hour
Audience: General
Subject(s): Teams, problem solving
Source: C. M. Consalvo (1996), *Changing Pace: Outdoor Games for Experiential Learning* (pp. 161-164). Amherst, MA: HRD Press. (800) 822-2801. www.hrdpress.com

New
JIGSAW

Five jigsaw puzzles are mixed up and placed in four boxes. Participants are divided into four groups, each with one box of puzzle pieces. The facilitator instructs the group to complete the puzzles, with no elaboration. An exchange area is set up in which a participant may offer one piece but may not ask for one. When all five puzzles are complete the group discusses the tendency toward competition and the necessity of collaboration in negotiations.

Author: Lorraine L. Ukens
Publication Date: 1999
Preparation: Mix up puzzle pieces

Space or Equipment Needs: Five simple jigsaw puzzles, four boxes
Number of Participants: 8 to 24
Time: 15 to 20 minutes
Audience: General
Subject(s): Negotiation
Source: L. L. Ukens (1999), *All Together Now! A Seriously Fun Collection of Training Games and Activities* (pp. 91-92). San Francisco: Jossey-Bass/Pfeiffer. (800) 274-4434. www.pfeiffer.com

JUNGLE ESCAPE

Jungle Escape is intended for existing teams but may be used by other people who want to learn about group dynamics, team leadership, and consensus. The exercise puts three teams in an imaginary jungle following a helicopter crash. To escape the jungle each team must assemble a new helicopter from 93 parts. An observer notes each team's planning and assembly to track the time spent on each process, the contribution of all team members, the problem-solving and decision-making systems, and the group's morale. A team successfully completes the assignment when its helicopter matches the facilitator's sample. During the debriefing, teams evaluate their dynamics to determine if they are fragmented, divergent, or cohesive. They learn the ideal dynamics of effective teams and discuss the changes they can make on real work projects. Includes 15 participant booklets, parts for three helicopters, audiocassette of rain forest sounds, and a *Facilitator Guide*.

Author: Rollin Glaser & Christine Glaser
Publication Date: 1981, 1984, 1985, 1988, 1990, 1993, 1995
Preparation: The facilitator needs 30 minutes to assemble the display helicopter, set up the room, and make transparencies
Space or Equipment Needs: Stopwatch for each observer, audiocassette player, flip chart or overhead projector, markers
Cost: $245; additional helicopter parts: $30; five extra participant booklets: $18
Number of Participants: 12 to 18
Time: 1-1/2 hours
Audience: Intact work groups
Subject(s): Group dynamics
Source: HRDQ. King of Prussia, PA. (800) 633-4533. www.hrdq.com

New
JUST MY TYPE: THE PERSONALITY GAME

Carl Jung's theory of personality types (*Psychological Types*, 1923) describes four pairs of contrasting personality dimensions, which address how we focus, gather information, make decisions, and take action. This game teaches participants about Jung's theory using playing cards divided into suits representing the four dimensions. Each card contains an adjective, such as "independent," "expressive," or "idealistic," that is related to a specific personality style.

In the game, each player is dealt a random hand of cards and must then discuss and trade cards with others to build a hand that best describes him or her. Participant workbooks provide information on the personality types, team discussion questions, and an opportunity for individual action planning.

Author: John Taylor
Publication Date: 1996
Cost: $125
Number of Participants: 16
Time: 45 minutes to 1 hour
Audience: General
Subject(s): Personality types
Source: HRDQ. King of Prussia, PA. (800) 633-4533. www.hrdq.com

New
KALEIDOSCOPE

This "soft-sell" activity makes its impact through the combined use of touch, sight, and hearing. Various sizes and types of kaleidoscopes are available around the training room, cafeteria, or other public space. They are appealing and accessible so that participants randomly pick them up, look, change the design, and look again. Nearby are various signs that supplement the theme of change. Participants are encouraged to discuss their changing views, which may serve as a springboard for a more complex discussion of change.

Author: Carolyn Nilson
Publication Date: 1995
Preparation: Set out kaleidoscopes, make signs
Space or Equipment Needs: A variety of kaleidoscopes, poster boards, and markers
Number of Participants: Any number
Time: 1 minute
Audience: General
Subject(s): Change
Source: C. Nilson (1995), *Games That Drive Change* (pp. 51-52). New York: McGraw-Hill. (800) 352-3566. www.bookstore.mcgraw-hill.com

New
KNOW ME

Based on the Johari Window model of Disclosure/Feedback (Luft, 1969), this game is designed to develop trust and build community by helping participants learn about themselves and each other. Players move around the game board selecting Ask and Tell cards at the Light-Hearted, Serious, and In-Depth levels. Points are earned by following directions on the cards, such as "Ask the group members what they think is most important to you," and "Tell the group how you feel talking about yourself." Facilitators can use blank cards to customize the game and optional Venture cards to introduce multiple-choice questions about the organization or players. The game comes with a set of Master cards designed to build trust and rapport, but additional sets of cards focusing on specific issues of career management, change and transformation, quality and service, and team building can also be ordered.

Author: Ric Matthews & Graham Bullen
Publication Date: 1994
Preparation: Photocopy handouts, print transparencies
Cost: $250
Number of Participants: 4 to 6
Time: 1 to 1-1/4 hours
Audience: Intact groups
Subject(s): Trust, group relationships
Source: HRDQ. King of Prussia, PA. (800) 633-4533. www.hrdq.com

New
LANDSLIDE

This exercise helps build teams by having participants assume roles as managers in a company that makes mountain climbing equipment. A group of ten volunteers out testing the equipment is trapped by a landslide and can only be rescued one at a time. Groups are given descriptions of the volunteers and must decide in what order they should be rescued. Afterwards participants discuss how and why they ranked volunteers and analyze the performance of their group in areas such as setting objectives, communication, and leadership.

Author: Martin Thompson
Publication Date: 1998
Cost: Participant booklets: $4.95; facilitator guide: $20
Number of Participants: Small groups
Time: 2 to 3 hours
Audience: General
Subject(s): Group consensus
Source: Organizational Learning Tools, Inc. Novi, MI. (800) 684-1190.

New
LEADERSHIP JAZZ

In Leadership Jazz participants develop individual and group skills using creative approaches. Their assignment is to make musical instruments out of ordinary objects such as combs for plucking, cans for blowing into, car keys for rattling, or spiral notebooks for strumming. Then each group chooses a few tunes, rehearses, and gives a performance. Groups are judged on their number and variety of instruments and the quality of their performance. A debriefing addresses the obstacles to creativity and creativity-enhancing strategies.

Author: Mark L. Lengnick-Hall & Cynthia A. Lengnick-Hall
Publication Date: 1999
Space or Equipment Needs: Objects to make musical instruments
Number of Participants: Groups of 5
Time: 1 to 1-1/4 hours
Audience: General
Subject(s): Creativity

Source: M. L. Lengnick-Hall & C. A. Lengnick-Hall (1999), Leadership Jazz: An exercise in creativity, *Journal of Management Education, 23*(1), 65-70. Sage Publications, Inc. Thousand Oaks, CA. (805) 499-9774. www.sagepub.com

New
LEADERSHIP ROLE PLAYS: USING COACHING AND COUNSELING SKILLS

This exercise differentiates between coaching and counseling and provides a role play to practice each set of skills. A trio of supervisor, subordinate, and observer participates in a complex scenario of a troubled employee who needs to learn a new job skill. The supervisor attempts to meet all of the subordinate's coaching needs in ten minutes and counseling needs in the next ten minutes. Detailed instructions enable the observer to provide extensive feedback following the exercise.

Author: Cynthia L. Sutton & Katherine A. Karl
Publication Date: 1998
Preparation: Prepare handouts
Space or Equipment Needs: Paper
Number of Participants: Groups of 3
Time: 1 hour
Audience: General
Subject(s): Coaching
Source: C. L. Sutton & K. A. Karl in D. Marcic & J. Seltzer (1998), *Organizational Behavior: Experiences and Cases* (5th ed., pp. 163-164+). Cincinnati, OH: South-Western College Publishing. www.swcollege.com

New
LEADOUT

In small groups participants assume roles as land acquisition officers who are seeking parcels of land for growing grapes. Three of four requirements must be met: adequate rainfall, proper drainage, rich soil, and a gentle slope. A land board contains 144 covered squares representing the land parcels, some that meet the requirements and some that don't. Each group member has minimal information about which parcels are best. New information is distributed at several points throughout the game. Additional pressure is exerted through deadlines, competition from other groups, and attention to team performance. A trainer's guide contains instructions for administration and debriefing.

Author: C. L. Hosford
Publication Date: 1987
Space or Equipment Needs: Flip charts, markers, and masking tape
Cost: $495
Number of Participants: 15 to 120
Time: 2 hours
Audience: General
Subject(s): Problem solving, risk-taking
Source: Charles Hosford & Associates, 1507 S.E. 129th Avenue, Portland, OR 97233-1214. (503) 254-9868. www.leadout.com

LED LIKE SHEEP

This exercise focuses on the link between group decision-making schemes and the type of task assigned. Group decision making is viewed on a continuum relative to the amount of influence or persuasion necessary to arrive at a group decision. Tasks range from those with correct answers to those that have a preferred answer. Each small group is given four tasks that span this range. After completing all of the tasks the group members relate their observations about their groups and group processes given the different tasks.

Author: Diane Dodd-McCue
Publication Date: 1991
Number of Participants: 25 to 40
Time: 1-1/4 to 1-1/2 hours
Audience: General
Subject(s): Decision making, teams
Source: D. Dodd-McCue (1991), Led Like Sheep: An exercise for linking group decision making to different types of tasks, *Journal of Management Education*, 15(3), 335-339. Sage Publications, Inc. Thousand Oaks, CA. (805) 499-9774. www.sagepub.com

LIVING ETHICS: MEETING CHALLENGES IN DECISION MAKING

Participants are divided into four groups to study individually and as groups four scenarios of ethical dilemmas in the workplace: pirating a computer program, hiring a friend, a global executive-exchange program, and giving a problem employee a glowing recommendation so that she'll get a new job and become someone else's problem. With the help of a facilitator the groups discuss the critical factors in each ethical dilemma, consider possible resolution actions, and select resolutions that are most positive for all parties.

Author: Gilbert Joseph Duran, Erna E. Gomar, Marianne Stiles, Christina A. Vele, & Judith F. Vogt
Publication Date: 1997
Preparation: Photocopy handouts
Space or Equipment Needs: Newsprint, flip chart, markers, and masking tape; pencil, paper, and clipboard for each participant
Number of Participants: 16 to 24
Time: 1-1/4 hours
Audience: General
Subject(s): Ethics
Source: G. J. Duran, E. E. Gomar, M. Stiles, C. A. Vele, & J. F. Vogt in J. W. Pfeiffer, *The 1997 Annual: Volume 1, Training* (pp. 127-135). San Francisco: Pfeiffer (Jossey-Bass/Pfeiffer). (800) 274-4434. www.pfeiffer.com

New
MANAGERIAL PERCEPTIONS: WHAT DO EMPLOYEES REALLY WANT?

This exercise is based on research reported in K. Kovach (1995), Employee motivation: Addressing a crucial factor in your organization's performance, *Employment Relations Today*, 22(2), 93-107. The relative importance of these ten job factors is considered: pay, security, promotion, working conditions, interesting work, help with personal problems, loyalty, appreciation, tactful discipline, and feelings of inclusion. In step one participants rank the factors according to their perceptions of employees' motivation. In step two the facilitator reveals managerial responses from Kovach's research. Finally, the facilitator reveals Kovach's employee responses. Participants calculate the variation between perceived and actual importance of the ten job factors. The facilitator leads a debriefing.

Author: John Sample
Publication Date: 1998
Preparation: Photocopy handouts
Space or Equipment Needs: Flip chart and markers for facilitator; clipboards and pencils for participants
Number of Participants: Any number
Time: 1 to 1-1/4 hours
Audience: Managers
Subject(s): Motivation
Source: J. Sample in J. W. Pfeiffer, *The 1998 Annual: Volume 2, Consulting* (pp. 87-94). San Francisco: Jossey-Bass/Pfeiffer. (800) 274-4434. www.pfeiffer.com

New
MAROONED

This is a basic-level exercise in the Team Adventure Series™ of survival simulations. The scenario is a pleasure cruise through the French Polynesian Islands recreated by a color slide show. During a picnic on an uninhabited island a group wanders off and gets left behind—marooned. The group must plan its survival by ranking, individually and as a team, ten action alternatives. The Australian Army's priorities for surviving in a hostile environment are used to determine the expert rankings that provide a basis for comparison. Upon completion teams plot their scores to understand their achievement in the seven-step process that leads to team synergy. The *Facilitator Guide* provides background information, rationale for rankings, and guidelines for a debriefing on group behaviors. New teams can use this as an icebreaker.

Author: Rollin Glaser & Christine Glaser
Publication Date: 1993
Space or Equipment Needs: Slide projector is optional
Cost: Five participant booklets: $30; *Facilitator Guide*: $30; optional color slides: $32
Number of Participants: Groups of 4 to 6
Time: 1-1/2 hours
Audience: Intact work groups
Subject(s): Group consensus, decision making, teams
Source: HRDQ. King of Prussia, PA. (800) 633-4533. www.hrdq.com

MARS SURFACE ROVER

This exercise is based on a model of facilitative leadership presented in Rollin Glaser's *Facilitative Behavior Question-*

naire (HRDQ, 1991). The model illustrates a gradual growth from high directive leadership to facilitative leadership without becoming passive. Because this concept is difficult to grasp, Mars Surface Rover was created to provide a physical comparison between the three leadership styles. Participants are divided into three teams. Each team's leader receives instructions to behave in a traditional, passive, or facilitative way as his or her team builds a motorized vehicle to explore the surface of Mars. The traditional leader gives orders, while the passive leader offers no information at all. The facilitative leader shares information and encourages all team members to contribute ideas. When the completed vehicles race it is usually obvious that the one built by the team with a facilitative leader is the best product. Mars Surface Rover: Team Version showcases the benefits of true teamwork relative to group work.

Author: Eileen M. Russo & Matthew P. Eckler
Publication Date: 1995
Preparation: Make transparencies and set up team supplies
Space or Equipment Needs: Overhead projector, transparency marker, and masking tape; table and chairs for each team (a round table is best)
Cost: $395; five extra participant booklets: $28; extra parts: $85
Number of Participants: 12 to 18
Time: 2 hours
Audience: Managers
Subject(s): Leadership styles
Source: HRDQ. King of Prussia, PA. (800) 633-4533. www.hrdq.com

New
MBTI CHALLENGE CARDS

This card game helps participants understand the four personality preference scales of the *Myers-Briggs Type Indicator®*: introversion or extraversion, sensing or intuition, feeling or thinking, and perception or judgment. Half the cards contain a quote and half describe a behavior that represents one of the preferences. Teams discuss and gain consensus on which preference each card represents. An answer key provides correct answers.

Author: Davis/Neal & Associates
Publication Date: 1989
Cost: $12
Number of Participants: Small groups
Time: 30 to 45 minutes
Audience: General
Subject(s): Personality
Source: CAPT—Center for Applications of Psychological Type, Inc. Gainesville, FL. (800) 777-2278. www.capt.org

MEET DR. CLAY AND DR. GLASS

This exercise was developed as an exam for international exchange students in management. Because it requires creativity and divergent thinking this exercise benefits ESL students or managers working in cross-cultural situations.

The facilitator introduces two candidates for a CEO position, Dr. Clay (a lump of clay) and Dr. Glass (an empty bottle). Students are asked to write lists of leadership qualities present or absent in each candidate. For instance, Dr. Glass may be perceived as rigid, easily broken when stressed, and open to new ideas (through the hole in the top). Dr. Clay may be considered flexible and responsive. The facilitator leads a discussion about desirable leadership attributes.

Author: Robert Cunningham
Publication Date: 1997
Space or Equipment Needs: Lump of clay and an attractive, empty glass bottle
Cost: Cost of materials
Number of Participants: Any number
Time: 50 minutes or less
Audience: General
Subject(s): Creativity
Source: R. Cunningham (1997), Meet Dr. Clay and Dr. Glass: A leadership exercise, *Journal of Management Education, 21*(2), 262-264. Sage Publications, Inc. Thousand Oaks, CA. (805) 499-9774. www.sagepub.com

MINEFIELD

This exercise provides a learning experience with the same anxiety, excitement, and commitment that accompanies the start-up of an entrepreneurial venture. Students must cross a simulated 50-yard minefield by placing and stepping on anti-mines. The exercise requires students to create a shared vision, share resources, support each other, be persistent, learn from mistakes, keep morale high, and adjust to change—all behaviors that help entrepreneurs develop new ventures. The students also learn about false starts, lack of focus, and instability—challenges that entrepreneurs often encounter.

Author: Peter B. Robinson
Publication Date: 1996
Preparation: Gather flat rocks or cut wood six inches in diameter to make anti-mines
Space or Equipment Needs: One anti-mine for each participant
Number of Participants: 15 to 30
Time: 1-1/2 to 2-1/2 hours
Audience: Students
Subject(s): Creativity, change, entrepreneurial leadership style
Source: P. B. Robinson (1996), The MINEFIELD exercise: "The challenge" in entrepreneurship education, *Simulation & Gaming, 27*(3), 350-364. Sage Publications, Inc. Thousand Oaks, CA. (805) 499-9774. www.sagepub.com

NASA MOON SURVIVAL TASK

This survival exercise asks participants to imagine a crash landing on the moon 200 miles from their rendezvous point. Fifteen supply items survived the crash. Each individual ranks the importance of each item. Participants are then separated into small groups who discuss the possibilities and reach consensus on the rankings. During the discussion some participants will argue for their own position, cave in to pressure from others, or encourage compromise. The groups are scored on the quality of their decisions and do a self-analysis on their members' commitment, conflict, creativity, and consensus. Researchers at the Manned Spacecraft Center of NASA in Houston, Texas, reviewed the exercise and supplied the expert solution and rationales for each ranking.

Author: Jay Hall
Publication Date: 1963, 1986, 1989, 1994
Space or Equipment Needs: Large meeting room for whole group, small meeting rooms for small groups, flip chart, and markers
Cost: Participant booklets: $8.95 each
Number of Participants: Groups of 5 to 7
Time: 3 hours
Audience: General
Subject(s): Decision making, influence, group consensus
Source: Teleometrics International. The Woodlands, TX. (800) 527-0406. www.teleometrics.com

New
THE NATURE OF LEADERSHIP

Participants are divided into two pairs to prepare for and practice constructive controversy. In the first round the debate is whether leaders are pawns of history or creators of history. After both sides have presented persuasive cases, there is group discussion and the pairs switch positions. Again, the arguments must be thorough and persuasive. In the end the group must reach consensus on one position. The process is repeated with a new debate about whether leaders are born or made.

Author: David W. Johnson & Frank P. Johnson
Publication Date: 1997
Preparation: Prepare handouts
Number of Participants: Groups of 4
Time: 2 hours
Audience: General
Subject(s): Leadership theories
Source: D. W. Johnson & F. P. Johnson (1997), *Joining Together: Group Theory and Group Skills* (pp. 179-182). Needham Heights, MA: Allyn & Bacon. (800) 666-9433. http://vig.abacon.com

NETWORK™

NetWork is a group-operated drawing device used to teach team leadership, group decision making, the balance between control and support, and techniques for giving descriptive feedback. The device is constructed of a metal frame and control strings that guide a marker over a variety of targets. Participants each control one or two strings to draw together a series of designs such as a figure 8, the group's best guess at the direction of due north, a mathematical sum, or a rendition of the company logo. Variations of this activity include: giving the drawing instructions to

only one person who must act as leader, dividing the group into two competitive teams, and using a coach outside the group to provide information and instructions. Each drawing period is brief to allow time for discussion.

Space or Equipment Needs: Six-foot by six-foot indoor activity area
Cost: Floor model: $380; tabletop model: $280
Number of Participants: 4 to 8
Time: 20 minutes
Audience: Managers, intact work groups
Subject(s): Decision making, communication, teams
Source: Interel, Inc. San Francisco, CA. (415) 566-0554.

NEW COMMONS GAME

This game simulates a central problem of human society, which is that interdependent individuals can destroy the society by choosing only those actions that benefit them as individuals while making the world poorer. It demonstrates that people tend to opt for short-term, individual gain at the expense of the collective good. It illustrates the need for rules limiting freedom and autonomy. Players see that some actions are clearly more beneficial to themselves and they also quickly learn that the world suffers when they make self-serving choices. Even though players eventually learn that if enough other people choose the world-preserving action all can enjoy personal benefits without impoverishing the world, it is maddeningly difficult to get agreement on the rules to enforce this world-preserving option.

Author: R. B. Powers
Publication Date: 1993
Cost: $100
Number of Participants: 6 to 24
Time: 1-1/2 to 2 hours
Audience: Civic leaders, students
Subject(s): Ethics, power
Source: Educational Simulations. Oceanside, OR. (503) 842-7247.

New
NEWS ROOM: A GROUP-CONSENSUS TASK

Small groups become editors, writers, and producers for a news program and are under a strict deadline to write a fast-breaking news story. Each group receives a packet of index cards with selected "news" words on each card and has ten minutes to create a story. They must use at least as many words as there are group members, use no words more than once, and gain consensus from all members on their decisions. One suggested word group includes tremors, fire, buildings, collapse, warning, bystanders, wreckage, rubble, almost, forever, escape, sudden, and evacuation, which suggests a news story about an earthquake.

Author: Heidi Ann Campbell & Heather Jean Campbell
Publication Date: 1998
Preparation: Writing "news" words on index cards
Space or Equipment Needs: Index cards

Number of Participants: 24 to 30
Time: 50 to 55 minutes
Audience: General
Subject(s): Communication, group consensus
Source: H. A. Campbell & H. J. Campbell in J. W. Pfeiffer, *The 1998 Annual: Volume 2, Consulting* (pp. 59-62). San Francisco: Jossey-Bass/Pfeiffer. (800) 274-4434. www.pfeiffer.com

New
A NO-DOZE LEADERSHIP CLASS

This activity highlights the various leadership styles of members in a group who know each other—having worked together or observed each other in a course or program. The facilitator outlines a horizontal continuum with "wind" representing flexibility and "water" representing authority at the extremes. Participants place themselves along the continuum and are moved around by their fellow group members. The vertical continuum runs from "cool cucumber" to "red hot tamale." The process of self-placement and group opinion is repeated until members cover the four quadrants. From their various perspectives, they discuss the strengths, weaknesses, and leadership functions of each quadrant and the value of including multiple styles within a group.

Author: Molly Doran
Publication Date: 1998
Preparation: Place and label the continuum markers
Space or Equipment Needs: Tape, chalk, or rope to define the continuum
Number of Participants: Any number
Time: 1 hour
Audience: General, intact work groups
Subject(s): Leadership styles
Source: M. Doran in J. Gookin, R. Green, & M. Doran (Eds.), *1998 NOLS Leadership Education Toolbox* (pp. 7/2-7/4). Lander, WY: The National Outdoor Leadership School. (307) 332-8800. www.nols.edu

New
OOGLY: A METAPHOR FOR CHANGE

Oogly is a sticky mixture of cornstarch and water that serves as a hands-on metaphor for change. Oogly resists fast stirring and forceful poking. It will only respond to gentle molding. If handled with too much energy it fractures; too little energy and it drools back into its original form. Instructions are included for making the mixture and for achieving a balance of energy when handling change.

Author: Sam Sikes
Publication Date: 1995
Preparation: Mix cornstarch and water
Space or Equipment Needs: Large bowl, cornstarch, and water
Number of Participants: Any number
Time: 15 to 30 minutes

Audience: General
Subject(s): Change
Source: S. Sikes (1995), *Feeding the Zircon Gorilla and Other Teambuilding Activities* (pp. 110-113). Tulsa, OK: Learning Unlimited Corporation. Available from Jossey-Bass/Pfeiffer. San Francisco, CA. (800) 274-4434. www.pfeiffer.com

OURTOWN

Two community-based agencies are given the task of exploring their mission and purpose and developing a five-year strategic plan. In the middle of the process the agencies are merged unexpectedly and the two groups are instructed to continue the task as one group. The objectives of this exercise are to: 1) have participants experience change over which they have no control, 2) understand the characteristics of effective leadership before and after change, and 3) develop awareness of how to lead people as they pass through change-induced personal transitions. A variation of this exercise, Lakeview, is designed for public administrators.

Author: W. Christopher Musselwhite
Publication Date: 1991, 1996
Preparation: The facilitator must have experience running a simulation and managing a debriefing
Cost: Contact Discovery Learning for licensing or in-house delivery
Number of Participants: 8 to 14
Time: 2 hours
Audience: Managers, civic leaders, students
Subject(s): Change
Source: Discovery Learning. Greensboro, NC. (336) 272-9530. www.discoverync.com

OUTBACK!

This is an advanced-level exercise in the Team Adventure Series™ of survival simulations. The scenario is set in the enchanting but crocodile-infested Australian Outback. As the group ventures away from camp without a guide, it gets lost in the bush. With one member injured the team must stop wandering and make a plan for survival in the wild until they can be rescued. Participants rank individually and as a team ten items and ten action alternatives for survival. Expert rankings provide a basis for comparison. Upon completion teams plot their scores to understand their achievement in the seven-step process that leads to team synergy. The *Facilitator Guide* provides information for introducing the simulation, running it, and debriefing it. An optional set of mood-setting slides is available.

Author: Rollin Glaser & Christine Glaser
Publication Date: 1993
Space or Equipment Needs: Slide projector is optional
Cost: Five participant booklets: $30; *Facilitator Guide*: $30; optional color slides: $32
Number of Participants: Groups of 4 to 6
Time: 2-1/2 hours

Audience: Intact work groups
Subject(s): Group consensus, decision making, teams
Source: HRDQ. King of Prussia, PA. (800) 633-4533. www.hrdq.com

PAPER PLANES, INC.

Paper Planes, Inc. helps participants explore work redesign issues including participation, total quality, customer satisfaction, and systems thinking. In the simulation employees of a plane manufacturing company have the opportunity to sell as many planes as they can manufacture that meet given quality standards. The prescribed production design consists of a traditional functional division of labor. After evaluating the effectiveness of their efforts the workers are told to redesign the production process to their own specifications. Both production designs are compared for cost, quality, delivery time, and worker satisfaction.

Author: W. Christopher Musselwhite
Publication Date: 1993
Preparation: The facilitator must have experience with simulations and group facilitation
Cost: Contact Discovery Learning for licensing or in-house delivery
Number of Participants: Small groups
Time: 5 to 7 hours
Audience: Managers
Subject(s): Systems thinking, participatory leadership style
Source: Discovery Learning. Greensboro, NC. (336) 272-9530. www.discoverync.com

PAT HOWARD ROLE-PLAY

In a group of eight, four students assume roles as supervisors, each with a different leadership style. The other students assume roles as subordinates, each with different abilities, need for consideration, and task orientation. The role-play situation provides an opportunity for each supervisor to interact with each subordinate and practice using the four leadership styles described by the path-goal theory—supportive, directive, participative, or achievement oriented. Subordinates later rate each supervisor on his or her use of each of the four leadership styles.

Author: Joseph Seltzer & James W. Smither
Publication Date: 1995
Preparation: Photocopy handouts
Number of Participants: Groups of 8
Time: 1 to 1-1/2 hours
Audience: Students
Subject(s): Path-goal Theory
Source: J. Seltzer & J. W. Smither (1995), A role-play exercise to introduce students to path-goal leadership theory, *Journal of Management Education*, 19(3), 380-391. Sage Publications, Inc. Thousand Oaks, CA. (805) 499-9774. www.sagepub.com

New
PERSONAL BUSINESS AT WORK

The dilemma is briefly described as a manager who must deal with a valued employee who violates company policy when doing personal business at work. Participants individually rank six strategic options for managing differences in this situation: collaborate, smooth, maintain, dominate, bargain, and decide by rule. Then in small groups participants must reach consensus and calculate a group score. The debriefing reveals which of the six styles for managing differences was used by each group.

Author: Herbert S. Kindler
Publication Date: 1988, 1998
Cost: Participant booklets: $4.95
Number of Participants: 25 to 36
Time: 1 hour
Audience: General
Subject(s): Conflict management, group consensus
Source: Center for Management Effectiveness. Pacific Palisades, CA. (888) 819-0200. www.tools4trainers.com

PLASCO, INC.

This management simulation creates an environment for top-level executives to interact as they run a fictional plastics manufacturing company called Plasco. Participants assume roles as the CEO; CFO; presidents of three divisions; and vice presidents of products, marketing, administration, planning, operations, and technology. Over 200 items of information pass around the office. Not everyone is privy to all information—collaboration is necessary for success. Over 100 problems, some trivial and some titanic, need to be addressed. Each participant is given more work than can be accomplished. Manus-trained facilitators observe each participant's strategic thinking, problem solving, decision making, cooperation, and influence skills. At the end of the simulation, participants complete a questionnaire that describes what actions they chose to take and how they met their goals. Feedback from peers and the facilitator helps each participant learn about his or her ability to lead in complex environments. A variation of this simulation is Tower, geared to the insurance industry.

Author: Manus
Publication Date: 1994
Preparation: Facilitators must be certified by Manus; certification training is available
Space or Equipment Needs: Large meeting room to set up a conference room and 18 workstations; four flip charts, markers, and an overhead projector
Cost: Contact Manus for information
Number of Participants: 25 or fewer
Time: 3 days
Audience: Executives, intact work groups
Subject(s): Decision making, problem solving, communication, influence
Source: Right Manus. Stamford, CT. (800) 445-0942. www.rightmanus.com

PLASTIC WRAP

Participants explore issues related to boundaries, both real and assumed. First they are bound together snugly with several layers of plastic wrap around the entire group at waist level. Then they plan their movement across a 20-yard course. They attempt a crossing and their time is recorded. After each attempt they discuss possible process improvements. After several attempts the facilitator suggests that they stretch the plastic band that constrains them. The plastic expands significantly without breaking, allowing the team to make significant process improvements. In the debrief participants discuss the limiting effect of boundaries and creative ways to expand them.

Author: Beth Michalak, Steve Fischer, & Larry Meeker
Publication Date: 1994
Space or Equipment Needs: One roll of plastic wrap, stopwatch, paper and pencil, start and finish line markers such as orange cones
Number of Participants: Small groups
Time: 20 minutes
Audience: Teams
Subject(s): Teams, problem solving
Source: B. Michalak, S. Fischer, & L. Meeker (1994), *Experiential Activities for High-performance Teamwork* (pp. 35-38). Amherst, MA: HRD Press. (800) 822-2801. www.hrdpress.com

POLYGON PUZZLE

The group is divided into work teams who must coordinate to create a 28-piece three-dimensional polygon puzzle. Each work team receives clue cards with partial instructions for completing the shape. No work team has sufficient information to complete the puzzle alone. The solution requires that participants share information within their teams and with other teams. Includes a *Facilitator's Guide* and transparencies.

Author: Donna Reichmann
Cost: $199.95
Number of Participants: 8 to 30
Time: 45 minutes to 1 hour
Audience: General
Subject(s): Communication, team building
Source: Organizational Learning Tools, Inc. Novi, MI. (800) 684-1190.

POSITION POWER: EXPLORING THE IMPACT OF ROLE CHANGE

Changes in the roles of group members can often affect attitudes and performance. For this exercise each small group is given the same task to reduce their membership by one. Following the loss of one member they appoint one member to manager status. Each group is then instructed to create one symbol that best illustrates levels within an organization (worker, managerial, executive). The managers are unable to work directly on the task, and the members who were earlier excluded from the groups become the executive committee that decides which group has the winning symbol. Debriefing questions focus on the thoughts and feelings at each stage in the exercise.

Author: Phyliss Cooke & Lawrence C. Porter
Publication Date: 1986
Space or Equipment Needs: Newsprint, flip chart, masking tape, and markers for each group; a prize for the winning group
Number of Participants: 10 to 35
Time: 3 hours
Audience: Executives, managers
Subject(s): Power, change
Source: P. Cooke & L. C. Porter in J. W. Pfeiffer, *The 1986 Annual: Developing Human Resources* (pp. 51-54). San Diego, CA: University Associates (Jossey-Bass/Pfeiffer). (800) 274-4434. www.pfeiffer.com

PRECISION BICYCLE COMPONENTS: EXPLORING THE GLASS CEILING

Participants have to make both individual and group rankings of men and women candidates who are being considered to replace the retiring vice president of operations for the company. Each group has to reach consensus on who will be selected for this position. Following this step each group explains how it reached its decision; then the facilitator leads a discussion about the gender differences in managers' developmental job experiences.

Author: Linda M. Hite & Kimberly S. McDonald
Publication Date: 1995
Space or Equipment Needs: Flip chart and markers
Number of Participants: 8 to 40
Time: 1-3/4 to 2-1/4 hours
Audience: General
Subject(s): Gender diversity
Source: L. M. Hite & K. S. McDonald in J. W. Pfeiffer, *The 1995 Annual: Volume 2, Consulting* (pp. 97-116). San Diego, CA: Pfeiffer & Company (Jossey-Bass/Pfeiffer). (800) 274-4434. www.pfeiffer.com

PRISONERS' DILEMMA: AN INTERGROUP COMPETITION

Prisoners' Dilemma deals with the issues of trust, cooperation, competition, and interpersonal and intergroup relations. A team (acting the part of a prisoner charged with a crime) gets the highest payoff if it doesn't confess and the opposing team does confess, a mid-range payoff if both teams confess, a mid-range loss if neither team confesses, and a maximum loss if it confesses and the other team doesn't. The game is introduced as a "win as much as you can" process, but the competing teams usually interpret this to mean "beat the other team" rather than "maximize points."

Author: J. W. Pfeiffer & J. E. Jones
Publication Date: 1974
Preparation: Prepare debriefing material
Number of Participants: 16 or fewer
Time: 1 hour
Audience: General
Subject(s): Trust, teams
Source: J. W. Pfeiffer & J. E. Jones (1974), *A Handbook of Structured Experiences for Human Relations Training, Volume III* (pp. 52-56). San Diego, CA: University Associates (Jossey-Bass/Pfeiffer). (800) 274-4434. www.pfeiffer.com

PUMPING THE COLORS

In this highly interactive exercise, teams design and construct a working water-transfer system. Each participant performs a hands-on task that realistically simulates a real-world job but cannot be accomplished in the given time frame without successful teamwork. The learning outcome depends more on the objectives of the training session than on the final product produced. Possible objectives include team building, total-quality-management practices, assessing feedback and communication skills, and developing project management skills. A skillful facilitator is required to process the ongoing dynamics at predetermined "break times" during the simulation.

Author: R. Garry Shirts
Publication Date: 1991, 1999
Preparation: Facilitators must be trained by Simulation Training Systems
Space or Equipment Needs: Large break-out area, flip chart, and markers for each team
Cost: Price varies depending on the number of participants; call Simulation Training Systems for details
Number of Participants: Groups of 6 to 10
Time: 4 hours to 2 days
Audience: General
Subject(s): Communication, teams
Source: Simulation Training Systems. Del Mar, CA. (800) 942-2900. www.stsintl.com

PYRAMID™

Pyramid is an activity device that allows participants to practice two types of organizational behavior. The device is constructed of four ten-foot poles that suspend a grabber from 16 strings. In phase one participants assume hierarchical roles to move the grabber and manipulate an object. Information about the assignment flows from the CEO to functional managers, department managers, and finally to the string operators who are restricted in several ways. Problems arise from the executives' lack of operator skills and subsequent inability to give clear directions. In phase two all members receive the same instructions and string operator training. Comparing the two phases demonstrates the value of empowerment and self-directed teams. It is

recommended to allow at least one day between phases for classroom instruction.

Space or Equipment Needs: 16-foot by 16-foot indoor or outdoor activity area
Cost: $720
Number of Participants: 8 to 16
Time: 1-1/2 hours for each phase
Audience: Managers, intact work groups
Subject(s): Participatory leadership style
Source: Interel, Inc. San Francisco, CA. (415) 566-0554.

New
QUALITY CRUNCH AT ROCKPORT

This case presents a series of operational problems causing poor quality and low morale at the fictional Rockport automotive plant. Participants select from 30 strategic actions to improve competence. Then in small groups they reach consensus about the best strategies and their rationale. Scores are plotted to determine which strategies best improve collaboration, commitment, and creativity and the balance of these competencies. The case and scoring strategy are based on actual events.

Author: Jay Hall
Publication Date: 1991, 1995
Cost: Participant booklets: $9.95; *Leader's Guide*: $24.95
Number of Participants: Small groups
Time: 1-1/2 hours
Audience: Managers
Subject(s): Collaboration, commitment, creativity, group consensus
Source: Teleometrics. The Woodlands, TX. (800) 527-0406. www.teleometrics.com

RADMIS

RADMIS is an interactive behavioral learning activity that simulates a fast-paced research and development project. The project is the development of a superior-quality printing plate that must be ready for market within nine months. At a desktop computer the project team faces a variety of challenges via on-screen scenarios. They must decide on issues relating to strategy, competition, quality, price, schedule, human resources, and marketing. During the simulation and feedback participants learn skills to improve team interactions and to enhance strategic planning and problem-solving skills. An earlier version of this activity was titled BATEC.

Author: Discovery Learning
Publication Date: 1997, 1999
Space or Equipment Needs: PC and flip charts
Cost: Contact Discovery Learning for licensing or in-house delivery
Number of Participants: 5 to 7
Time: 1-1/2 days
Audience: Intact work groups
Subject(s): Decision making, teams

Source: Discovery Learning. Greensboro, NC. (336) 272-9530. www.discoverync.com

RHETORIC AND BEHAVIOR: THEORY X AND THEORY Y

Based on Douglas McGregor's delineation of two contrasting views of work motivation (workers are lazy and need to be controlled versus workers are responsible and eager to be involved), this exercise offers participants a chance to compare their X-Y rhetoric with their behavior. In the process they also have the chance to explore the assumptions (and the behaviors that demonstrate those assumptions) of Theory X and Theory Y. The exercise starts with participants completing an inventory of what they would say and another on what they would do. The participants compare behavior with rhetoric, explore the assumptions in each, then complete role plays to further demonstrate Theory X and Theory Y rhetoric and behavior.

Author: Maureen Vanterpool
Publication Date: 1991
Preparation: Prepare poster
Space or Equipment Needs: Newsprint and markers
Number of Participants: 12 to 20
Time: 2-1/2 hours
Audience: Managers
Subject(s): Communication
Source: M. Vanterpool in J. W. Pfeiffer, *The 1991 Annual: Developing Human Resources* (pp. 51-64). San Diego, CA: University Associates (Jossey-Bass/Pfeiffer). (800) 274-4434. www.pfeiffer.com

ROLE POWER: UNDERSTANDING INFLUENCE

This role-play exercise explores the types of power inherent in different group and organizational roles. It acquaints participants with power strategies that can be used in the decision-making process and helps them understand effective versus ineffective use of power. The role positions are: controller, director of merchandising, personnel director, promotion director, and operations director. In addition to a description of their particular role, all players get a "public knowledge" sheet that summarizes all positions; later in the role play they are each given a handout that describes the real political power possessed by the different roles.

Author: Patrick E. Doyle
Publication Date: 1984
Space or Equipment Needs: Paper, pencil, and clipboard for each observer
Number of Participants: 18 to 35
Time: 2 hours
Audience: General
Subject(s): Power
Source: P. E. Doyle in J. W. Pfeiffer & L. D. Goodstein, *The 1984 Annual: Developing Human Resources* (pp. 26-36). San Diego, CA: University Associates (Jossey-Bass/Pfeiffer). (800) 274-4434. www.pfeiffer.com

RUBICON

Rubicon is an intense simulation utilizing both indoor and outdoor activities to focus on leadership, teamwork, and the impact of values on achievement of results. The simulation offers the opportunity for participants to create an organization that supports a complex scenario involving the recovery of vital worldwide technology and the rescue of missing and injured persons. In establishing the organization participants must create a vision, build a structure, define values and philosophies for operating, develop strategies and plans, and implement rescue and recovery.

Author: John Schmidt
Publication Date: 1985
Cost: This is a proprietary simulation; contact Executive Expeditions for information
Number of Participants: 10 to 50
Time: 8 to 24 hours
Audience: Executives, managers, intact work groups
Subject(s): Teamwork, values
Source: Executive Expeditions. Roswell, GA. (678) 461-8880. www.executive-expeditions.com

THE RULES OF THE GAME

This is a role-playing exercise designed to help participants explore issues in hierarchical communication within complex organizations. Participants are assigned roles from production worker to president. Those role-playing each level are given a set of cards containing issues that they must rank in order of importance. Each group's goal is to have the issues they identify as most important dealt with at the appropriate organizational level. To do this they must communicate with the appropriate level either orally or in writing. Observers are assigned to help record interactions and process. A debriefing follows.

Author: Linda C. Lederman & Lea P. Stewart
Publication Date: 1991
Preparation: Prepare the message decks (samples are provided in the article)
Number of Participants: 11 or more
Time: 30 minutes to 1-1/2 hours
Audience: General
Subject(s): Communication
Source: L. C. Lederman & L. P. Stewart (1991), The rules of the game, *Simulation & Gaming, 22*(4), 502-507. Sage Publications, Inc. Thousand Oaks, CA. (805) 499-9774. www.sagepub.com

New
SEVEN SMARTS

This board and card game is based on Howard Gardner's theory of multiple intelligences (*Multiple Intelligences: The Theory in Practice,* 1993). Each deal of the game corresponds to one of the seven types of "smarts": linguistic-verbal, logical, mathematical, visual-spatial, body-kinesthetic, musical-rhythmic, interpersonal, and intrapersonal. Players move around the board according to how well they can match card statements to each type of intelligence. A *Feedback Table* provides official answers. Chance cards and die add challenge to the game. Includes a *Facilitator Guide*.

Author: Sivasailam Thiagarajan & Raja Thiagarajan
Publication Date: 1998
Cost: $89
Number of Participants: 2 to 16
Time: 30 to 45 minutes
Audience: General
Subject(s): Intelligence
Source: Workshops by Thiagi, Inc. Bloomington, IN. (800) 996-7725. www.thiagi.com

SHALOM/SALAAM: A SIMULATION OF THE MIDDLE EAST PEACE NEGOTIATIONS

Set in the context of a Middle East conflict, this exercise helps participants understand how differences in power can affect negotiation. They observe how the appearance of having greater power may not result in a better outcome. Several leadership styles and their impact on bargaining results are incorporated within the game. It involves multiparty negotiation, which can evolve into coalition negotiation.

Author: Gedaliahu H. Harel & Sandra Morgan
Publication Date: 1994
Preparation: The facilitator must photocopy handouts, make transparencies, and read articles on the general background of the Arab-Israeli conflict
Space or Equipment Needs: Conference room, three smaller meeting rooms, and overhead projector; each participant contributes $1
Number of Participants: 15 to 24
Time: 1-1/2 to 3 hours
Audience: General
Subject(s): Power, negotiation
Source: G. H. Harel & S. Morgan (1994), SHALOM/SALAAM: A simulation of Middle East peace negotiations, *Simulation & Gaming, 25*(2), 285-292. Sage Publications, Inc. Thousand Oaks, CA. (805) 499-9774. www.sagepub.com

New
A SIMPLE—BUT POWERFUL—POWER SIMULATION

Each participant contributes a dollar bill in this lesson on power dynamics. The collected money is divided into thirds. Participants are also divided into thirds—a top group, middle group, and bottom group. The top group receives two-thirds of the money, a private work space, and authority over the other groups. The middle group receives the remainder of the money and authority over the bottom group. Each group contributes to a decision about how to use the money, but ultimate responsibility is within the top group. Following the exercise representatives from each group discuss power structures, trust, justice, and methods for gaining increased power.

Author: Lee Bolman & Terrence Deal
Publication Date: 1998
Space or Equipment Needs: Three separate work areas, dollar bills
Number of Participants: 24 to 90
Time: 1 hour
Audience: Students
Subject(s): Power
Source: L. Bolman & T. Deal in D. Marcic & J. Seltzer (1998), *Organizational Behavior: Experiences and Cases* (5th ed., pp. 139-140). Cincinnati, OH: South-Western College Publishing. www.swcollege.com

SITUATIONAL LEADERSHIP SIMULATION GAME

The Situational Leadership Simulation Game has been designed to assist participants in understanding the situational leadership theory of four basic styles. Players receive a situation card from which they are to diagnose the maturity level of the group. Once the diagnosis has been made the players choose from a set of alternative actions. Points are awarded for choosing the most appropriate actions. The objective is to win enough points with correct answers to reach the end of a 28-square track.

Author: Paul Hersey, Kenneth Blanchard, & Lee Peters
Publication Date: 1977
Preparation: The facilitator must be familiar with the situational leadership model
Cost: $69.95
Number of Participants: 2 to 20
Time: 1 to 2 hours
Audience: General
Subject(s): Situational leadership style
Source: HRD Press. Amherst, MA. (800) 822-2801. www.hrdpress.com

New
SPACE ESCAPE

While wearing hula hoops around their waists participants must rearrange themselves from a triangular formation to a circle. The challenge comes from a set of nine rules distributed separately and randomly to various team members. To succeed in this activity members must share information and plan their movements. Observers watch for leadership patterns and violation of the rules.

Author: Carmine M. Consalvo
Publication Date: 1996
Preparation: If hoops look alike, change them with colored tape; prepare index cards and handouts
Space or Equipment Needs: Six hula hoops in different colors or designs, index cards
Number of Participants: 8 to 20
Time: 30 to 45 minutes
Audience: General
Subject(s): Teams, problem solving
Source: C. M. Consalvo (1996), *Changing Pace: Outdoor*

Games for Experiential Learning (pp. 35-38). Amherst, MA: HRD Press. (800) 822-2801. www.hrdpress.com

New
THE SPIDER WEB

This classic exercise challenges a team's ability to plan and solve problems. It involves passing all team members through the openings in a giant spider web. All openings must be used, whether they are large or small, low or high. Touching the web or frame is not allowed. Teams must plan carefully to determine who goes through which opening and who can provide adequate support for the first and last passes. In the debrief participants assess their planning, decision making, problem solving, and communication practices and discuss the value of diversity among team members. Safety issues of lifting and spotting are discussed.

Author: Beth Michalak, Steve Fischer, & Larry Meeker
Publication Date: 1994
Preparation: Construct frame and web
Space or Equipment Needs: Frame (trees or PVC pipes), small diameter rope
Number of Participants: 10 to 12
Time: 20 to 30 minutes
Audience: Teams
Subject(s): Teamwork, problem solving
Source: B. Michalak, S. Fischer, & L. Meeker (1994), *Experiential Activities for High-performance Teamwork* (pp. 39-44). Amherst, MA: HRD Press. (800) 822-2801. www.hrdpress.com

STAR POWER

This is a "new world" game in which participants progress from one level of society to another by acquiring wealth through trading. At one point the society is "frozen" by giving the group with the most wealth the right to make the rules of the game. This usually leads to further differentiation of power and rebellion by the disempowered group. Star Power underscores the use and misuse of power and the sometimes divisive influence of social systems.

Author: R. Garry Shirts
Publication Date: 1969
Cost: $275
Number of Participants: 18 to 35
Time: 2 hours
Audience: Managers, students, intact work groups
Subject(s): Power
Source: Simulation Training Systems. Del Mar, CA. (800) 942-2900. www.stsintl.com

New
STRANDED IN THE HIMALAYAS

The scenario for this survival simulation is a mountain trek in the Himalayas. One person wanders away from the camp without a Sherpa guide just as heavy snow begins to fall. The wanderer decides to find shelter for the night and descend the mountain alone in the morning. Participants must reach consensus on the best tactics for navigating rough terrain, staying warm and hydrated, and surviving an avalanche. Rationale for recommended answers and scoring tables are included. This consensus-building activity doesn't require a trained facilitator. Any member of the group may lead the activity.

Author: Lorraine L. Ukens
Publication Date: 1998
Cost: $6.95; *Leader's Guide*: $17.95
Number of Participants: 4 to 9
Time: 1-1/2 hours
Audience: General
Subject(s): Group consensus, decision making
Source: Jossey-Bass/Pfeiffer. San Francisco, CA. (800) 274-4434. www.pfeiffer.com

STRATEEGY CLASSIC

StraTEEgy Classic provides a simulated work process that allows participants to experience real-world work decisions and barriers. The scenario involves a design team working on a request from Wall Street. Using a desktop PC, maps, and architectural modeling materials, the team must design a new golf course, do detailed design and modeling of a "signature hole," and develop a computerized growth model of the neighboring urban community. Within this process participants practice strategy, teamwork, and negotiation skills. Results are quantified and a debriefing concludes the exercise.

Author: John Schmidt
Publication Date: 1995
Space or Equipment Needs: Desktop computer for each team
Cost: This is a customized, proprietary simulation; contact Executive Expeditions for information
Number of Participants: 8 to 250
Time: 3 to 4 hours
Audience: Executives, managers, intact work groups
Subject(s): Decision making, negotiation, cross-functional teams
Source: Executive Expeditions. Roswell, GA. (678) 461-8880. www.executive-expeditions.com

New
SUBARCTIC SURVIVAL SITUATION

Set in an isolated area of northern Canada, this group-decision exercise requires teams to rank the survival importance of 15 items they have salvaged, first individually, then as a group. Expert answers are provided by Canadian specialists in arctic and subarctic region rescue. Debriefing includes discussion of the methods and benefits of team decision making versus individual decision making.

Author: Human Synergistics
Space or Equipment Needs: VCR and viewing screen

Cost: Participant booklet: $4.25; *Leader's Guide*: $25; *Observer's Guide*: $5; video enhancement: $125
Number of Participants: Small groups
Time: 1-1/2 to 2-1/2 hours
Audience: General
Subject(s): Teams, decision making, group consensus
Source: Human Synergistics International. Plymouth, MI. (800) 622-7584. www.humansyn.com

New
SURVIVAL

Plastic parts snap together to build model vehicles in this set of survival simulations. In the Island Storm scenario, participants build a rescue helicopter before the tide rises. In Desert Storm, participants build a dune trike to help them escape a sandstorm in the Sahara Desert. During Apollo Rescue, a team of "astronauts" builds an escape shuttle before their capsule runs out of oxygen. In each scenario there is a challenging deadline and a need for teamwork. The instructions and models represent three levels of difficulty. Includes a *Facilitator's Guide* and masters for handouts.

Preparation: Prepare handouts
Cost: $395
Number of Participants: Small groups
Time: 2 to 3 hours
Audience: Intact work groups
Subject(s): Teamwork
Source: Organizational Learning Tools, Inc. Novi, MI. (800) 684-1190.

New
SWAMPED!

This is a basic-level exercise in the Team Adventure Series™ of survival simulations. The scenario is a canoe trip in the remote Boundary Waters of Minnesota enhanced with a color slide show. When a heavy storm swamps the canoes in icy waters one member suffers hypothermia, the paddles are lost, and most of the supplies sink. To make a survival plan participants rank individually and as a team ten items necessary for a return trip to civilization. Expert rankings determined by experienced Boundary Water canoeists provide a basis for comparison. Upon completion teams plot their scores to understand their achievement in the seven-step process that leads to team synergy. A *Facilitator Guide* provides background information, rationale for the rankings, and guidelines for a debriefing on team decision making. A new team could use this exercise as an icebreaker.

Author: Rollin Glaser & James Roadcap
Publication Date: 1992
Space or Equipment Needs: Slide projector is optional
Cost: Five participant booklets: $30; *Facilitator Guide*: $30; optional color slides: $32
Number of Participants: Groups of 4 to 6
Time: 1-1/2 hours
Audience: Intact work groups
Subject(s): Group consensus, decision making, teams

Source: HRDQ. King of Prussia, PA. (800) 633-4533. www.hrdq.com

New
SYSTEMS AND SYNERGY: DECISION MAKING IN THE THIRD MILLENNIUM

This exercise facilitates decision making through the understanding of interrelationships in organizations. It begins with an introduction of Bolman and Deal's four frames of reference—structural, human resources, political, and symbolic—as described in *Reframing Organizations* (1991). Play proceeds as a card game with each suit representing a particular frame. Each round of play involves a decision-making scenario typical in corporate life. Players choose a best frame (suit) to make the decision and assign a level of importance (face value of card). Scoring and discussion follow each round. The player with the highest score at the end of ten rounds is the winner. Appendices include the introduction to four frames, ten scenarios, and a scoring sheet.

Author: Hamilton Beazley & John Lobuts, Jr.
Publication Date: 1998
Preparation: Prepare handouts
Space or Equipment Needs: Two decks of standard playing cards, play description, and scoring sheets for each group
Number of Participants: Groups of 3 to 5
Time: 1-1/2 hours
Audience: General
Subject(s): Systems thinking
Source: H. Beazley & J. Lobuts, Jr. (1998), Systems and Synergy: Decision Making in the Third Millennium, *Simulation and Gaming*, *29*(4), 441-449. Sage Publications, Inc. Thousand Oaks, CA. (805) 499-9774. www.sagepub.com

TASK FORCE

This business case study deals with team dynamics within a real business situation. The case is based on a successful task force in a Fortune 100 company that was assigned the responsibility of developing a new customer-service department. Participants are given background information, including notes from the first meeting of the original task force. They are asked to rank individually and then as a group actions and issues in the areas of task force dynamics, equipment, staffing, and training. Scores are compared to the actual process used by the real task force. The real-world nature of this exercise differentiates it from many ranking-type exercises based upon hypothetical disasters.

Author: Richard Hill
Publication Date: 1994
Cost: Participant's exercise: $4.95; *Facilitator's Handbook*: $20
Number of Participants: Small groups
Time: 1-1/2 to 2 hours
Audience: General

Subject(s): Decision making, teams
Source: Organizational Learning Tools, Inc. Novi, MI. (800) 684-1190.

New
TEAM BUILDING BLOCKS

This set contains 14 wooden blocks and an activity manual with instructions for 18 exercises. Spelunking is a simulated cave expedition that mirrors the dynamics between a team vision and its implementation. Paradise Lost highlights the importance of information sharing and creative thinking. Bomb Squad encourages the empathetic ability to think like another person. Code-Breakers puts participants into an ethical and a time-critical decision-making situation. All activities include handouts, debriefing commentary, and suggestions for variations.

Author: Carmine Consalvo
Publication Date: 1995
Preparation: Varies
Space or Equipment Needs: Varies—may include index cards, dice, colored labels, graph paper, masking tape, flashlights, walkie-talkies, stopwatch, prizes, bandanas, rulers, manila envelopes, carpet squares, flip charts and markers, paper and pencils
Cost: $149.95
Number of Participants: 4 to 48
Time: 30 minutes to 1-1/2 hours
Audience: Teams
Subject(s): Teams, collaboration
Source: HRD Press. Amherst, MA. (800) 822-2801. www.hrdpress.com

New
TEAM NORMS

Teams and potential teams can use this activity to generate discussions about group norms and develop standard operating procedures for the team. Participants are given a list of 30 possible team norms such as vote on all decisions, start meetings on time, share leadership, and have fun. Each individual identifies the ten most important norms. Then the group uses consensus to develop a team list of important norms that can be used after the game in day-to-day work. The rankings can also be measured against an expert's "best practices" list.

Author: Ronald L. Potter & Thomas G. Webber
Publication Date: 1993
Cost: Participant activity: $6.95; facilitator guide: $20
Number of Participants: Small groups
Time: 2 to 2-1/2 hours
Audience: Intact work groups
Subject(s): Teams, group consensus
Source: Organizational Learning Tools, Inc. Novi, MI. (800) 684-1190.

New
TEAM PLAYERS

This board and card game explores a framework of team-player styles introduced by Glenn Parker (*Team Players and Teamwork,* 1996). The cards are dealt to correspond with the four styles of team player: contributor, collaborator, communicator, and challenger. Each player receives ten cards and picks one to match a specific style. Other players may object and debate the appropriateness of the selection. A *Feedback Table* provides official answers. Players move around the board according to their correct plays and objections. Chance cards and die add challenge to the game. Includes a *Facilitator Guide.*

Author: Glenn M. Parker, Sivasailam Thiagarajan, & Raja Thiagarajan
Publication Date: 1997, 1999
Cost: $89
Number of Participants: 2 to 16
Time: 30 to 45 minutes
Audience: General
Subject(s): Teams
Source: Workshops by Thiagi, Inc. Bloomington, IN. (800) 996-7725. www.thiagi.com

New
TEAM POKER

This game is played in two parts. In Team Poker I, each participant is given one playing card. After a "walkaround" to view all cards participants are given three minutes to form teams that yield the best poker hands. Team Poker II adds a cash incentive and forces teams to choose between players who have duplicate cards. The debriefing examines the team formation process. A reference handout explaining the value of poker hands is included.

Author: Sivasailam Thiagarajan
Publication Date: 1999
Preparation: Prepare handouts
Space or Equipment Needs: Two decks of playing cards, $25 (real or play money), timer, whistle
Number of Participants: 12 to 40
Time: 40 minutes to 1 hour
Audience: Teams
Subject(s): Team formation
Source: S. Thiagarajan (1999), Double jolt!, *Thiagi Gameletter, 2*(5), G1-G4. Jossey-Bass/Pfeiffer. San Francisco, CA. (800) 274-4434. www.pfeiffer.com

New
TEAM RING TOSS: AN EXPERIENTIAL EXERCISE

This exercise illustrates the effects of motivation on individual and group behavior. Teams examine a 14-foot tossing range to determine how well their designated member can throw rings onto a post. Successful throws earn points, which increase incrementally with distance and risk. Teams plan their risk strategies and set goals before each round. Typically teams that take moderate risks earn the most points. There are detailed suggestions for a debriefing on motivation.

Author: William P. Ferris & Russell Fanelli
Publication Date: 1998
Preparation: Prepare the tossing range
Space or Equipment Needs: Four plastic rings, a post, masking tape, and ruler
Number of Participants: Groups of 4 to 6
Time: 26 to 36 minutes
Audience: General
Subject(s): Group behavior, motivation, risk-taking
Source: W. P. Ferris & R. Fanelli in D. Marcic & J. Seltzer (1998), *Organizational Behavior: Experiences and Cases* (5th ed., pp. 82-85). Cincinnati, OH: South-Western College Publishing. www.swcollege.com

TEAMTREK™

TeamTrek is a group transport device used to teach communication and teamwork. Up to ten participants stand on a pair of 15-foot rubber treads and hold handstraps for control as they move along a course. The team is forced to communicate and compromise in order to move synchronously. Additional challenges may be introduced by blindfolding some members, having some face backwards, placing obstacles along the path, prohibiting speaking, and creating competition between two or more teams. One variation is PlanTrek in which teams must rescue one member from a distant island. Another is DiversiTrek in which team members adopt personal challenges such as sight or hearing impairments, language differences, breathing difficulties, or other physical limitations. Moderate physical activity is required with all TeamTrek activities, so participants who cannot trek may serve as coaches.

Space or Equipment Needs: 30-foot by 60-foot indoor or outdoor activity area and six markers such as orange cones; optional materials for challenges and variations include team bandanas, blindfolds, earplugs, face masks, ropes, plastic jugs, tables, or other barrier items
Cost: $390 per set of treads
Number of Participants: 5 to 10 participants per set of treads
Time: 25 minutes
Audience: Managers, intact work groups
Subject(s): Teams, communication
Source: Interel, Inc. San Francisco, CA. (415) 566-0554.

TEAMWORK

Teamwork is a puzzle-completion game designed to help participants define teamwork and appreciate how team success leads to individual success. It begins with a brainstorming session about teams and teamwork then continues with the playing of the game. In the recommended configuration there are two teams of six players each. Each person on a team takes ownership of one puzzle piece and the

teamwork principle associated with it and must try to fit that piece into the puzzle solution. There is a series of three such puzzles that must be solved. After each the facilitator reviews effective and ineffective team behavior. By the third round the two teams must work together to reach a win-win solution. Includes a facilitator's guide, an instructional video, transparency masters, and participant notebooks.

Author: Alban Associates, Inc.
Preparation: Make transparencies
Space or Equipment Needs: Overhead projector, VCR, and viewing screen
Cost: $395; additional participant notebooks: $49.95
Number of Participants: 13
Time: 3 to 3-1/2 hours
Audience: Intact work groups, students
Subject(s): Teams
Source: Jossey-Bass/Pfeiffer. San Francisco, CA. (800) 274-4434. www.pfeiffer.com

THUMBS UP, THUMBS DOWN: A CONFLICT-MANAGEMENT ICEBREAKER

This exercise is an icebreaker to open a lesson on conflict and cooperation. Participants pair off, hook fingers, and raise their thumbs. When the facilitator instructs them to get their partners' thumbs down, most participants assume that means to thumb wrestle. The facilitator explains another option, simple and obvious but often overlooked. This exercise teaches participants to approach conflict with a variety of choices.

Author: Roger Gaetani
Publication Date: 1997
Number of Participants: 6 to 50
Time: 15 minutes
Audience: General
Subject(s): Conflict management, collaboration
Source: R. Gaetani in J. W. Pfeiffer, *The 1997 Annual: Volume 1, Training* (pp. 65-67). San Francisco: Pfeiffer (Jossey-Bass/Pfeiffer). (800) 274-4434. www.pfeiffer.com

TINKERTOY POWER

In Tinkertoy Power participants explore issues of resource dependence, power, and ethics as they bargain for resources to build their structure. One of the four groups is considered resource rich and powerful, one resource poor and powerless, and the remaining two about average. Each group is awarded points for completing its structure. Debriefing discussions may focus on topics such as coalition building, win-win versus win-lose assumptions, group cohesion and competition, rules and innovation, and power and influence strategies.

Author: Cathy P. Lindsay & Cathy A. Enz
Publication Date: 1991
Space or Equipment Needs: Five sets of Tinkertoys
Cost: Cost of materials
Number of Participants: 12 to 40

Time: 1 hour
Audience: General
Subject(s): Power, ethics
Source: C. P. Lindsay & C. A. Enz (1991), Resource control and visionary leadership: Two exercises, *Journal of Management Education*, 15(1), 127-135. Sage Publications, Inc. Thousand Oaks, CA. (805) 499-9774. www.sagepub.com

New
THE TITANIC

A ship-sinking scenario encourages participants to collaborate rather than compete. Two mock ships each have two mock lifeboats. To get safely to shore participants stand on one lifeboat, pick up the other, and place it forward. Teams have a tendency to compete against each other for the fastest time to the shoreline. However, teams who share lifeboats can stand on three while moving the fourth and easily reach the shore quickly.

Author: Carmine M. Consalvo
Publication Date: 1996
Preparation: Make the ship shapes
Space or Equipment Needs: Plywood or carpet squares for lifeboats, rope for ships and shoreline
Number of Participants: 8 to 14
Time: 30 to 50 minutes
Audience: General
Subject(s): Teams, collaboration
Source: C. M. Consalvo (1996), *Changing Pace: Outdoor Games for Experiential Learning* (pp. 93-94). Amherst, MA: HRD Press. (800) 822-2801. www.hrdpress.com

TOWER BUILDING EXERCISE

Small groups make plans to build paper towers that will be judged on height, stability, beauty, and significance. During the planning and building phases, group dynamics become evident to observers. Who emerges as group leader? Is there any conflict? Does each member contribute? Does the group function well to produce a good product? After judging the completed towers the groups analyze their ability to succeed as self-managed teams.

Author: Dorothy Marcic
Publication Date: 1992
Space or Equipment Needs: Newspaper to build towers
Number of Participants: Groups of 6 to 8
Time: 50 minutes
Audience: General
Subject(s): Teams
Source: D. Marcic (1992), *Organizational Behavior: Experiences and Cases* (3rd ed., pp. 127-130). New York: West Publishing.

New
TOXIC WASTE

A pail of "toxic waste" must be transported to a target location. To avoid contact the pail is lifted by a device made of bungi cord and long ropes. Blindfolded team members handle the ropes while guided by sighted coaches. The goal is to secure, lift, carry, set down, and release the pail without spilling. To succeed, communication is required between blindfolded and sighted pairs and among all team members.

Author: Beth Michalak, Steve Fischer, & Larry Meeker
Publication Date: 1994
Preparation: Cut and tie rope sections to bungi cord, fill pail with water
Space or Equipment Needs: 12-inch circle of bungi cord, 64-foot rope, one half-gallon pail, bandanas, and a hula hoop
Number of Participants: 8 to 16
Time: 25 to 40 minutes
Audience: Teams
Subject(s): Teams, communication
Source: B. Michalak, S. Fischer, & L. Meeker (1994), *Experiential Activities for High-performance Teamwork* (pp. 23-24). Amherst, MA: HRD Press. (800) 822-2801. www.hrdpress.com

New
THE TROLLEYS

This outdoor exercise challenges teams to communicate and cooperate as they advance their trolley across a designated course. Standing in a line, eight team members put a foot on each trolley and hold rope handles. The only way to move the trolley is to engage in dialogue, reach consensus, and work together. Spotters are essential to help those who lose their balance. Additional challenges may be introduced when a member loses balance. Penalties for falling can include muting one member or starting over.

Author: Beth Michalak, Steve Fischer, & Larry Meeker
Publication Date: 1994
Preparation: Construct the trolleys, set up an obstacle course
Space or Equipment Needs: Two eight-foot trolleys constructed of 4"x4" lumber and rope, orange traffic cones
Number of Participants: 10 to 12
Time: 20 to 40 minutes
Audience: Teams
Subject(s): Teams, communication, collaboration
Source: B. Michalak, S. Fischer, & L. Meeker (1994), *Experiential Activities for High-performance Teamwork* (pp. 19-22). Amherst, MA: HRD Press. (800) 822-2801. www.hrdpress.com

New
TRUST WALK

Participants are paired for this exercise in trust and communication. One is blindfolded and the other cannot speak. Together they navigate a simple obstacle course, communicating only by touch and their chosen signals. When finished they reverse roles and the course is rearranged. This time they cannot touch but the sighted member may speak. The lesson learned is reliance on information provided by teammates.

Author: Beth Michalak, Steve Fischer, & Larry Meeker
Publication Date: 1994
Preparation: Set up obstacle course
Space or Equipment Needs: Blindfolds, tables, chairs, hula hoops, traffic cones, steps
Number of Participants: Any number of pairs
Time: 15 to 30 minutes
Audience: Teams
Subject(s): Teams, trust
Source: B. Michalak, S. Fischer, & L. Meeker (1994), *Experiential Activities for High-performance Teamwork* (pp. 75-78). Amherst, MA: HRD Press. (800) 822-2801. www.hrdpress.com

TURNAROUND

In this simulation, team members work, individually then as a group, to reverse the climate and fiscal position of a failing business. Survival of the company depends on the decisions the participants make in six key areas: assumptions and values, problem identification, establishing objectives, action steps, approach to management, and feedback and communication. A *Leader's Guide* provides a theoretical base as well as background and administrative information for simulation facilitators.

Author: Human Synergistics, Inc.
Cost: Four participant booklets: $21; *Observer's Guide*: $5; *Leader's Guide*: $25
Number of Participants: 4
Time: 3 to 4 hours
Audience: General
Subject(s): Decision making, problem solving, communication, teams
Source: Human Synergistics International. Plymouth, MI. (800) 622-7584. www.humansyn.com

TWELVE ANGRY MEN

This exercise uses the classic film *Twelve Angry Men* (1957) to learn about influence and group dynamics. Participants view a portion of the film to get acquainted with each juror, his attitudes, and his behavior. Each participant makes a private judgment about the impact each juror will have on the group to determine the final verdict in a murder trial. Then the class discusses the influence rankings and tries to reach consensus. They once again make individual judgments that may or may not align with their group's consensus. The rest of the film contains a dramatic lesson on the impact of one man's influence on a group. Following the film, participants measure their pre-discussion choices, group choices, and post-discussion choices against the film's results. They learn about their own levels of influence, coercion, and submission. The publisher recommends combining this exercise with the instrument *Group Barrier Analysis*, also available from Teleometrics.

Author: Jay Hall
Publication Date: 1970, 1986, 1994

Space or Equipment Needs: *Twelve Angry Men* video, VCR, and viewing screen
Cost: Participant book: $9.95; *Leader's Guide*: $24.95
Number of Participants: Any number
Time: 3 to 3-1/2 hours
Audience: General
Subject(s): Influence, group dynamics
Source: Teleometrics International, Inc. The Woodlands, TX. (800) 527-0406. www.teleometrics.com

UGLI ORANGE CASE

In this exercise students practice negotiating and learn about trust, influence, and interpersonal communication. Students are divided into groups of three—Dr. Jones, Dr. Roland, and an observer. Separately the two doctors read handouts that dictate their bargaining positions to buy the entire, but limited, supply of valuable Ugli oranges. Neither knows the other's budget or end product. To succeed both parties must share confidential information and give a little to gain a lot. Following negotiations the observers report on each party's level of trust and influence.

Author: Robert House
Publication Date: 1992
Preparation: Photocopy handouts
Number of Participants: Groups of 3
Time: 40 minutes
Audience: General
Subject(s): Negotiation, influence, trust
Source: R. House in D. Marcic & J. Seltzer (1998), *Organizational Behavior: Experiences and Cases* (5th ed., pp. 188-189+). Cincinnati, OH: South-Western College Publishing. www.swcollege.com

New
VACATION IN THE KEYS

This is a basic- to intermediate-level exercise in the Team Adventure Series™ of survival simulations. The scenario is set, with the help of color slides, on a fishing boat near the Florida Keys. When the boat explodes, one member is injured and most supplies are lost. The group is stranded on a deserted island and must make a survival plan while waiting for rescue. Participants rank individually and as a group the importance of 15 items. Several Navy and Marine officers and licensed boat captains contributed to the expert rankings that provide a basis for comparison. Upon completion teams plot their scores to understand their achievement in the seven-step process that leads to team synergy. The *Facilitator Guide* provides background information, rationale for the rankings, and a guideline for a debriefing on team effectiveness.

Author: Rollin Glaser & Christine Glaser
Publication Date: 1992
Space or Equipment Needs: Slide projector is optional
Cost: Five participant booklets: $30; *Facilitator Guide*: $30; optional color slides: $32
Number of Participants: Groups of 4 to 6

Time: 2 hours
Audience: Intact work groups
Subject(s): Group consensus, decision making, teams
Source: HRDQ. King of Prussia, PA. (800) 633-4533. www.hrdq.com

New
VALUE CARDS: CREATING A CULTURE FOR TEAM EFFECTIVENESS

One hundred cards are each imprinted with a work-related value statement such as "encouraging experimentation" or "fighting fires all the time." After the cards are dealt each team member selects one to review and place in the Value, Don't Value, or Not Sure pile according to team consensus. In the next round players use the cards in the Value pile to determine if the preferred attitudes and behaviors belong in the Happens, Doesn't Happen, or Needs to Happen More Often pile. The final round decides whether the undesirable attitudes and behaviors are happening or not. Discussion during and after each round reinforces team mission and valued behaviors. Blank cards are included for teams to add unique value statements. The game can be adapted for new groups trying to define their values or experienced groups who want clarification and reinforcement. The *Trainer's Manual* contains instructions and masters for handouts and transparencies.

Author: Alan Barlow
Publication Date: 1994
Preparation: Prepare handouts and transparencies
Cost: $99.95
Number of Participants: Small groups
Time: 4 hours
Audience: Intact work groups
Subject(s): Values
Source: Jossey-Bass/Pfeiffer. San Francisco, CA. (800) 274-4434. www.pfeiffer.com

VANATIN: GROUP DECISION MAKING AND ETHICS

The authors state that "the Vanatin case provides an opportunity for group members to struggle with questions of social responsibility and ethics in decision making. The case is centered around a medical product considered by experts to be injurious to the health of consumers—even to the point of possibly causing death." Seven corporate roles are assigned and the action takes place in a meeting called by the chairman of the board. Some specific alternatives are presented and discussed. After 45 minutes a group decision is recorded and a discussion follows.

Author: Roy J. Lewicki, Donald D. Bowen, Douglas T. Hall, & Francine S. Hall
Publication Date: 1988
Space or Equipment Needs: Name tags
Number of Participants: Groups of 7
Time: 1-1/2 hours
Audience: General
Subject(s): Decision making, ethics

Source: R. J. Lewicki, D. D. Bowen, D. T. Hall, & F. S. Hall (1988), *Experiences in Management and Organizational Behavior* (3rd ed., pp. 175-179). New York: Wiley. (800) 225-5945. www.wiley.com

VICE-PRESIDENT'S IN-BASKET: A MANAGEMENT ACTIVITY

This in-basket exercise focuses attention on communication priorities in organizations and increases awareness of the role of delegation. Participants work individually on the items in their in-baskets, having gotten instructions that they will likely not be able to finish in the two hours allotted and thus will need to assign priorities and decide what to delegate. After individual work is done participants meet in small groups to discuss their work and feelings. Following this the facilitator records the groups' priority setting, then shares the "correct" solution. A final discussion focuses on participants' delegating styles and work styles.

Author: Annette N. Shelby
Publication Date: 1983
Space or Equipment Needs: Felt marker and newsprint pad for the facilitator; ruled paper pads, paper clips, and pencils for each participant
Number of Participants: 4 to 25
Time: 3-1/2 hours
Audience: General
Subject(s): Communication, decision making
Source: A. N. Shelby in L. D. Goodstein & J. W. Pfeiffer, *The 1983 Annual for Facilitators, Trainers, and Consultants* (pp. 49-64). San Diego, CA: University Associates (Jossey-Bass/Pfeiffer). (800) 274-4434. www.pfeiffer.com

VISIT TO AN ALIEN PLANET

The objective of this game is to expand participants' understanding of the value of others who may differ from the majority culture on such dimensions as age, sex, religion, and cultural background. The scenario is a visiting alien from another planet who wants to take a number of Earth volunteers back to her planet. Because only six people may go on the trip, she has asked that a committee of Earth people (the simulation participants) make a decision on who should go. It is this committee and its negotiations, along with the wide diversity among the candidate group, that structure this simulation.

Author: Richard B. Powers
Publication Date: 1993
Preparation: Photocopy handouts
Number of Participants: 9 to 24
Time: 1 hour
Audience: Civic leaders, students
Subject(s): Multicultural diversity, communication
Source: R. B. Powers (1993), Visit to an Alien Planet: A cultural diversity game, *Simulation & Gaming, 24*(4), 509-518. Sage Publications, Inc. Thousand Oaks, CA. (805) 499-9774. www.sagepub.com

VMX PRODUCTIONS, INC.: HANDLING RESISTANCE POSITIVELY

This role-play exercise is designed to increase participants' understanding of the phenomenon of resistance, to explore and compare strategies for dealing with resistance, and to present to participants an effective method for handling resistance. Participants are divided into pairs and go through a series of activities and role plays to demonstrate personal power and resistance. At the end those who played "resister" roles are asked for their reactions to the power moves of their partners.

Author: H. B. Karp
Publication Date: 1988
Space or Equipment Needs: Flip chart and markers
Number of Participants: Any number of pairs
Time: 1-1/2 hours
Audience: General
Subject(s): Change
Source: H. B. Karp in J. W. Pfeiffer, *The 1988 Annual: Developing Human Resources* (pp. 43-49). San Diego, CA: University Associates (Jossey-Bass/Pfeiffer). (800) 274-4434. www.pfeiffer.com

New
WATER, WATER, EVERYWHERE

A team is challenged to fill to overflowing a barrel that has been riddled with holes. They must choose from among the options: 1) fewer holes or more buckets, 2) more team members or more time, and 3) more options to block the holes or less distance between the barrel and the water. Teams must reach consensus because they will directly experience the consequences of their decisions. Towels and dry clothes will be necessary for all.

Author: Carmine M. Consalvo
Publication Date: 1996
Preparation: Set up materials
Space or Equipment Needs: Two bags, 50 corks, four buckets of various sizes, a 55-gallon steel or plastic drum, and an abundant source of water
Number of Participants: 7 to 12
Time: 1 to 1-1/4 hours
Audience: Teams
Subject(s): Teams, problem solving, collaboration, group consensus
Source: C. M. Consalvo (1996), *Changing Pace: Outdoor Games for Experiential Learning* (pp. 97-98). Amherst, MA: HRD Press. (800) 822-2801. www.hrdpress.com

New
WE CONNECT™

The We Connect Model represents six areas of diversity: mental, physical, spiritual, relational, occupational, and societal. Dialogue cards ask participants to share personal perspectives and experiences within the model. Others in the group share similar thoughts, making a connection. Each connection is represented by a chain link until all group members are linked to one another. During play, when connections don't form naturally, skill cards are introduced to encourage active listening, enhancing trust, disclosure, and mediation. Includes a facilitator's guide. This exercise must be administered by an experienced trainer. One-day facilitator training and certification is available for $1,500.

Author: Jennifer Patrick
Publication Date: 1997
Cost: $749
Number of Participants: 25
Time: 30 to 45 minutes
Audience: Intact work groups
Subject(s): Diversity, trust, conflict resolution
Source: Global Lead Management Consulting. Cincinnati, OH. (800) 762-0882. www.globallead.com

WEB OF YARN: SIMULATING SYSTEMS

This exercise encourages systems thinking. Participants form a circle and toss a ball of yarn from person to person, holding on to a piece of yarn each time. After many tosses, a web forms to create a sensory experience of belonging to a system. Members yank their pieces of yarn, drop pieces, and add new members to the web to reinforce their connectedness and dependence on each individual within the system. They also learn about the importance of the flow of information throughout the system.

Author: M. K. Key
Publication Date: 1997
Preparation: Print and post two statements
Space or Equipment Needs: Ball of sturdy yarn, newsprint, marker, and masking tape
Number of Participants: 10 to 15
Time: 45 minutes
Audience: General
Subject(s): Systems thinking
Source: M. K. Key in J. W. Pfeiffer, *The 1997 Annual: Volume 2, Consulting* (pp. 25-28). San Francisco: Pfeiffer (Jossey-Bass/Pfeiffer). (800) 274-4434. www.pfeiffer.com

WHERE DO YOU DRAW THE LINE?

This game is designed to get a group involved in a provocative discussion of ethical issues. To play, participants are divided into small groups who make judgments about the ethical behavior of individuals and organizations as described in vignettes. These judgments become the basis of the group's "ethical system." In the second phase the decisions of all the groups are summarized, displayed, and discussed.

Author: R. Garry Shirts
Publication Date: 1977
Space or Equipment Needs: Overhead projector (optional)
Cost: $185
Number of Participants: 5 to 35
Time: 50 minutes

Audience: General
Subject(s): Ethics
Source: Simulation Training Systems. Del Mar, CA. (800) 942-2900. www.stsintl.com

New
WILDERNESS SURVIVAL

This is another example of a group consensus and decision-making survival-type exercise. The scenario puts participants on a canoe trip in Ontario's Quetico Provincial Park. Following a ride down the rapids the group is left with damaged canoes, injured team members, and limited supplies. Individuals rank the importance of 14 supply items, then work on reaching group consensus. A scoring system helps the group measure its synergy.

Author: Dorothy Marcic
Publication Date: 1998
Preparation: Prepare handouts
Number of Participants: Groups of 6 to 9
Time: 50 minutes
Audience: General
Subject(s): Teams, decision making, group consensus
Source: D. Marcic in D. Marcic & J. Seltzer (1998), *Organizational Behavior: Experiences and Cases* (5th ed., pp. 106-120+). Cincinnati, OH: South-Western College Publishing. www.swcollege.com

New
WILDERNESS SURVIVAL

This survival simulation poses 12 situations that could be encountered by someone lost in the wilderness. Participants must reach consensus on what to eat and drink; how to deal with snakes, bears, and snowstorms; and how to climb rocks and ford streams. Rationale for recommended answers and scoring tables are included. This consensus-building activity doesn't require a trained facilitator. Any member of the group may lead the activity.

Author: Jossey-Bass/Pfeiffer
Publication Date: 1989
Cost: $6.95; *Leader's Guide*: $17.95
Number of Participants: 4 to 9
Time: 1-1/2 hours
Audience: Intact work groups
Subject(s): Group consensus
Source: Jossey-Bass/Pfeiffer. San Francisco, CA. (800) 274-4434. www.pfeiffer.com

New
WINDSOCK, INC.

This simulation explores intergroup relationships. Participants are divided into four divisions of Windsock, Inc.: the Central Office, Product Design, Sales and Marketing, and Production. Each group has a defined purpose and must coordinate with other groups to achieve the mission of designing, producing, and advertising a new windmill prototype. At the end of 30 minutes each group makes a brief presentation of its work to "stockholders."

Author: Christopher Taylor & Sandra Taylor
Publication Date: 1998
Preparation: Prepare handouts
Space or Equipment Needs: 500 straws and 750 pins
Number of Participants: 4 or more
Time: 50 minutes
Audience: General
Subject(s): Teams, communication
Source: C. Taylor & S. Taylor in D. Marcic & J. Seltzer (1998), *Organizational Behavior: Experiences and Cases* (5th ed., pp. 121-123). Cincinnati, OH: South-Western College Publishing. www.swcollege.com

INSTRUMENTS AND EXERCISES VENDORS

The vendors in this directory offer a wide variety of training tools. A brief description of each vendor's specialization helps readers decide where to call to request a catalog or find more information about a product. Contact information is provided.

ACUMEN INTERNATIONAL, INC.

Acumen, a subsidiary of Human Factors, Inc., provides multi-rater instruments for career management and organizational change.

4000 Civic Center Drive, Suite 500
San Rafael, CA 94903
Phone: (415) 492-9190
Fax: (415) 479-5358
Website: www.acumen.com

BIRKMAN INTERNATIONAL, INC.

This organization creates assessment tools for selection, team building, coaching, and career guidance. Dr. Roger Birkman's instrument, The Birkman Method®, is the foundation of their work.

3040 Post Oak Boulevard, Suite 1425
Houston, TX 77056-6511
Phone: (713) 623-2760
Fax: (713) 963-9142
E-mail: info@birkman.com
Website: www.birkman.com

BLOCK PETRELLA WIESBORD

This organization provides simulations for learning about organizational change.

136 Central Avenue
Clark, NJ 07066
Phone: (800) 296-1279 or (732) 680-4300
Fax: (732) 680-4304
Website: www.bpwconsulting.com

CAPT—CENTER FOR APPLICATIONS OF PSYCHOLOGICAL TYPE, INC.

CAPT is an organization dedicated to the work of Carl Jung and Isabel Briggs Myers. They conduct research; publish (Mary McCaulley is founder and president); distribute books, tests, and other products related to the *MBTI*®; facilitate test administration and interpretation; and provide scoring services.

2815 N.W. 13th Street, Suite 401
Gainesville, FL 32609
Phone: (800) 777-2278 or (352) 375-0160
Fax: (800) 723-6284 or (352) 378-0503
E-mail: info@capt.org
Website: www.capt.org

CARLSON LEARNING COMPANY

Carlson produces learning tools around concepts such as innovation, leadership, diversity, and time management. Their products are available through certified trainers and consultants.

P.O. Box 59159
Minneapolis, MN 55459-8247
Phone: (800) 777-9897
Website: www.carlsonlearning.com

CENTER FOR CREATIVE LEADERSHIP® (CCL®)

CCL's goal to link theory with practice is reflected in its publication of training materials. Instruments are designed to measure competencies, development experiences, creativity, and culture. Certification training is available for those who administer CCL's instruments.

One Leadership Place
P.O. Box 26300
Greensboro, NC 27438-6300
Phone: (336) 286-4480
Fax: (336) 282-3284
E-mail: info@leaders.ccl.org
Website: www.ccl.org

CENTER FOR MANAGEMENT EFFECTIVENESS

The center offers training tools for self-discovery, interpersonal skills, stress management, and conflict management.

P.O. Box 1202
Pacific Palisades, CA 90272
Phone: (888) 819-0200 or (310) 459-6052
Fax: (310) 459-9307
E-mail: kindlercme@aol.com
Website: www.tools4trainers.com

CHARLES HOSFORD & ASSOCIATES

This is the source for the management training board game *Leadout*®.

1507 S.E. 129th Avenue
Portland, OR 97233-1214
Phone: (503) 254-9868
Fax: (503) 254-9868
E-mail: sales@leadout.com
Website: www.leadout.com

CIM TEST PUBLISHERS

CIM offers computer-assisted assessment tools for business psychologists and human resources managers. They include psychometric tests that measure emotional intelligence, personality, and management competency.

23 Dunkeld Road
Ecclesall, Sheffield S11 9HN UK
Phone: 44 114 236 3811
Fax: 44 114 235 3448
E-mail: cimtest@msn.com
Website: www.cimtp.com

CLARK WILSON GROUP, INC.

The Wilson Group publishes multi-rater surveys used for leadership development training to change behavior and improve effectiveness on the job.

4900 Nautilus Court North, Suite 220
Boulder, CO 80301
Phone: (800) 537-7249
Fax: (303) 581-9326
E-mail: info@cwginc.com
Website: www.cwginc.com

CONSULTING PSYCHOLOGISTS PRESS (CPP)

CPP publishes and distributes materials that help people understand themselves and others. Their materials are used for personality testing, career planning, human resources development, leadership development, and organizational development. Some materials are sold only to facilitators who have advanced degrees.

3803 East Bayshore Road
Palo Alto, CA 94303-4300
Phone: (800) 624-1765 or (650) 969-8901
Fax: (650) 969-8608
E-mail: custserv@cpp-db.com
Website: www.cpp-db.com

DEVELOPMENTAL ADVISING INVENTORIES, INC.

This organization supports Greg Dickson's research on student development through cocurricular programs.

P.O. Box 1946
Paradise, CA 95967-1946
Phone: (916) 872-0511

DISCOVERY LEARNING

Their hands-on learning products are designed to support training in creativity, conflict management, communication, change management, leadership development, and team building.

909 North Elm Street, Suite 200
P.O. Box 41320
Greensboro, NC 27404
Phone: (336) 272-9530
Fax: (336) 273-4090
E-mail: DLI@discoverync.com
Website: www.discoverync.com

EDUCATIONAL SIMULATIONS

This company produces simulations for learning about ethics and multicultural diversity.

P.O. Box 276
Oceanside, OR 97134
Phone: (503) 842-7247
Fax: (503) 842-4654
E-mail: rpowers@oregoncoast.com

EXECUTIVE EXPEDITIONS

Their four- to sixteen-hour organizational simulations mirror the complex interactions and work processes of service and manufacturing-based corporations.

24 Sloan Street
Roswell, GA 30075
Phone: (678) 461-8880
Fax: (678) 461-8870
E-mail: ee@execexp.com
Website: www.executive-expeditions.com

GLOBAL LEAD MANAGEMENT CONSULTING

Global Lead provides training services and products in the areas of corporate culture, change management, strategic planning, diversity management, continuous improvement, executive leadership, educational reform, and community development. One-day certification training is recommended for exercise facilitators.

Hillcrest Tower
7162 Reading Road, Suite 250
Cincinnati, OH 45237
Phone: (800) 762-0882 or (513) 366-8344
Fax: (513) 731-8702
E-mail: globallead@globallead.com
Website: www.globallead.com

GLOBAL OPTIONS

Global Options is the source for the Culture Clash simulation.

8160 Manitoba Street, #315
Playa del Rey, CA 90293-8640
Phone: (310) 821-1864
Fax: (310) 821-1864

HAY/McBER TRAINING RESOURCES GROUP

This subsidiary of the Hay Group of human resource consulting firms produces training materials to identify and develop leadership styles and competencies.

116 Huntington Avenue
Boston, MA 02116
Phone: (800) 729-8074 or (617) 425-4588
Fax: (617) 927-5060
E-mail: trg_mcber@haygroup.com
Website: trgmcber.haygroup.com

HR PRESS

HR Press supplies workshops, videos, exercises, instruments, company audits, books, calendars, and other tools for cultural diversity training.

P.O. Box 28
Fredonia, NY 14063
Phone: (800) 444-7139 or (716) 672-4254
Fax: (716) 679-3177

E-mail: hrpress@netsync.net
Website: www.hrpress-diversity.com

HRD PRESS

Among other human resource development training products, HRD Press distributes a line of Situational Leadership® products.

22 Amherst Road
Amherst, MA 01002-9709
Phone: (800) 822-2801 or (413) 253-3488
Fax: (413) 253-3490
E-mail: info@hrdpress.com
Website: www.hrdpress.com

HRDQ

Formerly known as HRD Quarterly, this vendor sells books, instruments, games, simulations, and case studies to support all areas of human resources development.

2002 Renaissance Boulevard, #100
King of Prussia, PA 19406-2756
Phone: (800) 633-4533 or (610) 279-2002
Fax: (800) 633-3683 or (610) 279-0524
E-mail: custserv@hrdq.com
Website: www.hrdq.com

HUMAN SYNERGISTICS INTERNATIONAL

Their products measure growth and improvement at the individual, team, and organizational levels. They offer a variety of survival and business simulations.

39819 Plymouth Road, C-8020
Plymouth, MI 48170-4290
Phone: (800) 622-7584 or (734) 459-1030
Fax: (734) 459-5557
E-mail: info@humansyn.com
Website: www.humansyn.com

INTERCHANGE INTERNATIONAL INC.

Interchange is the source for training products based on The Change Cycle™ model. Certified trainers use these products to teach skills and techniques for dealing with change in the workplace.

1001 G Street, N.W., Suite 200 East
Washington, DC 20001-4545
Phone: (800) 878-8422 or (202) 783-7700
Fax: (202) 783-7730
E-mail: info@changecycle.com
Website: www.changecycle.com

INTERCULTURAL PRESS

This is a publisher of books and games dealing with intercultural communication and problem solving in multicultural groups.

P.O. Box 700
Yarmouth, ME 04096-0700
Phone: (800) 370-2665 or (207) 846-5168
Fax: (207) 846-5181
E-mail: books@interculturalpress.com
Website: www.interculturalpress.com

INTEREL, INC.

Interel provides action learning devices to aid corporate productivity. The devices are used in training programs for developing leadership, coaching, systems thinking, and teamwork.

140 Carl Street
San Francisco, CA 94117
Phone: (877) 468-3735 or (415) 566-0554
Fax: (415) 566-8317
E-mail: sales@interel.com
Website: www.interel.com

JOSSEY-BASS/PFEIFFER

Formerly known as Pfeiffer and University Associates, this vendor offers a large selection of tests, exercises, videos, books, and CD-ROMs for training in leadership and organizational development.

350 Sansome Street, 5th Floor
San Francisco, CA 94104
Phone: (800) 274-4434 or (415) 433-1740
Fax: (800) 569-0443 or (415) 433-0499
E-mail: pfeiffer@jbp.com
Website: www.pfeiffer.com

LOMINGER LIMITED, INC.

Lominger is the source for The Leadership Architect® Suite of leadership development products. This set of instruments, cards, handbooks, and software supports job profiling, development, team building, and succession planning. Facilitators must be certified.

5320 Cedar Lake Road South
Minneapolis, MN 55416-1643
Phone: (952) 542-1466
Fax: (952) 544-0280
E-mail: business_office@lominger.com
Website: www.lominger.com

MANAGEMENT RESEARCH GROUP® (MRG)

MRG specializes in research-based assessment tools for selection and development in the areas of leadership, sales, customer service, career development, and personal growth. Facilitators must attend certification workshops. Regional and country-specific norms are available.

14 York Street, Suite 301
Portland, ME 04101
Phone: (207) 775-2173
Fax: (207) 775-6796

E-mail: info@mrg.com
Website: www.mrg.com

METRITECH, INC.

MetriTech specializes in the research and development of assessment and training products for industry and education. Purchasers must meet standards of educational background and professional certification.

4106 Fieldstone Road
P.O. Box 6479
Champaign, IL 61822-6479
Phone: (800) 747-4868 or (217) 398-4868
Fax: (217) 398-5798
E-mail: mtinfo@metritech.com
Website: www.metritech.com

MIND GARDEN, INC.

Mind Garden products support personal and team development, mentoring skills, and stress management.

1690 Woodside Road, Suite 202
Redwood City, CA 94061-3402
Phone: (650) 261-3500
Fax: (650) 261-3505
E-mail: info@mindgarden.com
Website: www.mindgarden.com

NCS WORKFORCE DEVELOPMENT

NCS publishes psychological assessments for behavioral counseling and organizational development.

9701 West Higgins Road, Suite 770
Rosemont, IL 60018-4720
Phone: (800) 221-8378 or (847) 292-1900
Fax: (847) 292-3400
E-mail: assessment@ncs.com
Website: www.ncs.com

ORGANIZATIONAL LEARNING TOOLS, INC.

This organization supplies questionnaires, games, simulations, newsletters, and how-to manuals for HRD trainers.

25715 Meadowbrook Road
Novi, MI 48735-1849
Phone: (800) 684-1190
Fax: (248) 735-8048

PERFORMANCE SUPPORT SYSTEMS

This organization provides affordable, easy-to-use tools for performance management.

11835 Canon Boulevard, Suite C101
Newport News, VA 23606
Phone: (800) 488-6463 or (804) 873-3700
Fax: (804) 873-3288
E-mail: sales@2020insight.net
Website: www.2020insight.net

PERSONAL STRENGTHS PUBLISHING®

This vendor's tools are designed to help individuals understand their own behaviors, motivations, relationships, and personal values.

P.O. Box 2605
Carlsbad, CA 92018-2605
Phone: (800) 624-7347 or (760) 730-7310
Fax: (760) 730-7368
E-mail: info@personalstrengths.com
Website: www.personalstrengths.com

PERSONNEL DECISIONS INTERNATIONAL (PDI)

PDI's assessments are designed to be used in their executive feedback and coaching programs. Certification training is available for facilitators.

2000 Plaza VII Tower
45 South 7th Street
Minneapolis, MN 55402-1608
Phone: (800) 633-4410 or (612) 339-0927
Fax: (612) 904-7120
Website: www.pdi-corp.com

PSYCHOLOGICAL ASSESSMENT RESOURCES, INC. (PAR)

PAR's products include assessment instruments, software, books, audiotapes, and videotapes for professionals in psychology, counseling, education, business, and human resources. Purchasers must meet qualification standards.

P.O. Box 998
Odessa, FL 33556
Phone: (800) 331-8378 or (813) 968-3003
Fax: (800) 727-9329
E-mail: custserv@parinc.com
Website: www.parinc.com

QED CONSULTING

QED aims to improve workplace performance by aligning people and processes with strategy. Their products raise awareness of change and diversity issues.

41 Central Park West
New York, NY 10023
Phone: (800) 724-2215 or (212) 724-3335
Fax: (212) 724-4913
E-mail: info@qedconsulting.com
Website: www.qedconsulting.com

THE RESOURCES CONNECTION

This organization is the primary source for products related to systems thinking, whole brain technology, open space technology, and *The Fifth Discipline*.

908 Niagara Falls Boulevard, Suite 530
North Tonawanda, NY 14120-2060
Phone: (800) 295-0957

Fax: (905) 473-4219
E-mail: info@resourcesconnect.com
Website: www.resourcesconnect.com

RIGHT MANUS

Right Manus produces simulations, 360-degree-feedback instruments, and complete training programs. They will provide facilitators or train the trainers at certification workshops.

100 Prospect Street, South Tower
Stamford, CT 06901
Phone: (800) 445-0942 or (203) 326-3880
Fax: (203) 326-3890
E-mail: manus@rightmanus.com
Website: www.rightmanus.com

SIMULATION TRAINING SYSTEMS

Their one- to two-hour simulations are intended to spark enthusiasm and change the pace in training sessions.

P.O. Box 910
Del Mar, CA 92014-0910
Phone: (800) 942-2900 or (858) 755-0272
Fax: (858) 792-9743
E-mail: sts@cts.com
Website: www.stsintl.com

SYMLOG CONSULTING GROUP

This is the source for SYMLOG® products that are used in leadership training and development, organizational development, team building, and total quality management.

18580 Polvera Drive
San Diego, CA 92128
Phone: (858) 673-2098
Fax: (858) 673-9279
E-mail: staff@symlog.com
Website: www.symlog.com

TELEOMETRICS INTERNATIONAL

Training themes are supported by feedback instruments, exercises, and videos. Materials are available in nine languages.

1755 Woodstead Court
The Woodlands, TX 77380-0964
Phone: (800) 527-0406 or (281) 367-0060
Fax: (281) 292-1324
E-mail: teleo.info@teleometrics.com
Website: www.teleometrics.com

WONDERLIC, INC.

Wonderlic tests are used primarily for selection and promotion evaluations.

1795 North Butterfield Road
Libertyville, IL 60048-1238
Phone: (800) 963-7542 or (847) 680-4900
Fax: (847) 680-9492
E-mail: contact@wonderlic.com
Website: www.wonderlic.com

WORKSHOPS BY THIAGI, INC.

This organization supports the training games and simulations designed by Sivasailam Thiagarajan. A variety of products are offered for sale—books, the monthly newsletter *Thiagi Game Letter*, board games, software, workshops— and for free on the website and via e-mail discussion groups. Thiagi also offers facilitation and instructional design services.

4423 East Trailridge Road
Bloomington, IN 47408-9633
Phone: (800) 996-7725 or (812) 332-1478
Fax: (812) 332-5701
E-mail: thiagi@thiagi.com
Website: www.thiagi.com

VIDEOS

In this section, there are videos of three different types: feature films, documentaries of actual people or events, and training films made especially for leadership development programs. Whenever possible, the descriptions include reference to support materials such as case studies, leader's guides, or articles that describe using a video in the classroom. Following each description is information about:

- release year—this indicates the release date of the original film, not the year in which the film became available on video
- runtime—the length of the film
- source
- cost
- type of program—feature film, documentary, or training film
- subject

The distributors are your appropriate contacts for copyright information and permission to use videos in the classroom.

THE ABILENE PARADOX

This classic film describes the Abilene paradox, in which people agree for the sake of agreement although everyone secretly disagrees. This lack of communication can move bad projects forward, commit people or funding irresponsibly, and cause frustration for all. Mismanaged agreement is as dangerous to organizational effectiveness as excessive conflict because it can lead the organization toward inappropriate goals.

Release Year: 1985
Runtime: 27 minutes
Cost: $845
Film Type: Training
Subject(s): Group decision making
Source: CRM Learning. Carlsbad, CA. (800) 421-0833. www.crmlearning.com

New
ABRAHAM LINCOLN: PRESERVING THE UNION

This A&E Biography examines Lincoln's life, describing his childhood, campaigns, presidency, marriage, and how his assassination made him an American martyr. Interviews with historians are used to analyze the difficult leadership choices Lincoln was faced with during his first term as president.

Release Year: 1997
Runtime: 100 minutes
Cost: $14.95
Film Type: Documentary
Subject(s): Political leadership; U.S. presidents: Lincoln, A.
Source: A&E Home Video. South Burlington, VT. (800) 625-9000. www.aetv.com

New
AIR FORCE ONE

Harrison Ford plays the hero/U.S. president whose plane is hijacked by terrorists in this action film. One reviewer recommends that executives watch this movie for lessons in leadership. K. Sheridan (1997, "All I really need to know about leadership, I learned in *Air Force One*," *Bank Marketing, 29*(10), 5) describes a scene in which the president learns about technology—cell phones and fax machines—to gain a competitive edge. With tongue in cheek, Sheridan explains how the president manages by wandering around, acts as a change agent, hires people smarter than himself, and knows when to let people go.

Release Year: 1997
Runtime: 125 minutes
Cost: $12.99
Film Type: Feature
Subject(s): Leadership effectiveness
Source: Columbia Tristar Home Video. Culver City, CA. (310) 244-4000.

AMERICA'S GREAT INDIAN LEADERS

This film uses archival photos, reenactments, and narration to tell the stories of four 19th-century Native American leaders: the Apache rebel, Geronimo; Comanche leader, Quannah Parker; Chief Joseph of the Nez Perce nation; and the great Lakota Sioux warrior, Crazy Horse. The stories describe the efforts of these leaders to save their land and their culture.

Release Year: 1994
Runtime: 65 minutes
Cost: $29.95
Film Type: Documentary
Subject(s): Native American leadership
Source: Questar Video, Inc. Chicago, IL. (800) 544-8422. www.questar1.com

New
THE AMERICAN PRESIDENT

Michael Douglas is the widowed U.S. president in this romantic comedy. Annette Bening is the lobbyist who catches the president's eye when she seeks support for an environmental bill. As reelection day approaches, the once-popular liberal president faces numerous ethical dilemmas. The environmental bill threatens his crime-reform bill upon which his platform is based. He's forced to make a deadly military response. And his conservative opponent launches a smear campaign against the romantically involved president. The former idealist resorts to decision making by popular opinion rather than by the strength of his convictions. When all appears lost, the president makes a passionate speech about character and firmly makes the noble decision.

Release Year: 1995
Runtime: 123 minutes
Cost: $16.95
Film Type: Feature
Subject(s): Political leadership, ethics, character
Source: Columbia Tristar Home Video. Culver City, CA. (310) 244-4000.

New
ANDREW JACKSON: A MAN FOR THE PEOPLE

This A&E Biography describes how Andrew Jackson redefined the role of the American president through his bold, aggressive leadership and his focus on "the common man." Although Jackson was wildly popular with the lower classes, he made many enemies who thought him too authoritarian and considered "King Andrew" a threat to democratic government.

Release Year: 1998
Runtime: 50 minutes
Cost: $14.95
Film Type: Documentary
Subject(s): Political leadership; U.S. presidents: Jackson, A.
Source: A&E Home Video. South Burlington, VT. (800) 625-9000. www.aetv.com

New
ANIMAL FARM

This allegory, based on George Orwell's 1945 book, is a political satire about the birth of communism. Live action is combined with animatronics to create an eerie representation of an animal revolution against abusive humans. The pig Old Major inspires his fellow animals with a vision of a farm on which all animals are created equal, a place where justice and freedom exist for all who walk on four legs. Upon Old Major's death, the wicked pig Napoleon usurps power and rewrites the vision to benefit himself, claiming that some animals are more equal than others. A few brave animals stand up to the injustice and manage to endure until the powermongers self-destruct. Jim Henson's Creature Shop and celebrity voices create convincing animal characters.

Release Year: 1999
Runtime: 91 minutes
Cost: $14.99
Film Type: Feature
Subject(s): Political leadership, ethics, leadership lessons from literature, power
Source: Amazon.com. Seattle, WA. (800) 201-7575. www.amazon.com

APOLLO 13

In *Apollo 13* it is not only the team in the air but the teams on the ground that have to work together to get the astronauts home alive. A life-threatening problem on the way to the moon engages everyone on board as well as at NASA in many aspects of teamwork. Everyone keeps working until a creative solution is found and the astronauts make it safely home.

Release Year: 1995
Runtime: 135 minutes
Cost: $14.98
Film Type: Feature
Subject(s): Creative problem solving, cross-functional teams
Source: Universal Studios Home Video. Universal City, CA. (818) 777-1000.

APOLLO 13 LEADERSHIP: DOWN-TO-EARTH LESSONS FOR YOU AND YOUR ORGANIZATION

Captain James Lovell, commander of the Apollo 13 mission, and author James Belasco describe the leadership strategies that safely brought the troubled spacecraft home. They explain how leaders can develop a vision, establish shared values, and teach teams to collaborate under stress.

Release Year: 1996
Runtime: 31 minutes
Cost: $595
Film Type: Training
Subject(s): Teamwork, collaboration, vision
Source: Media Learning Resources. Rosemont, PA. (800) 474-1604. www.medialearning.com

New
THE ART OF COACHING IN BUSINESS

A seven-part coaching model provides a framework for a video seminar on coaching. Successful leaders and coaches who relate their personal and professional experiences to the model are: Herb Kelleher, CEO of Southwest Airlines; Jack Nicklaus, Chairman of Golden Bear Golf; Mercedes Ellington, Artistic Director of Dance Ellington; Keith Lockhart, Conductor of the Boston Pops Orchestra; Lenny Wilkens, Head Coach of the Atlanta Hawks; Sarah Nash, Managing Director at J. P. Morgan; and Jim Flick, Director of Education at the Nicklaus/Flick Golf School. Includes *The Leader's Guide, The Participant's Guide*, and *My Coaching Quotient* self-assessment.

Release Year: 1998
Runtime: 35 minutes
Cost: $795
Film Type: Training
Subject(s): Coaching
Source: Greylock Associates. Tequesta, FL. (888) 279-4857. www.greylockassociates.com

New
AUGUSTUS: FIRST OF THE EMPERORS

This A&E Biography calls Augustus, Julius Caesar's adopted son, the first true Roman Emperor and describes how he led the empire while always presenting himself as first citizen, not as a ruler. Among his major accomplishments as emperor, Augustus led a major reconstruction campaign in Rome and restored peace in the empire after years of civil war.

Release Year: 1998
Runtime: 50 minutes
Cost: $14.95
Film Type: Documentary
Subject(s): Political leadership, military leadership, Roman history
Source: A&E Home Video. South Burlington, VT. (800) 625-9000. www.aetv.com

New
BABY BOOM

Diane Keaton is J. C. Wiatt, the yuppie executive working 70 hours a week toward her goal of partnership in an ad agency. Everything is under control thanks to time management and power lunches. When she inherits her recently deceased cousin's baby, she tries to remain in the rat race as a working mom. It doesn't work out and they move to the country. Compulsive Wiatt picks a bushel of apples to make applesauce, sells some to local shops, applies her business skills, and begins to build a successful gourmet baby food business. A scene at the end of the movie shows Wiatt involved in a decision-making process. Should she sell her business for a huge profit or keep her business at home and centered around her baby? She finds a way to succeed at business and enjoy her family, too.

Release Year: 1987
Runtime: 103 minutes
Cost: $14.95
Film Type: Feature
Subject(s): Work and family balance, women's leadership, decision making
Source: MGM/UA Home Video, Inc. Santa Monica, CA. (310) 449-3000.

New
BRAVEHEART

Mel Gibson directs and stars in this Oscar-winning epic about William Wallace, a 13th-century warrior who led the Scottish people to victory over the English. Based loosely on historical fact, the film shows how personal loss drove Wallace to a position of leadership, how he used creative methods to unite his people and create an army capable of defeating the established and organized English forces, and how he remained true to his ideals to the end.

Release Year: 1995
Runtime: 177 minutes
Cost: $24.95
Film Type: Feature
Subject(s): Leadership without authority
Source: Paramount Home Video. Los Angeles, CA. (213) 956-3952.

THE BRIDGE ON THE RIVER KWAI

In a World War II jungle POW camp, British prisoner Alec Guinness refuses to build a bridge for the enemy unless his officers supervise the work. After some grumbling the camp commander shrewdly relents, allowing Guinness to get his way while getting the bridge he wanted. Hartwick Humanities in Management Institute (800-942-2737) offers a case study and teaching guide based on this film.

Release Year: 1957
Runtime: 161 minutes
Cost: $19.95
Film Type: Feature
Subject(s): Charisma, vision, integrity
Source: Columbia Tristar Home Video. Culver City, CA. (310) 244-4000.

New
BUFFALO SOLDIERS

Danny Glover produced and starred in this story about an all-black cavalry unit who patrolled the West following the Civil War. Composed mainly of freed slaves, these buffalo soldiers suffered degradation at the hands of white officers. Their assignment to capture an Indian renegade included the slaughter of men, women, and children who refused to cooperate. Emerging leadership within their ranks questioned the morality of this order. The soldiers, recently freed from slavery, were torn between duty and humanity. Strength of character helped them to answer the moral dilemma with dignity.

Release Year: 1997
Runtime: 120 minutes
Cost: $13.99
Film Type: Feature
Subject(s): History, African American leadership, character
Source: Warner Home Video, Inc. Burbank, CA. (818) 954-6000.

New
A BUG'S LIFE

This animated film employs an ant colony as a metaphor for humanity. Flik is the misfit who suggests innovative methods and tools for collecting food and resisting attacks by villainous grasshoppers. However, the colony ridicules his strange ideas. As an outcast he happens upon a motley team of insects for hire. Flik thinks that they are the samurai warriors who will defend his colony, but they are actually unemployed actors from a flea circus. Together this band of "warriors" achieves success and convinces the colony that change and personal differences are good. *Antz* (1998) has a very similar story line.

Release Year: 1998
Runtime: 95 minutes
Cost: $18.99
Film Type: Feature
Subject(s): Innovation, group dynamics
Source: Walt Disney Home Video. Burbank, CA. (818) 562-3560.

C AND THE BOX: A PARADIGM PARABLE

Predictable behavior leads to predictable results. This brief session-starter may help people change from their predictable routines to more creative and innovative problem-solving ways. Based on the book of the same name by Frank Prince, it encourages viewers to break out of their self-imposed boundaries and to have fun doing it.

Release Year: 1993
Runtime: 7 minutes
Cost: $295
Film Type: Training
Subject(s): Creative problem solving
Source: Jossey-Bass/Pfeiffer. San Francisco, CA. (800) 274-4434. www.pfeiffer.com

CAN CONFLICT IMPROVE TEAM EFFECTIVENESS?

Based on the research of Center for Creative Leadership researcher Valerie Sessa, this program demonstrates how the effective handling of conflict can improve team performance. Learn how to use perspective taking and tools such as the Information Importance Grid to focus the group on the task instead of on people-oriented conflict.

Release Year: 1996
Runtime: 22 minutes
Cost: $495
Film Type: Training
Subject(s): Conflict management, teams
Source: corVision Media Inc. Buffalo Grove, IL. (800) 537-3130. www.corvision.com

CHALK TALK: STANFORD COACHES ON LEADERSHIP AND TEAM BUILDING

Nine Stanford University coaches share 14 strategies for building winning teams such as: inspiring others to believe in themselves, risk-taking, and overcoming obstacles. Includes an assessment tool to identify areas for improvement.

Release Year: 1995
Runtime: 20 minutes
Cost: $195
Film Type: Training
Subject(s): Teams, motivation
Source: LearnCom. Bensenville, IL. (800) 824-8889. www.lrncom.com

THE CHARGE OF THE LIGHT BRIGADE

This is a dramatization of events in the Crimean War. A power struggle between British officers, who are also brothers-in-law and sworn enemies, leads to a disastrous decision. The British cavalry meet their death in the ensuing battle with the Russian troops at Balaclava. Hartwick Humanities in Management Institute (800-942-2737) offers a case study and teaching guide based on this film.

Release Year: 1968
Runtime: 130 minutes
Cost: $19.98
Film Type: Feature
Subject(s): Power, decision making
Source: MGM/UA Home Video, Inc. Santa Monica, CA. (310) 449-3000.

New
CHIANG KAI-SHEK

Although Chiang Kai-shek was ultimately driven out of China by communist forces, he was a pivotal leader in Chinese history who helped bring down the imperial government and defeat Japan in World War II. This A&E Biography uses historical footage and interviews to describe his training, diplomatic experience, and the years he spent leading the fight against Chinese communism.

Release Year: 1998
Runtime: 50 minutes
Cost: $14.95
Film Type: Documentary
Subject(s): Political leadership in China; military leadership; cultural context: China
Source: A&E Home Video. South Burlington, VT. (800) 625-9000. www.aetv.com

CITIZEN KANE

Considered by many to be a perfect film, if not the best American film of all time, *Citizen Kane* is truly a cinematic masterpiece. The emotion-packed story of Charles Foster Kane (allegedly based on the life of William Randolph Hearst) is told with ever-shifting perspective. Directing his own vital performance as well as members of the famous Mercury Players, Orson Welles created an enduring classic of leadership and power. Hartwick Humanities in Management Institute (800-942-2737) offers a case study and teaching guide based on this black-and-white film.

Release Year: 1941
Runtime: 119 minutes
Cost: $19.98
Film Type: Feature
Subject(s): Leader-follower relations, ethics
Source: Movies Unlimited. Philadelphia, PA. (800) 668-4344. www.moviesunlimited.com

New
CLASH OF THE TITANS

Archival footage of newsreels and fresh insights from colleagues chronicle the adversarial relationships between four sets of powerful leaders. These *titans* are men who confronted each other during great conflicts of the 20th century: British Prime Minister Winston Churchill and Nazi leader Adolph Hitler during World War II, Nationalist leader Chiang Kai-shek and Communist leader Mao Tse-tung during a 50-year struggle for control of China, U.S. president John F. Kennedy and Soviet premier Nikita Khrushchev during the Cuban Missile Crisis, and Ho Chi Minh versus Richard Nixon during the Vietnam War. This video is part of the History of the 20th Century series hosted by Sir David Frost.

Release Year: 1996
Runtime: 48 minutes
Cost: $89.95
Film Type: Documentary
Subject(s): History, political leadership
Source: Films for the Humanities and Sciences. Princeton, NJ. (800) 257-5126. www.films.com

COACHING AND PERFORMANCE FEEDBACK

This tape is intended for self-study or group learning. There are eight scenarios of workplace problems that involve coaching or feedback dilemmas. Actors dramatize three possible solutions for each dilemma. HRD experts discuss the effectiveness of each solution and explain which solutions facilitate support, commitment, listening, and learning. An accompanying guide includes reproducible handouts so that participants can stop the tape, write out the impact and consequence of each solution, then return to the lesson.

Release Year: 1996
Runtime: 94 minutes
Cost: $425

Film Type: Training
Subject(s): Coaching
Source: Coastal Human Resources. Virginia Beach, VA. (800) 725-3418. www.coastal.com

New
CODE OF THE WEST: TIMELESS VALUES

The *Code of the West* series relates an old-fashioned code of conduct to current business behaviors and attitudes. Cowboy philosopher Red Steagall recites five story-poems to inspire employees. *The Maverick Way* tells of brave souls who are not afraid to step outside boundaries, change, or fail. *Ride for the Brand* describes a rich organizational culture full of trust and loyalty. *Born to This Land* focuses on the power of shared values and relationships. *The Fence That Me and Shorty Built* tells a story of personal accountability and pride in a job well done. *To an Old Friend* is about the relationship between a protégé and his old mentor. A *Facilitator's Guide* includes transcripts of the poems and suggestions for discussions about leadership. The individual videos are available for $225 each.

Release Year: 1995
Runtime: Five parts—5 minutes each
Cost: $895
Film Type: Training
Subject(s): Innovation, values, relationships, accountability, loyalty
Source: ChartHouse International Learning Corporation. Burnsville, MN. (800) 328-3789. www.charthouse.com

CONQUERORS

Military heroes throughout history are portrayed as men of charisma, vision, and fatal flaws. This film explores how the fate of a nation is impacted by the personality of its leader. Peter the Great and Alexander the Great are portrayed as inspired leaders and Napoleon as an idealistic yet self-serving leader.

Release Year: 1997
Runtime: Two tapes—120 minutes each
Cost: $29.95 for the set
Film Type: Documentary
Subject(s): Military leadership
Source: Discovery Channel Home Video. Florence, KY. (800) 889-9950. www.shopping.discovery.com

New
COURAGE UNDER FIRE

Denzel Washington is Lieutenant Colonel Nat Serling, who is assigned to investigate and approve a posthumous Medal of Honor. Meg Ryan is Captain Karen Walden, the Gulf War helicopter pilot who gave her life to save her crew. In this story Congress is eager to make the presentation, the first-ever Medal of Honor awarded to a female soldier. However, Serling's investigation uncovers differing accounts of the event. Each account is influenced by the gender and cultural background of the crew member telling the story. Serling faces the fact that war brings out the best and worst in humanity as he searches for the true act of courage that reaffirms his faith in humanity. Hartwick Humanities in Management Institute (800-942-2737) offers a leadership case study and teaching guide based on this film.

Release Year: 1996
Runtime: 117 minutes
Cost: $13.99
Film Type: Feature
Subject(s): Courage, gender diversity, ethnic diversity, military leadership, Gulf War
Source: Twentieth Century Fox Home Entertainment. Beverly Hills, CA. (888) 223-4360.

COURAGEOUS FOLLOWERS, COURAGEOUS LEADERS

This film is based on Ira Chaleff's book *The Courageous Follower: Standing Up To and For Our Leaders* (Berrett-Koehler, 1995). In several workplace scenarios it demonstrates how employees who are not in positions of power may engage in participatory leadership. They must have courage in four areas: serving their leaders by taking initiative, assuming responsibility, challenging their leaders, and leaving a situation in which they cannot support the leader.

Release Year: 1996
Runtime: 23 minutes
Cost: $845
Film Type: Training
Subject(s): Participatory leadership
Source: CRM Learning. Carlsbad, CA. (800) 421-0833. www.crmlearning.com

CRIMSON TIDE

Gene Hackman is commander of the submarine USS Alabama and Denzel Washington is the executive officer who challenges his authority. The two struggle for control of the sub's crew and nuclear missiles as they disagree about the authenticity of their order to fire the missiles.

Release Year: 1995
Runtime: 116 minutes
Cost: $19.99
Film Type: Feature
Subject(s): Power, military leadership
Source: Movies Unlimited. Philadelphia, PA. (800) 668-4344. www.moviesunlimited.com

New
THE CUBAN MISSILE CRISIS: A CASE STUDY IN DECISION MAKING AND ITS CONSEQUENCES

In 1962 the installation of nuclear missiles in Cuba 90 miles from the U.S. coast demanded a swift but careful response from President John F. Kennedy. His handling of this crisis serves as an example of the decision-making process at its best. Kennedy assembled a diverse team of experts, established an environment of openness and trust, and kept creative discussion alive until all action plans and their consequences were evaluated from every perspective. Photographs, audiotapes, television footage, and commentary from executive committee members document the nondirective leadership style and decision-making process that led to peaceful resolution rather than to nuclear holocaust.

Release Year: 1999
Runtime: 25 minutes
Cost: $795
Film Type: Training
Subject(s): Decision making
Source: Media Learning Resources. Rosemont, PA. (800) 474-1604. www.medialearning.com

DAVE

Kevin Kline is the presidential look-alike hired to cover for the unscrupulous and unconscious American President. His inside look at national politics inspires him to balance budgets, hold other officials accountable, expose the bad guys, and eventually run for office in his own identity.

Release Year: 1993
Runtime: 110 minutes
Cost: $19.98
Film Type: Feature
Subject(s): Charisma, situational leadership, ethics
Source: Warner Home Video, Inc. Burbank, CA. (818) 954-6000.

DEAD POETS SOCIETY

Robin Williams is a professor at an exclusive prep school who gets into trouble for encouraging his students to "seize the day." Management and organizational behavior professors may want to use this video to explore issues in leadership, such as ethics, role conflict, autonomy, risk-taking, stress, and organizational pressures toward conformity. Hartwick Humanities in Management Institute (800-942-2737) offers a case study and teaching guide based on this film.

Release Year: 1989
Runtime: 128 minutes
Cost: $19.99
Film Type: Feature
Subject(s): Contrasting leadership styles
Source: Movies Unlimited. Philadelphia, PA. (800) 668-4344. www.moviesunlimited.com

THE DEMOCRAT AND THE DICTATOR

In this part of the *Walk Through the Twentieth Century* series Bill Moyers examines the parallels between two charismatic leaders, Franklin Roosevelt and Adolf Hitler, both of whom came to national power in 1933 and died in 1945. Their presence and conflicting ideologies are revealed through their words and gestures.

Release Year: 1984
Runtime: 58 minutes
Cost: $59.95
Film Type: Documentary
Subject(s): Charisma; Roosevelt, F. D.; Hitler, A.; political leadership
Source: PBS Video–Educational Division. Alexandria, VA. (800) 344-3337. www.pbs.org

New
DIVERSE TEAMS AT WORK: CAPITALIZING ON THE POWER OF DIVERSITY

This video is based on the Gardenswartz and Rowe book by the same name (Irwin, 1995). A workplace scenario demonstrates the difficulty of meeting dual challenges—building a new team and valuing the diversity among team members. We watch a struggling new team develop along four dimensions: product focus, human dynamic focus, process intervention, and a shared bond. The team members learn that each individual has a unique personality and three types of filters through which they relate: internal filters such as race and gender, external filters such as religion and educational background, and organizational filters such as department or managerial status.

Release Year: 1995
Runtime: 25 minutes
Cost: $745
Film Type: Training
Subject(s): Diversity
Source: corVision Media, Inc. Buffalo Grove, IL. (800) 537-3130. www.corvision.com

DIVERSITY: FOOD FOR THOUGHT

Viewers visit the Diversity Diner where customers learn to appreciate differences on the lunch menu and among coworkers. Conversation revolves around a new "touchy-feely" human resources survey on diversity. After some initial resistance, diners recognize that there are obvious and not-so-obvious differences among members of any workforce. Valuing these differences can decrease discrimination and increase productivity. Includes a leader's guide and participant handbooks.

Release Year: 1997
Runtime: 20 minutes
Cost: $595
Film Type: Training
Subject(s): Diversity
Source: Coastal Human Resources. Virginia Beach, VA. (800) 725-3418. www.coastal.com

New
DWIGHT D. EISENHOWER: COMMANDER-IN-CHIEF

Eisenhower was a leader in both the military and political worlds, and this A&E Biography uses period news footage and interviews with family members and historians to profile the man and his legacy. The film describes his rise from West Point to Supreme Allied Commander in Europe during World War II to the presidency.

Release Year: 1995
Runtime: 50 minutes
Cost: $14.95
Film Type: Documentary
Subject(s): U.S. presidents: Eisenhower, D. D.; political leadership; military leadership
Source: A&E Home Video. South Burlington, VT. (800) 625-9000. www.aetv.com

New
THE EFFICIENCY EXPERT

Originally titled *Spotswood*, this is a story about an outdated manufacturing company doomed to failure. Anthony Hopkins is the consultant brought in to create a new vision. His idea of good management is mechanistic, running a company as efficiently as clockwork. However, his recommendations to decrease socializing and increase productivity don't work. Instead of changing the employees, they change the consultant. He learns about loyalty, trust, respect, and the importance of balancing work and personal life. From his fresh perspective, the consultant creates an innovative vision that saves the company and the dignity of its employees.

Release Year: 1992
Runtime: 97 minutes
Cost: $14.95
Film Type: Feature
Subject(s): Organizational culture, loyalty
Source: Paramount Home Video. Los Angeles, CA. (213) 956-3952.

New
ELEANOR ROOSEVELT: A RESTLESS SPIRIT

Eleanor Roosevelt transformed the role of First Lady from celebrity homemaker to social activist. This A&E Biography shows how she formed a staff, held press conferences, and defined a political agenda that included civil rights and women's issues.

Release Year: 1995
Runtime: 50 minutes
Cost: $14.95
Film Type: Documentary
Subject(s): Roosevelt, E.; women as leaders; social movements
Source: A&E Home Video. South Burlington, VT. (800) 625-9000. www.aetv.com

New
ELIZABETH

Cate Blanchett stars as Elizabeth I in this story of the 16th-century monarch's unlikely rise to power. As bastard daughter of Henry VIII, the Protestant Elizabeth isn't prepared to rule in Catholic England. However, the sudden death of her half-sister Mary Tudor places her on the throne. Subversive plots abound among her advisors, political allies and enemies, the church, and even her lover. Elizabeth survives and gains power through subversive maneuvers of her own and very persuasive speechmaking. By the end of the movie she has sworn off her dependence on men, claiming to be the virgin queen who is married to England.

Release Year: 1998
Runtime: 121 minutes
Cost: $13.99
Film Type: Feature
Subject(s): History, women's leadership, power
Source: Polygram Filmed Entertainment. New York, NY. (800) 825-7781.

New
THE ENCOURAGING MANAGER: HELPING EMPLOYEES FEEL EMPOWERED, INFORMED, AND INVALUABLE

With tongue-in-cheek scenarios this film illustrates the horrors that can occur in the workplace when managers shoot down ideas, foster rumors by withholding information, treat employees like children, hide behind company policy, and compete with other managers. Contrasting scenarios demonstrate managers who genuinely involve employees in the problem-solving process, keep employees informed, show genuine appreciation for employees by trusting their judgment, take ownership of corporate policies, and create a cooperative work environment. A *Leader's Guide* and *Participant Workbook* supplement the video.

Release Year: 1999
Runtime: 16 minutes
Cost: $625
Film Type: Training
Subject(s): Leader-follower relations, empowerment
Source: Star Thrower Distribution Corp. Saint Paul, MN. (800) 242-3220. www.starthrower.com

EVEN EAGLES NEED A PUSH

In a motivational way, David McNally presents five essential qualities that successful, confident, empowered people have in common: self-appreciation, vision, purpose, commitment, and contribution. His key message is that each of us can develop new strategies that will help us live the life we've always imagined for ourselves.

Release Year: 1992
Runtime: 24 minutes
Cost: $795
Film Type: Training
Subject(s): Motivation
Source: CRM Learning. Carlsbad, CA. (800) 421-0833. www.crmlearning.com

New
EVERYDAY CREATIVITY

Photographer Dewitt Jones uses personal stories and dramatic photographs to explain how to see something ordinary, change the lens, and view something extraordinary. On assignment for *National Geographic*, Jones takes 14,000 images to get 30 for an article. He's not afraid to make mistakes, to turn problems into opportunities, or to break his pattern. Jones says that when a perfected technique collides with a perfect moment, love happens. Passion is the essence of creativity. His message is stunningly delivered with examples of his creative work. Includes a *Leader's Guide* and *Workbook* for participants.

Release Year: 1999
Runtime: 20 minutes
Cost: $695
Film Type: Training
Subject(s): Creativity
Source: Star Thrower Distribution Corp. Saint Paul, MN. (800) 242-3220. www.starthrower.com

EXCALIBUR

King Arthur envisions Camelot, a kingdom in which power is used to benefit the common good, and the Round Table, a symbol of participatory leadership. Arthur is portrayed as a mortal who struggles with loyalty and betrayal, duty and power. Hartwick Humanities in Management Institute (800-942-2737) offers a case study and teaching guide based on this film.

Release Year: 1981
Runtime: 140 minutes
Cost: $19.98
Film Type: Feature
Subject(s): Charisma, vision, power
Source: Warner Home Video, Inc. Burbank, CA. (818) 954-6000.

THE EXCELLENCE FILES

Eight case studies demonstrate how innovative companies and a government agency are strengthening community and corporate culture, building teams, competing globally, and managing change. Includes profiles of: Southwest Airlines, Rubbermaid, Defense Personnel Support Center, USAA Property and Casualty Insurance, Timberland, Coca-Cola, Work/Family Directions, and Whole Foods Market.

Release Year: 1997
Runtime: 86 minutes
Cost: $795
Film Type: Training
Subject(s): Corporate leadership, government leadership
Source: Enterprise Media. Cambridge, MA. (800) 423-6021. www.enterprisemedia.com

EYES ON THE PRIZE: AMERICA'S CIVIL RIGHTS YEARS, 1954-1965

New national leaders emerged during the civil rights struggle. This inspiring six-part series is a comprehensive look at the people, events, and issues of those years.

Release Year: 1986
Runtime: Six tapes—60 minutes each
Cost: $250 for the set
Film Type: Documentary
Subject(s): Ethnic diversity, African American leadership, civil rights movement
Source: PBS Video–Educational Division. Alexandria, VA. (800) 344-3337. www.pbs.org

EYES ON THE PRIZE 2: AMERICA AT THE RACIAL CROSSROADS, 1965-1985

The second award-winning series by the same name continues the chronicle of the American civil rights movement. From community power in the schools to "Black Power" in the streets; from police confrontations in neighborhoods to political confrontation in city government; from Malcolm X to Martin Luther King; it depicts a period of great transformation.

Release Year: 1990
Runtime: Eight tapes—60 minutes each
Cost: $350 for the set
Film Type: Documentary
Subject(s): Ethnic diversity, African American leadership, civil rights movement
Source: PBS Video–Educational Division. Alexandria, VA. (800) 344-3337. www.pbs.org

New
FDR: THE WAR YEARS

This A&E Biography examines FDR's leadership during World War II, from his election to an unprecedented third term, through Pearl Harbor and the Yalta Conference. It ends with the mourning of the country at his death.

Release Year: 1995
Runtime: 50 minutes
Cost: $14.95
Film Type: Documentary
Subject(s): U.S. presidents: Roosevelt, F. D.; political leadership; World War II
Source: A&E Home Video. South Burlington, VT. (800) 625-9000. www.aetv.com

FEEDBACK SOLUTIONS

This series explains how to give and receive feedback through dramatizations and narrated lessons. The workplace scenarios feature a diverse cast of characters in supervisory and management positions. An accompanying workbook supports both classroom training and self-study.

Release Year: 1994
Runtime: Four tapes—60 minutes each
Cost: $495 each
Film Type: Training
Subject(s): Feedback
Source: Ash Quarry Productions, Inc. Studio City, CA. (800) 717-0777. www.ashquarry.com

THE FIFTH DISCIPLINE: DEVELOPING LEARNING ORGANIZATIONS

Peter Senge presents the importance of organizational learning. He discusses how to foster it through intrinsic rewards, and draws parallels between early individual learning and organizational learning.

Release Year: 1992
Runtime: 70 minutes
Cost: $69.95
Film Type: Training
Subject(s): Organizational learning
Source: ASTD. Valencia, CA. (800) 369-5718. www.mobiltape.com

THE FINEST HOURS

This tribute to Sir Winston Churchill documents his rocky diplomatic career and his inspiring passionate leadership in World War II, recalling his words, humor, family life, and patriotic fervor. Narrated by Orson Welles.

Release Year: 1964
Runtime: 116 minutes
Cost: $49.95
Film Type: Documentary
Subject(s): Churchill, W. S.; political leadership; World War II
Source: Amazon.com. Seattle, WA. (800) 201-7575. www.amazon.com

New
FISH! CATCH THE ENERGY, RELEASE THE POTENTIAL

The staff of Seattle's Pike Place Fish Company demonstrates how to take a job, any job, and turn it into a joy for workers and customers. With a playful, positive attitude and attention to customer service, the Fish team is creatively engaged in their work experience. Their four-part Fish philosophy is: 1) be there—stay focused, 2) choose your attitude, 3) play, and 4) make the customers' day. A set of bean bag fish is available for after-video exercises.

Release Year: 1998
Runtime: 17 minutes
Cost: $590
Film Type: Training
Subject(s): Motivation
Source: ChartHouse International Learning Corporation. Burnsville, MN. (800) 328-3789. www.charthouse.com

New
FISH! STICKS: KEEPING THE VISION ALIVE

This sequel to *Fish!* focuses on how the workers at Seattle's Pike Place Fish Company maintain the sense of joy and excitement they bring to their work. Pike Place's owner says that fish is only a vehicle for the company's real goal, which is to positively impact the quality of life in the world. The workers use three concepts to make this vision stick: commit, be it, and coach it. Practicing these principles gives employees a sense of responsibility for the business, encourages coaching among the employees, and helps new workers learn the organizational culture.

Release Year: 1999
Runtime: 17 minutes
Cost: $590
Film Type: Training
Subject(s): Vision
Source: ChartHouse International Learning Corporation. Burnsville, MN. (800) 328-3789. www.charthouse.com

FLIGHT OF THE PHOENIX

When a sandstorm forces a crash landing in the Arabian desert, a multinational band of survivors is stranded as a leaderless group. The pilot, played by James Stewart, is unprepared and unwilling to assume leadership for the group's rescue. A German businessman suggests building a new plane from damaged parts but is ridiculed and distrusted by the other survivors. When it becomes obvious that this plan is their only hope for survival, the group slowly cooperates, then embraces the vision of a new plane. There is prophetic dialogue about distrust of "newfangled" technology and the future of the world belonging to the "men with the slide rules." Hartwick Humanities in Management Institute (800-942-2737) offers a case study and teaching guide based on this film.

Release Year: 1965
Runtime: 147 minutes
Cost: $19.98
Film Type: Feature
Subject(s): Emergent leadership, group dynamics, innovation
Source: CBS/Fox Video. New York, NY. (877) 258-0794.

FRAMING THE FUTURE: LEADERSHIP SKILLS FOR A NEW CENTURY

Cultural anthropologist Jennifer James explains the technological forces causing turbulent change in today's workplace. She describes the skills needed to cope with change and embrace discovery.

Release Year: 1996
Runtime: 26 minutes
Cost: $695
Film Type: Training
Subject(s): Change

Source: CRM Learning. Carlsbad, CA. (800) 421-0833. www.crmlearning.com

THE FRONT OF THE CLASS: LEARNING TO LEAD

In this humorous take on basic leadership principles for the beginner, a man goes back to his sixth-grade teacher for advice when he has trouble in his first supervisory role. Together, they illustrate the four Fs that make your employees, and therefore you, succeed: First, Fair, Firm, and Flexible.

Release Year: 1995
Runtime: 29 minutes
Cost: $625
Film Type: Training
Subject(s): Leadership effectiveness
Source: Coastal Human Resources. Virginia Beach, VA. (800) 725-3418. www.coastal.com

GANDHI

Richard Attenborough's production and Ben Kingsley's award-winning performance highlight this dramatic account of the spiritual leader who inspired nonviolent resistance to British rule in India. The film follows Gandhi's life from his fight against racial inequality in South Africa to his unsuccessful attempts to unite Hindu and Muslim factions into an independent India. Hartwick Humanities in Management Institute (800-942-2737) offers a case study and teaching guide based on this film.

Release Year: 1982
Runtime: 188 minutes
Cost: $29.95
Film Type: Feature
Subject(s): Gandhi, M.; social movement; negotiation; spirit; cultural context: India
Source: Columbia Tristar Home Video. Culver City, CA. (310) 244-4000.

New
GEORGE WASHINGTON: THE MAN WHO WOULDN'T BE KING

This video from the American Experience series describes how Washington's early defeats as leader of the Revolutionary Army taught him to employ inventive strategies to defeat the British. After he became president, Washington refused to assume dictatorial power, establishing the American presidency as a democratic, not tyrannical, position.

Release Year: 1992
Runtime: 60 minutes
Cost: $19.95
Film Type: Documentary
Subject(s): U.S. presidents: Washington, G.; political leadership; military
Source: PBS Video. Alexandria, VA. (800) 344-3337 (Educational Division) or (800) 531-4727 (Home Division). www.pbs.org

New
GETTING TO YES: VIDEO WORKSHOP ON NEGOTIATION

This video is based on the book *Getting to Yes* (Fisher, Ury, & Patton, 1991). More than a dozen vignettes demonstrate a system for succeeding at interest-based negotiation. This system allows the negotiator to achieve personal interests while building long-term relationships.

Release Year: 1999
Runtime: Seven segments—20 minutes each
Cost: $1,495
Film Type: Training
Subject(s): Negotiation
Source: Harvard Business School Publishing. Boston, MA. (800) 988-0886. www.hbsp.harvard.edu

GETTYSBURG

Ted Turner's adaptation of the novel *The Killer Angels* is epic in scale. The greatest and bloodiest battle of the Civil War is realistically portrayed by an all-male cast including over 5,000 actors. In one moving scene a young Union commander delivers a powerful speech that persuades reluctant soldiers to recommit to the vision of a free America. The human cost of the war is emphasized. Hartwick Humanities in Management Institute (800-942-2737) offers a case study and teaching guide based on this film.

Release Year: 1993
Runtime: 254 minutes
Cost: $29.99
Film Type: Feature
Subject(s): Vision, military leadership, followership, Civil War
Source: Movies Unlimited. Philadelphia, PA. (800) 668-4344. www.moviesunlimited.com

GIVING LEADERSHIP AWAY

A new leader receives a jar of Lego building blocks as a lesson in team leadership. He learns that each decision is like a building block and that sharing decisions (blocks) can build a better project. Throughout the frustrating period of learning about leadership through trial and error, the jar of blocks reminds him to get out of people's way and trust others to make good decisions.

Release Year: 1996
Runtime: 19 minutes
Cost: $695
Film Type: Training
Subject(s): Team leadership, empowerment
Source: Video Visions. Atlanta, GA. (404) 521-3456.

GLORY

Glory is the story of the 54th Massachusetts, the first black volunteer regiment in the Civil War. The transformational leadership that emerges within the ranks and in their young, white commander contrasts with the authoritarian leadership outside the regiment. Hartwick Humanities in Management Institute (800-942-2737) offers a case study and teaching guide based on this film.

Release Year: 1989
Runtime: 122 minutes
Cost: $19.95
Film Type: Feature
Subject(s): Contrasting leadership styles, group dynamics, African American leadership, Civil War
Source: Columbia Tristar Home Video. Culver City, CA. (310) 244-4000. www.cthv.com

THE GOAL

This dramatization of an actual case concerns a plant manager with 90 days to turn around his losing operation or watch his department get downsized. At the same time, his family relationships are suffering and need attention. An old college professor reminds the manager about focusing on basic goals, using appropriate methods to achieve goals, and recognizing the gap between reality and goals.

Release Year: 1995
Runtime: 50 minutes
Cost: $895
Film Type: Training
Subject(s): Goal setting
Source: American Media, Inc. West Des Moines, IA. (800) 262-2557. www.ammedia.com

GREAT MINDS OF BUSINESS

The editors of *Forbes* present five case studies of innovative business leaders. Featured are Federal Reserve Chairman, Paul Volker; Intel CEO, Andrew Grove; marketing expert, Pleasant Rowland; FedEx leader, Fred Smith; and investment expert, Peter Lynch.

Release Year: 1997
Runtime: Five tapes—30 minutes each
Cost: $79.98 for the set
Film Type: Documentary
Subject(s): Corporate leadership
Source: PBS Video–Home Division. Alexandria, VA. (800) 531-4727. www.pbs.org

New
THE GREATEST SPEECHES OF ALL TIME

This collection of major speeches by this century's world leaders includes Franklin Roosevelt's State of the Union address after Pearl Harbor, John Kennedy's inaugural address, two speeches by Martin Luther King, Jr., an address given in Harlem by Malcolm X, and Richard Nixon's resignation speech.

Release Year: 1999
Runtime: 68 minutes
Cost: $19.95
Film Type: Documentary
Subject(s): Speeches, motivation, leaders in history

Source: PBS Video. Alexandria, VA. (800) 344-3337 (Educational Division) or (800) 531-4727 (Home Division). www.pbs.org

GROUNDHOG DAY

Bill Murray is Phil the Weatherman, caught in perpetual Groundhog Day and can't get out. In this complex but static environment he tries ingratiation and manipulation to achieve his short-term goals without much success. When he discovers his competencies and changes his interpersonal style, the spell breaks, he gets the girl, and he wakes up to a new day.

Release Year: 1993
Runtime: 103 minutes
Cost: $14.95
Film Type: Feature
Subject(s): Path-goal Theory, self-development
Source: Columbia Tristar Home Video. Culver City, CA. (310) 244-4000.

GROUPTHINK (REVISED EDITION)

Even empowered team players are at risk of experiencing groupthink: the natural tendency to agree just for the sake of unity. Groupthink symptoms and solutions are analyzed against a backdrop of historical events, including the Space Shuttle Challenger disaster where groupthink so tragically influenced the decision to launch.

Release Year: 1991
Runtime: 22 minutes
Cost: $845
Film Type: Training
Subject(s): Group decision making
Source: CRM Learning. Carlsbad, CA. (800) 421-0833. www.crmlearning.com

GUNG HO

Gung Ho is a comedy pertinent to discussions about cultural stereotypes and cross-cultural leadership. When a Japanese firm takes over a small U.S. auto factory, Michael Keaton tries to keep employees and management from killing each other during the misunderstandings that occur. Directed by Ron Howard.

Release Year: 1985
Runtime: 111 minutes
Cost: $14.95
Film Type: Feature
Subject(s): Multicultural diversity
Source: Paramount Home Video. Los Angeles, CA. (213) 956-3952.

New
GUNG HO!

Ken Blanchard and Sheldon Bowles host this dramatization of a workplace renewed. In the story, a Native American manager shares secrets from nature to create Gung Ho—a technique for managers to inspire higher morale and productivity. There are three principles: 1) the spirit of the squirrel—ensuring that people know their work is worthwhile; 2) the way of the beaver—giving people the control to achieve their goals; and 3) the gift of the goose—cheering each other on. Includes a participant's workbook and a *Leader's Training Guide.*

Release Year: 1998
Runtime: 29 minutes
Cost: $895
Film Type: Training
Subject(s): Motivation, spirit, Native American leadership
Source: American Media, Inc. West Des Moines, IA. (800) 262-2557. www.ammedia.com

HEART OF TIBET: THE 14TH DALAI LAMA

This profile of the spiritual leader and exiled political leader of Tibet was filmed during a 1989 visit to Los Angeles for a Tibetan Buddhist ritual. It includes an introduction by former president Jimmy Carter and footage of Chinese military abuse in occupied Tibet.

Release Year: 1991
Runtime: 60 minutes
Cost: $29.95
Film Type: Documentary
Subject(s): Political leadership, Dalai Lama
Source: PBS Video–Home Division. Alexandria, VA. (800) 531-4727. www.pbs.org

HENRY V

Kenneth Branagh portrays the young Hal who assumes the British throne and quickly develops into a transformational leader. He learns about the hopes and dreams of his troops and, in turn, gains their trust. His St. Crispian's Day speech before the battle at Agincourt inspires the few, weary foot soldiers to a spectacular victory against impossible odds. Hartwick Humanities in Management Institute (800-942-2737) offers a case study and teaching guide based on this film.

Release Year: 1989
Runtime: 138 minutes
Cost: $19.98
Film Type: Feature
Subject(s): Transformational leadership, trust, communication
Source: CBS/Fox Video. New York, NY. (877) 258-0794.

HERO

Dustin Hoffman is the reluctant hero who saves plane crash survivors from a fiery explosion. Andy Garcia is the charismatic impostor who takes credit for the heroic deed and infects society with goodness. Geena Davis is the reporter and crash survivor who makes a noteworthy speech about ethics in journalism and then learns firsthand about apparent and genuine heroism.

Release Year: 1992
Runtime: 116 minutes
Cost: $14.95
Film Type: Feature
Subject(s): Charisma, ethics, expectancy theory
Source: Columbia Tristar Home Video. Culver City, CA. (310) 244-4000.

New
HOOK

In this update of the Peter Pan legend, Robin Williams plays Peter Banning, a father and businessman who has forgotten he was once Peter Pan. When Captain Hook, played by Dustin Hoffman, kidnaps his children, Peter must return to Neverland to rescue them. The scenes where Peter rediscovers his magic and rallies the Lost Boys show how imagination, creativity, and a sense of play are necessary elements of leadership and teamwork. A discussion of how the film illustrates the effects of fatherhood on management style is found in I. Aaltio-Marjosola and J. Lehtinen (1998), "Male managers as fathers? Contrasting management, fatherhood, and masculinity," *Human Relations, 51*(2), 121-136.

Release Year: 1991
Runtime: 144 minutes
Cost: $14.95
Film Type: Feature
Subject(s): Creativity, leadership effectiveness
Source: Columbia Tristar Home Video. Culver City, CA. (310) 244-4000.

HOOSIERS

Gene Hackman stars in this movie about a small, in-the-dumps high school basketball team that manages to make it to the state finals. It is a classic sports-movie plot, but in this well-acted drama Hackman's character rings true and exemplifies the leadership and team-building power of inspiration and high expectations. Hartwick Humanities in Management Institute (800-942-2737) offers a case study and teaching guide based on this film.

Release Year: 1986
Runtime: 115 minutes
Cost: $14.98
Film Type: Feature
Subject(s): Transformational leadership, sports leadership
Source: Movies Unlimited. Philadelphia, PA. (800) 668-4344. www.moviesunlimited.com

HOW TO MAKE CROSS-FUNCTIONAL TEAMS WORK

Viewers learn how to set up cross-functional teams in this four-volume video program. Mark Howard shows how to use teams to break up bureaucracy, streamline processes, and solve problems. A facilitator's guide and participants' workbooks are available.

Release Year: 1994
Runtime: 188 minutes
Cost: $249.95
Film Type: Training
Subject(s): Cross-functional teams
Source: CareerTrack Publications. Boulder, CO. (800) 488-0928. www.careertrack.com

THE HUNT FOR RED OCTOBER

Sean Connery stars as a Soviet submarine commander who involves his crew and nuclear weapons in a plot to defect to the West. Scott Glenn as a U.S. Naval commander and Alec Baldwin as a military analyst complete a leadership triad that overcomes cultural differences to pursue a common goal. Hartwick Humanities in Management Institute (800-942-2737) offers a case study and teaching guide based on this film.

Release Year: 1990
Runtime: 137 minutes
Cost: $14.95
Film Type: Feature
Subject(s): Power, intuition
Source: Paramount Home Video. Los Angeles, CA. (213) 956-3952.

I KNOW JUST WHAT YOU MEAN! OVERCOMING ROADBLOCKS TO EFFECTIVE COMMUNICATION

Stephen Covey presents a satire to highlight common mistakes made in communication. The scene is a restaurant at lunchtime with several mini-dramas involving work and family issues. We see repeated instances of listening to evaluate, probe, advise, or interpret. It is obvious that communication could be improved by listening to understand instead. Includes a *Discussion Leader's Guide* and participant handouts.

Release Year: 1996
Runtime: 21 minutes
Cost: $695
Film Type: Training
Subject(s): Communication
Source: Franklin Covey. Salt Lake City, UT. (800) 654-1776. www.franklincovey.com

IF AT FIRST . . . OVERCOMING THE FEAR OF FAILURE

Fear of failure stifles many individuals and teams. *If at First* shows how to identify and move beyond the fear. Tony Buzan presents examples from 3M, sports, and the MacPhail Center for the Arts.

Release Year: 1994
Runtime: 26 minutes
Cost: $895
Film Type: Training

Subject(s): Motivation
Source: ChartHouse International Learning Corporation. Burnsville, MN. (800) 328-3789. www.charthouse.com

New
IMPLODE! BUILDING COMMUNICATION, TRUST AND TEAMWORK . . . WITH 10,000 TONS OF TNT

Controlled Demolition Inc. (CDI) explains the importance of teamwork as they prepare to implode a skyscraper in downtown Omaha, Nebraska. Each member of their tightly knit team is committed to the team's mission and success. As they so dramatically demonstrate, they have only one chance to get the job done and done right. The consequences of a bad job are unthinkable. The secrets of CDI's successful teamwork are communication and trust. An action guide transfers the video's message to teams in the workplace.

Release Year: 1999
Runtime: 15 minutes
Cost: $595
Film Type: Training
Subject(s): Teamwork, communication
Source: Enterprise Media. Cambridge, MA. (800) 423-6021. www.enterprisemedia.com

IN REMEMBRANCE OF MARTIN

This remarkable documentary chronicles the life of Martin Luther King, Jr. through personal comments from family members, former classmates, close friends, and advisors. Archival footage documents King's early civil rights efforts, including the "I Have a Dream" address on the steps of the Lincoln Memorial. Later events in King's life and a brief synopsis of key civil rights decisions of the 1950s and 1960s are also included.

Release Year: 1986
Runtime: 60 minutes
Cost: $19.98
Film Type: Documentary
Subject(s): African American leadership; civil rights movement; King, M. L., Jr.
Source: PBS Video–Educational Division. Alexandria, VA. (800) 344-3337. www.pbs.org

INNOVATIVE PROJECT TEAMS

Examples from Duke Power, Ethican Endo-Surgery, and the *Tallahassee Democrat* newspaper demonstrate the difficulties, risks, and benefits of teams. These companies overcame safety, product development, and marketing dilemmas through teamwork. Includes a presenter's guide.

Release Year: 1994
Runtime: 40 minutes
Cost: $595
Film Type: Training
Subject(s): Innovation, teams
Source: Harvard Business School Publishing. Boston, MA. (800) 988-0886. www.hbsp.harvard.edu

INTUITION IN BUSINESS

To remain competitive, organizations must learn to use intuition. In this two-part program Dr. Weston Agor discusses ways in which organizations can learn to accommodate intuitive styles. He also provides examples of how intuition can be used in different business settings. In part two he explores exercises that cultivate intuition in people and organizations.

Release Year: 1993
Runtime: 90 minutes
Cost: $49.95
Film Type: Training
Subject(s): Intuition
Source: Thinking Allowed. Berkeley, CA. (800) 999-4415. www.thinking-allowed.com

New
INVISIBLE RULES: MEN, WOMEN AND TEAMS

This video seminar is Pat Heim's sequel to *Dead-Even Rule* (1995) about men's and women's ways of working in teams. Heim believes that children grow up in separate male and female cultures. Men learn leadership and teamwork behaviors in hierarchical situations such as team sports. They learn a command-and-control style of leadership that is effective in time-bound situations and crises. Women learn in flat structures playing games of involvement and creativity. Heim explains gender differences to help men and women understand each other's cultures and communicate across invisible boundaries. Includes a discussion guide.

Release Year: 1996
Runtime: 34 minutes
Cost: $495
Film Type: Training
Subject(s): Gender diversity, teams
Source: corVision Media, Inc. Buffalo Grove, IL. (800) 537-3130. www.corvision.com

New
IT'S A WONDERFUL LIFE: LEADING THROUGH SERVICE

Margaret Wheatley, author of *Leadership and the New Science,* uses scenes from the classic movie to illustrate servant leadership. She identifies three major themes in the movie: leading through service to others, the importance of personal integrity, and developing a sense of community. Wheatley says that in order to leave a legacy in your community or organization, like George Bailey did, you must act to serve others, recognize when acts of courage are called for, speak truthfully, and be a colleague others can depend on.

Release Year: 1999
Runtime: 22 minutes
Cost: $795
Film Type: Training
Subject(s): Servant leadership

Source: Media Learning Resources. Rosemont, PA. (800) 474-1604. www.medialearning.com

New
JAMMING: THE ART AND DISCIPLINE OF BUSINESS CREATIVITY

Jazz musicians share the secrets of jamming to introduce John Kao's framework for fostering corporate creativity. Three successful businesses—IDEO, a design firm; Senco Products, a manufacturing firm; and Coca Cola—explain how jamming helps them to develop creative capital. Some of their lessons to the viewer are: conduct a creativity audit, allow ideas to bubble up, insulate creative activity, and enable talent. This video is based on Kao's book of the same name.

Release Year: 1998
Runtime: 25 minutes
Cost: $595
Film Type: Training
Subject(s): Creativity
Source: Coastal Human Resources. Virginia Beach, VA. (800) 725-3418. www.coastal.com

New
JOAN OF ARC

One recent story of Joan of Arc is this television miniseries featuring Leelee Sobieski as the 15th-century peasant-girl-turned-savior of France. The story introduces Joan as a child who hears divine voices. As she grows, the voices continue with the message that she is responsible for saving France from British invasion and returning France to God. Joan convinces the dauphin that he will be crowned king if she assumes leadership of the French army. After a few remarkable victories, Joan suffers defeat, is tried as a heretic, and is burned at the stake. The leadership lesson is in Joan's ability to rally an entire nation to action from a position of absolutely no authority. Other versions are *Messenger: The Story of Joan of Arc* (1999) and Ingrid Bergman's *Joan of Arc* (1948).

Release Year: 1999
Runtime: 140 minutes
Cost: $19.99
Film Type: Feature
Subject(s): Leading without authority
Source: Artisan Entertainment. Hanover Park, IL. (877) 848-3865. www.artisanent.com

JOSHUA IN A BOX

This is a short animated parable about freedom and control—and much more. A person imprisoned in a box eventually escapes—then becomes a box himself to control another creature.

Release Year: 1981
Runtime: 6 minutes
Cost: $295

Film Type: Training
Subject(s): Motivation, power
Source: CRM Learning. Carlsbad, CA. (800) 421-0833. www.crmlearning.com

New
THE KENNEDY ERA

This two-volume video examines the life of John Kennedy, one of this country's most charismatic leaders. Volume One describes Kennedy's youth and his early political career up through the 1960 Democratic convention. Volume Two describes his presidency and includes footage of his funeral.

Release Year: 1997
Runtime: 100 minutes
Cost: $29.95
Film Type: Documentary
Subject(s): Political leadership; U.S. presidents: Kennedy, J. F.
Source: PBS Video. Alexandria, VA. (800) 344-3337 (Educational Division) or (800) 531-4727 (Home Division). www.pbs.org

LAND OF O'S: COMPETING THROUGH DIVERSITY

Barry Stein talks us through this follow-up to *A Tale of "O,"* addressing real-world issues. He links diversity with productivity, competitiveness, and bottom-line results. He also shows how to leverage differences to the advantage of both the organization and the individual.

Release Year: 1995
Runtime: 28 minutes
Cost: $695
Film Type: Training
Subject(s): Diversity
Source: Goodmeasure Direct, Inc. Cambridge, MA. (617) 868-8662. www.goodmeasure.com

New
LEADERSHIFT: FIVE LESSONS FOR LEADERS IN THE 21st CENTURY™

Futurist Joel Barker uses a bridge-building metaphor to discuss new responsibilities of leaders as we cross over from the present paradigm to the future. The five most important lessons are: focus on the future, understand the nature of change, appreciate complex systems, learn how leadership style affects employee productivity, and create a shared vision. Motorola, the Y2K bug, the Delancy Street rehabilitation program, and the stock market serve as examples. The video is beautifully photographed at impressive bridge sites around the U.S. Includes a *Facilitator's Guide*, a *Participant's Workbook*, and a CD-ROM that contains Power Point overheads.

Release Year: 1999
Runtime: 29 minutes
Cost: $895
Film Type: Training

Subject(s): Future of leadership
Source: Star Thrower Distribution Corp. Saint Paul, MN. (800) 242-3220. www.starthrower.com

LEADERSHIP: REACH FOR THE STARS

Apollo 11 astronaut Buzz Aldrin hosts this film about the differences between managers and leaders. Lessons are dramatized by two brothers, one who seeks the answer and the other who has already learned the difference. Between lessons about communicating vision, raising expectations, gaining commitment, and building trust, Aldrin describes the leadership of the Apollo program. From President John Kennedy's vision to the commitment and creativity at every level, the Apollo program is an example of leadership that helps us realize extraordinary goals.

Release Year: 1997
Runtime: 20 minutes
Cost: $495
Film Type: Training
Subject(s): Vision, trust, transformational leadership
Source: Coastal Human Resources. Virginia Beach, VA. (800) 725-3418. www.coastal.com

LEADERSHIP: WHAT'S TRUST GOT TO DO WITH IT?

This film follows a team leader who is caught between corporate goals and unmotivated employees. He and his team members discover the importance of trust—of being honest, sharing information, keeping promises, and valuing each member's contribution.

Release Year: 1996
Runtime: 19 minutes
Cost: $695
Film Type: Training
Subject(s): Trust, team leadership
Source: CRM Learning. Carlsbad, CA. (800) 421-0833. www.crmlearning.com

LEADERSHIP AND THE NEW SCIENCE

In this video based on the popular book of the same name, Dr. Margaret Wheatley suggests a new approach for breaking out of limited perspectives and seeing chaos as a natural force for creating order. With insights into organizational life gleaned from such diverse fields as physics and biochemistry, she asks us to loosen the bonds of our own paradigms and consider other, more productive models for how we work with one another.

Release Year: 1993
Runtime: 23 minutes
Cost: $845
Film Type: Training
Subject(s): Chaos
Source: CRM Learning. Carlsbad, CA. (800) 421-0833. www.crmlearning.com

LEADERTALK

LeaderTalk is a series of video interviews with leadership scholars and practitioners. The 2000 series of nine programs includes: *Think Global, Act Local*; *Making Sense of the Knowledge Revolution*; *Leading Change*; *Shaping the 21st Century* (business's role in society); *Leadership in the Digital Age*; and *Storytelling: The Leader's New Art*. Produced for viewing on the PBS Business Channel, each segment is also available on video. A one-year subscription is available for $1,170. Some videos from previous years' series include: *Values Still Matter*; *Leadership on the Line: The Lessons of Crisis*; *Boomers Versus Busters: Managing the Emerging Generations*; and *Balancing a Successful Career with a Fulfilling Life*. Some videos come in two parts and run 58 minutes.

Release Year: 1998-2000
Runtime: 28 minutes each
Cost: $395 each
Film Type: Training
Subject(s): Leadership effectiveness
Source: LearnCom. Bensenville, IL. (800) 824-8889. www.lrncom.com

LEADING BY EXAMPLE: MENTORING AND COACHING FOR EFFECTIVE LEADERSHIP

Stephen Covey presents the story of Anne Sullivan to illustrate that a leader's legacy is reflected in the character and competence of followers. Sullivan was a teacher and mentor to only one student, Helen Keller. Through courage, vision, and patience Sullivan pioneered methods to help her student and other deaf and blind people find expression and purpose. Helen Keller makes an appearance and, through her interpreter, speaks with eloquence about teaching and leadership. Includes a *Leader's Discussion Guide* and participant handouts.

Release Year: 1996
Runtime: 20 minutes
Cost: $695
Film Type: Training
Subject(s): Teacher as leader; mentoring; women's leadership; Keller, H.
Source: Franklin Covey. Salt Lake City, UT. (800) 654-1776. www.franklincovey.com

LEADING WITH PERSUASION

In this video scenario a blue-collar manager learns to persuasively present his ideas. A mentor guides him through the process of preparation and presentation. To prepare, the manager must recognize his own value, focus on his idea and reduce it to one sentence, support the idea with evidence, and anticipate others' objections. During the presentation, the manager must establish credibility, be direct, and show conviction. When the manager learns to respond to emotional issues, he succeeds in persuading others to see his idea in the best light and give it a fair hearing. Includes a *Leader's Guide*.

Release Year: 1999
Runtime: 20 minutes
Cost: $695
Film Type: Training
Subject(s): Influence, blue-collar managers
Source: CRM Learning. Carlsbad, CA. (800) 421-0833. www.crmlearning.com

LESSONS FROM THE NEW WORKPLACE

A follow-up to *Leadership and the New Science*, this video uses examples from the U.S. Army, the DuPont Corporation, and a public school system to demonstrate the application of Margaret Wheatley's visionary models in organizations. The film stresses the importance of information, relationships, and vision to the new workplace. Includes a leader's guide.

Release Year: 1995
Runtime: 20 minutes
Cost: $845
Film Type: Training
Subject(s): Vision, corporate leadership, educational leadership
Source: CRM Learning. Carlsbad, CA. (800) 421-0833. www.crmlearning.com

LIFE AND WORK: A MANAGER'S SEARCH FOR MEANING

In this video version of the book by the same name (William Morrow, 1994), James Autry explains how to integrate life and work. He suggests that viewers nurture their inner selves through meditation and prayer, reading, walking, the arts, and sports. They should invite challenges and seek meaning in all they do. To support their employees and meet organizational goals at the same time, managers must provide a connection between their employees' personal sense of purpose and the organizational mission.

Release Year: 1995
Runtime: 30 minutes
Cost: $695
Film Type: Training
Subject(s): Spirit, work and family balance
Source: VideoLearning. Bryn Mawr, PA. (800) 622-3610. www.videolrn.com

LIFE IS SHORT

This workplace dramatization is accompanied by music only, no dialogue. We see a manager who is too busy with his tasks to "waste" time talking to others. As a result, he and his staff are ineffective. A phone call from his doctor is obviously bad news and the manager believes he has only a short time left to live. He reevaluates his relationship and task priorities. The staff notices an improved manager who listens to others' concerns, communicates his expectations, acknowledges others' efforts, and gives others his whole attention.

Release Year: 1998
Runtime: 7 minutes
Cost: $395
Film Type: Training
Subject(s): Relationship versus task orientation, communication
Source: Coastal Human Resources. Virginia Beach, VA. (800) 725-3418. www.coastal.com

LORD OF THE FLIES

When a group of schoolboys are stranded on a remote island, they regress into primitive behavior. The story is one of power struggles and abuse of power as the group wrestles between the immediacy of survival and the long-range plans for building a new society. Hartwick Humanities in Management Institute (800-942-2737) offers a case study and teaching guide based on this film.

Release Year: 1992
Runtime: 90 minutes
Cost: $19.95
Film Type: Feature
Subject(s): Group dynamics, values, power
Source: Columbia Tristar Home Video. Culver City, CA. (310) 244-4000.

LOVE AND PROFIT: THE ART OF CARING LEADERSHIP

This is the video version of James Autry's book by the same name (William Morrow, 1991). Through poetry and lecture Autry injects some feeling to the cold business environment. He shows that the qualities of honesty, trust, courage, and self-awareness help turn leadership into an art, filled with mistakes and triumphs but capable of dealing with the whole range of human experience, from bad to good.

Release Year: 1993
Runtime: 30 minutes
Cost: $695
Film Type: Training
Subject(s): Spirit, self-development
Source: VideoLearning. Bryn Mawr, PA. (800) 622-3610. www.videolrn.com

New
MADELEINE ALBRIGHT: FIRST LADY OF STATE

This film in the A&E Biography series follows Albright's life from her birth in Prague through her political career and tenure as U.S. Ambassador to the United Nations to her appointment as the first female Secretary of State. Interviews with her friends and children help describe how she became a respected diplomat and an established leader in American foreign policy.

Release Year: 1999
Runtime: 50 minutes
Cost: $14.95
Film Type: Documentary
Subject(s): Political leadership; women as political leaders; Albright, M.
Source: A&E Home Video. South Burlington, VT. (800) 625-9000. www.aetv.com

New
MAHATMA GANDHI: PILGRIM OF PEACE

This film in the A&E Biography series follows the life of one of the leaders of Indian independence, describing how Gandhi used a campaign of nonviolent noncooperation to end British colonial rule. Both Gandhi's personal life and his historical achievements are described, and interviews with his grandson, Arun Gandhi, and the Dalai Lama are included.

Release Year: 1998
Runtime: 50 minutes
Cost: $14.95
Film Type: Documentary
Subject(s): Social change; Gandhi, M.; peace
Source: A&E Home Video. South Burlington, VT. (800) 625-9000. www.aetv.com

A MAN FOR ALL SEASONS

This film is a biographical drama concerning 16th-century Chancellor of England, Sir Thomas More, and his personal conflict with King Henry VIII. More chose to die rather than compromise his religious beliefs. It is an exquisitely rich portrayal that received several Academy Awards.

Release Year: 1966
Runtime: 120 minutes
Cost: $19.95
Film Type: Feature
Subject(s): Integrity; More, T.; history; political leadership
Source: Columbia Tristar Home Video. Culver City, CA. (310) 244-4000.

THE MAN WHO PLANTED TREES

The award-winning animated version of Jean Giono's book is inspiring. It beautifully illustrates the importance of individual action on larger goals: the small wins that lead to big successes. It is the story of a widowed peasant who plants 100 trees a day for 30 years, even though he knows only a tenth will survive. His devotion to detail and his generosity of heart turn a wasteland into a living ecosystem.

Release Year: 1987
Runtime: 30 minutes
Cost: $95
Film Type: Training
Subject(s): Goal setting, motivation
Source: Direct Cinema Limited. Santa Monica, CA. (800) 525-0000.

THE MAN WHO WOULD BE KING

Rudyard Kipling's story explores a clash of cultures in 19th-century India. Sean Connery and Michael Caine are British con men who travel to nearby Afghanistan to pose as kings and loot the local riches. When Connery convinces himself that he really is Alexander the Great reincarnated, his deception is revealed. Hartwick Humanities in Management Institute (800-942-2737) offers a case study and teaching guide based on this film.

Release Year: 1975
Runtime: 129 minutes
Cost: $19.98
Film Type: Feature
Subject(s): Situational leadership, charisma
Source: CBS/Fox Video. New York, NY. (877) 258-0794.

New
MANAGERS AS MENTORS

Based on Chip Bell's 1996 book of the same name, this video describes the SAGE model for mentoring. Four stages—Surrendering, Accepting, Gifting, and Extending—make up the mentoring partnership. In ideal partnerships there are six characteristics: balance, truth, trust, abundance, passion, and courage. There is a self-assessment in the accompanying *Leader's Guide* to help viewers evaluate their potential for serving as mentors.

Release Year: 1999
Runtime: 23 minutes
Cost: $695
Film Type: Training
Subject(s): Mentoring
Source: corVision Media, Inc. Buffalo Grove, IL. (800) 537-3130. www.corvision.com

New
MANAGING GENERATION X

Bruce Tulgan reports on his research of Generation X in the workplace. Xers, who are defined as Americans born between 1963 and 1977, are often stereotyped as slackers who feel no company loyalty, have short attention spans, and crave immediate gratification. Tulgan busts the slacker myth by viewing life and work through an Xer's lens. He presents four strategies for managers who want to retain and develop the rising stars in their young workforce. Includes a pocket-size version of Tulgan's book by the same title.

Release Year: 1997
Runtime: 30 minutes
Cost: $99.95
Film Type: Training
Subject(s): Emerging leaders, communication
Source: HRD Press. Amherst, MA. (800) 822-2801. www.hrdpress.com

MANDELA'S FIGHT FOR FREEDOM

Nelson Mandela's life is documented, from his early years as a protester against racial injustices in South Africa to his 26-year imprisonment and election as president of a new democracy in 1990. Mandela's early leadership helped to create the Youth League of the African National Congress and inspired the black political movement that eventually ended apartheid.

Release Year: 1995
Runtime: 150 minutes
Cost: $29.95
Film Type: Documentary
Subject(s): Political leadership; Mandela, N.; cultural context: South Africa
Source: PBS Video–Home Division. Alexandria, VA. (800) 531-4727. www.pbs.org

MARTIN LUTHER KING, JR.: FROM MONTGOMERY TO MEMPHIS

This black-and-white film surveys the career of Martin Luther King, Jr. and the nonviolent civil rights movement under his leadership—from the 1955-1956 bus boycott in Montgomery to his assassination in Memphis.

Release Year: 1969
Runtime: 26 minutes
Cost: $199.95
Film Type: Documentary
Subject(s): African American leadership; civil rights movement; King, M. L., Jr.
Source: Phoenix Coronet. St. Louis, MO. (800) 221-1274. www.phoenix-bfa-coronet.com

MAURITIUS: CELEBRATING DIFFERENCES

Stephen Covey takes viewers to the small island of Mauritius, an African nation where five distinct societies live, work, and govern together with respect for the diversity among them. They find synergy in their common values while cherishing the richness of their differences. Includes a *Leader's Discussion Guide* and participant handouts.

Release Year: 1995
Runtime: 26 minutes
Cost: $695
Film Type: Training
Subject(s): Multicultural diversity
Source: Franklin Covey. Salt Lake City, UT. (800) 654-1776. www.franklincovey.com

New
MAVERICKS OF SCIENCE

The scientists who have made the most important contributions to our world—including Copernicus, Da Vinci, and Einstein—were often considered dreamers or eccentrics in their own time. This video profiles four present-day scientists who are making revolutionary discoveries—despite their unusual methods—in their studies of hammerhead sharks, lightning, grizzly bears, and gray whales.

Release Year: 1999
Runtime: 47 minutes
Cost: $19.95
Film Type: Documentary
Subject(s): Entrepreneurs, innovation, science and technology
Source: Discovery Channel. Florence, KY. (800) 889-9950. www.shopping.discovery.com

MAX AND MAX: UNLEASHING THE POTENTIAL IN PEOPLE . . . AND DOGS!

Stephen Covey presents a humorous vignette about the parallel experiences of Max, the new employee, and Max, the new hunting dog. Both enter their new situations ready to put their training and innovative ideas to work. But an authoritarian leader imposes limits and stifles their initiative. Covey suggests that creating conditions to release their potential would yield better results for Max and his company and for Max and his owner. Includes a *Discussion Leader's Guide*.

Release Year: 1996
Runtime: 23 minutes
Cost: $695
Film Type: Training
Subject(s): Empowerment
Source: Franklin Covey. Salt Lake City, UT. (800) 654-1776. www.franklincovey.com

MEETINGS, BLOODY MEETINGS

This updated John Cleese video takes a humorous look at meetings that take too much of a manager's time and accomplish too little. It demonstrates, through whimsical drama, techniques for conducting meetings that are shorter and more productive.

Release Year: 1993
Runtime: 30 minutes
Cost: $870
Film Type: Training
Subject(s): Meetings
Source: Coastal Human Resources. Virginia Beach, VA. (800) 725-3418. www.coastal.com

New
MICHAEL COLLINS

Liam Neeson stars as Michael Collins, the Irish patriot and leader of the Irish Republican Army. This grassroots leader formed a bloody resistance to oppressive British rule in the early 20th century. After becoming a national hero he rejected violence and used negotiation to help his country achieve limited home rule known as the Irish Free State. This violent social movement may be contrasted to the nonviolent civil disobedience portrayed in the film *Gandhi* (1982).

Release Year: 1996
Runtime: 138 minutes
Cost: $16.99
Film Type: Feature
Subject(s): Social movements; cultural context: Ireland; political leadership
Source: Warner Home Video, Inc. Burbank, CA. (818) 954-6000.

THE MILAGRO BEANFIELD WAR

When a poor citizen kicks the water cutoff that separates the poor New Mexican town of Milagro from its wealthy neighbor, he accidentally irrigates his father's farmland. What ensues is a battle of legal rights, ethics, and a community's will to survive. Sonia Braga displays courage and persistence as she rallies the townspeople of Milagro to demand legal rights to the local water supply.

Release Year: 1988
Runtime: 118 minutes
Cost: $9.98
Film Type: Feature
Subject(s): Citizen leadership, Hispanic leadership
Source: Universal Studios Home Video. Universal City, CA. (818) 777-1000.

THE MISSILES OF OCTOBER

The Cuban missile crisis of October 16, 1962, is presented in this dramatic reenactment. The film follows the tensions and decisions faced by President Kennedy during the 12-day period when the United States and the Soviet Union confronted each other with nuclear destruction.

Release Year: 1975
Runtime: 155 minutes
Cost: $19.98
Film Type: Feature
Subject(s): Political leadership; crisis management; U.S. presidents: Kennedy, J. F.; history
Source: MPI Home Video. Orland Park, IL. (708) 460-0555. www.mpimedia.com

MORE BLOODY MEETINGS

This is a companion film to *Meetings, Bloody Meetings*. Where the other film concentrates on the mechanics of meetings, this one focuses on the human factor, including controlling aggression, keeping the group focused on the objective, and preventing dominant group members from overpowering the rest of the group. John Cleese stars.

Release Year: 1986
Runtime: 27 minutes
Cost: $870
Film Type: Training
Subject(s): Meetings
Source: Coastal Human Resources. Virginia Beach, VA. (800) 725-3418. www.coastal.com

New
MR. HOLLAND'S OPUS

Richard Dreyfuss is the high school band teacher who puts his family on hold as he dedicates attention to his students. He also neglects his passion—composing a symphony. His creative teaching style shocks and offends school administrators but he persists. After 30 years he wonders if his life's work has been worthwhile. A moving ending demonstrates the enormous appreciation his school, students, and family have for his creativity and his powerful influence. Hartwick Humanities in Management Institute (800-942-2737) offers a case study and teaching guide based on this film.

Release Year: 1995
Runtime: 142 minutes
Cost: $14.99
Film Type: Feature
Subject(s): Teacher as leader, musician as leader, work and family balance, organizational culture
Source: Movies Unlimited. Philadelphia, PA. (800) 668-4344. www.moviesunlimited.com

MR. SMITH GOES TO WASHINGTON

This black-and-white Frank Capra film features James Stewart, Jean Arthur, and Claude Rains. Stewart stars as an idealistic young statesman who finds nothing but corruption when he takes his seat in the Senate. The film illustrates how leaders deal with ethical issues and adversity.

Release Year: 1939
Runtime: 130 minutes
Cost: $19.95
Film Type: Feature
Subject(s): Political leadership, ethics
Source: Columbia Tristar Home Video. Culver City, CA. (310) 244-4000.

MUTINY ON THE BOUNTY

Clark Gable stars in this black-and-white adaptation of the 18th-century case in which Fletcher Christian leads a mutiny against the sadistic Captain Bligh. There is also a 1962 version with Marlon Brando and Trevor Howard available from the same source. And there is a 1984 version called *The Bounty* starring Mel Gibson and Anthony Hopkins available from Verstron Video. Hartwick Humanities in Management Institute (800-942-2737) offers a case study and teaching guide based on the 1984 film.

Release Year: 1935
Runtime: 132 minutes
Cost: $19.99
Film Type: Feature
Subject(s): Theory X and Theory Y, Path-goal Theory
Source: Movies Unlimited. Philadelphia, PA. (800) 668-4344. www.moviesunlimited.com

New
THE NEW PIONEERS

In this video, as in the 1999 book by the same title, Thomas Petzinger, Jr. chooses not to use the term *empowerment*. He states that power has always existed in the hands of the workforce. It can be unleashed if management simply gets out of the way. Video case studies at Monarch Marking Systems, DaimlerChrysler Financial Services, and Rowe Furniture illustrate this point as employees solve problems creatively and increase productivity. Includes a *Leader's Guide*.

Release Year: 1999
Runtime: 30 minutes
Cost: $695
Film Type: Training
Subject(s): Innovation, creative problem solving, participatory leadership
Source: corVision Media, Inc. Buffalo Grove, IL. (800) 537-3130. www.corvision.com

THE NEW WORKPLACE

A Native American storyteller uses folktales to deliver the message that change is a positive force in the workplace. There are two versions of her message: one for employees and one for organizational leaders. Includes a facilitator's guide with handouts to be photocopied, discussion questions, group exercises, and a bibliography.

Release Year: 1993
Runtime: Two tapes—23 minutes each
Cost: $722.50
Film Type: Training
Subject(s): Native American leadership, storytelling, change
Source: Coastal Human Resources. Virginia Beach, VA. (800) 725-3418. www.coastal.com

NORMA RAE

Sally Field portrays a textile worker whose life is changed by the arrival of a union organizer. Norma eventually joins his cause and begins to exert strong leadership in her plant. Hartwick Humanities in Management Institute (800-942-2737) offers a case study and teaching guide based on this film.

Release Year: 1979
Runtime: 115 minutes
Cost: $19.98
Film Type: Feature
Subject(s): Emergent leadership, women's leadership
Source: CBS/Fox Video. New York, NY. (877) 258-0794.

New
NORMAN SCHWARZKOPF

Schwarzkopf's leadership of American forces during the Gulf War earned him the nickname "Stormin' Norman" and made him a symbol of the new American military. This A&E

Biography uses news footage and interviews with Schwarzkopf's wife, sisters, and fellow soldiers to show how his experiences at West Point and in Vietnam helped him become a leader in the U.S. armed forces.

Release Year: 1998
Runtime: 50 minutes
Cost: $14.95
Film Type: Documentary
Subject(s): Military leadership; Schwartzkopf, N.; Gulf War
Source: A&E Home Video. South Burlington, VT. (800) 625-9000. www.aetv.com

New
NOT FOR OURSELVES ALONE

Filmmaker Ken Burns tells the story of Elizabeth Cady Stanton and Susan B. Anthony, two of the founders of this country's women's movement. The film uses historical materials and commentary by modern-day historians to describe the friendship between the two and how they worked together to lead the fight for women's suffrage.

Release Year: 1999
Runtime: 210 minutes
Cost: $29.98
Film Type: Documentary
Subject(s): Social movements; women's leadership; Anthony, Susan B.; Stanton, Elizabeth Cady
Source: PBS Video. Alexandria, VA. (800) 344-3337 (Educational Division) or (800) 531-4727 (Home Division). www.pbs.org

New
OCTOBER SKY

This feature film tells the true story of Homer Hickman, a West Virginia boy who was awestruck by his first vision of the Soviet satellite Sputnik in 1957. The experience led to a dream of escaping his coal mining heritage to build rockets and explore space. Faced with overwhelming obstacles, Hickman convinced three friends and one teacher to join his dream. Thanks to persistence and creativity, the "rocket boys" launched a success and won the national science fair. For their efforts, all the boys received college scholarships and a future away from the coal mines. Hickman achieved his dream of joining the space program and spent his career as a NASA engineer. This film provides an inspiring leadership lesson in setting and communicating a bold vision and the reward for doing the hard work necessary to achieve the vision.

Release Year: 1999
Runtime: 103 minutes
Cost: $29.98
Film Type: Feature
Subject(s): Vision, persistence, creativity
Source: Universal Studios Home Video. Universal City, CA. (818) 777-1000.

New
OFFICE SPACE

This satire of office life targets the minutiae that make up today's corporate world, including laser printers that jam for no reason, annoying cubicle neighbors, smooth-talking bosses, and office birthday parties. The film takes special aim at management consultants. When the main character decides to stop going to work, the consultants hired to downsize the company decide he has "management potential" and recommend him for a promotion.

Release Year: 1999
Runtime: 90 minutes
Cost: $9.98
Film Type: Feature
Subject(s): Management satire, humor
Source: Twentieth Century Fox Home Entertainment. Beverly Hills, CA. (888) 223-4360.

ORPHEUS IN THE REAL WORLD: 26 MUSICIANS, 26 CONDUCTORS

This film documents the participatory leadership style of the New York City-based chamber orchestra, Orpheus. The musicians demonstrate in planning meetings, practice sessions, and concerts why they prefer to share leadership rather than follow the lead of a conductor. They believe that the artistry and energy that emerge from strong personal commitment far outweigh the difficulties of the democratic process. This film inspired the ensemble of researchers and authors of *A Social Change Model of Leadership Development* (Astin & Astin, 1996).

Release Year: 1995
Runtime: 56 minutes
Cost: $69.95
Film Type: Documentary
Subject(s): Participatory leadership
Source: Four Oaks Foundation. New York, NY. (212) 753-6677.

PARADIGM MASTERY SERIES

Futurist Joel Barker holds a video retreat to discuss the management of organizational change. Participants share their experiences and new revelations about identifying new trends, encouraging those who break out of the boundaries, and harnessing the enthusiasm around new ideas. The retreat is divided into five segments: Change and Leadership, The Paradigm Effect, The Paradigm Curve, Paradigm Partners, and Paradigm Hunting.

Release Year: 1997
Runtime: Five segments—30 minutes each
Cost: $1,485
Film Type: Training
Subject(s): Future of leadership
Source: Star Thrower Distribution Corp. Saint Paul, MN. (800) 242-3220. www.starthrower.com

A PEACOCK IN THE LAND OF PENGUINS

A fable based on the book by Barbara Hateley and Warren Schmidt (Berrett-Koehler, 1995) takes us to the Land of Opportunity, where workers and bosses don't waste time or energy pretending to be something they're not. They know many types of qualities and strengths are needed to succeed in turbulent times. They also know that the most important requirements for success are acceptance and trust, which allow each bird of a different feather to fly.

Release Year: 1995
Runtime: 10 minutes
Cost: $495
Film Type: Training
Subject(s): Diversity, parables
Source: CRM Learning. Carlsbad, CA. (800) 421-0833. www.crmlearning.com

New
PIGEON-HOLED IN THE LAND OF PENGUINS

In the animated "sea of organizations" the Land of Penguins celebrates its diverse workforce. Some non-penguins are even promoted to management positions. However, most birds are stereotyped, their assignments based on appearances and presumed talents. Declining productivity and scarce resources force the birds to tear down boundaries and maximize individual talents. When the penguins, pigeons, hawks, parrots, and swans work together they realize the unique skills that each bird brings to the task, they share ideas, and they learn from each other. Includes a *Leader's Guide*.

Release Year: 1999
Runtime: 10 minutes
Cost: $495
Film Type: Training
Subject(s): Diversity, cross-functional teams
Source: CRM Learning. Carlsbad, CA. (800) 421-0833. www.crmlearning.com

New
THE POWER DEAD EVEN RULE: AND OTHER GENDER DIFFERENCES IN THE WORKPLACE

In this video seminar Pat Heim describes the cultural differences between men and women that stem from childhood games and play out in the workforce. While most boys play competitive games and seek win-lose outcomes, girls play dolls and seek to build relationships. Boys learn to focus on goals and girls practice process. As adults in the workplace, men find hierarchies comfortable. Women prefer a flat structure in which everyone has dead-even power. Heim explains how to resolve the differences to improve everyone's communication and comfort. Includes a discussion guide.

Release Year: 1995
Runtime: 36 minutes
Cost: $495

Film Type: Training
Subject(s): Gender diversity
Source: corVision Media, Inc. Buffalo Grove, IL. (800) 537-3130. www.corvision.com

New
THE POWER OF FUTURE CONVERSATION

This film is based on Kim Krisco's book *Leadership and the Art of Conversation* (Prima, 1997). Work and family scenarios illustrate how conversation can be managed to effect desired change. "Speech acts" occur in one of three realms: past, the realm of history; present, the realm of action; or future, the realm of possibility. Shifting conversations from the past directly to the future energizes commitment before pulling back to plan action in the present. Includes a leader's guide.

Release Year: 1999
Runtime: 18 minutes
Cost: $695
Film Type: Training
Subject(s): Communication
Source: CRM Learning. Carlsbad, CA. (800) 421-0833. www.crmlearning.com

THE PRACTICAL COACH

This film is intended for self-study use by supervisors and middle managers. Through a simple message and a little humor, viewers identify good coaching experiences from their past to develop their own coaching style. The message is that if you let people know that what they do matters to you, coaching can be a rewarding experience for all parties.

Release Year: 1997
Runtime: 24 minutes
Cost: $625
Film Type: Training
Subject(s): Coaching
Source: CRM Films. Carlsbad, CA. (800) 421-0833. www.crmfilms.com

THE PRACTICALITY OF A RADICAL WORKPLACE

Peter Block explains how stewardship focuses on empowerment as it relates to individual and team ownership and responsibility. He also talks about choosing service over self-interest, partnership over parenting, adventure over safety, and defining the stewardship contract.

Release Year: 1994
Runtime: 90 minutes
Cost: $69.95
Film Type: Training
Subject(s): Empowerment
Source: ASTD. Valencia, CA. (800) 369-5718. www.mobiltape.com

RAINBOW WAR

An animated short film that won several awards, *Rainbow War* can illustrate issues dealing with differences, whether cultural, racial, or other. Three kingdoms—Blue, Red, and Yellow—fight a colorful battle for supremacy, but in the end all are winners. Confrontation is transformed into collaboration and the colors blend into the world's first rainbow.

Release Year: 1986
Runtime: 20 minutes
Cost: $295
Film Type: Training
Subject(s): Diversity
Source: Pyramid Media. Santa Monica, CA. (800) 421-2304. www.pyramedia.com

RESILIENCE

Daryl Conner, a specialist in change management, identifies five key characteristics that resilient people have in common. They are positive, focused, flexible, organized, and proactive. He also shows how to cultivate these qualities in yourself and your organization. Includes a leader's guide.

Release Year: 1993
Runtime: 17 minutes
Cost: $595
Film Type: Training
Subject(s): Change management, resilience
Source: Mentor Media. Pasadena, CA. (800) 359-1935. www.mentmedia.com

New
RIDING THE WAVE: STRATEGIES FOR CHANGE

Susan Campbell's book *From Chaos to Confidence* (Simon & Schuster, 1995) inspired this video about change. When change keeps coming like the waves of an ocean, we can adopt "security control mindsets" to resist the change or we can ride the waves like surfers. To adopt surfer attitudes and behaviors the video suggests six elements of "learning discovery": 1) learn to be comfortable with discomfort, 2) learn to learn in public, 3) let go of expectations about how things should be, 4) communicate with the intent to share learning, 5) think in terms of both/and, and 6) focus on essential personal and team values. Three workplace scenarios dramatize the movement from control mind-set to discovery learning.

Release Year: 1999
Runtime: 18 minutes
Cost: $695
Film Type: Training
Subject(s): Change
Source: CRM Learning. Carlsbad, CA. (800) 421-0833. www.crmlearning.com

ROBERT K. GREENLEAF: SERVANT-LEADER

This program introduces the viewer to Greenleaf and to the concept of servant leadership. Biographical information about Greenleaf and Greenleaf's own commentary put the subject in historical context and apply it to modern life.

Release Year: 1991
Runtime: 14 minutes
Cost: $25
Film Type: Training
Subject(s): Servant leadership
Source: The Robert K. Greenleaf Center. Indianapolis, IN. (317) 259-1241. www.greenleaf.org

New
ROCKING THE BOAT: WOMEN RACE FOR THE AMERICA'S CUP

This video chronicles America3 chairman Bill Koch's 1995 decision to use an all-woman team to defend the prestigious sailing trophy, the America's Cup. Doubters said that a women's team wouldn't have the physical strength or competitive spirit to be a dominant force in this male domain. However, Koch believed that the women could achieve extraordinary things if they had the right focus, teamwork, attitude, dedication, and technology. The team prevailed in winning the final race and placing second overall.

Release Year: 1995
Runtime: 32 minutes
Cost: $395
Film Type: Training
Subject(s): Women's leadership, teams
Source: corVision Media, Inc. Buffalo Grove, IL. (800) 537-3130. www.corvision.com

New
SAVING PRIVATE RYAN

Steven Spielberg's Oscar-winning World War II film is about a unit of men who survive the D-Day landing and are sent to rescue a soldier from behind enemy lines. Tom Hanks stars as Captain John Miller, whose quiet leadership holds his men together despite a near-suicidal mission. *Time* described the key to Miller's leadership as "the reserve beneath his openness, hinting at unspoken competencies that make . . . the troops he commands willing to follow."

Release Year: 1998
Runtime: 170 minutes
Cost: $24.99
Film Type: Feature
Subject(s): Military leadership, World War II, group dynamics
Source: Paramount Home Video. Los Angeles, CA. (213) 956-3952.

SISTER ACT

Whoopi Goldberg poses as a nun to escape her mobster boyfriend. While in hiding, her unique vision of music with "soul" jumpstarts the convent's tortured choir. In time, the music's energy revitalizes the connecting church and the surrounding community. Contrasting leadership styles are portrayed by the tyrannical former choir director, the peacekeeping priest, and the competitive Mother Superior.

Release Year: 1992
Runtime: 100 minutes
Cost: $19.99
Film Type: Feature
Subject(s): Contrasting leadership styles, spirit, women's leadership
Source: Movies Unlimited. Philadelphia, PA. (800) 668-4344. www.moviesunlimited.com

New
SITTING BULL: CHIEF OF THE LAKOTA

Sitting Bull, one of the last leaders of the Indian Resistance movement, gained fame for defeating Custer at Little Big Horn but spent some of his last years as a performer in Buffalo Bill's Wild West Show. This A&E Biography uses period accounts to describe how Sitting Bull improved Native American warfare strategies and led early fights against settlers.

Release Year: 1998
Runtime: 50 minutes
Cost: $14.95
Film Type: Documentary
Subject(s): Native American leadership, Sitting Bull
Source: A&E Home Video. South Burlington, VT. (800) 625-9000. www.aetv.com

New
SMALL WONDERS

This is a documentary about Roberta Guaspari-Tzavaras, the East Harlem music teacher who lost her job to budget cuts but found a new way to continue teaching violin. As founder of the nonprofit Opus 118 Music Center, she conveys to her students a love of music and appreciation for discipline. Some of the successes enjoyed by her students are playing the national anthem at a Knicks game and a Fiddlefest concert at Carnegie Hall. Isaac Stern and Itzhak Perlman make brief appearances. Guaspari-Tzavaras's story inspired the feature film *Music of the Heart* (1999).

Release Year: 1996
Runtime: 85 minutes
Cost: $16.99
Film Type: Documentary
Subject(s): Teacher as leader, musician as leader, commitment
Source: Movies Unlimited. Philadelphia, PA. (800) 668-4344. www.moviesunlimited.com

New
SOARING WITH THE PHOENIX: RENEWING THE VISION, REVIVING THE SPIRIT, AND RE-CREATING THE SUCCESS OF YOUR COMPANY

In this follow-up to *Flight of the Buffalo* James Belasco and Jerre Stead discuss how leaders can renew their organiza-

tions by recognizing and developing the power their employees possess. They advocate providing all employees with information on their individual work and the firm's performance, arguing that this instills a sense of accountability and leadership in all workers. Case studies from the U.S. Naval Depot and Ingram Micro, Inc. illustrate the importance of rewarding employees for customer service, providing learning opportunities, and leaving a legacy of empowerment.

Release Year: 1999
Runtime: 34 minutes
Cost: $695
Film Type: Training
Subject(s): Empowerment
Source: CRM Learning. Carlsbad, CA. (800) 421-0833. www.crmlearning.com

SOLVING CONFLICT

Solving Conflict addresses new managers on an important topic: interpersonal conflict. By dramatizing a conflict and its resolution, the video imparts basic conflict-management skills. Includes a workbook with role-play exercises.

Release Year: 1993
Runtime: 21 minutes
Cost: $695
Film Type: Training
Subject(s): Conflict management
Source: American Media, Inc. West Des Moines, IA. (800) 262-2557. www.ammedia.com

THE SPIRIT OF PERSONAL MASTERY

After Peter Senge's introduction, Joel Suzuki tells a story of a master violin maker who exemplifies personal mastery. Personal mastery is one of five disciplines that can transform an organization by increasing its capacity to learn. This story illustrates the concept by showing that the desire for a shared vision will only have depth and power if it embraces personal visions, those that are truly meaningful to each individual.

Release Year: 1994
Runtime: 7 minutes
Cost: $395
Film Type: Training
Subject(s): Vision, organizational learning
Source: ChartHouse International Learning Corporation. Burnsville, MN. (800) 328-3789. www.charthouse.com

STAND AND DELIVER

In this fact-based feature film, a high school mathematics teacher takes a class of potential dropouts and transforms them in one year into kids who want to learn and who do learn—at year's end 18 class members are able to pass a tough advanced-placement calculus exam. The story provides a dramatic exposition of the teacher as leader.

Release Year: 1988
Runtime: 105 minutes

Cost: $14.95
Film Type: Feature
Subject(s): Teacher as leader, transformational leadership, Hispanic leadership
Source: Warner Home Video, Inc. Burbank, CA. (818) 954-6000.

New
STAR TREK: FIRST CONTACT

In this eighth installment in the Star Trek series, Captain Picard and his crew must go back in time to stop the villainous Borg from changing history. Picard's history with the Borg makes it an especially personal mission, and in one pivotal scene the captain is forced to differentiate between leadership and vengeance. A discussion of the leadership qualities Picard displays, including focus, initiative, interdependence, and resilience, is found in B. Ross (1996), "'Make it so': Captain Picard offers lessons in leadership," *Electronic Media*, *15*(48), 18.

Release Year: 1996
Runtime: 111 minutes
Cost: $14.95
Film Type: Feature
Subject(s): Military leadership, initiative, resilience
Source: Paramount Home Video. Los Angeles, CA. (213) 956-3952.

SURVIVAL RUN

Harry Cordellos, a blind marathon runner, and a sighted partner run the grueling Dipsea course near San Francisco. This award-winning video shows a highly motivated team that overcomes seemingly insurmountable risks and difficulties to achieve its goal.

Release Year: 1979
Runtime: 12 minutes
Cost: $295
Film Type: Training
Subject(s): Motivation, teams
Source: Pyramid Media. Santa Monica, CA. (800) 421-2304. www.pyramedia.com

New
TACTICS OF INNOVATION

This video introduces five tactics to ensure that good, new ideas are well presented and well received. One can overcome others' resistance to change by: 1) focusing on the upside, 2) keeping it simple and taking small steps, 3) creating a clear message and a compatible fit, 4) using a credible messenger, and 5) reducing the costs and frustrations of trying new ideas. Includes a *Leader's Guide* and a *Participant Workbook*.

Release Year: 1998
Runtime: 25 minutes
Cost: $895
Film Type: Training

Subject(s): Innovation
Source: Star Thrower Distribution Corp. Saint Paul, MN. (800) 242-3220. www.starthrower.com

A TALE OF "O": ON BEING DIFFERENT

This revised edition provides an objective, animated look at diversity (being different in any way). Rosabeth Moss Kanter and Barry Stein explore the human problem of what it's like to be the few among many by using Xs and Os in an abstract and therefore widely applicable way. By explaining the impact on people's performance in work groups, it makes points that can defuse conflict, promote mutual understanding, and prevent problems before they occur. Includes a training manual. *Land of O's* (1995) continues the message.

Release Year: 1993
Runtime: 18 minutes
Cost: $695
Film Type: Training
Subject(s): Diversity
Source: Goodmeasure Direct, Inc. Cambridge, MA. (617) 868-8662. www.goodmeasure.com

TALKING 9 TO 5: WOMEN AND MEN IN THE WORKPLACE

Miscommunication can result in lower morale, lost productivity, and nonfunctional teams. Deborah Tannen shows how our natural conversational styles differ, affect our work, and affect how others perceive us. *Talking 9 to 5* will help increase awareness and understanding of the different conversational styles.

Release Year: 1995
Runtime: 29 minutes
Cost: $695
Film Type: Training
Subject(s): Gender diversity, communication
Source: ChartHouse International Learning Corporation. Burnsville, MN. (800) 328-3789. www.charthouse.com

TEAMS AND ORGANIZATIONAL CHANGE

Jon Katzenbach and Douglas Smith take viewers behind the scenes at the Ritz-Carlton, Magna Metals, and Sealed Air Corporation to show how they successfully implemented a team-based management structure. High-performance teams help failing businesses, improve customer service, and boost productivity in sustainable ways.

Release Year: 1994
Runtime: 40 minutes
Cost: $595
Film Type: Training
Subject(s): Teams, change
Source: Harvard Business School Publishing. Boston, MA. (800) 988-0886. www.hbsp.harvard.edu

TEARING DOWN WALLS: MANAGING CHANGE AND DISMANTLING BARRIERS TO BETTER TEAM AND ORGANIZATIONAL PERFORMANCE

Stephen Covey introduces a discussion about the Berlin Wall among those who lived on both sides. The citizens of the divided city explain their feelings of disbelief, anger, and sadness when they lost the freedom to visit family members, hold jobs, and worship on the other side. Over time, the frustration gave way to acceptance. When the wall came down, a deep chasm remained and will take many years to repair. Covey describes this as a metaphor for organizational barriers that create walls between people and departments. Includes a *Discussion Leader's Guide* and participant handouts.

Release Year: 1996
Runtime: 21 minutes
Cost: $695
Film Type: Training
Subject(s): Relationships, organizational barriers
Source: Franklin Covey. Salt Lake City, UT. (800) 654-1776. www.franklincovey.com

New
THEODORE ROOSEVELT: ROUGHRIDER TO RUSHMORE

This A&E Biography argues that Teddy Roosevelt redefined the role of the American president by aggressively leading antitrust fights, the development of the conservation movement, and the campaign to construct the Panama Canal. The film also shows the range of Roosevelt's leadership: although he gained early fame in the Spanish-American War, in 1906 he became the first American to win a Nobel Peace Prize.

Release Year: 1997
Runtime: 50 minutes
Cost: $14.95
Film Type: Documentary
Subject(s): Political leadership; U.S. presidents: Roosevelt, T.
Source: A&E Home Video. South Burlington, VT. (800) 625-9000. www.aetv.com

New
THOMAS JEFFERSON

This film by Ken Burns focuses on Jefferson's political life, describing how he helped create a new form of democratic government, became U.S. Minister to France, and rose through the ranks of national politics to become president. It also explains the conflicts he felt between his political career and his family responsibilities, and addresses the controversy surrounding Jefferson's status as a slave-owner.

Release Year: 1996
Runtime: 180 minutes
Cost: $29.98
Film Type: Documentary

Subject(s): Political leadership; U.S. presidents: Jefferson, T.
Source: PBS Video. Alexandria, VA. (800) 344-3337 (Educational Division) or (800) 531-4727 (Home Division). www.pbs.org

TWELVE ANGRY MEN

This film depicts a classic courtroom drama of a hasty jury and one member who quietly makes the others consider their preemptive decision. It is a study of personal conviction and courage under heavy pressure. Henry Fonda stars as the informal leader who eventually sways the others to listen to reason. Hartwick Humanities in Management Institute (800-942-2737) offers a case study and teaching guide based on this film.

Release Year: 1957
Runtime: 95 minutes
Cost: $19.98
Film Type: Feature
Subject(s): Influence, group dynamics, integrity
Source: Movies Unlimited. Philadelphia, PA. (800) 668-4344. www.moviesunlimited.com

New
TWELVE ANGRY MEN: TEAMS THAT DON'T QUIT

Margaret Wheatley hosts this dramatization of team decision making. Clips from the classic 1957 film *Twelve Angry Men* demonstrate the messy but necessary process of making thorough and fair decisions. Henry Fonda's character is the true leader of the 12-man jury that must decide a murder case. He is the lone voice of courage that opens discussion and encourages each juror to contribute to the process. Wheatley compares Fonda's leadership style, the necessity of conflict, and the benefit of diverse perspectives to the team decision-making process in the workplace.

Release Year: 1999
Runtime: 25 minutes
Cost: $795
Film Type: Training
Subject(s): Group decision making
Source: Media Learning Resources. Rosemont, PA. (800) 474-1604. www.medialearning.com

TWELVE O'CLOCK HIGH

A psychological drama that deals with the problems of an Air Force commander who must rebuild a bomber group whose shattered morale threatens the effectiveness of daylight bombing raids. An edited version (34 minutes) is now available, but if you have time for the unedited version, go with it. Hartwick Humanities in Management Institute (800-942-2737) offers a case study and teaching guide based on this film.

Release Year: 1949
Runtime: 132 minutes
Cost: $14.98

Film Type: Feature
Subject(s): Situational leadership, vision, goal setting
Source: CBS/Fox Video. New York, NY. (877) 258-0794.

New
THE UNIFIED TEAM: A LEADER'S PLAN FOR PROMOTING, PROTECTING AND RESTORING TEAM UNITY

This video refers to a team leader as a coach and describes that role in handling the feelings of team members. Although feelings can be messy and uncomfortable, they are the reasons that members commit to teams. Members need to achieve, to belong, and to contribute. Several workplace scenarios demonstrate how coaches assure that these needs are met. A video quiz sets the stage for a discussion of S.M.A.R.T. goals—Specific, Measurable, Ambitious, Reachable, and Time bound—that foster team unity. Includes a *Trainer's Guide.*

Release Year: 1998
Runtime: 26 minutes
Cost: $625
Film Type: Training
Subject(s): Teams, coaching
Source: corVision Media, Inc. Buffalo Grove, IL. (800) 537-3130. www.corvision.com

UNITED STATES PRESIDENTS

This series profiles U.S. presidents from George Washington to Bill Clinton from their youth to their early careers and the years in office. The world events that shaped each presidency and the legacies left by each man are examined.

Release Year: 1995
Runtime: Five tapes—60 minutes each
Cost: $99.98 for the set
Film Type: Documentary
Subject(s): Political leadership, U.S. presidents
Source: PBS Video–Home Division. Alexandria, VA. (800) 531-4727. www.pbs.org

New
THE VISION OF TEAMS: LEARNING TO WORK TOGETHER TO ACHIEVE A COMMON GOAL

Cross-country skier Ann Bancroft describes the challenge and adventure of leading her all-woman team across Antarctica to the South Pole. Several factors helped the team complete its 200-mile journey on icy terrain and in subzero temperatures. Bancroft built a cohesive team from four experienced but strong-willed women. Each was passionate about the goal, and during times of stress and fatigue each team member renewed her commitment. The team learned together from their mistakes and took action together to support each other's success. A *Leader's Guide* and *Participant Workbook* suggest training activities and discussion topics.

Release Year: 1998
Runtime: 24 minutes
Cost: $625
Film Type: Training
Subject(s): Team building, women's leadership
Source: Star Thrower Distribution Corp. Saint Paul, MN. (800) 242-3220. www.starthrower.com

WALL STREET

The characters in this drama are caught up in the unethical culture of insider trading. Neophyte stockbroker Charlie Sheen is torn between the glamour of his greedy mentor and the scruples of his blue-collar father. Hartwick Humanities in Management Institute (800-942-2737) offers a case study and teaching guide based on this film.

Release Year: 1987
Runtime: 126 minutes
Cost: $19.98
Film Type: Feature
Subject(s): Abuse of power, ethics
Source: CBS/Fox Video. New York, NY. (877) 258-0794.

New
WHO MOVED MY CHEESE?

This cartoon features two mice and two little people who love cheese (a metaphor that represents whatever we want in life). Every day they venture into the maze (the workplace) to find cheese. For a while they have a familiar path to a rich source of cheese but, in time, it disappears. The mice, with their simple brains and good instincts, set out to find another source through trial and error. The little people, with their complex brains and emotions, have trouble coping with the change. When one breaks free of his fear and embraces the new challenge, he discovers a better source of cheese and fulfillment. Throughout the maze he posts his revelations about change to serve as "writings on the wall" for his friend. A training package is available for $895 that contains ten participant workbooks, a presenter's guide, a CD-ROM with transparency masters, an audio book, and ten copies of Spencer Johnson and Kenneth Blanchard's 1998 book on which this film is based.

Release Year: 1999
Runtime: 13 minutes
Cost: $495
Film Type: Training
Subject(s): Resistance to change
Source: CRM Learning. Carlsbad, CA. (800) 421-0833. www.crmlearning.com

WIN TEAMS: HOW ONE COMPANY MADE EMPOWERMENT WORK

A successful turnaround at General Electric Mobile Communications is described. Team members and supervisors describe the Winshare program and its self-managed teams who have the authority to make job improvement and budget decisions. A leader's guide suggests how to use this film with hourly workers, supervisors, and managers.

Release Year: 1994
Runtime: 26 minutes
Cost: $595
Film Type: Training
Subject(s): Self-managed teams
Source: Video Visions. Atlanta, GA. (404) 521-3456.

New
WINNING WITH WOMEN: CHANGING THE WAY WE LEAD

Over 20 years' experience coaching championship soccer teams has taught Anson Dorrance about leadership and the differences between men and women. In this video he describes learning through trial and error as he coached men's and women's teams at the University of North Carolina. The naturally self-confident male players were motivated by the coach's criticism. Female players, naturally self-critical, were motivated by focusing on strengths instead of weaknesses. Men favored public praise, women preferred praise in private. Women responded to a caring style of coaching, men to intimidation. Men required intense physical practices and warm-ups. Women performed better when practices and warm-ups provided a time for social connection with teammates. The women also needed permission to compete against each other in practice without risking social acceptance. To sum up his experience, Dorrance says he taught his female players to compete and they taught him to relate. Includes a discussion guide.

Release Year: 1999
Runtime: 27 minutes
Cost: $395
Film Type: Training
Subject(s): Gender diversity, coaching, sports leadership
Source: LearnCom. Bensenville, IL. (800) 824-8889. www.lrncom.com

New
WOODROW WILSON: RELUCTANT WARRIOR

Although his pacifist beliefs made Wilson reluctant to involve the U.S. in World War I, his leadership during the war and in the international policy development that followed helped transform America's position in the world. This A&E Biography describes how his controversial domestic strategies were balanced by superior leadership in foreign policy.

Release Year: 1998
Runtime: 50 minutes
Cost: $14.95
Film Type: Documentary
Subject(s): Political leadership; U.S. presidents: Wilson, W.; World War I
Source: A&E Home Video. South Burlington, VT. (800) 625-9000. www.aetv.com

WORKTEAMS AND THE WIZARD OF OZ

Ken Blanchard draws lessons on group dynamics and team leadership from the classic film. Dorothy, the scarecrow, the tin man, and the lion have personal goals yet realize that joining forces will help them succeed. Together they learn about cooperation, mutual support, diversity, openness, facing obstacles, and creative risk-taking. Includes a leader's guide and participant's workbook.

Release Year: 1994
Runtime: 18 minutes
Cost: $695
Film Type: Training
Subject(s): Group dynamics
Source: CRM Films. Carlsbad, CA. (800) 421-0833. www.crmfilms.com

VIDEO DISTRIBUTORS

To buy or rent a video, contact the distributors listed in the directory. An address, phone, and fax number are provided for each. E-mail and website addresses are provided when available. These distributors are your appropriate contacts for copyright information and permission to use videos in the classroom.

A&E HOME VIDEO
P.O. Box 2284
South Burlington, VT 05407
Phone: (800) 625-9000 or (212) 210-1340
Fax: (802) 864-9846
Website: www.aetv.com

AMAZON.COM
1200 12th Avenue South, Suite 1200
Seattle, WA 98144
Phone: (800) 201-7575
Website: www.amazon.com

AMERICAN MEDIA, INC.
4900 University Avenue, Suite 100
West Des Moines, IA 50266-6769
Phone: (800) 262-2557
Fax: (515) 224-0256
E-mail: ami@ammedia.com
Website: www.ammedia.com

ARTISAN ENTERTAINMENT
6405 Muirfield Drive
Hanover Park, IL 60103
Phone: (877) 848-3865
Fax: (310) 470-3785
E-mail: orders@artisanent.com
Website: www.artisanent.com

ASH QUARRY PRODUCTIONS, INC.
12444 Ventura Boulevard, Suite 203
Studio City, CA 91604-2409
Phone: (800) 717-0777 or (818) 761-4448
Fax: (818) 761-7277
E-mail: info@ashquarry.com
Website: www.ashquarry.com

ASTD
Mobiltape Company Inc.
24730 Avenue Tibbitts, Suite 170
Valencia, CA 91355-4768
Phone: (800) 369-5718 or (661) 295-0504
Fax: (661) 295-8474
E-mail: sales@mobiltape.com
Website: www.mobiltape.com

CAREERTRACK PUBLICATIONS
3085 Center Green Drive
Boulder, CO 80301-5408
Phone: (800) 488-0928
Fax: (918) 665-3434
E-mail: customerservice@careertrack.com
Website: www.careertrack.com

CBS/FOX VIDEO
1330 Avenue of the Americas
New York, NY 10019-5400

Phone: (877) 258-0794 or (212) 373-4800
E-mail: foxstore-support@ivendor.com

CHARTHOUSE INTERNATIONAL LEARNING CORPORATION
221 River Ridge Circle
Burnsville, MN 55337
Phone: (800) 328-3789 or (612) 890-1800
Fax: (612) 890-0505
E-mail: info@charthouse.com
Website: www.charthouse.com

COASTAL HUMAN RESOURCES
3083 Brickhouse Court
Virginia Beach, VA 23452-6854
Phone: (800) 725-3418 or (757) 498-9014
Fax: (757) 498-3657
E-mail: sales@coastal.com
Website: www.coastal.com

COLUMBIA TRISTAR HOME VIDEO
SONY Pictures Plaza
10202 West Washington Boulevard
Culver City, CA 90232
Phone: (310) 244-4000
Fax: (310) 280-2485

CORVISION MEDIA INC.
1359 Barclay Boulevard
Buffalo Grove, IL 60089
Phone: (800) 537-3130 or (847) 537-3100
Fax: (847) 537-3353
E-mail: corvision@aol.com
Website: www.corvision.com

CRM LEARNING
2215 Faraday Avenue
Carlsbad, CA 92008-7295
Phone: (800) 421-0833 or (760) 431-9800
Fax: (760) 931-5792
Website: www.crmlearning.com

DIRECT CINEMA LIMITED
P.O. Box 10003
Santa Monica, CA 90410-9003
Phone: (800) 525-0000 or (310) 636-8200
Fax: (310) 636-8228

DISCOVERY CHANNEL HOME VIDEO
P.O. Box 6448
Florence, KY 41022-6448
Phone: (800) 889-9950
E-mail: DCOL_customer_service@discovery.com
Website: www.shopping.discovery.com

ENTERPRISE MEDIA
91 Harvey Street, 3rd Floor
Cambridge, MA 02140-1718
Phone: (800) 423-6021 or (617) 354-0017
Fax: (617) 354-1637
E-mail: stewart@enterprisemedia.com
Website: www.enterprisemedia.com

FILMS FOR THE HUMANITIES AND SCIENCES
P.O. Box 2053
Princeton, NJ 08543-2053
Phone: (800) 257-5126 or (609) 275-1400
Fax: (609) 275-3767
E-mail: custserv@films.com
Website: www.films.com

FOUR OAKS FOUNDATION
635 Madison Avenue, 16th Floor
New York, NY 10022-1009
Phone: (212) 753-6677
Fax: (212) 752-2483

FRANKLIN COVEY
2200 West Parkway Boulevard
Salt Lake City, UT 84119-2099
Phone: (800) 654-1776 or (800) 655-1492
E-mail: comments@franklincovey.com
Website: www.franklincovey.com

GOODMEASURE DIRECT, INC.
One Memorial Drive, 16th Floor
Cambridge, MA 02142-1313
Phone: (617) 868-8662
Fax: (617) 576-7671
E-mail: info@goodmeasure.com
Website: www.goodmeasure.com

GREYLOCK ASSOCIATES
283 River Drive
Tequesta, FL 33469
Phone: (888) 279-4857
Fax: (561) 748-6327
E-mail: garyr@greylockassociates.com
Website: www.greylockassociates.com

HARVARD BUSINESS SCHOOL PUBLISHING
60 Harvard Way, Box 230-5C
Boston, MA 02163-1001
Phone: (800) 988-0886
Fax: (617) 496-1029
E-mail: corpcustserv@hbsp.harvard.edu
Website: www.hbsp.harvard.edu

HRD PRESS
22 Amherst Road
Amherst, MA 01002-9709
Phone: (800) 822-2801 or (413) 253-3488

Fax: (413) 253-3490
E-mail: orders@hrdpress.com
Website: www.hrdpress.com

JOSSEY-BASS/PFEIFFER
350 Sansome Street
San Francisco, CA 94104-1342
Phone: (800) 274-4434
Fax: (800) 569-0443
E-mail: pfeiffer@jbp.com
Website: www.pfeiffer.com

LEARNCOM
714 Industrial Drive
Bensenville, IL 60106
Phone: (800) 824-8889 or (630) 227-1080
Fax: (630) 238-9088
E-mail: sales@lrncom.com
Website: www.lrncom.com

MEDIA LEARNING RESOURCES
919 Conestoga Road
Building II, Suite 304
Rosemont, PA 19010-1352
Phone: (800) 474-1604 or (610) 527-9400
Fax: (610) 527-9400
Website: www.medialearning.com

MENTOR MEDIA
275 East California Boulevard
Pasadena, CA 91106-3615
Phone: (800) 359-1935 or (626) 449-8900
Fax: (626) 449-2624
E-mail: info@mentmedia.com
Website: www.mentmedia.com

MGM/UA HOME VIDEO, INC.
2500 Broadway
Santa Monica, CA 90404
Phone: (310) 449-3000

MOVIES UNLIMITED
3015 Darnell Road
Philadelphia, PA 19154-3295
Phone: (800) 668-4344 or (215) 637-4444
Fax: (215) 637-2350
E-mail: movies@moviesunlimited.com
Website: www.moviesunlimited.com

MPI HOME VIDEO
16101 South 108th Avenue
Orland Park, IL 60467-5305
Phone: (708) 460-0555
Fax: (708) 873-3177
E-mail: klynch@mpimedia.com
Website: www.mpimedia.com

PARAMOUNT HOME VIDEO
Bluhdorn Building
5555 Melrose Avenue
Los Angeles, CA 90038-3197
Phone: (213) 956-3952

PBS VIDEO
1320 Braddock Place, Suite 200
Alexandria, VA 22314-1698
Phone: (800) 344-3337 (Educational Division),
   (800) 531-4727 (Home Division)
Fax: (703) 739-8131
E-mail: shop@pbs.org
Website: www.pbs.org

PHOENIX CORONET
2349 Chaffee Drive
St. Louis, MO 63146-3306
Phone: (800) 221-1274 or (314) 569-0211
Fax: (314) 569-2834
E-mail: phoenixfilms@worldnet.att.net
Website: www.phoenix-bfa-coronet.com

POLYGRAM FILMED ENTERTAINMENT
825 8th Avenue
New York, NY 10019
Phone: (800) 825-7781 or (212) 333-8000
Fax: (212) 603-7960

PYRAMID MEDIA
P.O. Box 1048
Santa Monica, CA 90406
Phone: (800) 421-2304 or (310) 828-7577
Fax: (310) 453-9083
E-mail: sales@pyramedia.com
Website: www.pyramedia.com

QUESTAR VIDEO, INC.
P.O. Box 11345
Chicago, IL 60611-0345
Phone: (800) 544-8422 or (312) 266-9400
Fax: (312) 266-9523
E-mail: info@questar1.com
Website: www.questar1.com

THE ROBERT K. GREENLEAF CENTER
921 East 86th Street, Suite 200
Indianapolis, IN 46240-1841
Phone: (317) 259-1241
Fax: (317) 259-0560
E-mail: resources@greenleaf.org
Website: www.greenleaf.org

STAR THROWER DISTRIBUTION CORP.
26 Exchange Street East, Suite 600
Saint Paul, MN 55101

Phone: (800) 242-3220 or (651) 602-9630
Fax: (651) 602-0037
E-mail: info@starthrower.com
Website: www.starthrower.com

THINKING ALLOWED
2560 Ninth Street, Suite 123
Berkeley, CA 94710-2563
Phone: (800) 999-4415 or (510) 548-4415
Fax: (510) 548-4275
E-mail: thinking@ThinkingAllowed.com
Website: www.thinking-allowed.com

TWENTIETH CENTURY FOX HOME ENTERTAINMENT
P.O. Box 900
Beverly Hills, CA 90213
Phone: (888) 223-4360 or (310) 369-3900
Fax: (310) 369-5811

UNIVERSAL STUDIOS HOME VIDEO
100 Universal City Plaza
Universal City, CA 91608-9955
Phone: (818) 777-1000
Fax: (818) 866-1483
E-mail: store@universalstudios.com

VIDEOLEARNING
850 Lancaster Avenue
Bryn Mawr, PA 19010
Phone: (800) 622-3610 or (610) 526-9100
Fax: (610) 525-2563
E-mail: training@videolrn.com
Website: www.videolrn.com

VIDEO VISIONS
P.O. Box 42185
Atlanta, GA 30311-0185
Phone: (404) 521-3456
Fax: (404) 755-2054

WALT DISNEY HOME VIDEO
500 South Buena Vista
Burbank, CA 91521
Phone: (818) 562-3560

WARNER HOME VIDEO, INC.
4000 Warner Boulevard
Burbank, CA 91522
Phone: (818) 954-6000

WEBSITES

The Internet is a favorite source among information seekers. However, it is also a rapidly changing medium in which addresses change and sites disappear without warning. That said, we offer here some unique sites that provide free resources, search tools, and links that are useful to the leadership educator. Each of these sites was verified in March 2000. Websites for organizations, conferences, journals, and vendors are listed elsewhere in the book and are not repeated in this section.

ACADEMY OF MANAGEMENT ONLINE

In addition to Academy of Management membership information, there are 17 listserver discussion groups open to all interested people. Topics include Conflict Management, Entrepreneurship, Gender Issues in Organizations, the Public and Nonprofit Sector, International Management, Social Issues in Management, and Service Learning. Follow the links for descriptions and subscription information. There is also a directory of listserver discussion groups hosted by other organizations.

Address: www.aom.pace.edu/lists
Subject(s): Listserver discussion groups

ADVANCING WOMEN IN LEADERSHIP

This is a refereed online journal about women in society in general, and in leadership positions specifically. Full-text articles identify barriers faced by professional women and functional approaches to dismantling these barriers. Also available on the award-winning Advancing Women home site are a chat room, women's news, financial advice, a career center for job searches and résumé posting, and links to related sites for professional women.

Address: www.advancingwomen.com/awl/awl.html
Subject(s): Women's leadership

New
AMERICA'S LEARNING EXCHANGE

The U.S. Department of Labor offers this site, which allows users to search databases of training programs, providers, seminars, and certification and licensing requirements. Private companies can register their programs on the site, specifying their location and the type of training services they offer. Free demos of some programs are available, and the site also includes information on testing and career development.

Address: www.alx.org
Subject(s): Leadership programs

New
BIG DOG'S BOWL OF BISCUITS

Starbucks employee Don Clark maintains this award-winning site that is loaded with information about leadership, human resources development, training, performance, coffee, and computer technology. On Big Dog's Leadership Page, there is an online study guide that reviews major leadership theories and behaviors in 17 lessons. There is also an outline for a more detailed course with lesson plans for 26 modules. Other features are: a glossary of leadership terms, quotations by and about leaders, links to other leadership-related websites, and a bibliography of reading materials. Visitors are invited to submit questions and expect a response from Clark within a few days.

Address: www.nwlink.com/~donclark/index.html
Subject(s): Training resources

BIOGRAPHY

Sponsored by A&E Television networks and *Biography Magazine*, this searchable site contains brief biographical sketches of 25,000 people. Visitors may search by name or index to find information about celebrities, business people, scientists, authors, politicians, athletes, artists, musicians, and even mythical and fictional characters. Many of the brief descriptions contain links to more detailed information. Some items have video clips.

Address: www.biography.com
Subject(s): Biographies, leaders in history

New
CENTER FOR THE STUDY OF WORK TEAMS

The website for this center, located at the University of North Texas, includes online access to student papers, research articles, conference proceedings, and the archives of the *Work Teams Newsletter*. Extensive lists of links are organized by topic, including teaming, human resources, facilitation, conflict management, leadership and management, training and individual development, and virtual teams. The site also offers online resources for job hunters and describes the center's current research.

Address: www.workteams.unt.edu
Subject(s): Teams

New
CONSORTIUM FOR RESEARCH ON EMOTIONAL INTELLIGENCE IN ORGANIZATIONS

The consortium is a group of individuals and organizations dedicated to studying emotional intelligence in the workplace, and many of their findings and reports are on this site. Among the documents available for downloading: guidelines for best practice, a business case for emotional intelligence, and descriptions of model programs. The site also includes a list of instruments commonly used to measure emotional intelligence, a recommended reading list, links to other organizations working with emotional intelligence, and an online discussion group.

Address: www.eiconsortium.org
Subject(s): Emotional intelligence

CREATIVITY WEB

The Creativity Web is a source for articles, ideas, products, and quotations about creativity and innovation. There are basic descriptions of brain theories, mind mapping, and creative thinking techniques. An idea bank invites visitors to "deposit" problems, which are "withdrawn" by others and "redeposited" when solved. A Genius Gallery provides examples of creative genius throughout history. Puzzles, exercises, and suggested resources are intended to help teach creativity in the workplace.

Address: www.ozemail.com.au/~caveman/Creative
Subject(s): Creativity

New
CRITICAL THINKING COMMUNITY

Sponsored by several nonprofit organizations, this site is designed for educators and offers resources for elementary, secondary, and college instructors. Extensive online articles on critical thinking include a basic history, a recommended reading list, information on Socratic questioning, and a glossary of critical thinking terms. Lesson plans for K through 12 and sample college syllabi that use critical thinking techniques are also available. Includes information on ordering books and videos and on conferences and workshops.

Address: www.criticalthinking.org
Subject(s): Critical thinking

New
DIVERSITYWEB

This site describes itself as an interactive resource hub for leaders in higher education and organizes its resources around seven Campus Diversity Priorities: institutional vision, leadership, and systemic change; curriculum transformation; faculty and staff involvement; student involvement and development; campus and community connections; research evaluation and impact; and policy and legal issues. The resources provided include articles, scholarly papers, reading lists, model policies and syllabi, and more. The site also includes discussion groups and institution profiles of over 100 college and universities.

Address: www.inform.umd.edu/EdRes/Topic/Diversity/Response/Web/index.html
Subject(s): Diversity

New
ERIC CLEARINGHOUSE ON ADULT, CAREER, AND VOCATIONAL EDUCATION

This ERIC site provides full-text research reports on adult education issues, links to related organizations, and information on online education journals. Documents available here include practical application briefs, ERIC digests, trend alerts, and a series exploring myths and realities. Users can also search ERIC's full database of document and article citations.

Address: www.ericacve.org
Subject(s): Trainer resources

ERIC/AE TEST LOCATOR

This searchable database contains brief descriptions and source information for more than 10,000 tests and test reviews including leadership-related items. Users can search the ETS Test Collection, The Buros Institute of Mental Measurements directory, and a database of the names and addresses of over 900 major commercial test publishers.

Address: www.ericae.net/testcol.htm
Subject(s): Assessments

THE EUROPEAN CASE CLEARING HOUSE (ECCH)

ECCH is a nonprofit organization that acts as a source of case study material for management education and training. This site provides links to the world's business schools and their case collections. There are more than 14,000 titles searchable by subject.

Address: www.ecch.cranfield.ac.uk
Subject(s): Trainer resources

New
EXPLORING MULTIPLE INTELLIGENCES

Run by a research and training organization called New Dimensions of Learning, this site provides information on Gardner's theory of multiple intelligences. In addition to basic definitions, the site offers exercises for exploring each intelligence, links to schools and organizations that apply this theory in their work, and a description of a framework for staff development.

Address: www.multi-intell.com/mi_home.htm
Subject(s): Intelligence

New
HR WORLD

This award-winning site contains information for managers of human capital. All visitors may access online polls and words of wisdom. HR professionals may register for free access to HR/PC—an online magazine, a job bank, discussion forums, and an HR bookstore. Vendors may register for a fee to showcase their products in the resources directory.

Address: www.hrworld.com
Subject(s): Human resources professionals

New
HUMAN RESOURCES LEARNING CENTER

This site offers full-text articles on human resource issues including salaries, retention, information systems, and coaching. Users can view information about benchmarking and best practices studies and request executive summaries through e-mail. Links to other websites providing general HR information, legal data, recruitment and retention networks, and sites for HR organizations are also provided.

Address: www.human-resources.org
Subject(s): Human resources development

New
INTERACTIVE KNOWLEDGE FOR NONPROFITS WORLDWIDE

This site serves as a directory for nonprofit leaders looking for online information. Links are organized into twelve topics of concern for nonprofits: business services, education, fringe benefits, fund-raising, governance, human resources, legal issues, legislation, marketing and media, strategic planning, and volunteerism. The resources are divided into more specific groups within these categories, and include short news articles, bibliographies, FAQs, research reports, and online newsletters.

Address: www.iknow.org
Subject(s): Nonprofit leadership

New
LEADER EZZAY LIST

This site offers more than 100 "ezzays," short, provocative articles addressing the issues leaders are thinking about today. Writers including Warren Bennis, Peter Senge, and Frances Hesselbein have contributed articles on topics such as coaching, building community, and corporate culture. New ezzays are added throughout the year and readers are encouraged to respond directly to the authors via e-mail.

Address: www.mgeneral.com/3-now/now_list.htm
Subject(s): Leadership effectiveness

New
LEADER-VALUES

Leader-Values is maintained by Mick Yates, manager of a Fortune 50 Transnational corporation with responsibilities across the Asia-Pacific region. He dedicates this nonprofit site to furthering knowledge and discussion about leadership and values, particularly cultural values. Business leaders and students are invited to submit articles and participate in discussions. Yates posts his conference presentations and his values analyses of leaders throughout history.

Address: www.leader-values.com
Subject(s): Values

New
LEADERNET

Sponsored by the University of Maryland's James MacGregor Burns Academy of Leadership, the goal of LeaderNet is to use Internet technology to connect young leaders around the world. Users can contribute articles, book reviews, and papers, and can participate in online discussions. A database of members can be searched by country or interest areas and members can contribute their events to a calendar of leadership activities. LeaderNet also sponsors essay contests and provides links to over 200 governmental, nonprofit, and corporate websites that address youth leadership, civic action, and international networking.

Address: www.leadernet.org
Subject(s): Youth leadership

LISZT

Liszt is a searchable directory of discussion lists around the world. Its purpose is to help visitors identify, research, and join discussion lists in their areas of interest. Data are verified on an ongoing basis to maintain currency. A sample search for "leadership" yielded a match of 54 discussion lists.

Address: www.liszt.com
Subject(s): Listserver discussion groups

MANY PATHS QUOTES ON LEADERSHIP

Many Paths offers 400 quotations to inspire personal and spiritual growth. Visitors may search by keyword or use the index to find quotations on leadership, learning, human nature, problem solving, integrity, and life management. Words of wisdom are from such varied sources as Winston Churchill, Frederick Nietsche, William Penn, Frank Lloyd Wright, and Booker T. Washington.

Address: www.net-quest.com/~gdotao
Subject(s): Quotations

NATIONAL SERVICE-LEARNING CLEARINGHOUSE

This site provides information on organizations, people, publications, and information sources related to service learning, primarily at the K through 12 level. Includes a bibliography organized by subject, back issues of newsletters, a listserver discussion group, searchable databases of programs and events, and links to over 100 other service sites on the Internet.

Address: www.nicsl.coled.umn.edu
Subject(s): Service learning

New
THE OBTC RING HOME PAGE

This web ring, which links the homepages of management professors who teach organizational behavior and organizational psychology, is dedicated to improving teaching methods through sharing information. The pages in the ring include syllabi, course assignments, case studies, exercises, and learning activities faculty members are currently using. The ring structure allows users to browse a number of these related sites quickly.

Address: www.muohio.edu/~snavelwb/obtc.html
Subject(s): Leadership educators

New
OSU LEADERSHIP CENTER PUBLICATIONS

The Ohio State University Extension Leadership Center offers access to two publications through its website. *Leadership Link* is a quarterly publication of in-depth articles on leadership that are available both in printed form and in online archives. *Leadership Moments* is a weekly e-mail newsletter that offers short, inspirational readings on leadership topics, and can be subscribed to from this site.

Address: www.ag.ohio-state.edu/~leaders/publications.htm
Subject(s): Self-development

Leadership Resources: A Guide to Training and Development Tools (8th Edition)

New
PERFORMANCE MEASUREMENT RESOURCES

The Zigon Performance Group maintains this website of online performance measurement resources, including information on performance management, the balanced scorecard, teams, 360-degree assessment, and training. The site offers sample performance measurements, in-depth articles, recent news stories about performance measurement, and a bibliography of recommended books and articles. An extensive links page includes information on discussion groups, and the site even includes a page called "Performance Measurement Humor."

Address: www.zigonperf.com/performance.htm
Subject(s): Performance

QUOTATIONS

This collection contains over 23,000 quotations organized by topic, including a section on leadership, and a selection of quotes by great leaders such as Winston Churchill, Henry Ford, and Martin Luther King, Jr. More quotes are added regularly.

Address: www.geocities.com/~spanoudi/quote.html
Subject(s): Quotations

THE SOCIETY FOR ORGANIZATIONAL LEARNING (SOL)

The SoL USA site is based on the integrated theories and practices of leading, learning, and working together. There is an Idea Exchange where visitors may contribute original ideas and comment on others'. The Practice field leads visitors to news about projects, teaching tools, and a lexicon of organizational learning concepts. The Research section contains a bibliography of working papers, research proposals, and summaries. The Community section links to practitioners and scholars in the field of organizational learning.

Address: www.sol-ne.org/ne.html
Subject(s): Organizational learning

New
TECHNOLOGY TRANSFER AND ECONOMIC DEVELOPMENT PROGRAM

This site, operated by the U.S. Department of Energy (DOE) and the Westinghouse Electric Company, allows users to download adult education, training, development, and human resource materials developed by DOE. Organizations can then modify the material, reproduce it for internal distribution, or turn it into a commercial product. Some of the materials available include an Employee Appraisal and Development System, a Leadership Development Needs Assessment, a Management Training and Development Needs Analysis, and information on writing winning grant proposals.

Address: www.t2ed.com
Subject(s): Trainer resources

New
TIME'S 100 MOST IMPORTANT PEOPLE OF THE TWENTIETH CENTURY

Over the course of 1999, *Time* magazine named 100 of the century's most influential people in five areas: leaders and revolutionaries, artists and entertainers, builders and titans, scientists and thinkers, and heroes and icons. This site contains photographs and profiles of each person, ranging from Nelson Mandela to Mother Teresa. Links to related articles and sites are included.

Address: www.time.com/time/time100
Subject(s): Leaders

TRAINING AND DEVELOPMENT COMMUNITY CENTER

This site aims to be a "virtual" gold mine of resources for the human resources development (HRD) community. There is a bookstore for viewing recommended titles as well as a link to Amazon.com for direct ordering. There is also a career center for résumé and job postings, glossaries of HRD terms, and links to related sites.

Address: www.tcm.com/trdev
Subject(s): Human resources development professionals

THE TRAINING REGISTRY

An online training catalog, this site contains links to training providers, products, facilities, supplies, associations, job opportunities, publications, popular speakers, and more.

Address: www.trainingregistry.com
Subject(s): Trainer resources

New
TRDEV-L

This site introduces TRDEV-L, a moderated discussion group for professionals in human resources training and development. This list generates a lot of mail, but it is indexed in folders so that subscribers may easily select messages to read or ignore. Old discussion threads are archived for easy access.

Address: http://train.ed.psu.edu/TRDEV-L
Subject(s): Listserver discussion group

New
UNIVERSITY-BASED CENTERS FOR MANAGEMENT AND EXECUTIVE DEVELOPMENT

This site provides links to the websites of over 140 university-based organizations offering executive development programs. While most of the programs are American, links to centers in Australia, Spain, Canada, the United Kingdom, Portugal, India, France, and Mexico are included.

Address: www.geocities.com/Athens/Oracle/5228
Subject(s): Executive education

New
WEB OF CULTURE

The reference section of this site contains in-depth articles and quick tips on cross-cultural communication. Practical information for the business traveler includes exchange rates, locations of U.S. embassies and consulates, time zones, and international weather. The site also addresses more generally how managers can improve their cross-cultural communication through information such as descriptions of gestures used in different countries, advice on how to make web pages culturally competent, and links to international news sites.

Address: www.webofculture.com
Subject(s): Cross-cultural communication

WORKSHOPS BY THIAGI, INC.

This site contains free training games from prolific game designer Sivasailam "Thiagi" Thiagarajan. There are e-mail games, puzzles, and free software. Thiagi shares suggestions for using games to improve human performance in organizations and a checklist for evaluating training games.

Address: www.thiagi.com
Subject(s): Games

WORLD LECTURE HALL

Maintained by the University of Texas at Austin, this is a link to online course materials in many disciplines. There are 40 links to management courses, including Michael Usrey's Management of Research and Development at the University of Colorado, K. B. Massingill's Managerial Communications at Abilene Christian University, and Anthony F. Chelte's Organizational Theory and Behavior at Western New England College. Other disciplines with course offerings include communication, education, and cultural studies. Non-English course materials are included.

Address: www.utexas.edu/world/lecture/man
Subject(s): Leadership course syllabi

ORGANIZATIONS

The organizations in this section support leadership education as member associations, institutes, executive education providers, and funding sources. Descriptions include:

• the organization's mission or purpose
• the audience it serves
• examples of programs offered or programs funded
• publications
• meetings
• contact information
• subject

New
ADVENTURE LEARNING ASSOCIATES, INC.

This is a global network of providers who offer corporate experiential learning programs and professional coaching services. Programs include: Leadership Development, Team Development, Action Learning, and Leadership Trek in the Himalayas. Adventure Learning Associates also offers train-the-trainer sessions and provides action learning equipment such as a portable climbing mountain.

Address: P.O. Box 6062, Brattleboro, VT 05302
Phone: (800) 551-3210 or (802) 254-6160
Fax: (802) 254-3852
E-mail: info@alrna.com
Website: www.alrna.com
Subject(s): Adventure education

New
THE AFRICAN AMERICAN LEADERSHIP INSTITUTE (AALI)

AALI grew from a model program designed to enhance the performance of established, emerging, and potential African American leaders. In addition to the management and leadership training program, the institute conducts research, provides access to technical resources, and provides networking opportunities. Through these efforts, AALI aims to improve the quality of life and civic engagement of African Americans.

Publications: *African American Leadership*; other books and working papers
Meetings: Annual leadership training seminars
Address: James MacGregor Burns Academy of Leadership, University of Maryland–College Park, Room 0101 Taliaferro Hall, College Park, MD 20742-7715
Phone: (301) 405-2601
E-mail: AALI@academy.umd.edu
Website: www.academy.umd.edu/scholarship/AALI
Subject(s): African American leadership

AMERICAN LEADERSHIP FORUM (ALF)

ALF is a nonprofit organization dedicated to joining and strengthening community leaders. Local chapters provide year-long training that covers diversity issues, a wilderness challenge, visionary leadership, systems theory, moral dimensions of leadership, and collaborative problem solving. A recent initiative, Collaborative Leadership in Action, brought ALF chapters together with thought leaders for an exploration of leadership and collaboration. A new initiative, the African Leadership Forum, takes the one-year program to chapters in Africa but with a focus on the traditional African values of harmony and unity.

Publications: *Systems Thinking in Action* series; *Collaborative Leadership in Action (CLIA) Initiative Final Report*
Address: P.O. Box 3689, Stanford, CA 94309-3689
Phone: (650) 723-6127
Fax: (650) 723-6131

E-mail: mail@alfnational.org
Website: www.alfnational.org
Subject(s): Community leadership

New
AMERICAN SOCIETY FOR PUBLIC ADMINISTRATION (ASPA)

ASPA is a member association that aims to advance excellence in public service and foster professional growth in the field of public administration. Local chapters, seminars, awards, and online discussion groups encourage members to recognize and share best practices. The Center for Accountability and Performance measures government performance and produces research-based resources to facilitate high performance in federal, state, and local offices.

Publications: *Public Administration Review* journal; *PA Times* newsletter; *Performance Measurement Concepts and Techniques*; *Applying Standards and Ethics in the 21st Century*; other books; research reports; case studies
Meetings: Annual conference
Address: 1120 G Street, N.W., Suite 700, Washington, DC 20005
Phone: (202) 393-7878
Fax: (202) 638-4952
E-mail: info@aspanet.org
Website: www.aspanet.org
Subject(s): Public leadership

AMERICAN SOCIETY FOR TRAINING AND DEVELOPMENT, INC. (ASTD)

ASTD is an international association for people with training and human resource development responsibilities in business, industry, government, and public service. Organized in 1943, ASTD has over 70,000 members in chapters throughout the world. Members are encouraged to join a professional practice network and an industry group to receive information on activities of specific interest. There are benchmarking services, tools, and discussion forums to help organizations measure training effectiveness against industry peers. ASTD's free and fee-based library services to members and nonmembers include statistics, reading lists, and customized search services.

Publications: *Training & Development* monthly magazine; *Human Resource Development Quarterly*; *INFO-LINE* monthly publication for trainers; *Learning Circuits* webzine; *ASTD Buyer's Guide*; books; reports
Meetings: National and regional conferences
Address: 1640 King Street, Box 1443, Alexandria, VA 22313-2043
Phone: (800) 628-2783 or (703) 683-8100
Fax: (703) 683-1523
E-mail: info@astd.org
Website: www.astd.org
Subject(s): Training

AMERICAN YOUTH FOUNDATION (AYF)

The American Youth Foundation is a nonprofit organization whose purpose is to develop the leadership capacities of young people by helping them achieve their personal best, lead balanced lives, and serve others. Programs for K through 12 students include summer resident and day camps in Michigan and New Hampshire and the STREAM Urban Adventure Center in St. Louis, complete with a climbing wall and group challenge course. The Youth Leadership Compact program shares action learning curricula among high schools throughout the U.S. Each year, the *I Dare You* Leadership Award recognizes high school juniors and seniors who demonstrate personal integrity, balanced living, and leadership potential.

Publications: *I Dare You* book
Meetings: Annual International Leadership Conference
Address: 1315 Ann Avenue, St. Louis, MO 63104-4111
Phone: (314) 772-8626
Fax: (314) 772-7542
E-mail: mail@ayf.com
Website: www.ayf.com
Subject(s): Youth

New
ASHRIDGE MANAGEMENT COLLEGE

This independent center for management and organization development offers an executive MBA, conducts management research, and provides executive education programs. Among the one- to three-week programs are: Advanced Development for Developers, Ashridge Leadership Programme, Business Leadership for Women, Developing Business and Leadership Skills, Influencing Strategies and Skills, The Manager as Coach, and Strategy and Leadership.

Address: Berkhamsted, Hertfordshire HP4 1NS UK
Phone: 44 (0) 1442-841000
Fax: 44 (0) 1442-841036
E-mail: info@ashridge.org.uk
Website: www.ashridge.org.uk
Subject(s): Leadership programs

THE ASPEN INSTITUTE

The institute is an international, nonprofit educational institution dedicated to enhancing organizational and societal values through informed dialogue. There are leadership forums for those in public administration and corporate management as well as for women, minorities, emerging leaders, and global leaders. Policy programs examine current issues such as international security and self-governance for the Internet. Executive education programs include Leadership in the Digital Age, Leadership Values in China, and Leading Corporate Change.

Publications: Reports from policy programs and strategy groups
Meetings: Seminars and forums
Address: One Dupont Circle, N.W., Suite 700, Washington, DC 20036
Phone: (202) 736-5800
Fax: (202) 467-0790
Website: www.aspeninst.org
Subject(s): Leadership programs

ASPIRA ASSOCIATION, INC.

In Spanish, *aspirar* means to aspire to something greater. In that spirit, the Latino organization ASPIRA is dedicated to promoting youth leadership and education for Puerto Rican and other Latino youth. ASPIRA clubs in 400 schools offer the Youth Leadership Development Program that teaches the process of awareness, analysis, and action. Students participate in culturally enriching activities and organize community service projects. Other programs gain parent involvement, work on dropout prevention, enhance math and science skills, and provide opportunities for entrepreneurship. Over 25,000 Latino youth and their families are touched by ASPIRA programs in six states, Puerto Rico, and Washington, DC.

Publications: *ASPIRA News* quarterly newsletter; training manuals; reports
Meetings: Annual Latino Education Conference
Address: 1444 I Street, N.W., Suite 800, Washington, DC 20005-6543
Phone: (202) 835-3600
Fax: (202) 835-3613
E-mail: info@aspira.org
Website: www.aspira.org
Subject(s): Hispanic leadership, youth leadership

ASSOCIATION FOR EXPERIENTIAL EDUCATION (AEE)

AEE is a nonprofit organization with roots in adventure education, committed to the development, practice, and evaluation of experiential learning. Members from 25 countries join special interest groups to share information on facilitating programs for corporate managers, teams, students, community groups, and people with disabilities. Awards are presented each year to creative and outstanding educators and practitioners. AEE accredits adventure programs.

Publications: *Journal of Experiential Education; Adventure Program Risk Management Report; Manual of Accreditation Standards;* other books; directories
Meetings: Annual regional and international conferences
Address: 2305 Canyon Boulevard, Suite100, Boulder, CO 80302-5651
Phone: (303) 440-8844
Fax: (303) 440-9581
E-mail: info@aee.org
Website: www.aee.org
Subject(s): Experiential education

ASSOCIATION OF LEADERSHIP EDUCATORS (ALE)

ALE is a professional organization for those who design and deliver leadership development programs in higher education and the corporate sector. Its goals are to enhance the leadership competencies of these professionals and to strengthen the multidisciplinary base that supports leadership research and teaching. Two awards each year recognize outstanding programs and distinguished service.

Publications: *ALE Newsletter* quarterly; conference proceedings; membership directory
Meetings: Annual conference
Address: c/o Jon E. Irby, Treasurer, USDA/CSREES, 1400 Independence Avenue, S.W., Stop 2225 USDA/CSREES/F4-HN, Washington, DC 20250-2225
Phone: (202) 720-5345
Fax: (202) 690-2469
E-mail: jirby@reeusda.gov
Website: www.aces.uiuc.edu/~ALE
Subject(s): Leadership education

MARY REYNOLDS BABCOCK FOUNDATION, INC.

The foundation concentrates on assisting people in the Southeastern U.S. to build just and caring communities that nurture people, spur enterprise, bridge differences, foster fairness, and promote civility. It provides funds in two areas. The Community Problem Solving Program assists local communities with rebuilding efforts. The Grassroots Leadership Development funding area supports grassroots efforts to influence state policy.

Publications: Annual report; guidelines
Address: 2522 Reynolda Road, Winston-Salem, NC 27106-5123
Phone: (336) 748-9222
Fax: (336) 777-0095
E-mail: info@mrbf.org
Website: www.mrbf.org
Subject(s): Funding for leadership programs

New
BABSON SCHOOL OF EXECUTIVE EDUCATION

Babson offers executive education programs and consortiums that combine training with information sharing among senior executives. Programs include: The Babson Entrepreneurial Leadership Program for Information Technology Professionals, The Babson Program on Corporate Entrepreneurship, Leadership and Influence, and The Senior Leadership Forum for Franchise Executives.

Publications: *Executive Outlook Newsletter; Executive Education News*
Address: Babson College, Wellesley, MA 02457-0310
Phone: (800) 882-3932 or (781) 239-4354
Fax: (781) 239-5266
E-mail: exec@babson.edu
Website: www.babson.edu/see
Subject(s): Leadership programs

New
BRECKENRIDGE OUTDOOR EDUCATION CENTER

This nonprofit organization integrates classroom learning with outdoor adventures. Their programs are for people of all abilities, including disabilities, and at-risk populations. Professional Challenge programs include half-day to multi-day programs that teach leadership and teamwork concepts utilizing a ropes course and a climbing wall. River rafting and rock climbing options are also available. Breckenridge offers internships and volunteer opportunities to help facilitate programs.

Address: P.O. Box 697, Breckenridge, CO 80424
Phone: (800) 383-2632 or (970) 453-6422
Fax: (970) 453-4676
E-mail: pcprog@boec.org
Website: www.boec.org
Subject(s): Experiential education

THE JAMES MacGREGOR BURNS ACADEMY OF LEADERSHIP

The academy fosters future generations of political leaders through education, service, and research. Founded to encourage political participation at all levels, it is an academically sanctioned program to support emerging leaders seeking public office. Programs include the College Park Scholars in Public Leadership, the Rising Stars High School Leadership Conference, Team Maryland—a scholar-athlete leadership program, political campaign training, and for-credit courses.

Publications: *Boundary Crossers: Community Leadership for a Global Age*; *Cutting Edge: Leadership 2000*; curriculum guides
Meetings: Symposia and conferences
Address: University of Maryland, College Park, MD 20742-7715
Phone: (301) 405-6100
Fax: (301) 405-6402
E-mail: Academy@academy.umd.edu
Website: www.academy.umd.edu
Subject(s): Public leadership, leadership research

New
THE ANNIE E. CASEY FOUNDATION

The foundation is a private charitable organization that fosters public policies, human-service reforms, and community supports that meet the needs of vulnerable children and families. One initiative is the year-long Children and Family Fellowship Program that builds the leadership capacity of midcareer professionals in family-serving institutions.

Publications: *Kids Count Data Book; ADVOCasey Online*
Address: 701 St. Paul Street, Baltimore, MD 21202
Phone: (800) 222-1099 or (410) 547-6600
Fax: (410) 547-6624
E-mail: webmail@aecf.org

Website: www.aecf.org
Subject(s): Funding for leadership development

CATALYST

Catalyst is a nonprofit organization with a dual mission—to enable women in business and the professions to achieve their maximum potential and to help employers capitalize on the talents of their female employees. Research is conducted on workplace barriers, leadership development opportunities, women's representation on corporate boards, and women as organizational change agents. Advisory staff work with organizations wishing to implement work/life supports, mentoring programs, and flexible work arrangements. Catalyst's Corporate Board Placement, a confidential service, helps companies identify and recruit women board members. An Information Center screens periodicals, books, and statistical fact sheets to compile data on women's workplace issues. Each March, the Catalyst Award is presented to corporations or professional firms that demonstrate outstanding achievement in promoting women's career and leadership development.

Publications: *Perspective* monthly newsletter; *Mentoring: A Guide to Corporate Programs and Practices*; *Advancing Women in Business: The Catalyst Guide*; *Women of Color in Corporate Management: Opportunities and Barriers*; *Creating Women's Networks: A How-To Guide for Women and Companies*; research reports
Meetings: Regional conferences cosponsored by major corporations
Address: 120 Wall Street, New York, NY 10005-3904
Phone: (212) 514-7600
Fax: (212) 514-8470
E-mail: info@catalystwomen.org
Website: www.catalystwomen.org
Subject(s): Women's leadership, leadership research

New
CENTER FOR APPLICATION OF PSYCHOLOGICAL TYPE, INC. (CAPT)

CAPT is a nonprofit organization dedicated to the accurate understanding, measurement, ethical use, and practical application of Jung's theory of psychological types. The organization's work centers around the use of the *Myers-Briggs Type Indicator*® in education, organizational development, counseling, and research. In addition to provision of the instrument and scoring services, the organization provides training for facilitators, manuals for interpretation, translations, and normative data. CAPT houses the Isabel Briggs Myers Memorial Library.

Publications: *Atlas of Type Tables*™; *Portraits of Type: An MBTI Research Compendium*; *The Workplace Report: Looking at Type in the Workplace*
Meetings: CAPT Education Conference
Address: 2815 N.W. 13th Street, Suite 401, Gainesville, FL 32609
Phone: (800) 777-2278

Fax: (800) 723-6284
E-mail: info@capt.org
Website: www.capt.org
Subject(s): *Myers-Briggs Type Indicator*

THE CENTER FOR CREATIVE CHURCH LEADERSHIP

Founded with the vision of developing more effective church leaders, the center serves clergy and lay leaders from all denominations. Five-day intensive training and extended programs are based on the Creative Church Leader Model, which includes modules on leadership behavior, credibility, personality, creative thinking, ethical fitness, and psychological hardiness. This model is adapted for educational and corporate audiences.

Address: Long View House, 1722 Niblick Avenue, Lancaster, PA 17602-4826
Phone: (717) 299-5811
Fax: (717) 299-5588
E-mail: sixhats@aol.com
Subject(s): Religious leadership

CENTER FOR CREATIVE LEADERSHIP (CCL)

CCL is an international, nonprofit educational institution whose mission is to advance the understanding, practice, and development of leadership for the benefit of society worldwide. There are offices in New York, San Diego, Colorado Springs, and Brussels and headquarters in Greensboro, North Carolina. The center's research focuses on assessment for development, learning and the lessons of experience, executive development, leadership and creativity, teamwork, and simulation design. The Leadership Development Program (LDP)® enables leadership growth by developing personal awareness. Other programs include The African-American Leadership Program, Developing the Strategic Leader, Foundations of Leadership, Leadership and High Performance Teams, Leadership at the Peak, Leading Creatively, The Looking Glass Experience: Leadership in Action, Tools for Developing Successful Executives, and The Women's Leadership Program.

Publications: *Leadership in Action* journal; *The Center for Creative Leadership Handbook of Leadership Development*; guidebooks; research reports; instruments; simulations
Meetings: Periodic conferences
Address: One Leadership Place, P.O. Box 26300, Greensboro, NC 27438-6300
Phone: (336) 545-2810
Fax: (336) 282-3284
E-mail: info@leaders.ccl.org
Website: www.ccl.org
Subject(s): Leadership development, leadership research

CENTER FOR EFFECTIVE ORGANIZATIONS (CEO)

CEO is a research center that conducts intensive studies of key management issues, organizational diagnosis, and experimental programs with corporate sponsors. Its objective is to bridge the gap between theory and practice of the design and management of work organizations. Areas of interest include leadership, labor-management relations, organizational development and design, work design, employee involvement, and reward systems.

Publications: Books and articles for general and technical/academic audiences
Meetings: Human Resource Executive Seminars
Address: Marshall School of Business, University of Southern California, 3670 Trousdale Parkway, BRI 204, Los Angeles, CA 90089-0806
Phone: (213) 740-9814
Fax: (213) 740-4354
E-mail: ceo@usc.edu
Website: www.marshall.usc.edu/ceo
Subject(s): Corporate leadership, leadership research

CENTER FOR LEADERSHIP STUDIES

This nonprofit research and educational institution aims to contribute to the understanding of and to identify the importance of a full range of leadership and its applications. The center focuses on the evolution from a transactional style to a transformational style of leadership. The Executive Series of Leadership Development Programs includes one- to six-day workshops offered internationally. The center is currently examining shared leadership in combat units with the Israeli Defense Forces and developing a web-based learning system for leadership development.

Publications: *Bass and Stogdill's Handbook of Leadership*; *Full Range Leadership: Building the Vital Force in Organizations*; other books and research reports
Address: Binghamton University, P.O. Box 6015, Binghamton, NY 13902-6015
Phone: (607) 777-3007
Fax: (607) 777-4188
E-mail: cls@binghamton.edu
Website: cls.binghamton.edu
Subject(s): Transformational leadership, leadership research

CENTER FOR STRATEGIC URBAN COMMUNITY LEADERSHIP

The center is dedicated to the improvement of urban communities throughout the Northeastern U.S. by educating leaders about community-academia partnerships for dealing with race relations and urban development. The future of urban communities belongs to leaders who break the political, social, and cultural barriers that have previously impeded their access to leadership positions. The Hispanic Women Leadership Institute begins with self-examination, then shifts to community concerns. The Leadership Management for Urban Executives Institute trains African American, Latino, and Asian fellows who aspire to careers in key national, state, and regional programs. The Latino Fellows Public Policy Summer Leadership Institute provides ten

weeks of leadership development and public-policy training to Latino students enrolled in New Jersey colleges.

Publications: *The Center Focus* quarterly newsletter
Address: School of Social Work, Rutgers – The State University of New Jersey – Camden Campus, 327 Cooper Street, Camden, NJ 08102-1519
Phone: (609) 225-6348
Fax: (609) 225-6500
E-mail: gloriabs@crab.rutgers.edu
Website: www.camden.rutgers.edu/Camden/CFSUCL
Subject(s): Community leadership

CENTER FOR WOMEN'S GLOBAL LEADERSHIP

The center seeks to develop an understanding of the ways in which gender affects the exercise of power and conduct of public policy internationally. Its goals are to build international linkages among women in local leadership, and to promote visibility and increase participation of women in public deliberation and policy-making. The center sponsors an annual two-week Women's Global Leadership Institute for female leaders at the grassroots and national levels, runs human rights education programs, and cosponsors regional workshops.

Publications: *Global Center News* newsletter; *Local Action, Global Change: Learning About the Human Rights of Women and Girls*; other books and reports
Address: Douglass College, Rutgers – The State University of New Jersey – New Brunswick Campus, 160 Ryders Lane, New Brunswick, NJ 08901-8555
Phone: (732) 932-8782
Fax: (732) 932-1180
E-mail: cwgl@igc.org
Website: www.cwgl.rutgers.edu
Subject(s): Women's leadership, global leadership

New
COLUMBIA BUSINESS SCHOOL

Executive education programs are based on research conducted at the Columbia Business School and School of International and Public Affairs. Programs include: Emerging Leader Development Program, Leading and Managing People, Leading Organizational Change and Renewal, and Managing Interpersonal and Group Dynamics.

Address: Columbia Business School, Executive Education, 2880 Broadway, New York, NY 10025
Phone: (800) 692-3932 or (212) 854-3395
Fax: (212) 316-1473
E-mail: exec@claven.gsb.columbia.edu
Website: www.gsb.columbia.edu/execed
Subject(s): Leadership programs

THE CONFERENCE BOARD (TCB)

The Conference Board's twofold purpose is to improve the business enterprise system and to enhance its contribution to society. To accomplish this, TCB organizes councils for executives from all industries to exchange ideas on business policy and best practices. More than 100 councils address such topics as business conduct around the globe, learning and knowledge management, balancing work and life issues, and electronic business strategy. The Ron Brown Award for Corporate Leadership is given each year to honor companies for outstanding achievements in employee and community relations. Affiliate branches are located throughout North America, Europe, and Asia.

Publications: *Across the Board* magazine; *The Ron Brown Award for Corporate Leadership*; *Diversity: An Imperative for Business Success*; research reports on human resources and performance, global corporate citizenship, and economic issues

Meetings: Organization of the Future; Leadership Conference on Global Corporate Citizenship; Linking Human Capital with Strategy; The Business Ethics Conference—Maintaining Credibility; Leadership Development—Present Challenges, Future Opportunities; Leadership Redefined: Leveraging the Talent of Women in Your Business; other conferences

Address: 845 Third Avenue, New York, NY 10022-6679

Phone: (212) 759-0900

Fax: (212) 980-7014

E-mail: info@conference-board.org

Website: www.conference-board.org

Subject(s): Corporate leadership, leadership research

CONGRESSIONAL YOUTH LEADERSHIP COUNCIL

This educational organization is committed to fostering and inspiring young people to achieve their full leadership potential through experiential training programs in the nation's capital. Learning activities include a "Model Congress" that proposes and debates legislation, a simulated international crisis, and a mock Supreme Court case. Over 400 members of the U.S. Congress serve on the Board of Advisors, volunteer their time to lecture, and provide some students with short-term work experience in their offices.

Meetings: National Young Leaders Conference and Global Young Leaders Conference

Address: 1110 Vermont Avenue, N.W., Suite 320, Washington, DC 20005

Phone: (202) 638-0008

Fax: (202) 638-4257

E-mail: cylc@cylc.org

Website: www.cylc.org

Subject(s): Youth leadership

New
CONSORTIUM FOR RESEARCH ON EMOTIONAL INTELLIGENCE IN ORGANIZATIONS

The consortium is a group of scholars who are dedicated to advancing research and practice related to emotional intelligence in organizations. They seek and share information on programs that address some or all of the five dimensions—self-monitoring, self-regulation, self-motivation, empathy,

and social skills—described in Daniel Goleman's books *Emotional Intelligence* (1995) and *Working with Emotional Intelligence* (1998). The consortium offers a set of best-practice guidelines and partners with organizations to measure and promote emotional intelligence. Model program descriptions, guidelines, and technical reports are available on the website.

Meetings: Conferences

E-mail: emerling@rci.rutgers.edu

Website: www.eiconsortium.org

Subject(s): Emotional intelligence

New
CORNELL UNIVERSITY

Executive education programs at the Johnson Graduate School of Management include: Building High Performance into Existing Teams, Strategic Decision Making and Critical Thinking, Leading Organizational Change, Executive Leadership—Shaping the Future, and Leadership Development Program. Cornell University's School of Industrial and Labor Relations also offers executive education programs. They include: Creating Competitive Advantage through People and the International Human Resource Executive Development Program.

Address: Sage Hall Executive Education Center, Johnson Graduate School of Management, Cornell University, Ithaca, NY 14853-6201

Phone: (607) 255-4251

Fax: (607) 255-0018

Website: corporate.cornell.edu/ExecEd

Subject(s): Leadership programs

New
CRANFIELD UNIVERSITY SCHOOL OF MANAGEMENT

Many of Cranfield's research-based executive education programs focus on international management issues. Some of their programs are: The Alchemy of Leadership, The Director as Strategic Leader, High Performance Leadership, Human Resource Management—Policies and Practices, Human Resource Strategy Workshop, Leading Transnational Teams, Multi-source Feedback, Strategic International Human Resource Management, and the Women as Leaders Workshop.

Address: Cranfield, Bedford MK43 OAL UK

Phone: 44 (0) 1234-751122

Fax: 44 (0) 1234-751806

Website: www.cranfield.ac.uk/som/executive

Subject(s): Leadership programs

CREATIVE EDUCATION FOUNDATION, INC. (CEF)

The foundation encourages and stimulates creativity in learning and decision making through conferences, public programs, contract education, publishing, grant making, and an online bulletin board for members. Special programs for youth include an adapted version of the Creative Problem Solving Institute, the Global Odyssey, and the Leadership and Creativity Camp.

Publications: *Journal of Creative Behavior* quarterly journal; *Creativity in Action* monthly newsletter; *Source Book for Creative Problem Solving*; other books; videos; audiotapes
Meetings: Annual Creative Problem Solving Institute
Address: 1050 Union Road, Buffalo, NY 14224-3402
Phone: (800) 447-2774 or (716) 675-3181
Fax: (716) 675-3209
E-mail: cefhq@cef-cpsi.org
Website: www.cef-cpsi.org
Subject(s): Creativity, educational leadership

THE PETER F. DRUCKER FOUNDATION FOR NONPROFIT MANAGEMENT

The foundation believes that a healthy society requires three sectors: a public sector of effective governments, a private sector of effective businesses, and a social sector of effective community organizations. To this end, the foundation helps the social sector achieve excellence in performance and build responsible citizenship through seminars and video teleconferences. Guided by the writing of Peter Drucker, it helps nonprofits convert good intentions into results and make innovation part of all strategy. The Peter F. Drucker Award for Nonprofit Innovation is presented each year to a nonprofit organization that has demonstrated innovation in a program or project.

Publications: *Leader to Leader* journal; *The Drucker Foundation News* newsletter; *Leading Beyond the Walls*; other books; videos; audiotapes
Meetings: Two conferences each year
Address: 320 Park Avenue, 3rd Floor, New York, NY 10022-6839
Phone: (212) 224-1174
Fax: (212) 224-2508
E-mail: info@pfdf.org
Website: www.pfdf.org
Subject(s): Public leadership, nonprofit leadership

EUROPEAN FOUNDATION FOR MANAGEMENT DEVELOPMENT (EFMD)

This is a forum of European business school educators and HRD professionals who advocate innovation and best practices in management education. They conduct international benchmarking and auditing, support teachers' training, and develop teaching materials. They strive to identify distinctively European approaches to management education and development and share those approaches with partners worldwide. In 1997 efmd established EQUIS, the European Quality Improvement System, for assessment and accreditation of management development institutions.

Publications: *efmd Bulletin; efmd FORUM; Management Development Associations Around the World; efmd Euro-*

pean Executive Education Directory 2000; other management education guides
Meetings: Periodic conferences
Address: 88 rue Gachard, 1050 Brussels, Belgium
Phone: +32-(0)2-629 08 10
Fax: +32-(0)2-629 08 11
E-mail: info@efmd.be
Website: www.efmd.be
Subject(s): Management education, global leadership

New
EXPERIENTIAL TRAINING AND DEVELOPMENT CONSORTIUM

This consortium grew from the 1997 DEEP (Definition, Ethics, and Exemplary Practice) Task Force organized by professionals in the field of experiential training and development. They continue to identify best practices and professional behaviors. Task Force findings and new initiatives are described on the website.

Meetings: Periodic summits
E-mail: info@etdconsortium.com
Website: www.etdconsortium.com
Subject(s): Experiential learning

J. W. FANNING INSTITUTE FOR LEADERSHIP

This organization recognizes leadership development as the driving force of local development and quality-of-life issues facing each community, region, state, and beyond. It is a collaborative effort with the University of Georgia, Carl Vinson Institute of Government, Cooperative Extension Service, Georgia Center for Continuing Education, Institute of Community and Area Development, and Small Business Development Center. Its mission is to facilitate leadership development through a central source of information, identification of leadership needs and trends, program development, applied research, and education of community leaders. Among the many local and statewide programs are: Adult Community Leadership Program, Youth Leadership in Action, Leadership PLUS, and High Performance School Teams Leadership Institute.

Publications: *Leadership INSIGHTS* newsletter
Address: The University of Georgia, 1234 South Lumpkin Street, Athens, GA 30602-4350
Phone: (706) 542-1108
Fax: (706) 542-7007
E-mail: information@fanning.uga.edu
Website: www.fanning.uga.edu
Subject(s): Community leadership

GRASSROOTS LEADERSHIP

Grassroots Leadership provides leadership training to traditionally disempowered communities in the South. Programs include year-long training for individuals and custom-designed projects for organizations.

Address: P.O. Box 36006, 1515 Elizabeth Avenue, Charlotte, NC 28236-6006
Phone: (704) 332-3090
Fax: (704) 332-0445
E-mail: alfreda.barringer@together.org
Subject(s): Community leadership

New
GREEN CORPS

Green Corps provides leadership training to recent college graduates who are pursuing careers in the environmental movement. Twenty-five candidates are selected for salaried positions in the one-year Environmental Leadership Training Program. Classroom instruction is combined with experience in recruiting, training, and supervising volunteers; working with the media; raising funds; and mobilizing grassroots support. Graduates are placed in permanent positions with organizations such as the Sierra Club, the Rainforest Action Network, and the Greenbelt Alliance.

Address: 29 Temple Place, Boston, MA 02111
Phone: (617) 426-8506
E-mail: apply@greencorps.org
Website: www.greencorps.org
Subject(s): Environmental leadership

THE ROBERT K. GREENLEAF CENTER

The center's goals are to deepen the ideas of Robert K. Greenleaf and the principles of servant leadership through the preservation and promotion of his writings. This is intended to fundamentally improve the caring and quality of all institutions. The servant leader concept emphasizes increased service to others, a holistic approach to work, and promoting a sense of community and the sharing of power in decision making. Programs include: Putting Servant-Leadership Into Practice Where You Live and Work, Distributing Organizational Power Through Servant-Leadership, Ten Characteristics of Servant-Leadership, and the Leadership Institute for Higher Education.

Publications: *The Servant Leader* newsletter; *Insights on Leadership*; *On Becoming a Servant-Leader* by Robert K. Greenleaf; other books; videos; audiotapes
Meetings: Annual international conference; symposia
Address: 921 East 86th Street, Suite 200, Indianapolis, IN 46240-1841
Phone: (317) 259-1241
Fax: (317) 259-0560
E-mail: greenleaf@iquest.net
Website: www.greenleaf.org
Subject(s): Servant leadership

New
HARVARD UNIVERSITY

Research-based executive education programs at the Harvard Business School include: Leadership in Professional Service Firms, Making Corporate Boards More Effective, Strategic Human Resource Management, What's Next and So What?—Leading in the 21st Century, and Women Leading Business. John F. Kennedy School of Government programs include: Effective Decision Making, Leadership Educators Program, Managing People for Maximum Performance, Promoting Innovation and Creativity, Strategies for Enhancing Executive Influence, and Strategies of Persuasion.

Publications: *Harvard Business Review* and other periodicals; *Results-Based Leadership: How Leaders Build the Business and Improve the Bottom Line*; *Breaking Through: The Making of Minority Executives in Corporate America*; *John P. Kotter on What Leaders Really Do*; other books; case studies; videos; audiotapes
Address: Harvard University, Soldiers Field, Boston, MA 02163
Phone: (617) 495-6555
Fax: (617) 495-6999
E-mail: executive_education@hbs.edu
Website: www.exed.hbs.edu
Subject(s): Executive education

HEARTLAND CENTER FOR LEADERSHIP DEVELOPMENT

The center developed as an outgrowth of Visions from the Heartland, a grassroots futures project. Community leaders throughout North America attend the center's workshops and are eligible for assistance with long-term projects. Helping Small Towns Succeed is an intensive, five-day training program for professionals working in small-town and rural community development. Graduates of that program may attend the Skill Building for Stronger Communities workshop for more advanced leadership training.

Publications: *Clues to Rural Community Survival*; *The Entrepreneurial Community: A Strategic Leadership Approach to Community Survival*; other field research reports
Address: 941 O Street, Suite 920, Lincoln, NE 68508-3649
Phone: (800) 927-1115 or (402) 474-7667
Fax: (402) 474-7672
E-mail: heartcld@aol.com
Website: www.4w.com/heartland
Subject(s): Community leadership

HIGHLANDER RESEARCH AND EDUCATION CENTER

The Highlander Center is a nonprofit organization that helps people to take democratic leadership toward fundamental social change in communities throughout Appalachia and the Deep South. Based on the principle that institutional change can only be effective when solutions come from the people experiencing the problem, it provides educational programs that allow people to analyze their problems, test their ideas, learn from the experiences of others, and strengthen their organizations. The Southern and Appalachian Leadership Training program is designed to serve emerging leaders who are actively working on social justice issues. The Young and the Restless workshop trains youth and young adults. Latino workshops serve the growing Latino population throughout the Southeast. Technical assistance, fellowships, participatory learning, and peer interaction help participants to learn from collective experience.

Publications: *Highlander Reports* newsletter; *Citizen Power: Stories of America's New Civic Spirit*; other books; working papers; songbooks; videos; audiotapes
Address: 1959 Highlander Way, New Market, TN 37820-4939
Phone: (423) 933-3443
Fax: (423) 933-3424
E-mail: hrec@igc.apc.org
Subject(s): Community leadership

New
HUMAN RESOURCE INSTITUTE (HRI)

This nonprofit organization aims to develop human resources managers who are change-sensitive and have an enhanced ability to think strategically. The institute surveys human resources professionals and scans the environment to identify emerging issues among practitioners. The results provide a foundation for the institute's programs and products.

Publications: *The Generations at Work*; *The Future of Leadership*; *Ethics in Business*; other research reports and white papers
Meetings: Annual Issue Management Conference; Burning Issues in People Management periodic conferences
Address: Eckerd College, 4200 54th Avenue South, St. Petersburg, FL 33711
Phone: (727) 864-8330
Fax: (727) 864-1432
E-mail: info@hri.eckerd.edu
Website: hri.eckerd.edu
Subject(s): Human resources development

HUMAN RESOURCE PLANNING SOCIETY (HRPS)

This nonprofit organization is dedicated to providing current perspectives on complex and challenging human resource and business issues. Members are scholars, HRD practitioners, and consultants around the world. They have access to competency and certification workshops as well as research reports on high-performance work systems and future challenges in the field. Workshops such as Succession Planning and Leadership Development are open to members and non-members.

Publications: *Human Resource Planning* quarterly journal; *1999 HRPS State-of-the-art and Practice* report
Meetings: Annual HRPS conference
Address: 317 Madison Avenue, Suite 1509, New York, NY 10017-5201
Phone: (212) 490-6387
Fax: (212) 682-6851
E-mail: info@hrps.org
Website: www.hrps.org
Subject(s): Human resources development

INDEPENDENT SECTOR (IS)

IS encourages the philanthropy and volunteer action that impact the educational, scientific, health, welfare, cultural, and religious life of the nation. To preserve and enhance this nonprofit initiative, IS educates the public about the role of the nonprofit sector and conducts research on its usefulness to society. It engages in government relations to gain public-policy support and encourages effective leadership of nonprofit organizations. Several awards are presented each year for volunteer leadership and service—the John W. Gardner Leadership Award to individuals and the Leadership IS Award to organizations.

Publications: *Give Five* and *Leadership IS* newsletters; books; research reports; videos
Meetings: Annual conference
Address: 1200 18th Street, N.W., Suite 200, Washington, DC 20036
Phone: (202) 467-6100
Fax: (202) 467-6101
E-mail: info@IndependentSector.org
Website: www.indepsec.org
Subject(s): Nonprofit leadership

New
INSEAD

INSEAD's mission is to educate business leaders of the world, accelerate innovation, and build intellectual capital. As a model for international management, this organization provides executive development programs in addition to research and development. Some programs offered in Europe and Asia are: The Challenge of Leadership—Developing Your Emotional Intelligence, Human Resource Management in Asia, Joint Venture Management—The Human Factor, Management of People—Creating High-performing Organizations, and Managing Change and the Change of Management in Asia.

Publications: *IN* newsletter
Address: Boulevard de Constance, 77305 Fontainebleau, Cedex, France
Phone: 33 (0)1 60 72 42 90
Fax: 33 (0)1 60 74 55 00
E-mail: exec.info@insead.fr
Website: www.insead.fr
Subject(s): Management education, leadership research

INSTITUTE FOR CONSERVATION LEADERSHIP

The mission of the institute is to train and empower volunteer leaders and to build volunteer institutions that protect and conserve the earth's environment. To accomplish this mission, the institute develops and conducts training programs, and designs and facilitates meetings, retreats, and conferences. It also provides consulting and technical assistance to help groups and individuals address critical leadership and organizational development needs such as fund-raising, board development, strategic planning, and recruiting and involving volunteers.

Publications: *The Network* newsletter
Address: 6930 Carroll Avenue, Suite 420, Tacoma Park, MD 20912-4432
Phone: (301) 270-2900
Fax: (301) 270-0610
E-mail: icl@icl.org
Website: www.icl.org
Subject(s): Environmental leadership

INSTITUTE FOR CREATIVE DEVELOPMENT (ICD)

The institute is a nonprofit think tank and educational center dedicated to the use of creative systems thinking as a tool for solving society's problems. A major focus is to explore and teach new leadership skills to meet the challenges of the future. The institute's broad definition of leadership includes parents, service people, executives, and educators. All program participants face questions of purpose—both personal and cultural—to grow personally and professionally and to contribute to society. The institute's Creative Systems Theory is taught in a year-long workshop over ten weekends and in five-day workshops.

Publications: *The Creative Imperative*; *Necessary Wisdom*; other books; articles; videos
Address: P.O. Box 51244, Seattle, WA 98115-1244
Phone: (206) 526-0580
Fax: (206) 526-0580
E-mail: info@creativesystems.org
Website: www.creativesystems.org
Subject(s): Creativity

INSTITUTE FOR EDUCATIONAL LEADERSHIP, INC.

Programs at national, state, and local levels support and enhance the capabilities of educators and policymakers. The institute acts as an educational forum for information exchange among government, nonprofit, and business sectors. Seminars are designed to train education leaders in federal policy processes.

Publications: *Directory of Leadership Development Training Resources*; *Business Leaders and Communities Working Together for Change*; other reports; newsletter
Address: 1001 Connecticut Avenue, N.W., Suite 310, Washington, DC 20036-5541
Phone: (202) 822-8405
Fax: (202) 872-4050
E-mail: iel@iel.org
Website: www.iel.org
Subject(s): Educational leadership

New
INTERNATIONAL INSTITUTE FOR MANAGEMENT DEVELOPMENT (IMD)

IMD provides executive education around the world and organizes a global learning network for member companies to exchange ideas on management development. Faculty research is presented at short workshops called Discovery Events. Executive education programs include: Human Resources Leadership in Global Organizations, Leading Corporate Renewal, Leading the Family Business, Mobilizing People, and Orchestrating Winning Performance.

Publications: Books; articles; case studies
Address: 23 chemin de Bellerive, P.O. Box 915, Lausanne, CH-1001 Switzerland
Phone: 41 (0) 21-618-0111
Fax: 41 (0) 21-618-0707
E-mail: info@imd.ch
Website: www.imd.ch
Subject(s): Leadership programs

New
INTERNATIONAL LEADERSHIP ASSOCIATION (ILA)

ILA is an association for professionals involved in the field of leadership. The group meets once a year and continues dialogue in five special interest sections: leadership scholarship, leadership education, multicultural leadership, community organizing, and leadership development. Their goals are: 1) to generate and disseminate cutting-edge work in theory and practice; 2) to strengthen ties among those who study, teach, and exercise leadership; and 3) to serve as a forum for sharing research, resources, and ideas.

Publications: Section reports
Meetings: Annual conference
Address: c/o Center for the Advanced Study of Leadership, James MacGregor Burns Academy of Leadership, University of Maryland, College Park, MD 20742-7715
Phone: (301) 405-7920
Fax: (301) 405-6402
E-mail: ila@academy.umd.edu
Website: www.academy.umd.edu/ila
Subject(s): Leadership education

New
INTERNATIONAL SOCIETY FOR PERFORMANCE IMPROVEMENT (ISPI)

ISPI is a nonprofit organization dedicated to improving individual and organizational performance in the workplace through a systemic approach called Human Performance Technology (HPT). Members from around the world include trainers, human resources managers, and organizational development consultants. The society conducts workshops; facilitates discussion forums on HPT; and presents excellence awards for research, design, and implementation of performance improvement initiatives.

Publications: *Performance Improvement Journal*; *Performance Improvement Quarterly*; *The Handbook of Human Performance Improvement*; other books
Meetings: Annual conference
Address: 1300 L Street, N.W, Suite 1250, Washington, DC 20005
Phone: (202) 408-7969
Fax: (202) 408-7972

E-mail: info@ispi.org
Website: www.ispi.org/
Subject(s): Human resources development

THE INTERNATIONAL UNIVERSITY CONSORTIUM FOR EXECUTIVE EDUCATION (UNICON)

UNICON is a nonprofit organization dedicated to advancing the field of university-sponsored executive education through innovative processes for developing leaders and their organizations. Educational institutions and corporate representatives share dialogue on leadership development informally and at annual meetings. Their focus is on benchmarking and best practices, staff development, return on investment, and market research. UNICON members are located in North America, Europe, Australia, and Asia.

Publications: Member directory
Meetings: Annual spring and fall conferences
Address: 123 Cross Hill Road, Millington, NJ 07946-1412
Phone: (908) 903-1180
Fax: (908) 903-1180
E-mail: ExecDir@uniconexed.org
Website: www.uniconexed.org
Subject(s): Corporate leadership

KAUFFMAN CENTER FOR ENTREPRENEURIAL LEADERSHIP

This center established by the Ewing Marion Kauffman Foundation is dedicated to stimulating the growth and development of entrepreneurship in both the for-profit and nonprofit sectors. Their Entrepreneurial Training Institute teaches strategic development to existing or emerging entrepreneurs and also teaches about the free-enterprise system to students from kindergarten through high school. Through grants, the institute supports applied research, curriculum development, and evaluation.

Publications: *Attracting and Retaining Awesome People Toolbox*; *Entrepreneurship 2000*; research reports
Address: 4801 Rockhill Road, Kansas City, MO 64110-2046
Phone: (816) 932-1000
Fax: (816) 932-1100
E-mail: info@emkf.org
Website: www.emkf.org/entrepreneurship/vision.cfm
Subject(s): Entrepreneurship

W. K. KELLOGG FOUNDATION

The foundation helps people help themselves and improve their quality of life. It provides seed money to organizations and grants to persons and programs concerned with the application of existing knowledge. It supports emerging and existing leaders by providing them with broadened perspectives about local and national issues, improving their skills, and facilitating creative solutions. Its two signature fellowship programs are the Kellogg National Leadership Program and the Kellogg International Leadership Program.

Publications: *Developing Leadership in an International Context: A Summary of the Final Evaluation Report of the Kellogg International Leadership Program II*; *International Journal*; annual report; program guidelines
Address: One Michigan Avenue East, Battle Creek, MI 49017-4058
Phone: (616) 968-1611
Fax: (616) 968-0413
E-mail: communications@4sq.com
Website: www.wkkf.org
Subject(s): Funding for leadership programs

LEADERSHAPE, INC.

LeaderShape, Inc. is a nonprofit organization committed to developing young adults who will lead with integrity. The LeaderShape Institute is a six-day session in which students create visions, build teams, implement action plans, utilize ethics in decision making, and evaluate their personal strengths and weaknesses. Students create LeaderShape Projects to work on when they leave to effect extraordinary improvement in their organizations within the following year. Carpe Diem is a one-day course based on the same principles but in an abbreviated format.

Address: 1801 Fox Drive, Suite 101, Champaign, IL 61820-7255
Phone: (217) 351-6200
Fax: (217) 355-0910
E-mail: lead@leadershape.org
Website: www.leadershape.org
Subject(s): Student leadership

LEADERSHIP AMERICA, INC.

This nonprofit organization is dedicated to developing women's leadership at the state level. Participants are senior-level female executives in the corporate, nonprofit, and public sectors; educators; and entrepreneurs. The 50 by 20 initiative aims to replicate the program in 50 states by 2008, the 20th anniversary of Leadership America. Leadership training and networking is offered through the American Issues Forum and a mentoring program.

Meetings: Annual conference
Address: 700 North Fairfax Street, Suite 610, Alexandria, VA 22314-2040
Phone: (703) 549-1102
Fax: (703) 836-9205
E-mail: info@leadershipamerica.com
Website: www.leadershipamerica.com
Subject(s): Women's leadership

New
LEADERSHIP FOR ASIAN PACIFICS, INC. (LEAP)

This nonprofit organization exists to develop Asian American leaders in all sectors of society. LEAP offers separate leadership training institutes for Asian Americans in business, education, and community groups. A series of one-day workshops addresses visibility, networking, career planning, and collaborative problem solving. All programs contain a heavy emphasis on personal understanding and public awareness of Asian Pacific cultural values. A summer paid-internship program for college students puts emerging leaders to work in community-based organizations.

Publications: Research reports
Meetings: Annual awards dinner
Address: 327 East Second Street, Suite 226, Los Angeles, CA 90012
Phone: (213) 485-1422
Fax: (213) 485-0050
E-mail: leap@leap.org
Website: www.leap.org
Subject(s): Asian American leadership

MANDEL CENTER FOR NONPROFIT ORGANIZATIONS

The center is sponsored by four graduate schools of Case Western Reserve University: applied social sciences, management, law, and arts and sciences. The mission of the Mandel Center is to foster excellence in the education and leadership of nonprofit organizations. It conducts research and training for students, staff, and trustees in human services, the arts, education, community development, and religion. Programs include the Master of Nonprofit Organizations, an advanced professional degree; the Certificate in Nonprofit Management for the practicing manager; the Executive Education program of workshops for practicing managers; and the Nonprofit Management and Governance Clinic for the local nonprofit community.

Publications: *Nonprofit Management and Leadership* quarterly journal; *Nonprofit Notes* newsletter; discussion paper series; book chapters; journal articles
Address: Case Western Reserve University, 10900 Euclid Avenue, Cleveland, OH 44106-7164
Phone: (216) 368-2275
Fax: (216) 368-8592
E-mail: def2@po.cwru.edu
Website: www.cwru.edu/msass/mandelcenter
Subject(s): Nonprofit leadership, leadership research

New
THE MASIE CENTER

The Masie Center conducts research and provides services that link human resources training to technology. Founder Elliott Masie presents skills seminars for online trainers, suggests strategic models for organizational learning, and reviews other organizations' products prior to launch. Many of Masie's articles, keynote speeches, and interviews with training gurus are archived on the website in text and audio formats.

Publications: *Learning Decisions* interactive newsletter; *TechLearn TRENDS* free electronic newsletter
Meetings: Annual conference and periodic videoconferences

Address: P.O. Box 397, Saratoga Springs, NY 12866
Phone: (800) 986-2743 or (518) 587-3522
Fax: (518) 587-3276
E-mail: emasie@masie.com
Website: www.masie.com
Subject(s): Technology as a training tool, learning competence

New
MENNINGER LEADERSHIP CENTER

As a part of the Menninger Clinic, a mental health organization, the leadership center aims to apply Menninger's knowledge of human behavior and motivation to improve work relationships, creativity, and achievement. Programs for corporate and government executives include: Motivation and Behavior, and Personal and Interpersonal Dimensions of Leadership. There are also personal development programs for physicians.

Address: P.O. Box 829, Topeka, KS 66601-0829
Phone: (800) 288-5357
Fax: (913) 648-3155
E-mail: info@menningerleadership.net
Website: www.menningerleadership.net
Subject(s): Leadership programs

New
MONASH MT. ELIZA BUSINESS SCHOOL

In addition to original programs developed at the school, Monash Mt. Eliza is licensed to provide a variety of leadership programs from vendors around the world. Serving managers from Australia and the Asian Pacific, Monash Mt. Eliza's programs include: Business Leadership Program, Business Leadership for Women, Coaching for Performance, Innovation and Creativity—Strategies for Success, Leadership Development Program, The Looking Glass Experience: Leadership in Action, Leading High Performance Teams, Negotiation and Influence Strategies, and Strategic Leadership.

Address: Kunyung Road, Mt. Eliza, Victoria 3930 Australia
Phone: 61 3 9215 1100
Fax: 61 3 9572 3691
E-mail: progmkt@mteliza.edu.au
Website: www.mteliza.edu.au
Subject(s): Leadership programs

CHARLES STEWART MOTT FOUNDATION

The major concern of this foundation is maintaining the well-being of a community through partnerships among individuals, families, neighborhoods, and governments. Fundamental to Mott's grant making is nurturing strong individuals to ensure a well-functioning society, encouraging responsible citizen participation, promoting the empowerment of all individuals, and respecting the diversity of life. Leadership development initiatives that received funding in recent years are the American Leadership Forum's Collaborative

Leadership in Action, National Urban Coalition's Executive Leadership Program, and the Institute for Educational Leadership, Inc.

Publications: *Philosophy, Programs & Procedures* foundation guidelines; *@mott.now* and *InFocus* newsletters; brochures; annual report
Address: 1200 Mott Foundation Building, Flint, MI 48502-1851
Phone: (810) 238-5651
Fax: (810) 766-1753
E-mail: infocenter@mott.org
Website: www.mott.org
Subject(s): Funding for leadership programs

New
NATIONAL ACADEMY OF PUBLIC ADMINISTRATION

This independent, nonpartisan organization serves to enhance excellence in public management and administration. The academy is chartered by Congress and consists of 480 fellows who are current or former members of Congress or are public managers or scholars. In addition to problem solving, innovation, and research, the academy is a public education institution for traditional and emerging issues of governance. The Management Studies Program analyzes and evaluates managerial and performance issues in public institutions. The Center for Human Resources Management is a consortium within the Academy providing information and services for human resource professionals.

Publications: *Public Objective* newsletter; research reports; case studies
Address: 1120 G Street, N.W., Suite 850, Washington, DC 20005
Phone: (202) 347-3190
Fax: (202) 393-0993
Website: www.napawash.org
Subject(s): Public leadership

NATIONAL ASSOCIATION FOR CAMPUS ACTIVITIES (NACA)

Nearly 1,200 institutions of higher learning and associate members share ideas for the development of extracurricular and cocurricular activities, including student leadership development. NACA maintains a library and a hall of fame, compiles statistics, and bestows awards. It serves as a resource for scholarships that are awarded to outstanding student leaders. NACA Educational Foundation conducts leadership education research and hosts a National Summer Leadership Symposium.

Publications: *Programming* magazine; *Student Leadership Development: Approaches, Methods and Models*; other books and program resources
Meetings: Annual convention
Address: 13 Harbison Way, Columbia, SC 29212-3401
Phone: (803) 732-6222
Fax: (803) 749-1047

E-mail: shelbyw@naca.org
Website: www.naca.org
Subject(s): Student leadership

NATIONAL ASSOCIATION FOR COMMUNITY LEADERSHIP (NACL)

Local community-leadership programs and individuals in the U.S. and abroad join NACL to share ideas for transforming communities through leadership development. The network headquarters in Indianapolis creates, gathers, and distributes information, and provides training. A toll-free hotline connects members to a clearinghouse for advice and materials from successful programs. Two awards are given each year to recognize excellence in community leadership— The Distinguished Leadership Award to a program graduate and the Preceptor Award to a program director.

Publications: *Leadership News* newsletter; *Taking Leadership in Hand: The Program Development Guide*; *Leading the Way: A Guide to Changing Community Leadership*; other books and program resources
Meetings: Annual conference; seminars
Address: 200 South Meridian Street, Suite 250, Indianapolis, IN 46225-1015
Phone: (317) 637-7408
Fax: (317) 637-7413
Website: www.communityleadership.org
Subject(s): Community leadership

NATIONAL ASSOCIATION OF SECONDARY SCHOOL PRINCIPALS (NASSP)

The association serves leaders at the secondary school level—administrators, educators, and students. A resource center develops and distributes leadership training guides, professional education programs, and student activity materials. Assessment and development programs for administrators include: Democratic Leadership, Selecting and Developing the 21st Century Principal, Succession Planning for School Leaders, and the Quality School Leaders series. NASSP also sponsors scholarships, awards for outstanding leadership, international exchange programs for administrators and students, and summer leadership camps for students.

Publications: *NASSP Resource Guide; NASSP Bulletin; NASSP NewsLeader; Leadership for Student Activities;* books; research reports; videos; curriculum guides
Meetings: Annual conference; seminars
Address: 1904 Association Drive, Reston, VA 20191-1537
Phone: (703) 860-0200
Fax: (703) 476-5432
E-mail: nassp@nassp.org
Website: www.nassp.org
Subject(s): Educational leadership

NATIONAL CENTER FOR NONPROFIT BOARDS (NCNB)

NCNB's mission is to improve the effectiveness of nonprofit organizations by strengthening their boards of directors. The Board Development Program helps nonprofits design and conduct workshops and retreats. The Board Information Center provides information and advice on nonprofit governance. The membership program offers significant discounts on publications, workshops, and board development programs; a subscription to NCNB's periodical; and toll-free access to the Board Information Center.

Publications: *Turning Vision Into Reality*; *Board Members* newsletter; books; the Nonprofit Governance Series; videos; audiotapes; resource kits
Meetings: Annual National Leadership Forum; other conferences and seminars
Address: 1828 L Street, N.W., Suite 900, Washington, DC 20036-5104
Phone: (800) 883-6262 or (202) 452-6262
Fax: (202) 452-6299
E-mail: ncnb@ncnb.org
Website: www.ncnb.org
Subject(s): Nonprofit leadership

NATIONAL CLEARINGHOUSE FOR LEADERSHIP PROGRAMS (NCLP)

The goal of this organization is to have on file a copy of every higher education leadership course and program in the U.S. All educators are invited to send in their materials, and NCLP members are eligible to receive copies upon request. Their publications board invites educators to send papers on program evaluation, civic leadership, and other topics of interest for the Leadership Education and Leadership Scholar Series.

Publications: *Concepts & Connections: A Newsletter for Leadership Educators*; *Leader Scholar Series*
Meetings: Leadership Symposium annual conference
Address: 1135 Stamp Student Union, University of Maryland, College Park, MD 20742-7174
Phone: (301) 314-7164
Fax: (301) 314-9634
E-mail: nclp@union.umd.edu
Website: www.inform.umd.edu/OCP/NCLP
Subject(s): Leadership education

NATIONAL COMMUNITY FOR LATINO LEADERSHIP (NCLL)

Organizations that support leadership development for Latino youth, college students, and midcareer professionals form this network. NCLL acts as a clearinghouse for leadership models and community advocacy programs, and it submits policy analysis to the electronic network, LatinoNet. NCLL evaluates the impact of leadership development programs in the U.S. and Puerto Rico. Most of the programs sponsored by NCLL member organizations address civic education, analytical and communication skills, and internships with policy-making or advocacy groups.

Publications: National directory of Latino leadership programs
Meetings: Regional and national meetings
Address: 1701 K Street, N.W., Suite 301, Washington, DC 20006
Phone: (888) 464-6255 or (202) 721-8290
Fax: (202) 721-8296
E-mail: ncll@latinoleadership.org
Website: www.latinoleadership.org
Subject(s): Hispanic leadership

NATIONAL FORUM FOR BLACK PUBLIC ADMINISTRATORS (NFBPA)

NFBPA is a professional membership organization dedicated to the advancement of African American leadership in the public sector. Through research, networking, training, and mentoring programs, it strengthens the position of African Americans in public administration and grooms young, aspiring administrators for senior positions. Special programs like the Executive Leadership Institute polish the managerial skills of successful black managers seeking executive appointments in public service. The Mentor program matches emerging leaders with seasoned executives to facilitate career planning, skills enhancement, and networking support. The Bridges Summer Internship Program provides exposure to state and local government agencies for students planning careers in public service. Members gain access to a toll-free JOBS-HOTLINE which provides an up-to-date listing of public-management job opportunities in municipal and state agencies.

Publications: *The Forum* newsletter; membership directory
Meetings: Annual conference
Address: 777 North Capitol Street, N.E., Suite 807, Washington, DC 20002-4239
Phone: (202) 408-9300
Fax: (202) 408-8558
E-mail: nfbpa@erols.com
Website: www.nfbpa.org
Subject(s): African American leadership

NATIONAL HISPANA LEADERSHIP INSTITUTE (NHLI)

NHLI is a nonprofit organization committed to the education and leadership development of Hispanic women. Through the development of ethical leaders in a national network, it seeks to develop communities. The NHLI fellowship program is held in four segments over a nine-month period. The first, held in California, focuses on community building. The second, held at Harvard's Kennedy School of Government, presents an overview of public management. The third, held at the Center for Creative Leadership, focuses on creative goal setting and action planning. The final segment, held in Washington, DC, explores the national political agenda, policy development, and the legislative process.

Graduates of the program serve on local, state, and national boards and commissions, hold elected office, and act as mentors for other professional Hispanic women. Each year, the Mujer Award recognizes the sustained lifetime achievements of a Hispanic woman who has served her community and acted with justice, love, and the deepest of pride in her culture.

Publications: *NHLI News*
Meetings: Gala and leadership conference
Address: 1901 North Moore Street, Suite 206, Arlington, VA 22209-1706
Phone: (703) 527-6007
Fax: (703) 527-6009
E-mail: nhli@aol.com
Website: www.nhli.org
Subject(s): Hispanic leadership

NATIONAL INITIATIVE FOR LEADERSHIP AND INSTITUTIONAL EFFECTIVENESS (NILIE)

NILIE's purpose is to conduct research and disseminate information on leadership strategies in higher education. Its work links leadership to institutional effectiveness and promotes quality initiatives that improve student success. NILIE offers three customized organizational climate surveys and various organizational study instruments to community colleges, colleges, and universities throughout North America.

Publications: *Cultural, Environmental, Structural and Technical Assessment*; other assessment instruments
Meetings: Annual conference
Address: North Carolina State University, 300 Poe Hall, Box 7801, Raleigh, NC 27695-7801
Phone: (919) 515-6289
Fax: (919) 515-6305
E-mail: nilie@poe.coe.ncsu.edu
Website: www.ncsu.edu/cep/acce/nilie
Subject(s): Leadership research, educational leadership

NATIONAL LEAGUE OF CITIES (NLC)

The league's Leadership Training Institute exists to provide newly elected local officials with the knowledge and skills needed to help them respond proactively to the changing needs of their communities. Short-term seminars address developing a community vision, citizen involvement, ethics, media relations, and using technology as a leadership tool. Research initiatives, networking opportunities, and information sharing are available to local government leaders in cities that belong to the National League of Cities.

Publications: *Nations Cities Weekly*; *Issues & Options;* other reports
Meetings: Annual conferences and workshops
Address: 1301 Pennsylvania Avenue, N.W., Washington, DC 20004-1763
Phone: (202) 626-3000
Fax: (202) 626-3043

Website: www.nlc.org/ltiNST.htm
Subject(s): Public leadership

NATIONAL OUTDOOR LEADERSHIP SCHOOL (NOLS)

NOLS provides teenagers and adults with the opportunity to learn wilderness skills, leadership, and practical outdoor conservation. Mountaineering, kayaking, and horsepacking expeditions are conducted on public lands around the world—in the Rocky Mountains, Grand Canyon, Indian Himalayas, Australia, Alaska, Mexico, Chile, and Kenya. Courses for various ages and skill levels run ten days to three months. The curriculum in every course covers safety and judgment, leadership and teamwork, outdoor skills, and environmental studies. NOLS students may earn college credits at the University of Utah or by making arrangements for independent study at their home schools.

Publications: *The Leader* alumni newsletter; *1998 NOLS Leadership Education Toolbox*; guide books
Address: 288 Main Street, Lander, WY 82520-3140
Phone: (307) 332-5300
Fax: (307) 332-1220
E-mail: admissions@nols.edu
Website: www.nols.edu
Subject(s): Experiential education

NATIONAL SOCIETY FOR EXPERIENTIAL EDUCATION (NSEE)

As a community of individuals, institutions, and organizations, this society is committed to fostering the effective use of experience as an integral part of education, to empower learners, and to promote the common good. Its goals are: 1) to advocate the use of experiential learning throughout the educational system and the larger community, 2) to enhance the professional growth and leadership development of its members, 3) to disseminate information on principles of good practice and on innovations in the field, and 4) to encourage the development and dissemination of research and theory related to experiential learning.

Publications: *NSEE Quarterly*; *The National Directory of Internships*; *Program Evaluation Handbook*; other books
Meetings: Annual national conference
Address: 1703 North Beauregard Street, Suite 400, Alexandria, VA 22311-1714
Phone: (703) 933-0017
Fax: (703) 250-5852
E-mail: info@nsee.org
Website: www.nsee.org
Subject(s): Experiential education

NATIONAL YOUTH LEADERSHIP COUNCIL (NYLC)

The council develops service-oriented youth leaders by supporting individuals, organizations, and communities that encourage youth service and leadership. It coordinates the National Service-Learning Initiative that advises 34 model

K to 8 "Generator Schools" throughout the country. NYLC runs an annual summer camp, the National Youth Leadership Project, which trains young people to lead service learning initiatives in their own schools and communities, and offers one- to three-day Youth Leadership Development Seminars.

Publications: *The Generator* journal; *Growing Hope: A Sourcebook on Integrating Youth Service into the School Curriculum*; other books and curriculum guides
Meetings: Annual national conference
Address: 1910 West County Road B, St. Paul, MN 55113-5448
Phone: (800) 366-6952 or (651) 631-3672
Fax: (651) 631-2955
E-mail: nylcinfo@nylc.org
Website: www.nylc.org
Subject(s): Youth leadership

New
NORTHWESTERN UNIVERSITY

Faculty of the Kellogg Graduate School of Management teach executive education programs such as: Reinventing Leadership—A Breakthrough Approach, Value-based Management, and Leading High Impact Teams.

Address: Kellogg Graduate School of Management, Executive Programs, James L. Allen Center, 2169 North Sheridan Road, Evanston, IL 60208-2800
Phone: (847) 467-7000
Fax: (847) 491-4323
E-mail: ExecEd@nwu.edu
Website: www.kellogg.nwu.edu/exec_edu
Subject(s): Leadership programs

HUGH O'BRIAN YOUTH LEADERSHIP FOUNDATION (HOBY)

Founded in 1958 by actor Hugh O'Brian, HOBY seeks, recognizes, and develops leadership potential in high school sophomores by sponsoring state and international leadership seminars. Over 20,000 students each year attend the weekend workshops, which bring them together with recognized business and community leaders. Alumni are encouraged to continue their involvement through Community Leadership Workshops.

Publications: *Hugh O'Brian Youth Leadership Evaluation of Leadership Seminars: 1997 Evaluation and Training Institute*; annual report
Meetings: Annual World Leadership Congress
Address: 10880 Wilshire Boulevard, Suite 410, Los Angeles, CA 90024-4112
Phone: (310) 474-4370
Fax: (310) 475-5426
E-mail: hoby@hoby.org
Website: www.hoby.org
Subject(s): Youth leadership

OMICRON DELTA KAPPA

This national leadership honor society recognizes college students who exhibit superior scholarship, leadership, and exemplary character. Students must rank in the top third of their class and achieve distinction in athletics, campus or community service, social or religious activity, campus government, journalism, public speaking, or the creative arts. Society members are eligible to attend leadership workshops and for scholarships.

Publications: *The Omicron Delta Kappa Manual*; newsletter
Meetings: Biennial national convention; regional meetings
Address: University of Kentucky, 118 Bradley Hall, Lexington, KY 40506-0058
Phone: (606) 257-2110
Fax: (606) 323-1014
E-mail: odknhdq@pop.uky.edu
Website: www.odk.org
Subject(s): Leadership honor society

New
ORGANIZATIONAL BEHAVIOR TEACHING SOCIETY (OBTS)

This society's mission is to enhance the quality and promote the importance of teaching and learning across the management disciplines with a focus on the dynamics among individuals, groups, organizations, and cultures. Members share their experiences in the classroom, favorite resources, research projects, and innovative ideas. Each year, OBTS presents several awards to new and distinguished educators for excellence in teaching.

Publications: *Journal of Management Education*
Meetings: Annual conference; regional and international conferences
Address: Management Department, Colorado State University, Fort Collins, CO 80523-1275
Phone: (970) 491-6876
Fax: (970) 491-3522
E-mail: mccarthy@lamar.colostate.edu
Website: bernard.pitzer.edu/~obts
Subject(s): Organizational leadership

OUTWARD BOUND

This nonprofit educational organization uses experience-based programs to inspire self-esteem, self-reliance, concern for others, and respect for the environment. Students learn when they engage in and reflect on challenging environments, which require them to make choices, take responsible action, and work with others. Programs in five wilderness schools include dogsledding, rock climbing, whitewater rafting, and canyon exploration. There are also outdoor challenge programs in two urban centers, corporate team-building programs, and special courses for at-risk youths. Academic credit is available for many Outward Bound programs. The Kurt Hahn Leadership Center in North Carolina trains instructors of experiential and adventure-based education programs.

Publications: *Compass* alumni newsletter; course catalog
Address: 100 Mystery Point Road, Garrison, NY 10524-9757
Phone: (888) 882-6863 or (914) 424-4000
Fax: (914) 424-4280
Website: www.outwardbound.org
Subject(s): Experiential education

PEW PARTNERSHIP FOR CIVIC CHANGE

This national program is funded by the Pew Charitable Trusts to address problems in smaller American cities. It sponsors projects of collaboration between public, private, and nonprofit sectors in communities; identifies strategies for systemic change in urban issues; and suggests new models of citizen leadership for strengthening communities. The Pew Civic Entrepreneur Initiative helps participants learn about collaborative leadership among diverse groups and techniques to mobilize community assets.

Publications: *Community Matters* quarterly newsletter; *Leadership Collaboration Series* research reports
Address: 145-C Ednam Drive, Charlottesville, VA 22903-4629
Phone: (804) 971-2073
Fax: (804) 971-7042
E-mail: mail@pew-partnership.org
Website: www.pew-partnership.org
Subject(s): Public leadership, community leadership

PHI THETA KAPPA

Phi Theta Kappa is the international honor society for two-year colleges. With funding from the W. K. Kellogg Foundation, it has developed the Leadership Development Program, a humanities-based curriculum. Eleven skill modules incorporate readings from classic literature, films, discussion groups, and experiential activities. Additional modules teach students to identify their own leadership philosophies, maintain leadership journals, and create five-year plans. Although this program was created for junior-college students, Phi Theta Kappa encourages all leadership instructors and program directors to use this program in part or in full.

Publications: *Leadership Development Program Teacher's Manual*
Meetings: Annual convention
Address: 1625 Eastover Drive, Jackson, MS 39211-6461
Phone: (800) 946-9995 or (601) 957-2241
Fax: (601) 957-2625
E-mail: member.services@ptk.org
Website: www.ptk.org
Subject(s): Leadership honor society

POYNTER INSTITUTE FOR MEDIA STUDIES

This school promotes integrity among media professionals and encourages journalism that informs citizens and enlightens public discourse. Research, educational programs, and conferences support journalists and journalism students in all types of media—print, television, radio, photo, and online. A variety of leadership development programs focus on teamwork, ethics, diversity, and risk-taking.

Publications: *Poynter* newsletter; books; research reports; videos
Address: 801 Third Street South, St. Petersburg, FL 33701-4920
Phone: (888) 769-6837 or (727) 821-9494
Fax: (727) 821-0583
E-mail: info@poynter.org
Website: www.poynter.org
Subject(s): Leadership in journalism

PRINCETON CENTER FOR LEADERSHIP TRAINING

The center's mission is to increase opportunities for young people to succeed in school and in life. To achieve this mission the center helps students develop effective leadership skills and trains teams of educators, parents, and members of the community to work collaboratively to improve the education environment. Team Mentoring for Youth programs include The Peer Group Connection, which transforms peer pressure into a positive force, and Gesher L'Kesher, which helps Jewish adolescents build bridges connecting them to their heritage. The New Jersey Peer-to-Peer program helps to prevent substance abuse among middle school students. Programs are designed to reduce isolation, foster communication, improve morale, increase competence, and build confidence in all members of the school community.

Address: 12 Vandeventer Avenue, Princeton, NJ 08542-6921
Phone: (609) 252-9300
Fax: (609) 252-9393
E-mail: PrincetonCenter@juno.com
Website: www.princetonleadership.org
Subject(s): Youth leadership

PUBLIC HEALTH LEADERSHIP INSTITUTE (PHLI)

The institute is sponsored by the Centers for Disease Control and Prevention. Its mission is to strengthen America's public health system by enhancing the leadership capacities of senior public-health officials. Each year, a new class of city, county, and state health officials participates in the year-long program. Learning modules include: Personal Growth for Leadership Excellence, Leading Change for Public Health, Community Building and Collaborative Leadership, and Communications. The institute also holds interactive electronic seminars and writes case studies.

Publications: *Development of the 21st Century Workforce: Leadership, Commitment and Action—The Crucial Next Steps*
Meetings: American Public Health Association annual meeting
Address: 1204 Preservation Park Way, Oakland, CA 94612

Phone: (510) 986-0140
Fax: (510) 986-0146
Website: www.cfhl.org/phli/pimain.html
Subject(s): Public leadership, leadership in health care

PUBLIC LEADERSHIP EDUCATION NETWORK (PLEN)

PLEN is a consortium of women's colleges working together to educate women for public leadership. Students learn about the policy process in PLEN sessions in Washington, DC, and in programs on their own campuses. In the Women and Congress seminar, female members of Congress instruct students on the role of women in the lawmaking process. Women, Law, and Public Policy: A Public Leadership Career Conference introduces law students to women lawyers who use their legal education to influence public policy. Other programs include a Women and International Policy seminar and a Public Policy Internship semester.

Address: 1001 Connecticut Avenue, N.W., Suite 900, Washington, DC 20036-5524
Phone: (202) 872-1585
Fax: (202) 457-0549
E-mail: plen@plen.org
Website: www.plen.org
Subject(s): Public leadership, women's leadership

REFLECTIVE LEADERSHIP CENTER

Reflective leadership is informed by a sense of history, oriented toward the future, imbued with ethics and vision, and strong on follow-through and diversity. Reflective leadership is central to the Hubert H. Humphrey Institute's mission of education for public responsibility in a highly complex, specialized, and technical society. Seminars and workshops on leadership, public affairs, and societal change are designed for experienced practitioners with diverse ethnic and occupational backgrounds. All programs link theory and practice through role plays, simulations, small groups, journal writing, retreats, private study, presentations, and discussions.

Publications: *Leadership for the Common Good Fieldbook*; other books; articles; videos; audiotapes
Meetings: Leadership for the Common Good seminars held January through June
Address: Hubert H. Humphrey Institute of Public Affairs, University of Minnesota, 301 19th Avenue South, Room 55, Minneapolis, MN 55455-0429
Phone: (612) 625-7377
Fax: (612) 624-5756
E-mail: bcrosby@hhh.umn.edu
Website: www.hhh.umn.edu/centers/rlc
Subject(s): Public leadership, social responsibility

New
SOCIETY FOR HUMAN RESOURCES MANAGEMENT (SHRM®)

SHRM is a member association for those who practice and study human resources management. The nonprofit SHRM Foundation operates as the research and development arm of the organization. It conducts research and designs educational programs. Members network and develop skills in professional emphasis groups, through SHRM's information services, and at member forums.

Publications: *HR Magazine*; *HR News Online*; research reports
Meetings: Conferences
Address: 1800 Duke Street, Alexandria, VA 22314-3499
Phone: (800) 283-7476 or (703) 548-3440
Fax: (703) 535-6490
E-mail: shrm@shrm.org
Website: www.shrm.org
Subject(s): Human resources managers

New
SOCIETY FOR INDUSTRIAL ORGANIZATIONAL PSYCHOLOGISTS (SIOP)

SIOP is a division of the American Psychological Association for behavioral scientists who specialize in human behavior in the workplace. These professionals facilitate behavioral measurement and identify training needs. They advise organizations about communication, motivation, social interaction, and leadership issues.

Publications: *The Industrial/Organizational Psychologist (TIP)* journal; research reports
Meetings: Annual conference; symposia
Address: P.O. Box 87, Bowling Green, OH 43402-0087
Phone: (419) 353-0032
Fax: (419) 352-2645
E-mail: lhakel@siop.bgsu.edu
Website: www.siop.org
Subject(s): Psychology of leadership

THE SOCIETY FOR NONPROFIT ORGANIZATIONS

The society exists to foster the betterment of individual nonprofit organizations, regardless of their size and mission, and to foster a sense of community within the nonprofit sector. To promote excellence in leadership and governance practices, the society conducts research on emerging trends and provides training and information to its members. Resources available to members include a monthly funding alert on grant opportunities, tax and legal updates, a directory of services and products, and a professional network of colleagues throughout the voluntary sector. Society members are eligible for group discounts on publications, long-distance telephone charges, travel, office supplies, and other services.

Publications: *Nonprofit World* journal; *Nonprofit World Funding Alert*

Address: 6314 Odana Road, Suite 1, Madison, WI 53719-1141
Phone: (800) 424-7367 or (608) 274-9777
Fax: (608) 274-9978
E-mail: snpo@danenet.org
Website: www.danenet.org/snpo
Subject(s): Nonprofit leadership

New
SOCIETY FOR ORGANIZATIONAL LEARNING (SOL)

SoL is a global learning community for practitioners and scholars dedicated to the interdependent development of people and their institutions. Individual and organizational members collaborate on research projects, peer learning, and capacity-building workshops that integrate leading and learning.

Publications: *Reflections: The SoL Journal*; *Work-Based Learning: The New Frontier of Management Development*; other books and reports
Meetings: Annual conference
Phone: (617) 492-6260
E-mail: Contact@sol-ne.org
Website: www.sol-ne.org
Subject(s): Organizational learning

New
STANFORD UNIVERSITY

Stanford University takes advantage of its proximity to Silicon Valley and invites entrepreneurs from the nearby technology companies to serve as guest lecturers. Executive education programs include: Human Resource Executive Program—Leveraging Human Resources for Competitive Advantage, Leading and Managing Change, Managing Teams for Innovation and Success, and the Stanford Leadership Seminar.

Publications: *The Knowing-Doing Gap: How Smart Companies Turn Knowledge into Action*; *Stanford Business* alumni magazine
Address: Office of Executive Education, Stanford Graduate School of Business, Stanford, CA 94305-5015
Phone: (650) 723-3341
Fax: (650) 723-3950
E-mail: executive_education@gsb.stanford.edu
Website: www.gsb.stanford.edu/exed
Subject(s): Leadership programs

STENNIS CENTER FOR PUBLIC SERVICE

The mission of the Stennis Center is to promote and strengthen public service leadership in the U.S. The center provides training and development in three broad areas:
1) attracting talented young people to public service;
2) enhancing the ability and commitment of senior congressional staff to service the institution of Congress and its members in a world of rapid change; and 3) improving the quality, character, and performance of state, local, and other appointed and elected officials. The center is an independent agency of the federal legislative branch and is governed by a board of trustees appointed by the Democratic and Republican leaders in the U.S. House of Representatives and U.S. Senate.

Publications: Annual report; *Implications of a Global Economy for Congressional Operations: New Staff Roles to Foster Institutional Innovation & Effectiveness*; *Beyond Vicious Circles: Toward a Restoration of Stewardship and Public Trust in Congress*
Address: P.O. Box 9629, Mississippi State, MS 39762-9629
Phone: (662) 325-8409
Fax: (662) 325-8623
Website: www.stennis.gov
Subject(s): Public leadership

New
STRATEGIC LEADERSHIP FORUM (SLF)

Also known as the International Society for Strategic Management, this association aims to advance the understanding and practice of strategic management to improve organizational performance and global competitiveness. More than 4,000 members, primarily senior executives, participate in monthly chapter meetings and annual events for national and international networking. Every year SLF presents the Peter F. Drucker Strategic Leadership Award "to recognize an innovative and results-oriented leader who, through others, executes a vision with consistency, candor, and focus."

Publications: *Strategy & Leadership* magazine
Meetings: The annual International Strategic Leadership Conference; regional conferences
Address: 435 North Michigan Avenue, Chicago, IL 60611-4008
Phone: (800) 873-5995 or (312) 644-0829
Fax: (312) 644-8557
E-mail: cclark@bostrom.com
Website: http://rampages.onramp.net/~formac
Subject(s): Strategic leadership

TRUSTEE LEADERSHIP DEVELOPMENT (TLD)

TLD is a national nonprofit leadership center offering training and resources to nonprofit boards and executives. It provides coaching and customized workshops that assist participants in self-assessment and the inner work of leadership. Organizational development work includes cultural assessment, history, mission, and strategic planning.

Publications: *TLD Trustee Education Manual*; *TLD Individual and Community Trusteeship Manual*; videos include *Trustee Leadership Development: Building the Capacity to Serve and to Lead*
Address: 719 Indiana Avenue, Suite 370, Indianapolis, IN 46202-3176
Phone: (877) 564-6853 or (317) 636-5323
Fax: (317) 636-0266

E-mail: info@tld.org
Website: www.tld.org
Subject(s): Nonprofit leadership

UNITED NATIONAL INDIAN TRIBAL YOUTH, INC. (UNITY)

UNITY is a national organization serving Native American and Alaska Native youths ages 15 to 24. The UNITY Network, which consists of 147 youth councils in 29 states, develops leadership, instills cultural pride, and promotes self-sufficiency through conferences, regional training, work-shops, and seminars. Youth councils allow young people to develop leadership skills, help others, and become effective team players.

Meetings: Annual conference
Address: P.O. Box 25042, Oklahoma City, OK 73125
Phone: (405) 236-2800
Fax: (405) 971-1071
E-mail: unity@unityinc.org
Website: www.unityinc.org
Subject(s): Native American leadership

New
UNIVERSITY OF PENNSYLVANIA

Wharton's research-based executive education programs include: Critical Thinking—Real-world, Real-time Decisions, Executive Leadership Program, Executive Team Dynamics—When All Members are Leaders, Leading Organizational Change, and Managing People—Power Through Influence. A certificate of professional development is awarded to participants who successfully complete four courses within a four-year period.

Publications: *Leadership Digest* bulletin
Meetings: Annual leadership conference
Address: Wharton Executive Education, 255 South 38th Street, Philadelphia, PA 19104-6359
Phone: (800) 255-3932 or (215) 898-4560
Fax: (215) 386-4304
E-mail: execed@wharton.upenn.edu
Website: www.wharton.upenn.edu/execed
Subject(s): Leadership programs

New
UNIVERSITY OF VIRGINIA

Darden's research-based executive education programs include: Creating the Future—The Challenge of Transforma-tional Leadership, Leadership for Extraordinary Perfor-mance, and Power and Leadership. There are also a variety of industry-specific programs focused on leadership and change.

Address: Darden Executive Education, P.O. Box 6550, Charlottesville, VA 22906-6550
Phone: (877) 833-3974 or (804) 924-3000
Fax: (804) 982-2833
E-mail: Darden_Exed@Virginia.edu
Website: exed.darden.virginia.edu
Subject(s): Leadership programs

THOMAS J. WATSON FELLOWSHIP PROGRAM

The Thomas J. Watson Fellowship Program enables college graduates with leadership potential to spend a year of independent study and travel abroad. This opportunity for *Wanderjahr* allows students to thoroughly explore a particu-lar interest, test aspirations and abilities, and develop a sense of international concern. Fellowships of $22,000 are awarded to students who demonstrate integrity, potential for creative achievement, and excellence within a chosen field. Appli-cants must be nominated by one of 50 participating colleges.

Publications: Informational brochure
Address: 293 South Main Street, Providence, RI 02903
Phone: (401) 274-1952
Fax: (401) 274-1954
Website: www.watsonfellowship.org
Subject(s): Funding for leadership programs

WILDERNESS EDUCATION ASSOCIATION (WEA)

The purpose of the WEA is to promote the professionalism of outdoor leadership, thereby improving the safety of outdoor trips and enhancing the conservation of the wild outdoors. Strategies to achieve professionalism include the Outdoor Leadership Certification Program, curriculum development, program consulting, and research. Backpack-ing, rafting, and mountaineering courses are available for college credits, for trainer certification, and for short-term, low-impact sessions. Participants learn judgment and decision making, group dynamics, wilderness skills, environmental ethics, and emergency procedures.

Publications: *WEA Legend* newsletter; *The Backcountry Classroom: Lesson Plans for Teaching in the Wilderness*; catalog
Meetings: Annual conference
Address: 1101 Otter Creek Road, Nashville, TN 37220-1708
Phone: (615) 331-5739
Fax: (615) 331-9023
E-mail: wea@edge.net
Website: www.wildernesseducation.org
Subject(s): Experiential education

CONFERENCES

The conferences described here include regularly scheduled events that offer workshops, nationally recognized speakers, resource exhibitions, service learning opportunities, and presentations of scholarly papers. Information is provided about:

• the host organization
• audience
• when
• where
• cost, often based on previous conferences and intended only as an estimate to help with budget planning
• subject

Many conferences offer discounts for members, students, early registration, groups, and one-day tickets.

AEE INTERNATIONAL CONFERENCE

In addition to eight regional conferences throughout the year, AEE sponsors an annual international conference for professionals in experiential and adventure education. All conferences provide professional development renewal, networking opportunities, and workshops on outdoor adventure education programs. The annual conference includes an exhibition, more than 150 workshops, live entertainment, and numerous outdoor activities. For more information, contact Director of Conferences, AEE, 2305 Canyon Boulevard, Suite 100, Boulder, CO 80302-5651. (303) 440-8844. www.aee.org

Host Organization(s): Association for Experiential Education (AEE)
Audience: Educators and trainers
When: Each fall
Where: Location varies—2000 in Tucson, AZ; 2001 in Charleston, WV
Cost: $200 to $350
Subject(s): Adventure education

ALE ANNUAL CONFERENCE

ALE challenges educators to stretch beyond existing boundaries in practicing and teaching leadership, to bring ideas and enthusiasm to the conference, and to take home inspiration and personal renewal. The conference appeals to various interest groups with programs on graduate and undergraduate curricula, youth leadership development, business leadership, theory and concepts, and practical tips. Participants may attend concurrent sessions, workshops, papers presentations, roundtable discussions, an awards ceremony, and social events. Conference proceedings are published. For more information, contact Jon Irby, USDA/CSREES, 1400 Independence Avenue, S.W., Stop 2225 USDA/CSREES/F4-HN, Washington, DC 20250-2225. (202) 720-5345. www.aces.uiuc.edu/~ALE

Host Organization(s): Association of Leadership Educators (ALE)
Audience: Leadership educators
When: Each July
Where: Location varies—2000 in Toronto, ON
Cost: $125 to $160
Subject(s): Leadership education

AMA'S GLOBAL HUMAN RESOURCE CONFERENCE

This three-day conference addresses the real-world challenges faced by human resources professionals. Sessions offer practical solutions for harnessing cultural dynamics, linking HR services to corporate goals, aligning processes and systems to support change, using technology for communicating and motivating, developing leadership, and building global teams. Additional sessions encourage networking and discussion of hot topics. Includes a book shop. For more information, contact AMA, 1601 Broadway, 8th Floor, New York, NY 10019-7420. (800) 262-9699 or (212) 586-8100. www.amanet.org

Host Organization(s): American Management Association (AMA)
Audience: Human resources professionals
When: Each April
Where: Location varies—2000 in Nice, France
Cost: $2,400 to $3,200
Subject(s): Human resources management

New
ANNUAL CREATIVE PROBLEM SOLVING INSTITUTE® (CPSI)

This one-week conference features more than 200 sessions on creative thinking and creativity in the workplace. Music, dance, and other artistic sessions help to release the participants' creative spirits. A springboard session on the Osborn-Parnes Creative Problem Solving process is a prerequisite for four creative leadership programs. These advanced programs help facilitators to develop their leadership styles and to learn the tools and techniques for creative problem solving in groups. Innovative Champions, a cooperate networking group, meets each morning to discuss ways to apply the CPSI experience in the workplace. There are simultaneous sessions for creative young leaders ages 10 to 18. For more information, contact CPSI Registrar, Creative Education Foundation, 1050 Union Road #4, Buffalo, NY 14224-3402. (800) 447-2774 or (716) 675-3181. www.cef-cpsi.org

Host Organization(s): Creative Education Foundation
Audience: General
When: Each June
Where: Buffalo, NY
Cost: $660 to $825
Subject(s): Creativity

New
ANNUAL STORYTELLING AND BUSINESS EXCELLENCE SUMMIT

The Storytelling Foundation believes that storytelling is at the heart of the human experience. This three-day conference celebrates this age-old art and its application in the business world. More than 25 sessions teach business leaders how to maximize their companies' narrative assets. Some applications are: building an organization's identity, managing change through shared values, developing team spirit, sharing knowledge, connecting with customers, and encouraging innovation. For more information, contact Storytelling Foundation International, 116 West Main Street, Jonesborough, TN 37659. (800) 952-8392 or (423) 753-2171. www.storytellingfoundation.net

Host Organization(s): Storytelling Foundation International
Audience: General
When: Each spring
Where: Jonesborough, TN
Cost: $1,500 to $2,300
Subject(s): Storytelling

New
ANNUAL SYMPOSIUM ON INDIVIDUAL, TEAM, AND ORGANIZATIONAL EFFECTIVENESS

This three-day conference examines the *hows* and *whys* of team effectiveness. Practicing HRD managers participate as session discussants to translate theoretical ideas into the language of practice. Some of the session topics are team diversity, geographically dispersed teams, systems thinking, online collaboration, and team learning. For more information, contact the Center for the Study of Work Teams, University of North Texas, P.O. Box 311280, Denton, TX 76203-1280. (940) 565-3096. www.workteams.unt.edu

Host Organization(s): Center for the Study of Work Teams at the University of North Texas
Audience: Team leaders, human resources managers, trainers, coaches, and organizational development consultants
When: Each spring
Where: Denton, TX
Cost: $395 to $695
Subject(s): Teams

New
ASPA NATIONAL CONFERENCE

This four-day event has a strong focus on local government and citizen involvement. Nearly 100 workshops and concurrent sessions address such topics as ethics, collaboration, and communities of the future. Some presenters offer research reports, others offer career advice. Each year, the National Public Service Awards are presented to exceptional public servants. For more information, contact ASPA, 1120 G Street, N.W., Suite 700, Washington, DC 20005. (202) 393-7878. www.aspanet.org

Host Organization(s): American Society for Public Administration (ASPA)
Audience: Public administrators and educators
When: Each spring
Where: Location varies—2001 in Newark, NJ
Cost: $250 to $625
Subject(s): Public service leadership

ASTD INTERNATIONAL CONFERENCE & EXPOSITION

This conference is for HRD professionals interested in training and development issues, tools, and technology. There are more than 200 concurrent sessions in nine areas: career development, global issues, human performance improvement, learning technologies, evaluation, managing the training function, organizational development, training basics, and workplace issues. There are also plenary speakers, in-depth preconference workshops, and more than 500 booths exhibiting resources. For more information, contact ASTD, 1640 King Street, Box 1443, Alexandria, VA 22313-2043. (800) 628-2783 or (703) 683-8100. www.astd.org

Host Organization(s): American Society for Training and Development (ASTD)
Audience: Human resources professionals
When: Each spring
Where: Location varies—2000 in Dallas, TX; 2001 in Orlando, FL
Cost: $720 to $1,140
Subject(s): Training

New
THE COACHING AND MENTORING CONFERENCE

This four-day conference offers solutions to coaching and mentoring challenges. Participants take the *Coaching Assessment Instrument* to analyze their strengths and weaknesses. Then they attend Learning Labs that focus on the core competencies they would like to improve. Following presentations by experts in the field, participants reflect on their new learning and make action plans. Keynote speakers describe successful coaching efforts in corporations and the link between coaching and emotional intelligence. For more information, contact Linkage, Inc., One Forbes Road, Lexington, MA 02421. (781) 862-3157. www.linkageinc.com

Host Organization(s): Linkage, Inc.
Audience: HRD professionals
When: Each spring
Where: Location varies—2000 in Chicago, IL
Cost: $1,095 to $1,395
Subject(s): Coaching, mentoring

New
DIVERSITY SUMMIT

This three-day conference focuses on measuring, managing, and leveraging diversity in the workforce. Specific topics include: recruiting and retaining a diverse workforce, training the trainer, senior management buy-in, and global diversity. Companies with successful diversity initiatives lead discussion groups. Vendors demonstrate diversity training products. Conference proceedings are available on videotape. For more information, contact IQPC, P.O. Box 401, 150 Clove Road, Little Falls, NJ 07424-0401. (800) 882-8684 or (973) 812-5161. www.iqpc.com

Host Organization(s): International Quality & Productivity Center (IQPC)
Audience: HRD executives and trainers
When: Each fall
Where: Location varies—2000 in Scottsdale, AZ
Cost: $1,495 to $2,295
Subject(s): Diversity

THE DRUCKER FOUNDATION LEADERSHIP AND MANAGEMENT FALL CONFERENCE

This conference focuses on issues of importance to leadership in nonprofit organizations. Nationally recognized leaders from business, government, and the social sector share ideas on designing and delivering service, developing partnerships, and accountability. Each year, one organization with an exceptional program or project is recognized with the Peter F. Drucker Award for Nonprofit Innovation and a $25,000 prize. Most conference sessions are audiotaped and available for purchase after the conference. For more information, contact The Peter F. Drucker Foundation, 320 Park Avenue, 3rd Floor, New York, NY 10022-6839. (212) 224-1174. www.pfdf.org

Host Organization(s): The Peter F. Drucker Foundation for Nonprofit Management
Audience: Nonprofit organization executives and board members
When: Each fall
Where: Location varies—2000 in Dallas, TX
Cost: $300
Subject(s): Nonprofit leadership

New
THE EFMD ANNUAL CONFERENCE

This three-day conference offers opportunities for discussion and reflection on corporate management in the Global Information Age. In 2000, a renaissance theme includes presenters from the diverse fields of philosophy, music, literature, military, management, and biotechnology. Participants are asked to challenge traditional thinking and explore the complexities of leading in a changing world. The conference language is English. For more information, contact efmd, 88 rue Gachard, Brussels, 1050. +32-(0)2-629 08 10. www.efmd.be

Host Organization(s): European Foundation for Management Development (efmd), SDA Bocconi, ABB, HEC School of Management, University of Chicago Graduate School of Business, and Isvor Fiat
Audience: Business leaders and educators with European interests
When: Each June
Where: Location varies—2000 in Sardinia, Italy
Cost: $1,300 to $1,800 Euro (approximately $1,260 to $1,740 U.S.)
Subject(s): Global leadership

New
THE EMERGING LEADER PROGRAM

Participants at this three-day conference learn how organizations are successfully developing leadership. They may follow one of six learning tracks: advanced practice, succession management, world-class programs, nonprofit and government systems, skill building, and leadership at all levels. Learning sessions are interspersed with keynote speeches in which experts such as Warren Bennis, John Kotter, Marshal Goldsmith, and Ann Richards present their views. Vendors display training products and classroom resources in an exhibition hall. For more information, contact Linkage, Inc., One Forbes Road, Lexington, MA 02421. (781) 862-3157. www.linkageinc.com

Host Organization(s): Linkage, Inc. and The Global Institute of Leadership Development
Audience: Executives, HRD professionals, trainers
When: Each fall
Where: Location varies—2000 in San Diego, CA; 2001 in Palm Springs, CA
Cost: $995 to $1,395
Subject(s): Leadership development

New
FRIENDS OF THE CENTER LEADERSHIP CONFERENCE

This three-day conference engages participants in dialogue with CCL faculty and researchers as well as with other leadership scholars. Examining leadership challenges in small groups provides exposure to new ideas and the opportunity to share ideas with colleagues who face similar challenges. Minisessions cover such topics as spirit and leadership, the power of vulnerability, the impact of globalization, the art of coaching, and the use of visual exploration to make sense of complex challenges. For more information, contact Monica Mancuso, CCL, P.O. Box 26300, Greensboro, NC 27438-6300. (336) 545-2810. www.ccl.org

Host Organization(s): Center for Creative Leadership (CCL)
Audience: Corporate, educational, and nonprofit leaders
When: Each summer
Where: Greensboro, NC
Cost: $720 to $900
Subject(s): Leadership research

HRPS ANNUAL CONFERENCE

This four-day conference offers professional development opportunities for human resources professionals. Strategy forums focus on building partnerships with CEOs and executive teams, fostering organizational growth, and creating a learning culture. Thought leaders who speak at the forums include Steve Kerr, David Nadler, Nancy Adler, and Dan Goleman. Other sessions report on HRPS research and use case studies for in-practice application. For more information, contact Dillian Waldron, HRPS, 317 Madison Avenue, Suite 1509, New York, NY 10017. (212) 490-6387. www.hrps.org

Host Organization(s): Human Resource Planning Society (HRPS)
Audience: Human resources executives
When: Each spring
Where: Location varies—2000 in New York, NY
Cost: $1,450 to $1,800
Subject(s): Human resources management

New
ILA ANNUAL MEETING

This three-day conference provides a forum to share cutting-edge ideas in five areas—leadership scholarship, leadership education, leadership development, multicultural leadership, and community leadership. Most of the sessions encourage interactive dialogue among a panel of experts and the conference participants. Some session topics are: systemic leadership, program evaluation, social change, assessment, global leadership, and mediated dialogue as a leadership process. For more information, contact James MacGregor Burns Academy of Leadership, University of Maryland, College Park, MD 20742-7715. (301) 405-7920. www.academy.umd.edu/ILA

Host Organization(s): International Leadership Association (ILA)
Audience: Leadership scholars and practitioners
When: Each fall
Where: Location varies—2000 in Toronto, ON
Cost: $250 to $350
Subject(s): Leadership education

INTERNATIONAL CONFERENCE ON SERVANT-LEADERSHIP

This three-day conference addresses the link between servant leadership and business, education, healthcare, religious organizations, and personal growth. It offers time to "withdraw and reorient oneself . . . to sort out the more important from the less important." Speakers from "most admired companies" and "best companies to work for" explain how to apply servant-leader characteristics in real-life situations. Other speakers address organizational learning, creativity, and leadership. Preconference workshops offer orientation sessions for those not familiar with the work of Robert K. Greenleaf and the theory of servant leadership. For more information, contact Kelly Tobe, The Robert K. Greenleaf Center, 921 East 86th Street, Suite 200, Indianapolis, IN 46240. (317) 259-1241. www.greenleaf.org

Host Organization(s): The Robert K. Greenleaf Center
Audience: General
When: Each June
Where: Indianapolis, IN
Cost: $495 to $645
Subject(s): Servant leadership

New
INTERNATIONAL CONFERENCE ON WORK TEAMS

This three-day conference presents cutting-edge ideas on systems applications for teams. Audience participation is invited in most sessions to showcase best practices and to practice new hands-on approaches. Session topics include: cross-cultural issues, team and organizational alignment, emotional intelligence, and technology for geographically dispersed teams. For more information, contact the Center for the Study of Work Teams, University of North Texas, P.O. Box 311280, Denton, TX 76203-1280. (940) 565-3096. www.workteams.unt.edu

Host Organization(s): Center for the Study of Work Teams at the University of North Texas

Audience: Team leaders, human resources managers, trainers, and organizational development consultants
When: Each fall
Where: Location varies—2000 in Dallas, TX
Cost: $595 to $995
Subject(s): Teams

New
INTERNATIONAL PERFORMANCE IMPROVEMENT CONFERENCE AND EXPO

This three-day conference teaches the concept of Human Performance Technology (HPT), a systematic approach to performance improvement. HPT involves performance analysis, cause analysis, intervention selection and design, and evaluation. This process may be applied to individuals, groups, or entire organizations. Conference sessions offer models, tools, and techniques to implement HPT. For more information, contact Registration Department, ISPI, 1300 L Street, N.W., Suite 1250, Washington, DC 20005. (202) 408-7969. www.ispi.org

Host Organization(s): International Society for Performance Improvement (ISPI)
Audience: Human resources managers, trainers, and organizational development consultants
When: Each spring
Where: Location varies—2000 in Cincinnati, OH
Cost: $549 to $849
Subject(s): Human resources management

New
LEADERSHIP CONFERENCE

This two-day event examines new frameworks for developing leadership. Session topics include: research findings and their practical applications, coaching, global leadership, diversity in the executive ranks, leadership development throughout an organization, and web-based training. Companies with established leadership development processes share their models and success stories. For more information, contact The Conference Board, 845 Third Avenue, New York, NY 10022-6679. (212) 759-0900. www.conference-board.org

Host Organization(s): The Conference Board, Center for Creative Leadership, and corporate sponsors
Audience: Executives, managers, and human resources professionals
When: Each June
Where: New York, NY
Cost: $1,425 to $1,625
Subject(s): Leadership development

New
THE LEADERSHIP DEVELOPMENT CONFERENCE

This three-day conference is about the development of corporate leadership and the impact that such development can have on organizations. There is emphasis on building programs, tools, techniques, and development systems. Prominent keynote speakers include Colin Powell, John Kotter, Warren Bennis, and Ann Richards. Other leadership scholars and practitioners lead half-day workshops on such topics as emotional intelligence and return-on-investment. There are six conference tracks that allow participation in specialized areas and advanced levels. For more information, contact Linkage, Inc., One Forbes Road, Lexington, MA 02421. (781) 862-3157. www.linkageinc.com

Host Organization(s): Linkage, Inc. and corporate sponsors
Audience: Business leaders and HRD executives
When: Each June
Where: Location varies—2000 in Washington, DC
Cost: $1,095 to $2,285
Subject(s): Leadership development, corporate leadership

New
LEADERSHIP INSTITUTE FOR HIGHER EDUCATION

Educational institutions are encouraged to send partners— two people who hold positions of leverage—to this conference. During the conference, partners interact and reflect on their personal and institutional values. Their goal is to forge alliances for incorporating servant leadership practices at different levels within their institutions. In 2000, Margaret Wheatley was a featured speaker. For more information, contact Julie Beggs, The Greenleaf Center for Servant-Leadership, 921 East 86th Street, Suite 200, Indianapolis, IN 46240. (317) 259-1241. www.greenleaf.org

Host Organization(s): The Greenleaf Center for Servant-Leadership and W. K. Kellogg Foundation
Audience: College and university presidents, faculty, board members, deans, and other decision-makers
When: Each April
Where: Indianapolis, IN
Cost: $1,495 to $1,795
Subject(s): Educational leadership, servant leadership

NACL ANNUAL LEADERSHIP CONFERENCE

This conference aims to energize civic leaders for the roles they play in strengthening and transforming communities. Participants are encouraged to make new connections, to explore community trusteeship, and to enrich their personal and professional lives. Workshops cover a wide range of interests from program marketing and unique programs for special groups to program evaluation and a festival of training films. Highlights of each conference are a leadership resource fair, sharing of success stories, and an awards ceremony. Audiotapes of most sessions are available for purchase. For more information, contact NACL, 200 South Meridian Street, Suite 250, Indianapolis, IN 46225. (317) 637-7408. www.communityleadership.org

Host Organization(s): National Association for Community Leadership (NACL) and corporate sponsors
Audience: Community leaders
When: Each spring

Where: Location varies—2000 in Miami, FL
Cost: $330 to $555
Subject(s): Community leadership

NASPA INTERNATIONAL SYMPOSIUM ON STUDENT SERVICES AROUND THE WORLD

This conference offers interest sessions on a wide variety of subjects: diversity, international programs, student leadership, staff development, distance learning, and technology issues. A Mentor Dinner helps young professionals form alliances with experienced mentors. An Internship Fair helps students find institutions with experiential learning opportunities. There are also keynote speakers, workshops, a career services center, and a case study competition. For more information, contact NASPA, 1875 Connecticut Avenue, N.W., Suite 418, Washington, DC 20009. (202) 265-7500. www.naspa.org

Host Organization(s): National Association of Student Personnel Administration (NASPA) and National Council on Student Development (NCSD)
Audience: Student affairs officers, faculty, and professionals
When: Each spring
Where: Location varies—2000 in Indianapolis, IN
Cost: $235 to $395
Subject(s): Student leadership

New
NASSP ANNUAL LEADERSHIP ACADEMY

This six-day academy examines various models for educational change and school excellence. Some of the topics examined are: raising children in the 21st century, acknowledging multicultural students, and raising emotional intelligence in the classroom. Participants learn to apply the Baldrige Award criteria to improve student achievement and to implement school-based mentoring programs. For more information, contact NASSP, 1904 Association Drive, Reston, VA 20191-1537. (703) 860-0200. www.nassp.org

Host Organization(s): National Association of Secondary School Principals (NASSP)
Audience: Principals and other school leaders
When: Each summer
Where: Washington, DC
Cost: $525 to $575
Subject(s): Educational leadership

NATIONAL COMMUNITY SERVICE CONFERENCE

This is an annual training event for leaders in the field of volunteer management. There are more than 100 workshops on topics such as collaboration, community leadership development, diversity, employee volunteerism, mentoring, personal development, technology, and service learning. Participants may choose to attend introductory, intermediate, or advanced sessions. Outside the classroom, participants may visit local model programs and engage in community service projects. For more information, contact The Points of Light

Foundation, 1400 I Street, N.W., Suite 800, Washington, DC 20005. (202) 729-8000. www.pointsoflight.org

Host Organization(s): The Points of Light Foundation
Audience: Nonprofit organization staff and board members
When: Each June
Where: Location varies—2000 in Orlando, FL
Cost: $380 to $600
Subject(s): Community leadership

NATIONAL CONFERENCE ON GOVERNANCE

For over 100 years, the National Civic League has held an annual conference and membership meeting showcasing community-building efforts. The three-day conference is attended by leaders from the public, private, and nonprofit sectors to discuss current innovations in local and state governance. A keynote speaker and plenary sessions feature experts with community revitalization success stories to share. For more information, contact National Civic League, 1445 Market Street, Suite 300, Denver, CO 80202-1728. (303) 571-4343. www.ncl.org

Host Organization(s): National Civic League (NCL)
Audience: Policymakers and civic leaders
When: Each fall
Where: Washington, DC
Cost: $300
Subject(s): Public service leadership

NATIONAL LEADERSHIP FORUM

This three-day conference addresses the issues of importance to the management and governance of nonprofit organizations: board composition and structure, leadership development, fund-raising, and the changing nature of volunteerism. A journalistic account of the proceedings is featured in the December issue of *Board Member*. For more information, contact NCNB, 1828 L Street, N.W., Suite 900, Washington, DC 20036-5104. (800) 883-6262 or (202) 452-6262. www.ncnb.org

Host Organization(s): National Center for Nonprofit Boards (NCNB)
Audience: Executives, staff members, and board members of nonprofit organizations
When: Each November
Where: Washington, DC
Cost: $350 to $525
Subject(s): Nonprofit leadership

NATIONAL LEADERSHIP SYMPOSIUM

The National Leadership Symposium is a scholarly program designed to promote a greater understanding of critical issues and evolving models centered on college student leadership programs—curricular, cocurricular, and community-based. Participants are expected to read assigned books in advance to prepare for conference discussions. Scholars are invited to bring working papers on leadership topics of interest to share with colleagues. For more information, contact NACA

Foundation, 13 Harbison Way, Columbia, SC 29212-3401. (803) 732-6222. www.naca.org

Host Organization(s): National Association for Campus Activities (NACA) Educational Foundation and National Clearinghouse for Leadership Programs (NCLP)
Audience: Experienced leadership faculty and student affairs professionals
When: Each July
Where: Location varies—2000 in Richmond, VA
Cost: $425 to $490—includes meals and lodging
Subject(s): Leadership education

NATIONAL SERVICE-LEARNING CONFERENCE

This event promotes service learning as a way to build citizenship and academic skills while renewing communities. Conference features include an activities hall for service project displays and experiential activities, site visits to local service projects, salons, workshops, information toolboxes, and a town hall meeting on active citizenship. Young people are encouraged to get involved as planners, leaders, and participants. For more information, contact National Youth Leadership Council, 1910 West County Road B, Roseville, MN 55113. (651) 631-3672. www.nylc.org

Host Organization(s): National Youth Leadership Council
Audience: Educators, students, and community leaders
When: Each spring
Where: Location varies—2000 in Providence, RI; 2001 in Denver, CO
Cost: $215 to $425
Subject(s): Student leadership, service learning

NSEE NATIONAL CONFERENCE

This conference caters to those who are new to the field of experiential education as well as those who have many years of experience. Workshops and roundtables feature ways to build bridges between schools and communities, school-to-work initiatives, and academic skills in experiential programs. A resource center, site visits, and poster sessions with models on display run throughout the four-day conference. For more information, contact NSEE, 1703 North Beauregard Street, Suite 400, Alexandria, VA 22311-1714. (703) 933-0017. www.nsee.org

Host Organization(s): National Society for Experiential Education (NSEE)
Audience: Experiential education professionals
When: Each fall
Where: Location varies—2000 in San Antonio, TX
Cost: $295 to $495
Subject(s): Experiential education

SDSU LEADERSHIP INSTITUTE

An intensive weekend program exposes students and advisors to issues on leadership, current affairs, and personal and professional growth. Workshops on motivation, creativity, meeting management, vision, goal setting, communication, and multicultural diversity encourage participants to find leadership opportunities in their own communities. For more information, contact SDSU Leadership Institute, San Diego State University, 5500 Campanile Drive, Mail Code 7440, San Diego, CA 92182-7440. (619) 594-5221. www.sa.sdsu.edu/src/leadership/leadership_home.html

Host Organization(s): San Diego State University (SDSU)
Audience: Student leaders and advisors from the western U.S.
When: Each fall
Where: San Diego, CA
Cost: $80 to $100
Subject(s): Student leadership

SHRM ANNUAL CONFERENCE

Since 1948, this conference has brought HRD managers together for professional development activities and a resources exposition. Masters series sessions are for senior HR executives. Strategic thinking sessions examine tools for critical thinking and strategic planning. More-to-life-than-work sessions help participants enhance their personal and professional experiences. There are also sessions focused on talent retention, rewards, and employment legal issues. Keynote speakers at the 2000 conference included Jay Leno, Edward Lawler III, Bertrice Berry, David Ulrich, and Archbishop Desmond Tutu. For more information, contact SHRM, 1800 Duke Street, Alexandria, VA 22314. (800) 283-7476 or (703) 548-3440. www.shrm.org

Host Organization(s): Society for Human Resource Management (SHRM)
Audience: Human resources professionals
When: Each June
Where: Location varies—2000 in Las Vegas, NV
Cost: $780 to $1,130
Subject(s): Human resources management

New
SIMMONS GSM LEADERSHIP CONFERENCE

Women's issues receive intense focus at this one-day conference. Featured speakers and session leaders are prominent leaders in business, politics, and social issues. In 2000, they included Her Majesty Queen Noor of Jordan; Katie Couric, anchor of NBC's Today Show; Lea Rabin, former First Lady of Israel; and Pulitzer Prize-winning author Frank McCourt. Between speakers, there are skill-building workshops on topics such as communication, entrepreneurship, and work/life balance. For more information, contact Simmons College Graduate School of Management, 409 Commonwealth Avenue, Boston, MA 02215. (800) 597-1622 or (617) 521-3840. www.simmons.edu/gsm

Host Organization(s): Simmons Graduate School of Management Alumnae Association and corporate sponsors
Audience: Female leaders
When: Each May
Where: Boston, MA

Cost: $375 to $500
Subject(s): Women's leadership

New
SIOP ANNUAL CONFERENCE

Three days of this conference are devoted to research reports and presentation of conceptual models. Topics include systemic leadership development, merging organizational cultures, multicultural team dynamics, and cognitive reactions to performance feedback. Panelists discuss career opportunities and professional standards in the field of industrial and organizational psychology. Also discussed are the use of assessment instruments, their validity studies, and a comparison of paper-and-pencil tests to online versions. One day of preconference workshops offers 16 choices of half-day continuing education programs for an additional fee. For more information, contact SIOP, P.O. Box 87, Bowling Green, OH 43402-0087. (419) 352-2645. www.siop.org

Host Organization(s): The Society for Industrial and Organizational Psychology (SIOP) and corporate sponsors
Audience: Industrial and organizational psychologists
When: Each April
Where: Location varies—2001 in San Diego, CA; 2002 in Toronto, ON
Cost: $65 to $155
Subject(s): Psychology of leadership

STUDENT LEADERSHIP TRAINING CONFERENCE

This one-day conference includes keynote speakers and breakout sessions on such topics as advising challenges, communication skills, ethical leadership, follow-through, innovation, motivation, service learning, and team building. *New Student Leader* and *Seasoned Student Leader* awards are presented to conference participants nominated by their advisors. For more information, contact Colleen Daly, Office of Leadership Training Programs, University of South Carolina, Russell House University Union 043, Columbia, SC 29208. (803) 777-6688. www.sa.sc.edu/stlife/leader/lead.htm

Host Organization(s): University of South Carolina–Columbia
Audience: Student leaders and advisors from the southeastern U.S.
When: Each spring
Where: Columbia, SC
Cost: $20 to $35
Subject(s): Student leadership

New
THE SUMMER INSTITUTE FOR INTERCULTURAL COMMUNICATION (SIIC)

This conference offers a range of workshops for novice to experienced facilitators in multicultural education and training. Three sessions over a three-week period offer lessons in valuing diversity and leading global corporations.

Some lessons offer comparisons between European and American or between Asian and Western cultures. Other lessons cover cross-cultural team building and conflict management. There are internship opportunities to support the conference faculty and experience multicultural teamwork in action. For more information, contact The Intercultural Communication Institute, 8835 S.W. Canyon Lane, Suite 238, Portland, OR 97225. (503) 297-4622. www.intercultural.org

Host Organization(s): The Intercultural Communication Institute
Audience: Educators and trainers
When: Each summer
Where: Portland, OR
Cost: $1,285 to $1,440
Subject(s): Cross-cultural communication

WEA NATIONAL CONFERENCE FOR OUTDOOR LEADERSHIP

This annual three-day conference focuses on existing wilderness-education programs and provides a forum to display and examine them. Workshops are offered in outdoor leadership, skill development, design of programs, and career issues. The Paul Petzoldt Award is presented each year to a professional who has made an outstanding contribution to the field of wilderness education. Preconference certification workshops are available for an extra fee. For more information, contact WEA, P.O. Box 158897, Nashville, TN 37215. (615) 531-5174. www.wildernesseducation.org

Host Organization(s): Wilderness Education Association (WEA) and university or state park cohosts
Audience: Educators, students, and trainers
When: Each winter
Where: Usually at a university campus or state park
Cost: $75 to $165
Subject(s): Adventure education

New
WHARTON LEADERSHIP CONFERENCE

Wharton School faculty members partner with other leadership scholars and corporate leaders to examine leadership issues at this one-day conference. There are nine one-hour lectures on such topics as cross-cultural issues, the speed of change, and technology as a leadership tool. One session features an improvisation group demonstrating creativity at work. A drawing for prizes awards copies of books by conference presenters and free attendance at a Wharton Executive Education program. For more information, contact Rita Gorman, Center for Human Resources, The Wharton School, University of Pennsylvania, Vance Hall, Room 309, 3733 Spruce Street, Philadelphia, PA 19104-6358. (215) 898-5605. www-management.wharton.upenn.edu/leadership

Host Organization(s): Wharton Center for Human Resources and Wharton Center for Leadership and Change Management at the University of Pennsylvania
Audience: Executives and researchers
When: Each May
Where: Philadelphia, PA
Cost: $750 to $975
Subject(s): Leadership development

New
THE WOMEN IN LEADERSHIP SUMMIT

This three-day event features seven keynote addresses by dynamic women in corporate leadership, world politics, sports, social movements, technology, and the space program. Between keynote speeches, participants may attend workshops to build leadership skills and learn to balance work and family challenges. One session outlines the ATHENA Leadership Model that celebrates relationships, community service, and balance. For more information, contact Linkage, Inc., One Forbes Road, Lexington, MA 02421. (781) 862-3157. www.linkageinc.com

Host Organization(s): Linkage, Inc. and corporate sponsors
Audience: Female executives
When: Each winter
Where: Location varies—2000 in San Francisco, CA
Cost: $1,495
Subject(s): Women's leadership

INDEXES

AUTHOR INDEX

Greenberger, D. B., *A test of vision training and potential antecedents to leaders' visioning ability*, 98

Greene, D., *Defining the leadership role of school boards in the 21st century*, 14

Greenleaf, R. K.
> *On becoming a servant leader*, 70
> *The power of servant leadership*, 70
> *Servant leadership: A journey into the nature of legitimate power and greatness*, 70

Greenstein, F. I.
> *The president who led by seeming not to: A centennial view of Dwight Eisenhower*, 48
> *The two leadership styles of William Jefferson Clinton*, 49

Greer, J. T., *Leadership in empowered schools: Themes from innovative efforts*, 39

Gregersen, H. B.
> *The importance of savvy in global leaders*, 157
> *Participative decision-making: An integration of multiple dimensions*, 57

Gresso, D. W., *Cultural leadership: The culture of excellence in education*, 15

Griego, O. V., *An extension of the theory of margin: A framework for assessing readiness for change*, 72

Griesinger, D. W., *Board performance and organizational effectiveness in nonprofit social services organizations*, 21

Griffith, J., *The school leadership/school climate relation: Identification of school configurations associated with change in principals*, 22

Grint, K., *Leadership: Classical, contemporary, and critical approaches*, 5

Grobler, P. A., *In search of excellence: Leadership challenges facing companies in the new South Africa*, 149

Groff, L., *Culture Clash: An Ethical Intercultural Simulation*, 227

Gronn, P., *Substituting for leadership: The neglected role of the leadership couple*, 6

Grose, P. G., Jr., *Case teaching and why it works in leadership education*, 124

Grove, A. S., *Only the paranoid survive: How to exploit the crisis points that challenge every company and career*, 22

Grude, K. V., *The project manager as change agent: Leadership, influence and negotiation*, 98

Gryskiewicz, S. S.
> *Leading renewal: The value of positive turbulence*, 70
> *Positive turbulence: Developing climates for creativity, innovation, and renewal*, 71

Guardia, J., *Global Service Provider: Managing Change*, 234

Guastello, S. J., *Facilitative style, individual innovation, and emergent leadership in problem solving groups*, 105

Guest, C. W., *Leadership Skills*, 205

Guillet de Monthoux, P., *Good novels, better management: Reading organizational realities in fiction*, 115

Gullatt, D. E., *Teachers taking the lead*, 22

Gundry, L. K., *The leadership focus of women entrepreneurs at start-up and early-growth stages*, 22

Guns, B., *The faster learning organization: Gain and sustain the competitive edge*, 175

Guntern, G., *The challenges of creative leadership*, 71

Gustafson, S. B.
> *Perceived Leader Integrity Scale*, 209
> *Perceived Leader Integrity Scale: An instrument for assessing employee perceptions of leader integrity*, 63

Guthrie, V. A., *Coaching for action: A report on long-term advising in a program context*, 121

Guzman, N., *Ethical considerations in the development of the interdisciplinary leadership studies program*, 121

Gyatso, T. (Dalai Lama XIV), *Freedom in exile: The autobiography of the Dalai Lama*, 49

Gyr, H., *The dynamic enterprise: Tools for turning chaos into strategy and strategy into action*, 68

H

Haass, R. N., *The power to persuade*, 22

Hackel, S. W., *The staff of leadership: Indian authority in the missions of Alta California*, 149

Hackman, M. Z.
> *Ethical considerations in the development of the interdisciplinary leadership studies program*, 121
> *Leadership: A communication perspective*, 71

Haeckel, S. H., *Adaptive enterprise: Creating and leading sense-and-respond organizations*, 175

Hagan, C. M., *Management practice, organization climate, and performance: An exploratory study*, 94

Hagberg, J. O., *Real power: Stages of personal power in organizations*, 71

Halal, W. E., *The infinite resource: Creating and leading the knowledge enterprise*, 176

Hale, G. A., *The leader's edge: Mastering the five skills of breakthrough thinking*, 71

Hall, D. T.
> *The career is dead—long live the career: A relational approach*, 122
> *Choosing a Leadership Style: Applying the Vroom and Yetton Model*, 225
> *Effective Delegation*, 230
> *Experiences in management and organizational behavior*, 112
> *Vanatin: Group Decision Making and Ethics*, 255

Hall, F. S.
> *Choosing a Leadership Style: Applying the Vroom and Yetton Model*, 225
> *Effective Delegation*, 230
> *Experiences in management and organizational behavior*, 112
> *Vanatin: Group Decision Making and Ethics*, 255

Hall, G. E., *Becoming a principal: The challenges of beginning leadership*, 33

Hall, J.
> *Conflict Management Survey*, 198
> *The Harwood Dilemma*, 235
> *NASA Moon Survival Task*, 241
> *Power Management Inventory*, 209
> *Quality Crunch at Rockport*, 246
> *Twelve Angry Men*, 254

Hallam, G. L.
> *The adventures of Team Fantastic: A practical guide for team leaders and members*, 168
> *Campbell-Hallam Team Development Survey*, 196

Hambleton, R. K., *Leader Behavior Analysis II*, 203

Hambrick, D. C., *Navigating change: How CEOs, top teams, and boards steer transformation*, 71

Hammer, A., *Fundamental Interpersonal Relations Orientation-Behavior*, 201

Hammer, A. L., *MBTI manual: A guide to the development and use of the Myers-Briggs Type Indicator*, 130

Hamson, N., *After Atlantis: Working, managing, and leading in turbulent times*, 72

Handley, P. G., *Insight Inventory*, 201

Handy, C.
> *Gods of management: The changing work of organizations*, 176
> *Looking ahead: Implications of the present*, 5
> *Waiting for the mountain to move: Reflections of work and life*, 6

Hanges, P. J., *Culture specific and cross-culturally generalizable implicit leadership theories: Are the attributes of charismatic/transformational leadership universally endorsed?*, 146

Hanpachern, C., *An extension of the theory of margin: A framework for assessing readiness for change*, 72

Hansen, M. C., *Geographically dispersed teams: An annotated bibliography*, 171

Hardy, C.
> *Managing organizations: Current issues*, 173
> *The power behind empowerment: Implications for research and practice*, 72

W

Waclawski, J., *Influence behaviors and managerial effectiveness in lateral relations*, 60

Wagner, S., *Leadership: Lessons from the best*, 20

Waiguchu, J. M., *Management of organizations in Africa: A handbook and reference*, 163

Waite, B., *Putting together a world-class team*, 170

Walberg, H. J., *Childhood traits and experiences of eminent women*, 100

Waldman, D. A.
  CEO charismatic leadership: Levels-of-management and levels-of-analysis effects, 100
  Has 360-degree feedback gone amok?, 139
  A qualitative analysis of leadership and quality improvement, 109

Waldroop, J., *The executive as coach*, 139

Walker, A., *Comparative educational administration: Developing a cross-cultural framework*, 17

Walker, D., *Delivering on the promise: How to attract, manage, and retain human capital*, 68

Wall, S. R., *ERA*, 231

Wallis, M., *Mankiller: A chief and her people*, 50

Walsh, D. F., *Governing through turbulence: Leadership and change in the late twentieth century*, 44

Walsh, K., *Grassroots leaders for a new economy: How civic entrepreneurs are building prosperous communities*, 23

Walter, G. M., *Corporate practices in management development*, 139

Walton, A. E., *Discontinuous change: Leading organizational transformation*, 179

Walton, R. E., *Managing conflict: Interpersonal dialogue and third-party roles*, 100

Wanke, J., *Women are citizen leaders: The citizen leadership training program*, 131

Warech, M. A., *Self-monitoring and 360-degree ratings*, 139

Warren, R. A.
  Leadership Skills, 205
  Leadership WorkStyles, 205

Washington, J. M., *I have a dream: Writings and speeches that changed the world*, 53

Watkins, K. E., *Understanding support for innovation in a large-scale change effort: The manager-as-instructor approach*, 100

Watkins, M., *Right from the start: Taking charge in a new leadership role*, 60

Watson, M. A., *Learning theory in the practice of management development: Evolution and practice*, 83

Watson, T. R., *Corporate Communication Assessment*, 199

Weaver, G. R., *Culture, communication and conflict: Readings in intercultural relations*, 164

Webber, A. M., *Learning for a change*, 183

Webber, T. G., *Team Norms*, 251

Weber, C., *Creating a significant and sustainable executive education experience: A case study*, 127

Weber, J.
  Creating a significant and sustainable executive education experience: A case study, 127
  Influences upon managerial moral decision making: Nature of the harm and magnitude of consequences, 100

Weed, F. J., *The MADD queen: Charisma and the founder of Mothers Against Drunk Driving*, 100

Weeks, J. R., *Styles of success: The thinking and management styles of women and men entrepreneurs*, 164

Weems, L. H., Jr., *Church leadership: Vision, team culture, and integrity*, 44

Wegemer, G. B., *Thomas More on statesmanship*, 53

Weick, K. E., *Sensemaking in organizations*, 183

Weiner, B. J., *Dynamics of upward influence: How male and female managers get their way*, 154

Weisbord, M. R., *Discovering common ground: How future search conferences bring people together to achieve breakthrough innovation, empowerment, shared vision, and collaborative action*, 164

Weisinger, H., *Emotional intelligence at work: The untapped edge for success*, 101

Welch, E., *Public administration in a global context: Bridging the gaps of theory and practice between Western and non-Western nations*, 45

Wellins, R. S.
  High-involvement leadership: Changing roles for changing times, 74
  Leadership trapeze: Strategies for leadership in team-based organizations, 171

Wells, S., *From sage to artisan: The nine roles of the value-driven leader*, 10

Wentling, R. M.
  Current status and future trends of diversity initiatives in the workplace: Diversity experts' perspective, 164
  Women in management: A longitudinal study of their career development and aspirations, 164

Westphal, J. D., *Board games: How CEOs adapt to increases in structural board independence from management*, 45

Wheatley, M. J.
  Leadership and the new science: Learning about organization from an orderly universe, 10
  A simpler way, 183

Wheelan, S. A., *The role of informal member leaders in a system containing formal leaders*, 109

Whelan, K. S., *Successful professional women in midlife: How organizations can more effectively understand and respond to the challenges*, 149

Whicker, M. L., *Toxic leaders: When organizations go bad*, 101

Whitaker, G. P., *Improving city managers' leadership*, 45

White, M. C., *CEO succession: Overcoming forces of inertia*, 45

White, R. E., *An organizational learning framework: From intuition to institution*, 174

White, R. P.
  Breaking the glass ceiling: Can women reach the top of America's largest corporations?, 157
  Four essential ways that coaching can help executives, 140
  The future of leadership: Riding the corporate rapids into the 21st century, 45
  Seekers and scalers: The future leaders, 10

Whitney, D. M., *Looking inside the fishbowl of creativity: Verbal and behavioral predictors of creative performance*, 92

Whitney, G., *Border Dispute*, 223

Whittington, J. L., *A field study of a cognitive approach to understanding transformational and transactional leadership*, 109

Wiggerhorn, W., *The evolution of learning strategies in organizations: From employee development to business redefinition*, 110

Wildemeersch, D., *Strategies in organizing work-related learning projects*, 90

Wilkes, S. B., *Building Trust in Pairs: An Obstacle Course*, 223

Wilkinson, D., *The role of story-telling in organizational leadership*, 68

Williams, E. A., *Does leadership matter in the political arena? Voter perceptions of candidates' transformational and charismatic leadership and the 1996 U.S. presidential vote*, 34

Williams, M. L., *Substitutes for Leadership Scale—Revised*, 211

Williams, S. U., *The long-term impacts of leadership development: An assessment of a statewide program*, 116

Williamson, M. L., *Practicing leadership: Principles and applications*, 9

Wills, G.
  Certain trumpets: The call of leaders, 53
  Lincoln at Gettysburg: The words that remade America, 101

Wilson, C. L., *Survey of Leadership Practices*, 212

Wilson, J. M., *Leadership trapeze: Strategies for leadership in team-based organizations*, 171

Wilson, M. G., *Putting the "team" into teamwork: Alternative theoretical contributions for contemporary management practices*, 169

Wilson, M. S.
  International success: Selecting, developing, and supporting expatriate managers, 164
  Managing across cultures: A learning framework, 165
  What every leader should know about expatriate effectiveness, 165

TITLE INDEX

SUBJECT INDEX

J

jazz music as metaphor for leadership, 64 (De Pree), 77 (Kao), 93 (Schrage)
justice, 159 (Plato), 172 (Beugre)

K

Kappa Omicron Nu, 129 (Mitstifer)
Kauffman Center for Entrepreneurial Leadership, 316
Kellogg Foundation, 316
Kennedy, J. F., 280 (*The Kennedy Era*), 284 (*The Missiles of October*)
King, M. L., Jr., 278 (*In Remembrance*), 283 (*Martin Luther King, Jr.*)
knowledge management, 176 (Halal), 180 (Pasternack), 180 (Rajan)

L

leader portrayed as
    actor, 70 (Gardner)
    artist, 34 (Pitcher), 64 (De Ciantis)
    change agent, 77 (Katzenbach), 87 (Nadler), 98 (Turner), 108 (Spreitzer), 123 (Karp)
    musician, 64 (De Pree), 77 (Kao)
    peacemaker, 49 (Gyatso), 69 (Frost), 282 (*Mahatma Gandhi*)
    teacher, 13 (Bolman), 22 (Gullatt), 33 (Palmer)
LeaderShape, Inc., 316
Leadership America, Inc., 316
leadership development
    books and articles
        guidelines, 128 (McCauley), 140 (Woodall)
        higher education, 21 (Green)
        job assignments, 117 (Eichinger), 127 (McCauley), 128 (McCauley), 133 (Ruderman)
        learning process, 112 (Brungardt), 117 (Eichinger), 132 (Posner)
        organizational systems, 98 (Townsend), 110 (Avolio), 114 (Conger), 127 (Maxwell), 139 (Vicere)
        personal growth, 111 (Barker), 123 (Kaplan), 131 (Palus)
        personality and, 130 (Myers), 105 (Fitzgerald)
        training, 114 (Conger), 120 (Fulmer)
        women and, 100 (Walberg), 107 (Proehl), 114 (Cook), 123 (Kaufmann), 130 (Nemerowicz), 131 (Oberst), 162 (Thackray), 163 (Thorp)
    conferences
        The Emerging Leader Program, 330
        Leadership Conference, 331
        The Leadership Development Conference, 331
        Wharton Leadership Conference, 335
    instruments
        Benchmarks, 196
        COMPASS: The Managerial Practices Survey, 198
        Executive Success Profile, 200
        Voices, 214
    journals
        Leader to Leader, 190
        Leadership in Action, 190
    organizations, Center for Creative Leadership, 309
leadership education
    books and articles, 39 (Shoemaker), 69 (Fritz), 121 (Gookin), 122 (Howe), 124 (Kelly), 130 (Newell), 134 (Schwartz), 163 (Thorp)
    conferences
        ALE Annual Conference, 328
        ILA Annual Meeting, 330
        National Leadership Symposium, 333
    journals
        Concepts and Connections, 186
        The Journal of Leadership Studies, 189
    organizations
        Association of Leadership Educators, 308
        International Leadership Association, 315

leadership education (*continued*)
    organizations (*continued*)
        National Clearinghouse for Leadership Programs, 319
        Organizational Behavior Teaching Society, 321
    websites
        The OBTC Ring Home Page, 302
        World Lecture Hall, 304
leadership effectiveness
    books and articles
        challenges, 3 (Bennis), 5 (Farson), 8 (Kouzes)
        Generation X, 9 (Tulgan)
        golf and, 4 (Cottrell)
        intelligence and, 5 (Gardner)
        personality and, 6 (Hogan)
        relationships, 6 (Hesselbein), 7 (Kellerman), 8 (Kouzes)
        research, 4 (Clark), 10 (Yukl)
        self-awareness, 126 (Lee)
        students, 7 (Komives)
    instruments
        Campbell Leadership Index, 197
        Denison Leadership Development Survey, 199
        Leader Reward and Punishment Questionnaire, 203
        Leadership Effectiveness Analysis, 204
        Leadership/Impact, 204
    videos
        Air Force One, 266
        The Front of the Class: Learning to Lead, 275
        Hook, 277
        LeaderTalk, 281
    websites, Leader Ezzay List, 302
Leadership for Asian Pacifics, Inc. (LEAP), 316
leadership overviews, 3 (Bass), 3 (Boone), 3 (Burns), 4 (Campbell), 4 (Clark), 4 (Cleveland), 4 (Covey), 4 (Culp), 4 (Daft), 5 (Du Brin), 5 (Fairholm), 6 (Hesselbein), 7 (Kellerman), 7 (Kotter), 8 (Krass), 8 (Nahavandi), 8 (O'Toole), 8 (Reckmeyer), 9 (Rost), 9 (Sayles), 9 (Shepard), 9 (Shriberg), 10 (Vaill), 10 (Vecchio), 10 (Wells), 10 (Wren), 96 (Smith)
leadership without authority
    videos
        Braveheart, 268
        Joan of Arc, 279
learning
    books and articles
        action learning, 92 (Rothwell), 117 (Dotlich)
        competence, 55 (Barrie), 55 (Barth), 57 (Bierma), 61 (Coad), 61 (Confessore), 72 (Hayes), 76 (Kamoche), 83 (Mailick), 90 (Poell), 101 (Wofford), 159 (Reed)
        experiences, 64 (Daudelin), 75 (Hughes), 82 (Lindsey), 83 (McCall), 99 (Van Velsor)
        job assignments, 127 (McCauley), 128 (McCauley)
        service learning, 46 (Zlotkowski)
    instruments
        The Choices Architect Talent Management Tool, 197
        Job Challenge Profile, 202
        Learning Styles Questionnaire, 205
        Learning Tactics Inventory, 206
        Prospector, 210
    journals, *Management Learning: The Journal for Managerial and Organizational Learning*, 190
    organizations, The Masie Center, 317
    See also organizational learning
literature—lessons in
    books and articles, 5 (Grint), 32 (Nice), 47 (Clemens), 47 (Corrigan), 50 (Krause), 51 (McNeilly), 114 (Clemens), 115 (Czarniawska-Joerges)
    videos
        Animal Farm, 267
        Lord of the Flies, 282

CENTER FOR CREATIVE LEADERSHIP
New Releases, Best-sellers, Bibliographies, and Special Packages

NEW RELEASES

IDEAS INTO ACTION GUIDEBOOKS

Ongoing Feedback: How to Get It, How to Use It Kirkland & Manoogian (1998, Stock #400) .... $6.95 *

Reaching Your Development Goals McCauley & Martineau (1998, Stock #401) .... $6.95 *

Becoming a More Versatile Learner Dalton (1998, Stock #402) .... $6.95 *

Giving Feedback to Subordinates Buron & McDonald-Mann (1999, Stock #403) $6.95

Three Keys to Development: Using Assessment, Challenge, and Support to Drive Your Leadership Browning &
   Van Velsor (1999, Stock #404) $6.95

Feedback That Works: How to Build and Deliver Your Message Weitzel (2000, Stock #405) $6.95

Communicating Across Cultures Prince & Hoppe (2000, Stock #406) $6.95

Choosing Executives: A Research Report on the Peak Selection Simulation Deal, Sessa, & Taylor (1999, Stock #183) $20.00

Coaching for Action: A Report on Long-term Advising in a Program Context Guthrie (1999, Stock #181) $20.00

The Complete Inklings: Columns on Leadership and Creativity Campbell (1999, Stock #343) $30.00

Executive Coaching: An Annotated Bibliography Douglas & Morley (2000, Stock #347) $20.00

Geographically Dispersed Teams: An Annotated Bibliography Sessa, Hansen, Prestridge, & Kossler (1999,
   Stock #346) $20.00

High-Performance Work Organizations: Definitions, Practices, and an Annotated Bibliography Kirkman, Lowe,
   & Young (1999, Stock #342) $20.00

The Human Side of Knowledge Management: An Annotated Bibliography Mayer (2000, Stock #349) $20.00

Internalizing Strengths: An Overlooked Way of Overcoming Weaknesses in Managers Kaplan (1999, Stock #182) ... $15.00

Leadership and Spirit Moxley (1999, Stock #2035) $30.95

Leadership Resources: A Guide to Training and Development Tools (8th ed.) Schwartz & Gimbel (2000,
   Stock #348) $49.95

Positive Turbulence: Developing Climates for Creativity, Innovation, and Renewal Gryskiewicz (1999,
   Stock #2031) $32.95

Selecting International Executives: A Suggested Framework and Annotated Bibliography London & Sessa (1999,
   Stock #345) $20.00

Workforce Reductions: An Annotated Bibliography Hickok (1999, Stock #344) $20.00

BEST-SELLERS

The Adventures of Team Fantastic: A Practical Guide for Team Leaders and Members Hallam (1996, Stock #172) .. $20.00

Breaking Free: A Prescription for Personal and Organizational Change Noer (1997, Stock #271) $25.00

Breaking the Glass Ceiling: Can Women Reach the Top of America's Largest Corporations? (Updated Edition)
   Morrison, White, & Van Velsor (1992, Stock #236A) $13.00

The Center for Creative Leadership Handbook of Leadership Development McCauley, Moxley, & Van Velsor
   (Eds.) (1998, Stock #201) .... $65.00 *

CEO Selection: A Street-smart Review Hollenbeck (1994, Stock #164) .... $25.00 *

Choosing 360: A Guide to Evaluating Multi-rater Feedback Instruments for Management Development
   Van Velsor, Leslie, & Fleenor (1997, Stock #334) .... $15.00 *

A Cross-National Comparison of Effective Leadership and Teamwork: Toward a Global Workforce Leslie &
   Van Velsor (1998, Stock #177) $15.00

Eighty-eight Assignments for Development in Place Lombardo & Eichinger (1989, Stock #136) .... $15.00 *

Enhancing 360-degree Feedback for Senior Executives: How to Maximize the Benefits and Minimize the Risks
   Kaplan & Palus (1994, Stock #160) .... $15.00 *

Evolving Leaders: A Model for Promoting Leadership Development in Programs Palus & Drath (1995, Stock #165) . $15.00 *

Executive Selection: A Look at What We Know and What We Need to Know DeVries (1993, Stock #321) .... $20.00 *

Executive Selection: A Research Report on What Works and What Doesn't Sessa, Kaiser, Taylor, & Campbell
   (1998, Stock #179) .... $30.00 *

Feedback to Managers (3rd Edition) Leslie & Fleenor (1998, Stock #178) .... $60.00 *

Four Essential Ways that Coaching Can Help Executives Witherspoon & White (1997, Stock #175) $10.00

A Glass Ceiling Survey: Benchmarking Barriers and Practices Morrison, Schreiber, & Price (1995, Stock #161) $15.00

High Flyers: Developing the Next Generation of Leaders McCall (1997, Stock #293) $27.95

How to Design an Effective System for Developing Managers and Executives Dalton & Hollenbeck (1996, Stock #158) .... $15.00 *

If I'm In Charge Here, Why Is Everybody Laughing? Campbell (1984, Stock #205) .... $9.95 *

If You Don't Know Where You're Going You'll Probably End Up Somewhere Else Campbell (1974, Stock #203) .... $9.95 *

International Success: Selecting, Developing, and Supporting Expatriate Managers Wilson & Dalton (1998, Stock #180) .... $15.00 *

The Lessons of Experience: How Successful Executives Develop on the Job McCall, Lombardo, & Morrison (1988, Stock #211) $27.50

A Look at Derailment Today: North America and Europe Leslie & Van Velsor (1996, Stock #169) .... $20.00 *

Making Common Sense: Leadership as Meaning-making in a Community of Practice Drath & Palus (1994, Stock #156) .... $15.00 *

Managerial Promotion: The Dynamics for Men and Women Ruderman, Ohlott, & Kram (1996, Stock #170) $15.00

Managing Across Cultures: A Learning Framework Wilson, Hoppe, & Sayles (1996, Stock #173) $15.00

Maximizing the Value of 360-degree Feedback Tornow, London, & CCL Associates (1998, Stock #295) .... $42.95 *

The New Leaders: Guidelines on Leadership Diversity in America Morrison (1992, Stock #238A) $18.50

Perspectives on Dialogue: Making Talk Developmental for Individuals and Organizations Dixon (1996, Stock #168) .... $20.00 *

Preventing Derailment: What To Do Before It's Too Late Lombardo & Eichinger (1989, Stock #138) $25.00

The Realities of Management Promotion Ruderman & Ohlott (1994, Stock #157) .... $15.00 *

Selected Research on Work Team Diversity Ruderman, Hughes-James, & Jackson (Eds.) (1996, Stock #326) $24.95

Should 360-degree Feedback Be Used Only for Developmental Purposes? Bracken, Dalton, Jako, McCauley, Pollman, with Preface by Hollenbeck (1997, Stock #335) .... $15.00 *

Take the Road to Creativity and Get Off Your Dead End Campbell (1977, Stock #204) .... $9.95 *

Twenty-two Ways to Develop Leadership in Staff Managers Eichinger & Lombardo (1990, Stock #144) $15.00

BIBLIOGRAPHIES

Formal Mentoring Programs in Organizations: An Annotated Bibliography Douglas (1997, Stock #332) $20.00

Management Development through Job Experiences: An Annotated Bibliography McCauley & Brutus (1998, Stock #337) $20.00

Selection at the Top: An Annotated Bibliography Sessa & Campbell (1997, Stock #333) .... $20.00 *

Succession Planning: An Annotated Bibliography Eastman (1995, Stock #324) .... $20.00 *

Using 360-degree Feedback in Organizations: An Annotated Bibliography Fleenor & Prince (1997, Stock #338) .... $15.00 *

SPECIAL PACKAGES

Executive Selection (Stock #710C; includes 157, 164, 179, 180, 321, 333) $85.00

Guidebook Package (Stock #721; includes 400, 401, 402) $14.95

HR Professional's Info Pack (Stock #717C; includes 136, 158, 169, 201, 324, 334, 340) $125.00

New Understanding of Leadership (Stock #718; includes 156, 165, 168) $40.00

Personal Growth, Taking Charge, and Enhancing Creativity (Stock #231; includes 203, 204, 205) $20.00

The 360 Collection (Stock #720C; includes 160, 178, 295, 334, 335, 338) $100.00

Discounts are available. Please write for a Resources catalog. Address your request to: Publication, Center for Creative Leadership, P.O. Box 26300, Greensboro, NC 27438-6300, 336-545-2810, or fax to 336-282-3284. Purchase your publications from our on-line bookstore at **www.ccl.org/publications**. All prices subject to change.

*Indicates publication is also part of a package.

ORDER FORM

Or E-mail your order via the Center's on-line bookstore at www.ccl.org

Name _____ Title _____

Organization _____

Mailing Address _____
(street address required for mailing)

City/State/Zip _____

Telephone _____ FAX _____
(telephone number required for UPS mailing)

Quantity	Stock No.	Title	Unit Cost	Amount

CCL's Federal ID Number
is 237-07-9591.

Subtotal	
Shipping and Handling (add 6% of subtotal with a $4.00 minimum; add 40% on all international shipping)	
NC residents add 6% sales tax; CA residents add 7.75% sales tax; CO residents add 6.1% sales tax	
TOTAL	

METHOD OF PAYMENT
(ALL orders for less than $100 must be PREPAID.)

❏ Check or money order enclosed (payable to Center for Creative Leadership).

❏ Purchase Order No. _____ (Must be accompanied by this form.)

❏ Charge my order, plus shipping, to my credit card:
    ❏ American Express ❏ Discover ❏ MasterCard ❏ VISA

ACCOUNT NUMBER: _____ EXPIRATION DATE: MO. _____ YR. _____

NAME OF ISSUING BANK: _____

SIGNATURE _____

❏ Please put me on your mailing list.

Publication • Center for Creative Leadership • P.O. Box 26300
Greensboro, NC 27438-6300
336-545-2810 • FAX 336-282-3284

6/00

fold here

CENTER FOR CREATIVE LEADERSHIP
PUBLICATION
P.O. Box 26300
Greensboro, NC 27438-6300